CAMBRIDGE SOUTH ASIAN STUDIES

PRIVATE INVESTMENT IN
INDIA 1900–1939

CAMBRIDGE SOUTH ASIAN STUDIES

These monographs are published by the Syndics of the Cambridge University Press in association with the Cambridge University Centre for South Asian Studies. The following books have been published in this series:

PRIVATE
INVESTMENT IN
INDIA 1900-1939

AMIYA KUMAR BAGCHI

CAMBRIDGE
AT THE UNIVERSITY PRESS
1972

Published by the Syndics of the Cambridge University Press
Bentley House, 200 Euston Road, London N.W.1
American Branch: 32 East 57th Street, New York, N.Y.10022

© Cambridge University Press 1972

Library of Congress Catalogue Card Number: 79–152631

ISBN: 0521 07641 2

Printed in Great Britain by
Western Printing Services Ltd, Bristol

CONTENTS

v

TABLES

FIGURES

PREFACE

The aim of the present book is to provide a statistical framework for the determinants of private investment in India during the period 1900–39 and to provide an analysis of the data contained within that framework. Some readers may feel that in my impatience to arrive at meaningful conclusions I have not pushed on to perfect statistical series as much as I could have done. The apology I would offer is that selection of the data and their arrangement made sense to me only in reference to the questions I was asking. Hence I stopped refining the series at the point at which further refinement did not seem to have any bearing on the answers to those questions. There was also the danger that the book would not have been finished at all if it had not been finished now.

Like all authors of such an enterprise, I have accumulated a very large, tangible debt to other workers in the field, and to a wide circle of friends and critics. I have given references to the work of other people that I have drawn upon in different places of the book and so perhaps it is unnecessary and invidious to mention a selected few here. My biggest intellectual debt is to Professor Joan Robinson who carefully read the penultimate version and had very valuable comments to make on the theoretical framework. Dr Krishna Bharadwaj also read the general chapters very carefully and helped to weed out faults of logic and construction.

Among the people who helped with suggestions or comments on one or more chapters of the book are: Esra Bennathan, Dhiresh Bhattacharya, Pramit Chaudhuri, Ashin Dasgupta, Ashok Desai, Moses Finley, R. M. Goodwin, Edmund Leach, M. V. Posner, K. N. Raj, W. B. Reddaway, A. K. Sen and Daniel Thorner. To them all I am very grateful. I also owe a debt of gratitude to Atish Dasgupta and Mrs Ena Desai who assisted in my research at an early stage.

I am grateful to the Government of West Bengal for granting me leave from Presidency College, Calcutta, and the Faculty of Economics and Politics, University of Cambridge and Jesus College, Cambridge, for providing the academic atmosphere and the facilities which enabled me to complete the book. I am particularly indebted to Professor Tapas Majumdar of Presidency College, Calcutta for putting up cheerfully with my many demands and to Mr B. H. Farmer, Director of the Centre of South Asian Studies at the University of Cambridge, for prodding me into completing the book. My thanks go to Dr Sunanda Sen who helped in proof-reading and to Mrs Leonard and Mrs Weis who typed the manuscript. The officers of the Cambridge University Press have saved me from numerous errors through their persistent questioning and patient subediting of the manuscript.

For most of my materials, I depended on the following libraries: Bengal Chamber of Commerce Library, Calcutta, the library of the Bombay Shareholders' Association, Bombay, the British Museum, the Cambridge University Library, the India House Library, London, the India Office Library, London, the Indian Institute Library, Oxford, the library of the London School of Economics and Political Science, the National Archives of India, New Delhi, the National Library, Calcutta and the office of the Registrar of Joint-Stock Companies, Calcutta. To the librarians and other staff of all these libraries, and in particular to Miss W. Thorne and Miss M. Travis of the India House Library and to Mr C. Vickrey of the official publications section of the Cambridge University Library I am sincerely grateful. My thanks are also due to the officials and directors of several commercial firms who let me use the official histories of their firms. In the way of sources I owe a special debt to Dr S. D. Mehta, who very kindly handed over to me the materials he had collected for his two books on the Indian cotton-textile industry.

My wife managed to give me full 'logistic support' in the middle of writing her doctoral thesis, managing a house and looking after a child; I shall follow the custom of old-fashioned Indian families and not presume to thank one who is so near.

None of the persons mentioned in this preface bears any responsibility for any errors – of opinion, fact or logic – remaining in the book.

Presidency College,
Calcutta

A. K. BAGCHI

ABBREVIATIONS USED IN THE BOOK

CISD	(Government of India) Commercial Intelligence and Statistics Department
IFLC	Indian Factory Labour Commission
IIC	Indian Industrial Commission 1916–18
IISCO	Indian Iron and Steel Company Limited
IIYB	*Investor's India Year-Book*
IJMA	Indian Jute Mills Association
ILO	International Labour Organization
IPG	Indian provincial government
ITB	Indian Tariff Board
ITJ	*Indian Textile Journal*
JPE	*Journal of Political Economy*
JRSA	*Journal of the Royal Society of Arts*
JRSS	*Journal of the Royal Statistical Society*
JSA	*Journal of the Society of Arts* (*JSA* became *JRSA* in the first decade of the twentieth century)
PP	U.K. Parliamentary Papers
RC	Royal Commission
SCOB	Steel Corporation of Bengal
TISCO	Tata Iron and Steel Company Limited
UP	United Provinces of Agra and Oudh

PART I.

GENERAL – THEORETICAL FRAMEWORK

1

INTRODUCTION

In 1900, India, 'the brightest jewel in the British Crown', was one of the poorest nations of the world. Lord Curzon, the then Viceroy, and imperial proconsul *par excellence*, in answer to the critics of British rule, during the debate on the budget for 1901–2, proclaimed India prosperous at Rs. 30 or £2, of income per head per year.[1]

The viceregal statement did not go unchallenged: William Digby produced a massively documented indictment claiming that the average Indian was even less prosperous than Lord Curzon had made him out to be, and that he was getting poorer every year, directly as a result of British rule.[2] F. J. Atkinson, in an attempt to vindicate Curzon's estimate, produced a detailed calculation showing that the income per head of an average subject of British India was Rs. 39·5, or about £2. 13s. 0d. per year in 1895.[3] The best available estimate for Great Britain in 1901, by contrast, puts the income per head at £52 per year.[4]

Atkinson's estimate for 1895 has been confirmed by Sivasubramonian, who found that the income per head in India (including native states) at current prices was Rs. 42·1 in 1900–1 and Rs. 41·5 in 1901–2.[5] Atkinson also claimed that there was a sizeable improvement in the standard of living of an ordinary Indian between 1875 and 1895: the income per capita had increased from Rs. 30·5 in 1875 to Rs. 39·5 in 1895. This claim was, however, based on questionable assumptions. Atkinson's data for 1875 were much more fragmentary than his data for 1895. In arriving at the figure for the increase in per capita income between the two dates, he had assumed that productivity per acre had increased for all the major Indian crops (including rice), as a result of extension of irrigation and improvement in techniques. Although a measurement of productivity change during the period 1875–95 has not been attempted, later records of changes in

---

[1] In this book 'India' is used as a shorthand expression for 'India and Pakistan' prior to partition unless otherwise indicated.

[2] William Digby: *'Prosperous' British India* (London, 1901), especially Chapter II.

[3] F. J. Atkinson: 'A statistical review of the income and wealth of British India', *JRSS*, LXV, Part II, June 1902, pp. 209–72.

[4] Phyllis Deane and W. A. Cole: *British Economic Growth 1688–1959* (Cambridge, 1967), p. 282. The estimates of national income for British India and for Great Britain are at current prices.

[5] See S. Sivasubramonian: *National Income of India, 1900–01 to 1946–47* (mimeographed, Delhi School of Economics, Delhi, 1965), Table 6.1.

productivity do not support Atkinson's claim that, although an ordinary Indian was poor in 1895, he was getting distinctly richer over time.[6]

Most of the investigators who have tried to chart the course of national income in India over the subsequent forty years or so, have concluded that the rate of growth of real national income per head was very small, if not actually negative.[7] The rate of growth of population over this period must be considered moderate by modern standards: the total population was 285 million in 1901 and 389 million in 1941, which yields a rate of growth of considerably less than 1% per year over the same period,[8] so a very high rate of growth of population can hardly be blamed for the relative stagnation of incomes. The rate of growth of total agricultural production and the rate of growth of industrial production were both low during these years; and the failure of the industrialization process to get going at an appreciable rate is reflected in the relative stability of the occupational structure. Between 1901 and 1931, the share of industrial workers in the total working force hardly changed, and although there was no detailed occupational census taken for 1941, the evidence available from other sources indicates that the share of the working force employed in industry could not have changed significantly over the decade of the 1930s.[9] Finally we have the 'puzzling fact' that India was ' "the first of the oriental countries to feel the impact of industrialism" and yet never completed the transition; whereas Japan, starting later and starting with fewer resources, did complete it'.[10]

It is the aim of this book to document and analyse one of the basic reasons for the slowness of economic growth in India, viz., the sluggishness of private investment. Modern industry in India meant, barring a few ordnance factories and a few pigmy-sized demonstration factories, private industry. Hence an enquiry into the pattern of industrial investment is tantamount to an enquiry into the pattern of private industrial investment. This enquiry

[6] For a contemporary critique of Atkinson's estimate, see William Digby's discussion on Atkinson: 'Statistical review', *JRSS*, LXV, Part II, June 1902, pp. 272–5. For a discussion of later trends in income and the productivity of land, see Chapters 3 and 4 below.

[7] Daniel Thorner: 'Long-term trends in output' in Daniel and Alice Thorner: *Land and Labour in India* (London, 1962), pp. 82–112; S. J. Patel: 'Long-term changes in output and income in India' in S. J. Patel: *Essays on Economic Transition* (London, 1965), pp. 33–50; and Sivasubramonian: *National Income of India, 1900–01 to 1946–47.* Sivasubramonian's estimate, which is the most comprehensive one yet to be made, puts income per capita in India as a whole, at Rs. 49.4 in 1900–1 and Rs. 61 in 1939–40, at 1938–9 prices, which gives a rate of growth of less than 0.5% per year. Both Patel and Thorner were inclined to put the figure even lower.

[8] Kingsley Davis: *The Population of India and Pakistan* (Princeton, N.J., 1951), p. 27.

[9] Daniel and Alice Thorner: ' "De-industrialisation" in India' in Daniel and Alice Thorner: *Land and Labour in India*, pp. 70–81.

[10] Davis: *Population of India and Pakistan*, p. 214. The quote within the quote is from Herbert Heaton, 'Industrial revolution' in *Encyclopaedia of the Social Sciences*, Vol. VIII (New York, 1935), pp. 3–13, at p. 9.

is conducted here at two levels: an attempt is made first to assess the influence of macroeconomic factors on the fortunes of private investment. Secondly, the major manufacturing industries are taken up one by one to find out which factors were specific to those industries and which affected all industries to more or less the same extent.

A major factor influencing private investment in any country is the attitude of the government to industry and the operational content of government policy towards industry. The operational content of government policy in an economy embarking on industrialization under the auspices of private industry is largely, though not wholly, determined by the tariff policy of the government. From this point of view, the history of private investment in India over the period 1900–39 divides naturally into two epochs; up to 1914, there was virtually completely free trade as far as imports into India from other countries were concerned; there was during the First World War some increase in import duties and a shortage of shipping, making trade between India and the rest of the world much less free than before; then in 1923, the Government of India adopted the policy of discriminating tariff protection towards Indian industries, which clearly marked the end of the era of free trade, and the beginning of the epoch of growth of industry under tariff protection.

Hence in this chapter we devote some attention to the major influences on the pattern of private investment in India during the two epochs, assuming for the most part that the constraints on the supply of capital or of other factors of production are not the decisive influence in most cases. The discussion has been kept largely theoretical in order to bring the framework of analysis of later chapters into clearer focus, but concrete illustrations are given for most of the substantive points made.

I.I INVESTMENT IN THE EXPORT INDUSTRIES

Before the First World War, the Indian economy was as open as any in the world had ever been. India's exports consisted of raw materials and foodgrains, and simple manufactures such as jute goods, cotton yarn and coarse cotton piecegoods, and plantation products – mainly tea.[11] Her imports consisted mainly of manufactured commodities, and these imports made up the major fraction of her consumption of these commodities.

Among the modern industries in which capital was employed on a large scale the most important were cotton manufactures, jute manufactures, coal and tea. Of these industries cotton and jute were the most important manufacturing (as opposed to mining or plantation) industries. While the cotton industry was concentrated mainly in the Bombay Presidency, that is,

[11] H. Venkatasubbiah: *The Foreign Trade of India: 1900–1940* (New Delhi, 1946), pp. 31–9 and P. K. Ray: *India's Foreign Trade since 1870* (London, 1934), Chapter 4.

in western India, all the jute mills worth mentioning were situated in or near Calcutta in eastern India. The two industries were dissimilar in many respects. While the cotton industry was controlled mainly by the Indians, the jute industry was almost the exclusive province of European (mainly British) businessmen. India held a monopoly of raw jute production, whereas she was only one of the major producers of raw cotton; thus while the supply of raw jute in India was a major factor in determining its price, the supply of raw cotton in India had only a negligible influence on its price, which was dominated (on the supply side) by the output of raw cotton in the U.S.A. Jute manufactures were mainly in the nature of capital or intermediate goods, whereas cotton manufactures were primarily intermediate (cotton yarn) or consumption goods (cotton cloth). Finally, while one could visualize a future in which the Indian cotton industry catered entirely to the domestic market, one could not visualize such a future for the jute industry without there occurring a major economic revolution in India.

But before the First World War the two industries had also a number of features in common. More than 90% of the output of jute goods was sold abroad. Similarly, in the case of cotton mills, the major portion of the output of yarn produced by the mills in Bombay City and Island was exported; Bombay City and Island had more than 50% of the total number of spindles and looms located in India at the beginning of the century. The picture was complicated by the fact that Bombay mills also provided cotton yarn and cloth for domestic consumption, and that other centres, of which Ahmedabad was the most vigorous, mainly produced yarn for use by handloom weavers in India and cloth for domestic consumption. But the export market was extremely important for the major centre of industry, viz., Bombay City and Island. Furthermore, although both the cotton and jute industries absorbed domestically produced raw materials, the major fractions of both raw cotton and raw jute were exported; thus the effects of any increase or decrease in the output of cotton or jute manufactures on incomes generated in India were generally swamped by movements in exports of raw cotton and raw jute. Again, both the industries were almost entirely dependent on imports of machinery from abroad, primarily from the U.K. Lastly, although these two industries were the most important ones in the modern manufacturing sector, their contribution to the total national income or the growth of national income was insignificant in relation to the contribution made by the agricultural and small industrial sector, and more particularly, by the exports of raw materials and food-grains. Thus to use some currently fashionable jargon, both the backward and forward linkage effects of the jute and cotton manufacturing industries were rather weak.

It is thus possible to trace the course of investment in these two industries separately, and ignore any feedback effects which the growth of these industries may have had on national income, cost of raw materials or demand for their own products, without vitiating the conclusions too much. Furthermore, since these two manufacturing industries were the most important ones as far as the modern industrial sector was concerned and usually accounted for more than half of the total imports of machinery and mill-work for use by the modern industrial sector before the First World War, once we have accounted for investment in the jute and cotton manu-facturing industries, we have accounted for the major part of changes in aggregate industrial investment. In order to complete the picture, we also have to take into account developments in the sugar, paper, iron and steel, and cement industries, but the stories of their growth before the First World War are very much special cases and are treated as such in the chapters concerned with the respective industries.

The pattern of investment in the jute industry can be largely explained by following the course of sales of jute goods in foreign markets. The output of the Bombay spinning mills can also be explained by the course of yarn sales to China. It is, nevertheless, rather difficult to fit a rather simple model linking the sales of jute goods and of cotton yarn to the annual levels of investment in the respective industries.

First, let us assume that all entrepreneurs perceive the opportunities for making profit in the same way, that is, that they have more or less had the same experience in terms of sales and costs in the recent past and that they form their expectations on the basis of this experience in the same way. In that case, unless the plans of all the entrepreneurs are co-ordinated their aggregate response to any change – particularly to a favourable change – is likely to be exaggerated. The degree of exaggeration cannot be predicted without detailed knowledge of the financial position of each of the firms and, what is more important, the degree to which a favourable change induces the entry of new firms. One can argue that if the firms try to preserve the same shares of the total market as before, and if all of them correctly anticipate the aggregate change in demand then even without co-ordination of plans the total investment should vary directly with the total increases in sales in the recent past (assuming that reasonable profits are earned), and there need not be any exaggeration of the response to changes in sales or profits on this score. But this assumes that there is no entry of new firms which try to encroach on the market of other firms. The British managing agents interested in the jute industry in India were homogenous enough in their social and business outlook and in their access to information, finance and markets for them to be able to regulate current output in accordance with changes in demand in relation to the supply of jute goods in world markets. But no one managing agency house was in a position to dominate the industry, and several large managing agency houses were trying through a high rate of investment to capture as much of the growing market as possible. Furthermore some new managing agency houses also entered the field. Thus neither of the assumptions required to guarantee a close conformity of investment to desired capacity for the industry as a whole was fulfilled.

Secondly, let us assume more realistically that the experience, the expectations and the financial position of different firms do differ. In this case, without detailed knowledge of the way the expectations of different firms are formed, it is not possible to predict the investments of individual firms. However, if expectations follow some simple laws, and if the deviations of expectations of individual firms are distributed around the mean or modal expectations according to some simple rule, then the aggregate result might be predictable even if the distribution of the aggregate investment among different firms is not.[12]

Since with the data at our disposal it is not even possible to form an idea of the law governing the statistical distribution of reactions of individuals to a change in a macroeconomic variable such as total sales of jute goods in foreign markets, we have to be content with very roughly correlating the direction of change in jute sales with the direction of change in the desired stock of capital in the jute industry. One approximation to the 'desired stock of capital' for the industry as a whole would be the amount of expected sales multiplied by the marginal capital–output ratio; however, the aggregate result of the plans of individual firms will normally exceed or fall short of such a desired stock of capital by a substantial margin because of lack of co-ordination of plans among the different firms, and because of possible differences in technical conditions of different firms.

However, the jute industry in India was in a special position. By any criterion it had a substantial lead over its nearest rival, the jute industry of Dundee, in respect of production costs, and this lead was reflected in its growing share in the world market for jute goods. The industry was also formally organized in the Indian Jute Manufacturers' (later Mills) Association and informally organized through a dozen or so British managing agency houses controlling the whole industry. The actions of the jute mills of Calcutta had a substantial impact on the prices of jute goods in the world market. Hence the industry could reasonably take the growth of its own sales into account in making its investment plans assuming that, while it need not fear the sudden disappearance of its major markets abroad through the actions of competitors, it could not also encroach upon the markets of industries located in other countries without inviting retaliation, very often in the form of increased tariffs.

[12] See in this connection, R. Ferber: 'The anatomy and structure of industry expectations in relation to those of individual firms', *Journal of the American Statistical Association*, Vol. 53, June 1958, pp. 317–35; and Earl O. Heady and Donald R. Kaldor: 'Expectations and errors in forecasting agricultural prices', *Journal of Political Economy*, Vol. 62, February 1954, pp. 34–47.

The rate of growth of the share of the Indian jute industry in the world jute sales was limited by (1) the existence of jute industries in other countries which could carry on so long as the price of jute goods could at least cover the average variable cost of production, since the fixed capital was already there and was quite specific and had a small scrap value, (2) the threat that severe price-cutting by the Indian industry would invite retaliation in the form of increased tariffs on imports of jute goods by consumers of jute and jute goods with jute manufacturing industries of their own, particularly when such price-cutting threatened the survival of the less efficient manufacturing industries, and (3) possible reluctance on the part of British managing agents to encroach too fast on the markets of Dundee. The firms composing the industry would also have reasonably similar expectations because of the similarity in the background of their decision-makers and because of the similarity in the channels of contact with foreign markets (mostly Australia, the U.S.A. and South America). Hence any favourable change in sales and profits evoked similar reactions on the part of most of the firms; this led to a bunching of investment in one period followed by a period in which sales would fall short of output at prevailing prices, leading to a building up of stocks and a fall in profits. The Indian Jute Manufacturers' Association then generally succeeded in restricting hours of work, and the process of sales overtaking capacity would start again, given an expanding world market for jute goods and given the favourable position of the Indian jute-mill industry.

The other major manufacturing industry in India in which investment was taking place on a large scale was the cotton-mill industry. As I have indicated above, Bombay was the main centre for production of yarn for exports, and the Bombay spinning mills depended substantially on the exports of yarn to China. In the nineties of the last century, in spite of foreign exchange troubles and political instability in China, the total exports of cotton twist and yarn from India had increased from 143·2 million lb. in 1889–90 to 242·6 millon lb. in 1899–1900. There was then a very sharp break in 1900–1 because of the plague in Bombay when total Indian exports declined to 119·3 million lb.; the total of exports of cotton twist and yarn recovered and reached 298·5 million lb. in 1905–6. But after that a definite stagnation set in; exports of cotton twist and yarn from India were 152·3 million lb. in 1911–12 and 198·9 million lb. in 1913–14.

In contrast to this, the domestic demand for cotton piecegoods in India was increasing steadily except for periods of famine in 1896–7 and 1899–1900, and domestic mill production of cotton piecegoods was also increasing. There was thus a strong incentive even for the Bombay mills to pay greater attention to the domestic market. Since cotton manufacture accounted for more than 36% of total imports of commodities into India between 1900–1 and 1913–14,[13] and since cotton mills and handlooms together supplied only about 34% of the total domestic consumption of piecegoods in 1900–1,[14] there was enormous scope for substitution of imports by domestic production. There was also room for substitution of imports from Great Britain by yarn spun in Indian mills. Hence the potential new investment in the Indian cotton-mill industry was governed by three factors: first and foremost, displacement of imported cotton piecegoods, secondly, the defence of the market for Indian yarn in China against Chinese and Japanese competition, and thirdly, the supply of yarn spun in Indian mills in the place of imported yarn for the use of Indian handlooms. A pattern of specialization emerged among the Indian cotton mills corresponding to these three factors governing potential investment. Bombay continued to export yarn to the Chinese market and the investment in the mill industry there continued to be strongly influenced by the rate of the yarn exports to China; the centres away from western India mainly catered to the demand of handloom weavers for coarse yarn; and Ahmedabad within the Bombay Presidency concentrated mainly on supplying cotton piecegoods to the Indian market. But in all the three types of centres the dominant influence was that of the domestic market for cotton piecegoods.

Industrialists and politicians were well aware of the prospect of displacing a very large proportion of imported cotton piecegoods by those produced in India.[15] But before the First World War, the Indian mill owners could not reasonably have aimed at producing the whole of the internal demand for mill-made cotton piecegoods for the following reasons: (a) Lancashire was assumed to have a decided advantage in spinning the finer counts of yarn and weaving the finer varieties of cloth. (b) The major portion of the trading network in manufactured goods was geared to the import of Manchester piecegoods. Indian piecegoods would have to overcome considerable prejudice when they invaded a preserve of Manchester goods. This applied particularly to the market supplied by Calcutta, which was the biggest single

---

[13] Venkatasubbiah, *Foreign Trade of India*, p. 28.

[14] See Table 7.1 pp. 226–7 below.

[15] Dadabhai Naoroji and M. G. Ranade were among the eminent public figures advocating and predicting the displacement of foreign piecegoods by those produced in India. See M. G. Ranade: *Essays on Indian Economics* (2nd ed.: Madras, 1906) and S. D. Mehta: *The Cotton Mills of India: 1854–1954* (Bombay, 1954), Chapter 7. The Swadeshi movement after the partition of Bengal in 1905 gave this advocacy a directly political turn. But mill-owners had been conscious of the possibility of spinning higher-numbered counts of yarn and weaving finer cloth at least as early as 1901. See the speeches of the Chairman and of Bomonjee D. Petit in Mill-owners' Association, Bombay: *Annual Report 1901* (Bombay, 1902), pp. 72–3. Bomonjee D. Petit as Chairman of the Bombay Millowners' Association for 1903 came back to the same theme: 'For the last three or four years I have been constantly urging along with my other colleagues that the out-turn of our mills ought to be made to meet the demands of our own country for goods of finer counts which, besides being large, ensure us a ready and profitable market.' Millowners' Association, Bombay; *Annual Report 1903* (Bombay, 1904), p. 170.

cotton piecegoods market in the East and which was entirely dominated by British managing agency houses with close connection with Great Britain. (c) The cotton grown in India was mostly of the short-staple variety, and was unsuitable for the spinning of finer counts of yarn.

Of these obstacles the last one was the least important. It was the differential advantage in labour costs which gave Indian industry an edge over Lancashire in respect of coarser yarn and cloth. The transport cost of long-staple cotton from Egypt to India or to Great Britain would not be very different; Great Britain had a freight advantage in respect of American cotton. But transport costs were very low in relation to the cost of raw cotton anyway. If Indian mill-owners could convince themselves that Indian labour could spin finer counts of yarn at least as efficiently as they spun the coarser counts, then the long-staple cotton could be imported and woven in Indian mills. The lack of any tariff protection on either cotton yarn or cotton piece-goods and the presence of very definite prejudices against Indian piecegoods in comparison with Lancashire piecegoods of the finer variety meant that Indian mills would have to push ahead cautiously. Some tariff protection would have made all the difference, because then the mills could have tried out new counts of yarn and new varieties of piecegoods on a wider scale. The greater premium placed on long-staple cotton in Indian markets might also have induced Indian cotton-growers to plant the long-staple varieties in larger quantities. Without tariff protection, only the mills of Ahmedabad and an isolated mill or two in Bombay were trying out the production of finer varieties of piecegoods.[16]

Total imports of cotton piecegoods into India increased during the period from 1900–1 to 1913–14 by about 50%. It would be tempting to suggest that the target for Indian mills was to satisfy the increment in demand, assuming that the established imports of Manchester goods would remain undisturbed. However, during this period the proportion of better-quality goods in total imports went up substantially and the Indian cotton mills also turned out yarn of finer counts (above 20s) which was largely used for weaving cloth in the mills, but the proportion of yarn above 40s to total yarn output remained very small. In view of this one can reconstruct the history of new investment in the cotton-mill industry in this period by assuming that Indian mills took as their target the production of goods which could be woven with yarn up to 40s; the speed with which this target was approached depended on the resistance of the maufacturers of Manchester goods and their distributors in India, the financial experience of the bigger Bombay companies involved in sales of yarn to China and the experience of the mills which tried to spin finer counts of yarn and weave finer qualities of piece-goods.

From the middle of the First World War import tariffs were imposed on

[16] For documentation and further discussion of the points made, see Chapter 7 below.

the major consumer goods and on some producer goods; after the war, there were several years of uncertainty, and then qualified official sanction was given to the protection of industrial infants by the policy of discriminating protection. This sanction was made more effective from the beginning of the 1930s primarily because of the financial needs of the government. It is therefore important to analyse the effects of tariff protection on the rate of growth and efficiency of private manufacturing industries. This analysis is attempted in the next section and in the Appendix to this chapter.

1.2 TARIFF PROTECTION AND EFFICIENCY OF INDUSTRY IN AN UNDER-DEVELOPED COUNTRY

Most of the literature on tariff protection assumes pure competition, zero investment and full employment of resources, and compares positions of full equilibrium before and after tariff protection. The conclusions derived from such an analysis can provide an ideology but hardly a guideline for policy in the real world, particularly in an under-developed country.

One of the conclusions that can be derived from a static analysis of this kind is that if all the other industries are obeying all the conditions for competitive efficiency, then the higher the degree of protection for the remaining industry, the greater is the departure from the position of Pareto optimality for the economy as a whole, assuming that consumers' preferences are well-behaved (with no saturation points) and are not altered by the fact of protection as such. However, such a conclusion does not at once dictate a policy of free trade even if policy-makers are not concerned with economic growth, and even if all the scarce resources of the economy are fully employed. For, as Bickerdike had shown as long ago as 1906,[17] an individual country may gain by imposing a positive level of tariffs on one or more of the imported commodities. When we introduce economic growth as an explicit objective and take into account the existence of unemployed resources, the relevance of the neoclassical arguments in favour of free trade is even more drastically restricted. First, assuming constant returns to scale and no gains in efficiency through experience, it may be that with a rise in the level of tariff protection the total amount of investment in the given industry also rises; if the potential savings tapped in this way are new, then they constitute an addition to the total capital stock. If capital is the limiting factor, then the net addition to total national income is equal to the net addition to the total output of the given industry, after allowing for the rise that may take place in the prices of the products because of the reallocation of total expenditure by consumers in response to increases in tariff rates, and hence prices, of the protected commodities.

[17] C. F. Bickerdike: 'The theory of incipient taxes', *Economic Journal*, XVI (4), December 1906, pp. 529–35.

Secondly, the ultimate effects of tariff protection will also depend on the degree to which learning by doing can improve efficiency in the protected industry and in the industries which are directly linked to it on the supply side. If the duty is high, the activities leading to improved skill both in the protected industry and in the supplying industries will receive an impetus, and the speed of diffusion of previously known technical improvements will be greater. If there are strongly increasing returns to scale in the particular industry, the effects of learning on the scale of production of the industry may lead to external economies, some of which may, of course, be internalized by the bigger firms. Whether all these improvements in the conditions of production lead to a fall in prices for consumers depends on the competitive structure of the industry at home (and, to a lesser extent, abroad). But there may be a net addition to the national product even without any actual fall in prices.

Three crucial factors will determine the extent to which the real value of national income can be increased by increased efficiency and output in a protected industry: (a) the degree to which potential savings[18] and complementary factors of production are employed; (b) the height of the 'barriers to new competition' in the protected industry, which in turn depends on the specificity of the skills or natural resources required, and the minimum size of a viable unit in the industry in relation to the total demand for the products in a given economy; and (c) the strength of the dynamic factors such as economies of scale and learning by doing in the protected industry and in the industries linked to it on the supply side.

1.3 INVESTMENT IN INDUSTRIES PRODUCING FOR AN INTERNAL MARKET UNDER TARIFF PROTECTION

If tariff protection is effective in shutting out the major portion of foreign manufacturers, then assuming that there is no limit on investment because of lack of savings, managerial talent or entrepreneurship, the total domestic consumption of the commodity in question before the introduction of tariff protection can become the target of production for industrialists investing in the economy, after allowing for any expected fall in consumption because of the rise in price. If we assume that the volume of investment in the given industry is proportional to the difference between the desired capital stock, which is equal to the volume of domestic consumption multiplied by the

---

[18] The objection can be raised that potential savings can be made actual only by decreasing the consumption of some commodity; as is well known, this is not true in an economy with unemployed resources. All that is involved is a raising of the investment schedule in the usual Keynesian cross of savings and investment schedules. Furthermore, imports of gold or luxury articles from abroad often provide the outlet for savings which do not materialize in investment because of lack of profitable opportunities. Tariff protection merely diverts expenditure from such items into domestic industrial activity.

marginal capital–output ratio, and the actual capital stock existing in the economy, and if the investment takes place with a time lag (determined by the delivery lags of suppliers of capital goods, gestation lags in construction and lags in recognition of the new opportunity for profit), then the path of investment in the given industry will look roughly as in Figure 1.1. The rationale of the shape of the curve in Figure 1.1, which is very similar to the graph of investment in the sugar industry of India over the period 1930–9, as given in Chart 1, is roughly as follows: as a new investment opportunity in the shape of possibilities of substitution of imports by domestic

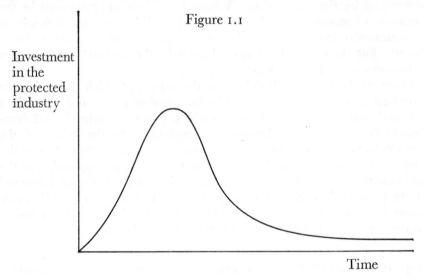

Figure 1.1

Investment in the protected industry

Time

production opens up because of, say, tariff protection, there is at first a rush for investment in the industry. Because of the time needed in the selection of sites, planning of the factory and selection of machinery and the transport of machinery from a foreign country (generally the U.K. in India's case), the peak in the imports of machinery is reached some time after the new opportunity opens up. (Since some machinery had already been ordered for replacement or extension by the more progressive firms, the investment in machinery is not zero between the date the opportunity opens up and the date when the machinery ordered in response to the new investment opportunity begins to arrive.) After a time – probably even before the actual peak in investment is reached – investors begin to realize that there is going to be more activity in the new field than they had at first calculated (some investors may have foreseen the rush in the first place); furthermore, good sites for the location of the plant become scarcer and more costly and the anticipated return from investment falls off, and so the investment also drops off. But some firms which had good management or were luckier than others realize higher-than-normal profits and hope to benefit, say, from better utilization of overheads, and continue to invest, so that the new investment does not fall abruptly but gradually tails off. Since the stock of capital after the major portion of the new investment has taken place is greater than before, the demand for replacement and therefore the level of normal gross investment to make up for wear and tear is generally greater

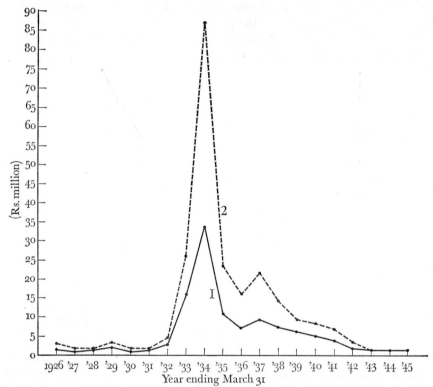

Chart: Money (curve 1) and real (curve 2) value of imports of sugar machinery into India

than it was before the new investment opportunity appeared, which is why the right-hand tail of the graph of investment in the Indian sugar industry is higher than the left-hand tail.

Whether, in fact, investment in all the industries follows paths which are similar to that in Figure 1.1, depends partly on the 'animal spirits'[19] of the entrepreneurs. One can argue that if the rate of investment is high and its rate of growth is high, then there will also be a high rate of growth of income leading to a high rate of growth of demand for all industrial products

[19] The phrase is due to J. M. Keynes: *The General Theory of Employment, Interest and Money* (London, 1949), p. 161.

and this in turn will justify the optimism of the entrepreneurs. Although the pattern of response of investors to any isolated increase in domestic demand for any particular product might follow a path similar to that of Figure 1.1, when domestic demand for the product goes on increasing at a steady proportionate rate, the total investment also will tend to increase at a steady proportionate rate. The actual investment taking place within a given period of time will be the sum of different streams of investment elicited by increases in domestic demand for the product anticipated in different periods in the past. If the levels of domestic demand for the products produced by all the industries enjoying protection increase at steady proportionate rates,

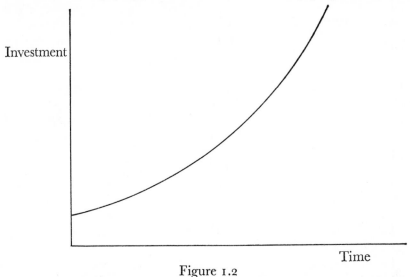

Figure 1.2

then levels of investment in particular industries and in the aggregate of industries enjoying protection will also show positive (though not necessarily steady) proportionate rates of growth in the long run. The graph of investment in particular industries and in the industrial sector enjoying protection will then look roughly as in Figure 1.2 (although the curve shows a steady exponential trend, this is only one of a large number of possibilities: it is the continued upward trend of investment, contrasting with its falling off in Figure 1.1, which should be noticed).

Although as a logical proposition it is all right to say that there exist high enough rates of investment in several industries, which, if maintained over a long period of time, will lead to a strongly positive rate of growth of demand, it is not very informative in the context of an existing under-developed economy. If the under-developed economy does not possess any large intermediate or capital goods industries and if no special measures are taken to foster them, then much of the initial expenditure in the protected consumer goods industries will leak out to foreign countries. If the total demand for the protected consumer goods industries is small in relation to total national income, and/or the marginal capital–labour ratios in the given industries are high, and/or the capitalists' share in the additional income generated is high and the marginal propensity to save is high, then the growth of the protected industries will have little noticeable effect on total national income because the multiplier effects will be small. In an under-developed economy agriculture generally accounts directly for half or more of the national income, and a large number of activities such as transport and trade in basic raw produce and consumer goods are dependent on the prosperity of agriculture. Hence if agriculture is depressed because of international or uncontrolled natural factors, the level of national income will also be depressed. If tariff protection is introduced (as a defensive measure against balance of payments deficits or deficits in the budget of the government caused by a fall in revenues from the sale of primary products) at a time when agriculture is depressed, the trend of income and demand for the protected commodity (or commodities) will be static. Under these circumstances, in order to sustain a rate of investment which might ultimately lead to a self-sustaining growth of industry, entrepreneurs will need not just buoyant animal spirits but a degree of foolhardiness which is inconsistent with a rational management of the protected industries. Further, in an under-developed economy, agriculture is generally subject to much severer constraints than industry, and an upsurge in industrial investment is often frustrated by a sharp turning of the terms of trade against industry.

The demand for the protected goods can also be kept up by an expanding government sector. If one could regard the economy as closed, and if the supplies of all the goods could be increased in step with the demand for them, then continually expanding government expenditure could provide the basic stimulus for the growth of the private industrial sector. If the marginal propensity to consume is as high as it is supposed to be in an under-developed economy, a unit increase in government expenditure will increase national income by several units. Of course, in a private enterprise under-developed economy with a large population, the growth in real income will be limited by the lack of factors of production such as capital goods and technical skill, and if the increase in demand oversteps the supply of goods from industry and agriculture, there will be problems of inflation; in an otherwise depressed international economy, this will lead to acute balance of payments problems and growth will be halted.

In practice, however, the Government of India before independence was wedded to classical balanced budget principles;[20] it was also highly depen-

[20] For a good exposition of such principles see Jesse Burkhead: 'The balanced budget', *Quarterly Journal of Economics*, May 1954, reprinted in Arthur Smithies and J. Keith Butters (eds.): *Readings in Fiscal Policy* (London, 1955), pp. 3–27.

dent on indirect taxes and therefore on income from agriculture. Hence a contraction of agricultural incomes in the thirties led to contraction of revenues for the government which led to deflationary rather than expansionary measures. Thus there is really no record of expansion initiated by government expenditures leading to an expansion of private industry and ultimately to balance of payments difficulties. One can in fact find a high degree of parallelism between the movement of private expenditures and of total public expenditure in India during the thirties as the figures in Table 1.1 show. For any *acceleration* of the rate of growth of national income stimulated by a rise in the government expenditure, one should have noticed a *rise*

TABLE 1.1   *The movement of private consumer and public expenditure, 1931–2 to 1937–8*

	Total gross public investment (Rs. million) (1)	Total gross public expenditure (Rs. million) (2)	Total consumer expenditure (Rs. million) (3)
1931–2	488.0	2,783.6	28,088
1932–3	337.6	2,487.6	25,947
1933–4	334.0	2,503.3	24,849
1934–5	340.4	2,519.1	24,434
1935–6	435.9	2,630.6	24,135
1936–7	358.8	2,523.5	25,171
1937–8	358.0	2,478.2	25,756

Sources: Columns (1) and (2) from M. J. K. Thavaraj: 'Capital Formation in the Public Sector in India: A Historical Study, 1898–1938' in V. K. R. Rao *et al.: Papers on National Income and Allied Topics,* Vol. 1 (Bombay, 1960), pp. 215–30; column (3) from R. C. Desai: *Standard of Living in India and Pakistan, 1931–32 to 1940–41* (Bombay, 1953), Ch. 16, Table 109.

in the ratio of government expenditure to consumer expenditure. However, one can argue that the *relative* inelasticity downward of total government expenditure in the face of a violent fall in agricultural incomes imparted some measure of stability to the national income. Moreover, a *fall* in the ratio of public investment to public expenditure in the thirties in relation to the twenties also meant that government expenditure had greater multiplier effects on the economy, since a lower proportion of government expenditure was spent abroad (for India had a very small capital goods sector). But this fall did have an adverse impact on the only capital goods industry then existing in India, viz., the iron and steel industry.

The issues relating to the relation of government economic policy to private industrial investment are examined in greater detail in Chapter 2. In the Appendix to this chapter the implications of our investment model – which makes the *demand* for the particular commodity the crucial variable –

are examined more rigorously. I also there take up the question of the degree to which course of investment in particular industries is affected by (a) the initial market structure of the industry and (b) the barriers to new competition in the industry imposed by indivisibility, economies of scale, limitation of the market and other such factors.

1.4 SUPPLY-ORIENTED HYPOTHESES FOR EXPLAINING LOW RATES OF INVESTMENT

In the sections above I have stressed factors working primarily on the side of demand in explaining the behaviour of aggregate and sectoral investment in modern industry in India. In the following chapters I shall try to substantiate the broad thesis that, before the First World War, it was the governmental policy of free trade, and after the war it was the general depression in the capitalist system combined with the halting and piecemeal policy of tariff protection adopted by the Government of India, that limited the rate of investment in modern industry.

Although no general model of Indian economic development covering the period 1900–39 is available in the literature, a set of hypotheses particularly favoured by economic historians or commentators writing on India[21] can be extracted from the generalizations that are from time to time made without much argument. This set of hypotheses singles out the factors on the supply side for explaining the slow rate of economic growth in India. The crucial limiting factor is alleged to be the scarcity of capital and, associated with it and reinforcing it, the scarcity of entrepreneurial talent. The theme of scarcity of capital as the limiting factor on development is expanded in two directions. Some interpretations stress the absolute scarcity of capital which was supposed to result from the very low level of income of the vast majority of the population and wasteful expenditure on conspicuous consumption by the small group of people with high incomes. Some other interpretations stress, not the absolute scarcity, but the 'shyness' of capital for modern enterprises. This was the view of many Indian students of development and of British publicists sympathetic to the cause of Indian industrialization. In a recent article,[22] Professor G. C. Allen writes: 'Finally, and this is probably the most powerful reason for the slowness of industrial

---

[21] See for example, Vera Anstey: 'Economic development' in L. S. S. O'Malley (ed.): *Modern India and the West* (London, 1941), pp. 258–304; P. P. Pillai: *Economic Conditions in India* (London, 1925), Chapter 10; P. S. Lokanathan: *Industrial Organization in India* (London, 1935); N. Das: *Industrial Enterprise in India* (London, 1938), Chapters 1 and 8; Sir Reginald Coupland: *India: A Re-statement* (London, 1945), pp. 52–70. For a restatement of the same set of views as applied to modern India see D. K. Rangnekar: *Poverty and Capital Development in India* (London, 1958).

[22] 'The industrialization of the Far East' in *Cambridge Economic History of Europe*, Vol. VI, Part II (Cambridge, 1965), pp. 909–10.

growth in India, the social traditions and institutions of India were un-congenial to native enterprise in modern large-scale industry; for Indian capital and Indian talent were drawn in quite other directions.' Perhaps the most virulent expression of the view that Indian economic development was limited by unsuitable Indian values and that British rule on balance hastened India's growth is to be found in a book by L. C. A. Knowles.[23] Two quotations may be given to illustrate the trend of the argument: 'Nor did the English ever have the same sense of values as the Indian peoples, whose outlook in life is essentially non-economic.'[24] Again: 'More might have been done perhaps to stimulate economic growth in India had England not believed so thoroughly in laissez faire for herself and for others, but a policy of Government development is expensive, and it would have meant increased taxation to be paid by the peasant, and it is doubtful whether a more energetic constructive policy would have been worth the financial pressure.'[25] We shall see in Chapter 2 how these twin policies of free trade and financial orthodoxy, both of which Knowles implicitly endorsed, were allowed to strangle governmental initiative in the field of modern industry time and time again. It is in most cases rather obscure how 'shyness' of capital is recognized. One could properly call capital 'shy' if an enterprise promised a reasonable rate of profit and yet capital was not forthcoming. It is very rare for the critics alleging the lack of enterprise of Indian capitalists to provide concrete examples where the rate of profit was reasonable and yet capital was not forthcoming for investment.

The proper definition of the degree of 'shyness' of Indian capital involves several problems which have rarely been faced. There is first the question of what rate of profit is considered 'reasonable' in the Indian economy. If it is claimed that the rates of profit expected by Indian capitalists from modern enterprises were too high, one could easily challenge that state-ment by showing that similar rates of profit were being earned in trade, money-lending, and banking, and even in some sectors of modern industries such as cotton-spinning and crude processing of raw materials for export or consumption at home. If one then claims that such rates of profit were inimical to industrial growth and *should not* therefore have been claimed by Indian industrialists then one is simply expecting them to be irrational in a systematic fashion. Entrepreneurs *qua* entrepreneurs will naturally be attracted to those activities which promise the highest rates of return on an average. If high rates of return are obtainable on money-lending or trade, there must be special reasons for the maintenance of such rates: these reasons have to do with the social and political structure sustaining a given pattern of distribution of incomes, assets and consumption.

For the strict purpose of explaining the failure of Indian entrepreneurs

---

[23] *Economic Development of the British Overseas Empire* (London, 1924).
[24] *Ibid.*, p. 267.   [25] *Ibid.*, p. 466.

to enter modern industry on a large scale, it is not necessary to delve deep into the structure of society in India. For the rates of return obtainable from most branches of modern industry were low not only in comparison with those obtainable from alternative avenues of employment of money in India, but also with rates of return expected by entrepreneurs in advanced countries. As far as the major British managing agency houses and the large Indian business groups were concerned, capital was abundant.[26] What was lacking was a market expanding sufficiently rapidly. The smaller Indian business houses in all regions and all Indian business houses in regions other than western India suffered from a special disadvantage since they did not have an easy access to organized banking. Thus British managing agency houses with access to the organized money market which charged a lower rate of interest were in a position to accept smaller rates of return; in the industries catering to export markets European business houses would also generally earn higher rates of return because of advantages in information, contact and shipping and banking services. But for both British and Indian entrepreneurial groups many fields of modern industry were barred because of the low levels of return that could be rationally expected. One then has to ask questions about domestic consumption of the commodities concerned, and about government economic policy affecting the growth of that consumption and of substitution of imports by domestic production. This is one line of enquiry which is pursued in Chapter 2 and in the chapters concerned with individual industries.

In the usual accounts of the economic development of India, the scarcity of Indian entrepreneurial talent is also stressed. Entrepreneurial talent by its very nature can be discovered only *ex post*: it is a combination of foresight and luck backed by adequate capital that produces a successful entrepreneur. But entrepreneurs also need information and access to markets. It is rarely recognized that the free-trade policy of the Government of India favoured only certain types of entrepreneurial activity, such as foreign trade and production for exports, in which Europeans had a natural advantage over Indians. Before the convention was adopted around 1919 that Indian fiscal policy would largely be determined by the Government of India without interference from the British Parliament, most of India's trade and industry was geared towards foreign markets. European businessmen thus enjoyed special advantages because of their contact with foreign countries. London was the centre of the world money market and Britain had the largest merchant navy; hence naturally British businessmen enjoyed considerable superiority over Indians in respect of financing and transport of exports and imports. Further, within India the railway network was geared primarily towards serving the ports, and was managed by British officers. There again European businessmen scored over the Indians because of their social

[26] See Chapter 6 below.

contact with railway officials and because of the cheaper freight rates on goods exported and imported rather than transported from one inland station to another.

Although, generally speaking, the scarcity of capital and of entrepreneurial talent is supposed to be the limiting factor on Indian economic development, the alleged immobility of labour and the supposed lack of adaptability of Indian peasants to changes in the profitability of different crops or to changed circumstances in general have also been mentioned in the literature[27] as further limiting factors. I would contend, however, that both the labour supply and the pattern of agricultural output adjusted to the changes in demand brought about by the limited degree of industrialization in India during the period 1900–39. The mechanisms by which the supplies of labour and of agricultural raw materials adapted or were made to adapt (through government policy) are examined in some detail in Chapters 5 and 4 respectively.

There is a more sophisticated version of the supply-oriented theory of industrial stagnation which follows more or less the lines of Arthur Lewis's model of economic growth with unlimited supplies of labour.[28] Here the supply of labour for industrial work is taken to be perfectly elastic at a given real wage in the long run. The volume of investment in industry (and in the advanced sector of agriculture) is dependent on the supply of savings which in turn depends on the capitalists' share in the national income and on their propensity to save. All savings are invested, and development is not limited in any way by deficiency of demand in the aggregate or in the major industrial fields. According to this version, the rate of investment was low because the share of the Indian capitalists in the national income was low. However, even with Indian capitalists having a small share of national income, the rate of growth of investment could have been higher if the rate of reinvestment of profits by European capitalists had been higher, at least before the First World War; for the latter group then dominated modern industry, foreign trade and organized finance. Hence, even in a model of growth along this capitalistic pattern, the political factors inhibiting the entry of Indian capitalists into modern industry and the reinvestment of surplus by the European capitalists could not be left out of account.

Some other features which had been mentioned earlier by economic historians can be easily incorporated into this more sophisticated version. The growth of Indian entrepreneurial talent can be made directly dependent on their control over capital and on the length of their apprenticeship in modern industry. The allegedly high rate of population growth which is

[27] See, for example, Coupland: *India: A Restatement*, pp. 59–63.
[28] W. A. Lewis: 'Economic development with unlimited supplies of labour', *The Manchester School*, XXII (1954).

often cited as a cause of arrested growth in India during this period,[29] can be taken as decreasing the volume of investible surplus in the economy. These additional features would not alter the mechanics of the model in a fundamental way.

The basic limitation of this model is the same as that of the supply-based complex of hypotheses that I discussed earlier. This model also fails to take into account the fact that investment in most fields of modern industry was limited not by the supply of savings but by the lack of profitability of domestic investment in those fields, whether undertaken by Indian or by European capitalists. In support of this charge we can refer to some microeconomic evidence such as statements of Indian and European capitalists denying the lack of capital for investment in industry and to such dramatic incidents as the raising of capital by the Tata Iron and Steel Company and the virtual cessation of foreign borrowing by the Government of India and the provincial governments in the 1930s. The microeconomic evidence is discussed in greater detail in Chapter 6. If industrial growth is limited by the lack of capital, we would expect this to be reflected in balance of payments crises and in internal inflation which cannot be attributed primarily to external causes. Neither of these developments came about during the period in question. With the sole exception of several years when the foreign exchange situation was affected by a virtual breakdown of the international payments mechanism and by short-sighted government economic policy, India had a surplus in the balance of trade and in the balance of payments throughout the period under consideration. Again, apart from several war and post-war years, there was little inflation in India which could not be attributed primarily to impulses transmitted from abroad. These macroeconomic developments are discussed in greater detail in Chapters 2 and 3.

Most of the supply-based hypotheses have an air of automaticity about them. If the supply of savings was inadequate this was primarily because the share of the Indian capitalists in national income was not high enough; if the wages of industrial labour were low, this was because the density of population was high and the rate of growth of population was also high; if the supply of raw materials did respond to increase in demand (in the more sophisticated versions of the hypotheses) this was because the peasants responded to the market mechanism. But no sustained enquiry has been made into the possible reasons for the smallness of the share of the Indian capitalists in the national income, such as the barriers to entry into trade and industry imposed by European dominance, the maintenance of a precapitalist form of social organization partly by deliberate imperial policy and partly by forces indigenous to Indian society. It is not recognized that the real wages of labour were affected by many forces other than those that

[29] See Anstey, 'Economic development' and *idem, The Economic Development of India* (London, 1957).

a model of pure competition would recognize,[30] and that the real wages moved very differently in different parts of the country. In particular, it is not recognized that if the supply curve of labour appeared perfectly elastic at a constant real wage in some parts of the country, such as eastern India, this might be because of deliberate policies pursued by the British managing agency houses assisted by the government at different levels and not just because of the demographic forces making for a larger and larger population subsisting at the same level. (In any case, between 1901 and 1921 the average rate of growth of population of India was low by the standards of Western Europe and the U.S.A. in the nineteenth century.)[31] Lastly, little account is taken of the research sponsored by the Government of India in making possible some technical changes in agriculture which allowed the peasants successfully to adapt to increasing demand for agricultural raw materials. Thus the supply-oriented theories place too much stress on the impersonal working of the market mechanism and too little stress on the British imperial and British Indian policies in hindering (and in some cases, assisting) Indian economic development during this period.

The complex of hypotheses that is put forward in this book starts from the other side and looks at the profitability of investment and ease of entry into different fields by European and Indian industrialists to explain the major changes in the levels and patterns of investment. This way of looking at the problem does not rule out the possibility that at some stages of the story supply factors could be important. In a dynamic sequence it is not always possible to assign primacy to one or the other set of factors. But it does take into account the observed fact that in macroeconomic terms there was a slack in the Indian resources for industrial development. It also recognizes the fact that investment is the father of further investment, particularly in the presence of unemployed resources. If the investible surplus commanded by European and Indian capitalists taken together or by Indian capitalists taken as a separate group was low in one period, it is because the opportunities for making profit through investment had been restricted in the previous periods. Putting it the other way round, if there had been a sustained growth of investment by Indian and European capitalists in India, fostered by deliberate government policies of the kind

[30] On the ways in which employer–labour relationships could deviate from the model of impersonal pure competition see Daniel Thorner: 'Employer-labour relationships in Indian agriculture' in Daniel and Alice Thorner: *Land and Labour in India*.

[31] The annual rate of growth of population per thousand was 9.9 for the whole of Europe, 9.6 for Great Britain and Ireland, and 13.2 for Germany between 1801 and 1900. See D. V. Glass: 'World population 1800–1950' in H. J. Habakkuk and M. Postan (eds.): *The Cambridge Economic History of Europe*, Vol. VI, Part I (Cambridge, 1965), pp. 56–138, at p. 62. The estimated population of the United States grew from 5,486,000 in 1801 to 76,094,000 in 1900. See U.S. Bureau of the Census, *Historical Statistics of the United States, Colonial Times to 1957* (Washington, D.C., 1960), p. 7. The estimated population of India by contrast increased from 285,244,000 in 1901 to 305,623,000 in 1921. See Davis: *Population of India and Pakistan*, pp. 26–7.

that had already been made familiar through the experience of Prussia, Japan and the U.S.A., to take the most notable examples, then the resources for further investment would also have expanded at a positive rate. If the fruits of investment and economic growth had not been completely restricted to the upper classes, then the markets for the various consumer goods would also have expanded faster; and finally a high rate of growth of investment would have made for a high rate of growth of capital and intermediate goods if appropriate policies had been pursued.

If it is urged that all these possibilities belong only to the realm of speculation, then on the same ground one can question the validity of the supply-oriented models of stagnation. For in order to generalize about Indian experience and single out particular aspects of the observed phenomena as causal factors, one must have specific theoretical constructs in mind. The empirical bases of those constructs must in turn be built up from the experience of other countries where the rates of economic growth were high. Thus it is legitimate to pick out those aspects of the Indian and social scene which distinguished India from advanced economies which were not enmeshed in the British imperial system. For, during the period from roughly 1880 to 1914, India was practically the only sizeable economy which was forced to pursue a policy of free trade and non-intervention in industry.[32] To overlook the nature of the political and social system in India and her special place in the British imperial system and single out such end-results of the working of the whole process as the continued stagnation of observed investment in industry and the continued poverty of ordinary people as causative factors is to mistake the symptoms for the cause of the disease.

APPENDIX TO CHAPTER 1

In this appendix we offer a more rigorous and more extended analysis of the issues that were raised in Section 1.3 (i.e. the section dealing with 'Investment in industries producing for an internal market under tariff protection').

We assume that after tariff protection has been introduced the domestic price of the protected commodity has reached an equilibrium determined by the market structure of the domestic producers and the conditions of world supply of the commodity (the prices of all other commodities remaining unchanged). Thus at the ruling post-protection price of the protected commodity, the quantity demanded is determined. Then the basic model of investment at time t in the industry enjoying tariff protection is

$$I(t) = \frac{dK(t)}{dt} = \lambda(\bar{K}(t) - K(t)) \qquad (1.1)$$

$$= \lambda(v\bar{Y}(t) - vY(t)),$$

---

[32] The state did engage in the construction of social overhead facilities, but this again was meant primarily to promote trade or military objectives (or in a limited number of cases, to prevent famines).

where $I(t)$, $K(t)$, $\Upsilon(t)$, $\bar{\Upsilon}(t)$, v, and λ, denote investment, the existing capital stock, the domestic output for domestic consumption, the total domestic demand, the marginal (=average) capital–output ratio, and the speed of response of investment in the protected industry, respectively. The rate of investment is thus proportional to the difference between the desired capital stock, $\bar{K}(t)$ and actual capital stock $K(t)$ in the protected industry. If total domestic demand, and therefore, the desired capital stock, is a constant, so that one can write $\bar{K}(t)=\bar{K}$, a constant independent of time, equation (1.1) has the solution

$$K(t)=\bar{K}-(\bar{K}-K(0))\ e^{-\lambda t} \qquad (1.2)$$
$$=K(0)\ e^{-\lambda t}+(1-e^{-\lambda t})\ \bar{K},$$

where $K(0)$ is the initial capital stock in the protected industry. It is obvious from equation (1.2) that investment in the protected industry declines exponentially over time (assuming, naturally, that $\bar{K}>K(0)$).

If we assume that domestic demand for the protected product increases at the proportional rate α over time, so that $\bar{K}(t)=\bar{K}(0)e^{\alpha t}$, then the growth of the capital stock in the protected industry follows the pattern given by

$$K(t)=\frac{\lambda}{\alpha+\lambda}\bar{K}(0)e^{\alpha t}+(K(0)-\frac{\lambda}{\alpha+\lambda}\bar{K}(0))e^{-\lambda t} \qquad (1.3)$$
$$=\frac{\lambda}{\alpha+\lambda}\ \bar{K}(0)\ (e^{\alpha t}-e^{-\lambda t})+K(0)e^{-\lambda t}.$$

In this case the long-term rate of growth of investment is the same as the long-term rate of growth of domestic demand for the protected product. The model has the implication that the absolute (though not the proportional) difference between 'desired' and actual capital stock grows exponentially over time, as one can see by computing

$$\bar{K}(\ )-K(t)=\bar{K}(0)e^{\alpha t}-K(t)$$

with the help of equation (1.3). This is not as disturbing as it sounds at first, because in a steadily growing economy, one would expect the sectoral rates of investment to be growing at the same rate as the respective components of demand. Suppose we have a steadily growing economy with all the sectors growing at the same rate. Then it is necessary that the expected demand in the next period should be higher than the demand in the current period by the same percentage as the rate of growth of the economy; it is also necessary for the steady growth of the output of the capital goods industry that the gap between the desired and actual capital stock should be widening at the rate at which the economy is growing.

It may be objected that whatever may be the needed behaviour for the growth of the economy at a steady rate, in real life entrepreneurs do learn and may catch up with actual demand, and the approach to the desired capital stock is not indefinitely postponed. While this is partially true – this, incidentally, is one of the more potent of the factors causing growth to be unsteady – this argument fails to recognize that entrepreneurs acting independently can learn and yet fail to catch up with actual demand, for each individual entrepreneur is faced by a small segment of the total demand. If they all increase their output by the same percentage as before, without new entry into the field, the gap between total demand and actual production will expand at the rate at which total demand is growing.

Although the investment function used here applies more naturally perhaps to an industry which enjoys effective tariff protection, it can also be used to explain the course of investment in the weaving section of the cotton-mill industry in India before the First World War. While the mill-owners of India tried to overtake 'desired capacity' in the fields (such as medium-quality printed goods and grey goods) which they considered to be their own, the 'desired capacity' itself was expanding with population growth, the rise in average per capita income and (perhaps) change in tastes, so that actual capacity did not catch up with the 'desired capacity'. One would under these circumstances expect both imports and domestic output of cotton piecegoods to grow. The higher rate of growth of domestic piecegoods may be explained by (a) learning on the part of Indian mill-owners which enabled them to weave finer varieties of cloth over time, and (b) (possibly) a higher rate of growth of demand for medium-quality cloth. The fluctuation in total investment in the cotton-mill industry is to be explained, as we have indicated in the body of Chapter 1, primarily in terms of the elimination of yarn exports as a factor governing investment.

This type of adjustment function has been used extensively in the literature on trade cycles and cyclical growth, particularly by R. M. Goodwin[33] and A. W. Phillips.[34] The adjustment function can be rationalized in several different ways. First, the larger the gap between 'desired capacity' and actual capacity, the

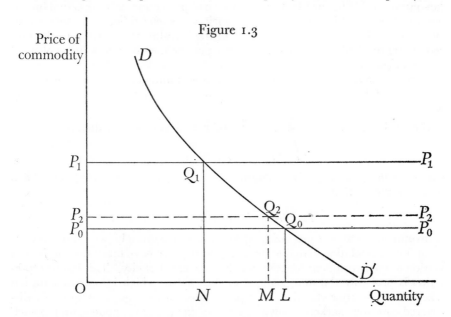

Figure 1.3

[33] 'Secular and cyclical aspects of the multiplier and the accelerator' in *Income, Employment and Public Policy* (New York, 1948); and 'The nonlinear accelerator and the persistence of business cycles', *Econometrica*, Vol. 19, 1951, pp. 1–17.

[34] 'Stabilisation policy in a closed economy', *Economic Journal*, LXIV, June 1954, and 'A simple model of employment, money and prices in a growing economy', *Economica*, Vol. 28, November 1961.

greater is the expectation of profit in the short run and therefore the larger is the amount of investment made by existing firms and by new entrants in the industry. This can best be seen if we draw a simple diagram (Figure 1.3) illustrating the effects on demand of the imposition of a protective tariff on a commodity. Suppose that the price of the commodity before tariff protection was introduced was that indicated by the line P_0P_0, and that immediately after the imposition of the tariff the price moves up to P_1P_1. At this price for the product a number of firms are attracted to the industry, but with increasing production, the price of the product moves down (assuming purely competitive conditions); as the price moves down, investment by the less efficient producers decreases, and some inefficient firms are forced out of production, until at a price of P_2P_2 only the most efficient domestic producers survive. At this price no importing can take place (because the minimum price at which importers can supply in the long period is given by P_1P_1) nor does any new investment take place. Our investment function implies that the approach of domestic sales (by importers and producers) from point Q_1 to point Q_2 (which indicates the equilibrium combination of price and output) will be slowed down over time.

The second rationalization of our investment function is in terms of a lag in the actual investment process. It is assumed that domestic producers correctly aim at producing the total domestic demand that will be forthcoming eventually (an output of OM in our Figure 1.3) after tariff protection. But the actual investment is distributed in a declining geometric series over time, the investment in every period being a constant fraction of the investment occurring in the preceding period. This lag in the investment process may be due to technological and financial reasons.

Finally, one can also interpret our adjustment function to mean that the expectations of domestic producers about further sales are formed in the following way:

If expected sales in period t are S_t^*, and actual sales are S_t, then

$$S_t^* - S_{t-1}^* = \beta(S_{t-1} - S_{t-1}^*),$$

where β is the coefficient of expectations adjusting actual to expected sales. Then it can be shown that

$$S_t^* = \beta S_{t-1} + (1 - \beta)\,\beta S_{t-2} + \cdots$$

If investors then aim at producing S_t^* and invest accordingly, we get our investment function relating actual to desired capacity (we have taken the continuous version of the investment function for the sake of simplicity). This last interpretation is probably the most natural in the case in which import substitution takes place not after effective tariff protection but as a response to newly-discovered cost and marketing advantages over the foreign suppliers; and as such this is the interpretation that comes closest to explaining the behaviour of investment in the weaving branch of the cotton-mill industry in India before the First World War.[35]

[35] For the various rationalizations of the investment function used, see A. R. Bergstrom: *The Construction and Use of Economic Models* (London, 1967), pp. 27–8. For an

If we assume that several industries engage in import substitution at the same time, and that they have no important interconnections between themselves on the supply side, then the total volume of investment can be found simply by adding the investments in all the industries:

$$\sum_{i=1}^{m} I_i(t) = \sum_{i=1}^{m} \lambda_i \left(\bar{K}_i(t) - K(t) \right),$$

where subscript i refers to the ith industry and m is the number of industries concerned. If the desired capacity of each of the industries remains the same, total net investment will eventually tail off. If the demand for industry $i(i=1,\ldots,m)$ is expanding at the proportional rate α_i $(i=1,\ldots,m)$, then the investment in the ith industry will eventually grow at the rate α_i, and the aggregate investment in the import-substituting industries will grow at a rate lying between the lowest and the highest of the α_i's $(i=1,\ldots,m)$.

If, however, there are important interconnections on the supply side between the different industries, then total investment will grow at a higher rate than will obtain if we consider import substitution in each of the industries separately. The larger the number of industries which are interconnected in this way, the larger will be the amount of income generated in the industrial sector, other things being equal. Of course, the mere existence of interconnections on the input side will not lead to the growth of intermediate and capital goods industries: the price relations have to be such that it is more profitable to use domestically produced intermediate or capital goods than to import such goods. The importance of economies of scale, the experience needed in producing these goods and the rapidity of technical change in such industries will determine how important state help will be in making possible the growth of large intermediate or capital goods sectors. Historical experience suggests that innovations originating in capital goods industries are a major source of technical change in advanced countries; but the capital goods industries generally need bigger markets, expanding at a positive rate, than consumer goods industries. This is particularly true if we contrast the conditions for efficient operation of, say, machinery-making industries and consumer goods industries producing relatively non-durable goods such as cotton textiles, sugar or paper. In order that the capital goods industries should be securely established and expanded, a continuous growth in investment in the other industries must take place and this presumes the existence of either developed capitalism or a state policy striving for economic growth in the long run. Mere protection for home industries in conditions of recession is not likely to lead to the growth of sophisticated capital goods industries.[36]

extended discussion of the class of adjustment functions to which the investment function used by us belongs, see Marc Nerlove: 'Time-series analysis of the supply of agricultural products' in E. O. Heady and others (eds.): *Agricultural Supply Functions – Estimating Techniques and Interpretation* (Ames, Iowa, 1961).

[36] On the role of capital goods industries in the generation of innovations and growth in capitalist countries, see Karl Marx: *Capital: A Critical Analysis of Capitalist Production* translated by Samuel Moore and Edward Aveling and edited by Frederick

Before we close this discussion two complications should be mentioned. First, our simplest adjustment function, equation (1.1) (on page 25), will lead to a path of investment which declines exponentially from the very beginning. Actually, however, the response of the industrialists to the discovery of investment opportunities will not be instantaneous but will take place after a delay of a finite period. It can be shown that this will lead to a path which is similar to the one shown in Figure 1.1[37] (on page 14).

The second complication is that we have implicitly assumed pure competition in the product markets. Suppose we remove this assumption and introduce the polar assumption that there is only one domestic producer of product i and there is no threat of entry of another producer. Then the only constraint on the price

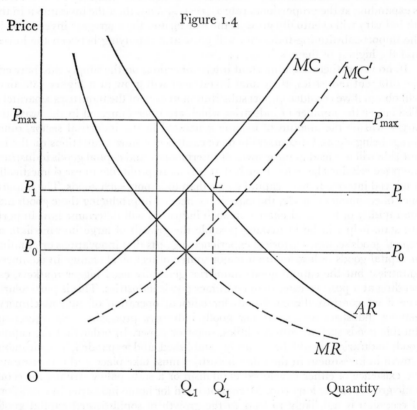

Figure 1.4

Engels (London, 1957), Part IV, Chapter XV, 'Machinery and Modern Industry'. On the conditions for exploitation of economies of specialization and of scale in capital goods industries with special reference to underdeveloped countries see Nathan Rosenberg: 'Capital goods, technology and economic growth', *Oxford Economic Papers*, N.S., Vol. 15, 1963, pp. 216–27, and the articles of J. R. Hicks, S. Kuznets and G. Stigler there referred to. For an attempt to measure technical change by giving due weight to innovations in capital goods industries see L. L. Pasinetti: 'On concepts and measures of changes in productivity', *Review of Economics and Statistics*, Vol. 41, 1959, pp. 270–86.

[37] See A. W. Phillips: 'Stabilization Policy and the Time-Form of Lagged Responses', *Economic Journal*, LXVII, June 1957.

that he may charge is that it must be equal to or lower than the import-preventing price P_1P_1 in Figure 1.3. In Figure 1.4, P_0P_0 is the world price for the product and P_1P_1 the price of the imported product after the tariff has been imposed. AR is the demand curve for the commodity and MR is the marginal revenue curve associated with it. Suppose MC is the marginal cost curve of the only domestic producer of the product. If this producer could effectively behave as a monopolist in a protected market without threat of entry, then the profit-maximizing price for him would be given by P_{max}, the price which corresponds to the output level at which the MR curve cuts the MC curve. If as a result of tariff protection the price is pushed above P_{max}, then the monopolist's best policy in the short run would be to fix the price P_{max}; of course, the monopolist could then also practise price discrimination, selling this output at a higher price in the protected domestic market and at a lower price in foreign markets. If the post-protection price is below P_{max}, the 'monopolist' can no longer take AR as the demand curve facing him; rather, the demand curve facing him is perfectly elastic at the post-protection price (such as P_1P_1 in the diagram) up to the point where the price line cuts AR, assuming that there is no collusion or oligopolistic interdependence among the major suppliers of the product. The output produced by the sole producer will thus be given at the point of intersection of the MC curve and the appropriate price line. The total amount of investment undertaken by the sole domestic producer will be determined by the difference between the initial and the post-protection outputs sold by him.

It is possible for the marginal cost curve of the domestic producer to cut the AR curve below P_1P_1 (the post-protection line). In that case, the effective marginal revenue curve facing the domestic producer will coincide with P_1P_1 up to point at which it cuts the AR curve (L in Figure 1.4) and then with the curve which is marginal to the AR curve. Thus there will be a large range of discontinuity in the effective MR curve corresponding to the kink in the effective demand curve (at L) of the domestic producer. So long as the marginal cost curve of the producer cuts the effective MR curve within the range of discontinuity (this possibility is illustrated by MC' in Figure 1.4), the most profitable price for the domestic producer will remain the post-protection price (or a price slightly below it to take account of xenophilia in consumption). The most profitable post-protection output will depend, thus, on the competitive conditions and the cost structure facing the producer. This analysis is valid only so long, of course, as the profit made by the domestic producer is 'normal' after allowing for both variable and fixed costs.

If we relax the assumption that there can be only one domestic producer, then as a first approximation we can say that the number of plants that can be profitably set up in the industry will depend on the extent of the domestic demand at the post-protection price (assuming that it is lower than P_{max}), on the importance of economies of scale in the industry and on the speed of response of investors to the creation of a protected domestic market through tariffs on imports. If there is a uniform post-protection price, and if the MC curves of different sellers are similar in shape and turn upwards, then the number of plants that can be supported profitably will be found to be the number (plus one, in case of there being a fractional part) obtained by dividing the total domestic demand by the profit-maximizing output of any one plant. One single firm may, of course, operate several plants. If investors react rapidly to the creation of the protected domestic market, then it is possible for there to be over-investment in the industry: the number of plants erected may be such that not all of them can break even at the post-protection price. Then a process of exit of some firms and of revaluation of capital will have to ensue: it is possible for equilibrium to be reached at a price which is lower than the immediate post-protection price and at an output which is higher than what could be sold in the domestic market immediately after the introduction of tariff protection. It is then possible for all imports to be cut off since it is impossible for any foreign producer to sell at the new price, which will have to cover both the costs of the foreign producer and the import tariff on the product. Thus we can see that even if there are no strong increasing returns to scale, or learning by doing in the domestic industry, the initial impulse given by tariff protection may lead to a situation where the increase in price due to tariff protection and the consequent decrease in domestic consumption are largely eliminated over time. It is also clear that if the speed of response of investors is directly proportional to the degree of tariff protection imposed, then with plausible values of the parameters of the cost curves and the degree of depreciation of capital in case of reinvestment, the best way of eventually getting rid of the evils of tariff protection is to impose a high rate of tariff protection to begin with.

Let us assume that there are already some producers of the product when an import tariff is imposed on the product. If the initial amount of investment required for a plant of an economic size (in the sense that below that size economies of scale are not exhausted) is large, then there may be little new investment if the initial rate of tariff protection is low: most of the investment will normally take the form of extensions undertaken by existing firms and the price for the protected product will be determined by the world price plus the premium covering the import tariff. If, however, the rate of tariff protection is high, then new entrepreneurs will be induced to set up plants with a large enough capacity. If in the normal course these plants embody more advanced techniques, then their eventual costs of production will be lower than the costs of the established producers with older plants. It can be argued that if the new producers are eventually able to produce at lower total costs than the established producers, then even without tariff protection they could come in and drive the established producers out of the market or at least force them to lower prices. But this argument does not hold if (a) the initial investment required is large and (b) there is a teething period during which the costs of the new entrepreneurs with plants of current vintage continue to be high. For either or both of these reasons the established producers will want a reasonable margin in the form of tariff protection or other types of government help in order to hedge against initial losses or against eventual failure because of competition from abroad.

The picture becomes more complicated when there are a few established producers who can through deliberate policy prevent the entry of new firms. If the product is homogeneous, then obviously the established producers cannot charge more than the price P_1P_1, which is the world price augmented by the tariff per unit of the imported product. However, the established producers can try to charge a price which is just below P_1P_1, meanwhile expanding their capacities so as to exploit economies of scale. If, because of limits on the availability of finance or limits to expansion imposed by geographical factors, the established producers cannot supply the whole domestic market and prevent the entry of new firms, they can try to enter into price-fixing and/or market-sharing agreements with the new firms and thus prevent prices from going below certain economic levels. These tactics will be more successful the greater the initial amount of investment required, the more imperfect the capital market, the more significant the economies of scale and the greater the costs involved in building up output to the capacity level and in learning by doing.[38]

The experience of the sugar and paper industries in India illustrates the cost-reducing potential of the entry of new firms with latest-vintage plants; the experience of the cotton industry shows how locational factors can alter the relative degrees of efficiency of established producers and new firms in new locations; and the experience of the iron and steel, and cement and paper industries shows how established producers can try to use price-fixing and market-sharing agreements to keep up their own profits and make it more difficult for new firms to encroach on their preserves. The increase in the degree of tariff protection for the cotton-mill industry and later the restriction of Japanese exports of cotton goods to India under a quota system may have led to a slowing down of technical change in the cotton-mill industry in the form of adoption of automatic looms.[39] But in all the cases considered the computation of the cost of tariff protection by taking the cost conditions in the Indian industry at the beginning of effective tariff protection and comparing them with world prices would almost certainly lead to an over-estimation of the ultimate cost of tariff protection to the consumer, granting that such comparisons do have a bearing on the right policy to adopt.

In the last few paragraphs I have indicated broadly under what circumstances we can expect an industry enjoying tariff protection to be dynamically efficient. The bigger the size of the market, the lower the barriers to the entry of a new producer, the less depressed the money-market conditions after the grant of tariff protection, and the less the degree of dependence of an industry on a continuous growth of demand in the economy in general for profitable expansion, the greater in general will be the degree of dynamic efficiency of the protected industry as measured by the fall in its cost of production over time. Tariff protection may in fact create the conditions under which new investment eliminates pockets of inefficiency by the replacement of obsolete methods and the expulsion of badly-managed firms. But tariff protection for some consumer goods industries alone, in an under-developed, poor economy such as India, cannot create the conditions for continuous economic growth which alone can keep the established or new industries abreast of their counterparts in more developed countries.

[38] Many of the issues raised in the above paragraphs have been discussed at a more abstract level by F. Modigliani in 'New developments on the oligopoly front', *JPE*, LXVI, June 1958, pp. 215–32. See also the criticisms of the Bain–Sylos–Modigliani model by F. M. Fisher, and D. E. Farrar and C. F. Phillips, Jr, and Modigliani's reply in *JPE*, LXVII, August 1959, pp. 410–19.

[39] See Chapter 7, the final section.

2

THE ECONOMIC POLICY OF THE GOVERNMENT OF INDIA

The behaviour of private investment depends as much on government policy affecting various sectors of the economy as on the general condition of the people and the state of development of techniques. Governmental policies in India were rarely conceived with a conscious view to affecting the economy as a whole, partly because the information available to the government was often very meagre. There were only some parts of the economic life of the country which chiefly occupied the attention of the bureaucrats ruling India. Nevertheless, other areas of the economy were affected, if only because some aspects of policy such as the encouragement of foreign trade or keeping up the reputation of the Government of India in the London money market would rule out certain options for the encouragement of modern industry. In order to study the impact of different aspects of government policy in different periods of the era we are covering, governmental policies are classified in accordance with the variables which were being immediately manipulated: we study under fiscal policy the major features of the expenditure policies of the Government of India, under commercial and industrial policy the impact of import tariffs or subsidies for the development of industry, and under monetary policy the impact of the banking organization and the currency system of India, both of which could be affected intimately by the actions of the government. The study of these policies is roughly broken up into the period up to the First World War and the interwar period, but the line of demarcation in real life was not always sharp. Commercial policy after the First World War cannot really be separated from fiscal policy and hence no separate section has been devoted to it. The industrial policy of the Government of India after the war, and particularly after the introduction of so-called provincial autonomy was more or less synonymous with the industrial policies of the different provinces taken together. Hence the relevant section concentrates on the latter. It is not implied that the different facets of government policy could be put together in any way one pleased: there would be organic relations between, say, the maintenance of a gold exchange standard with a stable value of the rupee and a rigid adherence to financial orthodoxy. It is only for expository convenience that we chose this particular taxonomic scheme, which does not preclude us from treating the relations of the various aspects of policy either in their intention or in their impact.

2.1 FISCAL POLICY UP TO THE FIRST WORLD WAR

Balancing the revenue account of the budget was the prime article of faith with all Finance Ministers (or Members) of the Government of India. Up to 1924–5, railway accounts were merged with the accounts of the Government of India, and the balance between revenue and expenditure was struck after including railway (and irrigation) revenues and expenditures in the general budget. This balance was quite uncertain during the nineties mainly because of (a) the operating deficit contributed by the railways, (b) the instability of the exchange (a fall in the value of the rupee contributing to an increase in the cost of home charges), (c) the tendency of the opium revenue to fall, and (d) the impact of the famine of 1896–7 on both the revenue and the expenditure of the government.[1] Out of eight financial years from 1890–1 to 1897–8 four produced surpluses and four deficits (the sum of the deficits exceeded the sum of the surpluses). The deficits were kept from growing larger only by increased taxes, including the import duty on cotton piecegoods and the countervailing excise duty imposed in 1895.

By contrast, the financial years from 1898–9 to 1913–14 produced a surplus in every year except in 1908–9. The deficit in the latter year was largely due to the transference of the major share of the provincial rates, that is, the rates levied chiefly for the construction and repair of roads, the upkeep of schools and dispensaries, village sanitation, and other local expenditure, on the annual rent or revenue of the land (the rates varying in different provinces), from the accounts of the Government of India to those of local bodies, whereas the costs of many local works were assumed by the central government.

The stability of the exchange value of the rupee under the gold exchange standard definitely contributed to the continuing surpluses of the Government of India, by eliminating losses (often unforeseen) owing to the sudden fall in the value of the rupee. However, there was an underlying buoyancy in the economy due primarily to the world-wide expansion of trade and production, particularly in the richer countries, and this buoyancy contributed both to the increasing revenues of the government and to the increasing exports and imports of India. The stability of the rupee under the gold exchange standard was the product of increasing exports, a favourable balance of trade and a substantial amount of foreign investment (in the

---

[1] See P. J. Thomas: *The Growth of Federal Finance in India* (Oxford University Press, Indian Branch, 1939), Part v; *Banking and monetary statistics of India* (Reserve Bank of India, Bombay, 1954), pp. 872–7; Speech of G. K. Gokhale in *Indian financial statement for 1904–5 and the proceedings of the Legislative Council of the Governor-General thereon* (PP 1904, LXIII, pp. 256–9).

sense of transfer of real resources from Europe) primarily under government auspices.[2]

With the emerging budget surpluses and the stability of the exchange value of the rupee, there were three basic fiscal alternatives before the Government of India: (a) to reduce taxation; (b) to increase expenditure on social services, particularly health and education; (c) to increase expenditure on public works, such as railways and irrigation works. There were advocates for all three courses of action. There was one school of thought comprising both British Government officials and nationalists, or sympathizers with the nationalists, which considered the land revenues to be too high.[3] There were some who considered the land revenue demands of the government to be reasonable in the aggregate but criticized them for being inflexible. Neither the prosperity of the government officials nor the major expenditures of the government were closely connected with the prosperity of the people, because land revenue demands did not vary proportionately with the incomes of the cultivators: thus in years of famine the land revenues had still to be paid, except when they were specially suspended or remitted.[4]

Without going into the question of the relative burden of taxation on the representative Indian, one can say that the tax system was quite regressive in the beginning of the century: land revenues contributed more than a third of the total revenues in the year ended 31 March 1900. Customs revenue and central excise, together contributed another 14% or so of total revenues; and these three groups of taxes made up about two-thirds of total tax-revenues. Income taxes which were assessed at very moderate rates at first on non-agricultural incomes (with special exemptions for salaries of military personnel) above Rs. 500 per year yielded only about 2–3% of total revenues. Since agricultural incomes were exempt from taxes, and since land revenue was assessed on the land rather than on the income of the holder of the land, the system was quite definitely regressive.

[2] The classic study of the gold exchange standard is J. M. Keynes: *Indian Currency and Finance* (London, 1913), Chapter 2; the best study of the mechanism of adjustment of the Indian balance of payments under the gold exchange standard is Y. S. Pandit: *India's Balance of Indebtedness, 1898–1913* (London, 1937), Part II.

[3] For the most provocative statement of this point of view, see Digby: *'Prosperous' British India*, particularly Chapter IV; for a better documented statement of the same point of view, see R. C. Dutt: *The Economic History of India in the Victorian Age* (first published London, 1904; Indian edition, Delhi, 1960), Preface, and Parts II and III. Dutt also argued that the periodic enhancements of state demands after new settlement surveys were inimical to agricultural progress and introduced a basic uncertainty about the rights and income of the cultivator. See also E. Thompson and G. T. Garratt: *Rise and Fulfilment of British Rule in India* (London, 1934), pp. 565–7, 593–5.

[4] For an able presentation of the case for flexibility of land revenues and against enhancement of demand after a new settlement see the note of Rai Bahandur B. K. Bose, official representative of the Central Provinces in the Imperial Legislative Council in *Indian financial statement for 1902–3 and proceedings* (PP 1902, LXX, Appendix I, pp. 299–306).

The government made some concessions to the group pleading for lower taxation, firstly, by remitting substantial amounts of land revenue in the years during and immediately after the famines of 1896–7 and 1899–1900, and by raising the exemption limit for income tax (in the budget for 1903–4) from Rs. 500 to Rs. 1,000. (This left untouched the fortunes of the ordinary Indian whose average income was Rs. 30 according to Lord Curzon's estimate but it pacified the rich traders, lawyers and industrialists.) Secondly the duty on salt was lowered successively from Rs. 2½ to Rs. 2 per maund in 1903–4, from Rs. 2 to Rs. 1½ per maund in 1905–6, and finally to Re. 1 per maund in 1907–8.[5]

The government also made slight concessions to the group pleading for greater expenditure on education and social services. Although Lord Curzon had recognized that the provision of more extensive and better quality education involved greater expenditure, only miniscule amounts were actually spent on education:[6] the amounts spent in 1903–4, 1904–5 and 1905–6 amounted, for example, to Rs. 20·46 million, Rs. 22·12 million and Rs. 24·49 million respectively, when total expenditure on the revenue account in all these years exceeded Rs. 840 million. The demand for more primary or secondary education did not find any strong political expression; the demand for higher education did find vocal expression both in the Legislative Council and outside it, but the government did not want to swell the ranks of political agitators by adding to the number of lawyers and unemployed or badly paid Arts graduates. As far as technical education was concerned, the lack of industrial development, and the existence of prejudice against Indians in the industries controlled by Europeans and in the Public Works Department of the Government of India, limited the number of possible jobs quite drastically; and the Government of India early recog-

---

[5] The official reason given for the retention of the salt tax in spite of its unpopularity was that it should prove convenient in the event of a major war. See Lovat Fraser: *India under Curzon and After* (London, 1911), p. 357. Indian nationalist opinion pointed to the elasticity of salt consumption with respect to changes in salt tax as evidence of the extreme poverty of ordinary people. See Gokhale's speech in the Imperial Legislative Council during the 1907–8 budget session, reproduced in R. P. Patwardhan and D. V. Ambekar (eds.): *Speeches and Writings of Gopal Krishna Gokhale* (Poona and London, 1962), p. 109. Most of the increase occurred in India excluding Burma since the salt tax was Re. 1 per maund in Burma throughout this period.
The total consumption of salt in India (including Burma) was as follows (in maunds):

1902–3	*1903–4*	*1904–5*	*1905–6*	*1906–7*
36,663,409	37,602,945	39,131,607	40,729,173	43,086,000

Source: Gov. India, Commercial Intelligence and Statistics Department (CISD), *Financial and commercial statistics of British India* (Calcutta, 1900–7).

[6] On the educational policy of the Government of India under Lord Curzon and subsequent Viceroys up to 1921, see Thompson and Garratt, *Rise of British Rule*, pp. 571–4; Fraser, *India Under Curzon*, pp. 175–200; for a short but good survey of the educational policy of the Government of India, see J. R. Cunningham, 'Education', in L. S. S. O'Malley: *Modern India and the West* (London, 1941).

nized the perils of increasing the number of dissatisfied technically qualified men.[7]

On the increase of expenditure on railways there was a clear divergence of opinion between the British mercantile community in India and Britain, and the Indian nationalists. The British businessmen definitely wanted the Government of India to spend more money on railways than they had been spending up to the end of the nineteenth century.[8] For a country of the size of India, Pakistan and Burma, less than 20,000 miles of railways were open up to 1895; and only 24,752 miles were open in 1900. There were vast tracts of land which were not served by any railways, major or minor. The famines of 1896–7 and 1899–1900 were aggravated by the lack of adequate railway communication in vast tracts of the country away from the ports. The railways as a whole had been making a loss up to 1899–1900; but this was partly because under the old guarantee system the government had to bear the entire losses of all losing systems and only had a small share in the surplus profits of the paying systems – so that there was a tendency for all paying systems to inflate their losses and for all losing systems to keep their ways unchanged – and partly because a sizeable proportion of the railways constructed at the end of the nineteenth century were strategic railways built mainly for military purposes.[9] With the improvement of trade and the buying off of some of the old companies' interests, the fortunes of the railways improved:[10] even in years of famine such as 1899–1900 and 1900–1, the railway revenues increased because of increased movement of grains from one part of India to another and from foreign countries to the affected parts (practically half) of India. Naturally with the improvement in railway and government finances, and increasing trade, merchants demanded better railway connections,

[7] See Lord Lansdowne's address to the University of Calcutta in 1889 and Government of India's *Review of Education in India* (1886), quoted in Cunningham, 'Education', pp. 164–5.

[8] For the views of Manchester merchants see A. Redford: *Manchester Merchants and Foreign Trade*, Vol. II: *1850–1939* (Manchester, 1956), Chapters III and IV; for the views of the Bombay Chamber of Commerce (largely but not exclusively representing British business opinion in Bombay) see R. J. F. Sulivan: *One Hundred Years of Bombay* (Bombay, c. 1937), Chapters XXII and XXIII; for the views of the Bengal Chamber of Commerce (representing the British businessmen of Eastern India) see G. W. Tyson: *The Bengal Chamber of Commerce and Industry, 1853–1953: A Centenary Survey* (Calcutta, 1953), p. 110; for the views of the Karachi Chamber of Commerce (representing the British businessmen of Sind and Punjab) see Herbert Feldman: *Karachi through a Hundred Years* (Karachi, 1960), Chapter V.

[9] See, for the history of the finances of Indian railways up to 1921, *Report of the Committee appointed by the Secretary of State for India to enquire into the administration and working of Indian Railways* (PP 1921, x), Chapter VII.

[10] One can see from *ibid.*, Appendix No. 3, that the improvement of railway finances owed greatly to the decrease in the guaranteed interest through the purchase of private companies by the state: in 1894–5 the guaranteed interest came to £5,233,064; by 1900–1, this had declined to £2,532,430.

and a better co-ordination of the programmes of different railways. The Government of India first appointed Thomas Robertson as a special commissioner to report on the administration and working of Indian railways. On Robertson's recommendation[11] the Railway Board was constituted to look after the interests of Indian railways as a whole and to prepare capital programmes of railways. Later, a committee was appointed under the chairmanship of Sir James L. Mackay (later Lord Inchcape) to enquire into the financing and administration of Indian railways. The Mackay Committee recommended a programme of capital expenditure of £12·5 million annually for the foreseeable future.[12] The railway construction programme certainly picked up in 1907–8, but there had been a gradual increase in capital expenditure on railways from 1898–9 onwards.[13] The actual capital expenditure did not reach the target of £12·50 million (Rs. 187·5 million) in most of the subsequent years as the figures in Table 2.1 will show.

TABLE 2.1   *The capital programmes of Indian railways* (Rs. million)

1908–9	150.0	1915–16	120.0
1909–10	150.0	1916–17	45.0
1910–11	163.0	1917–18	54.0
1911–12	142.5	1918–19	63.0
1912–13	135.0	1919–20	265.5
1913–14	180.0	1920–1	219.8
1914–15	180.0	1921–2	178.2*

* Including a sum of Rs. 28·2 million to cover loss by exchange.

Source: Report of the Committee appointed by the Secretary of State for India to enquire into the administration and working of Indian Railways (PP 1921, x), p. 21.

From the published official data, it is difficult to make out exactly the extent to which engineering firms in India benefited from the capital programmes of the railways: in some years, the ratio of total imports of railway plant and rolling stock to the total capital programme was less than half; in some other years (for example, 1913–14) the ratio was well above half of the capital programme and in fact, above half of total gross investment in railways. These fluctuations probably reflected variations in replacement of rolling stock and stock-building by the railway companies. One cannot

[11] Thomas Robertson (Special Commissioner for Indian Railways): *Report on the administration and working of Indian Railways* (PP 1903, XLVII, pp. 483–702).

[12] *Report of the Committee on Indian Railways finance and administration* (PP 1908, LXXV, p. 14).

[13] See, for estimates of total capital expenditure on the railways, M. J. K. Thavaraj: 'Capital Formation in the Public Sector in India: A Historical Study', in V. K. R. V. Rao *et al.* (eds.): *Papers on National Income and Allied Topics*, Vol. 1 (London, 1960), pp. 215–30. The capital programmes of the Indian railways, however, were lower than total gross investment in all railways in India, since the latter included capital programmes of railways not under the control of the Railway Board.

conclude that the gap between the total imports of railway plant and rolling stock and the gross investment in railways is a measure of the orders obtained by the engineering firms in India; for, apart from the items classified under railway plant and rolling stock, there were other items such as cement, and iron and steel, which went into railway investment. Furthermore, a major part of the construction work was done in railway workshops (in 1911, while factories classified as railway workshops employed 98,723 persons, those classified as machinery and engineering workshops employed only 23,147 persons).[14]

There is no doubt, however, that engineering industries depended to a considerable extent on railway programmes and that there was considerable pressure on the government to buy a larger and larger proportion of railway requirements in India.[15] In September 1905 the Railway Board issued instructions to the State Railways (a major part of the railways in India at that date were managed by companies) to call for tenders in India for the supply of 25% of any sanction for goods stock. But this was subject to the condition that most of the rolling stock supplied should be of *bona fide* Indian manufacture and not just an assembly of imported parts.[16] There were also other restrictions on the purchasing officers; in practice, not very much progress was made in the direction of purchase of Indian materials for the railways until the war. But the engineering firms benefited from construction, including bridge-work orders placed by the railways.[17]

It is easy to understand that Indian public opinion should not be as enthusiastic about railway construction as British business opinion was: only a fraction of the total railway expenditure was spent in India, and the firms which benefited from that fraction – whether situated at Bombay, Calcutta, Cawnpore, Madras or Mazaffarpur – were almost always controlled by European businessmen. Moreover, there was a feeling that railways were competing for funds with irrigation, which had been for long a rather neglected subject: in spite of the fact that irrigation yielded

[14] *Census of India, 1911*, Vol. 1, Part 1: *Report* (Calcutta, 1913), p. 444 (Subsidiary Table x).

[15] See the speech of A. A. Apcar (representing the Bengal Chamber of Commerce) during the budget session, 27 March 1907, in the Imperial Legislative Council. Apcar pointed out the acute shortage of railway wagons all over the country (quoting the President of the Bombay Chamber of Commerce), stressed the need for long-term programmes for railway rolling stock as well as construction of news lines, and pleaded the case for purchasing wagons at a steady rate from the two engineering firms in Calcutta (Burn and Company, and Jessop and Company) which had recently set up wagon-construction plant. According to Apcar, about 60% of the cost of wagons was spent on imported materials, and 40% on labour and materials in India. See *Indian financial statement for 1907–8 and proceedings* (PP 1907, LVII) pp. 196–9.

[16] See the speech of J. F. Finlay in *Indian financial statement for 1907–8 and proceedings* (PP 1907, LVIII), pp. 217; and the speech of W. L. Harvey in *Indian financial statement for 1908–9 and proceedings* (PP 1908, LXXIV), p. 207.

[17] See Chapters 9 and 10 below on the iron and steel industry and the engineering industry.

a positive net revenue, even after allowing for unproductive and protective works (whereas railways as a whole had incurred huge losses up to the end of the nineteenth century), the budgeted capital expenditure on irrigation was generally only a quarter or even less of the capital expenditure on railways. This discrepancy tended to widen rather than lessen in the years of surpluses of the Government of India; for in a year of a revenue surplus, the government pushed through a bigger programme of railway construction, whereas the capital expenditure on irrigation was increased only slightly, if at all. Before the famines of 1896–7 and 1899–1900, the government had been very reluctant to spend money on any works other than 'productive' works. Productive works were defined as those which would meet the working expenses, as well as the interest charge on the accumulated capital, within ten years from their initiation. As was pointed out later,[18] none of the railways could have met the rigid test laid down for productive irrigation works.

Indian public and official opinion urged that spending money on irrigation, particularly in areas of uncertain rainfall such as the Central Provinces and the Bombay Deccan, might be a better way of preventing the loss from famines, than constructing railways for carting grain once famine had occurred.[19] The Irrigation Commission of 1901–3 outlined a programme of major works which would cost Rs. 440 million and would be spread over a period of twenty years or so. They also recommended protective works – mainly in the form of storage tanks – in areas which were particularly susceptible to failure of rainfall and which did not have rivers with enough annual flow to sustain perennial irrigation canals.[20] The tempo of expenditure on irrigation seems to have picked up after the Report of the Irrigation Commission was published, but the percentage increase in public investment in irrigation between, say, 1900–1 and 1913–14 was lower than the percentage increase in gross public expenditure on railways: the figures of gross investment in the two years under the two heads are as follows:[21]

	Railways (Rs. million)	*Irrigation* (Rs. million)
1901–1	83.7	24.1
1913–14	230.6	48.4

[18] K. T. Shah: *Sixty Years of Indian Finance* (London, 1927), p. 323 n. On the history of irrigation in British India and its results in terms of revenue see Sir Bernard Darley: 'Irrigation and its Possibilities' in Radhakamal Mukherjee (ed.): *Economic Problems of Modern India*, Vol. 1 (London, 1939), pp. 148–67; Shah: *Sixty Years of Indian Finance*, pp. 318–30; *Report of the Indian Irrigation Commission, 1901–03*, Part I: *General* (PP 1904, LXVI), pp. 11–23.

[19] See the speech of Rai Bahadur B. K. Bose, official representative of the Central Provinces in the *Indian financial statement and proceedings* for the years 1900–1 and 1901–2 (PP 1900, LVII, pp. 200–3; and PP 1901, XLIX, pp. 246–52).

[20] *Report of the Indian Irrigation Commission, 1901–03*, Part I: *General* and Part II: *Provincial* (PP 1904, LXVI).

[21] Source: Thavaraj: 'Capital Formation in the Public Sector in India', p. 224.

One can argue that from the point of view of maximizing the revenue of the government or from the point of view of providing the overhead capital for the development of agriculture and trade, the expenditure policy of the Government of India was unduly conservative. Whereas the major irrigation works on an *average* yielded a net revenue of 7% and above, and whereas the major irrigation works at the margin yielded much more than 7%, the Government of India could raise loans in London at an average cost between 3% and 4% throughout the period; they could also raise loans in India at a slightly higher cost (between 3·5% and 4·5%). The Mackay Committee in 1908 went into the question of the safe limits of borrowing by the Government of India in London and found that they could borrow £9 million in normal years;[22] but the annual average of loans raised by the Government of India and the railways together in the London market works out to £6,303,233 for the 15 years from 1900 to 1914.[23]

It can be argued that further investment in railways and irrigation works before the First World War would have swollen total expenditure and therefore aggravated the problem of rise in prices. But this probably is not a compelling argument, for two reasons: in the first place, the stimulus for the rise in prices came to a considerable extent through the rise in prices of Indian exports, and it was not easy to see how, in general, an increase in expenditure in India could have affected export prices very much. In the second place, one can argue that a very large percentage (at least 50%) of the increased government expenditure would have leaked abroad in the form of increased imports of capital goods and in the form of salaries for technical personnel who habitually sent large fractions of their incomes to the U.K. For the very same reason, however, an increased capital expenditure by the government on railways and irrigation by itself would have exerted only a weak influence on the further development of Indian industries. The multiplier effects of government expenditure might still have been large, if the marginal propensity to consume was large, but the effects on further investment could not have been great, given the under-developed nature of most of India's domestic industries, and given the conditions of free trade under which they operated.[24] So one can see that those Indian publicists who wanted tariff protection for the new industries had a case in their favour after all.[25]

[22] *Report of the Committee on Indian Railways finance and administration* (PP 1908, LXXXV), p. 14.

[23] *Report of the Committee on the administration and working of Indian Railways* (PP 1921, x), p. 30 n.

[24] On the disappointing results of railway development in India compared with other countries with an extensive network of railways, and their causes, see Daniel Thorner: 'The Pattern of Railway Development in India', *The Far Eastern Quarterly*, XIV (2), February 1955, pp. 201–16.

[25] The concern for the effects of European competition on the few Indian industries that there were was not confined to Indians: the paper industry and the sugar refineries

2.2 THE FISCAL POLICY OF THE GOVERNMENT OF INDIA
FROM THE FIRST WORLD WAR TO THE
DEPRESSION OF THE THIRTIES

Since at first the war was expected to last for a short while, the Government of India did not raise taxes to meet the increased expenditure, for increased taxes were supposed to be needed only for permanently increased expenditure. But by the time of the budget session of 1916–17, it was clear that the war would go on; the Government of India also found it difficult to raise loans in England for the latter was hard pressed. Hence in 1916, the general tariff was raised from 5% to $7\frac{1}{2}$% *ad valorem*, and the duty on imported sugar to 10% to protect the local industry. The imports of some articles, including machinery other than that required for cotton spinning and weaving, railway materials, and ships, were to be taxed at $2\frac{1}{2}$%. Some other articles from the old free list were to pay the general tariff of $7\frac{1}{2}$%. Duties on iron and steel and on the other metals were also raised: exports of tea and raw and manufactured jute were subjected to tax. Slight increases were made in income tax rates for upper income brackets. Next year the duties on exports of raw and manufactured jute were raised. Further, cotton piecegoods were for the first time since 1894 brought under the general tariff of $7\frac{1}{2}$%. Thus were laid the foundations of the scheme of discriminating protection.

In the meantime the public debt and interest charges were increased by the Government of India's borrowings both for defraying the expenditure of the Indian Army in India and abroad (partly), and for contributing *ex gratia* to the British war effort £100 million in 1917 and a further £45 million in the last month of the war.[26] The war added Rs. 100 million to the interest charges of India, and it gave rise to an increase of about Rs. 250 million in the permanent military expenditure of India. Further, during the war the Government of India invested heavily in sterling securities, partly as a measure to stabilize the rate of exchange at 1s. 4d., and with an increase in interest rates and the rise in the Indian rate of exchange during the years from 1918 to 1920 the government sustained heavy losses.

were largely under British control, and British businessmen were naturally worried about their fate. See the speeches of Sir Montagu Turner in *Indian financial statement for 1903–4 and proceedings*, p. 167 (PP 1903, XLVI) and E. Cable (later Lord Cable) in *Indian financial statement for 1904–5 and proceedings*, p. 193 (PP 1904, LXIII). Turner applauded the countervailing duties on imported sugar imposed by the Government of India and hoped for their continuation; Cable deplored the excise duties on cotton piece-goods produced in Indian mills, particularly if they became a permanent impost, and expressed concern lest the paper industry of India were similarly burdened, when it was facing stiff competition in the Indian market from Austrian paper mills.

[26] For an account of the finances of the Government of India during the First World War, see Shah: *Sixty Years of Indian Finance*, pp. 415–39.

Thus the postwar period was marked by largely increased expenditures on current account while the revenues had not expanded correspondingly. Hence there was a large increase in the public debt of India over the years from 1918–19 to 1923–4, most of the increase having taken place in the debt registered in India.[27] Since these years were also marked by considerable uncertainty in exchange rates and inflation, private business regarded the increased government borrowings with great misgivings, particularly after the collapse of the boom. The Government of India appointed a Retrenchment Committee in 1922, consisting primarily of businessmen.[28] This committee recommended drastic cuts in expenditure which affected not only military and other current expenditure, but also capital programmes for irrigation and for the rehabilitation of railways which had been badly overworked for the last seven or eight years.[29]

It is interesting to ask why a committee of private businessmen should recommend drastic economies in the expenditure of the government, when normally increased public expenditure would add to private profits. The reasons were probably: first, that the businessmen also believed in the doctrine of balanced budgets along with the officials of the government; secondly, that the businessmen in India did not gain very much from increased capital expenditure on railways or defence; thirdly, that the government was competing with the bigger private businessmen in the organized money market for loans and raising the rate of interest; fourthly, that the businessmen feared that the alternative to curtailed expenditure must be an increase in indirect, and (from their point of view much more dangerously), in direct taxes, which were admittedly low in India; and finally, that there was an appreciation of the connection between total expenditure and the rate of rise in prices in an economy with rather inelastic supply schedules for most commodities.

From 1923–4 onwards, partly as a result of improvement in general economic conditions, the Government of India again managed to generate reasonably large surpluses in the current account. But the memory of the post-war years continued to dampen the courage of the government.[30] The

[27] The total deficits from 1917–18 to 1922–3 amounted to more than Rs. 980 million. See G. F. Shirras: 'Public finance in India', *The Annals of the American Academy of Political and Social Science*, Vol. 145, 1929, Part II, p. 117.

[28] The members of the Indian Retrenchment Committee, 1922–3, were Lord Inchcape (British India Steam Navigation Company), Sir Thomas S. Catto (later Lord Catto, at the time partner of Andrew Yule and Co.), Dadiba Merwanji Dalal, Sir R. N. Mookerjee (Martin Burn), Sir Alexander R. Murray (Chairman, Bengal Chamber of Commerce), Purshotamdas Thakurdas, and H. F. Howard (Secretary).

[29] *Report of the Indian Retrenchment Committee* (Delhi, 1923). The savings recommended by the committee amounted to Rs. 193 millions, the largest economies being effected in military expenditure, railways, and post and telegraphs.

[30] Shirras, in 'Public finance in India', wrote: 'The years 1917–18, and their immediate successors, were years of unbalanced budgets and are a real blot in the history of Indian finance' (p. 117).

Government of India was later criticized for being extremely timid in its borrowing policy and not borrowing enough money in London in the good years of the twenties. Even during the period of the thirties the 'credit' of the Government of India in the London money market and in India had not suffered much, in spite of the political disturbances and in spite of the 'nationalization' of the biggest company railways such as East Indian and Great Indian Peninsula Railways.[31] It was, however, during the thirties that the Government of India pursued the policy of 'sound finance' with a doctrinaire zeal as we shall see presently.

The policy of discriminating protection adopted by the Government of India in 1923 was a piecemeal one: no general policy of industrialization was ever adopted by the government at this time.[32] It did not escape the attention of the high officials of the Government of India that exports from India were expanding even during the twenties at a slower rate than the exports of advanced countries such as Canada or the U.S.A.,[33] and that the terms of trade between manufactures and agricultural products had changed drastically against the latter.[34] It was also sometimes recognized that the low productivity of agriculture in India prevented the growth of industries demanding a large home market. But the sole practical response of the Government of India to these difficulties in the 1920s was to adopt the principle of discriminating protection. The protection was to be afforded only to industries which (a) had natural advantages, (b) might not develop at all or might develop too slowly without protection, and (c) would eventually be able to face world competition without tariff protection.

The method of application of the policy of discriminating protection made it even more ineffective in operation. The government was not bound to refer every application for discriminating protection to a Tariff Board; the Tariff Board was not bound to submit its report within any specified period of time;[35] and finally, the government was not bound either to accept the recommendations of the Indian Tariff Board or the resolution of the Legislative Assembly if the latter ran counter to government pro-

[31] For views of politicians and businessmen in London about the borrowing policy of the Government of India, see the speeches of George Pilcher and Sir Campbell Rhodes at the meeting of the Royal Society of Arts at which Sir Basil Blackett (who had been Finance Member of the Viceroy's Executive Council) presented his paper, 'The Economic Progress of India', in the *JRSA*, LXXVIII, No. 4,028, 31 January 1930, pp. 312–36.

[32] See Pillai: *Economic Conditions in India*, Chapter XI; H. R. Soni: *Indian Industry and Its Problems*, Vol. I (London, 1932), Chapters VIII and IX; and Anstey: *Economic Development of India*, pp. 350–1.

[33] See, e.g. Blackett: 'The Economic Progress of India', p. 318.

[34] H. A. F. Lindsay (Indian Trade Commissioner in London): 'World Tendencies Reflected in India's Trade', *JRSA*, LXXV, No. 3,876, 4 March 1927, pp. 391–3.

[35] The time taken by the Government of India to come to a decision about whether or not to protect a particular industry was often very long; in the case of the cotton-textile industry it was thirty-one months. See *Report of the Fiscal Commission, 1949–50* (Delhi, 1950), pp. 50–1.

posals.[36] Furthermore, the period for which tariff protection was given was often far too short: new entrants into industry did not have the confidence that the government would come to their assistance in case of trouble from foreign competition.

In practice, during the twenties, the only major industries which were protected were the steel industry and some branches of mechanical engineering, paper and matches. There was a high import duty on sugar but it did not serve the purpose of protection. Subject only to the introduction of the policy of weak discriminating protection, the fiscal and industrial policy of the Government of India during the twenties was the same as before the First World War.[37]

When the depression of the thirties overwhelmed the capitalist world and its colonies, the Government of India clung even more closely to the principles of sound finance. A clear, if dogmatic, account of such principles can be derived from the budget speeches of the Finance Member (Sir George Schuster) of the Government of India during the years from 1929 to 1934. Here is a typical statement: 'I feel, moreover, most strongly, on general grounds, that this is not the time when, keeping in view our credit in the world, we ought to attempt any substantial diminution in our provision for reduction or avoidance of debt. Anything that savours of a "raid" on a public sinking fund is normally – and, I think, quite rightly – viewed with disfavour.'[38] Another quotation from the same source will reveal the general tenor of government economic policy at this time: 'The time has not yet come for panic measures or desperate experiments which might land us in unknown complications or endanger the efficiency of the whole machinery of Government. What we need rather is to give unremitting care to details, stick to principles of sound finance, to work hard, keep our heads, and pull together. Above all, it is necessary to be sound in our finance.'[39] Salaries of public servants were cut, and there were also some economies in defence services, and increases in customs duties, but the main burden of adjustment fell on capital expenditure, particularly on investment in railways and irrigation. The deflationary policy was so savagely pursued that the revenue account showed a deficit only in the years 1930–1 and 1931–2. The excuse for this policy could not be severe balance of payments difficulties, for India had a surplus in merchandise accounts in all the years of the thirties except for 1932–3, according to

[36] For the *modus operandi* of the policy of discriminating protection up to 1927, see Sir David T. Chadwick (who was a member of the Indian Fiscal Commission of 1922): 'The Work of the Indian Tariff Board', *JRSA*, LXXVI, No. 3921, 13 January 1928.

[37] A Minute of Dissent to the Report of the Indian Fiscal Commission recommended a policy of rapid industrialization through protection.

[38] See *Indian financial statement and budget of the Governor-General of India in Council for 1930–31* (PP 1929–30, XXIII), speech of the Finance Member in introducing the budget for 1930–1, p. 11.

[39] *Indian financial statement and budget for 1931–2* (PP 1930–1, XXII), Part II, p. 2.

statements prepared by the Government of India itself.[40] If we take the movements of 'treasure' into account we find a surplus in commodity transactions throughout the period.[41] In fact, the Government of India took advantage of the situation to repatriate large amounts of sterling debt. Nor can the reasons for the caution of the Government of India be found in the state of the capital market for public loans. Even if the Government of India might have felt it unsafe to borrow in the London money market for various reasons, it could borrow large amounts in India at low rates of interest: in May 1936, for example, the Government of India raised Rs. 120 million at par with a maturity up to 1948–52 at $2\frac{3}{4}\%$.[42] Thus the government seemed to have been too cautious, even judged by the usual canons of safe finance.

The curious thing is that the people at the top were aware of the needs of India for the purpose of long-term economic development. The same Finance Member who was the high priest of sound finance during his tenure of office, could later talk impressively about the need for co-ordinated long-term planning for the whole of India, and for balanced development of different regions of India, with industry brought to the countryside, rather than people being moved from agriculture to overcrowded urban slums.[43] The explanation for this hiatus between intellectual understanding and practice would take us outside the scope of this study, but it appears that paralysis of will as far as economic decision-making was concerned set in among the top British officials long before the transfer of power to the Indians had taken place.

2.3 THE COMMERCIAL AND INDUSTRIAL POLICY OF THE GOVERNMENT OF INDIA UP TO THE FIRST WORLD WAR

Before the First World War, the dominant policy pursued by the Government of India was one of free trade. Low revenue tariffs on cotton piece-goods were introduced in 1894; there were also duties on petroleum and salt. But in the case both of cotton piecegoods and of salt there were offsetting excise duties on Indian produce. A countervailing duty on bounty-fed sugar was introduced in 1899, and the rate was increased in 1902–3 to check the sale of beet sugar from Europe. But following the sugar convention of 1903 the duty was reduced again. One can say

[40] A. K. Banerji: *India's Balance of Payments* (London, 1963), Chapter 7.
[41] *Ibid.*, Chapter 5.
[42] Reserve Bank of India: *Report on Currency and Finance for the years 1935–6 and 1936–7* (Bombay, 1937), p. 3.
[43] Sir George Schuster: 'Indian Economic Life: Past Trends and Future Prospects', *JRSA* LXXXIII, No. 4306, 31 May 1935, pp. 641–69. See also Blackett: 'The Economic Progress of India', pp. 313–27.

that before the First World War there was no import duty which intentionally or unintentionally protected an Indian industry to a significant extent.

This, of course, was quite contrary to the trend in the rest of the world, including the British Dominions. Practically all the countries with any modern industry of any size had erected tariff walls against goods from other countries, and particularly against goods from Britain. India was the most important market for the most important export of the U.K., namely, cotton piecegoods.[44] The concern of Lancashire at any proposal to introduce the principle of protection in the Indian budget was therefore understandable. The U.K. was the most important source of supply of industrial goods for India, and also supplied between 61% and 66·7% of the annual imports of private merchandise of India during the years from 1901 to 1914.[45] This proportion would be larger if we added invisible trade, for the U.K. controlled practically the whole of ocean shipping and a slightly smaller fraction of coastal shipping; the important foreign exchange banks were all British; and the insurance services were also provided predominantly by British firms. The index of dependence of India on the U.K. for imports would be even greater if we took into account imports of government stores, for these were almost wholly of British origin.

On the other side, Britain was the largest purchaser of exports from India, but as against more than 60% of the visible imports of private merchandise (and a much larger percentage of total imports) coming into India from the U.K., only between 23·4% and 30·1% of Indian exports were taken by the U.K. over the years from 1901 to 1914. Even if we take the British Empire as a whole, the proportion of Indian exports going to it does not rise to 50% or more in any of the years except 1901 and falls to 37·7% in 1914.[46] This pattern of trade suited British needs quite well; for, on the one hand, Britain had a large market where her goods entered duty-free when other markets were closing against her. On the other hand, a large portion of Indian exports (primarily raw materials and manufactured jute) going to countries outside the Empire meant that India earned a large export surplus with continental Europe and with the hard-currency areas of America with which the U.K. had normally a large deficit.[47]

---

[44] S. B. Saul: *Studies in British Overseas Trade, 1870–1914* (Liverpool, 1960), Chapter VIII. The average values of imports of cotton piecegoods as a percentage of total Indian imports came to 38·8, 36·0, and 36·2 over the periods from 1900–1 to 1904–5, 1905–6 to 1909–10 and 1910–11 to 1913–14 respectively. See Venkatasubbiah: *Foreign Trade*, p. 28.

[45] Venkatasubbiah: *Foreign Trade*, p. 32.

[46] *Ibid.*, p. 33.

[47] Saul: *Studies in British Overseas Trade*, Chapter III, particularly pp. 62–3.

Thus contrary to the impression left by many commentators who were sympathetic to Indian businessmen or economists pleading for tariff protection, it was not only the interests of Lancashire that were served by a free-trade policy in India: it served the interests of the imperial system as well. It also probably goes to explain the opposition of Whitehall in view of frequent appeals for fiscal autonomy made by British and Indian businessmen and British officials in India.[48]

An interesting turn-of-the-century debate on the economic importance of India in the British imperial system and its relevance to questions of 'fiscal reform' in Britain was published in the *JSA*.[49] J. M. Maclean, a convinced free trader, wanted Britain and India to remain on the path of free trade. He pointed out the immense importance of India in imperial defence and the role of the Indian army in defending interests throughout the East, including China and East Africa. He laid stress on the thousands of Englishmen who found 'honourable and liberal employment' in India. He also pointed out that 'She remains the one market in the world which is perfectly open to us, and is by far the largest buyer Lancashire has for the produce of her looms.'[50] Maclean was afraid that any protective tariffs imposed by Britain or by India would invite retaliation by other countries against one or the other. It was admitted in the discussion, in which Sir Charles Elliott, Sir Edward Sassoon, Sir Henry Fowler, Sir Richard Temple and Sir Frederick Young took part, that in the usual debates on fiscal reforms India was left out of account, but this was because India was bound to obey whatever policy Parliament laid down. There was no question of reciprocity between Britain and India: when Britain imposed duties on coffee and tea, she did it without India's permission. It would have been difficult to find changes in tariffs which would benefit both India and Britain; but there were cases in which India could profitably bargain with other countries if she imposed protective tariffs on items imported from these countries (petroleum from Russia was cited as an example). However, the discussion left the impression that the fear of retaliation against British and Indian goods leading to the loss of hard-currency earnings was a factor in the policy of free trade pursued by the British Government before the war.

There was also the view that whatever the rest of the world might do, Britain, and India under her guidance, would stick to the true path of free trade and long-term prosperity. One could claim that the increasing

---

[48] For a survey of Indian political opinion on the issue of protection see Bipan Chandra: *The Rise and Growth of Economic Nationalism in India* (New Delhi, 1966), Chapters II, III, VI.

[49] J. M. Maclean: 'India's Place in an Imperial Federation', *JSA*, LII, No. 2, 665, 18 December 1903, pp. 81–90, and the discussion following Maclean's paper, *Ibid.*, pp. 90–5.

[50] *Ibid.*, p. 85.

trade of India was proof that she was doing well out of a system under which she produced raw materials and food-grains and bought manufactured goods from the U.K. When Sir Theodore Morison claimed to discover the signs of an economic transition in India similar to those that were to be found in England before the Industrial Revolution, he was rebuked by Keynes for wishing on India a course which was more likely to lead to loss for India than to prosperity.[51]

This does not mean, of course, that the Government of India believed in complete *laissez-faire* for India, outside the fields of investment in railways and irrigation.[52] A Department of Commerce and Industry was created by the Government of India in 1905 with a member of the Viceroy's council in charge of it. A Director of Commercial Intelligence was appointed and the *Indian Trade Journal* was launched under his control. It is doubtful how much active help the new department rendered to the growth of industries in India: there was no positive policy of assistance and difficulties were apparently experienced in filling the post of the member in charge of Commerce and Industry.[53]

More significant were the developments initiated by the Governments of Madras and the United Provinces. In Madras, Alfred Chatterton began experiments in the manufacture of aluminium vessels when he was appointed the Superintendent of the School of Arts. The encouraging results of the experiment led the Government of Madras to submit proposals for employing Chatterton for the purpose of furthering the progress of industrial and technical education in the Madras Presidency. These proposals having been approved by the Secretary of State for India, and Chatterton having succeeded in developing the manufacture of aluminiumware (with imported aluminium ingots and sheets), a department of industries was created in August 1906, though not under that name, and Chatterton was put in charge, with the title of Director of Industrial and Technical Inquiries. Chatterton was engaged in (a) the manufacture of aluminium in a pioneer factory (which was turned over in September 1903 to a European barrister, Eardley Norton, as a going concern, with half the net profit (which came to Rs. 60,000) made by the government handed over as a free gift to

[51] Sir Theodore Morison: *The Economic Transition in India* (London, 1911), Chapter VII. Morison spoke of Prussia as an example for India. Keynes reviewed the above book in *Economic Journal*, XXI, September 1911, pp. 426–31.

[52] For examples of the departures from *laissez-faire* made by the Government of India in the nineteenth century see S. Bhattacharya: 'Laissez Faire in India', *The Indian Economic and Social History Review*, II (1), January 1965, pp. 1–22.

[53] See Fraser: *India under Curzon and After*, pp. 307–8. Curzon's achievements in the fields of commerce and industry seem to have been the simplification of procedures in the Customs Houses of various ports, the reduction of charges for overseas and internal telegraph services, the revision of mining and prospecting rules (in 1899) to remove the obstacles which private prospectors had to face previously, and the encouragement of the manufacture of steel by the house of Tata.

the new company); (b) the introduction of improved methods of chrome tanning; (c) the improvement of methods of weaving handloom cloth; (d) the introduction of improved methods of lift irrigation with the help of oil engines, and (e) the digging with modern boring tools of deeper wells capable of using oil engines for pumping water. A factory at Salem was started for the purpose of training weavers in improved methods. The department also tried unsuccessfully to introduce pencil manufacture in the Presidency. Usually, the reasons for failure seemed to be inability to start on a large enough scale, to survey the local market or sources of materials adequately before beginning the work and to procure suitable experts. Good experts were unlikely to be attracted by the subordinate positions and salaries offered to them. Proposals to utilize the power from the Periyar dam for industrial development in Madras fell through owing to the opposition of the Inspector-General of Irrigation; proposals to start a wood-distillation factory were squashed as a result of opposition from a committee of non-official gentlemen who objected to a government factory of large enough scale to succeed, because it would interfere unduly with private enterprise.

Because of the same objection, all efforts at starting pioneer factories by the Government of Madras (and any other official body in India) were squashed by Lord Morley, who was then the Secretary of State for India, in his despatch dated 29 July 1910. In taking this step he seems to have been supported both by his own liberal principles and by the objections, raised earlier by European businessmen organized in the Madras Chamber of Commerce, to the proposals adopted in the Industrial Conference at Ootacamund, which had been convened by the Government of Madras.[54]

The efforts made by the Government of the United Provinces began later and were altogether more modest. They were initiated as a result of the proposals adopted at the Industrial Conference at Naini Tal, convened by the government in 1907; these included the appointment of a Director of Industries, who was also at first made the head of a technological institute; later the headship of the institute was separated and a scientist was put in charge of it. The government granted loans to several concerns, and appointed a Sugar Engineer, but the direct efforts of the latter were hamstrung by the unsuitability of the small plant on which the experiments were carried out, and by the fact that the borrowing concerns were not obliged to seek his help or put up with his inspection. The government also started a cottonseed-oil mill at Cawnpore under the management of a European agency firm but this mill was closed down, as a result of Lord

[54] For a description of the work done by the Department of Industries in Madras up to 1916, see *Report of IIC* (PP 1919, xvii), Appendix J; see also Pillai, *Economic Conditions in India*, pp. 311–12.

Morley's despatch, before it could show any results, positive or other-wise.[55]

Even after these efforts were restarted, primarily under the stimulus of the demand for direct and indirect military supplies created by the First World War, they were concentrated on developing small-scale industries and helping the small man through guidance rather than on giving any substantial financial help to large-scale industries. The money handled by the Department of Industries was also meagre: even in the most pro-gressive province, Madras, the total amount of private money handled by the Department of Industries in 1913–14 was Rs. 500,000.[56] A few years later we find the Director of Industries in Bombay objecting to the establish-ment of a state school for instruction in weaving because the annual cost would come to Rs. 1,500 as against the original estimated cost of Rs. 600 per annum.[57] P. J. Mead, the Director of Industries, was a senior collector in Bombay both before and after he held the post of Director of Industries. As a senior collector, he had a salary of Rs. 27,900 p.a. that is, more than Rs. 2,250 *per month*.[58] He proposed to employ part-time demonstrators of improved methods of weaving for the sake of economy. The next Director in the Report for 1918–19 pointed out that the use of part-time demon-strators had already been proved unsatisfactory in other provinces because weavers abandoned the new methods as soon as a difficulty cropped up. Weaving schools provided a more thorough instruction. Behind the small scale on which state aid to industries was conceived, there was an idea that the state was there only to awaken interest in small industries and guide the entrepreneurs in their first steps. There was no systematic policy of helping new industries by any active financial assistance or guarantee of the market.

Alfred Chatterton, the first *de facto* Director of Industries, Madras, was easily the most enthusiastic and most effective official advocating government help for industrial development. His views on the sources of

[55] For a short summary of the work done by the Department of Industries of the Government of the United Provinces, see *Report of IIC* (PP 1919, xvii), pp. 68–9; for an account of the history of the Nawabganj factory to which the Government Sugar Engineer was attached, see *Report of the Indian Sugar Committee* (Simla, 1920), pp. 269–273. The decision to appoint a Sugar Engineer in 1911 was a direct result of the demand of Indian opinion that indigenous sugar should be protected: instead of increasing duties on imported sugar, the government decided to appoint Mr Hulme as Sugar Engineer with the specific task of improving indigenous methods with small plant. The factory at Nawabganj was put up during the season 1914–15 for the manufacture of crystal sugar or alternatively *gur*. The mill could crush only 24 tons of cane a day as against the minimum crushing capacity of 1,000 tons a day recommended by the Indian Sugar Committee for a government pioneering factory in Upper India.

[56] See K. Tressler, Director of Industries, Madras: 'Industries' in S. Playne (compiler) and A. Wright (ed.): *Southern India* (London, 1915), p. 626.

[57] Department of Industries, Bombay: *Annual Report, 1917–18*, p. 2.

[58] See *India Office List for 1920* (London, 1920), pp. 213 and 654.

industrial growth were Smilesian, tinged with some degree of paternalism.[59] It was not only Indians who considered the scale of the effort made by the state up to about 1916 too small. See, for example, the evidence to the Indian Industrial Commission of Sir W. B. Hunter, Secretary and Treasurer, Bank of Madras. 'In my opinion it is very desirable that in this Presidency Government should pioneer industries and establish demonstration factories...I think the time has come when all energies and funds should be turned on to really big things allowing in the meantime small things to be promoted by private enterprise...above all there should be no limit of any kind whatever to the aid which may be given to enterprises because it competes with an established external trade.'[60]

2.4 INDUSTRIAL POLICIES OF THE PROVINCES OF INDIA

At about the end of the war, Departments of Industries cropped up in many provinces of India. Some of them suffered from the very beginning from a shortage of staff and (one suspects) lack of priority in official attention. The history of the Department in Bombay illustrates this to an extreme degree. It was started on 31 October 1917, with a senior Indian Civil Servant, P. J. Mead, in charge with a clerk and 'the usual belted attendant'. The first seven months were spent mainly in looking at similar work in the U.P. and Madras and in setting up an office. The new Department took over the work on handloom weaving from the Registrar of Co-operative Societies.[61] A new Director was appointed on 18 April 1919, and in May the new Director also took charge as Controller of Munitions, Bombay Circle. There was no full-time staff at the command of the Department. It relied for expert advice on the part-time services of officers of other departments, including professors at technical institutes and colleges. The Department lost its part-time expert on handloom weaving, the head of the textile section of the Victorian Jubilee Institute, through retirement early in 1919. In February 1920, a new officiating Director of the Department was appointed since the Director was on leave: he was handicapped because of his additional duties in connection with the winding up of munitions operations in Bombay. The Department acquired the services of a new Mechanical Engineer, who later acted as Assistant Director of Industries, Northern Division, Ahmedabad.[62] At the

[59] See for example, A. Chatterton [listed in Bibliography under *Official publications: Indian provincial governments*, hereafter abbreviated as IPG pub.]: *Note on Industrial Work in India* (Madras, 1905), particularly p. 8. See also Tressler: 'Industries', pp. 622–4.

[60] *Evidence (Report of IIC)*, Vol. III (PP 1919, XIX), p. 276.

[61] Department of Industries, Bombay: *Annual Report, 1917–18* (Bombay, 1919), pp. 1–2.

[62] *Idem, Annual Report, 1918–19* (Bombay, 1920), pp. 1–2.

end of 1920 the old Director, R. D. Bell, returned, and the acting Director, G. H. Thiselton-Dyer, a mechanical engineer, could revert to his duties as Deputy Director, but proceeded on leave. The Assistant Director of Industries, Northern Division, was entirely occupied until January 1921 in overhauling and repairing a dilapidated distillery plant belonging to the government.[63] Thiselton-Dyer took up his duties as Deputy Director on his return from leave in September 1921. All the officers had to perform duties hardly connected with the Department of Industries throughout 1921–2.[64] While the services of a marine biologist were obtained on loan from the Ministry of Fisheries and Agriculture, the posts of Superintendent of Fisheries and Assistant Marine Biologist (of which the latter had not been filled), were retrenched during 1921–2. In May 1923 a new Director was appointed. No new appointments were made during 1922–3; as a measure of retrenchment the Ahmedabad office of the Department was closed, and the officers continued to be occupied with duties not connected with the Department.

In view of the limited activities of the Department and a vote of the provincial Legislative Council in March 1924 to abolish the post of Director of Industries as a measure of retrenchment, the Department was closed in 1924. Most of its activities were distributed among other departments. The Dapuri engineering workshops, which had originally been organized under the Public Works Department, for war work, and which had been transferred to the Department of Industries in 1921–2, were transferred back to the Public Works Department, along with the Deputy Director of Industries.[65] The Dapuri workshops had been hampered in their operation by peculiar restrictions, so their transfer to the Public Works Department might not have been a great loss from the point of view of the development of public enterprise and might in fact have been a gain insofar as it re-established their close connection with government public works. Along with many private commercial concerns, the Dapuri engineering workshops also suffered large losses in 1920–1 and 1921–2.[66] When the Department was closed, the pioneer factories started by the government for manufacturing magnesium chloride at Kharaghoda and casein at Anand had to be closed down, for these also were unprofitable.[67]

The Department of Industries was re-started in July 1925 and it proceeded to act on more or less the same lines as Departments in other provinces. The main activities of the Department were:

[63] *Idem, Annual Report, 1920–21* (Bombay, 1921), p. 3.
[64] *Idem, Annual Report, 1921–22* (Bombay, 1922), p. 4.
[65] The transfer of the workshops had already been effected during the year 1922–3. See *idem, Annual Report, 1922–23* (Bombay, 1923), p. 4.
[66] *Idem, Annual Report, 1921–22, pp. 32–4.*
[67] *Bombay, 1923–24, a review of the administration of the Presidency* (Bombay, 1925), pp. 85–6.

'(1) Supply of commercial intelligence to private enterprises.
(2) Professional or technical advice and assistance to minor industries.
(3) Demonstration in cottage industries, especially in weaving.'[68]

Some years later (1 April 1931), technical education was transferred from the Directorate of Public Instruction to the Department of Industries. But there was no radical change in the scope of activities of the Department throughout the twenties and thirties.

This description of the conditions of the Department of Industries, Bombay, illustrates the difficulties under which the Departments of Industries of all the provinces suffered. While in some provinces, such as Madras or the Central Provinces, the Departments of Industries may have been more effective in helping the small industries, their role in fostering large-scale industries was at best marginal: they had neither the financial and administrative resources nor the control over matters of basic policy necessary to make a significant impact on the pace of development of large-scale industries.

The reasons for the failure of most of the efforts of the provincial departments to pioneer new industries or to spread industrialization through the provision of technical education and information can be illustrated with reference to the experience of Madras:

(1) Most often, the enterprises worked on too small a scale; this was, for example, the case with the glue-making factory started in Madras. Whereas the price of imported glue at Madras and therefore the price that the factory could charge was Rs. 38 per cwt. during 1923–4, the cost came to Rs. 51 - 12 - 0 including depreciation and overhead charges (the variable cost is not given in the report but that could not have been lower than Rs. 38), and there was a loss of Rs. 13 - 12 - 0 per cwt. of glue manufactured. The Retrenchment Committee recommended 'that the Glue Factory should be closed and further experiment to prove that glue can be manufactured at a commercial profit should be abandoned since they were satisfied after a further examination of the position that, as held by the Retrenchment Committee, the difficulty of manufacturing glue on a small scale at a competitive rate and of finding a market for the product could not be overcome by continuing the present experiments.'[69]

(2) Often, the market for the products produced by the pioneer enterprises was too small. For example, the Fruit Preserving Institute at Coonoor suffered from lack of demand during the year 1923–4, although there was no difficulty about the supply of suitable fruits for making into jam and

[68] *Bombay, 1924–25, a review of the administration of the Presidency* (Bombay, 1926), p. 100.
[69] *Report of the Department of Industries, Madras, for the year ended 31st March 1924* (Madras, 1925), pp. 33–4.

preserves. The factory therefore showed a loss of Rs. 23,158-8-5 after allowing only Rs. 500 as charges for direction.[70]

Similar difficulties affected the work in respect of technical education. Of the thirteen students who completed their course at the Leather Trades Institute, Madras, during the year 1922–3, three were unable to secure any employment. One of these proceeded to England for 'higher study' to mend his fortunes. Another lost his job as a result of retrenchment in his firm. Naturally there was a decrease in the number on the rolls during 1923–4.[71]

After the first few years of the 1920s, the provincial governments did not generally start any new pioneering factories. Some financial aid was given to small-scale industries and in some cases to large-scale industries, particularly in the provinces which had passed State Aid to Industries Acts. The aid to large-scale industries had often been quite fruitless because the plants established were poorly located and poorly managed. It is possible in some cases that if the provincial governments had been prepared to take a more active interest and to sustain the firms with financial aid for a longer period of time, the firms would not have failed.[72]

But the basic difficulty was that there was no all-India policy regarding the location of new industries. The disadvantages of location due to high costs of raw materials and limited local demand could only rarely be overcome by providing finance at low rates of interest, or by providing marginal facilities such as the grant of concessions in regard to rates for water, power or rent of land. If a particular location was suitable for an industry which could obtain a foothold in India under the prevailing conditions, generally there would be entrepreneurs with enough command over capital willing to utilize that location on their own, with or without positive encouragement from the provincial governments. Generally speaking, because of the attraction of easily accessible markets, ports and services for the supply of machinery or power, industries would be concentrated in

[70] *Ibid.*, p. 31. The do-it-yourself-and-show-the-neighbours enthusiasm with which some of these 'pioneering' factories were started is very well illustrated by the case of the fruit-preserving factory at Coonoor. 'The work was carried on in a room in Sir Frederick Nicholson's residence at Coonoor and the plant was domestic in character. Besides Miss Chaning Pearce, the lady manager, the staff consisted of a second-class cook and a very young *chokra* both entirely inexperienced in work.' 'The cost of the experiments (in fruit-preserving methods and recipes) does not include the pay (Rs. 850) of the lady manager for the period since it was paid by Sir Frederick Nicholson from the amount he received from Government on account of travelling allowance.' *Report of the Department of Industries, Madras for the year ended 31st March 1920* (Madras, 1921), pp. 29 and 30.

[71] *Report of the Department of Industries, Madras, for the year ended 31st March, 1924* (Madras, 1925), p. 60.

[72] Soni gives a list of the large-scale enterprises which had been aided by the various provincial governments up to around 1931, and all of these seem to have done badly. Soni, *Indian Industry*, pp. 395–6

the regions which were already developed, if industry was carried on under private auspices. This simple fact began to be recognized officially in 1938, when the Indian National Congress also set up an unofficial National Planning Committee.[73]

It would be misleading to suggest that before the setting up of this National Planning Committee there was no attempt at any co-ordination of the industrial policies of the different Provinces. Although it was known that under the Montague–Chelmsford reforms scheme, policy towards industries would become a provincial subject, the Government of India, guided by Sir Thomas Holland, convened in 1920, 1921 and 1922 an Industries Conference to which Provincial Directors of Industries were invited.

Although these conferences deliberated seriously on how to give effect to the recommendations of the Indian Industrial Commission and on the desirability of co-operation between the Provinces, and between the Provinces and the Government of India, nothing concrete was achieved in any of these directions. There was no follow-up of the action taken on various recommendations. For the next eleven years no other conferences were convened. In 1931 Sir Arthur Salter, then Director of the Economic and Financial Section of the League of Nations, stated in a report to the Government of India:

. . . the need for co-ordination of policy in India is greater than in countries with a centralised Government and the difficulties of securing it are also greater. Instead of co-ordination between different departments of a single administration, India needs co-ordination (a) between the departments of the Central Government, (b) between those of each Provincial Government, (c) between the Centre and the Provinces, (d) between the Provinces themselves, and (e) between British India and the States. It is a quintuple, not a single problem.[74]

From 1933 onwards the Industries Conferences were resumed again and took place regularly; but apart from the allocation between Provinces of grants made by the Government of India for the development of handlooms and sericulture and the exchange of opinion and knowledge, not much was achieved at these conferences. Without a long-term policy objective and the framework of a long-term plan, the work of the Provinces remained limited to the sustenance of cottage and small industries, and in some cases,

[73] For an example of official recognition of the tendency towards concentration of industry, see *Report of the Department of Industries, Madras, for the year ending 31st March, 1938* (Madras, 1939), pp. 12–13. It is interesting that this report spoke approvingly of the development of industries (and agriculture) in the U.S.S.R. under the economic policies pursued by the Soviet Government.

[74] Quoted by S. Lall, 'Industrial development in the Indian Provinces', *JRSA*, LXXXIX, No. 4,579, 24 January 1941, pp. 142–3.

the development of hydroelectricity, which benefited both agriculture and small-scale industries.[75]

2.5 THE MONETARY POLICY OF THE GOVERNMENT OF INDIA UP TO 1914

There was no central bank for India, properly speaking, before the establishment of the Reserve Bank of India in 1935. The Imperial Bank of India, formed by merging the three Presidency Banks in 1921, was a half-way house, since it was mainly a commercial bank and only secondarily a bankers' bank, and it did not have powers of note-issue, which were retained by the government. Up to 1935, the Government of India retained all the powers of a central bank in its own hands: it should be pointed out, however, that it practically never acted consciously so as to influence the rate of interest in the money market by any of the methods usually adopted by the central banks of today.

The Presidency Banks enjoyed certain definite privileges in relation to the government, the chief of which was the right to use the surplus cash balances of the government free of interest. Any influence that the Government of India had on the internal money market was exercised solely through the Presidency Banks. The Government of India, of course, had a predominant influence on the supply of money because it was the sole source of currency notes and silver rupees. The main concern of the government between the years 1898–9 and 1919–20 was the maintenance of the value of the rupee at the fixed rate of 1s. 4d. This ratio was maintained by the sale of Council Bills (in normal years, when India had a surplus in her balance of payments and the rupee was strong) in London, or by the sale of Reverse Council Bills in sterling (when the rupee was weak). The Government of India seems to have succeeded quite well before the war in the limited objective it had placed before itself, viz., the maintenance of the gold exchange standard.

The essentials of the gold exchange standard were, as Keynes put it, 'the use of a local currency mainly not of gold, some degree of unwillingness to supply gold locally in exchange for the local currency, but a high degree of willingness to sell foreign exchange for payment in local currency at a high maximum rate, and to use foreign credits in order to do this.'[76] India was but one of the many countries which had adopted the gold exchange standard, as Keynes made clear as early as 1913, and as was more widely recognized later on.[77] The smooth working of the system was facilitated not

[75] For a succinct review of the achievements and limitations of the Provinces in the field of industry see Lall, 'Industrial development', pp. 134–45, and the discussion following the article in the same issue of *JRSA*, pp. 145–7.

[76] Keynes: *Indian Currency*, p. 29.

[77] See League of Nations (Ragnar Nurkse and William Adams Brown, Jr): *International Currency Experience* (1944), Chapter II.

only by the fact that the Indian money market was directly linked to London, the chief money market of the world before 1914, but also by the fact that India habitually exported more than she imported before the First World War, and that there was no sudden spurt in imports because of demands generated by a noticeably accelerated rate of economic growth.

Within India, the supply of money was primarily determined by the supply of paper currency. This supply was in its turn primarily governed by the demands of trade, since notes were issued freely from Paper Currency offices in return for rupees or British gold coin; the notes were also encashable in rupees in government treasuries. This latter provision created some trouble for the Government of India around the end of the year; it also provided the rationale for the arrangements restricting the circulation of notes to within their circle of issue, India being divided into four currency circles and four sub-circles up to 1910, and seven currency circles from 1910 onwards. Even if this division of one country into what were effectively several currency areas can be justified,[78] it shows the limited nature of the economic integration which had taken place in India by 1914. The timidity of the Government of India is the more obvious because paper currency had become the main means of payment in the country by the beginning of the century.

Part of the confusion in the minds of the policy-makers regarding the willingness of Indians to accept paper currency may have been caused by the fact that India imported increasing amounts of gold and silver – mainly gold bullion and gold coins – from 1898–9 to 1913–14: the fluctuations in these imports were probably caused as much by regional factors as by aggregative ones.[79] The gold bullion imported was, of course, used primarily for hoarding in the form of jewellery, etc.; gold sovereigns imported were, however, used in the Punjab and Northern India as currency. The absorption of gold sovereigns seems to have been the highest in the Punjab, followed by Bombay and Bengal.[80] Furthermore, although there was some controversy about whether the use of sovereigns was really on the increase up to, say, 1910–11, according to a detailed enquiry conducted by the Accountant General of Punjab, the sovereign was becoming more popular as currency.[81] Thus, contrary to the view expressed by some economists and officials, the

[78] Keynes, *Indian Currency*, Chapter III: 'The limitation of the areas of legal tender and of the offices where the notes were encashable on demand greatly restricted the popularity of the notes. It might well have seemed worth while to popularise them, even at the expense of temporary loss.' (p. 43).

[79] For the record of imports of 'treasure' from 1898–9 to 1913–14, see Pandit: *India's Balance of Indebtedness*, pp. 34–5; also G. F. Shirras: *Indian Finance and Banking* (London, 1920), Tables 8–11.

[80] Gov. India, Finance Department: *Report of the operations of the Currency Department during the year 1911–12* (Calcutta, 1912), p. 14.

[81] *Ibid.*, p. 14; for evidence up to 1910–11, see *idem, Report upon the operations of the Paper Currency Department during the year 1910–11* (Calcutta, 1911), pp. 12–15.

imports of treasure did, to some extent at least, supplement the supply of money in the country; and insofar as one can postulate some stable relationship (in an economy without sophisticated banking arrangements) between the value of the means of payment and total expenditure, this may have been a factor contributing to the Indian inflation before 1914.[82]

The disturbing feature about the monetary arrangements of India up to the First World War (and probably right up to the period of the depression which curtailed Indian foreign trade drastically) was that they were geared almost entirely to the requirements of trade, particularly foreign trade, in staple commodities such as food-grains, raw cotton, raw jute and jute manufactures. Since there was little industry in comparison with trade, the rates of discount charged by the commercial banks moved not with changes in the industrial conditions but with the ebb and flow of trade. There was a busy season and a slack season in the demand for money: the former generally began in November and ended in April or May. During the period 1900–14, the extreme variations of the rates of interest charged by the Banks of Bengal and Bombay during the 1890s (when in some months their rates went up to 12% per annum) were avoided. But it was still quite usual for the rate of interest to vary from 4% to 7% or from 6% to 9% in one month.[83]

Since there was no industrial banking in India, where the commercial banks were allowed to engage only in short-term lending, it is doubtful whether the extreme variations in the short-term lending rates of the Presidency Banks affected long-term investment in industry to any significant extent. But these variations almost certainly pushed up the cost of working capital for major industries such as jute and cotton. The extreme prudence of the Presidency Banks with their bias towards trade and their refusal to look at any but sound established houses – which in the two Presidencies of Madras and Bengal meant only European business houses – may also have affected long-term investment insofar as a prospective investor might be able to raise the minimum long-term capital needed but might find it too costly to borrow the working capital.[84]

[82] See Keynes, *Indian Currency*, Chapter IV, 'The Present Position of Gold in India and Proposals for a Gold Currency.' On the reasons for the rise of prices see K. L. Datta [listed in Bibliography under *Official publications: Government of India*, hereafter abbreviated as Gov. India pub.]: *Report on the enquiry into the rise of prices in India*, Vol. I (Calcutta, 1914), Chapters V–IX, and 'A Resolution of the Government of India reviewing the Report' in the same volume, pp. i–xiv. The Government of India placed a greater emphasis than Datta had done on world factors causing a rise in prices.

[83] See Reserve Bank of India: *Banking and Monetary Statistics of India* (Bombay, 1954), pp. 690–3, for tables of the rates of interest charged by the Presidency Banks.

[84] On the lending policies of the Bank of Madras, see Sir W. B. Hunter's evidence before the Indian Industrial Commission in *Evidence* (*Report of IIC*), Vol. III (PP 1919, XIX), pp. 275–95, esp. pp. 275–9. According to Hunter, who was Secretary and Treasurer of the Bank of Madras, in the busy season the bank lent between Rs. 17.5 million and Rs. 20 million to industrial concerns; of this amount about Rs. 11 million went to

Of course, some Indian banks did spring up which supplied some long-term capital to new investors in the guise of indefinite extensions of short-term loans. One can point to the failure of many of these banks, such as the People's Bank, the Indian Specie Bank and the Credit Bank of India, during the banking crisis of 1913–15 as evidence of the basic soundness of the cautious policy pursued by the Presidency Banks and hence at one remove, by the government.[85] But actually these failures prove very little of the kind; they point to the vulnerability of small banks pursuing a policy which is not approved of by the leading banks to which they might have to turn for accommodation in a crisis; they are bound to occur in a situation where there is in effect no bankers' bank either to help the banks out when there is a temporary run on them, or to guide them in their ordinary business. These failures also prove that there are two requirements for the success of industrial banking: first, a sufficient number of sound business propositions to keep the rate of return above the short-term borrowing rate, and secondly, government backing for such ventures. Both these conditions were lacking in India. The Tata Industrial Bank, which was established in 1917, had to wind up its business in 1923 and merge with the Central Bank of India for basically similar reasons; because it was difficult to form an inspectorate for vetting industrial propositions without prohibitive cost; and because it was difficult to find worthwhile industrial propositions which could not be financed by the ordinary capital market and yet could be safely financed by an industrial bank.[86]

There was also some evidence before the war that the deposits raised by the foreign exchange banks in India tended to be utilized in their operations abroad, and that the foreign exchange banks relied on the system of telegraphic transfers of the Secretary of State for India to tide them over periods of crisis instead of raising money in the London money market, to which they had ready access.[87] Hence it is uncertain to what extent the foreign exchange

Indian concerns and Rs. 8 million to European ones. Hunter favoured the fostering of industry by the government by means of financial assistance and demonstration and pioneer factories.

[85] See Shirras: *Indian Finance and Banking* pp. 365–7; also S. V. Doraiswami: *Indian Finance, Currency and Banking* (Madras, 1915), Chapter VII, for a (rather emotional) Indian view of the problem.

[86] On the problems of financing the fixed capital of industries in pre-independence India and on the fate of commercial banks trying to finance industrial ventures see S. K. Muranjan: *Modern Banking in India* (Bombay, 1940), pp. 303–8. Muranjan discusses the causes of bank failure in Chapter IX. On the difficulties faced by the Tata Industrial Bank, see the speech of Sir D. J. Tata at the Annual General Meeting of the Tata Industrial Bank, quoted in *Capital* (Calcutta, 28 February 1919), pp. 483–7; and the speech of Sir Alfred Chatterton in *JRSA*, LXXIII, 26 June 1925, p. 745. One of the main causes of bank failures during the period 1913–17 was the extremely small ratio maintained by Indian banks between cash balances and deposits. Keynes had foreseen the dangers of this situation. See Keynes, *Indian Currency*, pp. 224–7.

[87] On the first point, see Keynes: *Indian Currency*, pp. 215–16; on the second point, see RC on Indian Finance and Currency: *Minutes of Evidence*, Vol. I (PP 1914, xx),

banks did actually add to the finance available to the organized banking system in India. The final source of inadequacy in the banking system before 1921 was the existence of three Presidency Banks. The amalgamation of the Presidency Banks would probably itself have increased the flow of short-term capital from banks to industry, so that a more even spread of resources would have been achieved.[88] Because of the division of territory between the three Presidency Banks, there was sometimes a surplus in one region while there were still shortages of funds in other centres. This tended to happen particularly with the Bank of Madras: hence both the rates of interest charged and the dividends declared by the Bank of Madras were lower than those of the other two Presidency Banks.

2.6   THE MONETARY POLICY OF THE GOVERNMENT OF INDIA AFTER THE FIRST WORLD WAR

The latter part of the First World War and the immediate post-war years witnessed one of the most bizarre incidents in the history of Indian currency, which also produced lasting effects on Indian economic life. Before the war, the external value of the rupee was geared to that of sterling, and was maintained by the sale of the so-called Council Drafts (Bills) and the Reverse Councils. The Council Drafts were sold by the Secretary of State in London to facilitate remittances to India and to defray the expenditure incurred by the Government of India through the India Office. This sale also expanded the gold or sterling base for the issue of currency in India. The sale of Council Drafts was consciously varied according to the demands for remittance to India. If there was a tendency for the exchange value of the rupee to fall below 1s. 4d., the situation was met by the sale of bills in India, which were known as 'Reverse Councils', to be cashed in gold or sterling in London.

The burden of adjustment of the external value of the rupee was, however, also shared by changes in the net import of gold and silver into India. During the five years from 1909–10 to 1913–14, for example, the total net imports of treasure into India had amounted to £120,242,000 and the total net sales of Council Drafts had amounted to £138,202,200.[89]

---

pp. 130–1, and RC on Indian Finance and Currency: *Appendices to the Interim Report of the Commissioners* (PP 1914, xx), Appendix xv.

[88] It was estimated in 1901 by Sir Edward Law (the member in charge of Finance in the Viceroy's Council) that the banking capital available in India for trade purposes was less than £10 million, after making allowances for the share of the capital of the exchange banks which was held outside India; the amount required was estimated as £12 million. See *Statement exhibiting the moral and material progress and condition of India during the year 1901–02, and the nine preceding years* (PP 1903, XLVI), pp. 146–8.

[89] 'Report of Committee on Indian Exchange and Currency, 1919' (Babington Smith Committee) para. 8, in Gov. India, *Reports of Currency Committees* (Calcutta, 1931), p. 240.

After the outbreak of the war, the exchange value of the rupee at first tended to decline and was shored up by the sale of Reverse Councils. But soon the virtual cessation of imports from Central and Eastern Europe, the curtailment of imports from the U.K., the large expenditures made by the Government of India on behalf of the Government of the U.K. (between 1914 and 1919 such expenditure amounted to £240 million)[90] produced large trading surpluses for India. At the same time owing to a drastic curtailment of the imports of treasure from abroad, caused by the curtailment of the supply of both gold and silver, and the commitment of the Government of India to issue rupees in exchange for notes on demand, the latter found itself in a position in which it was difficult to finance a balance of trade *surplus*. This position was really created by the breakdown of the pre-war mechanism of international transfers and by the inability of the Government of India to introduce a paper currency to replace the old silver currency.[91] But the burden of international adjustment was assumed unilaterally by the Government of India. In August 1917 the price of silver exceeded 43*d*. per standard ounce: this marked the point at which the exchange value of the rupee was equivalent to its bullion value.[92] After that the Government of India announced that the price at which Council Bills would be sold in future would be based roughly on the price at which silver could be bought. The external value of the rupee thus became linked to the soaring price of silver; it rose from 1*s*. 4*d*. to 1*s*. 4$\frac{1}{2}$*d*. and then to 1*s*. 5*d*. in 1917, and 1918 it rose further to 1*s*. 6*d*. This rate was maintained till 13 May 1919, when it rose further to 1*s*. 8*d*. in response to a rise in the price of silver. On 12 December 1919 it rose to 2*s* 4*d*.[93]

The Babington Smith Committee recommended that the external value of the rupee should be fixed at 2*s*. gold. This recommendation took no account of the changed circumstances after the war, with enormously increased imports from abroad. Further, there was a world-wide crisis with falling prices; there was a steep rise in imports into India in relation to her exports so that the Government of India soon found itself in trouble in trying to maintain the value of the rupee at the inflated figure. The government finally abandoned the attempt to hold the value of the rupee at 2*s*.

---

[90] *Ibid.*, p. 244.

[91] Keynes had already deplored the excessive cautiousness of the Government of India in experimenting with a paper currency for purposes of internal circulation. As far back as 1863, C. N. Cooke, the then Deputy Secretary and Treasurer of the Bank of Bengal, had pleaded for a paper currency, pointing out that the large, illiterate populations of Russia and Java used paper currency extensively and that in India itself the notes of the Bank of Bengal had a wide circulation, not only in Calcutta but also inland as far as Benares. C. N. Cooke: *The Rise, Progress and Present Conditions of Banking in India* (Calcutta, 1863), p. 37.

[92] 'Report of the Committee on Indian Exchange and Currency 1919', para. 18 in Gov. India, *Reports of Currency Committees*, pp. 246–7.

[93] *Ibid.*, pp. 250–1.

sterling on 28 September 1920. In 1921 the value of the rupee fell below 1*s*. 3*d*. sterling and 1*s*. gold. From January 1923 onwards, the external value of the rupee began to rise again, recovering first to 1*s*. 4*d*. sterling and then to 1*s*. 6*d*. sterling in October 1924. The Government of India maintained the external value of the rupee at that level and this policy was given statutory embodiment after the Royal Commission on Indian Currency and Finance of 1926 (the Hilton Young Commission) had recommended that the exchange value of the rupee should be pegged at 1*s*. 6*d*. sterling.

The main reason for this recommendation of the Hilton Young Commission was their 'conviction, . . . that, at the present exchange rate of about 1*s*. 6*d*., prices in India have already attained a substantial measure of adjustment with those in the world at large, and, as a corollary, that any change in the rate would mean a difficult period of readjustment, involving widespread economic disturbance, which it is most desirable in the interests of the people to avoid, and which would in the end be followed by no countervailing advantage'.[94]

There was little doubt in anybody's mind that a recurrence of the instability of the exchange rate of the years 1917–24 was to be avoided. The instability created an intolerable degree of uncertainty in an open economy like India; it created special difficulties for industrialists because they were so dependent on imported stores and machinery, and so vulnerable to the epidemic of currency depreciation which had started in continental Europe. It is surprising in fact that in spite of the extreme degree of uncertainty the boom in industrial investment should have assumed the proportions that it did during the years 1920–1 to 1923–4.[95]

However, Indian business opinion was almost unanimous in rejecting the exchange value of 1*s*. 6*d*. to the rupee; it contended that the 'true' exchange value should be 1*s*. 4*d*., the pre-war rate. Sir Purshotamdas Thakurdas, who was the representative of Indian business on the Hilton Young Commission wrote a minute of dissent recommending that an exchange value for the rupee of 1*s*. 4*d*. should be adopted.[96]

While various muddled arguments were employed by both sides, three points stand out. First, a *de facto* devaluation of the rupee (by about 11%),

---

[94] RC on Indian Currency and Finance, Vol. 1, *Report* (London, 1926), para. 176 (p. 68).

[95] For a survey of the currency troubles of the period 1914–30, see Ray: *Indian Foreign Trade since 1870*, Chapters V, VI and IX. See also Anstey, *Economic Development of India*, pp. 409–32.

[96] RC on Indian Currency and Finance, Vol. 1, *Report* (London, 1926), pp. 120–44. Sir Maneckji Byramji Dadabhoy was another Indian member who was an industrialist, but he had also been connected with officialdom before the First World War as an Additional Member of the Viceroy's Council. He signed the report of the majority without a minute of dissent. On the career of Sir Maneckji Byramji Dadabhoy, see *Debrett's Peerage*, 1930, p. 278.

through the lowering of the exchange value from 1s. 6d. to 1s. 4d., would have given the Indian manufacturers a significant advantage over foreign imports. In the middle twenties, when cotton-textiles producers were particularly hard-pressed by foreign competition such an advantage was not to be spurned. On the other hand, Indian exports, particularly of raw materials, faced an inelastic demand schedule in foreign markets, so that from the point of view of the trader, a higher exchange value was probably welcome. Secondly, there is some truth in the allegation of Indian businessmen and publicists that the exchange value of the rupee was maintained at the 1s. 6d. rate only by means of a dose of deflation. We have seen already that the Government of India, faced with a series of deficit budgets after the First World War, cut down both current and capital expenditure severely, until budgetary equilibrium was achieved (from 1923–4 onwards). This 'financial' deflation was accompanied by a 'monetary' deflation.[97] The rate of increase of currency circulation was greatly slowed, particularly after 1922. The total of notes in circulation fell from Rs. 1,724·8 million in December 1923 to Rs. 1,656·0 million in December 1926.[98] Some of this fall was probably just a reflection of the deflation caused by the fiscal measures: but some of the contraction of currency was quite deliberate and led to increases in the bank rate charged by the Imperial Bank of India.[99] If we look at the money supply in the organized money market we see that the total deposits of all commercial banks decreased from Rs. 2,299·3 million in 1921 to Rs. 2,124·3 million in 1927: the average annual rate of increase of deposits of commercial banks had almost always been higher both in absolute and in proportional terms before the war.[100] While one should not connect either the price level or the level of national income directly to these crude measures of money supply, nor deduce that there was a scarcity of capital in any absolute sense for industrial investment during the middle of the 1920s, it is clear that this severe dose of internal deflation combined with intense competition from abroad made the prospects of profitable investment in any but the most 'naturally protected' industries look extremely gloomy.

The third factor which stands out in the exchange rate controversy is the concern of the government with minimizing the sterling costs of its commitments abroad and with improving its image as a sound borrower in

[97] See Sir J. C. Coyajee: 'Money Reconstruction in India (1925–7)' *Annals of the American Academy of Political and Social Science*, Vol. 145, Part II, 1929, pp. 101–14, particularly pp. 106–8.
[98] Reserve Bank of India: *Banking and Monetary Statistics of India*, p. 657.
[99] See Appendix 98, 'Extracts etc., from telegraphic correspondence between the Secretary of State for India and the Government of India, Finance Department', in RC on Indian Currency and Finance, Vol. III, *Appendices* (London, 1926), pp. 624–30, at p. 648.
[100] Reserve Bank of India: *Banking and Monetary Statistics of India*, p. 7.

the eyes of the foreign investor.[101] A devaluation of the rupee would have led immediately to a significant increase in the costs of government and railway purchases from the U.K., thus endangering the balance of the budget and imparing the credit of the Government of India.

The policy of deflation was resumed in earnest with the onset of the depression of the thirties, as was pointed out in the section on fiscal policy above. The tightness of the money market was reflected in the extraordinarily high bank rates of the Imperial Bank of India and the high yields on the treasury bills of the Government of India. On 10 July 1930 the bank rate of the Imperial Bank came down to 5%, but it was 7% on 6 August 1931 and was pushed up to 8% in 1931, after Britain had gone off gold. The bank rate began to fall significantly only from 28 April 1932 when it was lowered to 5%.[102] The central government treasury bill rates on accepted tenders stayed above 5·5% throughout 1931, and climbed up to 7·25% from 2 October 1931; it began to fall again from the end of January 1932.[103] There were also complaints from industrialists that the government was siphoning off too much capital from the private sector by offering too high a yield on government securities. For example, in the early part of 1932, the Government of India floated a 5·5% loan at 98, whereas it was argued that a 5% loan at 95 would have been attractive enough.[104] The depression of the thirties would by itself explain part of the jitteriness in the capital market. But this jitteriness was certainly aggravated by the deflationary policy of the government, particularly when the latter chose this peculiar moment to pay off part of the sterling debt of India. One could argue that the stimulating effects of the measures of tariff protection adopted in 1930 and 1931 were largely smothered by the deflationary fiscal and monetary policy of the government. This is reflected in the fact that our series of nominal and 'real' values of imports of machinery and mill-work do not show an upturn until 1933–4 (admittedly, such an upturn was also partly caused by the beginning of a world recovery).[105]

The concern of the Government of India about its credit-worthiness in the London money market proved to be rather short-sighted: after 1935 it did not raise any loans at all on the London money market.

The other developments in the monetary institutions and policy of the Government of India were the creation of the Imperial Bank of India in 1921 and the Reserve Bank of India in 1935. Although these steps improved

[101] See, for example, RC on Indian Currency and Finance, Vol. 1, *Report* (London, 1926), pp. 81–3.
[102] Reserve Bank of India: *Banking and Monetary Statistics of India*, p. 693.
[103] *Ibid.*, p. 716.
[104] Bengal National Chamber of Commerce and Industry, *Report of the Committee for the year 1932* (Calcutta, 1933) (6) pp. 405–6 (Speech of Kumar S. N. Law, Chairman, at the first quarterly general meeting).
[105] See Table 3·1, p. 71 below.

the working of the organized money market, no significant difference was made to the policies of commercial bank lending to industry. The commercial banks continued to lend primarily on the basis of stocks of goods for short-term purposes; but they also extended short-term credit (known as 'cash credit') on the basis of the security of fixed assets of a reputable concern.[106] The Imperial Bank continued to be controlled primarily by Europeans, and there were complaints of discrimination, particularly because at first (up to 1935) it acted as a bankers' bank at the same time as it engaged vigorously in commercial banking. But neither the Imperial Bank nor the Reserve Bank could really exert sufficient influence on monetary policy for their rates to be considered separately from that of the Government of India. The regime of cheap money which came in after 1932 certainly preceded the creation of the Reserve Bank of India and was more likely to have been the *result* of other developments than the *cause* of increase in industrial investment.[107]

The widespread desire for the creation of industrial banks did not lead to any tangible results. The Tata Industrial Bank which had been floated in 1917 had to merge its business with the Central Bank of India in 1923, for it found that there were very few propositions of industrial investment which were profitable and yet were not being financed by the people with capital at their command.[108]

---

[106] N. G. Hunt: 'Banks and the Indian Cotton Industry', *The Indian Textile Journal Jubilee Souvenir, 1890–1940* (Bombay, 1941), pp. 39 and 233. See also ITB, Special Tariff Board: *Written Evidence recorded during enquiry regarding the level of duties necessary to afford adequate protection to the Indian cotton textile industry*, Vol. II (Delhi, 1937), p. 311, letter dated 16 January 1936 from the Imperial Bank of India, Calcutta, to the Special Tariff Board: 'The passing of the amending Act of 1934 has not modified, to any great extent, the former restrictions on our lending powers as regards advances and loans to Indian cotton mills... We would now be prepared to consider providing short-term finance to cotton mills on the security of marketable debentures of companies but still prefer the legitimate method of advances against stocks. In the case of the latter our standard margin is 25 %, but we are always prepared to consider a temporary reduction in the margin in special circumstances...'

[107] For analysis of the various aspects of the monetary and fiscal policy of India in the 1920s and 1930s, see Chapters XXVII, XXIX, XXX, XXXII, and XXXV in Radhakamal Mukherjee and H. L. Dey (eds.): *Economic Problems of Modern India*, Vol II (London, 1941). See also Muranjan: *Modern Banking*, Chapters IV and VIII.

[108] See Muranjan, *Modern Banking*, pp. 306–7; see also the references in Section 2.5 above.

3

THE RECORD OF AGGREGATE PRIVATE
INDUSTRIAL INVESTMENT IN INDIA, 1900–1939

The aim of the present chapter is to trace the broad history of private investment in manufacturing industries in India and relate it to broad movements of national product and external factors. Investment in mining and plantation industries is entirely excluded. Furthermore, the discussion is centred on movements of investment in large-scale rather than in small-scale industries. But no rigid distinction is drawn between large-scale and small-scale industries because the data do not allow such discrimination in every case.

In the beginning of the period only two large-scale manufacturing industries, viz., cotton and jute mills, employed more than 20,000 people. At the end of the period, several others, notably iron and steel, sugar and cement had been added to the list. But up to the end of the twenties the cotton and jute mills dominated the industrial field as indeed they did, although less completely, even in 1950. But at least public attention had been shifted to other fields by the latter date.

Even when data regarding manufacturing concerns are systematically collected, the measurement of investment is a tricky affair.[1] The problems arise out of changes in prices of the different constituents of the capital stocks of companies, which determine the correct level of depreciation, changes in the price levels of commodities in general and changes in rates of interest. For India during the period under review, the problems are even more difficult. Data relating to the capital stock of companies are hard to come by in most industries before the *Investor's India Year Book* (*IIYB*) began to be published. Even the *IIYB* covered mainly those public companies which had head offices in Calcutta or whose shares were normally quoted on the Calcutta stock exchange: hence its coverage of the cotton-mill industry particularly was incomplete. The *Statistical Abstract* (annual) of the Government of India provided figures of paid-up (or sometimes authorized) capital of different industries. But the values of paid-up capital are not at all a good index of the true values of fixed capital in the different industries. Moreover, the totals of paid-up capital often did not cover the capital of many companies, and almost always excluded the capital of private companies. Hence these figures cannot provide any

---

[1] See in this connection, Tibor Barna: 'On measuring capital', in F. A. Lutz and D. C. Hague (ed.): *The Theory of Capital* (London, 1961).

reliable picture of the movements of investment in the respective industries except in very special cases.

In view of these deficiencies I have mostly used the figures of imports of machinery of various kinds as indices of gross investment in fixed capital in the different industries. These figures are also incomplete in many cases, and I have had to use approximations. They are subject to obvious limitations as indicators of gross fixed investment: no adjustments can be made for price changes except in a very crude fashion; no adjustments at all can be made for quality changes; no distinction can be made between new and secondhand machinery. Fortunately, in two major industries – cotton and jute mills – very little basic change in techniques took place until the very end of the period. In other major industries too, changes in techniques were not too revolutionary during the period when the industries were of any importance in India. Wherever possible an attempt has been made to assess the importance of changes in the composition of capital goods for a particular industry, but such an analysis is unfortunately extremely incomplete. It should also be made clear that although we are concerned only with gross investment in fixed capital (the term 'fixed investment' will be used to denote this entity), the importance of the other major components of investment, viz., investment in stocks, is not denied. The major justification for ignoring the latter component is that data relating to it are even more scarce than data relating to fixed investment. Moreover, measures of investment in stocks are even more affected by price changes, many of which are seasonal or temporary in nature, and the price data are not always fine enough for it to be possible to separate the seasonal from the cyclical or secular components.

For the convenience of exposition we shall divide the period into two sub-periods (a) the period up to 1914; (b) the period from 1915 up to 1939.

3.1 PRIVATE INDUSTRIAL INVESTMENT UP TO 1914

In the closing years of the nineteenth century there occurred, in India, two of the worst famines of the century: the famines of 1896–7 and 1899–1900. These famines combined with plague to affect the rate of progress of the cotton textile industry, particularly in Bombay City and Island. In contrast to the nine new mills started in 1896 (and planned earlier), no new mills were started during the years from 1900 to 1904.[2] But the famine and plague did not affect all the centres of the country equally: some progress continued to take place in the centres of Ahmedabad, the United Provinces, Bengal and Madras. Moreover, it was not just the famine that affected the fortunes of the Bombay cotton-mill industry – the flooding of the Chinese markets with yarn, and the competition from Chinese and especially

[2] See S. M. Rutnagur: *Bombay Industries: The Cotton Mills* (Bombay, 1927), pp. 20–1.

Japanese mills played their part in checking the growth of the spinning section of the industry.

In contrast, the jute mills of Bengal were relatively little affected by the famines of 1896–7 and 1899–1900. This was partly because the famine affected the Bombay Presidency and the Bengal Presidency very differently. For instance, while the out-turn of winter rice (the major crop) for the Bengal Presidency was estimated at 95% of the normal crop and while the output of the *bhadoi* and *rabi* crops in the same province was estimated at 70% and 87% of the normal crops respectively,[3] within the Bombay Presidency the out-turn of both *kharif* and *rabi* crops in 1899–1900 as a percentage of that of the previous years (a more or less normal year) varied from 0·9% in the Panch Mahals to 47·6% in Kolaba.[4] The famine in Bombay directly affected the cotton crop, whereas the jute crop in Bengal was not severely affected. The reason for this difference lay partly in the markets for the jute and cotton mills. An overwhelming proportion of the output of jute mills was sold abroad, whereas in the case of cotton mills, the major proportion of piecegoods was sold inside the country. It is true that Bombay sold a large part of her yarn output abroad, but she was already shifting increasingly from yarn to piecegoods, and other centres, whether producing yarn or piecegoods, produced for the home market.

It is difficult to judge to what extent one ought to stress long-term influences and the influence of the national market on investment in industry during this period. There is plenty of evidence that investors in the cotton-mill industry often reacted to very short-term influences, such as a sudden upsurge in the demand for yarn in the Chinese market, by expanding the number of spindles installed, although it was pretty clear already in the face of the growth of the indigenous Chinese cotton mills and the competition from Japan that the future of yarn exports could not be very bright. However, at the same time the capacity for weaving piecegoods was expanding faster than the spinning capacity. Also, finer counts of yarn were being produced and Bombay was leading in the production of finer and coloured goods, although the overwhelming proportion of better-quality piecegoods was still supplied to India by Lancashire.[5]

In the same way, purely *local* influences can be detected in the expansion of the Indian industry. One of the barriers to the spinning and weaving of finer-quality yarn and piecegoods was the poor quality of Indian cotton, which was almost entirely of the short-staple variety at the beginning of the twentieth century. Furthermore, Bombay owners were often amazingly ignorant of the conditions in Indian markets which were far from Bombay.[6]

[3] *Report on the administration of Bengal, 1899–1900* (Calcutta, 1900), p. 122.
[4] *Report on the administration of the Bombay Presidency* (Bombay, 1901), Part 1, p. iii.
[5] S. D. Mehta: *The Cotton Mills of India: 1854–1954* (Bombay, 1954), pp. 80–1.
[6] Gov. India, Department of Statistics, *Review of the trade of India, 1899–1900* (Calcutta, 1900), pp. 23–4.

TABLE 3.1 *Imports of cotton piecegoods and twist and yarn into different ports of British India in the early twentieth century*

	Total over the period 1901–2 to 1903–4 (Rs. '000)			Total over the period 1911–12 to 1913–14 (Rs. '000)			Percentage change in the second period over the first (%)		
	Bengal	Bombay and Sind	Madras	Bengal	Bombay and Sind	Madras	Bengal	Bombay and Sind	Madras
Cotton twist and yarn	19,085	17,709	21,825	31,860	47,835	33,870	+67	+170	+55
Cotton piecegoods	440,183	298,141	62,551	744,735	591,945	108,225	+69	+99	+73

Source: Gov. India, CISD: *Annual statement of the seaborne trade of British India* for the relevant years, Vol. I (Calcutta).

But there is little doubt that with the spread of the railways and the establishment of the ascendancy of Indian cotton mills in the coarser counts of
yarn and the coarser varieties of cloth, a national network in demand and
supply of cotton goods was becoming well-established. Table 3.1 throws
some light on this question.

It is interesting to note that although Bombay Presidency was the centre
of the industry, imports of both cotton twist and yarn and cotton piecegoods
into Bombay and Sind expanded much faster than imports into the two
other ports. This throws doubt on the hypothesis that the Bombay mills
catered primarily to the surrounding areas and strengthens our belief in the
existence of a national network of supply and demand.[7] That imports of
twist and yarn expanded so much faster than imports of cotton piecegoods
into Bombay can be explained by the fact that the handloom weavers were
much harder hit than cotton mills by the famines at the turn of the century,
and that, conversely, the weaving of fine cloth benefited more from the
prosperity of the country on the eve of the First World War. Our table also
furnishes some evidence that the local mills of Madras were supplying a
larger proportion of the demand for yarn than previously.[8]

The record of investment in the jute industry was one of unfettered
expansion. Between 1896 and 1900, nine new mills were added. After a lull
of four years during which extensions were made to the existing mills, another nine mills were added. There was a slight break in prosperity between
1910 and 1912, but three new mills were added between 1910 and 1914.[9]
The number of looms as well as spindles expanded very much faster in the
jute industry than in the cotton industry. There was also a shift towards
the production of hessian rather than sacking. The stimulus for expansion
came entirely from the side of exports. The management of the new mills
was almost wholly in British hands. Moreover, the period also saw the
expansion and consolidation of the interests of the existing managing agents
such as Bird and Co., and Andrew, Yule and Co. Completely new names
among managing agents are rare, and some of the weaker mills were
eliminated in the crisis of 1910–12.

During this period technological developments outside India blighted the
prospects of the paper industry. The industry was adversely affected by the
new techniques of making paper from wood pulp in Europe, so that the

---

[7] See in this connection, Gov. India, CISD: *Statistical abstract for British India*
(7th issue), Vol. 1, *Commercial statistics* (Calcutta, 1915), pp. iii–v.

[8] According to A. C. Chatterjee, in 1905–6, 121,000 maunds of Indian yarn were
imported into the United Provinces from Bombay port and province, as against total
imports of 19,000 maunds of European twist and yarn, imported mainly through Calcutta.
The net imports of European piecegoods into the United Provinces in the same year came
to 775,000 maunds as against 111,000 maunds of Indian piecegoods imported (the bulk
of it was machine-made cloth). A. C. Chatterjee [IPG pub.]: *Notes on the industries of
the United Provinces* (Allahabad, 1908), pp. 5–6.

[9] D. R. Wallace: *The Romance of Jute* (London, 1928), pp. 63–9.

value of production of paper grew only from Rs. 6·241 million in 1899 to Rs. 8·037 million in 1913,[10] while the value of imports of paper and pasteboard rose from Rs. 4·113 million in 1899–1900 to Rs. 14·967 million in 1912–13 and Rs. 16·683 million in 1913–14. The paper industry would probably have suffered even more (as it is, there was little expansion in capacity) but for the government purchase of a part of its output.[11] The amount of sugar imported into India went on increasing from 1892–3 onwards with a few breaks (the imports increased almost sevenfold within twenty years). The main stimulus came from the improvement of techniques of refining and the increase in the productivity of beet in the continental European countries such as Austria, and of sugar-cane in Java, Mauritius, etc. In the later part of the period particularly, the transfer of consumption from *gur* to refined sugar (as a result of the growth in incomes of the richer section of the population) may also have been important. The prospects for the establishment of a sugar refining industry appeared rather dim in the face of the increasingly severe competition from abroad.[12]

The Indian economy before the First World War was an open one with very low import duties on a restricted range of commodities, geared primarily to the U.K. as far as its imports were concerned, but exporting raw materials and food-grains to many parts of the world, and contributing precious dollars to the pool of the sterling area centred on Britain.[13] Much of the stimulus to investment in industries such as jute manufacture, tea and coal (all dominated by British industrialists) came from expanding exports of these commodities. Both the total exports and total imports of India expanded by more than 100% over the period 1900–13 and the net and gross barter terms of trade improved considerably.[14] There was only one break in the progress of foreign trade during this period: this was caused by bad monsoons in 1908–9 coinciding with a trade depression the world over. There was also a substantial inflow of foreign capital over the same period, primarily on public account, for investment in railways and other social overhead capital.[15]

It is difficult to assess the progress of national income and purchasing

[10] Gov. India, CISD: *Statistical abstract for British India* (7th issue), Vol. I (Calcutta, 1915), pp. vii and 76.

[11] See in this connection the evidence of H. W. Carr, representing the Bengal Paper Mill Co. Ltd, Calcutta, in *Evidence (Report of IIC)*, Vol. II (PP, 1919, XVIII), pp. 140–1.

[12] F. Noel-Paton [Gov. India pub.]: *Notes on Sugar in India* (3rd ed., Calcutta, 1911) pp. 10–14, 32–40. See also H. H. Ghosh: *The Advancement of Industry* (Calcutta, 1910), pp. 93–116, for the various methods of manufacture of sugar prevailing in India at the beginning of the century.

[13] For a discussion of the position of India in the British imperial system see S. B. Saul: *Studies in British Overseas Trade, 1870–1914* (Liverpool, 1960), Chapters III, IV, and VIII.

[14] Y. S. Pandit: *India's Balance of Indebtedness, 1898–1913* (London, 1937). With 1898–9 as base, the net barter terms of trade (import price index/export price index) declined to 75 in 1913–14. See also Ray: *India's Foreign Trade since 1870*, Chapter IV.

[15] Pandit, *India's Balance*, Chapter V.

power of ordinary Indians over the same period. Throughout the period of our enquiry, the only firm data available are for the output of some large-scale industries and for incomes from government employment. Agricultural statistics were collected, but the coverage varied from year to year, and the data were notoriously unreliable for individual years, although the trend over a number of years could be guessed at. The basic series which one has to start with are those for what might be called 'material' production, that is, primarily outputs of industries, plantations, mines and agriculture. The figure for agricultural output was the dominating one throughout. There are now available very careful estimates of agricultural output for British India by George Blyn;[16] also estimates of agricultural output for the whole of India by S. Sivasubramonian.[17] On the basis of the data on material production two studies of the national income of India, S. J. Patel[18] and S. Sivasubramonian,[19] have been prepared.

Blyn's study shows that total food-grain supply (measured in thousands of tons) in British India went down drastically in 1907–8 (below even the level reached in 1899–1900, although it remained above that of 1896–7); the total food-grain supply was also relatively low in 1904–5 and 1905–6. Food-grain exports from British India were positive in all these years.[20] Sivasubramonian's 1960 study showed that the gross values of food-grain output (at 1938–9 prices) were low (in relation to levels reached in 1902–3 and 1903–4) in the years from 1904–5 to 1908–9 and that it reached its trough in 1908–9. Thus there seems to be some truth in the conclusion reached by K. L. Datta, in his monumental enquiry into the causes of the rise in prices in India, that the rise in prices was partly due to the fact that the supply of food-grains was not keeping up with the growth of population and hence with the demand for food-grains.[21] Even if the food-grain output in some years rose faster than the trend rate of growth of population (which was about 6% for the decade 1901–11),[22] the recurrent

[16] George Blyn: *Agricultural Trends in India 1891–1947: Output, Availability, and Productivity* (Philadelphia, 1966).

[17] S. Sivasubramonian: 'Estimates of gross value of output of agriculture for undivided India, 1900–01 to 1946–7', in V. K. R. V. Rao *et al.* (eds.): *Papers on National Income and Allied Topics*, Vol. I (London, 1960), pp. 231–44.

[18] S. J. Patel: 'Long-term Changes in Output and Income in India: 1896–1900' *Essays on Economic Transition* (London, 1965), pp. 33–50. Patel used Blyn's 1951 study giving agricultural output for India as a whole. The results of Blyn's study had been quoted by Daniel Thorner in his paper 'Long-term Trends of Output in India' in S. Kuznets *et al.* (eds.): *Economic Growth: Brazil, India and Japan* (Durham, N. C., 1955). For the justification of using material production as the primary basis of national income estimates in under-developed countries, see Patel, 'Long-term Changes', pp. 38–9.

[19] Sivasubramonian: *National Income.*

[20] Blyn, *Agricultural Trends*, Appendix Table 5c.

[21] K. L. Datta [Gov. India pub.]: *Report on the Enquiry into the Rise of Prices in India* (Calcutta, 1914), Chapter x and pp. i–xiv (the latter contains the government resolution on the report, playing down internal factors and stressing the external factors).

[22] Davis: *Population of India and Pakistan*, pp. 26–7.

food shortages can reasonably be expected to have exercised a constant upward pull and provided a varying lower limit to any decline in prices in years of good harvests and/or declining export prices for food-grains. The other major reasons for rising prices were rises in the prices of exports and a high level of public investment. To the extent that the rise in prices of food-grains affected the poorer income-groups more than the richer, the purchasing power of the poorer groups must have suffered.

K. L. Datta has constructed series on money and real wages for workers in different industries in different parts of India. According to his estimates, the index number of average real wages for workers in the jute industry of Calcutta rose from 101 in 1890 to 116 in 1900 and 119 in 1904, but then fell to 107 in 1912. The index number of real wages for workers in the cotton industry of Bombay fell from 105 in 1890 to 91 in 1900 and then rose to 98.[23] These results are consistent with the estimates of real wages of workers in the cotton and jute textile industries which have recently been prepared by professor K. Mukerji and which are discussed in greater detail in Chapter 5 below. However, K. L. Datta estimated that the real wages of workers in unorganized industries and of artisans, such as carpenters, masons and blacksmiths, increased much more than the real wages of workers in organized industries. But the estimates for changes in the wages of workers outside organized industries and outside large towns or cities are even more unreliable than the estimates for changes in wages of workers in organized industries.[24] Moreover, one suspects that the estimates of changes in the wages of blacksmiths, carpenters and general labourers may have been seriously biased upwards by a burst of public expenditure and investment during the period 1905–8,[25] and by the casual empiricism of non-working-class observers, affected by temporary shortages of semi-skilled or unskilled labour. On the basis of the evidence relating to real wages of workers in organized industries alone, one can infer at best a modest improvement in the standard of living of the general mass of workers.

However, there were other groups in the economy which benefited from the increasing exports of non-food-grains such as raw jute, raw cotton and oilseeds, generally at improving prices; there were also groups which benefited from higher exports of jute manufactures, and from the relatively high levels of public construction activity. There were also second-order effects of increasing investment in cotton and jute mills. The series constructed by Surendra Patel showed a very slight advance in per capita output (at 1952–3 prices) in the decade 1905–15 over the decade 1896–1906; but this probably obscures the growth over the years 1900–5 and

[23] See Datta [Gov. India pub.]: *Report on the Enquiry into the Rise of Prices*, Vol. III, pp. 4–7 and 194–7, and Table 5.2 below.
[24] On the unsatisfactory nature of wage statistics in general, see Datta [Gov. India pub.]: *Report on the Enquiry into the Rise of Prices*, Vol. I, Appendix G.
[25] See Thavaraj: 'Capital formation in the public sector', Table 3.

1910–14 when output was not affected by either food shortages or the war. Sivasubramonian's 1965 study showed a far more significant advance from Rs. 49·4 per capita in 1900–1 to Rs. 55·7 per capita in 1913–14, both at 1938–9 prices.[26] But on the ground that a large part of Sivasubramonian's 1965 estimates is far more conjectural than the estimates of Patel, one probably ought not to attach too much importance to this difference. Our estimate of total consumption of piecegoods in India shows that consumption rose from 2,831·0 million yards in 1900–1 to 5,101·9 million yards in 1913–1914. Since population grew by only about 10% during the same period, there was a sizeable expansion in consumption per capita, and hence, barring dramatic changes in tastes in favour of cotton piecegoods, and barring extremely large price-effects, this provides support for the hypothesis that per capita incomes did rise over the period. This rise in incomes supported the increasing investment in cotton textiles; but there was also a substantial degree of import substitution in cotton textiles, since the ratio of total domestic production to total domestic consumption of cotton piecegoods rose during the period.

The impact of government policy on industrial investment in this period was not very important. It probably did provide a suitable climate for the reinvestment of a part of the profits made by European enterprises in India and for investment by Europeans in India in industrial enterprises, by maintaining a stable rupee–sterling exchange rate. It also provided a minimal market for the paper industry by guaranteeing to purchase a certain quantity from it, but this did not lead to any significant expansion of the domestic industry. Finally, it may have encouraged the growth of handloom production by encouraging the introduction of improved methods, but the impact of this policy was felt only in some restricted areas. The major movements of industrial investment in India during this period were determined by her place in the economic system of the British Empire as a primary-producing country earning hard currency and providing an open market for the centre country, that is, Great Britain. The only important qualifications to this were the increasing importance of Indian cotton mills in supplying domestic needs, and the yarn exports of Indian mills to China, which played an important role in the earlier years in the triangular settlement between Britain, China and India.

The period before the First World War witnessed two of the largest pioneering schemes ever launched by private enterprise. They were both conceived by J. N. Tata, although they were completed after his death by his family and other business associates. Pig iron was successfully manufactured by the end of the nineteenth century by the Bengal Iron and Steel Company. But the attempt of the latter at manufacturing steel had ended in failure. The Tata Iron and Steel Company began producing steel in

[26] Sivasubramonian: *National Income*, p. 338.

1912 with a much bigger plant and a better supply of iron ore. Years were spent prospecting before the entrepreneurs controlling the Tata Iron and Steel Company were able to find good quality iron ore within a reasonable distance of coal and markets. The house of Tata was also responsible for promoting and launching the hydroelectric power stations for utilizing the rainfall on the Western Ghats and supplying power to Bombay. These two Tata enterprises were financed entirely by capital raised in India, and they probably represented the two biggest blocks of initial capital for a private company in India up to that date. (The initial share capital for the Tata Iron and Steel Company was £1,630,000 plus a debenture capital of £400,000; the initial capital for the hydroelectric scheme was Rs. 20 million.) It should be noted that in both the iron and steel enterprises, the government had helped with a guarantee of purchase of part of the output and in other ways (such as extending the railway lines and helping in the purchase of land).[27]

In some ways, the years between the end of the nineteenth century and the beginning of the First World War were the most hopeful ones for the growth of the Indian industry in a colonial context. This period was marked by a substantial reinvestment of profits made by British residents in India in Indian business and industry. The government's interest in industrialization was fitful and undirected: with the exception of the experiment in Madras, the government was unwilling to pioneer factories. It still pinned its faith mainly on self-help and small-scale enterprises, and was loath to commit itself to any large-scale enterprise. Of course, there were pressures in Great Britain and India checking any bold action on the part of the government; and in some cases, the help of a Secretary of State could be procured for Indian enterprise (as by J. N. Tata). But for the most part the government was prepared to let things alone so long as people seemed by and large to be satisfied with the condition of the economy.[28] A few native states, such as Mysore, and to a much lesser extent Travancore and Baroda, were more concerned with industrialization, but their resources were far too limited and their powers were hedged about in far too many directions for them to do anything for the growth of large-scale industries.[29]

[27] For an account of the promotion of the Tata iron and steel and hydroelectric schemes, see F. R. Harris: *Jamsetji Nusserwanji Tata: A Chronicle of his Life* (Bombay, 1958); for a short account of the history of the iron and steel industry in India up to about 1931, see D. H. Buchanan: *The Development of Capitalistic Enterprise in India* (New York, 1934), Chapter XIII; see also Chapter 9 below.

[28] See Section 2.4 above.

[29] The activities of the Mysore Government in promoting industrial and agricultural development are described in the evidence of C. Ranganatha Rao Sahib, the Assistant Director of Industries, Mysore State, *Evidence (Report of IIC)*, Vol. III (PP 1919, XIX), pp. 590–1; the total annual revenue of all the native states averaged Rs. 271,155,000 and the annual revenue of Mysore averaged Rs. 24,000,000 approximately over the years

3.2 DEVELOPMENTS DURING THE FIRST WORLD WAR
AND IN THE IMMEDIATE POST-WAR YEARS

The First World War brought to an end the limited prosperity of India, which was based on expanding exports, domestic production of agricultural products, and increasing consumption of essential goods such as cotton cloth and sugar. The consumption of cotton piecegoods declined continuously from about 5,102 million yards in 1913–14 to a disastrous low of about 2,899 million yards in 1919–20.[30] Similarly, the imports of refined sugar into British India (and in this period, despite some increase in internal production of refined sugar, imports were synonymous with domestic consumption) declined from about 17,937,000 cwt. in 1917–18 to 10,520,000 cwt. in 1918–19 and 9,639,420 cwt. in 1919–20.[31] A calculation made by the Government of India's Commercial Intelligence and Statistics Department in *Review of the trade of India in 1919–20* (pp. 65–6) showed that even in 1919–20, when the quantities imported and exported of most commodities were very much greater than in 1918–19 and in the last two years of the war, the value of exports at 1913–14 prices was Rs. 1,976,196,000 as against Rs. 2,442,015,000 in 1913–14 and the value of imports at 1913–14 prices was Rs. 1,012,864,000 compared with Rs. 1,832,479,000 in 1913–14. The value of machinery and mill-work of all kinds imported was Rs. 42,553,000 (at 1913–14 prices) in 1919–20 as against Rs. 82,626,000 in 1913–14 (at 1913–14 prices). The figure for machinery and mill-work imports in 1919–20 was, however, more than double that for 1918–19 (at 1918–19 prices). If we take the imports of machinery and mill-work as providing a very crude index of imports for private investment in modern industry in India, we can see that the war had practically eliminated all investment except what was absolutely necessary to keep the plant and machinery going, and the situation did not change until 1920–1.[32]

During the war investment in railways and in irrigation also practically ceased. Hence one can say that while the industrial capacity of India was intensively used during the war, nothing could be done either to

1901–2 to 1911–12. See *Moral and material progress and condition of India, 1911–12* (PP 1913, XLVI), pp. 29–30. As against this, the annual revenue of the central government of British India exceeded Rs. 900 million over the years 1901–2 to 1911–12. See Reserve Bank of India: *Banking and monetary statistics of India* (Bombay, 1954), pp. 872–3. (I have added the revenue of the central government on revenue account to the capital contributed by railways, etc. in the capital account.)

[30] These figures are derived from ITB: *Reports on the cotton textile industry* (1927, 1932 and 1936), and Gov. India, CISD: *Statistical abstract for British India* (Calcutta, annual) for the relevant years. The details are given in Chapter 7 below.

[31] Gov. India, CISD: *Annual statements of the seaborne trade of British India.*

[32] On the setback suffered by Indian trade during the First World War, see Ray: *India's Foreign Trade since 1870*, Chapter v.

replace the worn-out equipment or to repair the damage to the social infrastructure that was caused by the war.[33] The major modern industries in India, however, earned fabulous profits during the war. The jute industry probably led the rest in terms of its profitability because of the peculiar situation of jute in India. Before the war more than half of the raw jute produced in India was exported to foreign countries, particularly the countries of continental Europe. With the beginning of hostilities against Germany and Austria–Hungary and the desperate shortage of shipping space to and from Europe, these exports virtually ceased. The mills on the Hooghly had now a captive supply of jute and they also enjoyed the virtual monopoly of jute manufactures. As a result an enormous increase in the prices of jute manufactures in relation to the prices of raw jute took place leading to fantastic profits.[34] The cotton mills of Bombay also made very large profits because of the sudden drop in imports from the U.K. But the position of the cotton-mill industry was different from that of the jute industry; first of all, cotton prices were determined by world demand and not by Indian demand, since Japan, which was the biggest foreign consumer of Indian cotton before the war, continued to import large amounts of Indian cotton. Secondly, imports of cotton piece-goods from the U.K. continued, although on a much reduced scale, while Japan began to export large quantities of cotton goods to India. (The gross imports of cotton piecegoods from Japan during the period 1915–16 to 1919–20 averaged 109·6 million yards annually as against only 6·4 million yards annually over the period 1910–11 to 1914–15.)[35]

After the war, then, most of the companies in the modern industrial sector had enough liquid resources to finance substantial expansion, though in many cases the profits made during the war were frittered away in very large dividends which were not generally reinvested in modern industry. Allowance must also be made for the substantial volume of unsatisfied consumption demand which had built up during the war. Some of the potential demand was utterly destroyed by the famine and influenza epidemic of 1918–19. Still, there was a boom through the years 1919–20 to 1921–2, which was reflected in, among other things, the number of joint-stock companies registered and the capital involved in these companies.[36]

[33] Some railway equipment was in fact exported during the war to Mesopotamia.

[34] Gov. India, CISD: *Review of the trade of India for 1917–18* (Calcutta, 1918), p. 21; see also *idem*: *Review of the trade of India for 1915–16* (Calcutta, 1916), pp. 45–7.

[35] Source: Gov. India, CISD: *Review of the trade of India* (Calcutta, annual) for the corresponding years.

[36] The numbers of companies newly registered in 1919–20, 1920–1 and 1920–2 were 948, 1,039 and 717 respectively, as against 356 in 1913–14; the amounts of paid-up capital of these companies were Rs. 15,781,000, Rs. 31,505,000 and Rs. 19,013,000 in 1919–20, 1920–1 and 1921–2 respectively, as against only Rs. 7,694,000 in 1913–14. See Gov. India, CISD: *Joint-stock companies in British India and in the Indian States 1922–23* (Calcutta, 1925), p. i.

TABLE 3.2 *Imports of industrial machinery and mill-work into India, 1900–40*

Year	Value of imports of machinery and mill-work excluding agricultural machinery (Rs. '000)	Index nos. of textile machinery prices (not comparable between panels)	Index nos. of textile machinery prices on a comparable basis (1904 = 100)	'Real' value of machinery and mill-work imported into India (Rs. '000)
1899–1900	24,094			
1900–1	20,554			
1901–2	27,305			
1902–3	30,130			
1904–5	36,429	100.00	100.00	36,429
1905–6	45,919	98.29	98.29	46,718
1906–7	53,445	93.51	93.51	57,454
1907–8	62,940	95.41	95.41	65,968
1908–9	61,223	102.09	102.09	59,970
1909–10	44,901	100.68	100.68	44,598
1910–11	41,784	109.29	109.29	38,232
1911–12	41,021	107.54	107.54	38,145
1912–13	50,627	107.34	107.34	47,165
1913–14	72,524	103.67	103.67	69,957
1914–15	55,886	100.00	109.10	51,225
1915–16	43,926	110.14	120.16	36,556
1916–17	50,728	158.30	172.71	29,372
1917–18	41,037	218.28	238.14	17,232
1918–19	46,879	277.90	303.19	15,462
1919–20	84,155	265.42	289.57	29,062
1920–1	202,322	300.29	327.62	61,755
1921–2	315,205	339.23	370.10	85,168
1922–3	218,172	289.45	315.79	69,088
1923–4	171,816	223.96	244.34	70,318
1924–5	126,448	210.28	229.42	55,116
1925–6	126,776	194.40	212.09	59,775
1926–7	116,453	210.61	229.78	50,680
1927–8	131,738	222.05	242.26	54,379
1928–9	163,761	184.70	201.51	81,237
1929–30	161,677	180.88	197.34	81,928
1930–1	126,676	186.52	203.28	62,316
1931–2	95,888	100.0	216.68	44,253
1932–3	98,213	87.82	190.29	51,612
1933–4	119,948	84.70	183.53	65,356
1934–5	113,915	83.38	180.67	63,051
1935–6	125,311	98.64	213.73	58,631
1936–7	126,281	111.92	242.51	52,072
1937–8	170,414	112.47	243.70	69,928
1938–9	189,083	121.67	263.63	71,723
1939–40	144,761	136.44	295.64	48,965

Source: Accounts relating to the Seaborne Trade of British India.

Notes: The textile machinery prices are derived from the *Annual Statements of Foreign Trade of the United Kingdom*. The basic figures are those of various kinds of textile machinery exported to different parts of India. The quantities are measured in tons. The classification of textile machinery exports changed drastically between 1913 and 1914 and again between 1930 and 1931. Hence three different series have been constructed with current quantities as weights. (The price index of 1904 is applied to the imports of machinery and mill-work into India in 1904–5, that of 1905 is applied to the imports of machinery and mill-work in 1905–6, and so on. The justification for this is that in British trade accounts the calendar year is used whereas in Indian trade accounts years ended 31 March are used, and that it took normally a month or so for cargo to reach India from the United Kingdom.) The three different series are made comparable by the following device. The price of the last year of the first series (1913) is compared with the price of the first year for the second series (1914). For this purpose spinning and weaving machinery exports in 1914 are grouped together for Madras, Bombay and Bengal, so that prices and quantities then become comparable (though only approximately since figures of textile machinery exports up to 1913 include also textile machinery other than spinning and weaving machinery). The quantities used as weights are those for 1913. In a similar way, the prices of 1930 and 1931 are compared by grouping weaving and preparatory machinery together for all the ports for 1930 and 1931, since in 1931 weaving and preparatory machinery are distinguished but not the ports, whereas the opposite classification is used in 1930. Needless to say, the figures within the same panel with the same system of classification are more comparable than figures relating to years in two different panels. Up to 1918–19 an exchange rate of £1=Rs. 15 was used: for 1919–20 the exchange rate of £1=Rs. 10 was used following official practice. For all other years the figures of imports are given in rupees in the official accounts.

The real index of the boom was the amount invested in modern industry. While the declared annual values of imports of machinery and mill-work during the years 1919–20 to 1923–4 were more than double (and in 1921–2 more than four times) the money value of imports of machinery and mill-work in 1913–14, the year of the pre-war peak in imports, in real terms they must have been considerably less. In order to get some idea of the 'real' magnitudes involved, we have deflated the values of imports of machinery and mill-work for India excluding Burma by an index of textile machinery prices. The results are presented in Table 3·2. It is probable that the resulting series understates to some extent the post-war 'real' values – particularly the values during the years 1919–20 to 1923–4. From the calculations made in the *Review of the trade of India in 1919–1920* (pp. 165–6) we get an implicit ratio of 225.21 of 1919–1920 prices to 1913–14 prices as against the crude textile machinery price index of 265·42 (with 1914 as the base year) here used. Secondly, there is evidence (see Table 12.2 below) that the prices of sugar refining machinery (measured in weight) declined much more drastically between 1920 and 1933 than did textile machinery prices. Although it is true that no price indices can be derived for pre-war years and no valid comparison can be made between pre-war and post-war years, it can be said that, to the extent that imports of sugar machinery were more important after 1930 than after 1920, our figures understate the real value of investment during the depression years. But the fact remains that textile machinery imports were the most important imports of industrial machinery in practically all the years, and hence some special weight must be given to them.

There were no major changes in the technology of the jute or cotton-textile industry during the period.[37] Probably improvements in design and performance were important in metallurgical industries, such as the steel industry, and in chemical industries, such as sugar refining and paper and pulp making. But investment in these industries began to play an important part only during the late twenties and particularly during the thirties. This probably means that industrial investment during the depression is understated by the figures in Table 3.2. There is also reason to believe that import of machinery for modern industry was a more important component of total imports of machinery and mill-work during the depression than it had been earlier. Agriculture was abnormally depressed from 1929–30 onwards; as a result one would expect imports of machinery used in agriculture (but not classified as 'agricultural machinery') – such as oil engines for irrigation – to decline drastically. One would also expect imports of machinery for purposes of lighting or other work by local authorities to decline very much. On the other hand, we definitely know that there was a spurt in investment in sugar and paper industries in the early thirties. For all these reasons, we would expect the use of the gross figures for machinery and mill-work imports to understate the true orders of magnitude of investment during the early thirties in relation to the investment in earlier years.

The series, however, includes various kinds of electrical machinery, all kinds of prime movers (excluding the ones used by railways) and machinery used by small-scale and cottage industries (such as boot and shoe machinery, rice-mill machinery, sewing machines, and so on). But the items such as electrical machinery, prime movers, or 'other machinery' are troublesome: quite a large proportion of them must belong to the modern industrial sector, but it is difficult to form an idea of what the proportion should be. One can construct a series of imports of 'industrial machinery' but this would be quite misleading, since it might, for instance, include paper machines, but not the digesters, beaters, etc., which account for a large fraction of investment in the paper industry; similarly, it would have to leave out the boilers or steam engines used for various purposes in cotton or jute mills. Hence for the moment, we have left the series of imports of machinery and mill-work as it is, without any adjustment.

---

[37] The stagnation of the techniques used in the jute industry was described (and deplored) by Dr S. G. Barker in his report to the Indian Jute Mills Association in 1935, cited in Chapter 8 below. The increase in the proportion of hessian looms to sacking looms is unlikely to have affected the results very much. There were, however, some important changes in the cotton-mill industry in the *proportion* of different types of equipment used over the period considered. See S. D. Mehta: *The Indian Cotton Textile Industry: An Economic Analysis* (Bombay, 1953), Chapter 1.

It can be seen that the series does not display any pronounced trend throughout the period from 1919–20 to 1938–9. A major part of the increase in investment during the years from 1919–20 to 1923–4 must have been frittered away in increases in the prices of capital goods, leaving the real average levels of investment only a little higher than in 1913–14. The four years from 1924–5 to 1927–8 appear to have been lean years, but the years from 1929–30 to 1930–1 record surprisingly high levels of imports of machinery and mill-work in real terms. The figures of imports of machinery during the depression years are in fact much higher than one would have expected if one was familiar only with the history of advanced industrial countries.

But all this amounts to the statement that India's industrial investment was not hampered as much by the depression as one would have expected on the basis of the experience of the advanced capitalist countries during the same period. To offset this, there is no strong evidence of the steady upward trend in investment that one has come to associate with the advanced countries of today.

The First World War marked a major 'structural break' as far as the composition of private investment in modern manufacturing industry was concerned. In the post-war period, the level of investment in the cotton mill industry grew in relation to the level of investment in the jute-mill industry; and correspondingly the level of investment in western India rose relatively to that in eastern India. In Tables 7.10 and 7.11 (pp. 258 and 260 below) are shown estimates of the investment in the cotton mill industry of western India, and of the real value of cotton-textile machinery imports into India; Table 8.1 (p. 273 below) provides estimates of the real value of investment in the jute industry of Bengal (which accounted for more than 95% of investment in the jute industry of India; see column (3) of Table 7.11 and column (2) of Table 8.1).

In Table 7.11 ('Imports of cotton-textile machinery into India as a whole'), by comparing columns (3) and (4), we find that the ratio of the money values of cotton-textile machinery imports to those of jute-textile machinery imports increased substantially during the period after 1918 compared with the period before 1914. The ratio of the sum of cotton-textile machinery imports to the sum of jute-textile machinery imports was 1·37 for the period from 1905–6 to 1913–14 and 2·21 for the period from 1919–20 to 1930–1. This change was not caused primarily by a change in the relative prices of cotton and jute-textile machinery (see column (6) of Table 7.11 and column (3) of Table 8.1: textile machinery exported to Bombay consisted primarily of cotton-textile machinery, whereas textile machinery exported to Bengal consisted primarily of jute-textile machinery and reflected a change in the relative levels of real investment in the cotton and jute-textile industries). This change in the commodity-composition of investment was accompanied by a change in the relative levels of investment in eastern and western India. For, in spite of a major shift of the cotton industry away from western India to southern and northern India, the cotton industry of western India continued to dominate the cotton industry of India as a whole, and there was no shift of the jute industry away from Bengal at all. On the other side, the cotton and jute industries continued to be the single most important manufacturing industries of western and eastern India respectively.

Comparing columns (5) of Tables 7.10 and 8.1, we find that the ratio of the sum of the gross values of real investment in the cotton-mill industry of western India to the sum of the gross values of real investment in the jute industry of Bengal was 1·16 for the period from 1905–6 to 1913–14 and 1·41 for the period from 1919–20 to 1930–1. The really dramatic decline in the ratio of investment in the jute industry of Bengal to investment in the cotton-mill industry of western India took place, however, after 1930–31. Comparing the figures in columns (1) of Tables 7.10 and 8.1, we find that the ratio of the sum of cotton-textile machinery imports into Bombay to that of jute-textile machinery imports into Bengal rose to 2·34 during the period from 1931–2 to 1938–9. (For reasons indicated in the notes to the tables, it was not possible to construct the series of real values of investment in the jute- and cotton-textile industry for this period.) Even if there was some increase in the local fabrication of jute-textile machinery, compared with that of cotton-textile machinery, it is not likely to have been great enough to account for this decline in the imports of jute-textile machinery into Bengal compared with the imports of cotton-textile machinery into Bombay.

The rate of industrial growth of Bengal was drastically reduced after the First World War because of the decline in the rate of growth of the jute industry – its major manufacturing industry. This decline was in its turn linked to the tribulations of the advanced capitalist countries during the immediate post-war years and during the depression of the thirties. The other major industries of Bengal such as coal and tea were also, like jute, extremely dependent on export markets; hence the doldrums of the twenties and the depression of the thirties also hit these industries badly. Unlike jute goods, Indian cotton piecegoods were produced mainly for home consumption. The total consumption of cotton piecegoods in India continued to expand, though not continuously, after the First World War. What is more, the share of the Indian cotton mills in total domestic production and consumption increased after the First World War. Although there was a shift of cotton mills away from western India, and particularly away from Bombay City and Island, western India continued to share in this expanding market for Indian piecegoods. A considerable volume of investment continued to flow into the cotton-mill industry, and other smaller industries benefited from the external economies created by the growth of the cotton-textile industry.

The introduction of tariff protection for the cotton, sugar, steel and paper industries did help industrial growth in Bengal; but none of the other manufacturing industries could compete, in the size of their labour force or capital employed, with the cotton and jute industries. The sugar industry accounted for a very large volume of investment in one or two years in the early thirties. Most of the new sugar mills, however, were sited in Bihar and the United Provinces. While new cotton mills were set up in Bengal, the major movement of the cotton mills was towards southern and northern India rather than to eastern India.[38] Some new sugar mills also appeared in western India.[39] Hence the relative decline in the industrial importance of Bengal compared with western India (comprising modern Maharashtra and Gujarat), caused by the decline of the jute and other export-based industries, was not fully checked by the growth of other industries in eastern India.

3.3 EXPLANATION OF THE COURSE OF AGGREGATE PRIVATE INVESTMENT DURING THE INTERWAR PERIOD

The basic explanation of the relative stagnation of private investment in modern industry is to be sought in three sets of factors. First, India was caught in the world-wide crisis which involved the capitalist countries during the interwar period. The twenties were a period of prosperity for the U.S.A.; but for most European countries, including the U.K., the biggest single customer for Indian goods, and the biggest exporter of goods and services to India, the twenties were a period at best of fitful prosperity.[40] The first few years of the twenties were marked by widespread depreciation of national currencies, particularly in Western Europe. This resulted in intense competition for the few new industries which had been built up (on a rather small scale) in India during the First World War. The end of the twenties was a period of relative prosperity for the industrialized countries of Western Europe and North America. But the world agricultural depression had already set in by 1926: the total exports of India on private account, which had increased up to 1924–5, declined after that year and remained stagnant up to 1928–9, after which they declined

---

[38] See M. M. Mehta: *Structure of Indian Industries* (Bombay, 1955), p. 158.

[39] *Ibid.*, pp. 178–81.

[40] For the U.S.A., see J. A. Schumpeter: 'The Decade of the Twenties', *American Economic Review*, Supplement, May 1946; for the U.K., see A. C. Pigou: *Aspects of British Economic History, 1918–1925* (London, 1947); for the world as a whole, see W. A. Lewis: *Economic Survey, 1919–1939* (London, 1949).

TABLE 3.3   *Terms of trade for India, 1899 to 1940*

Year	Index numbers of prices of exported articles (1873 = 100)	Index numbers of prices of imported articles (1873 = 100)	Crude terms of trade (1873 = 100)
1899	100	87	115
1900	124	96	129
1901	116	96	121
1902	113	86	131
1903	103	88	117
1904	104	93	112
1905	116	96	121
1906	139	105	132
1907	145	116	125
1908	151	106	142
1909	133	99	134
1910	127	109	117
1911	136	113	120
1912	145	117	124
1913	154	117	132
1914	160	114	140
1915	155	146	106
1916	163	236	69
1917	170	262	69
1918	199	289	69
1919	277	274	101
1920	281	280	100
1921	239	228	105
1922	245	201	122
1923	224	193	116
1924	222	217	102
1925	233	211	110
1926	225	195	115
1927	209	185	113
1928	212	171	124
1929	216	170	127
1930	177	157	113
1931	125	134	93
1932	120	139	86
1933	118	128	92
1934	117	122	96
1935	128	122	105
1936	127	122	104
1937	133	144	92
1938	128	142	90
1939	133	137	97
1940	164	181	91

Source: Gov. India, CISD: *Index numbers of Indian Prices, 1861–1931* and *Statistical abstract for British India* for the relevant years (Calcutta, annual).

drastically.[41] Further, prices of agricultural commodities began to fall from 1926 onwards, so that India obtained lower values from her exports of agricultural staples such as raw jute, raw cotton and wheat. If one takes the crude indices of export and import prices published by the Government of India, the ratio between the two fell far below the pre-war value during the war and the post-war years up to 1924, and improved a little towards the end of the twenties, though the value attained in 1914 was never regained. The years of the First World War and the interwar years witnessed a drastic decline in the terms of trade of India compared with 1914, and even compared with 1899, when the terms of trade had been much lower than in 1914. The relevant figures are given in Table 3.3.[42] Although the terms of trade figures quoted are very crude since the underlying price indices are based on averages of unweighted prices, they do indicate the direction of change: there is probably a tendency to underestimate both a rise (borne out by a comparison of Pandit's estimates of gross and net barter terms of trade with our crude terms of trade figures) and a fall in the terms of trade, since the quantities and prices of agricultural commodities exported often moved together. The general estimate of a fall in the terms of trade during the interwar years is borne out also by detailed studies of prices of particular commodities.[43]

Although the basic commodity composition of India's trade remained unaltered, there were important changes in the structure of her foreign trade as far as relations with different countries were concerned. The percentage share of the U.K. in Indian imports declined during the 1920s (although she remained far and away the biggest exporter to India), and it continued to decline during the thirties, although the Ottawa Pact changed the situation temporarily. The United States of America and Japan increased their share of imports into India. On the side of Indian exports, Japan and the U.S.A. took a larger share than before, although the relative importance of exports to both countries was affected by the depression and the Ottawa Pact, when the shares of the U.K. and other British Empire countries went up again: the years from 1926 to 1931 had seen the lowest percentage shares of the U.K. in total Indian exports.[44] One cannot see that India obtained any substantial advantages by being linked a little more closely with the more 'dynamic' economies of the U.S.A. and Japan;

[41] See Banerji: *India's Balance of Payments*, p. 24 (Table II).

[42] See also D. N. Gurtoo: *India's Balance of Payments (1920–1960)* (Delhi, 1961), pp. 110–11. Gurtoo's figures of terms of trade cover only the period from 1927–8 to 1938–9, but they also show the same tendencies as our 'crude' terms of trade figures over the same years; for instance, the two deepest troughs of Gurtoo's series were reached in 1932 and 1938. Both our series and Gurtoo's series register a decline over the years from 1929 to 1939, compared with 1927–8.

[43] See, for example, H. A. F. Lindsay: 'World Tendencies Reflected in India's Trade', *JRSA*, LXXIV, No. 3,876, 4 March 1927, pp. 384–94.

[44] Venkatasubbiah: *Foreign Trade*, Part II.

in general, the advanced countries depended less on the raw materials that India could supply, and Japan's dependence on low-quality cotton was a temporary phenomenon at best and was bound to cease as soon as Japan began to compete with other countries in the better quality ranges of cotton goods. India probably derived some advantage during the depression from a closer link with the U.K., which had proved the least unstable of all the advanced economies, but against this must be set her deteriorating trade relations with Japan, resulting from Imperial preference and discrimination aimed mainly against Japanese goods.[45] India continued to play her role as a major earner of dollars for the sterling area, and there were proposals about an Imperial federation embracing India and the U.K., but they were not taken seriously.[46] India's position as an exporter of primary commodities made her extremely vulnerable to the depression which swamped the capitalist countries, and the policies pursued by the Government of India could counteract the effects only slightly.

The second factor contributing to the relative stagnation of private investment in modern industry was that, despite some industrialization, India remained primarily an agricultural economy during the twenties and thirties. The share of the factory industries in total national income hardly exceeded 6% in normal years. Normally the primary sector contributed 60% or more of total income;[47] but during the 1930s its share went down to about 50%. The gross current value of agricultural output was affected very drastically by the agricultural depression; even the gross value at constant 1938–9 prices remained more or less constant: it fluctuated between roughly Rs. 7,800 million and Rs. 8,400 million over the years from 1919–20 to 1930–40 with no clear trend upward or downward.[48] If all consumer goods had enjoyed tariff protection during the whole interwar period, and if the demand for consumer goods had been determined by the aggregate national income alone, private investment in modern industry would have levelled off after satisfying the internal demand.[49] The major consumer goods industries in fact enjoyed tariff protection only from

[45] On the trade relations of India and Japan, see C. N. Vakil and D. N. Maluste: *Commercial Relations between India and Japan* (Calcutta, 1937); on the shares of the principal foreign countries in the export and import trades of India, see Venkatasubbiah: *Foreign Trade*, Part II.

[46] See Schuster: 'Indian Economic Life'.

[47] Sivasubramonian, in his *National Income*, has computed sectoral income as well as national income figures at current prices. From these figures (pp. 255, 337), it appears that the share of 'manufacturing' in national income was high (8%) in 1920–1; in other years it fluctuated between 4% and 7%. Since the share of the factory sector in Indian national income in 1950–1 was only about 6%, one can see the degree to which the incomes generated in modern industries moved with total national income.

[48] Sivasubramonian: 'Estimates of gross value of output of agriculture'. Blyn, *Agricultural Trends*, pp. 349–50, finds that the all-crop output for British India at constant prices fluctuated around Rs. 10,000 million over the years from 1921–2 to 1940–1.

[49] See Chapter 1 and its Appendix in this connection.

1929–30 onwards. Apart from iron and steel, and heavy chemicals for a brief period, there was no tariff protection for capital goods industries, nor was there any definite government encouragement for the development of these industries. Hence the movement of total Indian national income was dominated by movements of the weather, and world factors affecting the demand for primary products, and private investment in modern industry was only partially insulated against the effect of adverse world factors.

Thirdly, as we have seen in Chapter 2, the Government of India pursued an extremely cautious economic policy: the only departure from the pre-war period was the policy of discriminating protection. This did not have any substantial effect on total private investment until the depression of the thirties had set in, endangering the balance of the budget of the Government of India, the existing industries of India and the position of Great Britain in Indian markets. The response to all the threats was to increase customs duties with preference in favour of imports from the British Empire. The revenues of the Government of India remained critically dependent on the state of Indian agriculture.[50] The Government of India refused to indulge in any deficit financing since this was taken to be a sure sign of incompetence. The balance of payments was not a real constraint on the policies of the government: after 1922–3 India was not plagued by balance of payments difficulties. Even during the thirties, the balance of trade on current account was in her favour. Special difficulties were created by the massive repatriation of British capital during the thirties but these were overcome through the exports of gold from India.[51] The Government of India could borrow in India at very low rates of interest during the thirties. But, as we have seen in Chapter 2 above, it refused to avail itself of these opportunities.

However, there is a problem about the trends of private investment and private industrial production during the thirties: aggregate private investment in real terms during some years of the depression was higher than during the middle years of the twenties, and the aggregate internal demand for certain commodities such as refined sugar and cotton piecegoods was surprisingly well-maintained. The explanation of this phenomenon would run roughly as follows: during the late twenties, the agricultural depression had already started, and internal industrial production was also affected by competition from abroad; thus both agricultural and industrial incomes

---

[50] For a clear description of the degree of dependence, see Lord Meston: 'Public Finance' in Sir John Cumming (ed.): *Modern India* (London, 1931), particularly pp. 220–1.

[51] See Gurtoo: *India's Balance of Payments*, Chapter VI; and Banerji, *India's Balance of Payments: Estimates*, pp. 191–6. Banerji estimates that about Rs. 1,492.3 million of India's external public debt were repaid during the period from 1921–2 to 1938–9; of this amount about Rs. 1,000 million were paid back during the five years from 1931–2 to 1935–6.

were adversely affected.[52] During the depression, the terms of trade between industry and agriculture turned sharply in favour of the former both because, in the world as a whole, prices of industrial commodities did not fall as drastically as the prices of agricultural commodities,[53] and because there were heavy import duties on industrial goods whereas there was little protection for agricultural commodities apart from an import duty on wheat. With the increase in industrial activity behind tariff walls, there was a relatively high level of investment in modern industry, and there was a higher level of activity in internal commerce. The distribution of income very probably turned in favour of the towns. The income elasticity of demand for industrial goods being relatively high, the demand for these goods in towns probably expanded considerably. On the other hand, since most of India's agricultural production consisted of food-grains, and a large proportion of that output was consumed in the villages themselves,[54] the real incomes of the farmers were not affected as drastically as the fall in prices by itself would suggest. If cotton piecegoods and sugar-cane can be regarded as necessities for the majority of farmers, then one would expect their consumption to be relatively inelastic downward with regard both to price and to incomes. However, the consumption levels were not maintained just out of the current incomes of the farmers. There is a large body of evidence to suggest that the degree of indebtedness of the peasants increased during the depression period. The dishoarding of gold was another factor helping the maintenance of the levels of consumption of essential commodities. Finally, the relative inelasticity of current government expenditure helped maintain the level of money incomes in India to some extent (see Chapter 2 above).

It can also be argued that from 1930 onwards, India's links with Great Britain paid off in two ways, assuming that India had to operate under capitalist conditions and had therefore to be closely linked to the world capitalist system. First, as was stated earlier, Great Britain was less affected than other advanced capitalist countries by this trade depression, and Indian exports to Britain contracted less than those to other advanced countries. This already showed itself in the larger share of Great Britain

[52] An additional factor was the deflationary policy pursued by the government of India during the years from 1923–4 to 1925–6, which resulted in balanced governmental budgets and a stable external value of the rupee (which was fixed at 1s. 6d. to the rupee). As we have argued in Section 2.6, while the higher exchange value of the rupee probably helped exporters of primary products, it also made the position of Indian producers of manufactured products more vulnerable to foreign competition at home and abroad. See, for example, the written evidence of Mysore Iron Works, dated 16 October 1928, in ITB: *Report on the removal of the revenue duty on pig iron including the evidence recorded during the enquiry* (Calcutta, 1930), p. 23.

[53] League of Nations: *The Causes and Phases of the World Economic Depression* (Geneva, 1931), pp. 156–70.

[54] See, for example, S. A. Husain: *Agricultural Marketing in Northern India* (London, 1937, Chapter IV.

in Indian exports in 1930 and 1931, compared with immediate pre-depression years. Secondly, the Ottawa Agreement signed between different members of the British Commonwealth did have the effect of ultimately increasing the British share in Indian exports even further. Initially, the Ottawa Agreement was necessitated by the departure of the U.K. from free trade in 1931 when under the Import Duties Act, duties were imposed by Britain on a large range of imports from India. India had already extended preference to British goods in various measures of protective and revenue tariffs, and her bargaining position was particularly poor because of the fact that agriculture was more severely hit than industry by the depression, even assuming that the Indian delegation, which was official, could have an independent policy. India extended preferences over about £55 million worth of imports from Britain (at 1929–30 values); in return, she received preferences over about £47 million worth of exports to the U.K.[55]

There were misgivings in India about the effect of the agreement: it was considered that protection might often be nullified because of preference for British goods; it was also feared that Japan might retaliate by boycotting Indian raw cotton (and pig iron) of which she was the biggest consumer. This latter fear did materialize and India had to enter into a separate agreement with Japan in 1934. But the bid of Japan to capture the Indian market was effectively foiled by (a) the further development of the Indian cotton-textile industry and (b) the formal and informal agreements with Britain. The Ottawa Agreement and Mody–Lees Pact, in respect of the maintenance of the market for Indian raw cotton in the U.K. and the market for British cotton goods in India, helped to increase the share of Indian agricultural exports to Great Britain. The Ottawa Agreement also improved the position of India as an exporter in other countries of the British Empire. To the extent that these developments helped maintain the incomes of cultivators in India, they also helped the modern industries which had been developing under the umbrella of tariff protection.[56]

[55] Sir Padamji P. Ginwala: 'India and the Ottawa Conference', *JRSA*, LXXXI, No. 4,175, 25 November 1932, p. 50.

[56] For an analysis of the effects of the Ottawa Agreement on Indo-British trade patterns see B. N. Adarkar: 'The Ottawa Pact' in Radhakamal Mukherjee: *Economic Problems of Modern India*, Vol. I. (London, 1939), pp. 378–95. The Ottawa Agreement, however, did not permanently check the fall in the British share of Indian imports. Whereas the British share in Indian exports moved up from 21.0% in 1930 to 27.5% in 1932 and 35.5% in 1940, the British share of imports into India changed from 42.8% in 1930 to 35.4% in 1932, 40.6% in 1935 and 25.2% in 1940. The reasons for such disparate movements are rather complex: they lie on the one side in India's quasi-monopolistic position in the case of some raw materials and agricultural goods exported to the U.K., which was strengthened by preferences. They also lie in the inability of Great Britain to compete with Japan, and of other countries of the British Empire to compete in the Indian market even with Imperial Preference. See Venkatasubbiah: *Foreign Trade of India*, pp. 54–70, for the statistical picture. See also H. A. F. Lindsay: 'Recent Ten-

It is interesting to recall that this was a period of large-scale repatriation of British capital from India. The effects of such repatriation on the supply side seem to have been more than counterbalanced by the floor provided to aggregate demand for Indian products through Imperial Preference and various bilateral and international control agreements.

dencies of Indian Trade', *JRSA*, LXXXI, 1933, p. 457; Sir David B. Meek: 'Indian External Trade', *JRSA*, LXXXIV, 1936, pp. 835–69, and 'World Economic Controls and India's Part in These', *JRSA*, LXXXVII, 1939, pp. 554–69; B. N. Ganguli: *Reconstruction of India's Foreign Trade* (New Delhi, 1946), pp. 20–4.

4

LAND AND THE SUPPLY OF RAW MATERIALS

The theories of under-development which emphasize the shortage of factors of production as the primary explanation generally follow the traditional grouping of factors of production under three heads: land, labour and capital. A further factor is generally added to account for the specific character of modern capitalism, viz., 'organization' (as in Marshall's *Principles*) or 'entrepreneurship' (as in Schumpeter's theory of economic development).[1] In the present chapter we are primarily concerned with the factor 'land': more specifically, we are concerned with the way in which peasant agriculture in India responded (or failed to respond) to the demands for raw materials (and less directly, food) generated by the limited development of modern industry in India up to 1939. One must here guard against two different kinds of fallacies: there is the fallacy which regards the illiterate peasant as essentially irrational in his responses to economic opportunities. The fallacy here is caused by deductive reasoning on faulty premises; illiterate peasants in under-developed countries have traditional value systems and are trapped in pre-capitalist social structures. Hence they are incapable of recognizing the most profitable course of action when faced with new economic opportunities or, even if they recognize the most profitable course, their social organization prevents them from following it. Empirical work has disposed of the major premises of such a syllogism. The peasants' value systems are rarely so irrational that they are incapable of smelling good opportunities of making money. Their social structure, however rigid, generally still leaves room for responding in the right direction when opportunities for making a profit change.

However, some economists are so surprised by this evidence of the basic rationality of peasants that they tend to extrapolate such rationality in an illegitimate fashion. This extrapolation usually takes two forms: the short-term rationality of peasants is extrapolated into long-term planning by peasants and farmers to preserve or improve the fertility of the soil and bring about an optimal allocation of the land and labour resources at their disposal. Secondly, the role of the supply of information or of new inputs by the government or other public authorities is minimized. In either of these cases what is not recognized is that even if peasants are individually rational,

[1] In the popular textbook by Professor C. P. Kindleberger: *Economic Development* (2nd ed.; New York, 1965) there are four consecutive chapters headed 'Land', 'Capital', 'Labour' and 'Organization'.

there are certain changes which can be brought about only by collective action, and a passive government or pre-capitalist (or capitalist) social structure can hamper long-term planning in the rural areas precisely by impeding such collective action (or the supply of information on a collective basis). In the following account of the response of Indian agriculture to the limited industrialization of India I have tried to bring out the element of rationality of peasants and farmers in adapting the crop pattern in the desired direction without, however, losing sight of the limits placed on such rationality by illiteracy and an agrarian structure which impeded individual or collective initiative by actual cultivators.

4.1　AGRARIAN BACKGROUND AND GENERAL TRENDS IN THE PRODUCTIVITY OF LAND

Of the industries we are concerned with, four were dependent on the supply of raw materials derived from agriculture. As such, the pattern of development of agriculture affected their fortunes quite closely. We shall be concerned primarily with the way in which the direct inputs into industry from agriculture behaved, although it is obvious that the development of agriculture also affected the state of internal demand for industrial products in India and the cost of the goods consumed by wage-earners, which in turn affected the levels of wages of the latter. The prices of agricultural commodities were primarily determined by world factors, and therefore the cost of wage-goods was also affected primarily by world factors. There was only one period of time, viz., the years of the First World War and the five or six years thereafter, when the cost of wage-goods rose abnormally; but this rise was generally more than counterbalanced by the rise in the prices of industrial goods. In general, industrialists did not face any problem of rising wages caused by a scarcity of food.

The low level of productivity per acre in Indian agriculture and therefore the low level of income per capita (since the land–man ratio was quite low) severely limited the market for most consumer goods. Since the distribution of incomes was extremely uneven, the market for mass consumption goods of better quality was even more limited.

The unit of cultivation all over India was the peasant family holding small plots of land; these peasants generally did not own most of the land they cultivated. A small group of *zemindars*, or rich farmers, generally owned a large percentage of the land, and a large body of poor peasants owned the rest, with a rather thin layer of comfortably-off farmers wedged between. Although there were differences in the legal form of land tenure in different regions of India, the ordinary cultivators all over India were poor, illiterate, and subject to coercion by money-lenders, upper-caste groups and landlords. A sizeable proportion of the peasantry were merely

TABLE 4.1 *Area and average productivity (per acre) in India, 1900–01 to 1939–40 (five-year averages)*

Period	Food crops			Commercial crops			All crops		
	Area (million acres)	Value of product (Rs. million)	Average productivity per acre (Rs.)	Area (million acres)	Value of product (Rs. million)	Average productivity per acre (Rs.)	Area (million acres)	Value of product (Rs. million)	Average productivity per acre (Rs.)
1900–1 to 1904–5	221.0	5,602.6	25.4	55.4	2,033.6	36.7	276.4	7,636.2	27.6
1905–6 to 1909–10	231.0	5,512.4	23.9	61.8	2,079.4	33.6	292.8	7,591.8	25.9
1910–11 to 1914–15	238.3	5,918.6	24.9	66.5	2,190.6	32.9	304.8	8,109.2	26.6
1915–16 to 1919–20	239.5	5,992.6	25.0	62.8	2,272.8	36.2	302.3	8,265.4	27.3
1920–1 to 1924–5	238.1	5,626.0	23.7	63.0	2,357.0	36.8	302.1	7,993.0	26.5
1925–6 to 1929–30	238.1	5,503.2	23.1	71.7	2,455.8	34.2	309.8	7,959.0	25.7
1930–1 to 1934–5	247.0	5,702.0	23.1	71.8	2,607.8	36.3	318.8	8,309.8	26.1
1935–6 to 1939–40	244.5	5,550.0	22.7	75.3	2,852.0	37.9	319.8	8,402.0	26.3

Source: The figures in the table were computed on the basis of Sivasubramonian: 'Estimates of gross value of output of agriculture', pp. 231–46.

Notes: (a) All values are measured in 1938–9 prices.
(b) Food crops include rice, wheat, *jowar, bajra*, barley, maize, *ragi*, grain and other foodgrains and pulses. Commercial crops include linseed, sesamum, rape and mustard, groundnut, castor seed, other oil seeds, sugar-cane, tea, coffee, tobacco, cotton, jute, indigo, opium and other crops.

TABLE 4.2 *Productivity per acre of different crops in India (Rs. per acre in 1938–9 prices)*

Annual average over the period	Rice	Cotton	Sugar-cane	Wheat	Jowar	Jute
1900–1 to 1904–5	42.49	15.04	137.33	22.92	11.97	83.26
1905–6 to 1909–10	37.64	14.64	132.30	22.45	16.61	68.30
1910–11 to 1914–15	40.48	14.62	152.65	23.98	17.05	81.84
1915–16 to 1919–20	39.76	15.79	163.81	23.22	27.83	84.10
1920–1 to 1924–5	37.44	18.42	162.64	23.18	22.20	76.76
1925–6 to 1929–30	36.91	18.18	166.01	21.56	13.89	84.47
1930–1 to 1934–5	37.65	17.03	207.03	21.11	13.37	87.34
1935–6 to 1939–40	35.08	19.28	202.69	24.45	13.53	81.41

Source: The figures were estimated from the data on area under cultivation and value of output of each crop given by Sivasubramonian, 'Estimates of gross value of output of agriculture'.

tenants-at-will and so had little incentive to invest in their holdings; another large fraction of the peasants did not have enough capital to be able to invest in new tools or fertilizers unless the latter yielded returns which were higher than the very high rates of interest that they had to pay on their loans.[2]

In spite of the extreme poverty of the majority of Indian peasants, and in spite of the fact that a very large proportion of the land was used for food production, the supply of raw materials for exports abroad and for use by industry increased almost continuously over the period 1900–40, as the figures in Table 4.1 will testify.

There are several features to be noted in Table 4.1: (i) the stagnation in the area under food crops between the years 1910–11 and 1929–30; (ii) the continuous fall in average productivity per acre of food crops from 1920–1 onwards and the fact that the average productivity of food crops per acre was distinctly lower during the last five years than during the first five years of our period; (iii) the rise in the proportions of the area and the value of commercial crops to total cultivated area and total value of agricultural output respectively; (iv) the relative stability of the productivity of commercial crops per acre over the period from 1915–16 to 1929–30, and the distinct rise in the same during the last ten years.

In order better to analyse the movements of productivity per acre the yields per acre of some individual crops for India as a whole and for individual provinces have been computed in Tables 4.2, 4.3 and 4.4. From these tables the decline in the yield per acre of rice is quite evident; so is the rise in the productivity per acre of raw cotton from 1920–21 onwards

[2] See Appendix to this chapter (p. 115) for references.

TABLE 4.3 *Yield per acre of sugar-cane in different provinces in India, 1912–13 to 1938–9 (figures in lb.)*

Annual average over the period	United Provinces	Madras	Bihar and Orissa*	Bombay including Sind†	Punjab	Central Provinces and Berar	Sind
1912–13 to 1913–14	1,813.5	4,085.0	2,464.0	5,343.0	1,679.0	2,383.0	n.a.
1914–15 to 1918–19	2,097.0	5,192.2	2,339.8	5,831.4	1,764.4	2,593.0	n.a.
1919–20 to 1923–4	2,172.0	6,054.2	2,370.0	5,429.2	1,801.6	2,654.0	n.a.
1924–5 to 1928–9	2,111.0	6,151.4	2,312.6	6,118.8	1,735.2	3,122.6	n.a.
1929–30 to 1933–4	2,848.0	6,296.0	2,592.4	6,088.4	1,668.6	3,536.8	n.a.
1934–5 to 1938–9	3,058.8	6,340.0	2,536.2	5,547.2	1,664.0	3,524.0	4,506.6

Source: Gov. India, CISD: *Estimates of area and yield of principal crops in India* (Calcutta, annual).

Notes: n.a. means 'not available'.

* Includes only Bihar from 1935–6 onwards: the average for 1934–5 to 1938–9 omits the yield for 1934–5 (yield per acre for Bihar *and* Orissa in 1934–5 was 3,388 lb.).

† Does not include Sind from 1933–4 onwards (the average for the period 1929–30 to 1933–4 omits the figure for 1933–4).

TABLE 4.4   *Yield per acre of cotton in different provinces in India,*
1912–13 to 1938–9 (figures in lb.)

Annual average over the period	United Provinces	Madras	Punjab	Bombay*	Central Provinces and Berar	Hyderabad	Sind†
1912–13 to 1913–14	135.0	46.0	107.0	87.5	81.0	43.0	162.0
1914–15 to 1918–19	99.2	61.0	100.0	79.2	79.0	65.2	122.0
1919–20 to 1923–4	122.0	71.6	114.2	86.0	85.8	103.6	n.a.
1924–5 to 1928–9	130.8	79.0	109.6	79.8	87.4	102.0	n.a.
1929–30 to 1933–4	117.4	79.8	123.6	72.0	74.8	60.2	n.a.
1934–5 to 1938–9	121.0	79.4	166.8	69.8	65.8	61.2	172.2

Source: Gov. India, CISD: *Estimates of area and yield of principal crops in India*
(Calcutta' annual).
Notes: n.a. means 'not available'.
* Includes Sind from 1914–15 to 1928–9.
† A princely state, included for the sake of comparison.
The yields per acre of cotton in all the provinces included increased again during the
period from 1939–40 to 1943–4 but the yield in Sind increased most dramatically, from
172.2 lb. for our last period to 210.2 lb. for the period from 1939–40 to 1943–4.

and of sugar-cane from 1925–6, and, more dramatically, from 1930–31
onwards.

George Blyn's study of trends in yields per acre in India[3] entirely confirms
our findings and the findings from Sivasubramonian's paper summarized
above. Taking all food crops it is found that there was a declining trend in
yield per acre, particularly after 1911. This declining trend was accounted
for by the declining trend in yield per acre of rice; although wheat had
a moderately increasing yield per acre, particularly up to 1911, its increase
was entirely swamped by the decline in rice yields, for rice output accounted
for about half the total food-grains output, and was about four times
greater than wheat output. For crops other than food-grains there was
a rising trend in yield per acre: the main components of this increase were
increasing yields per acre of tea, cotton and sugar-cane. There was hardly
any increase in the yield of jute per acre.

Taking the regional variations, it is found that the yield per acre of
all crops taken together showed a declining trend in Greater Bengal (i.e.
Bengal, Bihar and Orissa) throughout the period from 1911 to 1946.
Even in Greater Bengal there was a rising trend in yields per acre of
non-food-grains; but this latter trend was dominated by the rapid increase
in tea yield and by slightly increasing yields of oil-seeds and sugar-cane.
Among the other regions, Central Provinces also showed a decline in the
yield per acre of all crops taken together; there was a slightly rising trend

[3] Blyn: *Agricultural Trends*, Chapter VI, VIII, and VIII.

in the yield of crops other than food-grains. Greater Punjab and Madras showed rising trends in the yields of all crops and of non-food-grains and almost stationary trends in yields of food-grains, after some initial increases in yields per acre. In the case of Bombay–Sind and United Provinces, the trend in yields of all crops was stationary from 1911 onwards, a slowly declining trend in the yield of food-grains being offset by a rising trend in non-food-grains.

Analysing the evidence on both regional trends and trends in yields per acre, it appears that the former were more important in determining the basic pattern. Yields per acre may be deemed to be determined by the following factors: (1) improvements in the quality of crops produced; (2) increases in the supply of irrigation, which directly raises the yield in areas with scanty rainfall and allows a greater amount of complementary inputs to be used: (3) increases in inputs through private effort. The economic policy of the Government of India had an influence on all three sets of factors as we shall see in a moment.

4.2 SCOPE AND LIMITATIONS OF GOVERNMENT AGRICULTURAL POLICY: ROLE OF AGRICULTURAL RESEARCH

After the establishment of the Imperial Agricultural Research Institute at Pusa, a major part of the effort of the scientists connected with agricultural research went into the development of improved varieties of crops in India. Sir Albert Howard developed improved varieties of wheat, Dr Barber and his associates developed improved, high-yielding varieties of sugar-cane, and R. S. Finlow in Bengal tried to popularize an improved variety of jute known as *Kakya Bombai*.[4]

In the case of cotton, efforts had been made since before the middle of the nineteenth century to introduce long-staple varieties.[5] In the twentieth century special impetus had been given to the efforts when the British cotton industry experienced difficulties in securing adequate supplies of long-staple cotton from the U.S.A. during the First World War. (A similar impetus had been given to the efforts during the American Civil War.)[6]

---

[4] See J. MacKenna [Gov. India pub.]: *Agriculture in India* (Calcutta, 1915); Louise Howard: *Sir Albert Howard in India* (London, 1953); J. MacKenna: 'Scientific Agriculture in India', *JRSA*, LXIV, No. 3316, 9 June 1916, pp. 537–50; N. C. Choudhury: *Jute and Substitutes* (Calcutta, 1933).

[5] See Seth Leacock and David G. Mandelbaum: 'A Nineteenth Century Development Project in India: the Cotton Improvement Program', *Economic Development and Cultural Change*, III, No. 4, July 1955; David S. Landes: *Bankers and Pashas: International Finance and Economic Imperialism in Egypt* (London and Cambridge, Mass., 1958), pp. 71–4.

[6] See *Report of the Indian Cotton Committee* (Calcutta, 1919), Ch. 1; and B. L. Sethi [Gov. India pub.], 'History of Cotton', in B. L. Sethi *et al.*: *Cotton in India*, Vol 2 (Bombay, 1960), pp. 1–39, particularly pp. 13–18.

The Departments of Agriculture were from the beginning badly under-staffed. Since normally there was only one well-trained agricultural officer to a district (and sometimes not even that) with a handful of demonstrators under him, it was impossible for him to make any useful contact with even a substantial fraction of peasants in a district. The peasants often remained completely ignorant of the advances that had been made in techniques of cultivation even when the latter were within their means. Of course, the capital at the command of a peasant was normally quite meagre; hence it took a good deal of persuasion with actual examples before peasants would accept an innovation which would require the investment of capital.

Therefore the Agricultural Departments of the provinces pursued the policy of least resistance and tried to popularize new varieties of crops which could withstand the rigours of the uncertain Indian weather and which would bring in extra profits without substantially increased out-of-pocket expenses, although very often (as in the case of high-yielding varieties of sugar-cane) these improved varieties would require a much larger input of labour, particularly for irrigation. Compared with the investment that was made, this policy brought in remarkable returns in the form of a rapid spread of improved varieties of sugar-cane, wheat and cotton. But one area of effort which remained almost completely untouched was the introduction of new artificial fertilizers or the creation of demand for the older types of artificial or natural fertilizers already available in India. The experiments that were conducted with artificial fertilizers were often badly designed, and they were conducted in a very irregular fashion.[7] The Departments of Agriculture or the central research institute at Pusa could never spare enough money to conduct the experiments with artificial fertilizers under all the important combinations of soil types, rainfall and temperature; hence the results could not be used with any confidence to produce recommendations as regards the use of fertilizers. The Departments as a matter of routine often issued recommendations on the basis of a very small number of experiments, and the results were often disastrous, so that the peasants lost all confidence in the advice of the Departments of Agriculture.

In the meantime, some unhelpful advice was given about the usefulness of farmyard manure, and the wickedness of burning cow-dung as fuel.[8]

[7] On the unsatisfactory state of research in the economic effects of fertilizers and the reasons for it see the evidence of C. M. Hutchinson, late Imperial Agricultural Bacteriologist and in December 1926, Chief Scientific Adviser to the Fertilizer Propaganda of India, in RC on Agriculture in India: *Evidence*, Vol. iv, *Evidence taken in the Bengal Presidency* (Bombay, 1927), pp. 296–301.

[8] See, for example, the evidence of R. D. Anstead, Director of Agriculture, Madras, in RC on Agriculture in India: *Evidence*, Vol. iii, *Evidence taken in the Madras Presidency* (Calcutta, 1927), p. 43: 'I am inclined to think that the evil effects of using cowdung as fuel are apt to be exaggerated. A very large proportion of the cowdung thus

Under the price–cost relations prevailing, it was more economical over most parts of India to burn cow-dung than coal. Cow-dung was often practically a free commodity, whereas coal definitely was not. Moreover, even if the peasants did recognize the usefulness of cow-dung as a manure, there would not be enough of it in the country to make up even a fraction of the deficiency of nitrogen in Indian soils.

Furthermore, in some parts of the country in which sodium nitrate, bonemeal, or oilcakes were produced as fertilizers, there was little attempt by the government to see that these were used in India rather than exported, or that their prices did not go beyond the reach of ordinary peasants. While the Departments of Agriculture disapproved of the exports of these products, the government did not take any positive steps (such as finding more profitable ways of using the fertilizers, subsidizing their use, or discouraging the export of the fertilizers while encouraging their production by other means) to see that the amounts used by Indian farmers increased. See, for example, the evidence of R. D. Anstead, Director of Agriculture, Madras, before the RC on Agriculture in India:

The main drawback to the more extended use of natural manures is their cost. This has of late years increased so much that in many cases it has ceased to be profitable to use them . . . This is largely due to the fact that these manures (bones and oil-cakes) are being exported in large quantities every year and that there is a good demand for them, especially from the estates in Ceylon . . . Until this export is checked in some way it is not possible to extend the use of indigenous manures.

The use of artficial manures is increasing, but again it is largely a question of cost. Of late the price has been reduced and now sulphate of ammonia, for instance, is being used in very large quantities in this Presidency. If the price can be brought low enough to ensure a profit by their use, there is no particular difficulty in persuading the ryots to use manures.[9]

Saltpetre was produced on a large scale in the United Provinces and the Punjab. But most of it was exported. Atul Chatterjee wrote in 1908: 'Very little saltpetre is now used in the country as a fertilizer owing to its high cost in comparison with oilcakes.'[9a] around the end of the 1930s the consumption of artificial fertilizers in India as a whole was still very low, that of ammonium sulphate and other 'artificials' coming to 70,000 tons and 25,000 tons respectively. These figures included the consumption by the

used is collected from roads, etc., and would in any case have never reached the land as manure. Fuel of some kind must be had and people are not likely to buy wood, however cheap it may be, instead of using cowdung which they can get for nothing. I am of the opinion that nothing can be done to stop this practice and that it does not matter so much as is sometimes thought.'

[9] RC on Agriculture in India: Vol. III, *Evidence taken in the Madras Presidency* (Calcutta, 1927), p. 41–3.

[9a] A. C. Chatterjee [IPG pub.]: *Notes on Industries in the United Provinces* (Allahabad, 1908), p. 164.

plantation industries.[9b] Hence one of the most potent methods of raising agricultural yields in the world remained completely untapped in India up to 1929; after the world depression, it was quite useless to try to persuade the peasants to spend increased amounts on the business of farming.

4.3 CHANGES IN YIELDS OF SUGAR-CANE AND COTTON IN DIFFERENT REGIONS: IRRIGATION AS AN EXPLANATORY VARIABLE

The areas under different individual crops throughout the period responded quickly to changes in the relative prices of the crops concerned, as the studies of Dharm Narain, Raj Krishna, and Rabbani and the earlier studies of A. R. Sinha, H. C. Sinha and J. R. Guha Thakurta have clearly shown.[10] Further, the pre-war shift of area from food crops to non-food crops can be explained to a large extent by the strong foreign demand for such crops as raw cotton and raw jute when their prices relative to the prices of competing crops showed an upward trend.[11]

TABLE 4.5 *Area under sugar-cane and yield per acre of sugar-cane in India, 1930–1 to 1939–40 (excluding Burma)*

Year	Area under sugar-cane ('000 acres)	Area under improved varieties of sugar-cane ('000 acres)	Yield per acre of sugar-cane (in tons)
1930–1	2,905	817	12.3
1931–2	3,077	1,170	14.1
1932–3	3,425	1,846	14.6
1933–4	3,422	2,295	15.1
1934–5	3,602	2,446	15.1
1935–6	4,154	3,071	15.1
1936–7	4,584	3,452	14.7
1937–8	3,997	2,968	14.0
1938–9	3,270	2,673	11.0
1939–40	3,767	2,893	12.8

Sources: ITB: *Report on sugar* (Delhi, 1938), p. 18; *Reviews of the Sugar Industry of India* (Supplements to the *Indian Trade Journal*).

[9b] Sir Bryce Burt, 'Agricultural Progress in India during the decade 1929–1939', *JRSA*, xc, No. 4607, 20 February 1942, p. 214.

[10] Dharm Narain: *The Impact of Price Movements on Areas under Selected Crops in India, 1900–39* (Cambridge, 1965); Raj Krishna: 'Farm Supply Response in India-Pakistan', *Economic Journal*, LXXIII, September 1963; A. K. M. Ghulam Rabbani: 'Economic Determinants of Jute Production in India and Pakistan', *Pakistan Development Review*, Vol. 5 (1965), pp. 191–228; A. R. Sinha, H. C. Sinha and J. R. Guha Thakurta: 'Indian Cultivators' Response to Prices', *Sankhya: The Indian Journal of Statistics*, Vol. 1, Parts 2 and 3, May 1934; A. R. Sinha: 'Interrelation between Supply and Price of Raw Jute', *Sankhya*, Vol. 4, 1938–40, pp. 397–400; and *idem*, 'A Preliminary Note on the Effect of Price on the Future Supply of Raw Jute', *Sankhya*, Vol. 5, 1940–1, pp. 413–16.   [11] See Narain, *Impact of Price Movements*, Chapters IV and V.

But the yield per acre of commercial crops grown in the fields did not show any strong upward trend until after 1921.[12] This increase in yields was immediately associated with the introduction of improved varieties as shown by the figures for sugar-cane given in Table 4.5.

Similarly, in the case of cotton, the increase in measured yields per acre was largely associated with the spread of long-staple varieties of cotton (i.e. varieties with staple length of $\frac{7}{8}$ inch and above): while there had been an increase in the output of indigenous long-staple varieties (such as Tinnevelly cotton) even before the war, the proportion of long-staple varieties (particularly the American ones) increased significantly from 1926 onwards.[13]

During the four years from 1927–8 to 1931–2 the area under cottons below $\frac{7}{8}$ inch formed 75% of the area under cotton, and the area under medium to long staples ($\frac{7}{8}''$ to $1''$) formed 25% of the same. In 1938–9, the area under short-staple cotton was 63%, that under medium-staple 32·5% and that under long-staple ($1''$ and above) 4·5% of the total. According to the calculations of the Indian Central Cotton Committee the average yield of cotton in India during the five years from 1932 to 1937 was 108 lb per acre as compared with 96 and 95 lb. in the two preceding five-year periods.[14]

The increases in the yields of sugar-cane and raw cotton cannot be attributed only to the introduction of new varieties, however; far less can they be attributed to the *discovery* of new varieties of crops. Irrigation had a very important part to play: this becomes particularly clear if we look at the changes in yields of cotton in the different provinces. The yields registered the most dramatic increase in the three provinces of Madras, Punjab and Sind.[15] The public irrigation system had been most rapidly expanded in Punjab and Sind; around 1928 the areas irrigated constituted the highest percentages of the net sown area in the three provinces of Sind, Punjab and Madras in that order, if we exclude the North-West Frontier

---

[12] Blyn: *Agricultural Trends*, especially Fig. 7.3.

[13] ITB: *Report regarding the grant of protection to the cotton textile industry* (Calcutta, 1932), para. 34; ITB, Special Tariff Board: *Report on the enquiry regarding the level of duties necessary to afford adequate protection to the Indian cotton textile industry* (Delhi, 1936), para. 36.

[14] Burt: 'Agricultural Progress', pp. 206–7.

[15] There is reason to believe that the value of 162 lb. for average yield per acre in Sind for the years 1912–13 and 1913–14 is not very dependable, since the area under cotton was relatively small in the province at that time. In the decade preceding the opening of the Lloyd Barrage Scheme in 1932 the area under cotton in Sind was 320,000 acres whereas the area under American cotton was only 25,650 acres. During 1939–40 the area under cotton in Sind was 904,000 acres, of which about 664,000 acres were under American cotton. During the same year, of the total area of 2,641,105 acres under cotton in the Punjab, 93% was irrigated, and 54.2% was under Punjab-American cotton. See Indian Central Cotton Committee: *Annual Report for the year ending 31st August, 1940* (Bombay, 1941), pp. 75–6. According to Sir Bryce Burt, 'Agricultural Progress', the increase in yields due to improved varieties was greatest in the irrigated tracts.

TABLE 4.6 *Area under irrigation in British India excluding Burma, 1900–1 to 1938–9 ('000 acres)*

Province	1900–1		1910–11		1920–1		1930–1		1938–9	
	Area irrigated	Gross area cropped	Area irrigated	Gross area cropped	Area irrigated	Gross area cropped	Area irrigated	Gross area cropped	Area irrigated	Gross area cropped
Bengal	748	62,098	5,270	43,069	1,826	28,037	1,735	28,399	1,894	30,023
United Provinces:										
Agra	6,478	30,449	6,533	33,058	8,501	29,406				
Oudh	2,203	11,587	2,190	12,138	2,694	11,040				
Total	8,681	42,036	8,723	45,196	11,195	40,446	10,227	43,750	11,959	44,971
Punjab	9,446	28,570	10,094	28,597	12,954	24,561	14,814	30,265	16,544	28,845
Central Provinces	403	16,210	611	19,794	1,156	17,454				
Assam		4,687	87	6,028	205	6,339	579	6,646	655	7,487
Madras	5,971	27,850	9,906	38,202	9,369	37,606	9,153	39,192	8,444	35,958
Bombay	771	21,448	880	26,098	1,106	25,126	4,145	34,019	1,147	29,740
Sind	3,072	4,021	3,259	4,514	2,857	3,823			4,433	5,631
Berar	68	6,820	36	7,218	27	6,622				
Bihar									4,038	23,352
Central Provinces and Berar							1,130	27,658	1,060	27,438
North-West Frontier Province			844	2,783	889	2,035	973	2,432	1,032	2,453
Orissa										7,029
Eastern Bengal			64	19,966						
Bihar and Orissa					6,013	30,903	5,260	29,779		
British India	29,123	214,328	39,896	242,019	47,773	223,657	48,226	242,915	53,730	243,584

Source: Statistical abstracts relating to British India.

Notes: Bengal included Bihar and Orissa in 1900–1 and 1910–11 (partly); Bombay included Sind in 1930–1; Eastern Bengal was excluded from Bengal in 1910–11; there were various other differences in coverage; hence the absolute areas are not comparable between years except in the cases of Madras, the Punjab and the United Provinces, and even in these cases caution should be exercised.

Provinces.[16] The rates of expansion of irrigation in the different provinces of India are shown in Table 4.6.

The gross figure of areas irrigated is not a proper index of the effective value of irrigation. Irrigation brought more benefit to the areas with scanty rainfall than to the areas with heavy but uncertain rainfall; the area irrigated sometimes included the whole command area of a particular source of water, irrespective of whether that water was actually used or could be supplied when the normal source of water, viz., rainfall, proved insufficient or untimely. Measures of the area irrigated could not take account of the unevenness of the terrain, or the uneven intensity of irrigation. Finally, the official figures do not take account of the damage to the crops caused by faulty drainage, waterlogging and salinity, and excessive use of water by farmers.[17]

Nor should the figures of area irrigated by public works be taken as a proper index of area irrigated in all the regions of India. In the southern peninsula, particularly, private tanks and wells were extremely important as a source of irrigation and the exploitation or development of such sources was heavily influenced by economic factors, such as the increase in yields expected, the costs of excavation or of oil-engines and the prices of crops prevailing. It is reported that in Madras 'for a few years previous to the outbreak of [the First World War] the very high prices which were being obtained for most agricultural produce were reflected in the farming economy by a considerable increase in the number of wells'.[18]

Enough has been said above to indicate why we should not expect any simple correlation between the area irrigated and the effectiveness of sources of water supply other than rainfall, or between the proportion of the area irrigated and the rise in yields, or between expansion in the area irrigated and the rise in yields. But the proportion of the area effectively irrigated and the rise in yields are strongly related in that a high value of the former seems to have been a necessary though not a sufficient condition for the latter.

[16] H. H. Mann: 'The Agriculture of India', *The Annals of the American Academy of Political and Social Science*, Vol. 145, 1929, p. 75.

[17] For a discussion of the economic effects of irrigation, see H. H. Mann: 'The Economic Results and Possibilities of Irrigation', *Indian Journal of Agricultural Economics*, Vol. 13 (2), 1958, pp. 1–6; on the different problems and methods of irrigation in the alluvial plains of the Indo-Gangetic delta and the valleys of the Deccan, see A. V. Williamson: 'Irrigation in the Indo-Gangetic Plain', *Geographical Journal*, Vol. 65 (1925), pp. 141–53; and *idem*: 'Indigenous Irrigation Works in Peninsular India', *Geographical Review*, Vol. 21, October 1931, pp. 613–26. For a short review of irrigation works carried out by the Government of India under British rule see Sir Bernard Darley: 'Irrigation and Its Possibilities' in Radhakamal Mukerjee (ed.): *Economic Problems of Modern India*, Vol. 1 (London, 1939), pp. 148–67.

[18] D. T. Chadwick: 'Agricultural Progress' in Playne and Wright, *Southern India*, p. 748. The Department of Industries in Madras helped the farmers by lending the assistance of modern boring tools and experts in boring, and by giving loans for the purchase of oil-engines.

In Bihar and Orissa the yield of sugar-cane failed to rise significantly although the proportion of net sown area irrigated there was higher than in many other Indian provinces; in the United Provinces the yield of cotton failed to rise, although again a relatively high proportion of its net sown area was irrigated; in the Punjab the yield of sugar-cane failed to rise. In the case of the Punjab and United Provinces it was probably a matter of exploiting the differential advantage: while in the United Provinces sugar-cane became distinctly more profitable than cotton with the development of better varieties, in the Punjab it was American cotton which became much the more profitable crop. This led to the transfer of better-quality land from under sugar-cane in the Punjab and from under cotton in the United Provinces, thus producing the observed results.[19]

We are left with Bihar and Orissa, Bombay Deccan, Bengal and Central Provinces as the regions for which the trends in yields per acre cannot be explained just by substitution between different crops. In all these cases there was little public investment in the land, in the form of extension of irrigation. In the Central Provinces, in western Bengal and in southern Bihar and northern Orissa there was no easily accessible subsoil water which could be exploited by private means; there were also no rivers with gentle slopes which could be blocked to produce artificial reservoirs without considerable expenditure. In other words, costly public irrigation works on a large scale would have had to be constructed for an effective supply of water on a permanent basis. Such construction was ruled out by the policy of the Government of India that, generally speaking, only productive works would be constructed.

Productive irrigation works are expected within ten years after the probable date of their completion to yield sufficient revenue to pay their working expenses and the annual interest calculated at 4% on the capital invested. No project is now sanctioned as a productive public work unless it can be shown beyond reasonable doubt that when fully developed it will fulfil these conditions.[20]

While the Irrigation Commission of 1901–2 had recommended a programme of irrigation work costing Rs. 440 million, they had specifically ruled out irrigation projects which were not expected to bring in high returns.

---

[19] Narain: *Impact of Price Movements*, Chapters IV and VII, and Blyn: *Agricultural Trends*, pp. 283–97, give the areas under sugar-cane and cotton in the different regions of India. Blyn has apparently failed to realize the significance of the fact that in the Greater Punjab, including N.W.F. Province, while there was a very high rate of growth of the area under cotton, the area under sugar-cane was practically stagnant over the period from 1926–7 to 1940–1, and that in the United Provinces over the same period, while there was a high rate of growth of the area under sugar-cane, the area under cotton actually declined at a rapid rate, particularly after 1933–4.

[20] Gov. India, Public Works Department: *Review of Irrigation in India, 1911–12* (Simla, 1914), p. 1.

If we look at the pattern of changes in yields per acre we also observe that, generally speaking, the yield per acre of a particular crop increased only in those provinces in which the total production of that crop was rising. The trends in yields of, and areas under, sugar-cane in Madras, the United Provinces, and the Punjab clearly illustrate this point. There is also the case of jute, of which improved varieties were supposed to be introduced, but which did not experience any increase in yield over the interwar period. In 1937–8 the area under the varieties of jute recommended by the Departments of Agriculture was 1·76 million acres out of a total area under jute of 2·89 million acres,[21] but there was no appreciable trend in the yield per acre of jute. Of course, it may be the case that the so-called improved variety of jute was not suited to the cultivators' conditions,[22] but if one takes at their face value figures of spread of improved varieties and of increased profits from the improved varieties under experimental conditions, one has to look for a different factor. This factor may well be the depressed conditions of the jute market after 1927 and particularly after 1929. The cultivator might simply have decided that it was not worth his while to devote as much care and as great an amount of inputs (particularly those which he had to buy in the market) to the jute crop as before.

Of course, jute may have been involved in the general decline in the yield of the soil that seems to have occurred in Greater Bengal. But Blyn has pointed out that most of the decline in yields in Greater Bengal is to be ascribed to the decline in yields in Bihar and Orissa.[23] It is interesting to notice that the falling yield of rice in Bihar and Orissa was also connected with a sharp decline in the acreage under rice.[24] It is not very clear exactly what factors caused the deterioration in yield in Bihar and Orissa; the prevalence of lateritic soils, the high rate of soil erosion, and the absence of either private or public irrigation works in many parts of the province may have been responsible.[25]

[21] Burt, 'Agricultural Progress', p. 207.

[22] One of the best accounts of the problems associated with the introduction of improved varieties in India is contained in Albert Howard: 'The Improvement of Crop Production in India', *JRSA*, LXVIII, Nos. 3,530 and 3,531, 16 July and 29 July 1920. This paper is also valuable in focussing attention on the problem of assuring the proper use of water by the cultivator who often used to irrigate his crop far too freely and damage both the immediate yield by preventing proper aeration of the soil, and the long-term yield by creating waterlogged conditions.

[23] Blyn, *Agricultural Trends*, p. 174.

[24] Dharm Narain: 'Agricultural Change in India' (Review of George Blyn, *Agricultural Trends*), *Economic and Political Weekly* (Bombay), Vol. II, No. 6, 11 February 1967, pp. 359–60.

[25] For an account of soil erosion in the Damodar valley region which traverses eastern Bihar and western Bengal, see R. Maclagan Gorrie [Gov. India pub.]: *Forestry Development and Soil Conservation in the Upper Damodar Valley – A 15 year scheme* (Damodar Valley Corporation, Calcutta, c. 1954), pp. 10–15. For an account of soil erosion in western Bengal see the evidence of E. O. Shebbeare, Conservator of Forests, Bengal, in RC on Agriculture in India: *Evidence*, Vol. IV, *Evidence taken in the Bengal Presidency*

The decline in yields per acre of rice may also have some relation to the failure of the Departments of Agriculture to evolve varieties of paddy which could respond well to the use of artificial fertilizers under conditions of uncertain rainfall. The situation in Madras was different from that in Greater Bengal because the former had two monsoons and a much larger fraction of the area was irrigated, thus assuring a more certain supply of water. The yield of rice in Madras rose over the period from 1891 to 1911, and remained more or less constant over the period 1911–41. In both the United Provinces and Greater Bengal there was a declining trend in the yield of rice per acre; in the other regions the trend was erratic with a downward bias.[26]

There were also interregional variations in shifts in the area under food-grains and non-food-grains over the period (see Tables 4.7 and 4.8). Before the First World War all the regions except Greater Bengal and Greater Punjab experienced a rise in the ratio of the area under non-food-grains to the area under food-grains. In the case of Greater Punjab, of course, non-food-grains and commercial crops do not coincide, for wheat was exported in large quantities. During the war there was a check in the rise of this ratio, but after the war the ratio of the area under non-food-grains to that under food-grains again began to rise. The early years of the thirties again checked the rise but in most of the regions the rise was continued after about 1933–4. Ultimately, three regions – Greater Bengal, United Provinces and Central Provinces – ended up with a lower ratio of the area under non-food-grains to that under food-grains in 1938–9 than in 1913–14; the other three regions ended up with higher ratios. For British India as a whole the ratio in 1938–9 was marginally higher than in 1913–14.[27] The ratio of the output of non-food-grains to food-grains was distinctly higher in 1938–9 than in 1913–14 in British India as a whole and in the three regions, Madras, Greater Punjab and Bombay-Sind.

Reviewing the history of changes in the cropping pattern and in the yields of commercial crops per acre after the First World War, we can conclude that internal demand had a strong influence on them. In the case of cotton, in spite of sustained effort by the Departments of Agriculture, the areas under medium and long-staple varieties had failed to expand appreciably before the war, mainly because the *desi* varieties were more

(Bombay, 1927) pp. 206–24; for an account of soil erosion in Bihar and Orissa see the evidence of J. H. Lyall, Officiating Conservator of Forests, Bihar and Orissa, RC on Agriculture in India: *Evidence*, Vol. XIII, *Evidence taken in Bihar and Orissa* (Calcutta, 1928), pp. 416–29. There probably also occurred some deterioration in the fertility of the soil in the Gangetic delta because of the eastward shift of the lower branches of the Ganges and the consequent emergence of the 'moribund' delta. On the problems caused by changes in the direction of rivers see S. C. Majumdar: *Rivers of the Bengal Delta* (Calcutta, 1941), and K. Bagchi: *The Ganges Delta* (Calcutta, 1944).

[26] Blyn: *Agricultural Trends*, Appendix Table 3A and Figure 7.2.
[27] See Table 4.8 below, derived from *ibid.*, Appendix 4C.

TABLE 4.7   *Percentage of acreage and output of non-food-grains to all crops, and yield per acre of non-food-grains, in British India and the major regions, 1901–2 to 1939–40*

Year	British India (1)	(2)	(3)	Greater Bengal (1)	(2)	(3)	United Provinces (1)	(2)	(3)	Madras (1)	(2)	(3)
1901–2	16.26	24.54	77.2	14.47	24.20	116.4	15.97	26.94	85.2	13.91	16.54	66.4
1906–7	18.81	26.32	73.5	15.83	23.78	105.0	18.58	31.49	85.7	15.27	18.12	64.0
1911–12	19.95	24.08	67.7	14.48	20.50	112.5	20.55	29.24	75.0	18.14	17.16	62.3
1913–14	19.73	27.18	71.6	14.51	22.67	117.8	21.21	33.69	65.1	19.47	19.91	55.9
1916–17	18.25	24.72	78.1	13.85	21.24	120.7	18.41	26.14	78.0	19.78	21.57	73.0
1921–2	16.24	22.65	76.7	11.28	16.73	113.2	17.02	24.58	74.2	16.63	21.87	81.5
1926–7	20.11	30.67	82.3	15.56	29.59	132.0	18.62	30.65	85.8	21.95	29.16	81.5
1931–2	18.59	27.42	79.1	11.47	19.08	121.6	19.30	35.53	93.7	21.81	28.37	86.0
1936–7	20.10	33.51	94.7	13.61	27.51	154.7	20.77	45.15	125.1	25.10	33.30	87.2
1938–9	19.90	32.14	80.5	13.71	26.99	118.9	18.87	30.75	70.8	25.25	34.85	83.0
1939–40	20.00	33.75	92.5	13.79	29.40	145.6	19.02	33.61	94.8	24.95	33.52	93.0

Year	Bombay-sind (1)	(2)	(3)	Central Provinces (1)	(2)	(3)	Greater Punjab (1)	(2)	(3)
1901–2	18.03	26.42	34.1	29.78	37.95	48.8	13.66	22.64	57.0
1906–7	22.54	36.27	58.4	33.04	31.93	37.1	12.84	18.04	55.5
1911–12	24.87	33.55	37.3	35.89	32.38	34.7	14.65	16.82	46.9
1913–14	22.48	33.65	56.2	33.25	39.75	38.2	15.04	24.45	69.8
1916–17	21.51	32.55	52.9	31.01	26.00	31.2	10.74	21.40	70.4
1921–2	16.40	28.21	61.4	30.87	33.86	49.4	12.59	19.20	64.3
1926–7	22.78	33.33	50.8	30.71	32.16	39.7	15.82	24.14	61.3
1931–2	22.87	35.60	57.9	29.91	12.23	22.9	15.72	26.65	66.7
1936–7	23.25	42.03	34.9	27.69	30.17	41.7	17.89	36.70	104.6
1938–9	24.18	40.46	62.0	27.62	24.56	31.0	16.78	32.88	84.1
1939–40	24.75	43.39	60.6	25.84	29.32	40.6	18.10	31.00	82.5

Source: Estimated from George Blyn: *Agricultural Trends in India, 1891–1947: Output, Availability and Productivity* (Philadelphia, 1966), Appendix 4C.
Note: Columns (1), (2), (3) under each region denote the same magnitudes as the corresponding columns under British India. Yields per acre are in constant prices, which are averages of prices from 1924–5 to 1928–9.
Column (1) indicates the percentage of the area under non-food-grains to the area under all crops.
Column (2) indicates the percentage of the total yield of non-food-grains to the yield of all crops.
Column (3) indicates the yield per acre (Rs.) of non-food-grains.

TABLE 4.8 Ratios of acreage and yield per acre of non-food-grains to food-grains in British India, 1896–7 to 1940–1

Year	British India Acreage	British India Yield per acre	Greater Bengal Acreage	Greater Bengal Yield per acre	United Provinces Acreage	United Provinces Yield per acre	Madras Acreage	Madras Yield per acre	Greater Punjab Acreage	Greater Punjab Yield per acre	Bombay-Sind Acreage	Bombay-Sind Yield per acre	Central Provinces Acreage	Central Provinces Yield per acre
1896–7	0.17	1.73	0.15	2.41	0.18	1.60	0.15	1.01	0.14	1.68	0.19	1.64	0.26	0.94
1897–8	0.16	1.45	0.14	1.50	0.16	2.05	0.15	1.06	0.12	1.70	0.15	1.62	0.26	1.01
1898–9	0.16	1.45	0.13	1.42	0.16	2.08	0.13	10.0	0.12	1.47	0.17	1.90	0.27	1.15
1899–1900	0.16	1.32	0.13	1.44	0.17	1.72	0.14	1.10	0.14	1.54	0.15	4.36	0.26	0.59
1900–1	0.17	1.52	0.14	1.58	0.16	1.98	0.15	0.96	0.14	1.63	0.16	1.95	0.30	1.44
1901–2	0.16	1.68	0.14	1.89	0.16	1.94	0.14	1.23	0.14	1.84	0.18	1.63	0.28	1.12
1902–3	0.16	1.44	0.13	1.49	0.19	1.45	0.15	1.15	0.14	1.42	0.18	1.77	0.30	1.08
1903–4	0.18	1.34	0.15	1.59	0.18	1.45	0.16	1.07	0.15	1.41	0.22	1.65	0.33	1.00
1904–5	0.19	1.41	0.15	1.45	0.19	2.00	0.16	1.19	0.14	1.39	0.21	1.39	0.33	1.35
1905–6	0.18	1.46	0.15	1.58	0.19	1.75	0.15	1.28	0.14	0.85	0.22	1.55	0.33	1.03
1906–7	0.19	1.54	0.16	1.66	0.19	2.02	0.15	1.23	0.13	1.50	0.22	1.96	0.33	0.95
1907–8	0.19	1.57	0.16	1.90	0.20	1.52	0.16	1.17	0.14	1.90	0.22	1.62	0.32	1.06
1908–9	0.18	1.47	0.15	2.03	0.19	1.56	0.15	1.37	0.13	1.63	0.19	1.67	0.31	0.98
1909–10	0.18	1.35	0.14	1.29	0.19	1.51	0.16	1.15	0.13	1.77	0.21	2.02	0.30	1.10
1910–11	0.18	1.32	0.14	1.39	0.19	1.66	0.16	1.18	0.12	1.55	0.23	1.63	0.32	0.81
1911–12	0.20	1.27	0.14	1.52	0.21	1.60	0.18	0.93	0.15	1.18	0.25	1.52	0.36	0.86
1912–13	0.18	1.57	0.14	2.02	0.19	1.81	0.17	1.12	0.13	1.85	0.21	1.75	0.33	0.97
1913–14	0.20	1.52	0.15	1.73	0.21	1.89	0.19	1.03	0.15	1.93	0.22	1.75	0.33	1.32
1914–15	0.19	1.66	0.15	2.28	0.20	1.76	0.19	1.05	0.13	1.77	0.23	1.63	0.34	1.01
1915–16	0.17	1.53	0.13	1.63	0.18	1.63	0.16	1.27	0.11	2.06	0.18	1.72	0.29	1.07
1916–17	0.18	1.48	0.14	1.68	0.18	1.57	0.20	1.12	0.11	2.26	0.22	1.76	0.31	0.78
1917–18	0.19	1.40	0.14	1.64	0.19	1.44	0.20	1.28	0.13	1.74	0.22	1.67	0.32	0.72
1918–19	0.18	1.75	0.13	2.22	0.19	1.58	0.20	1.38	0.14	2.16	0.22	1.79	0.27	1.55
1919–20	0.18	1.53	0.14	1.88	0.19	1.70	0.17	1.26	0.13	1.96	0.20	1.75	0.30	1.21
1920–1	0.18	1.60	0.13	1.79	0.19	1.75	0.18	1.27	0.14	2.40	0.20	1.78	0.31	1.19
1921–2	0.16	1.51	0.11	1.58	0.17	1.59	0.17	1.41	0.15	2.37	0.16	1.99	0.31	1.14
1922–3	0.17	1.52	0.11	1.63	0.17	1.75	0.19	1.39	0.16	2.13	0.20	1.83	0.32	0.99
1923–4	0.19	1.70	0.14	2.10	0.18	1.90	0.21	1.33	0.13	1.65	0.24	1.88	0.33	0.99
1924–5	0.21	1.54	0.13	1.97	0.19	1.59	0.22	1.39	0.12	1.99	0.25	1.64	0.34	1.05
1925–6	0.20	1.65	0.14	2.02	0.19	1.79	0.24	1.35	0.14	2.02	0.26	1.79	0.31	0.97
1926–7	0.20	1.76	0.16	2.28	0.19	1.93	0.22	1.46	0.16	2.34	0.23	1.69	0.30	1.07
1927–8	0.20	1.94	0.15	2.41	0.19	1.80	0.24	1.56	0.14	1.52	0.24	1.84	0.32	1.46
1928–9	0.21	1.70	0.14	1.96	0.19	1.66	0.26	1.46	0.18	1.78	0.26	1.85	0.32	1.47
1929–30	0.21	1.66	0.14	1.41	0.19	1.84	0.24	1.44	0.15	2.05	0.25	1.73	0.30	1.25
1930–1	0.20	1.80	0.14	2.02	0.20	1.84	0.24	1.53	0.16	1.95	0.21	1.99	0.30	1.37
1931–2	0.19	1.65	0.11	1.82	0.19	1.82	0.22	1.42	0.15	2.10	0.23	1.86	0.30	0.63
1932–3	0.19	1.98	0.12	2.37	0.20	2.30	0.24	1.51	0.14	2.52	0.23	2.03	0.28	1.12
1933–4	0.19	1.89	0.13	2.52	0.20	2.80	0.26	1.48	0.16	2.24	0.23	2.13	0.29	0.99
1934–5	0.19	2.00	0.13	2.58	0.19	2.63	0.21	1.46	0.16	2.77	0.22	1.86	0.28	0.84
1935–6	0.18	2.46	0.12	3.09	0.19	2.62	0.23	1.45	0.18	2.67	0.24	2.12	0.28	0.96
1936–7	0.20	2.01	0.14	2.41	0.21	2.94	0.25	1.49	0.18	2.12	0.23	1.25	0.28	1.12
1937–8	0.21	1.93	0.13	2.34	0.19	3.14	0.29	1.43	0.17	2.42	0.24	2.21	0.29	0.98
1938–9	0.20	1.91	0.14	2.32	0.19	3.22	0.25	1.58	0.18	2.03	0.24	2.12	0.28	0.85
1939–40	0.20	2.04	0.14	2.60	0.19	1.91	0.25	1.66	0.18	2.12	0.25	2.33	0.26	1.19
1940–1	0.22	2.35	0.19	2.83	0.21	2.63	0.26	1.58	0.18	2.54	0.25	2.59	0.27	1.59

Source: Computed from Blyn, *Agricultural Trends*, pp. 316–25.
Note: The column headed 'Acreage' shows the ratio of the acreage under non-food-grains to that under *all* crops.
The column headed 'Yield per acre' shows the ratio of the yield per acre of non-food-grains to that of food-grains.

profitable, particularly in tracts which did not benefit from irrigation.[28] After the War, and particularly after the introduction of effective protection in 1930, the quality of yarn and cotton piecegoods produced in India improved, and this led to a growth in the local demand for better varieties of cotton.[29] This provided a stimulus for the farmers to put in the extra expenditure of effort for producing the longer-staple cottons.

Similarly, the growth of the yield of sugar-cane per acre coincided roughly with the period of protection, and unlike in the case of cotton, this was also associated with a sizeable increase in total area under the crop for British India as a whole.

Public investment in the form of irrigation provided the inputs which could be utilized for producing better varieties of crops: public investment in the form of research provided the basic information leading to the diffusion of the improved varieties; the speed of diffusion itself was far more influenced by the relative profitability of crops in different regions than by the mere fact of discovery of improved varieties by the Departments of Agriculture.

4.4 'LAW OF DIMINISHING RETURNS' IN AGRICULTURE, POPULATION GROWTH AND PRODUCTIVITY CHANGES

No attempt has so far been made to explain the changes in yields per acre and the changes in crop patterns for Indian agriculture as a whole. One could take as a starting point the picture of an agricultural system with stagnant techniques and with land as the dominating factor of production, in the sense that it is the quantity and quality of land which determines the cost of production of a crop.[30] In this model, at the point of equilibrium, the land will be distributed in such a fashion that the marginal value product of a given quality of land is the same in all uses,

[28] See *Report of the IIC* (PP 1919, xvii), Appendix B, especially pp. 327–8. In 1916–17, the area under medium- and long-staple cotton was 2,274,000 acres out of a total cotton area of 21,212,000 acres. *Ibid.*, p. 323.

[29] See Mehta: *The Cotton Mills of India, 1854 to 1954*, Chapter xii and N. S. R. Sastry: *A Statistical Study of India's Industrial Development* (Bombay, 1947), pp. 83–5 for an account of the improvement in the quality of yarn and piecegoods produced by Indian mills during the interwar period.

[30] When one introduces more than one crop, the grading of land is no longer independent of the factor prices and product prices, except under special assumptions. In ranking different qualities of land under a multi-product system, independently of the ratios of the prices of factors and products, we are making the (empirically testable) judgement that for the permissible ranges of variations in prices of factors and crops, the ranks of the different types of land in terms of their marginal value productivity will be the same in the production of all the crops under consideration. Hence our assumption does not rule out a drastic revision of the ranks of the different qualities of land if prices of factors and crops (including interest rates for different transactions) change drastically.

and in particular the marginal value product of the best land is the same in all uses. Hence if all other things remain the same, and if diminishing returns operate with about the same intensity for a given piece of land in all uses, then a major shift in the cropping pattern between two competing groups of products will usually mean a fall in the 'average' quality of land for the group which has gained. This will in turn mean a fall (rise) in the average yield per acre of the group the output of which has risen (fallen).[31]

One can protest that even under the simplest conditions this model requires some very special assumptions. Further, under Indian conditions over the period 1900–39 this model could not apply, for, first, the total area under cultivation increased slowly over the period, and secondly, the population increased fast; the second of these factors would tend to counteract the tendency of average productivity of land to fall, since the working population as a whole increased, and the proportion of working population engaged in agriculture did not change significantly. Some support for the view that the growth in average productivity per acre in the case of non-food-grains was mainly due to the growth of the working population can also be found in the fact that the rate of population growth rose after 1921 and much of the gain in productivity occurred after 1921. But the following considerations would tend to cast doubts on this view: first, there was a distinct decline in the rate of growth during the period 1911–21; one would have supposed that for work in agriculture, however much based on the family and help from women and children, it would be the increase in the adult working population which would be more relevant and the effects on adult working population of the acceleration of population growth after 1921 would not be felt significantly until the mid-thirties at the earliest. Secondly, if the gains from greater intensity of cultivation were to be distributed evenly between food-grains and non-food-grains, one would not expect the yield of food-grains per acre to remain constant or to decline. One can, of course, point out that while the increase in working population would increase the co-operating factors in agriculture (many of which are complementary to labour), this increase need not be distributed evenly over all the crops. In that case one has to stress such factors as changes in relative profitability of crops, and the basic determinants such as relative changes in demand for different crops. We can then use the growth in working population as one element in a model which stresses the changes on the demand side and the changes in the framework of agriculture brought about by public investment.

Thirdly, if the changes in working populations were the basic explanation of the changes in yield per acre one would expect the provinces with

---

[31] For a sophisticated but misleading application of the law of diminishing returns to problems of Indian agriculture see D. Ghosh: *Pressure of Population and Economic Efficiency in India* (New Delhi, 1946), Part II, particularly pp. 45–9.

higher rates of growth in population to show higher gains in productivity. Even a casual inspection of the figures in Table 4.9 shows that no close association exists between high rates of population growth and high rates of gain in productivity. Of course, even if such an association were established, this would not prove that it was the increase in working population which brought about the increase in output and yields; it might as well be that it was the prospect of increasing yields, output and

TABLE 4.9   *Variations in the population of major provinces of British India (figures in thousands)*

Province	Population in 1901	Change between			
		1901 and 1911	1911 and 1921	1921 and 1931	1931 and 1941
Madras	36,259	+2,870	+997	+4,079	+5,137
Bombay	15,319	+817	−124	+1,980	+2,858
Bengal	42,149	+3,342	+1,213	+3,412	+10,191
United Provinces	19,943	−506	−1,432	+3,034	+6,612
Punjab	19,943	−364	+1,106	+2,895	+4,838
Bihar	28,251	+1,097	−324	+3,345	+3,974
Central Provinces and Berar	11,843	+1,916	−17	+1,581	+1,491
Assam	5,726	+853	+880	+1,163	+1,582
North-West-Frontier Province	2,042	+155	+54	+174	+613
Orissa	7,127	+455	−231	+674	+703
Sind	3,211	+303	−234	+608	+648

Source: Census of India, 1941, Vol. I, India, Part I, Tables by M. W. M. Yeatts (Delhi, 1943), pp. 62–4.

employment that induced people to migrate, and that it was the actual increase in yields and output which allowed the population to grow faster, primarily through decreased mortality but also marginally through increased birth rates. Indeed, there is direct evidence about migration to the canal colonies of the Punjab, and more importantly to Assam and Bengal, precisely because of such reasons.[32]

Now that we have seen that the naive models, based on unchanged techniques in agriculture and stressing supply factors alone, provide an inadequate explanation of the observed patterns of yields, output and acreages of different crops, an attempt can be made to bring together our findings in a succinct fashion. The rice economy of India, particularly of

[32] Davis: *Population of India and Pakistan*, pp. 109–11, 117–21, and K. C. Zachariah: *A Historical Study of Internal Migration in the Indian Subcontinent, 1901–1931* (London, 1964).

eastern India, was involved in a process of deterioration because of un-changing varieties, lack of certainty of water supply, inadequate use of manures and fertilizers, and loss of fertility through soil erosion and silting-up of river beds. Within the food-grains group, wheat benefited from the introduction of improved varieties, and the extension of irrigation in the Punjab and Sind; the improved conditions on the supply side were matched on the demand side because of the pull of its export market and (to a much lesser extent) because wheat was granted tariff protection from 1931 onwards. Millets, the other large group among food-grains, benefited little from either improved varieties or extension of irrigation.

The demand factors acted continually in most regions of India to shift the areas under food-grains to non-food-grains. However, with changes in demand conditions and with the introduction of new varieties and extension of irrigation the relative profitability of different commercial crops[33] changed, so that even in a province which had an advantage in respect of irrigation, not all the commercial crops benefited to the same extent. It seems to be the case that the yield per acre of a commerial crop increased in a given region only when its total output in that region also increased. One explanation for this phenomenon is that when the farmers of an area found out that a given commercial crop was far more profitable than other crops in that region, they shifted the better lands to that crop and increased current inputs such as labour, manures and irrigation on areas under that crop at the expense of current inputs on areas under other crops. It could also, of course, be that as the farmers realized that the yields per acre of the most profitable crop were going up, they shifted part of the area under other crops to the most profitable crop.[34] As usual, in a dynamic sequence, it is difficult to separate the causes from the effects neatly without an elaborate model.

Thus as far as commercial crops were concerned, demand largely elicited its own supply, although with a lag: the effect on supply came about at first mainly through shifts of areas from food-grains to non-food-grains, but, after the war, also through increases in yields of com-mercial crops per acre. Thus the industries which could benefit from tariff protection and depended on indigenous agricultural raw materials were assured that they would not suffer from shortage of raw materials, except perhaps temporarily. Among the industries we have studied, jute was the one industry which depended on local agricultural raw materials and which could not benefit from tariff protection. Jute was also one of the commercial crops whose output or acreage failed to recover to the levels of the mid-twenties; it also happens to be one commercial crop which failed

[33] This explanation is confined to field crops, since the factors governing the output of plantation crops such as tea, coffee and rubber are outside our scope of enquiry.

[34] See Rabbani, 'Economic Determinants', pp. 201–2.

to show any increase in yield per acre in spite of an allegedly widespread introduction of improved varieties.

Finally, in the period under study, the supply of food-grains failed to keep pace with the growth in population; this did not apparently pose any problem for the new industries by way of a rise in real wages necessitated by a rise in the subsistence costs of labour. Part of the explanation lies in the fact that India was largely an open economy as far as food was concerned: so long as world supply was elastic, prices at home could not rise steeply. Partly, it may be that the small increase in industrial population did not pose any problems of increasing the marketable surplus. Partly, it may also have to do with the layers of society and regions from which industrial labour was drawn; the growth of industry may have shifted the distribution of income to the upper income groups, and the industrial labourers were only the more privileged among the lower income groups, the rest of which suffered while the real wages of industrial labour remained constant. In other words, the real wages of industrial labourers could remain constant *because* the demand for food in the economy as a whole could be kept within the bounds of the stagnant food supply, in spite of the rise in population, through a redistribution of income in favour of those groups whose income elasticity of demand for food was significantly less than unity.

APPENDIX TO CHAPTER 4

On the 'convergence' of various forms of land tenure in practice and on the basic organization of production in Indian agriculture, see H. H. Mann: 'The Agriculture of India', *Annals of the American Academy of Political and Social Science*, Vol. 145 (1929), reprinted in H. H. Mann: *The Social Framework of Agriculture: India, Middle East, England* (Bombay, 1966). On the situation in the United Provinces, see W. H. Moreland: *The Revenue Administration of the United Provinces* (Allahabad, 1911), and [IPG pub.] *Notes on the Agricultural Conditions and Problems of the U.P. and of its Districts* (Allahabad, 1913); H. Martin Leake: *The Foundations of Indian Agriculture* (Cambridge, 1923), particularly Parts III–V; W. C. Neale: *Economic Change in Rural India: Land Tenure and Reform in Uttar Pradesh 1850–1955* (New Haven, 1962); S. Misra and B. Singh: *A Study of Land Reform in Uttar Pradesh* (Calcutta, 1964), Chapters III and IV. On the peasant's condition and land tenure systems in Bengal see M. Azizul Huque: *The Man behind the Plough* (Calcutta, 1939); K. C. Chaudhuri: *The History and Economics of the Land System in Bengal* (Calcutta, 1927). On the peasant's condition and the condition of agriculture in the Punjab see M. L. Darling: *The Punjab Peasant in Prosperity and Debt* (London, 1928) and H. C. Calvert: *The Wealth and Welfare of the Punjab* (London, 1936), Chapters IX–XIII. On the land situation in western India see G. Keatinge: *Agricultural Progress in Western India* (London, 1921), Chapters III–V; and H. H. Mann: 'The Progress of Agriculture' in S. Playne (compiler) and Arnold Wright (ed.): *The Bombay Presidency, the United Provinces, the Punjab, etc.* (London, 1920), pp. 540–7. For an extremely interesting account of changes in some villages in the Bombay Deccan which were intensively studied between 1917 and 1926, see Dr Harold Mann's evidence in RC on Agriculture in India: *Evidence*, Vol. II, Part 1: *Evidence Taken in the Bombay Presidency* (Calcutta, 1927), pp. 1–16, 16(i)–16(viii). A. Mitra [IPG pub.]: *An Account of Land Management in West Bengal 1870–1950, Census 1951, West Bengal* (Alipore, 1953) is an interesting compilation of official documents on factors affecting land use in West Bengal. For southern India, see S. Srinivasa Raghavaiyangar [IPG pub.]: *Memorandum on the progress of the Madras Presidency during the last forty years of British administration* (Madras, 1893); G. Slater (ed.): *Some South Indian Villages* (London, 1918); D. T. Chadwick: 'Agricultural Progress' in Playne and Wright: *Southern India*, pp. 745–54. For a short account of the various efforts at reforming land tenure up to 1938, see Radhakamal Mukherjee, 'Land Tenures and Legislation' in Mukherjee (ed.): *Economic Problems of Modern India*, pp. 218–45. See also M. B. Nanavati and J. J. Anjaria: *The Indian Rural Problem* (Bombay, 1945), especially Chapter III.

5

THE SUPPLY OF UNSKILLED LABOUR

It was in the past considered by most writers on Indian economic affairs that Indian labour was immobile, difficult to discipline, and often scarce in a country with abundant population.[1] By implication or explicitly, therefore, the supply of labour was supposed to have been a serious constraint on the growth of industry in India in the recent past. Some of these ideas about the irrationality and intractability of the Indian labourer have fared no better than crude ideas about the irrationality of the Indian peasant, when faced with detailed research.[2]

But there is a danger that the myth of the agriculturist factory-worker of India may be replaced by the myth of the rootless Indian labourer, whose 'natural' supply price is the subsistence wage and whose condition is entirely governed by the high rate of population growth. The fact of the matter is that just as in other fields, so in the field of labour relations the *laissez faire* practised by the Government of India was a policy rather than the absence of one. Just as in the field of industrial production it 'naturally' led to the favouring of British or, rather, European traders and industrialists,[3] so in the field of labour supply it led to a policy of increasing the mobility of Indian labour with a view to pushing it into British-managed plantations and factories. On the other side, political factors and factors favouring the growth of trade union organization could to some extent at least modify the results one would expect on the basis of some neo-Malthusian theory of the determination of real wages. Since the policy of the Government of India regarding the supply of labour and the differential development of trade unions and certain

[1] On the supposed lack of mobility of Indian workers and their lack of response to economic incentives see Anstey, *Economic Development of India*, pp. 118–25, and 281–2; as regards the alleged recalcitrance of Indian labour, the views of Alexander Gerschenkron: *Economic Backwardness in Historical Perspective* (New York, 1962), although not based on first-hand research, are typical: 'creation of an industrial labour force that really deserves its name is a most difficult and protracted process. The history of Russian industry provides some striking illustrations in this respect . . . In our time, reports from industries in India repeat in a still more exaggerated form the past predicaments of European industrialization in the field of labour supply.' *Ibid.*, p. 9.

[2] See in particular, D. H. Buchanan: *The Development of Capitalistic Enterprise in India* (London 1966, reprint of the 1934 edition), Chapters xiv–xvii; C. A. Myers: *Labor Problems in the Industrialization of India* (Cambridge, Mass., 1958), Chapters iii and iv; and Morris David Morris: *The Emergence of an Industrial Labour Force in India* (Berkeley, 1965).

[3] See Sir Reginald Coupland: *India: A Restatement*, pp. 53–4.

immediately relevant political factors affected the cost of labour, and to a minor extent the market for industrial products, in different regions in different ways, we have therefore to devote some attention to both these sets of factors in the following sections. But we can properly assess the impact of these variables only if we consider them in conjunction with the agrarian and demographic base on which they operated.

5.1   THE STATISTICS OF POPULATION GROWTH AND VIEWS ABOUT THE SUPPLY OF UNSKILLED LABOUR

The population of India was 282 million in 1891, 285 million in 1901, 303 million in 1911, 306 million in 1921, 338 million in 1931, and 389 million in 1941. Taking 1901 as the base, the population increased by 36% over the period from 1901 to 1941. There was a net annual emigration of 69,500 persons from India over the period from 1901 to 1937.[4] According to one estimate, the number of persons supported by agricultural labour (as distinguished from cultivation of their own or rented land) increased from 52·4 million in 1901 to 95·9 million in 1931.[5] As against this the number of persons employed in organized industry was 2,105,824 in 1911 (including 810,407 in plantations) and 2,681,125 in 1921 (including 820,868 in plantations);[6] in 1931 the average daily number employed by the various industries excluding the plantations was 1,630,037.[7]

Although these figures of employment in industry relate to India including Burma and are not strictly comparable because of differences in definition and methods of collection of data, they still indicate quite clearly the small proportion of total industrial employment compared with the total population and the population of agricultural labour in three benchmark years within our period. Even the annual flow of net emigration from India was far greater than the annual increase in industrial employment. Taking all these factors into account, together

[4] Davis: *Population of India and Pakistan*, Chapters 4 and 13.

[5] Patel: *Essays on Economic Transition*, pp. 3–32 ('Agricultural Labourers in Modern India and Pakistan'); and *Census of India, 1931*, Vol. 1, *India*, Part 1, *Report* (Delhi), 1933, Chapter VIII. While the figure for 1901 relates to the number of persons supported by agricultural labour, the figure for 1931 (42.2 million) relates only to actual workers. The ratio of workers to non-working dependants (viz., 44.56) given in the Census Report for 1931 for Class I in the occupation table has been used to get a figure comparable to that for 1901.

[6] The figures are taken from the Industrial Census of 1911 and 1921, reproduced in *Census of India, 1911*, Vol. 1, *India*, Part 1, *Report* (Calcutta, 1913), p. 444, and in Gov. India, CISD: *Statistical Abstract for British India from 1911–12 to 1920–21* (Calcutta, 1923), pp. 648–53.

[7] Gov. India, CISD: *Statistical Abstract for British India from 1922–3 to 1931–2* (Delhi, 1934), Table Nos. 314 and 316.

with the extremely low productivity of work in agriculture, one would not normally expect industrialists to experience any difficulty in the supply of unskilled labour.

However, it had become an almost universally accepted proposition by the beginning of the 1920s, that not only was 'cheap' Indian labour dear because of its low productivity, but it was also scarce in relation to the needs of industry.[8] The doctrine of the scarcity of labour in India was enshrined in the Report of the Royal Commission on Labour in India in the following words:

Throughout the greater part of its history, organized industry in India has experienced a shortage of labour. A generation ago, this shortage was at times to become critical. Towards the end of the nineteenth century, after the plague epidemics, the difficulties of employers were acute, especially in Bombay; and in 1905 the complaints of employers in Bengal and the United Provinces led to an official enquiry into the causes of the shortage. Thereafter the position became easier in the factory industries, but even in these, before the war, few employers were assured of adequate labour at all seasons of the year.[9]

The explanation for the wide acceptance of such a view in a country with such a high density of population and low supply price of labour is to be sought in a combination of several factors. First, in some parts of India, notably East Bengal and Assam, there genuinely was a shortage of labour for agricultural operations almost throughout the period under observation. This shortage was reflected in the relatively high wages paid for agricultural labour in these parts, particularly during the seasons of sowing and planting and harvesting of the main crops – rice and jute.[10]

[8] See, for example, the foreword by Sir Stanley Reed to A. R. Burnett-Hurst: *Labour and Housing in Bombay* (London, 1925), p. v. 'The aged fiction that India is a land with an unlimited supply of cheap labour persists in England. Under ordinary conditions – periods of exceptional depression like the present excluded – the supply of labour in Indian industries, even in the staple agricultural industry, is never sufficient, and in relation to quality and quantity of output it is not cheap.'

[9] RC on Labour in India: *Report* (PP 1930–1, XI), p. 21.

[10] G. M. Broughton: *Labour in Indian Industries* (London, 1924), pp. 73–4; N. C. Chaudhury: *Jute and Substitutes* (Calcutta, 1933), pp. 45–7. Before the First World War, jute yielded a much higher gross revenue per acre than any other crop in India (with the possible exception of sugar-cane in South India) but it also demanded much more labour than the major competing crop, rice. See *Proceedings of the Inter-Provincial Jute Conference held at Calcutta from the 2nd to 4th August, 1915, with Appendices* (Calcutta, 1915), p. 3 (from the presidential address by B. Coventry, Agricultural Adviser to the Government of India) and pp. 19–20 ('Note on Jute' by R. S. Finlow, Fibre Expert to the Government of Bengal). The excess demand for agricultural labour in peak seasons was met by the (usually temporary) migration of labourers from Bihar and the United Provinces to Bengal, particularly the jute-growing districts of northern Bengal. See also *Census of India, 1911*, Vol. V, *Bengal, Bihar and Orissa and Sikkim*, Part I, *Report* (Calcutta, 1913), p. 66 (this report also remarks on the increase in the mobility of labour between different regions); Bengal District Gazetteers: *Santal Parganas* (Calcutta, 1910), pp. 192–3; Bihar District Gazetteers: *Santal Parganas* (2nd ed.; Patna, 1938), pp.

Secondly, the labour market was riddled with imperfections so that different rates of pay prevailed for the same operation in the same centre.[11] Since information about the state of the labour market was imperfect on the side of both the employer and the labourer, both depended to a large extent on the jobber for arrangements regarding employment, and the jobber could, in some cases and at least for short periods of time, create artificial scarcity by transferring labour from one mill to another, even when there might be an excess of labour supply in the market as a whole.

Thirdly, a condition of short-run shortage of labour often went hand in hand with a perfectly elastic supply of labour in the long run. India was a country of vast distances, the two major centres of industry, Calcutta and Bombay, being more than a thousand miles apart. While the figures of internal migration show labour to have been responsive to the demand from plantation and factory industries, it took time for the flow of migration to adjust to differential demands from different centres. This general condition of less-than-perfect mobility of labour which is to be observed in almost every settled country was aggravated by two other features in the Indian situation: (a) the wages and conditions of employment in the mines and plantations were unfavourable in comparison even with those in the factories of India, so that special arrangements had to be made for recruiting labour for the former; (b) Bombay and the upper part of the Indo-Gangetic plains were ravaged by plague from the year 1896

253–4. In the last two books, the source of the description of the migration (temporary or permanent) of the Santals is a report by the Deputy Commissioner of the district in August 1907, but it is added in the second edition: 'This account still holds good.' See, for the situation in the sugar industry of Bengal in the thirties, ITB: *Evidence (Report on sugar)*, Vol. II (Delhi, 1938), the evidence of the North Bengal Sugar Mills Co. Ltd, Rajshahi, and the Deshabandhu Sugar Mills Ltd, Dacca, pp. 270 and 277 respectively. The two mills complained that they had to import skilled labour at a high cost from the United Provinces and Bihar because of the unwillingness of local labour to work in the mills and their lack of training.

[11] For an example from the Bombay cotton mills and a thorough discussion of the problem of standardization of wages see Morris: *Emergence of an Industrial Labour Force*, Chapter IX. Some idea of the variation of wages between different jute mills and between mills producing different commodities such as jute goods, cotton yarn and cloth, paper and chemicals, in or near Calcutta, can be obtained by going through Indian Factory Labour Commission 1908: Vol. I, *Report* (Simla, 1908), Appendix F ('Inspection of notes'), pp. 19–26. As late as 1930, when the RC on Labour conducted its enquiry, no standardization of wages had taken place at all in the jute industry or in other industries in Calcutta. The argument provided for lack of uniformity was that conditions varied from place to place, but obviously no effort had been made by the Indian Jute Mills Association to standardize wages. The IJMA was in fact opposed to such a measure. (In Bombay, standardization of wages in cotton mills ultimately took place because of pressure from the government.) See the evidence of IJMA and its representatives, that of J. P. Mandelia, Secretary of the Birla Jute Manufacturing Company, and that of M. Dalmiya, Secretary and General Manager of the Kesoram Cotton Mills in RC on Labour in India: *Evidence*, Vol. V (London, 1931), Part 1, pp. 303, 430 and 421 and Part 2, pp. 163 and 171.

onwards and the effects of the plague were to decrease both the supply of labour at the source and the attractiveness of Bombay and Cawnpore as places to work in.[12]

One way of deciding whether the curve of supply of labour to Indian industries was perfectly elastic or not would be to look at the real wages of industrial labour during the period under consideration: a constant real wage of labour would provide a very strong presumption in favour of the hypothesis that Indian industry grew under conditions of an elastic supply of labour.

But there are formidable difficulties in the computation of a series of real wages for the whole of India: data on wages of different kinds of labour are scattered and anything but comprehensive; the composition of the labour force in terms of skill and physical labour required changed with a change in the composition of industry. Shifts of employment occurred between centres, thus changing the weights of wages paid in different industrial centres. The imperfection of the labour market, the fines imposed by mill-owners for breaches of discipline, and the high rates of interest paid by a large proportion of wage-earners on their debts render the task of constructing a representative wage series almost impossible of achievement.[13] Added to these uncertainties of basic data there are all the difficulties of constructing a cost-of-living index for all workers, or even for workers in specified centres. Hence one should interpret any results that are obtained with a great deal of caution.

5.2 DIFFERENTIAL MOVEMENTS OF REAL WAGES IN DIFFERENT INDUSTRIAL CENTRES

Recently, Dr K. Mukerji has tried to derive the long-period trend of real wages in the cotton mills of western India and in the jute mills of Calcutta from the information available in official publications.[14] His figures will be used for the purpose of our analysis, but the limitation of the figures must be stressed in order to get a proper perspective on the trends.

Apart from the well-known problems of constructing cost-of-living index

[12] For a short account of the spread and virulence of the plague epidemic in India, see Charles Creighton, M.D.: 'Plague in India', *JSA*, Vol. LIII, No. 2743, 16 June 1905, pp. 810–26, and the record of the discussion following the paper.

[13] It is interesting that, among American scholars, D. H. Buchanan writing in 1934, paid far greater attention to these difficulties than later scholars.

[14] K. Mukerji: (1) 'Trend in Real Wages in Cotton Textile Mills in Bombay City and Island, from 1900 to 1951', *Artha Vijnana* (Poona), Vol. 1, No. 1, March 1959; (2) 'Trend in Real Wages in Cotton Textile Industry in Ahmedabad from 1900 to 1951', *Artha Vijnana*, Vol. 3, No. 2, June 1961; (3) 'Trend in Textile Mill Wages in Western India: 1900 to 1951', *Artha Vijnana*, Vol. 4, No. 2, June 1962; and (4) 'Trend in Real Wages in the Jute Textile Industry from 1900 to 1951', *Artha Vijnana*, Vol. 2, No. 1, March 1960.

TABLE 5.1   *Real wages in the cotton- and jute-textile industries in India,*
1900–39

	Index of real value of average monthly wage in cotton mills in Bombay City and Island (1934=100) (1)	Index of real wages in the cotton-mill industry of Ahmedabad (1951=100) (2)	Index of real wages in the jute textile industry (1951=100) (3)
1900	43	31.5	62.3
1901	45	36.4	61.2
1902	47	37.6	60.3
1903	46	42.9	68.0
1904	51	42.9	68.4
1905	44	39.7	64.7
1906	47	36.6	57.9
1907	53	38.5	53.2
1908	52	34.5	48.7
1909	56	38.9	53.6
1910	55	42.0	58.3
1911	48	41.7	63.3
1912	50	38.5	55.0
1913	49	38.5	54.6
1914	56	35.3	55.1
1915	51	33.4	53.0
1916	49	33.0	52.7
1917	42	32.1	56.0
1918	49	28.8	52.0
1919	52	28.1	46.9
1920	56	29.9	48.7
1921	61	44.3	53.6
1922	70	51.3	54.4
1923	74	57.2	54.8
1924	70	54.9	53.9
1925	78	53.8	59.8
1926	82	57.5	61.2
1927	82	63.9	60.2
1928	86	67.2	56.0
1929	85	65.8	52.5
1930	93	73.4	51.0
1931	115	89.9	67.0
1932	116	88.7	62.3
1933	123	93.7	61.7
1934	100	95.0	67.7
1935	99	89.1	65.4
1936	99	89.1	78.6
1937	102	77.0	83.0
1938	111	87.8	86.8
1939	123	90.6	87.5

Sources: Column (1), K. Mukerji, *Artha Vijnana*, Vol. 1, No. 1, Table 6; column (2),
K. Mukerji, *Artha Vijnana*, Vol. 3, No. 2, 'Basic Tables'; column (3), K. Mukerji,
Artha Vijnana, Vol. 2, No. 1, 'Basic Tables'.

numbers and interpreting figures of real wages derived by deflating money wages by such numbers. Mukerji's estimates suffer from the difficulty that they rest on a very slender base, particularly for the period from 1900 to 1914. For these years, the source of data used by him is the official publication, *Prices and Wages in India*. The wage data given by this publication relate to one single cotton mill representing the cotton-mill industry of the whole of Bombay, and one single jute mill representing the whole jute mill industry of India. It is too much to expect that each of these mills would be representative in a statistical sense, particularly when it is known that conditions of work and wages could vary very widely within the same industry in the same locality. Mukerji's results are summarized in Table 5.1.

The series given by Mukerji is the only one which covers all the years in question. But for the years from 1900 to 1912 we have K. L. Datta's series of real wages, reproduced in Table 5.2. In the case of jute, the really important circle was the Calcutta circle; on the other hand, Calcutta was relatively insignificant in the case of cotton. We find a broad agreement between the trends in the series given by Mukerji and Datta for the years for which they overlap. Real wages seem to have increased both in Bombay and Ahmedabad (Gujarat in the case of Datta's series) and fallen very slightly in the case of the jute mills of Calcutta for the period from

TABLE 5.2 *Index numbers of average monthly real wages in different circles* and industries, 1900 to 1912*

| | Jute | | Cotton | | | Tea | Mining | |
	Calcutta	Bengal southern and western	Calcutta	Bombay	Gujarat	Assam	Bengal southern and western	Chota-nagpur
1900	116	101	118	91	76	92	100	159
1901	112	101	115	99	85	96	103	201
1902	116	108	124	101	87	94	111	210
1903	117	112	129	104	100	97	120	228
1904	119	122	131	103	99	99	125	222
1905	118	114	131	103	91	96	116	232
1906	107	102	123	98	86	90	106	212
1907	102	96	116	105	89	88	104	192
1908	99	97	112	98	80	85	108	165
1909	105	106	121	105	89	92	121	207
1910	109	109	129	105	96	98	130	224
1911	113	114	133	99	98	98	128	222
1912	107	104	148	98	89	95	121	207

Source: K. L. Datta: *Report on the Enquiry into the Rise of Prices in India*, Vol. III (Calcutta, 1914), pp. 194–7.

* 'Circles' were the regions into which Datta divided the whole of India for the purposes of his enquiry.

1900 to 1912. Referring to Table 5.1, we find that real wages declined
in both the jute- and cotton-mill industries during the First World War;
however, from 1921 onwards, the patterns of movements in real wages
in the jute mills of Calcutta and the cotton mills of Bombay and Ahmedabad
are quite different. Real wages moved up rapidly in the cotton mills of
Bombay and Ahmedabad between 1921 and 1930, whereas they remained
practically stagnant in the jute mills;[15] with the coming of the depression
and the drastic fall in prices of agricultural commodities, the real wages
of workers in the jute industry improved. But the total rise in real wages
in the jute mills from 1921 to 1939 was much less than in the cotton mills
of Bombay and Ahmedabad.

Apart from K. L. Datta's enquiry, and the wage data supplied by the
Labour Office, Bombay, there are very few published series against which
Mukerji's series can be checked. Many of the other apparently independent
sources turn out to be based on the same source – *Prices and Wages in
India* – which Mukerji has used.[16] Hence, in view of the limited information available, and bearing in mind the limitations of measured real wages
as an index of the welfare of wage-earners, we shall accept Mukerji's series
as giving a picture of the differences in wage movements between the
cotton mills of Ahmedabad and Bombay and the jute mills of Calcutta.

Looking at Table 5.1, we find that real wages in the Bombay cotton
mills rose by about a quarter between 1900 and 1914, showed a declining
tendency up to 1920 and then rose strongly up to 1933, declined during
the years 1934–6 and rose again up to 1939. In the Ahmedabad cotton
mills real wages rose slightly between 1900 and 1914 (by about 12%),
declined up to 1920 and then rose continuously up to 1934, declined
during the period 1935–7 and rose again in 1938 and 1939. In the jute-
textile industry (in or around Calcutta), real wages declined slightly (by
about 11.5%) between 1900 and 1914, declined further up to 1920, rose
up to 1926, declined up to 1930, rose temporarily (a freak produced by

---

[15] It is probable that for the years 1929 and 1930 Mukerji's series understate the
money and, therefore, the real wages of jute-mill workers; after the strike in 1929, an
increase of $7\frac{1}{2}$ to 10% was conceded, but this is not reflected in the money wage series
given by Mukerji in *Artha Vijnana*, Vol. 2 (1), March 1960, p. 67. For the results of the
strike of 1929, see the evidence of IJMA in RC on Labour in India: *Evidence*, Vol v
(London, 1931), Part 1, p. 302.

[16] For example, the data given in Gazetteers of the Bombay Presidency: [S. M.
Edwardes] Vol. 1, *Bombay City and Island* (Bombay, 1909), p. 323, are only a condensed
version of the figures for wages in the Manockji Petit Mills, Bombay, which were used as
the representative series by Gov. India, CISD: *Prices and Wages in India* (Calcutta,
annual). In Bengal District Gazetteers, *24 Parganas* (Calcutta, 1914), p. 141, the lowest
monthly wages in two jute mills (at Budge Budge and at Gauripur) are given for several
categories of workers in 1911. Since the exact composition of the working force and the
range of wages are both unknown, all one can check is whether the lowest wages could
be consistent with the average wage given by Mukerji for 1911, and it is found that they
are consistent.

the method of deflation) in 1931, fell in 1932 and 1933, and then rose during the period 1934–9 (with a temporary fall in 1935). In the case of the jute-textile industry, the upward movement, when it occurred, was rather feeble, and one suspects that much of the measured rise in real wages was due simply to the lag of measured money wages behind the cost-of-living index used during the years of the depression. For instance, workers in the jute-textile industry were earning less in real terms in 1933 than in 1900. By contrast, there is a strong upward trend in the series of real wages for workers in the Bombay and Ahmedabad cotton mills. Looking at the terminal years of the series, we find that between 1900 and 1939, the real wages of workers in the Bombay cotton mills rose by 186%, those of workers in the Ahmedabad cotton mills rose by 188%, and those of workers in the jute mills rose by only 40%. In the Bombay cotton mills workers had already made substantial gains before the First World War and in 1920 their real wages had recovered to the level reached in 1914; but still *most* of the gain in real wages was made between 1921 and 1933. In the Ahmedabad cotton mills, whereas workers had made some gain between 1900 and 1914, this had been completely eroded by the war-time lag of wages behind prices and all the gain made by them by 1939 was a post-war achievement. The contrast between this upward tendency of real wages in Bombay and Ahmedabad and the relative stagnation of real wages in Calcutta, where even in 1926 (a prosperous year for the jute industry) real wages had not recovered to the level they had attained in 1900, is sharp and clear.

Since, as we shall see in a moment, there are some doubts about the comparability of the deflating methods used by Mukerji in the case of different centres, we shall also compare the movements of money wages of workers in different centres. The figures are reproduced in Table 5.3 It is easily seen that according to this table the money wages of mill-workers increased between 1900 and 1939 by 188% in Bombay, 208% in Ahmedabad and 63% in Calcutta. Thus according to these figures the discrepancy between the rates of growth of wages in Bombay and Calcutta was less in money terms than in real terms, but the difference was still of a similar order of magnitude. Most of the conclusions reached in the paragraph above as regards changes in measured real wages thus remain unchanged when we discuss changes in money wages.

It would be useful to dispose of one possible explanation for the slower rate of growth of real wages in the jute mills of Calcutta than in the cotton mills of Bombay and Ahmedabad before we turn to more basic factors. This is the proposition that real wages might have risen more slowly in Calcutta than in the other two centres because they were initially higher and the stronger upward movement in Bombay and Ahmedabad was necessary to achieve some kind of parity in real wages in the different centres, given a reasonable degree of mobility of labour between the different parts of the country. This argument, however, is falsified by the limited amount of evidence that we do have. In Mukerji's series of money wages the average money wage per month in 1900 was Rs. 11·35 in

TABLE 5.3 *Average monthly money wages of workers in different centres, 1900 to 1939 (figures in Rs.)*

	Average monthly money wages of workers in Bombay cotton mills	Average monthly money wages of workers in Ahmedabad cotton mills	Average monthly money wages of workers in Cacutta jute mills
1900	12.29	11.35	12.0
1901	12.58	11.35	12.0
1902	12.59	11.35	12.0
1903	12.59	11.35	12.0
1904	12.59	11.35	12.7
1905	12.59	11.82	12.8
1906	12.59	12.44	12.8
1907	14.36	12.59	12.8
1908	15.36	12.76	13.5
1909	15.46	13.33	13.5
1910	15.46	13.45	13.5
1911	13.40	13.45	13.7
1912	14.11	13.45	13.2
1913	14.21	13.45	14.4
1914	16.37	13.45	14.5
1915	16.75	13.45	14.6
1916	16.78	13.45	14.6
1917	17.01	13.70	14.8
1918	21.08	17.70	14.8
1919	24.75	20.06	16.4
1920	30.75	22.77	18.4
1921	30.63	31.89	19.9
1922	31.69	32.58	19.9
1923	32.75	33.27	19.6
1924	32.75	33.44	19.4
1925	32.75	33.62	19.8
1926	34.56	33.80	19.2
1927	34.56	33.80	19.3
1928	34.56	33.80	17.7
1929	34.56	33.80	16.5
1930	34.56	33.80	14.3
1931	34.56	33.80	16.2
1932	34.56	35.69	15.4
1933	34.56	35.69	14.6
1934	27.25	35.69	14.6
1935	27.25	33.46	14.6
1936	27.25	33.46	16.9
1937	28.44	30.96	18.3
1938	32.13	32.98	19.6
1939	35.37	35.00	19.6

Sources: as for Table 5.1 above.

the Ahmedabad cotton mills, Rs. 12·29 in a cotton mill in Bombay City and Island, and Rs. 12·0 in a jute mill in Calcutta. These figures are based on the information supplied by only one mill in the case of Bombay and Calcutta and in the case of Ahmedabad on very crude and aggregative information provided by K. L. Datta's report. But the general impression that before the First World War while the (money) wages of textile workers in centres other than Bombay were lower than the wages of cotton-mill workers in Bombay or of jute-mill workers in Calcutta, the wages of cotton-mill workers might have been marginally higher or marginally lower than the wages of jute-mill workers, is not contradicted by other pieces of fragmentary evidence available.[17] Thus any 'catching-up' process would not explain the highly divergent movements of money and real wages in Bombay cotton mills and Calcutta jute mills.

Finally there remains one problem in comparing the levels or the rates of growth of real wages in different centres, which cannot be satisfactorily settled on the basis of the data available. This is the question of the housing of workers. Mukerji was unable to find any satisfactory item to represent the cost of housing in the case of Bombay; in the case of Ahmedabad also, at least for years earlier than 1927, the cost of housing does not seem to have been taken into account in constructing the cost-of-living index. In the case of Calcutta jute mills, prices of building materials were used to represent the cost of housing; this procedure is perhaps better than complete exclusion of housing from cost-of-living indices, but is not very reliable, particularly when a change in the price of land may be the major item in the change in the cost of construction of houses and – at a further remove – in the rent paid by workers. Hence a degree of incomparability is introduced in the real wage series derived by Mukerji for different centres.[18]

[17] Compare, for example, the 'Inspection Notes' for Bombay, Ahmedabad and Calcutta in Indian Factory Labour Commission 1908: Vol. 1, *Report* (Simla, 1908), Appendix F. This Report did say that the wages of jute-mill workers were 'rather higher' than the wages of operatives in cotton factories all over India (*ibid.*, p. 22), but the average wages for workers in cotton factories of all kinds and all over India were considerably lower than the average wages earned by cotton-mill workers in Bombay. G. K. Devadhar found from a survey (around 1913) of mill workers in two localities of Bombay (Chinchpokli and Tardeo) that the average monthly earnings of a man came to Rs. 20.17. See 'The Indian Mill Hands: A Movement on their Behalf', *ITJ*, October 1913, p. 32. This compares well (given the sex-ratio of workers in factories and the ratios of wages of men to those of women and children) with the average money wage for a jute mill of Rs. 14.4 in 1913 and Rs. 14.5 in 1914, and of Rs. 14.21 and Rs. 16.37 for a cotton mill in Bombay as found by Mukerji (see Table 5.3 above). It is possible that Mukerji's series slightly overstates the growth of real wages in Bombay before the First World War, particularly if we take 1914 rather than 1913 as the terminal year (compare with K. L. Datta's series given in Table 5.2 above) but this would not affect our basic argument in the text.

[18] The relative importance of housing can be roughly gauged from the fact that in the cost-of-living index prepared by the Bombay Labour Office from 1926 onwards, rent was given a weight of 13 in 100 (the items included accounted for 86.28% of the expenditure of a worker's family). See Labour Office, Bombay: *Wages and unemployment in the*

The little qualitative evidence that is available seems to indicate that initially the condition of housing of workers in the Calcutta jute mills was better than that of workers in the Bombay cotton mills.[19] One of the main reasons was that the cotton mills in Bombay were concentrated on Bombay Island, and it was very expensive to acquire land for constructing houses for the workers, whereas in Calcutta the mills were strung out on the Hooghly river and it was less expensive to provide houses. Before the founding of the Bombay Improvement Trust, mill managements near Calcutta may also have enjoyed another advantage.[20] The jute-mill owners were often able to use public money for the housing of workers through the 'Mill Municipalities', that is municipalities that were controlled by jute-mill managers.[21] But no systematic comparisons were ever made

Bombay cotton textile industry: Report of the Departmental Enquiry (Bombay, 1934) pp. 41–2.

[19] See G. O. W. Dunn's paper and the appended comment by Professor W. J. Simpson (late Health Officer of Calcutta) who 'could confidently say that there was nothing in Calcutta comparable with the dark, overcrowded, and foul tenements in Bombay': G. O. W. Dunn: 'The Housing Question in Bombay', *JRSA*, Vol. LVIII, No. 2989, 4 March 1910, p. 408.

[20] It is difficult to say whether it was definitely more profitable to build houses for workers in the jute mills than for mill workers in Bombay. In Calcutta, a jute mill was reported by the Indian Factory Labour Commission 1908 as earning 7% on 1,800 houses for operatives: Indian Factory Labour Commission 1908: Vol. I, *Report and Appendices* (Simla, 1908), Appendix F, p. 22. Fazulbhoy Currimbhoy Ibrahim, then Vice-Chairman of the Bombay Millowners' Association, in his evidence before the IFLC said that 'millowners could not become philanthropists at the expense of their share-holders, and build chawls for a 3% return when they could obtain 25% in other directions'. But he also mentioned that old chawls earned from 8% to 10% (presumably on their historic cost rather than on replacement value). Thus if the rate of return of 7% for the jute mill in Calcutta referred to the return on new houses, then the situation was definitely better than in Bombay (particularly if it was net rather than gross rate of return); otherwise one cannot come to any definite conclusion. In any case, the situation regarding private construction of tenements for workers in Bombay distinctly worsened between 1900 and 1914 as we find again from the evidence of Fazulbhoy Currimbhoy Ibrahim (who was both a large mill-owner and a wealthy landlord) before the Bombay Development Committee, 1914. In 1908, he thought that if the Bombay Improvement Trust borrowed the money at 4½% and built the chawls, the mill-owners would meet the loss on interest. But in 1914, although the Bombay Improvement Trust Act had come into force, and the mill-owners could borrow money from the Improvement Trust at 4% on the capitalized value of the houses and return the loan in 28 years, they could not profitably do so; for the cost of a chawl had doubled (to Rs. 680 per room) and presumably the mill-owners could not get an economic rent from the workers at that cost. See Indian Factory Labour Commission 1908: Vol. II, *Evidence* (Simla, 1908), p. 68 and *Report of the Bombay Development Committee 1914* (Bombay, 1914), pp. 44 and 243.

[21] See IJMA: *Report of the Committee for the year ended 31 December 1904* (Calcutta, 1905), p. iv (from the speech of the Chairman, J. D. Nimmo, at the Annual General Meeting): 'It is satisfactory to observe also that in several cases what may be called Mill Municipalities are taking advantage of the local Authorities' Loan Act to borrow from the Government for the purpose of introducing a filtered water-supply, better systems of drainage and like improvements.' (This was with reference to measures for controlling plague among mill workers.)

between the housing conditions of workers in Bombay and in Calcutta. G. M. Broughton wrote in 1924: 'It is believed that about one-third of the total number of jute-mill workers live in quarters provided by the mill-management. I have not been able to obtain reliable statistics on this point.'[22]

However, there is some evidence that the relative condition of the housing of workers in Bombay cotton mills may have improved over time. There were Improvement Trusts in both Calcutta and Bombay. The work of the Bombay Improvement Trust had a much more direct impact on the conditions of living of cotton-mill workers in Bombay than the corresponding work of the Calcutta Improvement Trust had on the standard of living of jute-mill workers in Calcutta, because the cotton mills were concentrated in a much smaller area in Bombay than were the jute mills in Calcutta.[23] If we compare the wage enquiry of the Bombay Labour Office in 1934 with the report of the Textile Labour Enquiry Committee relating to 1937 we find a slight increase in the number of tenements for workers provided by employers. Furthermore, the Bombay Improvement Trust constructed more than 16,000 tenements after 1920, and in 1937 the Government of Bombay undertook to spend Rs. 1·05 million on a phased programme of construction of cheap houses.[24]

The information available regarding housing conditions in the jute mills of Bengal is even more fragmentary. The Labour Investigation Committee, reporting in 1946, said:

The Indian Jute Mills Association in their reply have given the results of a very full survey which was made in 1937. Information obtained by the Association from 61 mills (out of a total number of 96 mills in 1937) shows that the percentage of workers housed by individual mills varied from 7·9

[22] G. M. Broughton: *Labour in Indian Industries* (London, 1924), p. 138. Broughton goes on to say on the same page: 'It is believed that the mill authorities would be willing to develop their housing scheme very considerably, but they are at present very much hampered by the difficulty of securing land in the vicinity of the mills. Compulsory acquisition cannot be resorted to under the present law and the owners of suitable land often ask prohibitive prices.' Thus it is clear that at least after the First World War mill-owners in Calcutta and in Bombay faced very similar problems in respect of the housing of workers.

[23] See C. H. Bompas: 'The Work of the Calcutta Improvement Trust', *JRSA*, LXXV, No. 3868, 7 January 1927, pp. 200–13. The Bombay Improvement Trust was formed in 1898 whereas the Calcutta Trust was formed only in 1912; in Bombay the trust had been able to start with undeveloped government land, whereas in Calcutta, because of the Permanent Settlement, there was no land at the disposal of the government, and all land had to be bought at inflated prices. After the war the work of the Calcutta Trust suffered because of a slump in building values.

[24] Labour Office, Bombay: *General Wage Census*, Part I, *Perennial factories, Third Report* (Bombay, 1937), pp. 61–4; *Report of the Textile Labour Enquiry Committee*, Vol. II, *Final Report* (Bombay, 1940), pp. 267–74. The population housed in the *chawls* of the Development Department in 1938 was over 63,000 persons, not all of whom were, however, textile workers. *Ibid.*, p. 272.

to 100 and the total number of rooms and quarters supplied by the mills for housing their workpeople comes to about 42,466.

Figures obtained during the present enquiry from 19 units providing housing accommodation to their workers shows that only 39% of the total labour force in these units was housed by the employers. When there are private *bustees* around the mills, the employers do not generally make any housing arrangements for their workers. Some of the mills situated outside Calcutta, however, have provided housing for about 50% of their employees as private housing was not easily available.[25]

The Committee then compared the housing conditions of jute-mill workers in or near Calcutta with those of factory workers in other industrial centres:

The Royal Commission on Labour in India have referred to the overcrowding and congestion in certain parts of Howrah as being unequalled probably in any other industrial area in India. Since then the housing conditions of jute-mill workers in Bengal have not improved materially . . . The *chawl* of Bombay or the *chatta* of Cawnpore is a mercy before some of the Bengal *bustees*.[26]

The Labour Investigation Committee also commented on the relative living standards of jute-mill workers in Bengal and cotton-mill workers in Bombay: 'as compared to the standard of living say, of cotton-mill workers in Bombay, the standard of living of jute-mill workers appears to be appreciably lower, as nearly three-quarters of their income has to be spent on food alone'.[27] Thus most of the evidence[28] – quantitative and qualitative – seems to point to the conclusion that the real wages of jute-mill workers in Bengal declined relatively to the real wages of cotton-mill workers in Bombay and Ahmedabad over the period from 1900 to 1939.

We shall now try to explain the differences in movements of real wages in the two main industrial centres – Bombay and Calcutta. Such an enquiry brings out some important differences in the political and social factors governing the supply of labour in different regions of India. Three main sets of factors appear to have governed the differential movements of real wages in Bombay and Calcutta, or more broadly, in industrial centres in western India, and industrial centres in eastern and northern India, such as Calcutta, Cawnpore and Jamshedpur. The first set can be grouped broadly under differences in the effective supply of labour in the respective regions and in the methods of recruitment in different industries. The second set of factors relates to the intensity of the workers' opposition to wage cuts and the support they received from the general public and the government.

[25] Gov. India, Labour Investigation Committee: *Report on an enquiry into conditions of labour in the jute mill industry of India* by S. R. Deshpande (Delhi, 1946), p. 29. Many of the tenements of the workers were *kutcha*, i.e. with mud walls and thatched or tiled roofing.

[26] *Ibid.*, p. 31.   [27] *Ibid.*, p. 27.

[28] See also Buchanan: *Development of Capitalistic Enterprise*, Chapters xv and xviii.

The third group is connected with the degrees of profitability of industry in the different centres, which might have influenced the degrees of resistance of the employers to demands for increasing wages.

5.3 INTERNAL MIGRATION AND DIFFERENCES IN DEMOGRAPHIC DEVELOPMENTS IN DIFFERENT REGIONS

Turning first to the effective supply of labour, we find that India had become, definitely by the end of the nineteenth century, and probably even earlier, an integrated economy as far as mobility of labour was concerned. The *actual* mobility of labour from one region to another was low because no region expanded fast enough to exert a very strong pull on labour from the rest of the country: the population of India was far too large and the rate of economic growth far too slow for this to happen. In addition, in a country of illiterate peasants and labourers, information about economic opportunities travelled slowly and imperfectly. Finally, there were also barriers erected by the influence of religious or social taboos, by local magnates who tried to prevent migration to other regions or other countries, and by conditions amounting nearly to slavery in some areas. Yet vast masses of population did move from one part of India to another, and out of India altogether. This movement was facilitated by the abolition of slavery, the construction of railways and active government assistance in the recruitment of labour for the plantations of Assam.[29]

The main flows of population during this period were from north and central India to Bengal and Assam, and to the canal colonies of the Punjab, from central and western India to Bombay, and from the north to the south.[30] Of these flows, the east–west one was the most significant in terms of numbers of men involved. The movement towards the eastern provinces was stimulated by new employment opportunities in plantations, mines, factories and agriculture. The movement towards Bombay seems to have been stimulated only by the growth of factories and to a lesser extent by new opportunities in agriculture. The following figures indicate the disparity in the effective supply of labour from net migration to Bombay, and to Bengal and Assam:

Total estimated number of net life-time migrants into Bengal, Assam and Bombay (in thousands)

	Bengal	Assam	Bombay
1911	1,285	757	272
1921	1,129	1,140	414
1931	762	1,241	424

Source: Zachariah: *Historical Study of Internal Migration*, pp. 203 and 210.

[29] For an account of the patterns of outward imigration and inland movement, see Davis: *Population of India and Pakistan*, Chapters 12–14.   [30] *Ibid.*, pp. 109–10.

These figures also indicate that after 1911, the *change* in net life-time migration into Bengal was negative (for both the decades 1911–21 and 1921–31), whereas the change in net life-time migration into Bombay remained positive throughout the period. The slackening of investment in the jute industry of Bengal, the rise of the sugar industry in Bihar and the United Provinces and the acceleration of the rate of population growth accentuated this development in the 1930s.[31] (The proportion of the labour force in the cotton mills of Bombay originating in the United Provinces seems to have increased over time.)[32]

The movement of population was caused at the source by precarious conditions of existence, particularly among landless labourers and among the tribal peoples of central and western India; in central India and Bihar, rainfall was scanty and uncertain, and irrigation facilities extremely meagre. The poorer peasants and landless labourers of the United Provinces also suffered from severe seasonal unemployment, and in bad years, from open unemployment even in the normal working seasons.[33]

The forces acting on the demand side of population movements were by and large matched by natural increases of population, particularly up to 1921, as Table 4.9 above would tend to show. According to a study by J. T. Schwartzberg,[34] there is also a remarkable degree of association between areas of high population growth and those with a high rate of growth in the number of agricultural labourers.

Thus, piecing all the aspects of the demographic situation together, one would expect the *natural* flow of labour to be directed towards the factories of eastern and western India from north, central and southern India. One would then expect to locate some sort of a boundary separating the areas from which labour migrated to the two major nodes of industrial development, lying somewhere across the middle of central India. It would at first

[31] Zachariah: *A Historical Study*, pp. 200–11.

[32] Morris: *Emergence of an Industrial Labour Force*, pp. 62–4.

[33] See, for example, Hari Har Dayal: 'Agricultural Labourers: An enquiry into their Conditions in the Unao District', in Radhakamal Mukerjee (ed.): *Fields and Farms in Oudh* (Calcutta, Bombay and Madras, 1929). There are few studies of the motives and prospects of labourers going to Bombay to work in the factories. In their study, *Land and Labour in a Deccan Village, Study No. 2* (London and Bombay, 1921), pp. 158–9, H. H. Mann and N. V. Kanitkar reported that as a result of the economic stress caused by the extremely uncertain rainfall in the village under study, Jategaon Budruk, large numbers of people emigrated to Bombay and other large centres for work. 'The usual plan is for the people to go from four to eight months in the year, except in a few cases when they remain permanently . . . The actual advantage to the village in reducing the pressure on the land is great, but there appears to be considerable doubt as to whether it received very much actual direct financial advantage . . . the people who had returned from Bombay were inclined to doubt whether they had benefited permanently very much – though, of course, it permitted them to enjoy luxuries for the time being . . . Only one such returned worker had bought land.'

[34] 'Agricultural Labour in India: A Regional Analysis with Particular Reference to Population Growth', *Economic Development and Cultural Change*, Vol. 11, July 1963.

sight appear superfluous to take into account differences in recruiting methods in explaining the relative degrees of scarcity of labour in western and eastern India.

5.4 DIFFERENCES IN METHODS OF RECRUITMENT AND IN GOVERNMENT POLICY APPLIED TO DIFFERENT REGIONS

The different methods of recruitment are, however, relevant in explaining the situation regarding supply of labour because: (a) the 'catchment area' for the supply of labour to Bombay and Ahmedabad was far more restricted than that for the supply of labour to the factories, mines and plantations of eastern India, (b) the factory population was derived to a far greater extent from the immediate locality in Bombay, Cawnpore or Ahmedabad than in Calcutta and its suburbs, and (c) even though the movement of population might ultimately respond to differing wage levels in different industrial centres, an efficient recruitment system could speed up the process. The recruitment of labour in the jute mills and other factories in and near Calcutta was more or less a by-product of the process of recruitment of labour for the Assam plantations, so we begin with a description of the methods of recruitment and retention of labour in the plantations.

The Government of India had from 1859 onwards passed a series of laws which allowed the tea plantations of Assam to recruit labour on an indenture system. Of these laws, the Workmen's Breach of Contract Act remained on the statute book from 1859 to 1926. The planters had at first the right of private arrest of the labourers, and workers were liable to be punished with imprisonment for breaches of contract. An attempt was made to lessen the rigours of the indenture system by Act VI of 1901 but the penal provisions for breaches of contract were not abolished until 1926 and in the case of Madras, where the system of recruitment was governed by the Madras Planters' Labour Act of 1903, not until 1929.[35]

The Assam Labour Enquiry Committee, which was appointed after serious rioting in the tea plantations of Assam in 1921, found many breaches of legal regulations on the part of the planters. At the time of the enquiry by the Royal Commission on Labour in India in 1929–30 the labourers were still found to believe that they were liable to punishment for 'absconding' from the plantations. Since the labourers were illiterate and poor and a long distance away from home, they were generally without any recourse except 'riots' against breaches of their personal freedom and inroads on their wages by planters. The Criminal Procedure Code was often invoked by the government against any 'outsider' trying to organize plantation labour.[36]

[35] R. K. Das: *Plantation Labour in India* (Calcutta, 1931), Chapters II–IV, and S. K. Bose: *Capital and Labour in the Indian Tea Industry* (Bombay, 1954), Chapters VIII–X.
[36] B. Shiva Rao: *The Industrial Worker in India* (London, 1939), Chapter IX.

On the other hand, the planters were organized in the Indian Tea Association which acted as a monopsonist as far as tea-plantation labour was concerned. The word used to describe the act of leaving a plantation by a labourer even after 1926 was 'absconding'. Strict watch was kept over the 'coolie lines' by the *chowkidars* who could bar any visitor from entering the workers' colonies or prevent any worker leaving the colonies without permission. The tea plantations would not allow any worker to leave one plantation and work in another, and would not employ any worker who might be suspected of having left another tea plantation in Assam.[37] It was pleaded before the Royal Commission on Labour in India that since recruitment by contractors had practically vanished and since workers' rights had come to be better protected by legislation, unrestricted recruitment of labour for tea plantations should be permitted. But the Government of Bihar and Orissa, one of the major areas of recruitment, would not agree;[38] and even the Government of Assam, though naturally more sympathetic to the planters' point of view, could not support free recruitment.[39] In the event the degree of supervision of recruitment was tightened to some extent by the Tea District Emigrant Labour Act of 1932, which created the office of Emigrant Labour Controller, and for the first time, gave the labourer the right to be repatriated. The system of recruitment prevailing up to 1930 and beyond depended on the plantation *sardar*, who was sent back to his own district by the plantation concerned for the purpose of recruiting labour. The plantation *sardars* had to have a certificate authorizing them to recruit labour. The work of these *sardars* was supervised by local agents in the districts, most of whom worked under the Tea Districts Labour Association. The Assam Labour Board, appointed by the government, generally supervised recruitment.[40] This Act was in operation throughout India except Bombay, and even in Bombay, the government allowed recruitment provided the emigrants were produced before a magistrate.[41]

This system of recruitment was mainly controlled by the British managing agency houses which had an interest in tea. In 1899, practically all the local agents who were empowered to recruit labour through contractors were British managing agency houses in Calcutta whose interests spanned tea, coal and jute, among other trades or industries.[42] For the mines or jute mills, no special recruiting machinery was in operation. The Government of

[37] RC on Labour in India: *Report* (PP 1930–1, XI), pp. 376–8.

[38] The Government of Bihar and Orissa pointed out, among other things, that a poor labourer could not really come back from the plantations once he had got there: 'It is cynical to point out the excellence of modern communications to a man whose only resort is to walk home.' RC on Labour in India: *Evidence*, Vol IV, Part I, *Bihar and Orissa with Coalfields* (London, 1931), p. 11.

[39] *Ibid.*, Vol. VI, Part I, *Assam and the Dooars*, pp. 5, 23–5, and 27–35.

[40] *Ibid.*, p. 4.   [41] *Ibid.*

[42] Gov. India, Department of Revenue and Agriculture: *Emigration*, October 1900, *A Proceedings*, Nos. 15 and 16, p. 796.

Bengal appointed a Commission in 1895 to find out the best means of supplying labour to the coal mines of Bengal which were increasing their output at a rapid rate. The Commission found that while the wages of mining labour were higher than the wages prevailing in Chotanagpur and the North-Western Provinces, they were generally lower than the wages of an able-bodied labourer in Burdwan – the district in which the richest coal mines of Bengal were situated.[43] The recommendation of the Commission that a special system of recruitment be instituted for mining labour as for plantation labour was not acted upon, as it proved unnecessary. The supply of labour from the Santal Parganas, from Chotanagpur and from among the Bauris of West Bengal proved ample; any shortages that occurred were temporary and were experienced mainly by the more inefficient of the coal mines, and by the manganese and mica mines which paid lower-than-average wages.[44]

The supply of labour to jute mills on the Hooghly was thus a part of the much larger stream of labour migrating from other provinces of India to the coal mines, plantations and factories of eastern India. The system of recruitment for the Assam tea plantations provided information to the managers of jute mills about the sources of labour supply; even more important, the regular flow of labour to mines and plantations provided the links with intending immigrants. Since conditions of work in jute mills were much better than in mines and plantations, and wages were higher, particularly for skilled workers, it was unnecessary for jute mills to make any special effort to recruit labour apart from ensuring that the eastward flow of labour continued. The jute mills did not want any special measures to be taken for recruitment of labour at the time of the labour enquiry of 1895; when in 1905 another enquiry was made into the problem of labour supply in Bengal and the United Provinces, the Chairman of the Indian Jute Mills Association concluded, after conferences with government officials, that a labour shortage occurred in all trades during the hot weather months and that so far as the jute industry was concerned, 'the question narrows itself down to one of overcoming what at present seems an inevitable shortage during about three months of the year'.[45]

[43] *Report of the Labour Enquiry Commission 1895* (Bengal) (Calcutta, 1896), pp. 7–16.

[44] The main sources of information for the supply of labour to the mines of eastern India are (a) Gov. India, Department of Mines: *Reports of the Inspection of the Mines in India* (annual; from 1901 onwards, *Reports of the Chief Inspector of Mines in India*), (b) *Report of the Labour Enquiry Commission* (Bengal) (Calcutta, 1896), (c) *Census of India, 1921*, Vol. v, *Bengal*, Part ii (Calcutta, 1923) and Vol. vii, *Bihar and Orissa*, Part ii (Patna, 1923), Table xxii, Parts iv and v in both volumes, and (d) RC on Labour in India: *Evidence*, Vol. iv, Part i, *Bihar and Orissa with Coalfields* (London, 1931), pp. 5–9. The methods of recruitment actually adopted by the mines are described in *ibid.*, pp. 9–11. See also Buchanan: *Development of Capitalistic Enterprise*, pp. 270–3.

[45] IJMA. *Report of the Committee for the year ended 31st December, 1905* (Calcutta, 1906), p. iii.

Thus the limitations of the local labour supply in Assam and Bengal did not prove to be a hindrance to the development of industry in Bengal. The jute mills in Bengal had at first employed mainly Bengali labour. However, as the industry expanded, a larger and larger proportion of the labourers, particularly in the mills in Calcutta and north of Calcutta, came to be composed primarily of labour from outside Bengal. A. R. Murray, Member, Provincial Industries Committee, Bengal, and later Chairman of the IJMA, gave the following figures for the composition of the work-force in four mills (two at Garulia, Shamnagar, and one each at Titaghur and Bhadreswar) in 1902 and 1916.[46]

	1902	*1916*
Total number of workers	17,110	31,841
Percentage of Bengali workers to the total number of workers	28	10
Percentage of local Bengali workers to the total number of workers	22	7

According to the Census of India, 1921, the composition of labour force in the jute mills of Bengal in that year was as follows:[47]

	Total no. of workers	*No. of workers born in Bengal*
Skilled workers	124,221	38,890
Unskilled workers	155,633	26,558

Thus the proportion of Bengalis was distinctly higher among the skilled workers (31%) than among the unskilled workers (17%).

We have already indicated the basic reason for the relative scarcity of Bengali labour in the factories, viz., the relative attractiveness of wages in agriculture in Bengal compared with the wages offered in factories, which were high enough to attract labour from the provinces of Bihar and Orissa, the United Provinces, the Central Provinces and Madras.[48]

In contrast with the situation in eastern India, Bombay recruited its labour force from a relatively narrow area around Bombay, particularly up to 1921; more than 55% of the mill-hands of Bombay up to 1921 had their birthplace within a distance of 200 miles from Bombay.[49] Ahmedabad

[46] A. R. Murray: 'Note on Industrial Development of Bengal', in *Evidence (Report of IIC)*, Vol. VI, *Confidential Evidence* (Calcutta, 1918), pp. 103–13, at p. 111.

[47] *Census of India, 1921*, Vol. V, *Bengal*, Part II (Calcutta, 1923), Table XXII, Parts IV and V.

[48] At the time of the enquiry by the IIC it was suggested that the main reasons for the drop in the proportion of the Bengalis in the workforce of jute mills were that 'the Bengalee asks higher wages', that 'he gets a jute crop' and that the price of jute had risen in comparison with the prices of other commodities (before the war). See *Evidence (Report of IIC)*, Vol. VI, *Confidential Evidence*, pp. 116–17.

[49] Morris: *Emergence of an Industrial Labour Force*, p. 63.

also drew the majority of its workers from the districts of Gujarat and Kathiawar.[50] The Bombay mill-owners never instituted any organized method of recruitment of workers from other parts of India in the years before the First World War,[51] and after the First World War they were beset with problems which were far more serious than those of labour supply. Finally, as we have already pointed out, the province of Bombay did not have the plantations or the mines which proved to be far bigger employers of labour than factories in eastern India, nor did it attract labour for agricultural purposes.[52]

Before going on to tackle the second group of factors, viz., the differences in the growth of workers' organizations and workers' resistance to wage-cuts in different industrial centres, as explaining the measured differences in real wages in different centres, we should refer to the differences in the natural rates of growth of population in Bengal and Bombay. Both the plague and the famine at the turn of the century and the influenza epidemic and famine in 1918–19 had a much severer impact on the natural rate of growth of population in Bombay than on that in Bengal; hence one would expect to find, given the same pattern of development of demand for labour, and abstracting from movement of labour from other provinces, a greater upward pressure on wages in Bombay than in Bengal. We cannot, however, conclude that these differences alone would be enough to explain the differences in movements of real wages in Bombay and Calcutta: labour mobility would in time smooth out differences in real wages which could not be attributed to skill or training. If it does not perform this function, then we have to look for 'imperfections' in the labour market. Secondly, the influenza epidemic and the famine of 1918–19 acted in opposite directions as far as the potential supply of labour was concerned. While the influenza epidemic removed vast numbers of people, particularly in northern, central and western India, the famine of 1918–19 and later crop failures in the twenties left the poorer people in an even more precarious position; the latter sought work in the plantations, mines and factories or in the more prosperous agricultural regions.[53] There was for a very short period a scare about the shortage of labour in the tea plantations because plantation wages failed to keep up with the rise in the cost of living during the War, and

---

[50] RC on Labour in India: *Evidence*, Vol. I, Part I, *Bombay Presidency* (London, 1931), pp. 4 and 275.

[51] J. N. Tata had proposed the institution of a recruiting system in 1888 and again in 1892, but the Bombay Millowners' Association had refused to do anything about it. See Morris, *Emergence of an Industrial Labour Force*, pp. 54–5.

[52] See Davis: *Population of India and Pakistan*, Chapter 14, and Zachariah: *A Historical Study*.

[53] R. K. Das: *Plantation Labour in India* (Calcutta, 1931), Chapters II and IV, and *Resolution on Immigrant Labour in Assam for the year ended 1920–21* (Shillong, 1921). The number of immigrants into Assam increased from 48,130 in 1916–17 and 19,407 in 1917–18 to 222,171 in 1918–19 and 102,089 in 1919–20.

consequently there was some exodus of labour; but the supply situation again became easy in the Assam plantations in the twenties.[54] Bombay is in fact nearer the Central Provinces, from which a great deal of tea plantation labour came, than are the tea plantations of Assam. Hence the demographic factors cannot by themselves explain the differential movements in real wages, particularly in the twenties.[55]

5.5 TRADE UNION ORGANIZATION AND POLITICAL FACTORS IN THE DIFFERENTIAL MOVEMENTS OF REAL WAGES

Whatever may have been the situation at the beginning of the twentieth century, or in the few years following the famine and the influenza epidemic of 1918–19, from the middle of the 1920s onwards there was little scarcity of labour – even of a short-term character – in any major industrial centre of India.[56] In view of this, one has to look for factors other than the potential

---

[54] *Reports on Immigrant Labour in the Province of Assam* for 1922–3 and 1923–4, (Shillong, 1923 and 1924), and RC on Labour in India, *Evidence*, Vol. VI, *Assam and the Dooars* (London, 1931), pp. 3–4. After recruiting vast numbers in 1918–19 and 1919–20, the tea industry experienced a depression in 1920–1 and 1921–2, so that the numbers demanded fell off. As soon as the industry recovered it began to complain of labour shortage to the government, which lent a sympathetic ear. The opening paragraph of the Resolution on Immigrant Labour in Assam for the year 1922–3 passed by the Government of Assam reads: 'Favourable conditions prevailed during the year under review. The Tea Industry, which employs most of the imported labour, was exceedingly prosperous, and the year was a healthy one. Nevertheless owing to good harvest in the recruiting districts and to the competition of other industries the number of immigrants was again small and the year ended with a further reduction in the strength of the imported labour force settled in the province. The shortage of labour is one of the most serious problems with which the Industry is faced, and the Governor in Council can only again give an assurance that the efforts made to open out fresh fields of recruitment and to offer greater attractions to possible immigrants have his sympathy and support. During the year the Government of Madras have opened the whole of the Presidency to recruitment for Assam.' Such solicitude on the part of the government was not wasted: the total number of immigrants into Assam went up from 21,654 in 1922–3 to 41,862 in 1923–4.

[55] Interesting information on the influence of famines and the development of transport in the heartland of India is provided by the evidence of the Industries and Labour Department of the Government of India before the Imperial Economic Committee: 'Tea, offering as it does a low cash wage no larger than that offered locally to the agricultural labourer, is forced to depend on seasons of famine and scarcity for the replenishment of its labour force. . . . (Good monsoon recently) . . . Further, the price of foodgrains has nearly doubled since the war and growing foodgrains is more than ever a paying proposition. The best recruiting districts have been found to be those with poor communications.' Gov. India, Department of Industries and Labour: Interprovincial migration files: File No. L-1420 of 1926, *Note on the Labour Position in the Assam Tea Gardens for the Imperial Economic Committee*, p. 3.

[56] S. Ghose and J. C. Mittra, representing the Bengal National Chamber of Commerce before the Indian Fiscal Commission of 1921–2, claimed that there was no paucity of labour for factory work in Bengal and that the drawing of labour from agriculture would not affect agricultural production in Bengal: *Evidence (Report of the Indian Fiscal*

supply of labour under competitive conditions to explain the divergence in the rates of change of real wages in different parts of India, particularly after the First World War.

We now ask whether the divergent movements of real wages in the cotton mills of Bombay and the jute mills of Calcutta can be attributed to the greater power of workers' organizations in Bombay than in Calcutta during the interwar period. There are difficulties in talking about the 'strength' of trade unions in the two centres, for before 1926, trade unions did not have much legal protection, and the registered trade unions were more in the nature of friendly societies or welfare societies for workers. But in spite of the absence of proper trade unions, strikes flared up all over India from 1918 onwards, and trade unions, which were primarily 'strike committees', were organized to co-ordinate the activities of workers. In Bombay, an attempt was made to co-ordinate the activities of the organized trade unions in the 'Central Labour Board' which was set up by F. J. Ginwalla and S. H. Jhabvala, two of the many 'outsiders' responsible for organizing the trade unions in the first place.[57] There were no stable and effective unions of textile workers in Bombay City until the Bombay Textile Labour Union was organized in 1926 by N. M. Joshi and R. R. Bakhale of the Servants of India Society, although an association called the Kamgar Hitwardhak Sabha had been set up in 1919.[58]

However, the situation in the Bengal jute mills was even worse from the point of view of workers' organization. The only registered union of the jute-mill workers at the time of the enquiry by the Royal Commission on Labour was the Kankinarrah Labour Union, which had been founded in 1920 by the Khelafatists with Maulvi Latafat Hossain as its first Secretary and Abdul Majid as its President.[59] Its membership in 1930 was 1,000

Commission), Vol. II (Calcutta, 1923), p. 405. The Government of Bombay in their written evidence before the Royal Commission on Labour in India pointed out that changes in wages upwards or downwards had little noticeable effect on labour supply because plenty of *badlis* (casual labour) were available, and workers tended to go back to the villages when they were unemployed: RC on Labour in India: *Evidence*, Vol I, Part I (London, 1931), pp. 78–9. For South India, the problem of shortage of labour for industry never arose. There was a net migration of labour from Madras to other parts of India and abroad throughout the period 1901–31, and the amount of net migration increased with time: Zachariah: *A Historical Study*, p. 207. Industrialists in South India corroborated the advantages of cheap labour. See, for example, *Issues advertised in the Times*, No. 15, January–June 1898, 23 May 1898, p. 217, advertisement for the Anglo-French Textile Company Limited of Pondicherry. See also the evidence of W. E. Winter and F. Stanes of Stanes and Company in *Evidence (Report of IIC)*, Vol. III (PP 1919, XIX), pp. 448–54. Similarly the United Provinces was a net supplier of labour to other regions: Zachariah, *A Historical Study*, p. 200. The Tata Iron and Steel Company experienced no difficulty in recruiting labour: RC on Labour in India: *Evidence*, Vol. IV, Part I (London, 1931), p. 160.

[57] A. R. Burnett-Hurst: *Labour and Housing in Bombay* (London, 1925), Chapter IX.

[58] RC on Labour in India: *Evidence*, Vol. I, Part I, *Bombay Presidency* (London, 1931), pp. 103–5.

[59] *Ibid.*, Vol. v, Part I, p. 271.

although it claimed to represent the 50,000 mill-hands in the jute mills in the Bhatpara municipality.[60] The major jute-mill strike of 1929 was led by the Bengal Jute Workers' Union, which claimed to represent all the jute-mill workers, but its claim was not supported even during the strike, for it split into two in the course of it.[61] No more than 4% of the workers in jute mills were organized in any trade union of a non-ephemeral character.

By contrast, in the Bombay cotton mills 42·50% of the operatives were organized in trade unions. In Ahmedabad the percentage fell to 28·52% and in Sholapur less than 5% were covered. The membership of some of the unions in Bombay was quite substantial as Table 5.4, giving the date of formation and membership of the trade unions in the cotton mills of the Bombay Presidency, shows.

TABLE 5.4 *Trade unions in the cotton mills of the Bombay Presidency: date of formation, and membership*

	Date of formation	No. of members on 1 March 1929
Bombay City		
The Girni Kamgar Mahamandal	Dec. 1923	1,200
The Bombay Textile Labour Union	Jan. 1926	6,749
The Bombay Mill Workers' Union	Mar. 1928	984
The Bombay Girni Kamgar Union	Mar. 1928	54,000
Ahmedabad		
The Weavers' Union	Feb. 1920	825
The Throstle Union	Feb. 1920	11,180
The Winders' Union	Jun. 1920	120
The Card Room, Blow Room and Frame Department Union	Aug. 1920	3,725
The Drivers' Oilmen's and Firemen's Union	Sept. 1920	525
The Jobbers' and Mukadams' Union*	Mar. 1926	700
Sholapur		
The Bombay Textile Labour Union Sholapur Branch		800

* This union was dissolved in 1922, and re-formed in 1926.
Source: RC on Labour in India, *Evidence*, Vol. I, Part 1, *Bombay Presidency* (London, 1931), p. 169.

The cotton textile workers of Delhi had no union at all.[62] At Cawnpore, workers from many industries were organized in a loose federation called the Mazdoor Sabha: while the total number of workers employed in the factories of Cawnpore in 1929–30 was 32,142, the membership of the

[60] *Ibid.*, Vol. v, Part 1, p. 261 and Vol. v, Part 2, p. 119.
[61] *Ibid.*, Vol. v, Part 1, p. 127.
[62] See the evidence of P. Mukerjee, W. R. Taylor and Shri Ram of the Upper India Chamber of Commerce in *ibid.*, Vol. II, Part 1, pp. 75–81 and Part 2, pp. 123–33.

Mazdoor Sabha was only 3,000.[63] Madras had led the trade union movement with the organization of the workers into the Madras Labour Union but the movement could not really flourish in a region with abundant labour, slow industrial growth, and employers who were determined not to make any concession to labour organizations. In the growth of the trade union movement and in the frequency or intensity of industrial disputes, political factors – including in the phrase the national, or rather racial, character of the employers, the degree of homogeneity among the workers, the relation of the workers to the other people in the industrial centre and the ideology of the leaders of the labour organizations – inevitably played a large role. One can claim that on the whole, in industries or centres dominated by European employers, trade unions were weak: The employers had a greater homogeneity among themselves and did not have the need to talk the workers' language for political purposes. This did not mean, however, that the European employers were able to prevent the disruption of the normal working of industry by strikes. It is clear, for example, that the major jute-mill strike of 1929 was to a large extent caused by the refusal of the employers to heed the warning of the only organized trade union in the industry – the Kankinarrah Labour Union – about possible trouble, or to meet representatives of labour to discuss the proposed increase of working hours from 54 to 60 per week without any increase in workers' earnings.[64] Again, in Madras, there were several strikes in the Buckingham and Carnatic Mills partly because of the unwillingness of the employers to concede that workers had any right to combine at all.[65]

The labour–management relations in Ahmedabad were unique: the Textile Labour Association controlled the several craft unions in the industry and negotiated with the employers for wage increases. In 1918, the first large-scale struggle between the workers and the employers was resolved primarily through arbitration by Mahatma Gandhi. The principle of arbitration was thenceforward recognized in the Ahmedabad cotton mills, and the Textile Labour Association was generally able to prevent strikes in the industry. The personality of Mahatma Gandhi has been rightly considered crucial for the success of the Ahmedabad experiment.[66] Ahmedabad, however, enjoyed special advantages because: (a) during the twenties at least, the cotton mills were able to offer increased employment to the workers even when wages were cut, and (b) the workers and the employers

---

[63] *Ibid.*, Vol. III, Part I, pp. 135 and 187.   [64] *Ibid.*, Vol. v, Part I, pp. 128–9.

[65] For descriptions of the causes and the course of the strike in the Buckingham and Carnatic Mills in 1920–1, see Gilbert Slater: *Southern India* (London, 1936), Chapter XXIX. Mahatma Gandhi apparently persuaded the workers of the Carnatic Mills to go back to work after a hopeless strike.

[66] C. A. Myers: *Labour Problems in Industrialization of India* (Cambridge, Mass., 1958), pp. 57–60; see also RC on Labour in India: *Report* (PP 1930–1, XI), pp. 336–7 and *Report of the Textile Labour Enquiry Committee*, Vol. II, *Final Report* (Bombay, 1940), pp. 370–1.

belonged to largely the same linguistic and cultural groups, and may have shared a common view about the goals and methods of the larger political struggle.

When such common goals did not exist, and when wage-cuts were accompanied by contraction in employment, costly strikes could and did result. The Bombay cotton mills experienced the highest intensity of strikes, particularly in 1928. Tables 5.5 and 5.6 bring out the contrast between Bombay and Bengal. Besides the factors mentioned above, the lack of linguistic homogeneity among the workers in the jute mills and the linguistic separation of the majority of workers from the surrounding Bengali community seem to have weakened the labour movement in Bengal both in respect of their power to organize in trade unions and in respect of their power to strike.[67]

TABLE 5.5 *Industrial disputes in jute mills in Bengal, 1921 to 1929*

	Number of strikes in jute mills	Number of men involved	Number of working days lost
1921	39	186,479	706,229
1922	40	173,957	1,079,627
1923	29	90,664	644,804
1924	18	69,488	346,756
1925	14	44,940	242,906
1926	29	38,042	794,384
1927	9	34,900	218,000
1928	18	56,524	1,508,708
Up to 30 June 1929	5	18,285	106,785
Subtotal	201	713,279	5,648,199
1 July 1929 to 30 Sept. 1929	n.a.	272,000	2,896,000

Source: RC on Labour in India, *Evidence*, Vol. v, Part i, *Bengal* (London, 1931), p. 126.

Note: The total number of working days lost in Bengal in industrial disputes from 1921 to 1929 was 16,510,669. *Ibid.* p. 121.

The bargaining power of the workers deteriorated significantly during the thirties, with the coming of the depression. Wage-cuts were enforced in practically all the major centres, but real wages did not always decline because the cost of living also went down substantially in most centres. Given the excess supply of labour, concerted action by trade unions was very difficult. Further, the Trades Disputes Act of 1929 made it a punishable

[67] The cotton-mill workers of Bombay had struck work when Tilak was arrested in 1908. See L. A. Gordon: 'Social and Economic conditions of Bombay workers on the eve of the 1908 strike', in I. M. Reisner and N. M. Goldberg (eds.): *Tilak and the Struggle for Indian Freedom* (New Delhi, 1966), pp. 471–544.

TABLE 5.6 *Industrial disputes in the Bombay Presidency, 1921 to 1929*

	Number of disputes	Number of workers involved	Number of working days lost
1921*	104	131,999	1,272,362
1922	143	173,386	756,747
1923	109	109,332	2,836,000
1924	50	179,522	7,559,401
1925	69	175,631	11,387,797
1926	57	29,314	78,113
1927	54	28,078	165,061
1928	114	326,196	24,629,715
1929†	38	161,587	5,249,096
Total of which spinning and weaving mills in the:	738	1,315,045	53,934,292
Presidency	612	1,233,170	52,450,814
Bombay City	n.a.	n.a.	48,259,737
Ahmedabad	n.a.	n.a.	2,604,737
Sholapur	n.a.	n.a.	1,214,434

* from 1 April to 31 December 1921. † from 1 January to 30 June 1929.

Source: RC on Labour in India, *Evidence* Vol. 1, Part 1, *Bombay Presidency* (London, 1931), pp. 117, 127.

offence to strike without sufficient reason and with an intention to cause harm to the public. With the industrial recovery in 1937 and with the introduction of Congress ministries in eight provinces of India, strikes broke out all over India, the main demands being that the cuts in wages made in the immediately preceding years should be restored, and that retrenchment should be stopped. The Government of the United Provinces appointed the Cawnpore Labour Inquiry Committee to recommend methods of improving the living conditions of workers and of collecting data bearing on the labour conditions, after strikes had broken out in several Cawnpore cotton mills. The Committee found the employers generally unco-operative in supplying information and extremely hostile to the only organized trade union – the Mazdoor Sabha. It found that the wages at Cawnpore were very much lower than in most other centres of industry in India, and considered the record of low wages to be unjustified by the level of profitability of most Cawnpore mills. The Committee suggested increments ranging from $2\frac{1}{2}$ annas in the rupee in the case of workers getting between Rs. 13 and Rs. 19 per month to half an anna in the rupee in the case of workers getting between Rs. 40 and Rs. 59 per month.[68] The employers, however, rejected the proposals of the Committee, and the workers came out in a

[68] *Report of the Cawnpore Textile Labour Inquiry Committee appointed by the Government of the United Provinces* (Allahabad, 1938), p. 40.

general strike, which was the biggest in the history of Cawnpore. The employers rejected mediation by the government in the subsequent disputes, but ultimately had to concede many of the demands of the workers.[69]

In Bombay, the strike of 1928 was followed by a long period of dwindling trade union membership and generally ineffective union resistance to wage-cuts, in the face of a dwindling volume of employment in the chief industry. The pressure of an excess supply of labour[70] was reinforced by the government action to discourage the growth of militant trade unions under communist leadership. The Trades Disputes Act, 1929, had originated with the Government of Bombay. After a desperate strike by cotton-mill workers in 1934 in a stand against repeated retrenchments and wage-cuts, the Government of Bombay passed the Trade Disputes Conciliation Act. The Act provided for the official appointment of a labour officer who came to usurp many of the functions of the trade unions. He also had the power to refer disputes to conciliation. Again, after the advent of a Congress ministry in Bombay in 1937 and the return of prosperity to the mill industry, there were a number of strikes involving a very large number of workers. The Government of Bombay appointed a Textile Labour Enquiry Committee which recommended in its interim report an 11·9% increase in wages. Simultaneously the government passed the Bombay Industrial Disputes Act, making conciliation compulsory, and at the same time strengthening the hands of unions fulfilling certain conditions in collective bargaining.[71]

Similarly, the Governments of Bihar, the Central Provinces and Berar, and Madras appointed labour enquiry committees in order to ascertain the facts behind the strikes of 1937–8 and recommend appropriate measures. In Bengal, however, the attitude of the government was less sympathetic to the striking workers. A very large number of workers (130,000) in jute mills lost their jobs during the depression which started in 1929. In February 1937, the workers struck work on the refusal of the mill-owners to restore the wage-cuts. The strike lasted until May, and compelled the employers to grant some of the workers' demands, including the recognition of the workers' union. In 1938 the workers went on strike again, and IJMA was largely able to crush the demands of the workers through concerted action. The Government of Bengal was on the whole more sympathetic to the management than to the workers during those disputes.[72]

---

[69] Radhakamal Mukerjee: *The Indian Working Class* (Bombay, 1945), p. 309; and R. P. Dutt: *India Today* (Bombay, 1949), p. 396.

[70] That there was considerable unemployment among the cotton-mill workers of Bombay even at the time of the enquiry by the Royal Commission is clear from the evidence of the Government of Bombay: RC on Labour in India: *Evidence*, Vol. I, Part I (London, 1931), p. 10 and pp. 78–9.

[71] See Morris: *Emergence of an Industrial Labour Force*, Chapter x.

[72] Dutt: *India Today*, pp. 395–6; IJMA: *Report of the Committee for the Year ended*

5.6 PROFITABILITY AND WAGES
IN DIFFERENT INDUSTRIAL CENTRES

It has sometimes been claimed that factory workers in under-developed countries are a privileged group who often enjoy a much higher standard of living than ordinary people, including peasants and agricultural labourers. What is more, the high profits made by entrepreneurs are shared with the workers. There is not much evidence of this profit-sharing in the case of either cotton or jute textile workers up to around 1920; most of the wage increases subsequently granted were meant to make up for the rise in the cost of living. There may have been some rise in the real wages in the Ahmedabad textile industry relative to those in the Bombay mills, because of the greater prosperity of the former. While in the twenties the wages of cotton-mill workers were higher in Bombay than in Ahmedabad, the position was reversed by 1934 as the figures in Table 5.7 show. It would, however, be wrong to attribute the higher level of wages in Ahmedabad

TABLE 5.7 *Daily wages and employment in cottons mills, 1934 and 1937*

		Bombay Rs. a. p.	Ahmedabad Rs. a. p.	Sholapur Rs. a. p.
Process operatives:	1934	1 - 1 - 9 (116,989)	1 - 5 - 11 (74,185)	0 - 11 - 6 (14,435)
	1937	1 - 1 - 4 (97,143)	1 - 3 - 0 (60,139)	0 - 11 - 3 (15,148)
Engineering operatives:	1934	1 - 2 - 9 (11,429)	1 - 3 - 11 (7,901)	0 - 12 - 6 (1,889)
	1937	1 - 2 - 8 (10,457)	1 - 2 - 3 (6,459)	0 - 11 - 6 (2,110)
All operatives:	1934	1 - 1 - 10 (128,418)	1 - 5 - 7 (82,086)	0 - 11 - 8 (16,324)
	1937	1 - 1 - 5 (107,600)	1 - 2 - 11 (66,598)	0 - 11 - 4 (17,258)

Source: Report of the Textile Labour Enquiry Committee, Vol. II, Final Report (Bombay, 1940), p. 57 (figures within brackets indicate the level of employment).

31st December 1938 (Calcutta, 1939), pp. 72–6. In Bombay the Mill owners' Association had already appointed a labour officer, R. G. Gokhale, to co-operate with the Government Labour Officer; see R. C. James: 'Labour mobility, unemployment, and economic changes: an Indian case', *The Journal of Political Economy (JPE)*, Vol. LXVII, No. 6, December, 1959, pp. 549–59; Morris: *Emergence of an Industrial Labour Force* pp. 125–127. The IJMA appointed (in 1938) as its first labour officer J. H. Mulcahy, a retired Assistant Commissioner of Police; because of its fear of the danger of 'communistic agitation' it appointed a second labour officer, B. Sinha, who retired from the Bengal Civil Service to take up this work and who was posted to the Budge Budge/Garden Reach area because of his 'first-class knowledge of that district', having been Sadar S.D.O. of 24 Parganas: IJMA: *Report of the Committee for the year ended 31st December 1938* (Calcutta, 1939), pp. 76–80.

Supply of unskilled labour

TABLE 5.8 *Annual wage per head (Rs.) and number of uncovenanted employees in the Tata Iron and Steel Company, 1912–13 to 1922–3*

	Coke ovens		Blast furnaces		Open-hearth		Blooming mill		28 inch mill		Bar mills		All departments	
	No.	Wage	No.	Wage	No.	Wage	No.	Wage	No.	Wage	No.	Wage	No.	Wage
1912–13	657	185.92	846	376.93	900	182.49	217	391.45	730	179.25	567	74.20	3,917	220.36
1913–14	628	207.25	810	339.48	860	242.27	198	414.98	648	185.23	541	106.29	3,685	236.95
1914–15	656	167.79	743	272.82	750	246.71	182	503.93	641	327.39	500	167.80	3,472	254.40
1915–16	713	167.90	915	206.54	980	236.35	224	483.55	791	370.07	620	288.57	4,243	264.03
1916–17	950	200.79	838	207.06	1,010	250.10	235	518.86	905	385.48	750	289.32	4,688	278.29
1917–18	1,120	198.66	1,040	198.33	1,490	258.54	260	522.95	1,090	395.91	980	286.86	5,980	278.03
1918–19	1,450	234.03	1,550	175.09	1,850	300.15	306	408.44	1,264	377.20	1,150	316.18	7,570	281.59
1919–20	1,910	235.93	1,993	162.64	2,070	205.31	325	393.99	1,315	378.35	1,170	287.90	8,783	246.18
1920–1	2,450	243.64	2,293	232.84	2,305	242.41	310	565.99	1,440	428.34	1,165	362.27	9,963	291.47
1921–2	2,353	255.47	2,306	272.12	2,360	239.82	332	595.98	1,543	401.68	1,030	356.99	9,924	300.28
1922–3	2,725	238.66	2,339	246.25	2,265	208.88	360	532.15	1,590	343.19	1,050	340.02	10,329	270.47

Source: ITB: *Evidence (Report on steel)*, Vol I (Calcutta, 1924), pp. 109–11.

Note: The figures for some of the departments in 1918–19 were reported as being related to a period of nine months only. But internal evidence suggests that the figures for *all* departments relate to a nine-month period. The figures of wages for 1918–19 were therefore adjusted by multiplying them all by 1.33. Some oddities result therefrom, as in the case of the open-hearth department; but according to the source the figure for this department definitely relates to a nine-month period.

merely to a higher degree of prosperity of the Ahmedabad industry. For a start, the Ahmedabad mills were also badly affected by the depression of the years 1923–33. Secondly, one must also take into account the more effective organization for wage negotiation which had been set up in Ahmedabad. We have already seen that while the cotton mills of Cawnpore had been profitable, the wages at Cawnpore had remained quite low. Similarly, the cotton-mill industry expanded fast in the Madras Presidency from the middle 1920s onwards; yet Madras and Comibatore mill-workers were paid the lowest wage rates in the country.[73]

When we come to a more 'modern' industry such as the iron and steel industry, the picture is not very different. Table 5.8 shows the wage rate of 'uncovenanted employees', that is Indian employees, in the Tata Iron and Steel works over the period 1912–23. During this period there was some substitution of European and American staff by Indian staff who were generally paid higher-than-average wages. Yet we find that wages per head did not rise steadily, and some compensation for increases in cost of living was made only after costly strikes in 1920 and 1922.[74] There was another big strike in 1928, caused primarily by the attempt of the Tata Iron and Steel Company to reduce its labour force. At the time of the enquiry by the Royal Commission on Labour it was found that while 'skilled' labourers at Jamshedpur earned a little more than elsewhere, the unskilled labourers earned very little more. Since the cost of living was higher there than in other towns or villages of Bihar, the real wages of unskilled labour were *lower* there than in other centres. Between 1922 and 1928, the wages of skilled and unskilled workers in the Tata Iron and Steel works remained almost stationary,[75] with the wages of unskilled labourers increasing very slightly; in the same town, the wages of workers of the Tinplate Company were generally higher than the wages of skilled workers of the same category in other factories in Bihar, such as the sugar works of Marhaura or the engineering works of Arthur Butler and Company, Muzaffarpur. But the wages of unskilled workers were about the same at Jamshedpur as at the Rice Mills, Dinapur or the Peninsular Tobacco Company, Monghyr, although they were a good deal higher than wages of the same category of workers at many other factories such as Arthur Butler and Company.[76] The cost of labour per head per annum at the Tata Iron and Steel works for 1927–33 is shown below (in Rs.):

[73] Mukerjee: *The Indian Working Class*, pp. 122–7.
[74] RC on Labour in India: *Evidence*, Vol. IV, Part I (London, 1931), p. 122. 'It is clear that the immediate cause of the strike (of 1920) was economic. The price of living had been increasing rapidly since the war all over India, and in the town of Jamshedpur there were conditions which made the cost of living higher than elsewhere at any time' (from a memorandum on the labour dispute in Jamshedpur by J. R. Davis, ICS).
[75] *Ibid.*, p. 67.
[76] *Ibid.*, pp. 65–7.

	1927–8	1929–30	1930–1	1931–2	1932–3
Covenanted employees	25,271	25,924	26,389	25,597	24,328
Monthly-paid employees	619	782	794	836	834
Weekly-paid employees	158	189	179	184	174

Source: ITB: *Statutory enquiry 1933, steel*, Vol. I (Delhi, 1934), p. 76.

The disparity in the wages of different groups of employees and the divergence in movements of wages of monthly-paid and weekly-paid employees may be noted. The subsequent history of wages at Jamshedpur up to 1939 was not very different. Thus the unskilled workers in this profitable industry did not gain any part of the increase of profits; because of the high cost of living and overcrowding combined with low wages, the unskilled and semi-skilled workers were naturally badly debt-ridden and strike-prone.[77] Profits were to a large extent shared with highly-paid European employees up to, say, 1933, and to a much lesser extent, with the Indian supervisory staff who replaced them, but not with ordinary workers.[78]

Thus the basic determinants of the movements of wages in India and therefore of the conditions of supply of labour were (a) the rate of growth of population as a whole, (b) the rates of growth of population in the particular regions in which the industries were situated, and (c) the rates of growth of landless agricultural labour in the different regions. This last factor was strongly correlated with the second, but probably also had something to do with the land-tenure system, the proportion of agricultural labour being generally higher in the regions with *zemindari* settlement. However, trade union resistance against wage-cuts and retrenchment did have some influence on the supply price, and in the last few years of the period, direct intervention by the provincial governments also played a part. The regions with European predominance were also generally the regions with low wages: this may have been simply because the Europeans had established themselves in the regions with a high density of population and a high rate of growth of that population. But there is also evidence that they were better able to organize among themselves and therefore could face unorganized labour with a monopsonistic organization. Their recruitment policies helped them to tap sources of cheap labour from the poorer regions, and tended to result in a heterogeneous labour force being employed in the factories. This hindered collective action by the workers, particularly when they were linguistically distinct from the local people, as in Bengal. By contrast, in places such as Ahmedabad and Bombay, the labour force

[77] Mukerjee, *Indian Working Class*, pp. 146–7; S. Kannappan: 'The Tata Steel Strike: Some dilemmas of Industrial Relations in a Developing Economy', *JPE*, LXVII, No. 5, October 1959, pp. 489–507, particularly pp. 501–4.
[78] See also in this connection, J. Kuczynski: 'Condition of workers (1808–1950)' in V. B. Singh (ed.): *Economic History of India, 1857–1956* (Bombay, 1965), pp. 609–37.

was more homogeneous, and employers were either unable to act monopsonistically, as in Bombay, or more willing to negotiate with workers' organizations, as in Ahmedabad.[79]

While at Cawnpore and Bombay, at the beginning of the twentieth century, there were occasional complaints of shortage of labour, a detailed investigation by Fremantle and Foley of labour supply for factories in Bengal and the United Provinces had failed to reveal anything that could be called a shortage.[80] The situation in Bombay may have been different for a few years because of the effects of plague and famine on the supply side, and large public works such as the construction of the docks on the demand side,[81] but this situation did not persist. While it would be inappropriate to say that the supply price of labour was constant over time because of the fact that real wages did not respond to a changed market situation at once and could be affected by trade union action, at least within limits, it would also be absurd to talk about a secular shortage of labour for industry.

Our discussion has primarily been confined to an analysis of movements of real wages as measured by deflating money wage series by crude cost-of-living index numbers. While the level of money wages in relation to the price of the product produced and, more doubtfully, the level of money wages in relation to the cost of living, can provide an approximation to the supply price of labour from the point of view of employers, neither of them can adequately measure the standard of living of workers. To judge the latter, the conditions of housing, the degree of indebtedness of workers, the legal or illegal deductions from pay made by employers of jobbers or money-lenders, and conditions of public health have all to be taken into account.[82] Even for housing, there are no unambiguous measures of consumption by workers in different centres, as we have already seen. It is possible that the higher rate of growth of real wages of workers in western India, combined with the higher rate of growth of import-substituting industries, contributed to a higher potential for economic growth in western

[79] Professor Morris David Morris has discussed the growth of the labour force in the Bombay cotton mills, and its organization, in great detail in *Emergence of an Industrial Labor Force*. He there emphasized repeatedly the elasticity of the labour supply to the Bombay cotton mills. He did not, however, attempt to explain the tremendous rise in the money wages of workers in the Bombay cotton mills or to reconcile such a rise with the thesis of a perfectly elastic labour supply. He also considered 'formal trade unionism' in the Bombay cotton mills to have been a failure (*ibid.*, pp. 196–7). Perhaps he would have been less categorical in his judgement if he *had* tried to explain the rise of real wages in the Bombay cotton mills. The fact is that a perfect elasticity of labour supply is consonant with rising real wages, but in order to reconcile the two one needs a more sophisticated model of the labour market than Professor Morris has employed in his book.

[80] S. H. Fremantle: 'The Problem of Indian Labour Supply', *JRSA*, LVII, No. 2,947, 14 May, 1909, pp. 510–19.

[81] *Ibid.*, p. 521 (discussion by T. J. Bennett).

[82] See in this connection, Buchanan, *Development of Capitalistic Enterprise*, Chapters XV and XVII.

India as compared with eastern India; but the proof or refutation of such a proposition needs a much more detailed analysis than we are able to provide in this book.

Most of the evidence, direct and indirect, points to the existence of surplus labour in several provinces of India (though not in all), which could be attracted to manufacturing industries whenever employment opportunities expanded there.[83] One of the consequences of the existence of disequilibrium in the labour market was that the formal rules of pure competition could not apply.[84] In most cases, employers were in a position to exploit the workers as monopsonists or oligopsonists. (European employers seem to have been more successful in these roles than their Indian counterparts.) Where the labourers were in a position to organize themselves and extract concessions from the employers, real wages went up, without noticeably hampering the growth of industry as a whole (though there may have been local difficulties because of rises in real wages), and without affecting the incentive to invest. It has already been argued in Chapter 1 that the rate of growth of modern industry in India was limited by the sizes of the effective markets for various industrial goods (as determined by internal demand and government policy) rather than by the supply of savings. Hence changes in real wages could not influence industrial growth through their effect on the investible savings of capitalists. Thus, in spite of the existence of an elastic supply of labour to modern industry in India, it would be inappropriate to apply Lewis-type models of industrial development to the case of Indian industry before independence for at least two reasons: (a) because investment in industry was limited by effective demand rather than by the supply of savings, and (b) because in a situation of excess supply of labour in rural areas, purely competitive models could turn out to be bad approximations to the mechanisms of determination of wages or service conditions of labour in rural or urban areas.

5.7 THE SUPPLY OF SKILLED LABOUR

In this chapter we have confined our attention mainly to the supply of unskilled labour. The supply of skilled labour and technically-trained personnel was dependent to a very large extent on the demand for such personnel. The demand in its turn was influenced by the rate of growth

[83] Professor T. W. Schultz had claimed to demonstrate with the aid of a test case – the influenza epidemic of 1918–19 – that there was no surplus labour in India. For a neat demonstration of the fallaciousness of Schultz's test, see A. K. Sen: 'Surplus Labour in India: A Critique of Schultz's Statistical Test', *Economic Journal*, Vol. LXXVII, March 1967, pp. 154–61.

[84] For a rigorous proof of this proposition in the general case, see K. J. Arrow: 'Towards a Theory of Price Adjustment', in Moses Abramovitz and others: *The Allocation of Economic Resources* (Stanford, California, 1959), pp. 41–51.

of industry and transport (primarily railways) and by the racial attitudes displayed by the British managers and industrialists controlling industrial and other modern productive enterprises. In general, British administrators and industrialists did not recruit Indians for positions of managerial responsibility. A distinction was made in this regard not only between Indians and Europeans but also between Indians and Anglo-Indians, that is, Eurasians. Thus the committee appointed to enquire into the system of state technical scholarships (instituted in 1904) reported: 'The prejudices of race and class which complicate so many Indian problems are not absent from industry. A large number of the most successful business concerns in India are in the hands of Europeans, and we were told that they were, as a rule, reluctant to offer employment to Indians!'[85] Although Sir R. N. Mookerjee, who was one of the few successful Indian collaborators of British businessmen in eastern India before 1914, assured the committee that this difficulty was on the point of being overcome, the evidence available about the employment of Indians in jute mills, for example, contradicts his statement.[86]

Recruitment of Indians to positions requiring technical knowledge in the railways and modern industry was blocked by racial prejudice. This applied also to the policy of the Government of India, which recruited in England most of the men needed for higher posts in public works and State railways. Side by side with this, it pursued a policy of severely limiting the facilities for technical education, because it was difficult to find jobs for the few men the engineering colleges turned out.[87] The government would not employ these men in supervisory posts in its existing commercial or industrial undertakings; it was against extending the traditional activities of the government in order to provide employment for the Indian graduates of technical institutions, and it would not interfere in any way with the recruitment policies of private firms; so what results could it expect except open or disguised unemployment for technically qualified Indians?

The case of the Royal Indian Engineering College starkly illustrates how severe and how wasteful the racial prejudices of the Government of India were. This college was established by the Government of India at Coopers Hill in England in order to train men to fill 'the superior ranks of the

---

[85] *Report of a Committee appointed by the Secretary of State for India to inquire into the system of State Technical Scholarships established by the Government of India in 1904* (PP 1913, XLVII), p. 25.

[86] See Chapter 8 below.

[87] For a good short survey of the educational policy of the Government of India, see J. R. Cunningham: 'Education', in O'Malley: *Modern India and the West*; for summary accounts of technical education in India, see R. I. Crane: 'Technical Education and Economic Development in India before World War I' in C. A. Anderson and M. J. Bowman (eds.): *Education and Economic Development* (London, 1966), pp. 167–201, and A. T. Weston: 'Technical and Vocational Education', *The Annals of the American Academy of Political and Social Science*, Vol. 145 (1929), pp. 151–60.

Public Works Department in India', and was maintained at the expense of the government which grew over time (it cost £280 a year to train a man in 1901). The prospectus of the college laid down, among other things, that candidates for admission must be 'British subjects of European race' – except that the President of the College could admit, in case of there being spare accommodation, up to two 'natives of India'.[88] Ultimately the College had to be closed down for the following reasons: (a) there were other institutions in the U.K. which had been imparting the same kind of training, (b) many of the men trained at the college did not want to serve in India, so that from the point of view of the Government of India, all the money spent on their training was wasted, (c) the college became too expensive, because there were not enough candidates who satisfied the requirements of admission, and (d) according a high degree of preference to students of the college for recruitment to posts in the Public Works Department made for inefficiency when the field of choice became much wider.

Even independently of the declared policy of the Government of India, systematic discrimination was practised by European (mainly British) officers of government and non-government establishments alike. For example, Brigadier-General H. A. Young, Director of Ordnance Factories in India from 1917 to 1921, stated in 1924: 'There has been little attempt to train Indians for posts of responsibility in the Ordnance Factories.'[89] This discrimination persisted after the First World War. F. S. Grimston, who had lately been Director of Ordnance Factories and Manufacture in India, speaking in 1931, could remember only one foreman and two assistant foremen at the metal and steel factory of Ishapore, and two assistant foremen at the harness and saddlery factory of Cawnpore, out of a total strength of 402 foremen in all Indian Ordnance factories, as being definitely Indians. There was not one Indian among the 49 gazetted officers in these factories.[90]

In private European enterprises no attempt whatsoever was made before the First World War to train Indians for managerial or supervisory positions. To take only one example out of many, in the Titaghur Paper Mills the supervision was entirely European; there were three Eurasians to look after the dispatching of manufactured articles and the receiving of raw materials. The mills never tried to substitute Indians for Europeans beyond a certain level, viz., the level of semi-skilled jobs, although Indian

---

[88] See *Report and correspondence relating to the expediency of maintaining the Royal Indian Engineering College* (PP 1904, LXIV) pp. 644–5, 649–51, and 665–6.

[89] 'The Indian Ordnance Factories and Indian Industries', *JRSA*, LXXII, 1 February 1924, p. 181.

[90] F. S. Grimston: 'The Indian Ordnance Factories and their Influence on Industry' *JRSA*, LXXIX, No. 4103, 10 July 1931, pp. 777–89, and discussion, pp. 789–92 (particularly pp. 778 and 790).

labour would have been much cheaper.[91] After the coming of discriminating tariff protection, under the goading of the Indian Tariff Board, some European firms already benefiting from tariff protection, or hoping to benefit from it, made half-hearted attempts at substituting Indians for European personnel, but in general the discrimination against Indians persisted among European firms. L. Zutshi, an Indian, speaking in 1932 during a discussion on a paper on Indian labour conditions said (the report is as summarized in the *JRSA*):

He could testify that racial prejudices were unfortunately rampant, particularly in Bengal. He remembered in 1925 asking a colliery manager for a job, stating that he had spent seven years at Indian universities and four years in London, having worked in various coalfields and mines all over the Continent. The manager had offered him a job at 50 rupees a month. On asking why he could not be offered more, with all his education and experience, the manager had replied, 'you have got to start where all these Anglo-Indian boys start, i.e. at 50 rupees a month.' These had passed (or not even passed) the matriculation examination of the Calcutta University.[92]

Technical education in a classroom had to be supplemented by practical training in a firm and then, after graduation, a man had to gain experience in an actual business before he could set up on his own or should claim to know his job properly.[93] If an Indian could obtain formal schooling in a technical subject, he could not get practical training, either because there were no suitable firms in India or because he was discriminated against in schemes of apprenticeship; he could often not obtain enough practical experience for the same reason. In Great Britain and the United States the growth of capital goods industries and, in particular, of the machine tool industry helped the process of skill formation immensely.[94] In Great Britain, locomotive factories were supposed to have acted as 'practical universities of mechanical engineering'.[95] In India, the Government of India steadily refused to grant tariff protection or substantial government assistance in any other form to any industry before 1923, and 'infant' capital goods industries were even more vulnerable to foreign competition than consumer goods industries. As late as 1924, the Peninsular Locomotive Com-

[91] See the oral evidence of W. L. Carey and J. Thomson (given on 4 December 1916) representing the Titaghur Paper Mills Co. Ltd in *Evidence* (*Report of IIC*), Vol. VI, *Confidential Evidence*, pp. 39–48, particularly pp. 42–5.

[92] See L. Zutshi's discussion at the end of the paper by Beryl M. le P. Power: 'Indian Labour Conditions', *JRSA*, LXXX, No. 4153, 24 June 1932, pp. 780–1.

[93] See the evidence of I. S. Mackenzie and of S. Deb in *Evidence* (*Report of IIC*) (PP 1919, XIX), pp. 34–51 and (PP 1919, XVIII), p. 50.

[94] See N. Rosenberg: 'Capital goods, technology and economic growth' and 'Technological change in the machine tool industry, 1840–1910', *Journal of Economic History*, Vol. XXIII, 1963, pp. 414–43.

[95] S. B. Saul: 'The Engineering industry' in D. H. Aldcroft (ed.): *The Development of British Industry and Foreign Competition, 1875–1914* (London, 1968), p. 196.

pany urged vainly the case for government help for a proposed locomotive factory in India, on the ground that it would help train mechanical engineers in India.[96]

At the beginning of the twentieth century private bodies – mostly actuated by the impulse of nationalism – financed technical education, in the belief that the efforts of the Government of India were inadequate in this field. The Association for the Advancement of Scientific and Industrial Education, founded in 1904 by Jogendra Chandra Ghosh, preceded the movement against the partition of Bengal in 1905; the foundation of the National Council of Education and of the Society for the Promotion of Technical Education coincided with the beginning of the antipartition movement.[97] These bodies set up technical institutions in India and granted scholarships for training in technical and scientific subjects in India and abroad. They definitely augmented the supply of technically-trained personnel, and insofar as these technical and science graduates filled supervisory positions in new Indian manufacturing firms or set up firms – usually small in size – themselves, this private effort contributed to the growth of skill and capital formation in India. The Government of India and provincial governments entered the field with the scheme of State Technical Scholarships for financing Indian students' technical education abroad. This scheme was continued in the interwar period as well. Meanwhile several engineering colleges produced graduates trained in India. The criticism was often made that many of the technical graduates – educated in India or abroad – had to work in fields other than those for which they had been trained, for the lack of suitable opportunities. In order to meet this criticism, the Government took the help of local Selection Boards who were asked to assess the scope of employment of foreign-trained graduates. Some provincial governments also awarded travel grants in the 1920s to actual industrialists for acquisition of technical skill abroad. Many governmental agencies sent men for training for jobs in which vacancies already existed.[97a] In spite of all this, there continued to remain in the interwar period an excess of supply of technical graduates in many fields.

[96] See ITB: *Evidence (Report on Steel)*, 1924, Vol. II, p. 280. Behind the refusal of the Government of India to assist the growth of a locomotive industry in India probably lay straightforward forces of 'economic imperialism' in the shape of interests of British locomotive firms which were the sole suppliers of locomotives to India. See F. Lehmann: 'Great Britain and the supply of railway locomotives to India: A case study of "Economic Imperialism" ', *The Indian Economic and Social History Review*, II, October 1965.

[97] See Sumit Sarkar: 'Swadeshi Movement in Bengal, 1903–1908' (thesis approved by the University of Calcutta in 1969 for the degree of D.Phil.), Chapter 3, and Haridas and Uma Mukherjee: *The Origins of the National Education Movement* (Calcutta, 1957), Part I, Chapters II and III. According to Weston: 'Technical and Vocational Education', the Association for the Advancement of Scientific and Industrial Education had given approximately 200 Indian students technical education abroad.

[97a] See A. G. Clow: *The State and Industry* (Government of India, Calcutta, 1928), Chapter V.

Since racial prejudice was much more of an effective barrier against the entry of Indians in the field of private industry or public enterprise than in the professional fields or even in the field of government civil and judicial service, and since a middle-class educated Indian had a much better chance of earning a competence or making a fortune in these latter fields than in industry, it was natural that his first choice would be the professions or civil or judicial service rather than service in industry. Contrary, in fact, to what is commonly supposed, the number of graduates produced by the Indian universities before the First World War did not exceed the number that could be gainfully employed in the public services and the professions. The annual output of graduates of all Indian universities in all subjects – arts, science, engineering and medicine – taken together and including licentiates of engineering only once exceeded 2,000 before 1907. The Madras University, serving a population of at least 50 millions, produced only 365 Arts graduates in 1900 and 331 in 1901. This illustrates the pitiful scale of effort in the field of higher education in India. The fifth quinquennial review of education in India stated:

Of the 1935 graduates of the Universities, 540 become Bachelors of Law, and in most cases proceed to the Bar. A return was made in 1903 of the number of higher posts in the public service held by Indians. This return took account only of posts at a pay of more than Rs. 75 a month, and this is a higher rate of pay than a young man would usually expect to receive immediately upon leaving the University. Consequently the return does not show the full extent of the demand for graduates in the public service; but it showed that Indians were employed in more than 16,000 posts at a pay exceeding Rs. 75.[98]

Thus the normal flow of educated Indians was either towards the civil and judicial branches of government service, where conditions were becoming more favourable,[99] or towards the professions, where Indians had a much better chance of earning high incomes than in modest positions as chemists or engineers in British firms, and where the racial discrimination practised by the British did not affect their prospects. Naturally when there was any sudden increase in demand for trained personnel, there might be a shortage of Indians meeting the needed qualifications. But these problems of shortage of skilled personnel were short-lived. When in the twenties and thirties, Indian-controlled enterprises sprang up in the iron and steel, engineering, sugar and paper industries, not much difficulty was experienced in replacing Europeans by Indians in managerial and supervisory positions. The initial cost of the training programmes was quite high in some cases,[100] but

[98] *Progress of education in India 1902–7*, Vol. I, *Fifth quinquennial review* (PP 1909, LXIII), pp. 34–5.

[99] The position in respect of employment of Indians in the civil service and in the railways is dealt with in Chapter 6 below.

[100] The cost of training a student at the Technical Institute of the TISCO during the years 1921–3 worked out to Rs. 250 per month: but this was probably unusually high

this cost was more than made up for by the fact that Indians could be paid lower salaries than Europeans with equivalent skill. Even before this, the cotton textile mills of Bombay, which were primarily under the control of Indian businessmen, had succeeded in largely replacing Europeans by Indians in supervisory positions with the help of formal training imparted in the Victoria Jubilee Training Institute (established in 1882), supported by schemes of apprenticeship in the mills. Already by 1895, of 245 men in superior posts in the Bombay cotton mills, only 104 were Europeans.[101] The proportion of Europeans to Indians continued to decline over time.

Thus, at the stage of industrial development which India had reached by the interwar years, the shortage of skill was not a fundamental bottleneck but was largely a reflection of the industrial backwardness of India and the policies of recruitment pursued by the British Government and British businessmen. Among ordinary workmen, the lack of development of skills was primarily due to their illiteracy.[102]

because the Institute had only recently been set up and was not yet working to its full capacity. See ITB: *Evidence (Report on steel)* (Calcutta, 1924), Vol. I, Statement No. IX (pp. 121–2).

[101] Mehta: *The Cotton Mills of India*, Chapter VIII, pp. 100–13, at p. 106.

[102] It was claimed that the low level of expenditure on primary and secondary education was due to the poverty of India, and more directly, to the paucity of the revenues of the Government of India. On this it is worth quoting the remarks of Miss Power, a member of the RC on Labour in India and Principal Officer, Ministry of Labour, His Majesty's Government, in 1932: 'Universal elementary education was not only a question of revenue; it was also a question of drive, enthusiasm and a real belief in the ultimate destiny of humanity: and on that she would say, "Look at Russia"'. See the discussion at the end of the paper by Beryl, M. le P. Power: 'Indian Labour Conditions', p. 782. See Chapter 7 below on effects of illiteracy on skill in the cotton-mill industry.

6

THE SUPPLY OF CAPITAL AND
ENTREPRENEURSHIP

In the literature on economic growth the suppliers of capital have always figured prominently as the prime movers in the process. Since, however, the removal of the ramifications of capital as a means of controlling productive agents and the immediate environment of production and its reduction to a simple factor of production left practically no indispensable function for the capitalist, he had to be smuggled in as the manager, the organizer, or the entrepreneur.[1] Under-developed countries, including India, are supposed to suffer from an acute shortage of capital not only in the tautological sense that the measured amount of capital located in these countries is small, but also in the functional sense that they are incapable of supplying the amount of capital demanded by the developmental process. This incapacity is supposed to spring from two sources, viz. the absolute poverty of ordinary people, and the unwillingness of the rich to invest money for worthwhile enterprises. In the vulgar sociology which some of these explanations affect, it is claimed further that the only effective suppliers of capital are businessmen, and that the feudal or other pre-capitalist remnants of upper-income groups which were preserved by the imperial power usually do not play any constructive part in the productive process. According to this view, the major dynamic element operating in the Indian economy was foreign enterprise which came endowed with the virtues of willingness to bear risk in industrial enterprises and the ability to innovate.[2] Most observers also noted the disproportionately large role played by the

[1] For examples of the way the growth of entrepreneurship is brought in to explain economic growth in a previously stagnant economy, see G. F. Papenek: 'The Development of Entrepreneurship' and the discussions on Papenek's paper by E. E. Hagen, A. M. Kamarck and F. C. Shorter in *American Economic Review*, Vol. LII, No. 2, May 1962, pp. 46–66.

[2] D. H. Buchanan, who was probably the most acute student of Indian industrial development during our period, noted among the important reasons for the dominance of Indian business by the British the following factor: 'Third, this period of industrial development and investment coincided with one in which business ability and capital were flowing from Europe, and from the British Isles in particular, out into various parts of the world – the United States, Canada, Australia, and South Africa, not to mention the West Indies, China and Malaysia. India could hardly fail to be touched, for it possessed large amounts of raw material, ready markets and an abundant supply of untrained but cheap and tractable labour. As Indians themselves were unfamiliar with the conduct of modern business, entrepreneurs and capital had to be imported. With pioneering and colonizing traditions, Englishmen and Scotsmen naturally came to fill the need.' Buchanan: *Development of Capitalist Enterprise*, p. 143.

Parsis in Indian industrial development; this phenomenon has usually been explained by the statement that Parsis were a special minority group and they acquired excellence *because* they were discriminated against by the rest of Indian society, or that they had cultural and religious values which were basically different from those of the Indians.[3]

In this chapter we analyse the supplies of capital and entrepreneurship in order to discover how they were influenced by the relatively tangible factors such as the colonial relationship of India with Great Britain, the differences in the degree of impact made by British rule on the trading or commercial classes of the different regions of India, the links of the trading classes with the upper strata of the pre-capitalist remnants and the role of the latter in industry. We also examine the barriers to entry which were erected by established British business groups against Indians: while economists have paid attention (in the context of developed economies) to the barriers to entry posed by such factors as control of the sources of raw materials, control of the transport services, control of the channels of distribution, economies of scale, and initial capital requirements,[4] they have not concerned themselves with the question of how political, social and racial factors can be used by established business groups to exclude challengers and select collaborators. Political, racial and social relationships between the rulers and the ruled did in fact play an important role in determining the relative performance of Indian and European business in India and the selection of Indian groups for collaboration with the British. Thus in examining the supply of capital and entrepreneurship we are led to discuss some rather obvious aspects of co-operation and conflict between European and Indian businessmen.[5]

6.1 PRIVATE FOREIGN INVESTMENT IN INDIA, 1900–14

At the beginning of the twentieth century, most of the capital employed in privately-owned enterprises employing modern techniques or modern methods of organization was under foreign – British – control. By 1939, the proportion of the capital invested in modern enterprises controlled by Indians had gone up substantially but foreign enterprises still

[3] For an example of the first view, see W. A. Lewis: *The Theory of Economic Growth* (London, 1960), pp. 89–90: 'Similarly in India the Parsees, being ineligible, because of their religion, for joining the governing classes, concentrated on economic activity, and became more expert at it than their hosts.' For an example of the second view see Robert E. Kennedy: 'The Protestant Ethic and the Parsis', *The American Journal of Sociology*, Vol. 68 (1962–3), pp. 11–20, reprinted in N. J. Smelser (ed.), *Readings in Economic Sociology* (Englewood Cliffs, N.J., 1965), pp. 16–26.

[4] See, for example, Joe. S. Bain: *Barriers to New Competition* (Cambridge, Mass., 1956).

[5] D. R. Gadgil: 'Indian Economic Organization' in *Economic Growth: Brazil, India, Japan* (Durham, N.C., 1955), pp. 448–63, and V. I. Pavlov: *The Indian Capitalist Class* (New Delhi, 1964) contain interesting accounts of the nature and origins of Indian entrepreneurial groups.

dominated some of the major industries such as jute mills, tea plantations, and coal mines.[6] It therefore becomes necessary to investigate the sources of the capital employed in private industry by Europeans in India, the means employed by the Europeans to retain control, and the methods employed by the Indians to wrest control of firms and industries from the Europeans, particularly after the First World War. We shall also try to see whether there were any essential differences in the quality of business leadership displayed by the Europeans and the Indians respectively either at the beginning or at the end of the period under consideration.

As in the case of other colonial areas with settled populations, most of the foreign investment in India was embodied in loans to the government, or in the railways and public utilities. Most of the remaining investment went into extractive or plantation industries aiming at export markets.[7] The only noticeable exception in the Indian case was British investment in the jute industry; however, although the jute mills did process domestic materials, more than 90% of the output was exported, and went primarily to the newly settled colonies.

The capital invested in the European-controlled enterprises was made up of the ploughed-back profits of these enterprises, and the capital raised from European residents in India; before the First World War, investment by Indians in these enterprises was probably not substantial. There was also little real transfer of resources from Europe (Britain) to India for investment in private enterprises. There was a tendency for proprietary concerns to be converted into companies; hence the figures for British 'private investments' in India (that is, investments made through channels other than the stock exchange) in Pandit's calculations were negative for all the years from 1898–9 to 1913–14 with the exception only of 1900–1 and 1905–6.[8] Political uncertainty after 1905–6 may have contributed to this development, as Pandit suggests,[9] but could not be the sole cause.

Sir Theodore Morison in 1910 thought that, in view of the fact that the

[6] Nurul Islam: *Foreign Capital and Economic Development: Japan, India and Canada* (Rutland, Vermont, and Tokyo, 1962), pp. 169–92; and A. Bose: 'Foreign Capital' in Singh: *Economic History of India, 1857–1956*, pp. 484–527.

[7] On the nature of capital investments in the colonial areas in the nineteenth century see H. W. Singer: 'The Distribution of Gains between Investing and Borrowing Countries', *American Economic Review*, XL, No. 2, May 1950, pp. 473–85; R. Nurkse: 'Some International Aspects of the Problem of Economic Development', *American Economic Review*, XLII, No. 2, May 1952, pp. 571–83; and *idem*, 'International Investment Today in the Light of Nineteenth-Century Experience,' *Economic Journal*, LXIV, December 1954, pp. 744–58. On the distribution of total foreign investment between the public and private sectors, see Y. S. Pandit: *India's Balance of Indebtedness, 1898–1913* (London, 1937), Chapter v. Pandit's term 'public investments' refers to investments financed by public loans in the stock exchange; but from Pandit's estimates and Hammond's estimates quoted by Pandit it seems pretty clear that foreign investments in the form of loans to the government, or embodied in railways and public utilities, accounted for considerably more than 50% of total foreign investment in India.

[8] Pandit: *India's Balance of Indebtedness*, p. 127.   [9] *Ibid.*, p. 126.

government usually failed to persuade European capitalists to invest in India without a guarantee, it would be 'a rash estimate' to put their investment at anything higher than £21 million sterling for the ten years from 1899 to 1909.[10] This estimate left out of account the private remittances made by British citizens resident in India. John Maynard Keynes, reviewing Morison's book, came to the conclusion that

during the ten years 1899 to 1909 the interest payable abroad on private capital invested in business or companies in India was approximately balanced by the private capital newly invested during the same period ... As an annual *average* for this ten-year period, I should place the amount of new capital privately invested at between £4,000,000 and £5,000,000 (including in this the trading capital of merchants and bankers), and the interest payable on former private investments at the same amount.[11]

This is consistent both with Pandit's indirect estimates of capital transfers between India and Great Britain, and also with Imlah's finding that, over the period from 1796 to 1913, the income from foreign investments by British citizens 'not only filled in whatever gaps were created by deficits on trade and services, but it also supplied most of the surpluses which were available for new investment abroad'.[12]

It is perhaps legitimate to ask, why was not more British capital invested in private industry? A recent computation by Matthew Simon shows that of the new British portfolio investment over the period 1865–1914, 14% went to Asia, 17% to South America, 11% to Africa, 11% to Australasia, 13% to Europe, and 34% to North America. Classifying countries by political status, Simon finds that only 40% of the total new portfolio investment went to the British empire countries.[13] The first argument that comes to mind is that demand in India was limited by extreme poverty.[14] This argument would explain a preference for investment in North America and Australasia, but not for investment in South America. The investments by the British public in Latin America had been outstandingly unprofitable, with defaulting governments, and battle-prone republics.[15] The following

[10] Sir Theodore Morison: *The Economic Transition in India* (London, 1911), Chapter VIII, particularly pp. 202–3.

[11] J. M. Keynes: *Economic Journal*, XXI, September 1911, p. 430.

[12] A. H. Imlah: *Economic Elements in the Pax Britannica* (Cambridge, Mass., 1958), p. 60.

[13] Matthew Simon: 'The Pattern of New British Portfolio Foreign Investment, 1865–1914' in J. H. Adler (ed.): *Capital Movements and Economic Development* (London, 1967), pp. 33–60.

[14] See, for example, J. E. O'Conor: 'The Economic and Industrial Progress and Condition of India', *JSA*, LII, No. 2691, 17 June 1904, esp. pp. 652–4.

[15] See J. Fred Rippy: *British Investments in Latin America, 1822–1949* (Hamden, Connecticut, 1966). In Chapter XV Rippy compares two samples of the most profitable British companies operating in Latin America, and in Asia and Africa respectively, and finds the latter uniformly more profitable than the former.

set of factors would seem to provide an explanation for the relatively low level of British investment in India: (a) the level of demand for domestic manufactures was low because of Indian poverty and because of the imperial policy of free trade when most other countries – including British Dominions – were abandoning it; (b) the British had more information about the present state of profitability and more control over future economic policy in India (and non-white countries in the Empire) and therefore there was less scope for speculative investment; (c) for the industries already existing in India, there were British firms resident in India in effective control of the sources of supply of materials or of the market, and hence there was less scope and less need for any real transfer of capital from Great Britain to India by other British firms.

At the beginning of our period then, the major sources of foreign capital invested in private industry were Indian companies managed by British citizens and British individuals resident in India. This can be verified by inspection of the place of registration of companies and of the history of company promotion in the major industries, such as jute, tea and coal, under European control. Most of the jute mills started after 1897 were registered in India.[16] Of the 128 joint-stock companies operating in the Indian coal industry in 1911, all but five were registered in India.[17] The situation apparently looks different in the case of tea: according to the Indian Tea Association, of the total nominal capital invested in the joint-stock companies producing tea in India in 1914, which amounted to Rs. 302·3 million, only about Rs. 43·1 million were accounted for by companies registered in India and the rest by sterling companies.[18] Two points must, however, be noted here. First, many of the plantations in India were privately owned and worked by managing agency houses or private planters in India and were not formed into joint-stock companies until later. Secondly, whether a company was registered in the U.K. or in India depended primarily on the convenience of the managing agents, and a sterling registration did not necessarily mean that much of the capital invested in the plantation was earned outside India. Plantations were generally first opened up by a firm doing business in India or by a planter who would then turn to a managing agency house for working capital and for additional fixed capital.[19] A planter might also open up a plantation and then sell it to a joint-stock company or a managing agency house at a

[16] See Chapter 8 below.

[17] *IITB, 1911*, First Annual Edition (Calcutta, 1911), p. 213.

[18] The figures are quoted in G. D. Hope, Chief Scientific Officer, Indian Tea Association, 'The Tea Industry of Bengal and Assam' in Playne and Wright: *Bengal and Assam, Behar and Orissa*, p. 387.

[19] See, for example, the prospectuses of the Cachar and Dooars Tea Company Limited and the East India and Ceylon Tea Company Limited in *Issues 1895 advertised in The Times* (London), No. 10, July–December 1895.

profit. The registration of the company was often a mere formality, since most of the capital was held by the partners of the managing agency firm and their close associates. Most of the large managing agency houses involved in the tea plantations in India were firms which had grown up with the tea industry in India or which had made money in other fields and then entered into the tea business as one of their many ventures: at the beginning of the century, Duncan Brothers and Company of Calcutta, Williamson Magor and Company, Alex Lawrie and Company and Davenport and Company were examples of the first type of concern, and Andrew Yule and Company, Shaw Wallace and Company, Jardine, Skinner and Company, and James Finlay and Company were examples of the second.[20]

James Finlay and Company was one of the few British managing agency houses which could trace its original roots in Great Britain and whose affairs seemed to be directed more from 'home' than from India. But even in their case the main focus of interest and source of profits shifted from Great Britain to India after the third quarter of the nineteenth century, when the firm started a jute company on the Hooghly (the Champdany Jute Company) and went into jute in a big way. The tea companies controlled by James Finlay and Company in India and Ceylon had a capital of £4,458,400 at the date of their formation (between 1896 and 1898), and had 74,000 acres under cultivation, employing 70,000 workers by the beginning of the century. Like many other managing houses in India, James Finlay and Company (Finlay, Muir and Company, or Finlay, Clark and Company in India) also lent money to indigo-planters, went into sugar when the trade in indigo collapsed and carried on an extensive trade in imports of Manchester piecegoods and exports of Indian raw produce. It was one of the few British managing houses to enter the cotton-mill industry.[20a]

6.2 SUPPLY OF CAPITAL TO EUROPEAN-CONTROLLED INDUSTRIES BEFORE 1914

When it comes to discovering the determinants of the supply of long-term foreign capital to other industries such as jute and coal, the managing

---

[20] On pioneering in the tea industry see H. A. Antrobus: *A History of The Assam Company 1839–1953* (Edinburgh, 1957); and *idem*: *The Jorehaut Tea Company Ltd* (London, 1949), particularly pp. 3–65. For a detailed description of the process of opening up and acquisition of plantations by a large managing agency firm see *The Duncan Group, Being a short history of Duncan Brothers & Co. Ltd, Calcutta and Walter Duncan & Goodricke Ltd. London 1859–1959* (London, 1959), Chapters 4 and 5; and Sir Harry Townend (compiler): *A History of Shaw Wallace & Co. and Shaw Wallace & Co. Ltd.* (London, 1965), chapter on tea by H. K. Stringfellow.

[20a] *James Finlay and Company Limited: Manufacturers and East India Merchants, 1750–1850* (privately published, Glasgow, 1951), esp. pp. 46–8, 85–8, and 90–5 and Chaper XVI. This last chapter discusses the problems of pioneering in the tea industry in some detail.

agency houses with interests in a number of industries are naturally of the greatest importance. Practically all the major managing agency houses were interested in trade as well as industry, and trade generally comprised all the major branches of exports and imports. There is a description of the activities of a typical managing agency – such as Jardine, Skinner and Company – in the middle of the First World War· They were managing agents for eight tea companies, some of which were registered in the U.K. and some in India, three coal companies, a timber producing and trading company, and two jute-mill companies; they were also the agents of several insurance companies, and several shipping lines operating in the Pacific. They also joined with the British India Steam Navigation Company Limited in operating a shipping line between India and China. In addition, they had a large trade in the import of Manchester piecegoods and in the export of gunnies and tea.[21] Jardine, Skinner and Company was one of the biggest managing agency houses in Calcutta; much of the capital of other managing agency houses also went into the jute-mill industry during the years 1900–1914. The tea industry suffered a depression from the middle of the 1890s when the rate of expansion of supply outstripped the rate of increase in demand, and it began to recover only after 1907 or so; by 1911 tea companies were beginning to declare normal dividends – and in case of very successful companies, dividends which were far above the normal rate.

Thus, because of the depression in the tea industry at the beginning of the century, it could not be considered a very serious competitor with the jute industry for the capital invested by the British managing agency houses of eastern India. But coal was at first sight a more serious competitor. The production of coal in India increased from 6·12 million tons in 1900 to 11·87 million tons in 1909.[22] This increase was stimulated by the growing demand for coal within India on the part of railways, public authorities, and jute and cotton mills, and by the increase in exports of coal to Ceylon, the Straits Settlements, Sumatra, and Hong Kong. There was a boom in the industry during the years 1906–8 when the price of Bengal coal f.o.b. increased from Rs. 3 - 8 - 0 per ton in 1905 to Rs. 4 - 10 - 0 in 1906, Rs. 6 - 4 - 0 in 1907 and Rs. 6 - 12 - 0 in 1908; this boom led to the registration of sixty-two coal companies in Bengal during the two years 1907 and 1908.[23]

However, it would be misleading to take this growth in the number of coal companies as evidence of a greatly increased investment of new capital in the industry by the managing agency houses of Calcutta: in the first place, 'a large number of these companies . . . merely took over existing collieries from private owners and have not added to any large extent to the total output'.[24] Secondly, the methods employed in the production of

[21] Playne and Wright: *Bengal and Assam, Behar and Orissa*, 'Jardine, Skinner and Company', pp. 128–31.
[22] *IITB, 1911*, p. 206.   [23] *Ibid.*, pp. 211–15.   [24] *Ibid.*, p. 215.

coal in India were generally extremely labour-intensive, human labour being employed on an extensive scale to hew and haul coal, and electrical equipment being practically unknown before the First World War. The coal was often very near the surface in thick seams, and, labour costs being extremely low, owners or managers did not feel called upon to use much mechanical or electrical equipment or power, except when they were taken in by the salesmanship of agents for machinery.[25]

The jute mills required much more fixed capital per unit of output, and as initial investment. To offset this, they possessed several advantages over coal mining and tea planting: jute mills could generally be supervised more easily from the Calcutta office; the production methods approximated much more to genuine industrial processes and therefore were far more subject to human control and could be made more uniform. *IITB, 1911* had the following comment to make for the benefit of the potential investor in coal shares:

In the case of a jute mill or a tea garden, it is possible to say with a fair degree of accuracy what the cost per loom or the cost per acre of a well-equipped garden should work out to, but, in the case of a coal property, it is a somewhat difficult matter to assess the capital value . . . It is not a very difficult matter to arrive at a fair estimate of the cost of opening out a particular property and providing it with the necessary plant, machinery, and siding accommodation to secure a certain output, though, unless a property has been very carefully and thoroughly tested, these estimates are often found to be not too reliable. But the difficulty is, with the fluctuations in the price of coal which have been witnessed of recent years, to arrive at the price which may be reasonably paid for the coal itself . . . Considering the risk and uncertainty which must in all cases exist in regard to the actual state of affairs below ground, which the development of any particular coal bearing property will ultimately disclose, the very lowest return which an investor in a new company may reasonably expect on his money may be taken at 10%.[26]

Further, India possessed practically a monopoly of jute and did not have to face any serious competition in the manufactured product from other countries except when world supply outran world demand: when it did so, and prices of jute goods fell below an economic level, the jute mills on the Hooghly were in a position (with the help of the right reaction from the peasants) to bring back supply to a better relation with demand through short-time working. Throughout the years before the First World War there was a high rate of increase in the demand for jute goods because of the increasing exports of raw produce from the old and new colonies or settlements of European countries. It is thus not surprising that in spite of the competing demands from the coal industry and the tea industry, there

[25] See Buchanan: *Development of Capitalistic Enterprise*, Chapter XII for a description of the methods employed in coal mining in India.
[26] *IITB, 1911*, p. 214.

should have been no difficulty in finding the capital for jute mills, which promised a much steadier though perhaps less spectacular return than the other two industries.

The long-term capital for all the ventures was mainly raised in the form of equities; but preference shares were also in favour, particularly for financing jute mills; the latter usually bore a rate of interest (sometimes cumulative) of 7%. Debentures usually bore a rate of interest of 5–6% per year.

Apart from Europeans interested in trade, banking and industry, the other investors were employees of the government, banks and offices, or in the army. The salary of a European (excluding the Viceroy) in India before the First World War ranged from about £300 to about £7,000 a year: making the conservative assumption that the distribution of incomes among the Europeans was lognormal, and taking the geometric mean as the appropriate average, we get £1,450 as the average income of a salaried European. Since all highly-paid jobs in British India were practically a monopoly of the Europeans, it is small wonder that most European industrialists in fact did not consider capital to be scarce.[27]

It is much more difficult to find out the source of the short-term capital of British industrialists in India. The managing agency houses engaged in trade could find some of the working capital themselves, but there is little doubt that a major portion came from the Presidency Banks, from other British-controlled Indian banks such as the Allahabad Bank and the Alliance Bank of Simla, and the so-called Exchange Banks. We shall see later that most of the capital in the organized banking sector in India up to the First World War was controlled by Europeans.

6.3 OFFICIAL OR SEMI-OFFICIAL MEASURES OF DISCRIMINATION AGAINST INDIAN BUSINESSMEN

The dominance of modern industry by European business houses before the First World War was supported and reinforced by a whole set of administrative, political, and financial arrangements within India. The European businessmen very consciously set themselves apart from 'native' businessmen; they claimed a cultural and racial affinity with the British rulers of India which was denied to the Indians who might compete with them.[28]

For the Europeans, whether civil servants or military officers or business-

[27] See, for example, the evidence of L. P. Watson of Cooper, Allen and Co., Cawnpore, and of W. A. Ironside, partner in the firm of Bird & Co., Calcutta in *Evidence (Report of IIC)*, Vols. I and II (PP 1919, XVII and XVIII), p. 65 and p. 869 respectively.

[28] See, for example, the evidence of R. Steel, representing the Bengal Chamber of Commerce, in RC on Opium: *Minutes of Evidence taken between 18 November and 29 December 1893, with Appendices* (PP 1894, LXI), p. 161. The phrases 'white man's burden' and 'black town' recall the racial basis of moral and physical demarcation from the 'natives'.

men, 'society' consisted of other Europeans, mostly other Britons (including Irishmen).[29] Their clubs generally admitted only Europeans. Although there were many clubs which admitted only European government officers, there were other clubs which admitted all Europeans of a minimum social standing. Thus the Bengal Club, the oldest social club in India, and one of the most influential, had many partners of mercantile houses as its Presidents.[30] As late as 1938, Murray's *Handbook for Travelling in India, Burma and Ceylon* (fifteenth edition, 1938) pointed out specifically that among the clubs listed (numbering 12 in Bombay, 10 in Calcutta and 9 in Madras), only the Calcutta Club was open to Indians and Europeans, though Willingdon Club in Madras was open to Indian and European ladies. The import of this togetherness among Europeans and the resultant discrimination against Indians was well understood by Indian businessmen as is shown by the following quotation:

Given their much larger world connection and experience, these concerns [non-Indian concerns in India] are able to compete on more than equal terms with the corresponding Indian concerns in the same field. They obtain all the fiscal and financial advantages open to Indians: in addition, they have the silent sympathy from the mystic bond of racial affinity with the rulers of the land, which procures them invisible, but not the less effective, advantage in their competition with their indigenous rivals. This device cannot be too strongly opposed.[31]

However, this social discrimination was complemented and supported by political, economic, administrative and financial arrangements which afforded European businessmen a substantial and systematic advantage over their Indian rivals in India.

There was, first of all, India's position in the imperial system, as the supplier of raw materials and the chief source of non-sterling exchange with which to balance Britain's deficits with the United States of America and with China.[32] The encouragement of a steady, or rather, increasing flow of exports and imports and support of the foreign exchange market for maintaining a stable external value of the rupee hence became crucial elements in the economic policy of the Government of India.

[29] For a selection of the views of Europeans who travelled or served in India before independence, see Hilton Brown: *The Sahibs* (London, 1948), particularly the chapters on 'Society' and 'Hospitality'.

[30] Prominent businessmen who were also Presidents of the Bengal Club included J. J. J. Keswick (1882–5), A. A. Apcar (1886–8, 1910), T. B. G. Overend (1906, 1908–9), and J. C. Shorrock (1912–13). See H. R. Panckridge: *A Short History of the Bengal Club (1827–1927)* (Calcutta, 1927), Appendix B.

[31] The All-India Manufacturers' Organization: *Indian and International Economic Policies*, Statement on the Agenda of the International Business Conference at Tye, New York, mid-November 1944, p. 41. (Quoted in M. Kidron: *Foreign Investments in India* (London, 1965), p. 67.)

[32] See Chapter 2 above.

The railway system had been built up primarily to link the inland centres of trade with the ports rather than with one another, and the railways generally charged much lower rates of freight on transport of materials from inland centres to the ports than between different inland centres.[33] Thus, external trade assumed an enormous importance in the economy of India: the prosperity of the country was often judged in official circles with reference to increasing or declining volumes of external trade. With the sole exception of Bombay, the Europeans (mainly the British) were in firm control of the external trade in all the ports. Even in Bombay, probably the major part of the trade passed through their hands. At the beginning of the

TABLE 6.1   *External trade of the major ports of India, 1901–2 to 1905–6*

	Gross imports (Rs. '000)		Gross exports (Rs. '000)	
	Private account	Government account	Private account	Government account
Bengal				
1901–2	32,81,96	3,44,11	55,20,20	16,82
1902–3	32,82,89	3,22,81	53,67,42	13,67
1903–4	33,64,54	3,73,78	59,75,01	6,81
1904–5	38,61,59	2,67,56	64,08,34	5,38
1905–6	41,90,14	3,61,49	70,42,49	1,78
Bombay				
1901–2	28,31,52	1,96,06	35,29,26	7,48
1902–3	27,61,19	1,55,84	36,08,90	37,11
1903–4	29,92,49	2,10,28	46,12,00	41,86
1904–5	32,99,37	2,41,19	41,54,45	10,13
1905–6	36,51,94	1,97,43	45,73,66	5,71
Madras				
1901–2	7,73,09	26,78	11,77,04	2,37
1902–3	7,20,36	39,84	13,01,59	1,08
1903–4	7,51,48	33,68	15,00,74	77
1904–5	8,45,56	31,03	14,66,43	1,09
1905–6	7,77,47	36,56	15,45,56	32
Sind				
1901–2	6,43,96	1,28,15	8,42,75	8
1902–3	5,18,81	1,62,24	7,62,69	12
1903–4	5,47,56	1,46,64	12,93,57	16
1904–5	7,70,37	2,00,08	17,58,78	11
1905–6	8,69,45	2,78,71	11,06,22	5

Source: Gov. India, CISD: *Annual statement of the seaborne trade of British India* (Calcutta annual).

[33] On government policy towards the railways and the policy of the railways towards trade, see Daniel Thorner: (a) 'Great Britain and the Development of India's Railways', *Journal of Economic History*, XI, No. 4, Fall 1951, pp. 389–402; and (b) 'The Pattern of Railway Development in India', *Far Eastern Quarterly*, XIV, No. 2, February 1955, pp. 201–16.

century the total trade of Bengal (that is, Calcutta mainly) far exceeded the total trade of Bombay (excluding Sind), as is evident from Table 6.1. This is even more true of exports than of imports. Calcutta was the major port for exporting tea, jute, jute manufactures, and opium.[34] Calcutta was also the biggest market for Manchester piecegoods in the east. Thus the control of external trade, supported by a practical monopoly of ocean and coastal shipping, gave British businessmen the lion's share of the profits from the commerce of India.

The senior administrative personnel in the public services, banks and railways were all almost exclusively British. Enquiries by two Royal Commissions on the public services of India in 1887 and 1914 produced the figures shown in Table 6.2 about the participation of Indians and Anglo-Indians in the public services.

TABLE 6.2   *Salaries of civil-service officers, 1887 to 1913*

Officers drawing per month	Europeans	Anglo-Indians	Indians and Burmans	Percentage of Indians and Burmans to total number of officers
Rs. 200 and over				
1887	4,836	1,001	3,003	34
1913	4,898	1,593	4,573	42
Rs. 500 and over				
1887	3,163	83	427	12
1913	3,691	351	942	19
Rs. 800 and over				
1887	1,637	7	77	4
1913	2,153	106	242	10

Source: RC on the Public Services in India, *Report* (PP 1916, VII), p. 26.

What was as striking as the low proportion of Indians and Burmans among officers drawing Rs. 800 and over was the extremely uneven distribution of Indian and Burman officers among the services in 1913: their proportion in provincial civil service (executive) was 87% and in provincial civil service (judicial) was 98%. Since these two services accounted for 2,432 officers drawing Rs. 200 and above, it follows that the proportion of Indians and Burmans in other services was much lower than the average figure of 42%. This was particularly true of the elite service, the Indian Civil Service, of

[34] On the importance of opium in the British imperial payments system and in the revenue system of the Government of India, see G. H. M. Batten: 'The Opium Question', *JSA*, XL, 1 April 1892, pp. 444–67. The discussion at the end of the paper (pp. 467–94), together with RC on Opium, *Evidence* (PP 1894, LX, LXI, LXII), illustrates both the strength of the opposition to the export of opium to China and the conviction of administrators and businessmen that 'good business' cannot be bad on moral grounds. The RC on Opium in effect agreed with the latter point of view.

whose officers only 5% were Indians, and of the technical or commercially important services, such as the Geological Survey, the Survey of India, customs, public works, mines, mint and assay, factory and boiler inspection, and pilots (Bengal) – the number of Indian and Burman officers in the last four services being zero.[35]

The situation was even worse in respect of employment of Indians in 'railways, State and private; the State railways had a higher percentage of Indians in the superior posts than the railways managed by companies. The Acworth Committee found, as late as 1921 that 'None of the highest posts are occupied by Indians; very few even of the higher'.[36] It found that on the principal railways of the country, out of 1,749 posts classed as superior, 182, or rather more than 10%, were filled by Indians. Of the 182 Indians, 158 occupied posts as assistant district officers in the various departments and only 24 reached the grade of district officers, and nobody reached any higher position. While the proportion of Indians and Burmans in superior posts on State lines (mostly concentrated in the Traffic Department) was 14.6%, in the Great Indian Peninsula Railway it was under 5%, and on the Burma Railways only 3%. In most company-managed railways the proportion was between 3% and 14.6%.[37]

The racial and political affinity of the European (British) businessman with the administrators and their shared prejudices against the Indians placed the latter at an enormous disadvantage in matters of business. The ranks of the European businessmen were often reinforced by the entry of senior administrators and politicians: Lord George Hamilton, who was Secretary of State for India from 1895 to 1903, joined the Court of the Chartered Bank of India, Australia and China in 1908 and served until 1926.[38] Sir John Hewett, who was Governor of the United Provinces and the first Commerce Member of the Viceroy's Council, joined the Board of the National Bank of India in 1915 (he had retired from the Indian Civil Service in 1912) and served on it until 1941.[39]

There were other aspects of government policy which also favoured Europeans against Indians. Although the economic policy of the Government of India was sometimes described as amounting to 'socialism' or at the other extreme as following strictly the doctrines of the Manchester School, it fitted into neither category. The building of the social overhead capital was taken to be a public responsibility. The building of railways or

[35] RC on the Public Services in India: *Report* (PP 1916, VII), p. 24.

[36] *Report of the Committee appointed by the Secretary of State for India to enquire into the administration and working of Indian Railways* (PP 1921, X), p. 58.

[37] *Ibid.*, p. 58 and Appendix No. 2. For a discussion of how the technical training of Indians was affected by government policies and the recruitment practices of British businessmen, see Section 5.7 above.

[38] Sir Compton Mackenzie: *Realms of Silver* (London, 1954), p. 178.

[39] G. W. Tyson: *100 Years of Banking in Asia and Africa* (London, 1963), p. 231.

port facilities required much lobbying and public pressure in which European Chambers of Commerce had a natural advantage over the Indian businessmen who were nowhere near as well organized or as well represented on public bodies. Port Trusts, Improvement Trusts, municipal bodies, particularly in towns dominated by European businessmen, not only had European officials as chairmen but also generally had a majority of European members. In the few cases in which the government helped in a pioneering industry, as in the iron manufacturing enterprise of Heath at Barakar, the aluminium-ware manufacturing enterprise of Alfred Chatterton at Madras, or the army boot and equipment manufacturing firm of Cooper Allen & Co. at Cawnpore, it was a British firm which benefited. When the stores purchase policy of the Government of India began to be relaxed in favour of Indian manufactures, it was the European engineering firms or the European paper or woollen goods manufacturing firms which benefited from such changes in policy.

6.4 EUROPEAN COMMERCIAL ASSOCIATIONS AND EUROPEAN DOMINATION OF INDUSTRY AND FINANCE

The European businessmen in their turn had erected organizations and institutions for building up their advantages and protecting them against intruders all over India. They were organized in Chambers of Commerce to which very few Indians were admitted. The Bengal, Madras and Upper India Chambers of Commerce had practically no Indian members before the First World War. Only the Bombay Chamber of Commerce had Indians – all Parsis in the beginning[40] – as members from the start but the predominantly European character of the organization was preserved. These Chambers of Commerce looked after the interests of a host of trade associations. In eastern India, the jute trade was almost entirely in European hands, and traders were organized into associations whose general interests were looked after by the Bengal Chamber of Commerce. For other commodities and other regions, barring western India, the same situation obtained. Some of the associations had explicit clauses barring Indians from membership. But most of them did not need such clauses, for any aspiring Indian could be barred by the existing members. The Chambers of Commerce and Trade Associations provided excellent means for adjusting the interests of different groups to one another, and for eliminating unnecessary competition. The European traders and businessmen were great believers in reasonable compromise and mutual accommodation among themselves, however much they might believe in the virtues of competition for others. The compromises were often facilitated by recognition of one association as

[40] R. J. F. Sulivan: *One Hundred Years of Bombay* (Bombay, 1937), Chapter II.

the leader for the group of trades: for instance, IJMA normally acted as the spokesman for both the jute trade and the jute industry.[41]

Thus in most fields, the European businessmen were well organized to maintain something approaching collective monopoly. This collective monopoly in most industrial fields and most regions of India could also fight off new entry, for the lockgates to the various channels of trade were under European control. Ocean shipping was in predominantly European hands; so was most of coastal and inland shipping. It was only in Bombay that there still were ships owned by Indians or Asians.[42]

As we have pointed out earlier, most of the external trade was in European hands, including the most lucrative trades in opium, tea, jute, and later on coal. (The trade in cotton and cotton yarn and in opium produced in western India, was, however in Indian hands.) There were few challenges to the European monopoly in shipping, and these were easily beaten off by companies which had much larger financial resources than their challengers, and which enjoyed patronage from public authorities and from the most powerful private firms.[43] The European shipping companies plying along the coast and across the oceans enjoyed mail subventions from the Governments of India and the U.K. During the First World War, the British Government subsidized British shipping companies in other ways, but attempts to get the Government of India to protect Indian shipping against unfair competition failed.[44]

The near-monopoly of Europeans in foreign trade was supplemented and buttressed by their control of the organized money market. The Banks of Bengal and of Madras never had an Indian Director on their Boards between 1876, when they were constituted as Presidency Banks, and their amalgamation into the Imperial Bank of India in 1921, except for a year

[41] Although Indian businessmen later on organized Chambers of Commerce and Mill-owners' Associations, the latter were far less successful than their European counterparts in getting collective agreements about prices, short-time working, wages or recruitment policies. See L. A. Joshi: *The Control of Industry in India* (Bombay, 1965), Chapter II.

[42] The Bombay Steamship Company Limited, registered in 1906, had a board of directors in 1914 consisting of two Europeans, one Jew (Sir David Sassoon), one Parsi and four other Asians; it had acquired the navigation business known as Shepherds Steamers from the owner and vendor Haji Ismail Hassum. *IITB, 1914,* (Calcutta, 1914), pp. 400–2.

[43] See the story of the ruin of the steamship company of an elder brother of Rabindranath Tagore by the (European) Flotilla Company, in Rabindranath Tagore: *My Reminiscences* (London, 1917), pp. 252–5; see also George Blake: *B. I. Centenary* (London, 1956), p. 170. Jamsetji Tata's attempt to break the monopoly of European liners in the carrying trade between India and China failed, owing to drastic rate-cutting extending even to 'the unusual offer of carrying cotton to Japan free of charge' by the P. & O. and its associates; see Harris: *Jamsetji Nusserwanji Tata*, Chapter V. Similar tactics were employed by the inland steamship companies.

[44] S. N. Haji: *State Aid to India Shipping* (Indian Shipping Series, Pamphlet No. 1, Bombay, 1922) and the memorandum of the Indian National Steamship Owners' Association, Bombay, in *Evidence (Report of the Fiscal Commission, 1949–50),* Vol. III (Delhi, 1952), pp. 185–276.

or two at the very end. But the Bank of Bombay had Indian directors on its board and the latter often had a majority. The Presidency Banks had the right to use deposits from the government and other public bodies free of interest: these deposits constituted in 1900 about a fifth of their total deposits.[45] Of the Presidency Banks, the Bank of Bengal was easily the biggest. The other major joint-stock banks such as the Mercantile Bank, the Alliance Bank of Simla and the Allahabad Bank were controlled by Europeans, although the last-named bank had originally been organized by Indians. Not only the directors of these banks, but also the senior officials, were almost without exception Europeans: thus the bias in favour of European business was very heavily built into the financial structure. It was only from 1906 onwards that large Indian joint-stock banks came into existence: of these only the Punjab National Bank and the Bank of India achieved any prominence before the First World War and survived.[46]

TABLE 6.3   *Transactions of Exchange Banks and others* (£'000)

	Capital reserve and rest	Deposits in India	Cash balances in India
Presidency Banks			
1900	3,731	10,458	3,363
1910	4,607	24,387	7,567
Exchange Banks			
1900	—	7,000	1,600
1910	—	16,200	2,900
Indian Joint-Stock Banks			
1900	850	5,380	790
1910	2,510	17,110	1,870

Source: J. M. Keynes: *Indian Currency and Finance* (London, 1913), Chapter VII.

All the so-called foreign-exchange banks which also received deposits and lent money in India were in European hands.[47] The total weight of the European-controlled banking institutions can be gauged roughly from the figures shown in Table 6.3.

In 1900, there were practically no Indian-controlled joint-stock banks of any importance: taking the Bank of Bombay as representing an institution

[45] *IIYB, 1911*, pp. 43–8.

[46] The Central Bank of India, organized mainly by the Parsi businessmen of Bombay, ultimately became the largest Indian-controlled private joint-stock bank, but it had not achieved such prominence before the First World War. Another large Bombay bank controlled by Indians was the Indian Specie Bank, but it crashed in 1913, primarily because it became involved in speculation in silver.

[47] The National Bank of India originated in 1863 as the Calcutta City Banking Corporation, with three European and four Indian directors. But its head office was transferred to London in 1866 and the Indian directors lost their seats on the board. See Tyson: *100 Years of Banking in Asia and Africa*, Chapters II and III.

jointly controlled by Europeans and Indians, we find that the total deposits of that bank in that year came to £3,471,049, out of a national total amounting to £22,830,000. Even in 1910, the total deposits of the Bank of Bombay, Bank of India, Central Bank of India (the figure of deposits for 1912 was used), People's Bank, Indian Specie Bank, Bombay Merchants' Bank, Bengal National Bank, Benares Bank, Oudh Commercial Bank, Punjab Banking Co., Punjab National Bank and Punjab Co-operative Bank amounted to about Rs. 26,62,32,000 or about £17,748,000, out of total deposits of £57,697,000 for all the banks together.[48] This figure if used as an index of Indian control over the organized banking sector will almost certainly exaggerate it, since two of the most important banks included in our calculation, viz., the Indian Specie Bank and the People's Bank, crashed in 1913.

It is not easy to discover the extent to which European industry borrowed its working capital from the banks; but from old share registers and evidence given before the ITB, it appears that most European managing agency houses had arrangements for cash credit or overdrafts for the companies under their control with the Presidency Banks, or with other European-controlled banks when the Presidency Banks did not have conveniently-situated branches. Indian industry also borrowed a substantial proportion of its working capital in Madras from the Bank of Madras, even before the First World War, according to the evidence of Sir W. B. Hunter before the Indian Industrial Commission.[49] No comparable figures were available for other banks before the war. According to the evidence given by Norman Murray, one of the Managing Governors of the Imperial Bank of India, before the Royal Commission on Indian Currency and Finance of 1926, the advances by the Imperial Bank to purely industrial concerns were distributed between regions and communities as shown in Table 6.4.

TABLE 6.4 *Advances by Imperial Bank to purely industrial concerns* (*Rs. '000*)

	Indian	European	Total
Bengal	374	574	948
Bombay	850	65	915
Madras	90	131	221

Source: RC on Indian Currency and Finance, Vol. IV, Minutes of Evidence taken in India before the RC on Indian Currency and Finance (London, 1926), p. 479.

[48] The figures were taken from *IITB, 1911*, and *IITB, 1914*.
[49] According to Hunter, during the busy season between Rs. 17.5 and Rs. 20 million was lent to industrial concerns (including cotton mills, rice mills, cotton gins and presses, oil mills and sugar factories). He also claimed that of this amount about Rs. 11 million were lent to Indian concerns and about Rs. 8 million to European concerns. See *Evidence (Report of IIC)*, Vol. III (PP 1919, XIX), pp. 275–6.

These figures obviously related to advances over a short period of time and may or may not be average figures, but it is fair to judge that the situation must have been more biassed in favour of European concerns before the war, when the Banks of Bengal and Madras had been under purely European management, and when Indian industrial control was even weaker.[50]

There were formal or informal links between the Presidency Banks, exchange banks, and the managing agency houses. The Chairmen of the Presidency Banks and many other members of the Boards of Directors belonged to leading managing agency houses. Similar links existed between the British managing agency houses in India and the exchange banks: Sir Montague Cornish Turner was a partner of Mackinnon, Mackenzie and Company, and became Chairman of the Chartered Bank of India, Australia, and China; Sir James L. Mackay, later Lord Inchcape, of the firm of Mackinnon, Mackenzie and Co., was a director of the same bank for the years from 1893 to 1897.[51] Similarly, the National Bank of India had on its Board at various times partners of Jardine, Skinner and Company, Hoare Miller and Company, Binny and Company, Duncan Brothers and Company, Begg, Dunlop and Company, George Henderson and Company, James Finlay and Company, Bird and Company, Kilburn and Company, and Alex Lawrie and Company.[52]

6.5 EUROPEAN CONTROL OF BUSINESS IN EASTERN INDIA

We now turn to the regional differences in the control of industry by Europeans and Indians. This analysis is necessary not only because India was a large country which displayed different patterns of development in different parts, but because such analysis may also illuminate the reasons for the domination of industry by Europeans before the First World War.

Even at a superficial glance, western India, and in particular Bombay and Ahmedabad, differed from other centres of trade and industry in India in that they had a much larger proportion of Indians controlling trade and industry. The pioneers of the largest industry under Indian control – the cotton-mill industry – were a Parsi from Bombay, C. N. Davar, and a Brahman from Ahmedabad, Ranchhodlal Chhotalal.[53] 'The sagacity,

[50] From a written statement submitted by Norman Murray it also appears that Europeans as a community accounted for a much larger fraction of total advances than of total deposits; this discrepancy is the most extreme in Bengal. See RC on Indian Currency and Finance: Vol. II, *Appendices to the Report* (London, 1926), Appendix No. 48. This is, of course, what one would expect in a situation where there was a larger fraction of businessmen among Europeans than among ordinary Indian depositors.

[51] Mackenzie: *Realms of Silver*, pp. 178–9.

[52] Tyson: *100 Years of Banking in Asia and Africa*, pp. 228–36.

[53] On pioneering in the cotton-textile industry, see S. M. Edwardes: *Memoir of Rao Bahadur Ranchhodlal Chhotalal, C.I.E.* (Exeter, 1920), Chapter IV; Mehta: *Cotton Mills*

activity, and commercial enterprise of the Parsis' of western India were considered 'proverbial in the East';[54] on the other side, it was said that 'practically a plutocracy has arisen in Gujarat and the Vania is often socially more important than the Brahman'.[55] Nothing like this combination of industrial enterprise and social respectability of business was found in any other part of India before the First World War. We shall first therefore contrast the situation in Calcutta and Bombay, the two major industrial 'nodes' of India, and then describe briefly the course of the rise of entrepreneurship in Cawnpore and Madras.

India was a very poor country in 1900,[56] and even though about 25,000 miles of railways had been built by that date, the interior parts were still largely unconnected with one another except through the ports. The currency system of India, with different notes for different 'currency circles' also led to the fragmentation of economic space. Hence if in an industry some protection against foreign competition existed, in the shape of transport costs from abroad or in the interior, or in the form of some public patronage, it was easy to set up a regional monopoly in the product, since the local market was small. Of the three major ports of India, Calcutta commanded the largest trade. One result of the greater European involvement in the commerce of India in eastern India was the greater relative difference between exports and imports in that part than in other parts of India. One other result was that the Europeans had a very much bigger base for the accumulation of capital than the Indian businessmen in Bombay. The fact that the seat of government was in Calcutta also meant a much bigger share of government patronage for Calcutta than for Bombay – at any rate, until the irrigation works of Sind demanded a much larger amount of construction in that part of India.

We have already referred to the facility with which European businessmen arrived at compromises minimizing competition and the threat of challenges from outside. This had quite tangible results in major industrial fields: IJMA organized short-time agreements whenever the need arose, from 1885 onwards, until the arrangements broke down under the dual stress of the depression of the thirties and the entry of new, primarily Indian-controlled, firms. The jute-mill companies regularly negotiated collective agreements with the steamship companies of eastern India for the carriage of jute and jute goods. The steamship companies themselves entered into a

of India, Chapter II, and H. Spodek: 'The "Manchesterisation" of Ahmedabad', *Economic Weekly* (Bombay), 13 March 1965, pp. 483–90.

[54] A. Fuhrer: 'Parsees or Parsis', *Encyclopaedia Britannica* (9th ed.; Edinburgh, 1885), Vol. XVIII, p. 327.

[55] *Census of India, 1911*, Vol. VII, *Bombay*, Part I, *Report* by P. J. Mead and G. Laird Macgregor (Bombay, 1912), p. 307.

[56] The income per capita was between £2 and £3, according to the calculations of Lord Curzon and F. J. Atkinson, as we have pointed out in Chapter I, p. 3.

series of agreements with one another for the division of the market and the fixing of rates and fares. The two major European-controlled paper mills of eastern India entered into agreements about prices before the First World War, and such co-operation continued throughout the inter-war period.

The straddling of different fields by the same managing agency house, and the concentration of capital in the hands of a few European managing agency houses, facilitated the maintenance of individual or collective monopolies, and British businessmen fully appreciated the advantages of such monopolies for themselves. Thus when Parry and Company, in conjunction with the Commercial Bank of India, floated the East India Distilleries and Sugar Factories Limited, the prospectus claimed: '. . . the Company will . . . secure the practical control of the Spirit and Sugar Trade throughout the Madras Presidency'.[57] The substance of this claim lay in the monopoly in supplying sugar to the troops stationed in the Madras Presidency and Burma, and in supplying spirits to Mysore, and the control of all big sugar- and spirits-producing factories in the Madras Presidency, except one that was managed by Binny and Company. This last obstacle to the exercise of effective monopoly was removed when Binny and Company had to hand over the management of the Deccan Sugar and Abkhari Company Limited to Parry and Company in 1902, because of large losses sustained mainly in the sugar trade.[58] Similar local European monopolies existed in the case of breweries in north and north-western India, and in the field of supply of army boots, blankets and other equipment: these monopolies were often based on an initial government patronage.[59]

More important perhaps than the domination of individual industries by individual companies or managing agency houses was the domination of all the major industries by a small group of European managing agency houses in eastern, southern and northern India. An analysis of the rupee companies listed in *IIYB, 1911* (see Table 6.5) revealed that the seven managing agency houses: Andrew Yule and Company; Bird and Company; Begg, Dunlop and Company; Shaw Wallace and Company; Williamson, Magor and Company; Duncan Brothers; and Octavius Steel and Company controlled 55% of the jute companies, 61% of the tea companies, and 46% of the coal companies. Andrew Yule and Company and Bird and Company alone controlled 14 out of 29 rupee jute companies, and their control increased during the decade 1910–20, though the inclusion of sterling com-

[57] *Issues 1897 advertised in The Times*, No. 14 (London, July–December 1897), p. 269.

[58] Hilton Brown: *Parry's of Madras: A Story of British Enterprise in India* (Madras, 1954), pp. 162–5.

[59] The Murree Brewery Limited, and E. Dyer and Company Limited, both connected with the Dyer family, controlled the trade and manufacture of spirits in north and north-western India: S. Playne (compiler) and A. Wright (ed.): *The Bombay Presidency, the United Provinces, the Punjab etc.* (London, 1920), pp. 157–64, 566–8, and 633–8. On government patronage enjoyed by factories at Cawnpore, see Section 6.7 below.

TABLE 6.5 *Control of joint-stock companies registered in India and working in the tea, coal and jute industries around*

Name of managing agents or secretary	No. of joint-stock companies controlled in		
	tea	coal	jute
Andrew Yule and Co.	10	11	6
Begg, Dunlop and Co.	10	—	2
Bird and Co.	—	11	8
Shaw Wallace and Co.	2	11	—
Williamson, Magor and Co.	10	5	—
George Henderson and Co.	2	—	—
Planters' Stores and Agency	1	—	—
Kilburn and Co.	6	2	—
Octavius Steel and Co.	10	2	—
Gillanders, Arbuthnot and Co.	1	—	1
Kettlewell, Bullen and Co.	1	—	1
J. Mackillican and Co.	2	—	—
C. A. Stewart	4	—	—
Duncan Bros.	12	—	—
Davenport and Co.	8	—	—
Hoare, Miller and Co.	1	3	—
Jardine, Skinner and Co.	2	2	2
McLeod and Co.	3	5	2
Barry and Co.	3	—	1
Macneill and Co.	—	5	—
H. V. Low and Co.	—	4	—
F. W. Heilgers and Co.	—	7	2
Stanley, Oakes and Co.	—	1	—
Apcar and Co.	—	—	1
Anderson Wright and Co.	—	2	1
Ernsthausen Ltd.	—	1	2
Balmer Lawrie and Co.	—	4	—
Martin and Co.	—	3	—
Lyall, Marshall and Co.	—	1	—
N. C. Sircar and Sons	—	7	—
Total	88	87	29

Source: IIYB, 1911 (Calcutta, 1911).

panies would tend to decrease the degree of concentration measured by control over capital and number of looms.[60] Most of the coal companies were rupee companies, and the biggest of them, such as Bengal Coal Company and Burrakur Coal Company, were controlled by Andrew Yule, and Bird respectively. In the tea industry, the inclusion of sterling companies would seem to make a material difference to our measurement of the degree

[60] An analysis of data from *IIYB, 1911*, and *Capital* (Calcutta), 5 January 1911 and 4 January 1912, shows that out of the total number of 32,711 looms in the jute mills in 1910, Bird and Company controlled 4,707, Thomas, Duff and Company controlled 3,724, Andrew Yule and Company controlled 3,302, Jardine, Skinner and Company controlled 2,177 Ernsthausen controlled 2,150 and George Henderson controlled 2,040 looms.

of concentration: according to an estimate we have already quoted, in 1914, out of a total nominal capital of Rs. 302·3 million of joint-stock companies registered in India only Rs. 43·1 million were accounted for by rupee companies.[61] However, a scrutiny of the list of sterling tea companies registered by 1914, and operating in India, published by the Mincing Lane Tea and Rubber Share Brokers' Association Limited and the Indian Tea Share Exchange Limited (see Table 6.6), reveals that out of 124 companies so listed, 42 were controlled by George Williamson and Company, Octavius Steel and Company, Walter Duncan and Company, and R. G. Shaw and Company, which were the London correspondents of four firms appearing in our list of the top seven managing agency firms in Calcutta.[62]

The seven listed firms were probably not the biggest ones; in terms of influence and involvement, possibly Jardine, Skinner and Company, Martin and Company, and F. W. Heilgers and Company would be bigger than some of the seven firms cited. Nor does the control of the jute, coal and tea industries alone give a proper measure of concentration. The same group of British managing agency houses also controlled other fields: Andrew Yule were important in the field of steam navigation, Bird, and Martin in the field of engineering, and Gillanders, Arbuthnot, and Martin in the field of railways. F. W. Heilgers and Balmer Lawrie controlled the two important paper mills in India before 1914. The degree of concentration cannot be measured by a mere listing of the companies or their capital under the control of the managing agency houses: there was an enormous degree of interlocking of boards of directors under the control of different managing agency houses.[63] Apart from the formal and informal associations and clubs of which the companies under the control of British managing agency houses and their managers were members, this interlocking of directorates also facilitated the smooth working of various types of price agreements or market-sharing arrangements.

It is not suggested that this degree of concentration of control was unusual in the field of Indian industry: although no rigorous estimate of changes in the degree of concentration of economic power has been worked out,

[61] Hope: 'The Tea Industry of Bengal and Assam', p. 387.

[62] *Tea Producing Companies 1914* (London, 1914) and *Tea Producing Companies 1923–4* (London, 1924). The latter publication was utilized in those cases in which a company had been registered by 1914 but for some reason had been omitted from the earlier publication.

[63] The Bank of Bengal itself was controlled by the leading managing agency houses. According to an article in *Capital* (Calcutta), 2 September 1909, 'the directorate of the Bank of Bengal has always been a very close borough, confined to certain favoured firms, some sixteen in number'. Of these sixteen again, nine had ceased to operate, so that the directors were drawn from only seven firms, of which two firms, Jardine, Skinner and Gillanders, Arbuthnot, had had directors on the Board of the Bank of Bengal over the previous half-century at least. The relevant extract from the article is given in RC on Indian Finance and Currency: *Appendices to the Final Report of the Commissioners* (PP 1914, xx), p. 649.

TABLE 6.6 *List of managing agency houses or secretaries controlling more than one sterling tea company in 1914*

Name of managing agency or secretary	Number of tea companies managed
George Williamson and Co.	18
Octavius Steel and Co.	13
Planters' Stores and Agency	6
Walter Duncan and Co.	6
James Finlay and Co.	5
F. A. Roberts and Co.	5
McLeod, Russel and Co.	5
R. G. Shaw and Co.	5
C. A. Goodricke and Co.	4
P. R. Buchanan and Co.	4
Alex. Lawrie and Co.	4
F. A. Bond and Co.	3
A. R. Warner	3
Harrisons and Grosfield	3
J. E. A. Sissmore	2
Thomas Hoare	2
W. E. Neish	2
Geo. G. Playfair	2
E. G. Rock	2
Jas. B. Leckie and Co.	2
Rowe, White and Co.	2
Companies or secretaries managing one tea company each	26
Total	124

Source: Tea Producing Companies 1914 and *Tea Producing Companies 1923–24* (London, 1914 and 1924), compiled by the Mincing Lane Tea and Rubber Share Brokers' Association Ltd and the Indian Tea Share Exchange Ltd.

all indications point to the conclusion that the 1920s witnessed a further increase in the concentration of control in the hands of the top British managing agency houses.[64] But the supremacy of the group of British managing agency houses began to be challenged seriously with the entry of new Indian entrepreneurial groups into the industrial field.

The control of the managing agency houses over the resources of eastern and northern India also extended to the supply of labour, as we have seen in Chapter 5. The existence of an elaborate agency for the recruitment of labour for the tea plantations meant that it could also be utilized for recruiting labour for jute mills and coal mines. The legal machinery of the government and the monopolistic position of the British managing agency houses were effectively utilized by the latter to ensure a supply of

[64] A merger of the interests of Bird and Company with those of F. W. Heilgers and Company was probably the single most important factor in this: the take-over of Burn and Company, the biggest engineering complex in India outside the works of the Tata Iron and Steel Company, by Martin and Company, was another important event.

cheap labour to the factories, mines and plantations from all over India, even though local labour supplies were relatively extensive.

Most of the big managing agency houses in Calcutta made their money in trade or as labour contractors: Andrew Yule started in trade and entered the fields of coal and steamships before they took up the jute industry. Bird and Company made their money first as labour contractors for the East Indian Railways.[65]

The major managing agency houses all over India continued to have large export and import departments after they had entered industry in a big way.[66] Among items of trade, imports of Manchester piecegoods remained extremely important among the operations of British managing agency houses; as we have mentioned earlier, Calcutta was the largest single piecegoods market of the East, and the control of the import trade by European businessmen conferred upon them a virtual monopoly of the wholesale trade in cotton piecegoods in ports other than Bombay. The imports of machinery and hardware constituted an important item. Among the exports, raw jute, jute goods, opium, leather, oilseeds, indigo, tea, coffee, and spices were important although both opium and indigo exports became less important over time.[67]

Two other points are to be noticed about the British managing houses in eastern India. First, most of the big firms had been started primarily by traders, contractors and financiers. Very few of the pioneering planters, apart from those who were involved with the early stages of the Assam Company and had managed to buy up large amounts of land suitable for tea cultivation, went on to become industrialists. The indigo planters remained primarily large farmers with the usual features of Indian landlords – receiving rent and doing very little to help change the methods of cultivation of the tenants. Apart from Martin and Company, no engineering firm by itself grew up to absorb or launch firms in other fields.

The second point to stress again is that the managing agency houses with large industrial interests continued to have strong interests in trade. In fact,

[65] Godfrey Harrison: *Bird and Company of Calcutta. A History produced to mark the firm's centenary 1864–1964* (Calcutta, 1964), Chapters II, III, IV. The labour department of the firm, dealing with two railway companies, two steamer companies, and the Port Commissioners of Calcutta, continued to be one of the most important departments. *Ibid.*, pp. 50–3.   [66] Playne and Wright: *Southern India*, pp. 135–9.

[67] Although both W. R. Macdonald, representing the Bombay Chamber of Commerce, and R. Steel, representing the Bengal Chamber of Commerce before the Royal Commission on Opium, claimed that they personally had nothing to do with opium, the official position of both the Chambers was in favour of continuation of the opium policy of the Government of India, including unrestricted export of opium to China: RC on Opium: *Evidence, with Appendices*, Vol. II (PP 1894, LXI), pp. 160–2 and 439–52 and RC on Opium: *Evidence, with Appendices*, Vol. IV (PP 1894, LXII), pp. 314–16. By far the largest proportion of opium exports (two-thirds or more of the total) were shipped from Calcutta after public auctions of opium produced in farms licensed and supervised by the government, so it is natural to suppose that European traders had the major share of the profits.

sometimes it was the industrial interest which led to an interest in trade in the raw material.[68]

The engineering firms generally also dealt in imported engineering stores and hardware.[69] One of the results of this combination of interests was that the attitude of the different managing houses to questions of tariff protection or State aid were often ambivalent. This ambivalence turned to definite opposition to protectionist policies in the case of those firms whose primary interests lay in the field of exports and imports and which had little to do with producing industrial goods for the domestic market.[70]

6.6 INDIAN AND EUROPEAN BUSINESSMEN IN WESTERN INDIA

If we turn our attention to Indian entrepreneurship in western India, the contrast with eastern and northern India could hardly have been greater. The British interests were there in strength, buying raw cotton, cleaning it in ginning presses, and baling it for export; spinning yarn out of cotton; and in the case of the Finlay and Swan mills and the mills under the control of Indio-British managing agency houses, weaving cloth for the Indian market. Killick, Nixon and Company were one of the leading managing agency houses of Bombay, developing and managing light railways all over India. The exchange banks of Bombay were exclusively in European hands, until the Eastern Bank was organized under the leadership of E. D. Sassoon and Company.[71] The senior officers of the administration and the railways of Bombay and Sind were European, as in other parts of India. The Bombay Port Trust was also European-controlled.

But the Indians had a toehold in the export business. They had been shipowners and also ship-builders until the activities of the Bombay dockyard had been discontinued by governmental decision.[72] The cotton

---

[68] Playne and Wright: *Bengal and Assam, Behar and Orissa*, 'Birkmyre Brothers', p. 85. The Birkmyre brothers had owned a small jute mill at Greenock and had dismantled the works and started in 1874 a highly successful jute company, the Hastings Jute Mills, near Calcutta. 'Recently Birkmyre Brothers have given their attention to the baling of their own marks of jute for export to Dundee and the Continent, and they have already been successful in introducing these to the favourable notice of spinners'.

[69] Martin and Company, for example, were described in *ibid.*, p. 157, as being in all probability the leading importers of engineering tools and plant. This firm was at that time also the managing agent for the Bengal Iron and Steel Company, whose interests definitely lay in getting tariff protection.

[70] See the written evidence of Turner, Morrison and Company and the oral evidence of W. S. J. Wilson of the same company in *Evidence (Report of Indian Fiscal Commission)*, Vol. II (Calcutta, 1923), pp. 381–8.

[71] With the shift of the main business interests of the Sassoon group to London and Shanghai, the Eastern Bank also passed under British control.

[72] See Edwardes, *Gazetteer of Bombay City and Island*, I (Bombay, 1909), pp. 390–1; also Pavlov: *The Indian Capitalist Class*, pp. 146–54. D. F. Karaka: *History of the Parsis*, Vol. 2 (London, 1884), listed a number of Parsi shipowners.

trade was mainly in Indian hands;[73] the Indians also had a hand in the opium trade, particularly since the opium of western India originated in native states where the Indians had a little more say in the conduct of political and commercial affairs than in British territory.

This difference in the position of the Indians is reflected not only in the greater percentage of industrial capital under Indian control, but also in the greater degree of collaboration between Indian and European businessmen. As we mentioned above, the Bombay Chamber of Commerce was primarily a European organization but it also had several Indian members. The Bank of Bombay had an Indian majority on its board of directors, although the President was generally an Englishman. There was often an Indian majority on the boards of directors of companies under the control of managing agency houses such as Bradbury and Company, and Killick, Nixon and Company.[74]

Table 6.7 brings out the differences in the degrees of control exercised by Indians and Europeans on industry in different parts of India around 1911. The table is obviously incomplete: one does not know how the 'more important industrial concerns' were chosen, and there are glaring omissions. For example, cotton spinning and weaving mills are excluded from the Central Provinces and Berar, the United Provinces (not reproduced here) and Madras, although all of these provinces contained large cotton mills – primarily under Indian control in the first province and primarily under European control in the last two provinces. Still it does show some important features which are unlikely to be vitiated by the incompleteness of coverage. The proportions of companies controlled by Indian directors are very different in Assam, Bengal, Bihar and Orissa taken together and in Bombay, and the Central Provinces and Berar taken together; plantations are dominated by Europeans; so are engineering and machinery workshops, and railway workshops. One reason for European control of engineering and machinery workshops was that government and railway patronage was important for most of them; when the patronage of private industry – for reasons of prejudice or common 'racial' background – was added to government and railway patronage, it was very difficult for any new Indian enterprise to compete with the European enterprises in this field.[75]

---

[73] See M. L. Dantwala: *Marketing of Raw Cotton in India* (Bombay, 1937), *idem*: *A Hundred Years of Indian Cotton* (Bombay, 1948) and Frank Moraes: *Sir Purshotamdas Thakurdas* (Bombay, 1957) for information on the organization of the cotton trade in western India.

[74] See for example, the companies listed under 'Railways' and 'Cotton' in *IIYB, 1914*.

[75] Among the pioneers of the engineering industry in India were Sorabji, Shapurji & Co.; the founder of the firm, a Parsi, established the first foundry and engineering works in western India, but neither this nor any other Indian firm was among the leading engineering firms of western India in, say, 1919. Sorabji, Shapurji and Co. became primarily importers of machinery from the U.K. See Playne and Wright: *The Bombay Presidency*, pp. 337–8, and S. M. Rutnagur: *Bombay Industries: The Cotton Mills*

TABLE 6.7 *Particulars of ownership and management of the most important industrial concerns*

Province and nature of factory, etc.	Number owned by companies of which the directors are			Number privately owned		Number managed by	
	Europeans and Anglo-Indians	Indians	Of both races	Europeans and Anglo-Indians	Indians	Europeans and Anglo-Indians	Indians
Assam							
Tea plantations	494	12	—	55	48	536	73
Bengal							
Tea plantations	158	18	—	46	18	193	47
Collieries	53	6	21	7	43	66	63
Jute presses	50	16	—	7	36	64	45
Jute mills	49	—	—	1	—	50	—
Machinery and engineering workshops	22	—	—	4	7	30	7
Brick and tile factories	7	3	4	10	136	8	153
Oil mills	4	4	—	—	118	4	115
Printing presses	11	4	1	17	65	32	71
Bihar and Orissa							
Indigo plantations	12	—	—	93	14	117	2
Collieries	80	11	5	6	99	87	112
Mica mines	10	—	1	4	37	14	38
Lac factories	1	—	—	1	46	2	46
Bombay							
Cotton, etc. ginning, cleaning and pressing factories	13	92	13	—	194	10	304
Cotton, etc. spinning, weaving and other mills	12	92	25	—	18	43	106
Flour and rice mills	1	14	3	—	39	6	51
Machinery and engineering workshops	5	—	2	4	2	10	3
Printing presses	8	8	—	5	36	16	45
Railway workshops	13	—	—	—	—	12	1
Central Provinces and Berar							
Manganese mines	15	3	—	1	21	20	20
Cotton ginning, cleaning and pressing mills	5	56	1	—	91	7	146
Madras							
Coffee plantations	30	6	1	56	11	86	18
Tile factories	7	9	—	2	23	10	30
Rice mills	2	23	—	—	57	3	78
Railway workshops	23	—	—	—	—	23	—
Printing presses	11	16	1	1	19	15	36
Tanneries	3	26	—	1	36	3	64

Source: Census of India, 1911, Vol. I, *India,* Part 1. Report by E. A. Gait (Calcutta, 1913), Subsidiary Table XII (p. 446).

Note: 'Europeans and Anglo-Indians' also included Armenians.

In interpreting this table it is important to remember that in most fields the joint-stock companies controlled the bigger enterprises, although there were exceptions, particularly in case of engineering workshops, plantations and the industries demanding smaller units in general. No detailed figures for the distribution of directorships among various Indian communities are available. But the following analysis of the figures of ownership of privately-owned factories – that is factories which were not owned by joint-stock companies or by public authorities – and of management of all factories in the Bombay Presidency in 1911 will give some idea of the wide distribution of ownership and management among the different Indian communities.[76] Of the total number of 798 factories covered, 453 were privately owned. Of these 20 were owned by Europeans or Anglo-Indians, 125 by Vanis (Banias), 85 by Zoroastrians (Parsis), 40 by Bohoras, 31 by Brahmans, 21 by Kunbis, 14 by Kumbhars, 13 by Memons, 13 by Shaikhs, 9 by Khatris, and 5 by Jews. None of the 194 privately-owned ginning, cleaning and pressing factories belonged to Europeans: 84 of them were owned by Vanis, 34 by Zoroastrians, 20 by Bohoras, 12 by Brahmans, and 12 by Kunbis. Only 19 out of 148 spinning, weaving and other mills (textile groups) were privately owned. Of these 5 were owned by Vanis, 3 by Zoroastrians and 2 by Bohoras.[77]

Among the managers of spinning, weaving and other mills, the Parsis (45) outnumbered both the Europeans and Anglo-Indians (43) and the Vanis (28); but 149 of the managers of ginning, cleaning and pressing factories were Vanis as against 46 Zoroastrians, 44 Brahmans, 16 Kunbis, 10 Europeans and Anglo-Indians, and 10 Lingayats. Of the total number of managers of the 798 factories analysed, 135 were Europeans and Anglo-Indians, 233 Vanis, 150 Zoroastrians, 86 Brahmans, 32 Kunbis, 22 Bohoras, 18 Kumbhars, 17 Shaikhs, 16 Khojas and 12 Memons.

From these figures, and from the information obtained from other sources, such as the *IITB 1914*, it apears that the Parsis controlled a larger fraction of the bigger enterprises, particularly in the cotton-mill industry, than did the other Indian communities, including the Vanis. The lead of the Parsis over the Vanis in the management of cotton mills was only partially

---

(Bombay, 1927), pp. 671, 725. No Indian firm in western India figured among the list of firms approved by the Government of India in 1922. See Sen: *Studies in Economic Policy*, pp. 227–8.

[76] The figures are taken from *Census of India, 1911*, Vol. VII, *Bombay*, Part II, Imperial Tables by P. J. Mead and G. L. Magregor (Bombay, 1912), pp. 518–21 (Table xv, Part E, Parts III and IV).

[77] It is an interesting illustration of the obsession of official India with caste that the writers of the report on Bombay concluded in defiance of the evidence that 'with the exception of the Parsees – the caste which is concerned with a certain handicraft is most intimately connected with the same craft when it has become a large commercial concern'. *Census of India, 1911*, Vol. VII, *Bombay*, Part I, Report by P. J. Mead and G. L. Macgregor (Bombay, 1912), pp. 324–5.

due to the larger degree of control exercised by the former; it was also due to the lead the Parsis had in general education, and in particular, in technical education, over the other communities. We shall discuss the other reasons for Parsi pre-eminence in a later section.

6.7 REASONS FOR EUROPEAN PREDOMINANCE IN BUSINESS: THE CASE OF CAWNPORE

One does not have to believe in either a 'conspiracy' theory of entrepreneurial dominance or a theory of absolute superiority of European businessmen in all fields of activity in order to be able to explain their extraordinary degree of control over the economy of eastern and northern India. One could explain the growth of European managing agency houses easily by reference to the essential interdependence of the fields of industry that they did control. That it was Europeans rather than Indians who did the controlling was due to a large extent to political factors, as we shall argue more fully later. This theory of expansion by 'one thing leading to another' is well illustrated by the case of Andrew Yule and Company. In the first few years of the Company in India, in the 1860s, the main interests had been the agencies for Horrocks's longcloth, and for three insurance companies.[78] Soon the firm moved into the fields of jute, cotton, tea and coal. In 1883 Andrew Yule and Company formed the Inland Flotilla Company primarily for the transport of jute and tea from East Bengal and Assam; this company was later absorbed by the India General Steam Navigation Company in order to 'avoid the severe competition which was proving ruinous to both, and George Yule joined the Board of India General'.[79] In 1895 David Yule of Andrew Yule and Company formed the Bengal Assam Steamship Company Limited, to operate on the waterways of eastern India. He then went on to form the Port Shipping Company 'which became Calcutta's largest lighterage Company'.[80] In the same way Bird and Company began by supplying labour under contract to the East Indian Railway and then gradually expanded into the coal and jute industries. Because of its interest in coal, the firm started an engineering works at Kumardhubi to produce such items as coal tubs and pithead frames for the collieries in the district; it started a pottery and firebrick works at Kumardhubi because of the presence of a deposit of the raw material – fireclay – at the site. These two works became the centre of a large development of secondary industry at Kumardhubi.[81]

[78] Andrew Yule & Co.: *Andrew Yule & Co. Ltd* (printed in Great Britain for private circulation, 1963), p. 5.
[79] *Ibid.*, p. 11. See also *IIYB, 1911*, pp. 310–11.
[80] Andrew Yule & Co.: *Andrew Yule & Co. Ltd*, p. 11.
[81] Harrison: *Bird and Company of Calcutta*, Chapters II–V.

The initial advantages of the British businessmen in most fields of industry could not be doubted; they were after all in touch with the world's pioneer industrializing country. But the systematic maintenance of those advantages definitely depended on erecting barriers to the entry of Indians into their preserves: the control of external trade would to a large extent have served as an effective barrier to entry because the stimulus to any development that occurred there was provided by the impact of the expanding world trade. But to the control of external trade was added an almost exclusive monopoly of government patronage and a remarkable degree of understanding among European traders and industrialists about the ineligibility of Indians as equal partners, particularly in those areas where British political and economic dominance had prevailed for a longer period of time. No industrial city displays these factors supporting the maintenance of European control better than Cawnpore (Kanpur in modern spelling) and so to Cawnpore we turn for the next development of our story.

An agency and a cantonment of the East India Company were established in Cawnpore in 1778, and the town grew rapidly to become the biggest marketing centre of the Doab.

The construction of the Ganges canal and the metalled road to Lucknow, added to the incentive afforded by the presence of a large military arsenal, removed all doubts as to the predominance of Cawnpore; and a further stimulus to commerce was provided by the completion of the East Indian Railway, which synchronised approximately with the opening of the first of the great tanneries and cotton mills.[82]

One of the first modern factories – if not the first modern factory – to be set up in Cawnpore was the Government Harness and Saddlery Factory, the need for which arose directly out of the difficulty of securing supplies of harness and saddlery during the Mutiny of 1857. A young artillery officer, Captain John Stewart, was authorized to make experiments in improving the quality of leather made at Cawnpore: for this purpose the services of soldiers who had worked at tanyards in England were utilized, and the commissariat cattle were slaughtered. The experiments proving successful, the Harness and Saddlery Factory was established in 1863. This factory was in a sense the parent of the Army Boot and Equipment Factory which was established in 1880 (or 1881) by Mr (later Sir) W. E. Cooper who joined with Sir George Allen to establish the firm of Cooper Allen and Company, the proprietors of the Army Boot and Equipment Factory.

[82] District Gazetteers of the United Provinces of Agra and Oudh, Vol. xix, *Cawnpore*, (Allahabad, 1909) p. 75.

The firm in 1883 secured their first boot contract from Government, and obtained a large advance of money on the understanding that they were to build pits and carry out the manufacture of leather after the methods employed in the Government factory. It now holds the contract for the supply of boots to the whole British army in India... The factory also does a very large trade with other Government departments in addition to a most flourishing private business...[83]

Cooper Allen and Company also became in 1904 the managing agents of the North-West Tannery Company Limited, which had erected a factory around the beginning of the 1890s.[84]

Another enterprise which catered to the needs of the army was the Cawnpore Woollen Mills and Army Cloth Manufacturing Company Limited, which was formed as a private concern by Dr J. Condon and Messrs Gavin Jones and Petman, but was sold to a limited company in 1882. It apparently did not receive the degree of government patronage that the founders had hoped for. 'A little Government aid and patronage in its early struggling career would have saved years of valuable time and pecuniary loss, but this assistance was not forthcoming, and the pioneers had to bear the whole burden of proving their faith and eventually establishing the industry on a sound basis', complained Mr Gavin Jones.[85] But the government purchase still formed 86·88% of its total sales in 1885 and 41·63% in 1890.[86] Both the Cawnpore Woollen Mills and the New Egerton Woollen Mills Co. Ltd, which was formed in 1890 to take over the property of the defunct Egerton Mills at Dhariwal in the Punjab,[87] flourished under the management of Sir Alexander McRobert.

The first cotton mills in Cawnpore, Elgin Mills, owed their origin to the scarcity of cotton goods and the rise in the price of Indian cotton, for which Cawnpore was a large market, caused by the American Civil War. The firm was founded in 1863 by a group of commissariat officers with financial aid from their wealthy contractors and commissariat *gomasthas* (Indians); but it was badly managed, and was reconstructed in 1864 on the lines suggested by Gavin Jones, who had been brought over to build and manage the original mill. Gavin Jones went on to establish the Muir Mills Company Limited in 1874. The Cawnpore Cotton Mills Company Limited was started in 1882 by J. Harwood, an employee of the Elgin Mills. A weaving master of Elgin Mills, Atherton West, established the Victoria Mills in 1885 in co-operation with Sheo Prasad, a well-known banker and trader, who already had a small spinning and weaving concern. In 1897 Gavin Jones set up the Empire Engineering Company Limited, which engaged in general structural engineering work for local needs,

[83] *Ibid.*, pp. 78–9.   [84] Playne and Wright: *The Bombay Presidency*, p. 475.
[85] Gavin Jones in 'The Rise and Progress of Cawnpore', in *ibid.*, p. 497.
[86] Sen: *Studies in Economic Policy*, p. 38.   [87] *IIYB, 1914*, p. 435.

manufactured well-boring and other boring tools, and a large portion of whose work was 'devoted exclusively to the out-turn of general municipal and sanitary requirements'.[88]

The most important managing agency house of Cawnpore during the period 1900–30, Begg, Sutherland and Company, did not enter the industrial field in a major capacity until 1894 when they set up the Cawnpore Sugar Works Limited. The factory began producing sugar in 1895 by processes which were acceptable to the orthodox Hindu community (that is, without using bone charcoal or other contaminating animal products).[89] The firm then started the Champaran Sugar Company Limited in 1905 and the Ryam Sugar Company Limited in 1913. In 1914 the firm was also the managing agent for Elgin Mills, and for Brushware Limited, and the local agents for the sterling company, the Indian Electric Supply and Traction Company Limited.[90]

Begg, Sutherland and Company had begun in Cawnpore in 1856 as Begg, Christie and Company (there was an earlier connection with a firm called John Kirk and Company, which had been established as merchants in Cawnpore before 1842).[91] Dr David Begg, one of the founders of the firm, came to India from the U.K. towards the end of the 1830s as an assistant to Dr Charles MacKinnon, who was the indigo and sugar-cane planters' doctor in Bihar. Begg gradually bought up large interests in indigo concerns, and then started Begg, Christie and Company in Cawnpore and Begg, Dunlop and Company in Calcutta.[92] Before 1894, the main business of Begg, Sutherland and Company was confined to indigo seed and general merchandise. It also acted as agent for indigo planters, mostly Europeans, and moved into sugar production in a large way, particularly after indigo had been badly hit by the discovery of aniline dyes by the Germans.

6.8   BUSINESS ENTREPRENEURSHIP IN SOUTHERN INDIA UP TO 1914

As in Bengal, so in Madras, the whole of the export and import trade was in European hands. The Bank of Madras, one of the three Presidency Banks, never had an Indian director from its inception in 1876 until its amalgamation in the Imperial Bank of India in 1921.[93] The Madras

---

[88] Playne and Wright: *The Bombay Presidency*, p. 447.   [89] *IITB, 1914*, p. 413.
[90] Playne and Wright: *The Bombay Presidency*, p. 426; District Gazetteers of the United Provinces of Agra and Oudh, Vol. XIX, *Cawnpore*, pp. 81–2.
[91] Playne and Wright: *The Bombay Presidency*, p. 426.
[92] Antrobus: *The Jorehaut Tea Company Ltd.*, p. 64.
[93] The exclusion of Indians from business on a large scale was self-justifying; according to Sir W. B. Hunter, the Secretary of the Bank of Madras, there was no Indian in Madras who managed firms of the same importance as the big European concerns and who could therefore qualify to be a Director of the Bank of Madras. *Evidence (Report of IIC)*, Vol. III, *Madras and Bangalore* (PP 1919, XIX), pp. 285–6.

Chamber of Commerce as late as 1923 had only two Indian members, the Honourable Sir S. R. M. Annamalai Chettiar and H. M. Ebrahim Sait.[94]

The whole of South India remained extremely backward industrially compared with Bombay and Bengal throughout the period; but in the latter part of the period there was some acceleration of development of industry. There were tea and a few coffee plantations, a few cotton mills, and a few engineering establishments, rice mills, and cotton gins and presses and that was about all. What little industry there was up to the First World War was controlled mostly by British businessmen with some Indian collaboration in a few cases.[95]

The leading business houses of the Madras Presidency before 1914, such as Best and Company, Binny and Company, Parry and Company and A. and F. Harvey had mostly started in trade. Best and Company specialized in the export of hides and skins, groundnut kernels and other oilseeds, and in the import of Manchester piecegoods. They acted as the agents of Anglo-French Textile Company Limited, which was registered as a sterling company in 1898. They also held the agencies, among others, of the P. & O. Steam Navigation Co. Ltd, the Anchor Line, the Barrakur Coal Co. Ltd, the Mysore Gold Mining Co. Ltd, and other mining enterprises (mostly gold mines), the Kolar Mines Power Station Ltd, the Kolar Gold Fields Electricity Department, and Nobel's Explosives Ltd.[96] Binny and Company were in 1914–15 'perhaps the largest general merchants in the City of Madras, and they had a banking establishment for the furtherance of business transactions with their many clients. As agents of the British India Steam Navigation Co. Ltd, Messrs Binny and Co. had acquired a flotilla of boats, and they ... handled a very considerable proportion of the imports of Madras.'[97] The firm was the landing agent for the Madras Port Trust, and in this capacity it owned a fleet of cargo boats and steamers, a dockyard for repairing the boats, and a transport service 'owing to the increasing difficulty of carting goods from exporters' godowns to the harbour'.[98]

Binny and Company were probably the pioneers of the cotton-mill industry in the Madras Presidency. The Buckingham Mill Company Ltd, for which the firm acted as secretaries, was registered in India in 1876

[94] *Report of the Proceedings of the Madras Chamber of Commerce, January–December 1923.* In 1917, the chamber had only one Indian member. See the evidence of Mr Gordon Fraser in *Evidence (Report of IIC)*, Vol. III, p. 313. The Madras Chamber of Commerce apparently had only two Indian members when it started in 1836. By a curious coincidence (according to the history of Parry's), it had again only two Indian members in its centenary year: Brown: *Parry's of Madras*, p. 66.

[95] *Evidence (Report of IIC)*, Vol. III, p. 88 (evidence of K. Suryanarayanamurti Nayudu, proprietor, Messrs Innes and Company, Cocanada); and Playne and Wright: *Southern India*, pp. 614–16 ('Innes & Co.').

[96] *Ibid.*, pp. 135 and 598.   [97] *Ibid.*, pp. 135–9.   [98] *Ibid.*, p. 139.

and its factory started working as a spinning mill in 1877, but weaving was introduced in 1890. The Carnatic Mill Company Limited, for which Binny and Company were also treasurers, was registered in India in 1881, and started working as a spinning and weaving mill. These two mills became two of the most profitable in the whole of India: at first their products were sold only locally but after the Swadeshi movement they were sold all over India. They consolidated their position by going over to high-quality goods for which they used the longer-staple local cottons, particularly the so-called Cambodia cottons.[99] The firm also acted as agents, secretaries and treasurers to the Bangalore Woollen, Cotton and Silk Mills Co. Ltd, at Bangalore. This firm was started in 1884 to take over the business of the Bangalore Woollen Mills (which had been founded in 1879) and to add thereto the manufacture of cotton yarn and goods; Binny and Company became agents in 1886. The Bangalore Mills Company doubled in size between 1886 and 1914; it sold superior quality yarn in the open market, and army blankets and *jhools* to the government. In 1913 practically the whole of the output of army blankets (nearly 1 million lb.) was sold to the army and government departments.[100] Binny and Company were also agents for the Madras Electric Supply Corporation of India Ltd, a number of cotton-press companies, and a large number of insurance companies.

Parry and Company had been started around the end of the eighteenth century; they had lent money to Colonel Cullen, who had experimented with indigo, and 'Sugar' or Edward Campbell, who had tried to cultivate indigo and had then become obsessed with sugar. But Parry and Company moved into the sugar industry only after equalization of tariffs in 1836 on sugar imported into England from the West Indies and from India. After the abolition of tariffs on all sugar imported into England in 1845, most of the new Indian sugar concerns vanished. Only the factories of Parry and Company in South Arcot and of Binny and Company at Aska survived. The sugar refinery of Parry's in South Arcot grew into the East India Distilleries and Sugar Works Limited (registered in England), which also absorbed Arcot Sugar Works and Distilleries. Parry and Company became virtual monopolists in the field of sugar and spirits in South India when in 1902 Binny and Company handed over to them the control of the Deccan Sugar and Abkhari Company because of financial difficulties caused by the losses sustained by the Deccan Sugar and Abkhari Company. Parry and Company also became the largest manufacturers of manure and fertilizers in South India.[101]

---

[99] *Ibid.*, p. 139; Slater: *Southern India*, p. 114.
[100] Playne and Wright: *Southern India*, pp. 139 and 212.
[101] The above account is based on Brown: *Parry's of Madras* and Playne and Wright: *Southern India*, pp. 166–9.

The firm of A. and F. Harvey had been founded in 1879, purely as a cotton-exporting firm. It set up the Tinnevelly Mills at Ambasamudram in 1884, the Coral Mills at Tuticorin in 1889 and the Madura Mills in 1892; the last mills became the largest in South India, with 100,536 spindles. All the mills remained purely spinning mills at least until 1914.[102]

Another British firm which was interested in the cotton-mill industry was T. Stanes and Co. Ltd. Robert Stanes, the founder of the firm, and his family started as planters of coffee in the Nilgiris, established a coffee-curing works, and became established at Coimbatore. They formed the Coimbatore Spinning and Weaving Factory, in conjunction with Arbuthnot and Company of Madras, and on the failure of the latter firm in 1907 assumed entire control of the factory. They later took over the management of the Coimbatore Mall Mills Company Limited.[103]

Finally, we have a group of engineering firms, such as Massey and Company and the Crompton Engineering Company (a branch of a firm with head offices in England) which depended largely on railways and public works departments for their steady work. Engineering in the Madras Presidency appears to have been entirely monopolized by Europeans. The first pioneering enterprise of the Government of Madras, the manufacture of aluminium utensils, was handed over to Eardley Norton, a barrister of Madras, and a subsidy was given in the initial purchase price.[104]

Although some cotton mills had been set up in Delhi and the Punjab, and there were breweries and carpet factories in the same region, the hinterland of Karachi, which had overtaken Madras as the third largest port of India even before the First World War, remained almost completely agricultural. The breweries were controlled by various branches of the Dyer family; E. Dyer started the industry at Kasauli to supply the military establishments in India, and became the manager of the first large-scale brewery at Murree in 1860. When the Punjab Government decided to stop manufacturing spirits, two brothers started the Amritsar distillery in 1898. The initial advantages of the chain of breweries controlled by the Dyer family and their associates were consolidated through long government contracts at first and later on through a practical monopoly of all government contracts – on a shorter-term basis – for supplying spirits.[105]

[102] Playne and Wright: *Southern India*, pp. 481–4.
[103] *Ibid.*, p. 414.
[104] *Ibid.*, p. 152 and *Report of IIC* (PP 1919, xvii), Appendix J.
[105] See Playne and Wright: *The Bombay Presidency*, pp. 566–8, 602 and 633–8.

6.9 CHANGE IN THE RELATIVE STRENGTH OF
EUROPEAN AND INDIAN ENTREPRENEURS
AFTER THE FIRST WORLD WAR

The grip of European businessmen on the economy of India was loosened by the impact of the First World War. Many European assistants all over India volunteered for the war.[106] The import trade in cotton piecegoods was affected by the involvement of Great Britain in the war and by the shortage of shipping. The export trade in jute and other staples was also similarly affected. On the other side, the cotton-mill industry under Indian control was stimulated by the growth of demand; many Indian concerns sprang up in engineering and other trades supplying the army and the navy. The end of the war witnessed a permanent shift in the trade relations of India with the external world, and in particular with Great Britain: Indian imports of cotton piecegoods shrank and over the interwar period dwindled to insignificance. In other fields also, such as iron and steel, paper and cement, India began to supply more and more of her own requirements.

But the effect of the war on the control of the Europeans over existing units was probably not very significant. Although claims were made that Indians controlled 'not less than 60% of the shares of the Jute Mills',[107] they were difficult to substantiate in the absence of detailed studies of shareholders' lists.[108] With the exception of Bangur and a few other names on the boards of directors of jute companies controlled by European firms, there is no evidence of Indian control of a substantial block of shares in the jute mills before the end of the Second World War.[109] No jute mill passed from European to Indian control during the interwar years. Around 1932, the percentage of ordinary share capital held by Indians in the Titaghur Paper Mills (controlled by the Bird-Heilgers group) was 56%, but the percentages of preference (old issue), preference (new issue), and deferred shares held by Indians were only 39, 33 and 28 respectively.[110]

[106] See G. W. Tyson: *The Bengal Chamber of Commerce and Industry 1853–1953: A Centenary Survey* (Calcutta, 1953), p. 112, and Herbert Feldman: *Karachi through a Hundred Years, the Centenary History of the Karachi Chamber of Commerce and Industry 1860–1960* (Karachi, 1960), p. 131.

[107] *Evidence (Report of Indian Fiscal Commission)*, Vol. II (Calcutta, 1923), p. 419 (written statement of the Marwari Association, Calcutta).

[108] The shareholders' lists which were deposited in the Office of the Registrar of Companies, Calcutta, have been destroyed because of lack of space: lists are now preserved only for the ten or fifteen years preceding the current date.

[109] Even in 1951, foreign investors held about three-fifths of the total capital of the companies under the control of the Bird-Heilgers group and 46% of the capital under the control of the Andrew Yule group: See Hazari: *Structure of the Corporate Private Sector*, pp. 117 and 122.

[110] ITB: *Evidence (Report on paper and paper pulp)*, 1932, p. 162.

At the same date, Indian shareholders held 43% of ordinary shares (value Rs. 387,000), 58% of 7% cumulative preference shares (value Rs. 116,000) and 25·5% of 7% A cumulative preference shares (value Rs. 102,000) in the Bengal Paper Mill, controlled by Balmer Lawrie and Company.[111] In Pat Lovett's book, *The Mirror of Investment* (Calcutta, 1927), the bulk of the shares in companies controlled by European managing agency houses was shown to be held by the managing agents or their associates in India or the U.K. Earlier on, W. A. Ironside had informed the Indian Industrial Commission that in the case of jute companies '148 lakhs of rupees are held by Europeans and 25 lakhs by Indians'.[112]

It is probable that British managing agency houses managed a much larger amount of industrial capital than was owned by British shareholders. But the effective control over most of the companies which they had floated remained firmly in their hands. This is borne out also by data from other parts of India. Sir Clement Simpson of Binny and Co. stated in his evidence before the IIC that Indian shareholders held about one-tenth of the shares in the Buckingham Mill.[113] One of the few shareholders' lists to have survived in the office of the Registrar of Companies, Calcutta, up to 1967 pertained to the Ryam Sugar Company. This company was registered in 1913 and controlled by Begg, Sutherland and Company. Of the total number of 39,585 shares of face value Rs. 10 each on 8 September 1914, only 4,025 were held by Indians (including Indian brokers) and the rest were held by British residents in India or the U.K. The total number of shares held by Indians in the same company was 3,625 on 23 August 1919, 5,675 on 21 August 1920, 4,425 on 17 October 1925 and 6,000 on 30 August 1932 (the total number of shares was 40,000 during all these years). The situation changed radically only after the Second World War, when Indians came to hold the majority of shares, the number of which had doubled in the meantime. Taking all this evidence together, one has to conclude that not only did the existing firms under the control of British managing agency houses before the First World War continue to be controlled by them during the interwar period, but the capital in those firms also continued to be owned largely if not predominantly by British residents in India and the U.K.[114]

The other pieces of indirect evidence – the profitability of jute mills up to 1927, the inflow of private foreign capital during the years from 1921–2 to 1925–6, the profitability of British-controlled paper and sugar mills during the thirties – support the above conclusion. There was probably some amount of repatriation of private foreign capital during

---

[111] *Ibid.*, p. 397.
[112] *Evidence (Report of IIC)*, Vol. II (PP 1919, XVIII), p. 881.
[113] *Evidence (Report of IIC)*, Vol. III (PP 1919, XIX), p. 204.
[114] See also Banerji: *India's Balance of Payments*, pp. 176–81.

the thirties, but most of the repatriation was on public account.[115] Thus on the eve of the Second World War, in traditional industries such as tea, jute and coal, European firms controlled much more than 50% of the total capital employed.[116]

In new enterprises, however, Indians began to play a larger role during the interwar period. The post-war boom during the years from 1919–20 to 1921–2 was abruptly checked by increased foreign competition, and many Indian and British enterprises collapsed. In a way, the twenties were a period of stalemate. There was one major breakthrough by Indian capital during this period, namely the consolidation of the position of the Tata Iron and Steel Company Limited after 1924. The hydroelectric projects under the management of the house of Tata also came to fruition during this period; there were difficulties because of the enormous amount of capital involved, and because of poor utilization of the capacity during the twenties, caused by the troubles of the Bombay cotton-mill industry, including the strike of 1928. From 1929 onwards the management of the company was shared between the house of Tata and an American company, the American and Foreign Power Company Incorporated.[117] Several Indian firms also entered the jute industry; it was chiefly Indian firms again which invested in the cement industry during the twenties, so that India's needs were supplied mainly by domestic production.

But the British firms in established manufacturing industries continued

[115] *Ibid.*, pp. 186–96. In Chapter 5 and its Appendices A, B and C, Banerji has provided an exhaustive account of the information available for arriving at a direct estimate of foreign investments. He comes to the conclusion, after analysing the evidence of witnesses before various commissions of enquiry, that 'if not in all cases, at least over a very appreciable field of its operations, as compared with capital contributed by Indian nationals, non-Indian capital was predominant in units with rupee capital managed by non-Indian agents, etc., at least up to the late twenties'. *Ibid.*, pp. 180–1. His 'direct estimate' of foreign investment in India showed a total of Rs. 7,084,700,000 in 1921 and Rs. 8,850,900,000 in 1938, an increase of Rs. 1,766.2 million over the relevant period. Banerji also estimated the cumulative net annual flow of capital into India on the basis of known borrowing and repayment of capital in the London money market. This came to a total of Rs. 1,830 million. Finally, the 'indirect estimate' of net capital inflow which was arrived at by totalling all the net credit and debit items in the balance of payments yielded a figure of Rs. 2,170 million. Bearing in mind the incompleteness of the data on foreign holdings of capital in rupee and – to a lesser extent – sterling companies, and the fact that the estimated foreign investment figures reflect par values and not market values, the twin sets of figures are remarkably consistent and hence lend support to the conclusion in the text about the continued preponderance of foreign ownership and control in certain industries.

[116] For some representative figures indicating the degree of control exercised see Michael Kidron: *Foreign Investments in India* (London, 1965), pp. 3–11.

[117] Harris: *Jamsetji Nusserwanji Tata*, Chapter xi; Alfred Dickinson: 'Water Power in India', *JRSA*, Vol. lxvi, No. 3,417, 17 May 1918, pp. 418–22; A. T. Cooper: 'Recent Electrical Progress in India', *JRSA*, Vol. lxxvii, No. 3,994, pp. 747–8; Sir Frederick James: 'The House of Tata – Sixty Years' Industrial Development in India', *JRSA*, Vol. xcvi, 27 August 1948, p. 616.

to expand; in the jute industry the number of looms controlled by the larger British managing agency houses worked out as follows in 1928:

Bird and Heilgers	8,215
Jardine, Skinner	5,896
Andrew Yule	5,296
Thomas Duff	4,937
Total number of looms (including others)	49,491

The total number of looms controlled by Indian firms came to only 2,166.[118] In 1936, the situation had not changed very much: out of a total number of 54,200 looms, the top four managing agency houses controlled the following number:

Bird and Heilgers	8,839
Andrew Yule	8,030
Jardine, Skinner	6,540
Thomas Duff	6,334

Thus these four houses controlled more than 50% of the looms both in 1928 and in 1936. In 1936, the Indian managing agency houses controlled 3,743 looms and thus had marginally improved their share of the total number of looms in jute mills, but this share was still quite small.[119]

On the other side, the biggest industry under Indian control, the cotton-mill industry, was going through an extremely difficult period during the twenties, particularly in Bombay. The thrust of Indian entrepreneurship tended to come thus from regions other than Bombay.

Apart from cement, Indian entrepreneurship began to make itself prominent in other fields only with the coming of effective protection for most of the simple consumer goods industries. In cotton textiles, Delhi had already during the twenties begun to develop as a major centre, and Ahmedabad was forging well ahead as the second largest centre of the cotton industry in the subcontinent. In sugar, the imposition of high tariffs was followed by the launching of a very large number of firms, most of which had no previous connection with the industry. In paper, the biggest advances were made not by the established British producers but by firms set up by new Indian entrepreneurs such as Birla Brothers, Karam Chand Thapar and Dalmia Jain. As the importance of exports and imports in the commerce of India decreased, the scope of Indian entrepreneurs who were primarily oriented towards supplying the domestic market expanded.

---

[118] IJMA: *Report of the Committee for 1928* (Calcutta, 1929), p. 273.
[119] IJMA: *Report of the Committee for 1936* (Calcutta, 1937), Statement XII.

6.10   COLLABORATION AND CONFLICT BETWEEN EUROPEAN AND
INDIAN BUSINESSMEN

Because we have concentrated our attention on the most important feature of the relationship between European and Indian capital during the period under consideration, viz., their basic antagonism, it must not be supposed that Indian businessmen never co-operated either with European business groups or with the British rulers. Insofar as British rule had sapped, if not completely destroyed, the power of the pre-capitalist rulers of India, it had created the ground for the emergence of Indian capitalists as the dominant class. The contradiction lay in the facts that European businessmen were in a privileged position in exploiting the resources of India and that the full development of productive forces was thwarted by the actual or imagined requirements for the stability of the imperial system. Despite this contradiction (and partly *because* of it), many individual Indian business groups found it profitable to collaborate both with British business groups and with British rule in general.

In the nineteenth century the Parsis were the most important collaborators with British enterprise and administration: Sir Jamsetjee Jejeebhoy, the first Indian knight and (later) baronet, was in partnership with Jardine, Matheson and Company in the opium trade with China; he was also connected with the initial floating of the Great Indian Peninsula Railway Company, which constructed the first railway line in India.[120] There were Parsi contractors responsible for the construction of large stretches of the railway.[121] There was the famous house of Wadias, master ship-builders for the East India Company until the Bombay dockyard was closed in the middle of the nineteenth century. There were other Parsi businessmen connected with British mercantile houses in Bombay.[122]

[120] J. N. Sahni: *Indian Railways, One Hundred Years 1853 to 1953* (New Delhi, 1953), p. 2.
[121] See, for example, the biography of Jamsedjee Dorabjee Naigaumwala in N. K. D. Naigamwalla: *Stars of the Dawn: A Historical Memoir* (Bombay, 1946). Jamsedjee Dorabjee had partners, such as Sorabjee Kharshedjee Thoonthi, Cooverjee Pallonjee, Pestonjee Rustomjee Kanga and Rustomjee Ratanjee Billimoria – all Parsis. *Ibid.*, p. 24.
[122] Framjee Nusserwanjee Patel (born 1804) was a partner first in the firm of Wallace and Company, which he himself helped to found (in 1844) and then in the firm of Framjee, Sands and Company (founded in 1858): Playne and Wright: *The Bombay Presidency*, p. 181. Wallace and Company (Wallace Brothers in London) came later to found and control the Bombay Burmah Trading Corporation Limited, the company which became the biggest owner of forest rights and the biggest timber merchants of South-East Asia. Significantly enough, Wallace and Company did not have any Indian partners after Framjee Patel had severed his connection. See A. C. Pointon: *The Bombay Burmah Trading Corporation Limited, 1863–1963* (London, 1964), pp. 2–3, and 133.
   The pioneer of the cotton-mill industry in Bombay, Cowasjee Nanabhoy Davar, and his father, had been brokers to British companies. Another pioneer of the cotton-mill industry, Maneckjee Petit, had been at first an apprentice in the agency house of Messrs Sutton

The collaboration between British and Indian businessmen in the sphere of business was not confined to the Parsis or to western India. Premchand Roychand, a Hindu, for instance, was a broker to the firm of Ritchie, Stewart and Company in Bombay.[123] In eastern India, Dwarakanath Tagore in the early part of the century and Neel Comul Sen in the later part were associated in business with Europeans. One can perhaps detect a change in the degree of association between European and Indian business over the nineteenth century, particularly in eastern India. As industrial capitalism changed the face of Britain and – aided by financial and political arrangements – tightened its grip over the Indian market, the European gains from collaboration with Indians on something approaching equal terms lessened. Dwarakanath Tagore was the most famous and the most enterprising Indian in eastern India to have had European businessmen as partners in the 1830s and 1840s: he has been claimed as the originator of the managing agency system which has hitherto been taken to be a peculiarly British invention.[124] After the death of Tagore and the failure of the Union Bank, Indian enterprise in eastern India suffered a definite setback. The confidence of the wealthy Indian in the benefits of collaboration with the British had already been shaken by the failure of the European agency houses in the early years of the 1830s when Indian creditors were very badly hit. However, even in 1860, one finds the firm of M. M. Bysack and Brothers as partners in the jute export business of Playfair, Duncan and Company, the parent company of Duncan Brothers and Company.[125] In 1863 four Indian businessmen in partnership with three Europeans founded the Calcutta City Banking Corporation, which was the original name of the National Bank of India.[126] But the further development of London as the centre of the world money market, and of eastern India as the major supplier of exports to Europe and the new colonies, helped European businessmen to oust Indians from positions of partnership. By the end of the nineteenth century, apart from Sir Rajendranath Mookerjee, there is practically no Indian in eastern India who is a partner of a large British Indian firm.[127] In

Malcolm and Company and then a broker to Messrs Dyren, Hunter and Company. The family surname, 'Petit', was acquired through business connection with the French. See Mehta: *Cotton Mills of India*, Chapter II, and S. M. Rutnagur: *Bombay Industries: The Cotton Mills* (Bombay, 1927), pp. 10, 705 and 720. The connection with European businessmen did not amount to subservience to them, for both Davar and Petit did a large trade on their own account. Cowasjee's father was elected a member of the Committee of the Bombay Chamber of Commerce.

[123] Playne and Wright: *The Bombay Presidency*, p. 192.

[124] See Blair Kling: 'The Origin of the Managing Agency System in India', *The Journal of Asian Studies*, XXVI, No. 1, November 1966, pp. 37–48 and N. K. Sinha: 'Indian Business Enterprise: Its Failure in Calcutta (1800–1848)', *Bengal Past and Present*, Diamond Jubilee Number, July–December 1967, pp. 112–23.

[125] *The Duncan Group*, pp. 23–4.

[126] Tyson: *100 Years of Banking in Asia and Africa*, Chapter II.

[127] The Calcutta Jute Dealers' Association: *Report of the Committee from 1st January*

Bombay, however, Indian businessmen soon emerged as industrialists in the field of cotton mills and the terms of collaboration between British and Indian business remained more equal than in the rest of India.

After the First World War, with the strengthening of the national movement and the weakening of British imperial power, the Government of India was prepared to make concessions to Indian businessmen in order to enlist their support against 'extremist' elements. Hence Indian businessmen no longer had to woo the favours of the government so directly. This was obviously not true of all industries or all business groups. The house of Tata, for example, became very dependent on government protection in the field of iron and steel. The board of directors of the Tata Iron and Steel Company in 1925 consisted of the following men: Sir D. J. Tata, Sir Sassoon David, Bart, Sir Cowasjee Jehangir, Bart, Sir Fazulbhoy Currimbhoy, R. D. Tata, Narottam Morarjee, the Hon. Mr Lalubhai Samaldas, F. E. Dinshaw, the Hon. Mr Pheroze C. Sethna, Sir Purshotamdas Thakurdas, and Sir Prabha-Shankar D. Pattani.[128] Lalubhai Samaldas and Pheroze C. Sethna were both later knighted. Thus most of the directors had proved their loyalty to the British rulers in the past. Furthermore, the Tata organization embarked on a systematic policy of recruiting former British civil servants or former officers of the Railway Board, who often presented their case to the Indian Tariff Board. J. C. K. Peterson, I. C. S., was Controller of Munitions and Director of Industries, Bengal, before he joined Tata Sons Limited as a director in 1919. S. K. Sawday was also in the Indian Civil Service before he joined the TISCO in 1919. R. H. Mather had served as technical adviser to the Indian Tariff Board in its first enquiry into the case for protection to the steel industry before he joined the TISCO as assistant general manager (in 1927). Later Sir Frederick James, a representative of British business, was similarly recruited and was put in charge of the Delhi office of Tata Sons Limited during the Second World War.[129] Sir Alfred Chatterton served briefly as an adviser to the Tata Industrial Bank. On the other side, Sir Jwala Prasad Srivastava represented the Upper India Chamber of Commerce, which was dominated by European businessmen, in the United Provinces Legislative Council from 1926 to 1936 and was elected again in 1937 from the same constituency to the new United Provinces Legislative Assembly.[130]

---

to 31st December 1927 (Calcutta, 1928), p. 21, lists the names of assistant brokers of the members of the Association; these turn out to be all Indians, most of them Bengalis. But the articles of association (pp. 12–17 of the *Report*) restricted membership to European dealers.

[128] *IITB, 1925–26* (Calcutta, 1925), pp. 401–2.

[129] Part of the information about James, Mather, Peterson and Sawday was supplied by Tata Limited, London; the rest is derived from the *Industrial Handbook 1919* of the Indians Munitions Board, the *Reports and Evidence* of the ITB, the JRSA. and from *Evidence (Report of the Indian Fiscal Commission)*.

[130] See the *Indian Year-Book, 1939–40*, Vol. xxvi (Bombay, 1939), p. 1085.

In eastern India, in the jute industry, and in export and import trade in general, the competition between Indian and European businessmen became acute after the First World War; furthermore, government help in any direct form was of limited value in the case of commodities of which the main consumers were ordinary Indians rather than the government or the railways. Hence we find in this region evidence of a more direct conflict between Indian and European businessmen than elsewhere.[131]

As Indian businessmen became more conscious of their potential power and opportunities in India, their attitude towards foreign capital became ambiguous. When they found that European-controlled business competed directly with Indian firms they took up a hostile attitude towards all foreign capital. However, since they were not yet strong enough to control the state apparatus and were conscious that other classes and groups might come to succeed the British, they were ever eager to make it easy for British rulers to hand over power gradually. Finally, when the first steps towards the control of major industries had been taken by Indian businessmen, they found that their financial and technical resources did not measure up to the standards of advanced capitalism. They were thus eager to welcome foreign investment from all advanced capitalist countries. This last phase of development, however, began only during the Second World War.[132]

6.11 SOCIAL ROOTS OF INDIAN BUSINESSMEN AND THEIR POLITICAL INTERESTS

We now turn to the social, national and regional roots of entrepreneurship in India. The European entrepreneurs who entered industry on a large scale generally made their money in trade, labour contracts or the financing of indigo or tea planters, as the examples of Bird and Company, Andrew

[131] See for example, the evidence of D. P. Khaitan and of the Marwari Chamber of Commerce in *Evidence* (*Report of the Indian Fiscal Commission*), Vol. ii (Calcutta, 1923), pp. 419–36. Successful collaborators represented in the Fiscal Commission, such as Sir R. N. Mookerjee and Sir Maneckjee Dadabhoy, were alarmed at the extreme protectionist stand taken by Khaitan. Khaitan was a member of the Birla group and became general manager of Birla Brothers Limited: *Indian Year-Book, 1939–40*, Vol. xxvi, p. 1029. In practice, of course, Indian traders sold British cotton piecegoods in spite of exhortations from Mahatma Gandhi at the height of the non-co-operation movement, because it was profitable for them to do so. In Bombay the representatives of the mill-owners in the assembly were generally opposed to the civil disobedience movement, although they obviously profited by it. The Bombay–Lancashire pact of 1933 was seen by Nehru and many other Indians (including businessmen like Birla) as a betrayal of the Indian nationalist cause. See J. Nehru: *An Autobiography* (London, 1936), p. 367.

[132] Michael Kidron, in *Foreign Investments in India* (London, 1965), pp. 19–26, and pp. 65–73, has surveyed Indian attitudes to foreign capital before independence. He does not, however, stress the ambiguity in the attitudes of Indian capital towards British rule and towards capital from advanced capitalist countries even before independence. The change from hostility to foreign capital to eager collaboration with it was not as clear-cut as he makes it out to be.

Yule, Binny and Company and Begg, Sutherland and Company show. The tea planters or indigo planters themselves rarely graduated to become managing agents in industry.[133] Nor did any European owners of specialized engineering firms come to control any large section of industry. The one apparent exception is Martin and Company; but Martin and Company had a very large business as building contractors and enjoyed extensive government patronage. They were ultimately able to acquire the interests of Burn and Company Ltd, who had specialized in railway engineering and who were hard hit by the contraction in railway investment in the early twenties.[134]

The European managing agency houses combined the interests of trading, agency, industry and financing of planters all through our period, and there was no sharp distinction between commercial and industrial interests. The Indian managing agency houses which followed them and became large industrialists were also generally involved in a large number of fields; in the case of a firm such as the house of Tata the industrial interests were, however, mixed up with ordinary trading or contracting interests to a far lesser degree.

Among the Indian competitors of European firms for the control of trade and industry the community of the Parsis achieved early prominence. It has been claimed that the Parsis were endowed with Protestant values and that it was these values which enabled them to emerge as industrial entrepreneurs.[135] However, as we have seen earlier, in western India, Indian industrialists in general, and not just Parsis, were in control of manufactur-

---

[133] Although the indigo planters – who later turned to sugar-cane when synthetic dyes ruined the indigo trade – operated much larger farms than ordinary *ryots* and often used fertilizers on a large scale, they did not bring about any 'revolution' in agriculture. Many of them leased out their land to tenants and found that they could reap a higher profit this way than by adopting capitalist methods of production. Thus they are best regarded as improving *zemindars* rather than as a vanguard of the capitalist revolution in agriculture. See Playne and Wright: *Bengal and Behar, Assam and Orissa*, pp. 296–9 ('The Doulatpur Concern') and p. 329 ('Naraipur Zemindary'); RC on Agriculture in India: *Evidence*, Vol. xiii, *Evidence Taken in Bihar and Orissa* (Calcutta, 1928), pp. 429–40 (evidence of N. Meyrick, General Secretary, Bihar Planters' Association Ltd); and ITB: *Oral Evidence (Report on Sugar)*, Vol. ii (Calcutta, 1932), pp. 288–92 (Evidence of E. C. Danby and W. W. Murray of the Behar Planters' and Cane Growers' Association). Both the Doulatpur concern and the Naraipur *zemindary* leased out land and became *zemindars*; Meyrick estimated that for operations on a scale which he would consider economic (1,000 acres), Rs. 300,000 would be required; Danby's estate covered 2,500 acres and Murray's covered 1,400 acres. They used both motor tractors and bullock ploughs and no steam tackles. On the paucity of research in the Indian indigo industry – either on the agricultural or on the manufacturing side – before it was hit by synthetic dyes, see D. J. Reid: 'Indigo in Behar', in Playne and Wright: *Bengal and Behar, Assam and Orissa*, pp. 257–8.

[134] Playne and Wright: *Bengal and Behar, Assam and Orissa*, pp. 154–7; K. C. Mahindra: *Sir Rajendra Nath Mookerjee* (Calcutta, 1962), p. 123, and *Growth and Perspective* (Martin Burn, Calcutta, 1968), p. 11.

[135] R. E. Kennedy: 'The Protestant Ethic and the Parsis', *The American Journal of Sociology*, 1962–3, pp. 11–20, reprinted in N. J. Smelser (ed.): *Readings in Economic Sociology* (Englewood Cliffs, N.J., 1965), pp. 16–26.

ing industry. If it was a Protestant value-system which alone enabled the Parsis to emerge as captains of industry, what enabled the banias and the Brahmans of Ahmedabad to emerge as pioneers of the cotton-mill industry? Why is it that Parsis were never able to play an important role in the Ahmedabad cotton-mill industry?[136]

The emergence of the Parsis in the field of business is explained better in terms of a special set of circumstances which started with the coming of the European merchants to India by sea. Before the Parsis began to find themselves useful as go-betweens between various groups of European merchants and Indian rulers or as brokers' agents or interpreters for British or Dutch merchants, they had lived for more than nine hundred years in India as a community primarily dependent on land.[137] If the values of the Parsis *were* important they were probably important more because they marked them out in the eyes of the Europeans as collaborators in trade than because they made their possessors intrinsically more enterprising.[138] When the British established a port and factory at Bombay, many Parsis followed them there. As at the end of the eighteenth century Surat declined, and Bombay emerged as the largest port in the west of India, the Parsis also prospered.[139] They accumulated their capital first from the opium trade,[140] and then from the cotton trade, particularly during the American Civil War.

However, in spite of their 'special relationship' with the British rulers,[141]

---

[136] Howard Spodek: 'The "Manchesterisation" of Ahmedabad', *Economic Weekly* (Bombay), xvii, No. 11, March 1965, pp. 483–90.

[137] Dosabhai Framji Karaka: *History of the Parsis* (London, 1884), Vol. 2, pp. 1–13.

[138] 'Either the Parsis had the knack of ingratiating themselves in the favour of Europeans or they were selected by them for their intelligence, business habits, and integrity, for certainly the closest confidence and most cordial relations were soon established.' *Ibid.*, p. 9. Again: 'There is one trait in their character for which the Parsis are remarkable, and that is loyalty to their Government', *Ibid.*, p. 50.

[139] On the decline of Surat as a port, see Gazetteers of the Bombay Presidency: Vol. ii, *Surat & Broach* (Bombay, 1877), pp. 166–77.

[140] The founder of Jamsetjee Jejeebhoy and Sons was Jamsetjee Jejeebhoy, the first Parsi (and Indian) baronet and the wealthiest Parsi of his time. The firm was the Bombay correspondent of Jardine, Matheson and Company, which was one of the largest British firms trading with China. See Michael Greenberg: *British Trade and the Opening of China* (Cambridge, 1951), pp. 146–51 and 164. Matheson described the Parsi firm as 'the best-managed business this side of the Cape'; *Ibid.*, p. 164n.

[141] The following quotation from a book written by a Parsi admirer of British rule, R. P. Masani, about another loyal Parsi, N. M. Wadia, reaches almost poetic heights in describing the fervour of Parsi loyalty: 'Fifty-six enthusiastic leading citizens of Bombay sent a requisition to the Sheriff of Bombay (12-10-1837) for convening a public meeting to send an address to the girl-queen (Victoria), felicitating her on her accession to the throne. Forty-two of them were Europeans, thirteen Parsis and only one Hindu. The name of one of the Parsi signatories is of peculiar interest to us today – Maneckji Nowrojee Wadia . . . Had he a premonition that Queen Victoria would be loved, esteemed and adored as the queenliest of queens throughout the British Empire, and that his wife and son would be two of her most fervent admirers amongst her Indian subjects?' R. P. Masani: *N. M. Wadia and His Foundation* (Bombay, 1961), p. 1. Not all Parsis were loyal in the same way. Dadabhai Naoroji, who probably has the greatest

the Parsis would not have been able to accumulate capital out of trade in a big way and to acquire the experience of markets which comes through external trade, had western India fallen under British sway in the days of rapacious conquest and plunder by the East India Company. With the exception of the Sikhs, the Marathas resisted the British longest of all; even when the Peshwa was finally overthrown in 1818, large areas remained under the rule of the four Maratha chieftains, the Scindia, the Gaekwad, the Holkar and the Bhonsla, although the territory of the last ruler was later absorbed into British India. During the struggle with the Marathas, the British needed the Parsis as collaborators and sometimes as financiers; the British traders had less time to establish themselves in western India, and by the beginning of the nineteenth century, wider political considerations had already begun to moderate the trading methods of European businessmen. Finally, the hinterland of Bombay was nowhere near as extensive as that of Calcutta, and before the coming of the railways it was pretty inaccessible. The British could not establish indigo or tea plantations in the relatively arid Deccan plateau, nor did they find any rich mines comparable to those of Bengal and Bihar. For all these reasons not only Parsis but other Indian trading communities also faced much less competition from European businessmen than in eastern India. The indigenous trading classes could also count to some extent on the patronage of the native principalities. The merchants of Ahmedabad and Baroda also had a share of the profits of the opium trade, which was known as the Malwa trade,[142] though probably these profits were much smaller than those that were made from the trade that passed through Bombay.

The Parsis thus were only a section – though in the nineteenth century the most important section – of the trading and business communities of western India which later entered industry. They did have some special advantages over the others: they had no caste system, and no gainful occupation was shameful to them. A Parsi family – the Wadias – had been master ship-builders to the East India Company until the closure of the Bombay dockyard. The Parsis had had no inhibitions against journeys overseas. All these factors probably made them more flexible in their trading methods, and conferred some initial advantage on them in technical education. Certainly one finds the Parsis outnumbering other Indian communities separately (and often together) in the supervisory jobs in cotton mills even in 1925.[143]

The Parsis also had a remarkably developed sense of civic life. Under Sir Pherozshah Mehta, the administration of Bombay became a model of

claim to be considered as the father of political (as distinct from cultural) nationalism in India, was a Parsi.

[142] Gazetteers of the Bombay Presidency: Vol. IV, *Ahmedabad* (Bombay, 1879), p. 64.

[143] S. M. Rutnagur: *Bombay Industries: The Cotton Mills* (Bombay, 1927), pp. 298–311.

municipal administration. They also donated money for civic purposes on a very large scale: in spite of initial congestion, Bombay thus became a much better-developed city than Calcutta;[144] for while the British owners of jute mills might be prepared to erect barracks for their coolies or riverside bungalows for their managers, very few of them gave away any money for public purposes at all.[145] Granted all these advantages, one has still to attribute the leadership of the Parsis in industry as much to their location in a particular region of India as to their initial advantages and their special qualities as a community.

We have already noticed the contrast between eastern and western India in terms of the control of industrial capital by Indians and Europeans. It was, and it still is, sometimes contended that the late emergence of Indian industrial entrepreneurship in eastern India was due to one of three factors: (a) the Bengali middle classes were averse to trade and industry and preferred the liberal professions; (b) the Indian businessmen in general were interested only in trade or banking and would not enter industry because it did not promise a quick return;[146] (c) the big merchants of eastern India had been eliminated by the Permanent Settlement and eastern India had been converted into 'a landlords' paradise' so that investment in land was much more attractive than other types of investment.[147]

Taking the last point first, one has to observe that while the Permanent Settlement was probably very important in converting Indian merchants of eastern India into landlords, the scope of their operation had already become limited by the trading activities of the East India Company and its servants. Further, the Permanent Settlement did not satisfactorily dispose of the

---

[144] On Parsi munificence for civic and charitable purposes, see L. R. Windham Forrest: 'The Town and the Island of Bombay – past and present', *JSA*, XLIX, No. 2534, 14 June 1901, pp. 579–80; Masani: *N. M. Wadia and His Foundation*, Ch. 10; and J. R. P. Mody: *Jamsetjee Jejeebhoy – the first Indian Knight and baronet* (Bombay, 1959), Ch. 7 and 8.

[145] Sir Percy Newson was apparently the first British merchant of Calcutta – and remained practically the only one – to give away any substantial amount of money (Rs. 1 million) for public purposes. 'The opportunities of helping their own poorer folk, of showing their gratitude to so tender an adoptive mother as India are spread round them in profusion, but they turn aside and remit the money not invested to Blighty, eagerly snatching at the advantage of a rising rupee.' 'Ditcher's Diary' in *Capital* (Calcutta), 3 January 1920, p. 11.

[146] For an authoritative statement of the first two propositions see Report of *IIC* (PP 1919, XVII), pp. 64–5; for an earlier statement of a similar kind by one of India's foremost historians, see Jadunath Sarkar: *The Economics of British India* (Calcutta, 1911), particularly the preface ('To my countrymen'), and Chapters 2 and 7. For a modern, if not very sophisticated, statement of the second proposition, in a widely-used textbook, see R. Chatterji: *Indian Economics* (Calcutta, 1959), p. 134.

[147] For a contemporary exposition of this view, applied to the whole of India, see Barrington Moore, Jr: *Social Origins of Dictatorship and Democracy* (London, 1967), pp. 345–70. For a description of the process of conversion of the Indian merchants into landlords, see N. K. Sinha: *The Economic History of Bengal*, Vol. I (Calcutta, 1961), and Vol. II (Calcutta, 1962), particularly Chapters 7–9 of Vol. II.

problem of native financiers from the point of view of the servants of the East India Company and the early European merchants. The Bank of Bengal was established specifically with the objective of minimizing the dependence of the East India Company and European merchants on Indian bankers and traders for finance. There was one Indian director of the Bank of Bengal at its very beginning (it was established in 1806 under another name); afterwards no Indian sat on the board of directors until the end of the First World War.[148]

There were later efforts by Indian – specifically Bengali – traders to make a breakthrough in industry. The failure of the European agency houses in the early 1830s ruined many Indians associated with them, whereas the original partners of the agency houses were often safely overseas with their profits. In 1829, Dwarakanath Tagore organized the Union Bank in association with European merchants; he went on to become one of the pioneers of the coal industry in Bengal (the mines acquired by his company later formed the nucleus of the Bengal Coal Company, the biggest coal company of India); he was also a pioneer of steam navigation on the rivers of India.[149] The India General and Navigation Company owed its inception to the efforts of Tagore and his European associates. As we mentioned earlier, Blair Kling has now credited him with originating the managing agency system.[150] But after Tagore's death in 1846 and the failure of the Union Bank in 1847, this phase of Indian entrepreneurship was ended. During the next sixty years and more, Bengal and Bihar became the suppliers of raw materials – jute and indigo – and of the new beverage – tea – to the expanding European and North American markets. The hold of British entrepreneurs on the economy was probably also tightened through the control of all channels of trade and organized banking. The Calcutta City Banking Corporation, originally established in Calcutta in 1863 with four Indian and three European directors, was converted into a sterling company, the National Bank of India, in 1866 with no Indian directors at all.[151] Finally, the confident advance of capitalism in Britain after 1840, with the final victory of the power loom and the steam locomotive, completed the process of turning India, along with other colonies, into farmyards for the British factories and industrial towns.

The above analysis is almost certainly over-simplified, and tries to telescope too much of history into a few paragraphs. But it should still be a

[148] C. N. Cooke: *The Rise, Progress and Present conditions of Banking in India* (Calcutta, 1863); H. Sinha: *Early European Banking in India* (London, 1927), and A. Tripathi: *Trade and Finance in the Bengal Presidency* (Calcutta, 1956).

[149] Kishori Chand Mitra: *Dwarakanath Tagore* (Calcutta, 1962) (Bengali translation of the book published in 1870). See also N. K. Sinha: 'Indian Business Enterprise: Its Failure in Calcutta (1800–1848)', *Bengal Past and Present*, Diamond Jubilee Number, July–December 1967, pp. 112–23.

[150] B. Kling: 'The origin of the managing agency system in India'.

[151] Tyson: *100 years of banking in Asia and Africa*, Chapters 1–3.

corrective to the usual brands of 'explanation' which relegate all responsibility for the relative obscurity of Indian entrepreneurship in eastern India on to 'values' or caste restrictions. Even if the Bengali middle classes were not keen entrepreneurs, the Marwaris and Vaisyas from upper India were. To say that they did not enter industry because they were interested mainly in trade does not solve the problem, for we have seen that British managing agents also had a large stake in trade. Furthermore, how did the same group of Indian traders emerge as aggressive entrepreneurs, after the First World War? The answers must lie at least partly in (a) the thorough orientation of eastern India to the raw-material-supplying function associated with a colony and (b) the persistent advantages enjoyed by the Europeans not only because of their early start and acquaintance with external markets but also because of the racial alignment of government patronage and the financial and other services supporting and reinforcing European control over trade and industry.

That this racial feeling was there is confirmed by the evidence of contemporary observers, including British administrators.[152] It found concrete expression in the legal system, in the different degrees of punishment inflicted on Europeans and Indians for the same offence, particularly when the offence was committed by a European against an Indian or an Indian against a European. We have already referred to the social barriers erected by Europeans against Indians. This had tangible results in the different degrees of facility enjoyed by the Indians and Europeans in respect of the handling of goods by the railways, most of whose superior officials were Europeans. Finally, this was also reflected in the racial discrimination practised by European businessmen against Indians in respect of appointment to responsible positions.[153] Since even people trained in a technical institution very much needed further practical training whether in India or in England,[154] this effectively barred Indians from acquiring technical experience suitable for business. This was reflected in, among other things, the

[152] See, for example, C. E. Buckland: 'The City of Calcutta', *JSA*, LIV, No. 2,776, 2 February 1906, pp. 275–94, at p. 292: 'Racial feeling is never absent from Calcutta. It is impossible to assert that friendly relations exist between the different races, as has been claimed to be characteristic of Madras . . . Social intercourse between the Europeans and natives makes but little progress.' For a remarkable example of rationalization of the feeling of superiority on the part of the Europeans see Slater: *Southern India*, p. 332. On the racial bias of law and justice in British India, see B. B. Misra: *The Indian Middle Classes* (London, 1961), pp. 377–9.

[153] See, for example, *Report of a committee appointed by the Secretary of State for India to inquire into the system of state technical scholarships established by the Government of India in 1904, with Appendices* (PP 1913, XLVII), p. 25.

[154] See section 5.7 above. At first non-official associations organized by Indians were established in Bengal, South India, Malwa, and other parts of India to send Indian scholars to be trained in modern science and technology. Then the native states of Baroda, Hyderabad and Mysore and the Government of India granted scholarships to Indian students for training abroad in branches such as mining and textile technology. But these Indian students often faced discrimination in the U.K. The committee which

virtually complete absence of Indians from supervisory posts in jute mills, as contrasted with the staffing of cotton mills mainly by Indians from the 1920s onwards, in spite of the fact that cotton mills almost certainly required a greater degree of technical expertise.[155]

The Indian entrepreneurial groups which emerged after the First World War generally came from trading castes or communities. Before the First World War, many Indian doctors and lawyers had tried their hand at industrial enterprise. Landlords were often associated in these enterprises. Dr Nilratan Sarkar in Bengal had started the National Tannery; Dr P. C. Roy had started the Bengal Chemical and Pharmaceutical Works.[156] In Bombay Dr Balchandra Bhatwadekar (Dr Balchandra Krishna) and Laxmanrao Kirloskar had been associated intimately with industrial enterprises: Kirloskar was probably one of the most imaginative industrial entrepreneurs of the country. In the Punjab, Lala Harkishan Lal, an Arora by caste and a lawyer by training, was the founder of Bharat Insurance, and a promoter of a host of companies including cotton mills and the Lahore Electric Supply Company Limited.[157] In Bengal again, Maharaja Manindra Chandra Nundy started the Calcutta Pottery Works in collaboration with Baikunthanath Sen.[158] In the United Provinces, the Raja of Baraon started a sugar factory which failed;[159] a little later the Raja of Baneli (in Bihar) started the Kirtyanand Iron and Steel Works Limited, which manufactured iron and steel castings and turned out to be an ill-fated enterprise when the government refused to protect steel castings by tariffs or bounties.[160] During and before the First World War many Indian traders started match factories and glass factories. Indeed, there was no shortage of entrepreneurship among Indians if 'entrepreneurship' means the willingness to commit capital for a risky industrial enterprise.[161] What was lacking mostly was the proper

was appointed by the Government of India in 1913 to review the working of state technical scholarships was told by Mr Levinstein (in England): 'We do not want Indians, but there is a certain amount of patriotism, and we will help England to help India'. It was told by Sir William Mather: 'I do not think it is possible to meet the case except by the council of India in London making it a matter of patriotic duty on the part of employers in certain industries to contribute to the welfare of India by affording opportunities for some of these well-selected fellows.' The *ITJ*, February 1914, p. 169.

[155] See Chapter 8 below.

[156] *Evidence (Report of IIC)*, Vol. II (PP 1919, XVIII) pp. 34–52, 78–88, 335–47.

[157] Playne and Wright: *The Bombay Presidency*, 'Bharat Insurance Company Limited'.

[158] H. Ghosh: *The Advancement of Industry* (Calcutta, 1919), p. 90.

[159] Playne and Wright, *The Bombay Presidency*, p. 423.

[160] ITB: *Evidence (Report on steel)* (Calcutta, 1924), Vol. II, p. 257.

[161] See, for example, the evidence of C. A. Innes, the then Director of Industries, Madras, in *Evidence (Report of IIC)*, Vol. III (PP 1919, XIX), p. 149. Commenting on the failures of Indian glassworks Alfred Chatterton wrote: 'The industry seems to have had a peculiar fascination for Indians, who undeterred by the failures of comparatively large concerns run by Europeans, started 16 glass factories on a smaller scale between the years 1906 and 1913.' Indian Munitions Board, *Industrial Handbook 1919* (Calcutta, 1919), p. 262.

environment for investment in the industries chosen and experience on the part of the entrepreneurs with markets and the patient business of management. Since the firms had to compete in a free market with industries from advanced countries, they also needed considerable amounts of capital to survive.

It was the creation of a more suitable environment for industrial investment, on however restricted a scale, which induced Indian trading communities to enter modern industry in a big way, first in the twenties and in much more significant numbers in the thirties. The case of the Chettiars can be cited to illustrate our point. The Nattukottai Chettiars came from the districts of Ramnad and the State of Pudukottai in Madras; they had a very highly developed agency system for money-lending and trading and were the chief banking and money-lending community in Madras.[162] They were also extremely important in the internal trade and finance of the whole of South-East Asia.[163] Furnivall estimated the capital employed by them in Burma alone to be Rs. 750 million in 1930.[164] But they did not enter large-scale industry in significant numbers until protective tariffs had been imposed on the import of cotton textiles, and the grip of the Europeans on the economy of southern India had been loosened in other ways.[165]

During the twenties many of the early Indian entrepreneurs with small capital or with no experience in trade or finance were weeded out, and the degree of concentration of industry probably increased in spite of the entry of new groups. We have already adduced some evidence for the jute mills of Calcutta which supports this. The evidence from Bombay is a little ambiguous. For on the one hand, in the depression of the early 1930s, the Currimbhoy group of mills, controlling probably the largest number of looms and spindles under a single business group, failed. But on the other

[162] See the Madras Provincial Banking Enquiry Committee, Vol. I, *Report* (Madras, 1930), pp. 186–7, and Vol. III, *Written Evidence – Contd.* (Madras, 1930), pp. 1101–18, (evidence of the Nattukottai Nagarathars' Association and of C. A. C. Kasinathan Chettiar) for their business methods. According to the *Report*, the capital of the Chettiars had increased from Rs. 100 million in 1896 to Rs. 800 million in 1930, and the capital employed by them (including borrowed capital) at home and in Madras came to Rs. 750 million, which is equal to what Furnivall claimed to be the capital employed by them in Burma alone. But since both the estimates are guesswork, one cannot easily judge the truth of either claim.

[163] For information on the role of the Chettiars in Ceylon, see Compton Mackenzie: *Realms of Silver: One Hundred Years of Banking in the East* (London, 1954), p. 90; for their part in Burma see J. S. Furnivall: *An Introduction to the Political Economy of Burma* (Rangoon, 1931); for their role in Malaya, the Straits Settlements and the Dutch East Indies see G. C. Allen and A. G. Donnithorne: *Western Enterprise in Indonesia and Malaya* (London, 1957). For further details on their operations in India see Madras Provincial Banking Enquiry Committee, Vol. I, *Report* (Madras, 1930), Chapter XIII.

[164] Furnivall: *An Introduction to the Political Economy of Burma*, pp. 119–24.

[165] For the industrial enterprises of the Chettiars and their organization, see Shoji Ito: 'A Note on the "Business Combine" in India – with special reference to the Nattukottai Chettiars', *The Developing Economies* (Tokyo), Vol. IV, No. 3, 1966, pp. 367–80.

hand, the Bombay Shareholders' Association submitted a list in 1932 showing the number of directorships held by some individuals which showed an astonishing degree of interlocking of directorships:[166]

Name	Number of companies of which directorships were held
F. E. Dinshaw	65
Sir Purshotamdas Thakurdas	42
Sir Pheroze C. Sethna	34
H. P. Mody	14
Sir Fazulbhoy Currimbhoy Ebrahimbhoy	26
Sir Lalubhai Samaldas	26
N. B. Saklatwala	29

Of these names, that of Sir Fazulbhoy can be left out of consideration, since the enterprises mainly under the control of his family failed soon after. Of the others, F. E. Dinshaw was a solicitor and financier; Sir Purshotamdas Thakurdas was known as 'King Cotton', and his interests in the companies rarely included any financial stake.[167] Thus in many cases, the control was exercised through expertise in marketing and finance rather than through a personal financial stake.

However, in other parts of India in the thirties new business groups, which sometimes already had a small stake in industry, emerged in strength, generally controlling large-sized firms or many firms at the same time. Most of them belonged to the trading or banking communities. In Delhi, Lala Sri Ram, who made the Delhi Cloth and General Mills the nucleus of a large business group, came from an old banking family.[168] The Narangs, who controlled a large number of sugar mills, had been led by Dr G. C. Narang, who had a training in law and was a Vaishya by caste.[169]

In eastern and central India the house of Birla had established itself in the jute and cotton-mill industries.[170] It entered the sugar industry and the paper industry in the thirties. Sir Sarupchand Hukamchand who belonged

---

[166] ITB: *Cotton Textile Industry*, Vol. II, *Views of the Local Governments, Collectors of Customs, and written statements submitted by Associations and Committees* (Delhi, 1934), pp. 242–8.

[167] Frank Moraes: *Sir Purshotamdas Thakurdas* (Bombay, 1957), pp. 164–5. Apart from the family business in raw cotton Sir Purshotamdas had a personal financial stake in only one cotton mill, and that also for a short period only.

[168] See Punjab District Gazetteers: Vol. VA, *Delhi District with Maps* (Lahore, 1913), p. 77; Playne and Wright: *The Bombay Presidency*, pp. 659–60; *ITJ, 1890–1940, Jubilee Souvenir* (Bombay, January 1941), p. 326.

[169] *Debrett's Peerage, Baronetage, Companionage, etc.*, 1941, p. 1166.

[170] The Kesoram Cotton Mills, the Birla Cotton Mills, the Birla Jute Manufacturing Company – all in or near Calcutta – and the Jiyajirao Cotton Mills in Gwalior had been registered between 1919 and 1921: *Joint-Stock Companies in British India and in the Indian States of Hyderabad, Mysore, Baroda, Gwalior, Indore and Travancore, 1929–30* (Calcutta, 1932). The Birlas like other entrepreneurs had made their money in trade. Raja Baldev Das Birla apparently started in business at the age of eleven, and founded a

to a Jain trading family of Marwar and central India and had accumulated capital in the opium trade,[171] in banking and in trade in cotton, grain and ready-made goods, entered the jute trade in Calcutta, established one of the first Indian-controlled jute mills and also put his money into a factory producing steel castings by means of the electric process. In the thirties the house of Juggilal Kamlapat Singhania became prominent at Cawnpore, setting up cotton gins and oil and flour mills before the war and later starting cotton and sugar mills and diversifying into several other fields.[172] This family like the others seems to have been established at Cawnpore in trade and banking long before it entered the field of industry.[173] At about the same time the Dalmia Jain family started sugar mills and provided a strong challenge to the Associated Cement Companies on the one hand and the European-controlled paper mills on the other, by setting up new mills which were expected to have a significant impact on the market.[174] Among the older Indian enterprises of Calcutta, the firm of Sir Rajendranath Mookerjee, Martin and Company, emerged as leaders in the production of pig iron and steel.

In southern India industrial growth was slow during the twenties; the new enterprises were practically all cotton mills. With a higher degree of tariff protection for cotton piecegoods, the rate of growth of looms and particularly spindles in the south (primarily in Coimbatore, Madras and Madura) was

firm in Bombay with his father at the age of fifteen (in 1879). He moved to Calcutta in 1901 and retired from business in 1920. His son Ghanshyam Das Birla, who was probably the most influential spokesman of the 'nationalist' wing of Indian businessmen (which did not prevent him, however, from co-operating with the government in the Indo-British trade negotiations of 1936–7), joined the family business at the age of 12 and started independent trade as a jute and gunny broker at the age of 16 (round about 1910). See G. D. Binani and T. V. Rama Rao: *India at a Glance: A Comprehensive Reference Book on India* (Calcutta, 1954), pp. 1703–4. It is symptomatic of the close alliance between trade, industry and landlordism in India that G. D. Birla was described as 'mill-owner, merchant and *zamindar*' in *Indian Year Book, 1939–40*, Vol. xxvi, p. 988.

[171] He was reputed to have made a profit of more than 10 million rupees in three years from trade in opium: Playne and Wright: *The Bombay Presidency*, pp. 898–901.

[172] Hazari: *Structure of the Corporate Private Sector*, p. 152, and *Report of the Monopolies Inquiry Commission 1965*, Vols. i and ii (Delhi, 1965), pp. 61–3.

[173] UP District Gazetteers: Vol. xix, *Cawnpore*, p. 74; the UP Provincial Banking Enquiry Committee 1929–30: Vol. iv, *Evidence* (Allahabad, 1931), pp. 65–74 (evidence of Parshotamdas Singhania of Messrs. Seth Amritlal Gulzarilal of Firozabad, district Agra); S. D. Tripathi: *The Kanpur Money Market* (Delhi, 1966), pp. 11–16. The partners of Seth Amritlal Gulzarilal, with the same surname (Singhania) as that of Juggilal Kamlapat, were mainly bankers, but also owned a glass-works and traded in glass goods. According to Hazari: *Structure of the Corporate Private Sector*, p. 152, the family of Juggilal Kamlapat migrated from Bikaner to Cawnpore in the middle of the nineteenth century.

[174] The founder, R. K. Dalmia, joined the firm of his uncle in Bombay at the age of 11, and started independent work very early. He apparently retired to Dinapore in 1929, but with the imposition of tariff protection on sugar in 1931, he started several sugar factories simultaneously, and thus his 'retirement' ended. See the *Indian Year-Book, 1939–40*, Vol. xxvi, p. 1218. For some obscure reason, Dalmia alone among businessmen finds his place in this *Year-Book* among 'Indian Nobles'.

higher. Among the new entrepreneurs were Chettiars as we have already mentioned. But there were other communities also involved in the flotation of enterprises. The introduction of cheap electric power through hydroelectric schemes, such as the Pykara Hydroelectric scheme, helped the industrialists who already had an abundant supply of cheap labour and – in the case of cotton piecegoods and cotton yarn – a large market near at hand.[175] Another factor which encouraged the growth of industry was the agricultural depression leading to an extreme degree of indebtedness of peasants: many men with liquid capital to employ found lending to peasants unprofitable and thus transferred their attention to industry. Then there was the patronage of the Mysore state government which helped both state-controlled and private enterprises with cheap loans, cheap or free land and other special privileges.[176]

In the other native states of India, such as Gwalior and Baroda, cotton mills multiplied apace, sometimes with direct state help but more often without it: the attractions were very often lower income and other taxes than in British India, cheaper labour and free or cheap land.[177] Since in most of the central Indian states the major trading community was the Marwari Hindu or Jain community,[178] naturally enough many of the new entrepreneurs came from their ranks.

In Bombay, the Parsis continued to be the dominant entrepreneurial group, but apart from the house of Tata no remarkable examples of successful daring in business are to be found. Perhaps Walchand Hirachand (a Marwari) should be considered an exception to this generalization. In collaboration with Kilachand Devchand and Narottam Morarjee, he founded the Scindia Steam Navigation Company in 1919, which became the first Indian shipping company of any size to survive the competition of the established British shipping companies. This it did in spite of the lack of State patronage (which the British shipping companies enjoyed), although

[175] The growth of the load on the Pykara hydroelectric system, which was commissioned in 1933 or so, was much faster than had been originally anticipated. By 1937–8 the system was earning over 14% of the capital outlay: *Madras, adminstration report 1937–38* (Madras, 1939), p. 181. The Mettur dam directly gave rise to the Mettur Chemical Works. The growth of cotton mills in south India was of course induced by the remarkable profitability of south-Indian mills even in times of depression. In 1934 and 1935, for example, the leading cotton mills of Bangalore and Madras continued to pay out reasonable dividends even though mills in most other parts of India were doing very badly indeed. See *Indian Finance Year-Book*, 1936, p. 256.

[176] G. B. Baldwin: *Industrial Growth in South India* (Glencoe, Illinois, 1959) provides a comprehensive account of industrial growth in south India – particularly in Mysore.

[177] To take only one example, whereas Baroda had only one cotton mill in 1905–6, it had 16 mills by 1937–8: Gov. India, CISD: *Financial and commercial statistics of British India*, 13th Issue (Calcutta, 1907).

[178] The Central India State Gazetteer Series: *Gwalior State Gazetteer*, Vol. I, *Text and Tables* (Calcutta, 1908), p. 77; *Indore State Gazetteer*, Vol. II, *Text and Tables* (Calcutta, 1908), p. 217; *Bhopal State Gazetteer*, Vol. III, *Text and Tables* (Calcutta, 1908), p. 55.

the Indian Mercantile Marine Committee had recommended various measures of State help for Indian shipping, and had stipulated that the Indian coastal trade should be reserved for 'ships the ownership and controlling interests of which are predominantly Indian'.[179] Walchand Hirachand's group later took over the Premier (originally, Tata) Construction Company which was the biggest company of its kind in western India. They also moved into sugar manufacturing in the thirties. The Walchand group was one of the top twenty business houses at the time of the enquiry by the Monopolies Inquiry Commission in 1965.[180] Among the Parsis who made a mark in business in the interwar period, F. E. Dinshaw was a successful solicitor and a financial wizard and master-minded many schemes for helping struggling mills and concerns, and finished his career by bringing about the cement merger scheme which led to the birth of the Associated Cement Companies. Sir Ness Wadia made the Bombay Dyeing and Manufacturing Company one of the best cotton mills in India. Other examples of Parsi entrepreneurship in Bombay are to be found. But apart from the Tata enterprises at Jamshedpur, and some cement companies, the enterprises of Parsis – like the enterprises of other business communities – remained confined to the regions where they were most heavily concentrated. There were few Parsi traders in the central Indian states of Gwalior, Indore or Bhopal. In Ahmedabad Kasturbhai Lalbhai and Ambalal Sarabhai made their names and fortunes in the management of both cotton mills and other new enterprises which they floated. Hence Indian entrepreneurship in the older centres did not exactly atrophy, but the greatest impact was made by the trading communities which found that investment in industry had become more profitable than traditional trade, at least up to a point.

In the above account we have stressed the different degrees of European domination of the different regions as providing the major explanation for the different degrees of Indian participation in business and industry. An alternative explanation would run in terms of the different systems of land tenure in the different regions of India. It could be argued that in the areas of *zemindari* settlement, it was profitable for businessmen to buy up land and set up as landlords rather than invest in industry; hence we would find more businessmen buying *zemindaries* in Bengal, Bihar or Madras than in, say, Bombay or the Punjab. This explanation, as it stands, cannot be accepted, because, assuming a reasonable degree of competitiveness in the

---

[179] Seth Narottam Morarjee: 'Indian Mercantile Marine', *Annals of the American Academy of Political and Social Science*, Vol. 145, Part II, 1929, p. 69. See also *Bombay Investors' Yearbook 1940* (Bombay, 1940), pp. 58–66 (Walchand Hirachand: 'Why Indian shipping does not grow').

[180] *Bombay Investors' Yearbook 1940*, pp. 71–2 (Lalchand Hirachand: 'Indian sugar industry'), and pp. 75–7 (Ratanchand Hirachand: 'Constructional engineering in India'). See also Hazari, *Structure of the Corporate Private Sector*, pp. 202–3; *Report of the Monopolies Inquiry Commission 1965*, pp. 117–18, 120.

market for titles to *zemindaries*, one would expect the net return on land as an asset to come close to that on other assets, such as real estate in towns, stocks of commodities held for speculative purposes or government paper. One would also have to explain how the surplus realized on the *zemindaries* was utilized. In terms of the argument which has been developed above it would appear that in areas dominated by European capital the room for investment of such surplus was small, so that businessmen faced a steeply declining schedule of net returns when they tried to move out of their traditional patterns of trade and asset-holding.

In testing the alternative hypothesis in terms of land tenure systems we face the familiar problem of interdependence among the explanatory variables. The areas with *zemindari* settlements were also areas with European domination of trade and industry: in Bengal the conversion of many businessmen into landlords went hand in hand with their displacement by Europeans, particularly in the fields of banking and external trade. We do find businessmen from Bengal and Madras complaining before the Indian Industrial Commission that because investment in land as an asset was so safe and profitable it was difficult to raise capital for industry.[181] But these businessmen were relatively small capitalists and in an imperfect capital market one is bound to come across such complaints. We do not meet any such complaint from the European capitalists of these areas nor from the big capitalists from Bombay.[182] Furthermore, we find that in provinces such as the United Provinces or Sind, where land was not generally held under the Permanent Settlement, the Europeans were dominant in the field of trade and industry before the First World War.

We have not discussed above the question of whether real investment in land rather than purchase of zemindaries as an asset was more profitable in Bengal than in, say, Bombay. There is very little direct evidence bearing on this question. On the other hand, we do know that in the absence of irrigation facilities it was difficult to plan cultivation in a capitalistic fashion. Only the indigo plantations and later the sugar-cane plantations of Bengal, Bihar and the United Provinces, displayed some characteristics of capitalistic agriculture. However, as we pointed out earlier (p. 200n) these planters were not really capitalistic farmers: they often used the same methods of cultivation as the peasants whose lands they had taken over, they made advances to the peasants on more or less the same conditions as prevailed for loans from landlords or money-lenders in other parts of India, and they themselves became heavily indebted to the agency houses.[183]

---

[181] See, for example, the evidence of Rai Sitanath Ray Bahadur of Bengal and of Rao Bahadur K. Suryanarayanamurti Nayudu of Madras in *Evidence (Report of IIC)*, Vol. II (PP 1919 XVIII), p. 279, and Vol. III (PP 1919 XIX), p. 88 respectively.

[182] See, for example, the evidence of C. N. Wadia, representing the Bombay Mill-owners' Association, in *Evidence (Report of IIC)*, Vol. IV (PP 1919, XIX), pp. 1–17.

[183] See Benoy Chowdhury: *Growth of Commercial Agriculture in Bengal (1757–1900)*,

There was another aspect of the land revenue system which affected the profitability of capital formation in land. In the areas of *ryotwari* settlement, the government took a direct interest in the cultivation of land because the revenues of the government were supposed to vary directly with the revenues of the peasants. The government regularly lent large sums of money as *taccavi* loans; in Bengal, however, there was very little direct lending by the government. Government expenditure on other schemes for the improvement of agriculture was also meagre.

Apart from the tenurial conditions one must also look at facilities for irrigation to discover the profitability of capital formation: there is some evidence that fertilizers were used more extensively in Madras than in other parts of India, particularly from the twenties onwards. How far this was due to government propaganda and expenditure for improvement of agriculture (for instance, through the installation of pumps and engines for lifting water), how far to the propaganda of Parry's, who began to manufacture manures and fertilizers at Ranipet before the First World War, and how far to the extension of irrigation and hydroelectricity in south India in the twenties and thirties, it is difficult to say. But again there is little evidence that entrepreneurship in agriculture provided a stepping stone to industry.[184]

The land revenue and land tenure systems prevailing in British India, and the primitive autocracies of the native states of India, definitely had an impact on the distribution of income and on the disposal of the surplus that was generated. But their impact cannot be separated from other aspects of British rule, and in particular from the policy of 'free trade' pursued by the government coupled with an informal quota system acting in favour of European traders and industrialists and against Indian traders and businessmen. The most significant results for our purpose were the impoverishment of the ordinary cultivator whatever system of land tenure he lived under,[185] and the contraction of the market for industrial goods. The princelings and *zemindars* were notorious for conspicuous consumption. Such wastage of the economic surplus was at least partly functional from the point of view of the British imperial system. The maintenance of a large number of retainers cushioned the impact of the introduction of bourgeois laws of property and personal relations, and helped stabilize an archaic social structure buffeted by the advance of capitalist imperialism. Furthermore, the failure of the

Vol. 1 (Calcutta, 1964), and D. J. Reid: 'Indigo in Behar', in Playne and Wright: *Bengal and Assam, Behar and Orissa*, pp. 255–8.

[184] There were examples of big cultivators in India entering industry. For example, a group of cultivators from the Deccan who were taken on a tour of sugar factories in the United Provinces in 1932 by the Deputy Director of Agriculture, Bombay, came back and started the Saswad Mali Sugar Factory Limited, Sholapur. See ITB: *Evidence (Report on sugar)* (Delhi, 1938–9), Vol. v, *Oral Evidence*, p. 33. But the enterprises were generally small and did not provide a base for building up a business group controlling large amounts of capital.

[185] See Chapter 4 above on the convergence of land-tenure systems.

wealthier classes to accumulate productive capital reduced the threat of competition for British businessmen in India and Britain, and widened the market for the shoddy luxury goods exported by Britain (and other European countries) to India, although the latter effect was probably of minor significance. The Government of India encouraged the luxury consumption of the *zemindars* or princelings, for they were regularly decorated for extending lavish hospitality to British officials or royal personages, and for giving away money for the benefit or amusement of British civil and military officers (in the form of benefactions for hospitals or clubs or race courses, primarily or solely meant for the use of Europeans).

The system was made economically viable by the combination (often in the same person) of the functions of the money-lender, the trader and the landlord.[186] The trader was willing to move into industry when opportunity offered. The landlord often had surpluses which he was anxious to invest given a profitable opportunity; complaints against the free-trade policy of the Government of India or its lack of interest in industrial development were not confined to industrialists.[187] Hence opposition between the interests of the landlord trader and the industrialist was not often witnessed. We find as two of the more notable though not perhaps more significant examples of collaboration, the Zemindar Farmers' Association, District Moradabad (United Provinces), and the Bihar Planters' Cane Growers' Association pleading the case for tariff protection in the sugar industry in 1930.[188] We find, on a more exalted plane, the Gaekwad of Baroda, the Scindia of Gwalior and the Holkar of Indore setting up state enterprises and helping Indian capitalists to set up factories within their territories.[189] In the south the states of Travancore-Cochin and Mysore helped in similar ways. The rulers of the native states also invested on a large scale in enterprises run by

[186] For an interesting example of a fortune based on three functions and steadfast loyalty to British rule see the description of the firm of Sitalprasad Kharagprasad in Playne and Wright: *Bengal and Assam, Behar and Orissa*, pp. 686–91. The firm moved into cotton spinning when the Bharat Abhyuday Mills, floated by more enterprising but less prudent and perhaps less wealthy promoters, were bought by them.

[187] Sir Rameshwara Singh, the Maharaja of Durbhanga, said during the budget session of 1905: 'I can assure your Excellency that there is plenty of money available: and the Indian capitalists' unwillingness would be largely overcome, if he can be convinced that his money is required for investment and not for speculation. An appreciable impetus would be given to the opening out of the country by the development of railways undertaken by private enterprise, if the Railway Board could see its way to formulating a scheme for the guaranteeing of interest': *Indian financial statement and proceedings* (PP 1905, LVII), p. 228.

[188] ITB, *Evidence (Report on sugar)* (Calcutta, 1932), Vol. I, pp. 242–9, and Vol. II, pp. 288–92.

[189] For the policies of the Scindia see H. M. Bull and K. N. Haksar: *Madhav Rao Scindia of Gwalior 1876–1925* (Gwalior, 1926), pp. 255–60. For Baroda see J. Alva: *Men and Supermen of Hindustan* (Bombay, 1943), pp. 75–88 and Gazetteers of Bombay Presidency: Vol. VII, *Baroda* (Bombay, 1883), Chapters V and VI. For other central Indian states see the Central Indian State Gazetteer Series quoted in footnote 178.

capitalists in British India,[190] although sometimes they were prevented from doing so by the Government of India.[191] The effect of rule by the native princes may have been detrimental to ordinary people; but insofar as the native states provided a market and some capital for the development of Indian enterprise, the effect on industrial growth was positive. The political separateness of the native states from British India was more important for industrial growth than the semi-feudal structure of administration within many of those states, given the discrimination practised against Indian businessmen under the imperial system.

During the 1920s, in the Legislative Assembly debates, a cleavage between the views of big landlords – particularly those who came from the more industrially backward provinces – and the views of businessmen or representatives of professional groups on questions of tariff protection can be noticed. But this rarely led to a showdown between the two groups, particularly because the Viceroy and his Executive Council had anyway the final say on most important questions. In the 1930s, with agricultural depression and widespread urban unemployment, the landlords and the businessmen came much closer in their views. At no stage does one find a difference in views comparable to that in the United States between the southern planters and the northern manufacturers before the Civil War. There was dissatisfaction particularly among the representatives of the Punjab about what was considered to be the dominance of the interests of Bombay, but this dissatisfaction had its origin in the relative backwardness of other parts of India within a capitalist framework: rarely did it imply any desire to go back to pre-capitalist relations.[192]

6.12 CONCLUSION

In summary, the conflict between European and Indian entrepreneurs was often hidden by short-term collaboration, particularly before the First World War. The most notable collaborators with British businessmen were the Parsis; but as other men from other Indian business groups emerged into prominence, they were also given the accolade of recognition through

---

[190] The case of the Scindia of Gwalior who invested in the Tata enterprises and helped them at critical moments, is well-known. Many of the native states invested their balances regularly through the same bankers and brokers in Bombay. See the evidence of Lalji Naranji of Kikabhai Premchand in Royal Commission on Indian Currency and Finance: *Evidence*, Vol. IV, pp. 244 and 251.

[191] See the evidence of Rao Bahadur R. N. Mudholkar in *Evidence (Report of IIC)*, Vol. II (PP 1919, LVIII), p. 468.

[192] One of the few thinkers to have realized that British rule automatically geared even the pre-capitalist relations towards money-making along capitalist lines and weakened what he called 'feudalism' beyond repair was D. D. Kosambi. See his review of the *Discovery of India* by J. Nehru, 'The Bourgeoisie comes of age in India', *Science and Society*, Vol. x, 1946, pp. 392–8.

the Honours List. (This was, of course, often a mark of political rather than economic collaboration.) In eastern India something like an open conflict between British and Indian businessmen developed after the First World War, particularly in the jute trade; but here again there was enough to be gained from public patronage for the hostility of the big businessman not to be turned into open hostility against British rule.

The relative importance of European and Indian entrepreneurship changed over time. On the whole, European businessmen had a relative advantage in the exploitation of export markets, and Indian businessmen in the exploitation of internal markets. Before the First World War this naturally gave the European businessmen the dominant position in trade and industry. It is noticeable that Greaves, Cotton and Company, which had grown to be the biggest group of spinning mills before the First World War, catering primarily to the Chinese market for yarn, failed to gear its production to the weaving of cloth for the Indian market when the export trade in yarn became increasingly unprofitable. The counter-example to this is found in South India where mills under European management mainly served the Indian market for cloth and yarn.

After the First World War, and much more clearly after the coming of protection, Indian entrepreneurs took the lead in the development of industries such as cement, paper and sugar, although the biggest firms in the last two fields had earlier been controlled by British managing agency houses. Indian entrepreneurs came from groups with connections in trade: very few professional, westernized Indians emerged as big industrialists. The major reasons for the relative inactivity of the Europeans in the interwar period were probably (a) political uncertainty connected with the gathering strength of the nationalist movement and the concessions made by the British Government to it, (b) the greater attractiveness of investment in the Far East (illustrated by the pulling out of the Sassoon interests from India), and (c) the difficulties faced by the British economy, which led to a massive repatriation of British capital (mainly public) in the early thirties.

Both Indian and European entrepreneurs suffered from the industrial backwardness of the economy in one major respect: neither group can be credited with any major technical innovation in our period. The low proportion of industrial investment to the national income and the small share of the capital goods industry in the modern industrial sector both told against such innovations. Thus at least during the period we are studying there is little evidence of technical dynamism brought in the wake of foreign investment.

PART II

STUDIES OF MAJOR INDUSTRIES

7

THE DEVELOPMENT OF THE COTTON-MILL INDUSTRY

7.1 HANDICRAFTS AND MILL PRODUCTION IN THE COTTON INDUSTRY

The textbook story of development of capitalist industry goes as follows: Given a blue-print of techniques, with a rise in wages a more capital-intensive technique than the one hitherto in use becomes profitable. Hence if a weaver was operating by hand only one loom it becomes profitable to add some device to speed up the production on the loom, thus increasing the amount of capital per weaver; the logical culmination becomes the displacement of the handloom by a powerloom. The *speed* of the change is not, however, dictated by the extent of rise in wages; it is determined by the rate of investment which in turn is dictated by the capitalists' share in income and their propensity to save.[1]

One can adapt this story to the Indian case and argue that there occurred a rise in the standard of living of the Indian worker at the end of the nineteenth century; this was induced by the increase in the prosperity of the peasant through the greatly increased exports of primary products. The rise in the wages of workers combined with the removal of the barriers to free competition imposed by an inefficient transport system, to bring about a situation in which the powerloom became a more profitable implement than the handloom.

If one was unwilling to attribute the superiority of the powerloom over the handloom to a rise in the standard of living of the Indian worker (because this alleged rise was difficult to prove), one stressed the absolute superiority of the new power-driven spindles and looms to the old spinning wheel and handloom in the sense that the former would be profitable whatever the relative prices of capital and labour. According to this version of the story, it was only a matter of time before powerlooms would win over handlooms in India, and since this development was associated with the

---

[1] D. Bensusan-Butt in his book *On Economic Growth* (Oxford, 1960) incorporates the capital-intensifying effect of a rise in wages into a story in which the volume of investment undertaken by the capitalists is the primary agent of change; the capitalists conquer one industry after another, the sequence leading from less capital-intensive to more capital-intensive industries. But in fact (as Professor Joan Robinson has pointed out) capitalists launch their attack on handicraft or 'simple commodity' production on several fronts.

advanced countries of Europe, it was to be welcomed, although it might involve temporary suffering for a sizeable fraction of the population.[2]

However, at the beginning of the twentieth century there were observers who realized that the story of the displacement of the handloom by the powerloom in Britain was not going to be repeated in every detail in India. One part of the story had already been repeated practically all over India, viz., the displacement of hand-spun yarn by machine-spun yarn. Although as late as 1885 most of the yarn used by handloom weavers in the Punjab was said to be spun at home,[3] hand-spinning suffered a rapid decline.[4] The earnings from hand-spinning round about 1900 came to only about an anna a day, so it was only old women or women in purdah who still carried it on. The cotton mills in India grew up primarily in order to supply the demand for coarse yarn on the part of handloom weavers in India and China, the higher counts of yarn being supplied by Lancashire. The move to powerloom weaving and to better handlooms became pronounced only after the initial stages had already been mechanized. In this there is a similarity to the British development since, apart from Kay's flying shuttle, invented in 1733, most of the technical developments in the cotton industry in Britain occurred in the spinning department until Cartwright invented the powerloom in 1785.[5]

But the situation appears to be quite different in the case of the relationship between handlooms and weaving mills. Although the weaving mills did expand their production much faster than did the handlooms throughout the period from 1900 to 1939, the handlooms also experienced a slow growth. From the point of view of profitability alone, handlooms in India did enjoy certain advantages at the beginning of the century: coarse handloom cloth was considered by the average Indian villager to be more durable than mill-made cloth. Handlooms produced multi-coloured saris which the Indian mills could not imitate, at least before the First World War; there were also local specialities in which the individual skill of the weaver and his associates was the critical factor. The mill industry might have been technically capable of producing fine Dacca muslins or intricate Kashmir shawls, but it would not have been economic for it to do so;[6] in any case the

[2] For an able statement of this view see Sir Theodore Morison: *The Economic Transition in India* (London, 1911), particularly Chapters VI and VII.

[3] Elijah Helm: 'An International Survey of the Cotton Industry', *Quarterly Journal of Economics*, 1903, pp. 417–37.

[4] See, for example, Chatterjee [IPG pub.]: *Notes*, pp. 2–3; and *Census of India*, 1911, Vol. I, *India*, Part I, *Report* by E. A. Gait (Calcutta, 1913), p. 418: 'As compared with 1901 there has been a decrease of 6.1% in the number of persons supported by textile industries (which together supported 2.6% of the *total* population in 1911). This is due mainly to the almost complete extinction of cotton spinning by hand.'

[5] W. Woodruff: *Impact of Western Man* (London, 1966), p. 207; H. H. Ghosh: *The Advancement of Industry*, pp. 142–4.

[6] The Imperial Gazetteer of India: *The Indian Empire*, Vol. III, *Economic* (Oxford, 1907), pp. 197–8.

Indian cotton mills had still to learn how to weave, bleach and print the finer varieties of cloth.

The workers in handlooms also enjoyed the advantage of working with low-cost capital and with family labour, so that the family rather than the wage labourer alone formed the economic unit; they also enjoyed special advantages in the 'sizing' of yarn.

But it would be a mistake not to stress the disadvantages of the Indian weaver which tied him down to the profession. In most parts of India, except western Punjab, weavers formed a low caste in the Hindu hierarchy, and in some cases, also in the Muslim hierarchy; they tended to be physically weak because of their sedentary occupation.[7] Very often they would work for wages that were lower than those earned by agricultural labourers.[8] They were often at the mercy of middlemen and money-lenders who supplied them with cotton or yarn and bought the cloth from them; the prices obtained for this cloth were often lower than what it really fetched in the market, which was often uncertain, and the weaver was often ignorant of market conditions.[9]

British officials, such as E. W. Collin in 1890, A. Chatterton in 1905 and A. C. Chatterjee and J. G. Cumming in 1908 had observed the persistence of the handloom weaver and his depressed condition.[10] Under the auspices of

[7] Chatterjee [IPG pub.]: *Notes*, p. 21; A. Latifi [IPG pub.]: *Industrial Punjab* (Bombay and Calcutta, 1911), p. 2.

[8] See Sir Theodore Morison: *The Industrial Organization of an Indian Province* (London, 1911), Appendix to Chapter VIII, which quotes evidence on the condition of artisans from the 'Inquiry into the Economic Condition of the Agricultural and Labouring Classes of the North-Western Provinces and Oudh', 1888. Whereas a weaver earned about an anna a day when he was employed, casual labour earned anywhere between 6 and 8 pice, that is about 50% to 100% more than a weaver. See *ibid.*, p. 193 and pp. 208–9.

[9] See, for instance, Chatterjee [IPG pub.]: *Notes*, p. 21; see also H. J. Tozer: 'The Manufactures of Greater Britain – III. India', *JSA*, LIII, No. 2,741, 2 June 1905, particularly pp. 754–6. Tozer pointed out the variability of the conditions of weavers in different parts of India. They appeared to have been harder hit in Bengal and the United Provinces than in Madras or Assam. They were said to earn about $2\frac{1}{2}$ annas a day or less in the United Provinces and up to between 6 and 10 annas a day for weaving fine cloth in Madras. But it was difficult to find out whether these earnings included the imputed earnings of other family members who helped with the work; the number of days worked in a year was also not known. Tozer, however, pointed out that most weavers were full-time workers and not agriculturalists who took up weaving as a part-time profession and that hand-weaving was a mainly urban profession. The demand for hand-woven cloth in most parts of India came either in the form of demand for coarse, durable cloth or in the form of demand for finer varieties of cloth with local popularity.

[10] E. W. Collin [IPG pub.]: *Report on the Arts and Industries of Bengal* (Calcutta, 1890), para. 28. Alfred Chatterton [IPG pub.]: *Note on Industrial Work in India* (contributed to the Industrial Conference held at Benares on 30 December 1905); A. Chatterton: 'Weaving in India', *Hindustan Review*, Vol. XV, No. 91, March 1907, pp. 235–49. He was quoted by Chatterjee [IPG pub.]: *Notes*, p. 22, with approval. Chatterjee estimated that handlooms manufactured at least one-third (by weight) of the cloth consumed in the United Provinces around 1908. J. G. Cumming [IPG pub.]: *Review of the Industrial Position and Prospects in Bengal in 1908 with Special Reference to the Industrial Survey of 1890* (Calcutta, 1908), particularly pp. 7–10.

Christian missionaries on the west coast, the Salvation Army, other private organizations and later, government Departments of Industries, efforts were made to improve the condition of the weaver. These attempts mainly took the form of introducing an improved loom – generally the ordinary hand-loom with a fly-shuttle sley – and of improving the preparatory processes – particularly warping.[11] Indian weavers' methods of sizing were generally admitted to be superior to those of the cotton mills. Many of the attempts were amateurish, made by people who knew little about either the economic or the technical problems of handloom weaving, and the improvements were too costly for the weaver. But a pitloom with a fly-shuttle used extensively in Madras came to be recognized as a suitable improved handloom, allowing the weaver to increase his daily output by between 50% and 200% (generally the wider the cloth, the greater was the gain from the use of a fly-shuttle loom).[12]

It is difficult to form an idea of the speed of diffusion of improved methods in handloom production: the Departments of Industries in the various provinces were too small and had too many interests to look after (including, for instance, providing industrial or commercial intelligence for enquiring businessmen and carrying out research work in the industrial use of Indian materials) for them to be able to provide a good survey of the improvements adopted. Since most weavers were illiterate and ignorant of the technical possibilities and the state of the market, one can hazard the guess that diffusion would have been slow even if the financial and demand conditions were favourable, unless the government took a really vigorous and continuous interest in such diffusion. But many government officials in high places, including Lord Curzon, the Viceroy, were not convinced either of the feasibility or of the utility of preserving the handloom industry.[13] It was left primarily to middle-level officials such as A. Chatterton in Madras, J. G. Cumming and E. B. Havell in Bengal, and A. C. Chatterjee in the United Provinces, and to non-official bodies, such as the Salvation Army or other Christian missionaries, and individuals such as P. N. De and Theogaraya Chetty, to try to introduce improved methods of weaving, warping and sizing among the weavers. A large part of the small-scale official effort was under a virtual moratorium after Morley's despatch of 1910 forbidding the setting up of government pioneering factories; under this interdict, for instance, the Salem weaving factory was closed.[14]

[11] At first it was considered doubtful whether the fly-shuttle loom could be at all profitable without an improvement in the warping methods used by the Indian weaver. See *Madras, a review of the Administration of the Presidency, during the year 1903–1904* (Madras, 1904), p. 112.

[12] See A. Chatterton: 'The Weaving Competitions in Madras' in *Indian Trade Journal*, Vol. IX, No. 106, 9 April 1908, pp. 54–7; and Chatterjee [IPG pub.]: *Notes*, pp. 22–7.

[13] E. B. Havell: 'Art Administration in India', *JRSA*, 4 February 1910, p. 278. For a survey of the early efforts at the improvement of handloom weaving, see Ghosh: *The Advancement of Industry*, pp. 6–8, 140–77.   [14] *Report of IIC* (PP 1919, XVII), Appendix J.

Apart from the official apathy, the handloom weavers suffered from lack of finance (many of them could not even afford to buy the English looms costing above Rs. 10), lack of demand for their products, and indebtedness to the middleman who supplied them the yarn and bought the cloth manufactured by them.[15] While the demand for mill-made cloth was countrywide, the demand for handloom cloth was local, the network of agencies for selling various kinds of cloth was extremely inadequate, and handloom weavers by themselves did not have the resources to develop them. It is fair to say that the same factors that kept the handloom weaver poor and socially depressed also prevented him from taking advantage of the improved methods to the fullest extent.

In spite of all these difficulties, the use of fly-shuttle looms did spread, often more through intercommunication among the weavers than through official propaganda.[16] A survey of fly-shuttle looms in Madras in 1911 revealed the existence of 6,528 looms with fly-shuttle sleys; the use of such sleys was practically confined to the coastal districts north of Madras, where roughly 40% of the weavers had adopted the new methods of plying the shuttle.[17] It was estimated around 1914–15 that more than 25,000 fly-shuttle looms had been introduced in Madras through the work of peripatetic parties sent out by the Department of Industries of the province.[18] Madras was probably not typical of the whole of India, since it had well-known specialities such as Madras handkerchiefs and *lungis* woven on handlooms. The Departments of Industries in the other provinces were not generally as organized or as enthusiastic for handloom work as in Madras. Hence the progress in the rest of India in this respect could be expected to be slower (unless, of course, diffusion through private effort and example was much more rapid in other parts, which seems *prima facie* doubtful). Again, the First World War, which interrupted the growth in handloom production because of the drastic decline in yarn imports from the U.K., also impeded the spread of fly-shuttle looms; the glut in the piecegoods market during the unsettled trade conditions of 1919–20 and 1920–1 aggravated the problem from the demand side and many weavers in the northern districts of Madras, who had earlier adopted improved methods, reverted to the old methods.[19] According to a census of handlooms carried out concurrently

---

[15] On problems imposed by the lack of demand see Alfred Chatterton's paper on the Salem weaving factory, contributed to the Surat Industrial Conference, December 1907, quoted in Chatterjee [IPG pub.]: *Notes*, p. 25; see also *Census of India, 1921*, Vol. XIII, Madras, Part I, *Report* (Madras, 1922), p. 196. Sir Alfred Chatterton in 1925 remarked on the futility of trying to increase the output per weaver when the demand for the products that can be turned out on old country looms is often deficient. See A. Chatterton; 'The Industrial Progress of the Mysore State', *JRSA*, Vol. LXXIII, 26 June 1925, p. 731.

[16] Cumming [IPG pub.]: *Review*, p. 9.　　　　[17] *Report of IIC* (PP 1919, XVII), p. 412.

[18] K. Tressler, Director of Industries, 'Industries' in Playne and Wright, *Southern India*, p. 627.

[19] *Census of India, 1921*, Vol. XIII, *Madras*, Part I, *Report* (Madras, 1922), p. 196.

with the Industrial Census in Bengal in 1921, out of a total of 213,886 handlooms in the province, 53,168, or roughly 25%, were fitted with fly-shuttles. The proportion was higher in districts such as Hooghly, Howrah, Jessore, Khulna, Dacca, Bakargunj, Malda, and Burdwan, but much lower in Midnapore, Murshidabad, Bankura, Mymensingh and all other districts generally. There were practically no fly-shuttle looms in Tripura State and Chittagong Hill Tracts, two districts with the largest numbers of handlooms per million of the population.[20]

Twenty years later, the Fact-finding Committee (Handloom and Mills) found that out of a total of 2 million handlooms in India, about 64% were throw-shuttle looms, 35% fly-shuttle looms, and only 1% came under other categories. Excluding Assam, the proportion of fly-shuttle looms was 44% for all India; this proportion was higher in Travancore (81%), Madras (81%), Mysore (78%), Cochin (73%), Bengal (67%) and Bombay (55%). The Committee commented: 'As we have no statistics for earlier periods, no comparison is possible. It is certain, however, that twenty years ago the number of fly-shuttle looms was far less.'[21]

Table 7.1 indicates a growth in handloom production from 1900–1 to 1914–15 with some wide fluctuations. There is a bunching of high rates of production during the years from 1904–5 to 1908–9, suggesting that the Swadeshi movement was responsible for some growth in handloom production. Contemporary accounts suggest that most of the gains from the Swadeshi movement were picked up by the mill industry, particularly since there was active campaigning against foreign yarn, which was used by handlooms; there are, however, statements suggesting that the Swadeshi movement (which preceded the political boycott movement) was responsible for the rebirth of moribund handloom centres, particularly when the movement was accompanied by an attempt to improve the technique of the weaver.[22] One should probably also attribute some of the growth to the discrimination in favour of handlooms embodied in the 1896 measure which placed an excise duty of $3\frac{1}{2}\%$ on Indian mill-made cloth to offset the duty of $3\frac{1}{2}\%$ imposed on imported cotton piecegoods for revenue purposes. Furthermore, our figures suggest that the effect of the Swadeshi movement was at best temporary, since handloom production fell again after 1908–9, not to recover fully until 1914–15. J. G. Cumming reported in 1908 that the more prosperous Serampore weavers (earning up to Rs. 30 a month) themselves wore mill-made cloth because of its cheapness, and A. C. Chatterjee reported in the same year that many of the weavers of the United

[20] *Census of India, 1921*, Vol. v, Bengal, Part 1, *Report* (Calcutta, 1923), pp. 400–2.

[21] *Report of the Fact-finding Committee (Handloom and Mills)* (Delhi, 1942), p. 31. The proportion of fly-shuttle looms was low in the provinces with a large number of looms, such as Assam, Punjab and the United Provinces; Madras was the sole exception.

[22] See, e.g. Bengal District Gazetteers, *Hooghly*, by L. S. S. O'Malley and Monmohan Chakravarti (Calcutta, 1912), pp. 182–3.

Provinces had not even heard of the increased demand caused by the Swadeshi movement.[23]

The pre-war growth in handloom production, to which attention was drawn during the enquiry by the IIC,[24] was definitely checked during the First World War. This is brought out both by the figures of yarn consumption by handlooms for all of India and for provinces such as Madras, and by the fall in the number of people dependent on cotton spinning, sizing and weaving in 1921 as compared with 1911.[25]

It is very difficult to form an idea of the change in handloom weavers' incomes over the period. A very large proportion of them were at best formally self-employed; another large fraction worked on piece-rates; only in the more organized centres with handloom factories were they paid definite money wages per day. Hence their daily earnings have very often to be worked out from other data. The wage data collected by the Department of Statistics and later on by the Department of Commercial Intelligence were generally defective, since the method for arriving at the daily earnings depended very much on the investigator, and the season in which the earnings were determined. In view of the considerable under-employment among weavers, there were bound to be wide fluctuations in the earnings from one season to the next. But from the admittedly incomplete and unsystematic data published in various issues of *Prices and wages in India*[26] one can see that before the First World War, generally speaking, weavers were just a cut above common labourers in urban centres as regards wages; while the lower limit of weavers' wages was reached by common labourers, the upper range was not. But during the war, the position of weavers seems to have deteriorated in a number of centres, in that common labourers were often earning more on an average than the weavers or at least the lower-paid among the weavers. Since in handloom weaving exceptional skill must have a premium, one suspects that the upper limit of weavers' earnings was applicable to only a small section. Both before and during the war, weavers were definitely paid lower wages than other skilled workers such as workers

[23] Cumming [IPG pub.]: *Review*, p. 9, and Chatterjee [IPG pub.]: *Notes*, pp. 30–1.

[24] *Report of IIC* (PP 1919, xvii), Appendix 1, Statistical Evidence Regarding the Development of Handloom Weaving. This appendix found the evidence from the various censuses on the number of persons dependent on hand-spinning and weaving quite unreliable. But it noticed a growth in the total consumption of mill-spun yarn consumed by the handlooms; it also presented evidence showing a growth in the imports of grey yarn of counts over 40 and in the Indian exports of handkerchiefs and shawls (both handloom products).

[25] *Census of India, 1921*, Vol. xiii, *Madras*, Part 1, *Report* (Madras, 1922), pp. 189–95. The Madras Report showed a rise in the number of handlooms in 1921 as compared with 1900. When set against the very marked fall in the number of weavers, etc. in the Presidency, this indicates a considerable increase in under-employment of the capital equipment, and perhaps also of the remaining weavers.

[26] See, for instance, Gov. India, CISD: *Prices and wages in India*, 35th Issue (Calcutta, 1920), Tables 20 and 21.

TABLE 7.1   *India: Mill production, handloom production, net imports and exports of cotton piecegoods, 1900–1 to 1938–9*

Years	Production of cotton piecegoods by Indian mills (million yards) (1)	Change in Indian mill production of cotton piecegoods over previous year (million yards) (2)	Net imports (imports— re-exports) of cotton piecegoods into India (million yards) (3)	Handloom production of cotton piecegoods (million yards) (4)	(1)+(4) (domestic production) (million yards) (5)	(1) as a percentage of (5) (6)	Exports of Indian piecegoods (million yards) (7)
1900–1	420.6		1,875	646.4	1,067.0	39.4	111
1901–2	506.7	+86.1	2,042	827.2	1,333.9	38.0	120
1902–3	521.0	+14.3	1,986	904.8	1,425.8	36.5	109
1903–4	578.4	+57.4	1,903	826.8	1,405.2	41.2	125
1904–5	664.4	+86.0	2,152	937.2	1,601.6	41.5	135
1905–6	693.1	+28.7	2,335	1,033.2	1,726.3	40.2	129
1906–7	702.7	+9.6	2,193	1,101.6	1,804.3	38.9	115
1907–8	803.0	+100.3	2,401	1,050.4	1,853.4	43.4	112
1908–9	817.4	+14.4	1,870	1,066.1	1,883.5	43.4	113
1909–10	975.1	+57.7	2,073	845.6	1,820.7	53.6	126
1910–11	1,042.0	+66.9	2,162	868.0	1,910.0	54.6	134
1911–12	1,137.6	+95.6	2,262	994.8	2,132.4	53.4	118
1912–13	1,214.1	+76.5	2,847	990.8	2,204.9	55.5	125
1913–14	1,171.1	−43.0	3,042	1,018.8	2,189.9	53.5	130
1914–15	1,175.9	+4.8	2,327	1,136.0	2,311.9	50.8	110
1915–16	1,496.1	+320.2	2,019	943.2	2,439.3	61.4	161
1916–17	1,606.1	+210.0	1,771	645.6	2,251.7	71.3	309
1917–18	1,615.6	+9.5	1,505	741.2	2,356.8	60.1	234
1918–19	1,481.8	−133.8	955	890.0	2,371.8	62.5	187
1919–20	1,630.0	+148.2	936	506.0	2,136.0	76.3	239
1920–1	1,563.1	−66.9	1,405	931.2	2,494.3	62.7	170
1921–2	1,716.0	+152.9	980	938.0	2,654.0	64.7	187
1922–3	1,720.8	+4.8	1,467	1,084.0	2,804.8	61.3	186

1923–4	1,696.9	−23.9	1,374	816.8	2,513.7	67.5	201
1924–5	1,935.9	+239.0	1,710	1,010.8	2,945.7	65.7	230
1925–6	1,964.6	+28.7	1,529	888.4	2,853.0	68.9	165
1926–7	2,265.7	+301.1	1,759	1,216.8	3,482.5	65.1	197
1927–8	2,370.9	+105.2	1,939	1,210.8	3,581.7	66.2	169
1928–9	1,859.4	−511.5	1,913	973.2	2,832.6	65.6	149
1929–30	2,356.5	+497.1	1,897	1,282.4	3,638.9	64.8	133
1930–1	2,480.8	+124.3	873	1,257.2	3,738.0	66.4	98
1931–2	2,872.8	+392.0	760	1,332.4	4,205.2	68.3	105
1932–3	2,982.7	+109.9	1,203	1,519.2	4,501.9	66.3	66
1933–4	2,767.6	−215.1	771	1,262.0	4,029.6	68.7	56
1934–5	3,135.7	+368.1	933	1,255.6	4,391.3	71.4	58
1935–6	3,240.8	+105.1	936.6	1,450.4	4,691.2	69.3	72
1936–7	3,322.1	+81.3	753.2	1,265.2	4,587.3	72.4	102
1937–8	3,661.5	+339.4	579.5	1,293.2	4,954.7	73.9	241
1938–9	3,905.3	+243.8	631.4	1,703.2	5,608.5	69.6	177

Notes: In the above table the conversion of yarn into cloth, for both mills and handlooms, has been made on the following basis:
 1 lb. of yarn = 4 yards of cloth (in the case of handlooms).
 1 lb. of yarn = 4.78 yards of cloth (in the case of mills).

Notes on sources: Figures for columns (1), (4) and (5) are derived from *Report of the Fact-finding Committee (Handloom and Mills)*, (Delhi, 1942). Figures for column (3) are derived from *ITB Reports on the cotton textile industry* (Delhi, 1927, 1932 and 1936); and Gov. India, CISD: *Statistics of British India* for the relevant years (Calcutta, annual).

in iron and hardware, carpenters, and masons and builders, but the difference in wages seems in most cases to have widened during the war.

At the time of the enquiry by the IIC, handloom factories employing weavers as wage-earners were growing up in South India: P. Theagaraya Chetty, who was one of the pioneers in the use of fly-shuttle looms in India, seems also to have been one of the first to organize handloom factories. But in large hand-weaving centres such as Coimbatore the domestic system seems to have prevailed: the traders supplied yarn as well as gold thread and silk to the weavers and paid them wages at piece-rates when the commissioned product was turned out.[27]

According to the Fact-finding Commitee (Handloom and Mills) the proportion of independent weavers had fallen in most parts of India by 1940, and the power of the *mahajan* lending money to the weavers on the domestic system and of the *karkhanadar* employing weavers in small factories had increased since the IIC enquiry: hence the proportion of wage-earners among weavers had definitely increased. The committee computed earnings (on the basis of piece-wage rates and nature and intensity of employment) of weavers in the busy and slack seasons. The slack season lasted from three to six months in various parts of India. Taking the handloom weaver of Madras, we find that earnings per month in the busy season of a weaver working under a master-weaver or in *karkhanas* varied from Rs. 6 - 8 - 0 to Rs. 15 - 0 - 0. Madras, however, was a prosperous province as far as weavers were concerned. In Assam, these wages varied from Rs. 5 - 0 - 0 to Rs. 10 - 0 - 0 and in Bombay from Rs. 4 - 8 - 0 to Rs. 12 - 0 - 0 per month.[28] When assessing the real value of these wages we should note that the handlooms (except in Assam) were concentrated in urban areas, where the cost of living was generally higher than in villages. The evidence on what happened to the wages of the handloom weavers during the thirties is fragmentary. But it is almost certain that they fell a good deal more than the wages of factory-workers, and that the weavers' earnings approximated to those of unskilled labourers.[29]

---

[27] See the evidence of Rao Bahadur P. Theagaraya Chetty and the evidence of N. Giriya Chettiyar in *Evidence (Report of IIC)*, Vol. III, *Madras and Bangalore* (PP 1919, XIX), pp. 51–63 and 444–8 respectively. According to N. Giriya Chettiyar, the weavers in the town of Coimbatore were much better off than in the villages because the latter produced mainly coarse goods, were paid less for piece-work and could not keep back unused yarn or silk and gold thread as the weaver in the town could. He also added that although weavers were generally indebted, an attempt to organize an industrial co-operative among them had failed. When he was asked: 'Are the weavers here in such flourishing conditions that they do not want any financial help?', he replied: 'Weavers are not in such a flourishing condition, but the traders are in a somewhat flourishing condition.' *Ibid.*, p. 445.

[28] *Report of the Fact-finding Committee (Handloom and Mills)* (Delhi, 1942), Chapter IV.

[29] See, for example, V. K. R. V. Rao: 'Handloom *vs* powerloom', *ITJ, 1890–1940, Jubilee Souvenir* (Bombay, January 1941), p. 63. Rao pointed out that the prices of cloth

7.2 THE DEVELOPMENT OF THE COTTON-MILL INDUSTRY IN
INDIA UP TO THE FIRST WORLD WAR

The controversy over the customs duties on cotton yarns and piecegoods and the countervailing excise duty on cloth manufactured in Indian mills brought out many features of the nature of competition between Indian cotton mills and the mills of Lancashire at the end of the nineteenth century.[30]

First, only about 6% of total Indian production of yarn consisted of counts over 24; secondly, of the total of 373 million lb. of yarn produced in India in 1893–4, 170 million lb. were exported, 129 million lb. sold to hand-looms and only 74 million lb. used for mill weaving. These 74 million lb. produced 84·5 million lb. of cloth of which 70·5 million lb. were sold at home. Of the total amount of yarn exported from India the counts above 24 formed considerably less than $\frac{1}{2}$%.

Of yarns imported into Bombay much less than 18% (by weight) was of counts of 24 and under. Practically no imported yarn was used in Indian mills. There was thus little direct competition between Indian mills and Lancashire in respect of yarns below 24s. The cost of spinning 1 lb. of 20s yarn in a Lancashire mill and in a Bombay mill in 1895 came to 8 annas 4·46 pies and 6 annas 2·98 pies respectively when the prices of American and Indian cotton were normal, and to 6 annas 10·57 pies and 4 annas 11·18 pies respectively when the prices of cotton had fallen to low levels. In either case, India had a decided advantage over Lancashire in the spinning of 20s counts with Indian cotton. Lancashire used very little Indian cotton since it went in for much finer counts of yarn.

In the case of cotton cloth, the line of demarcation was not so easily determinable, since piecegoods were not classified in terms of the counts of yarn used in them. But from information supplied by the representatives of Lancashire mills it came out that out of all the articles exported to India

woven on handlooms fell by between 48% and 81% for different centres of Bombay and different varieties of cloth between 1925 and 1938. *The administration report of the Department of Industries, United Provinces, for the year ending 31 March 1937* (Allahabad, 1937), p. 5, claimed that the cotton weavers under the sphere of influence of the government handloom scheme (which primarily provided co-operative or government marketing facilities at selected centres) earned on an average 6 annas a day while the earnings of those elsewhere ranged between 2 and 3 annas only.

[30] *Indian tariff and the cotton duties: papers relating to the Indian Tariff Act and the Cotton Duties 1894*, and *Representations made to the Government of India, in March 1894, against the exclusion of cotton manufactures from import duties, by Chambers of Commerce and other Public Bodies in India* (PP 1895, LXXII); and (*Papers relating to the*) *Indian Tariff Act, 1896, and the Cotton Duties Act, 1896* (PP 1896, LX). See in particular J. Westland's note in the 1895 volume, pp. 7–14, and the notes of R. E. Enthoven, First Assistant Collector of Customs, Bombay and John Marshall, Secretary, Bombay Mill-owners' Association, in the 1896 volume, pp. 106–58.

only drills used yarns of 20s and under, and drills accounted for about 2%
of the total imports of cotton piecegoods into Bombay and probably for
not more than $\frac{3}{4}$% of the total imports of cotton piecegoods into India.
But in the case of the better-class Indian cloths while the weft might be
of 25s or above, the warp was often of a count not exceeding 20. Since
the weft yarn represented about one-third of the weight of the cloth and
the rest was sized warp, and the product was acceptable as good cloth
to the consumer, there was potential for competition between Indian
and imported goods in this area. It is not, however, possible to determine
exactly what proportion of grey goods imported used yarns of 30s and
above which were produced in minuscule quantities in India.

In the case of bleached, dyed or printed goods Indian mill competition
in 1896 was totally ineffective because of the complete absence of bleaching
facilities.[31] There were only three dye-works, and their capacity was very
small. Hence without further investment in ancillary facilities, Indian mills
could not effectively invade the fields of dyed and bleached cloth. Since
dyeing and printing added from 30 to 70% to the total value of cotton
piecegoods[32] and since the home market in coloured piecegoods was large,
this was an obvious field for investment by Indian businessmen, but the
opportunity was not properly exploited until after 1905.

The spinning of higher counts also presented difficulties, which are best
described by a quotation from Westland's note.

In the preparatory stages i.e. up to the 'roving' stage the mill at full work
turns out a certain number of pounds of cotton. There are certain variations . . .
which have to be introduced even in these preparatory stages with reference
to the count of the final outturn, but generally speaking, the machinery at full
work will turn out a fixed number of pounds per day. Now in the spinning
department the outturn at full work depends on the number of revolutions so
that the full outturn is a certain length of yarns. If the mill is spinning 30s,
this will use up only two-thirds of the number of pounds that it would use if
it were spinning 20s, so that it can take off only two-thirds of what the
preparatory stages can produce. In other words, if a mill which is adapted for
spinning 20s is used for spinning 30s, one third of the machinery of the
preparatory stages must be kept idle. This effect is aggravated by the
consideration that for the finer counts the mills have to be run somewhat
slower.[33]

As things turned out, during the eighteen years between the imposition
of the countervailing excise duty $3\frac{1}{2}$% on mill-made cotton piecegoods and

[31] The Ahmedabad Manufacturing and Printing Company was apparently the only
company up to that date to print cloth, and it had given up doing so in 1896. See
Enthoven's note in (*Papers relating to*) *the Indian Tariff Act, 1896* (PP 1896, LX),
p. 495.   [32] *Ibid.* (PP 1896, LX), pp. 110–11.
   [33] *Indian tariff and the cotton duties* (PP 1895, LXXII), pp. 7–8. See also Mehta: *The
Indian Cotton Textile Industry.*

the outbreak of the First World War, the Indian mills found it easier to extend their production to coloured or printed goods than to bleached yarn of higher-numbered counts, or bleached goods using finer yarn. When Mr (later Sir) James Westland wrote his minute, only the Petit group of mills were experimenting with spinning finer counts of yarn, using Egyptian cotton to do so. In 1912 there were still only 20,000 spindles spinning finer counts of yarn in India.[34] But as is shown in Table 7.2, the total Indian mill output of yarn of counts up to 40, and of yarn of counts from 21 to 30, and from 31 to 40, expanded much faster than the imports of corresponding ranges of counts of yarn from abroad (mainly from

TABLE 7.2   *Imports and production of cotton yarn in mills in British India excluding Burma, 1899–1900 to 1913–14*

	1899–1900 to 1901–2 ('000 lb.)	1911–12 to 1913–14 ('000 lb.)
A. Quantity of yarn imported into British India		
Mule and water – counts:		
1 to 20	886	1,834
21 to 25	74	638
26 to 30	9,565	8,101
31 to 40	27,394	28,996
Above 40	9,158	18,896
Orange, red and other colours – counts:		
1 to 20	1,264	410
21 to 25	1,046	28
26 to 30	2,580	2,411
31 to 40	39,377	44,813
Above 40	1,870	2,140
Unspecified descriptions	5,980	16,864
Total	98,195	124,994
B. Quantity of yarn produced in mills		
Counts:		
1 to 20	1,187,373	1,371,708
21 to 30	181,579	446,655
31 to 40	30,618	58,055
Above 40	4,298	7,815
Total	1,404,468	1,886,277

Sources: Gov. India, CISD: *Financial and commercial statistics of British India* (Calcutta, annual) and *Statistical abstract for British India from 1911–12 to 1920–21* (Calcutta, 1922). While the figures of imports in the tables relate practically to the whole of India, those of yarn production in cotton mills relate only to British India, excluding native states. The latter territory accounted for only a small fraction of total production in either period.

[34] Mehta: *The Indian Cotton Textile Industry*, p. 10 (Mehta quotes *International Cotton Statistics* in support of his figure).

Great Britain).[35] It is not possible to compare the imports and Indian mill output of different categories of cotton piecegoods directly, since they were not classified in the same way in official statistical returns. It may be noted, however, that the imports of white (bleached) and of printed or coloured goods expanded faster than the imports of grey (unbleached) goods, and that the Indian mill output of grey goods and of figured, coloured and miscellaneous goods each expanded faster than the imports of the corresponding category of cotton piecegoods. Further, the Indian mill output of figured, coloured and miscellaneous goods expanded by almost five times between the period 1899–1900 to 1901–2 and the period 1911–12 to 1913–14 whereas the Indian mill output of grey goods expanded by a little over 100% over the corresponding interval.[36] Thus the relative

TABLE 7.3 *Imports and production of cotton piecegoods in mills in British India excluding Burma, 1899–1900 to 1913–14*

	1899–1900 to 1901–2	1911–12 to 1913–14
A. Imports of piecegoods ('000 yards)		
Grey (unbleached)	3,625,053	4,229,285
White (bleached)	1,395,471	2,054,035
Coloured, printed or dyed	1,128,416	1,888,170
Total piecegoods	6,149,940	8,171,490
B. Output of piecegoods ('000 lb.)		
(a) Grey goods	257,821	577,558
(b) figured, coloured and miscellaneous goods	48,082	191,593

Source: as in Table 7.2.

substitution of foreign imports by Indian mill production occurred over a broad front, although it was true even at the beginning of the First World War that finer-quality cotton piecegoods or yarn formed a much larger proportion of total imports of cotton piecegoods or yarn than of Indian mill output.

Soon after 1900 bleaching and dyeing facilities began to be established by the more dynamic mills.[37] After 1905, when the movement towards the use of Indian cloth was stimulated by the political movement connected

---

[35] See Table 7.2.   [36] See Table 7.3.

[37] Apparently the Khatau Makanji Spinning and Weaving Company Limited was the first firm to have its own bleaching and dyeing works. It was followed in 1905 by the Currimbhoy Ebrahim group of mills. See Playne and Wright: *The Bombay Presidency*, pp. 234 and 164.

with the partition of Bengal, it became usual for the larger weaving mills of Bombay to have their own bleaching and dyeing works. This development received a push also from the fact that after a temporary but brisk boom in yarn exports to China during the years from 1901–2 to 1905–6, they declined by a large percentage, never to recover fully.[38] The result of the decline in yarn exports was reflected in a drastic decline in the profitability of purely spinning mills and a marked improvement in the relative profitability of mills which wove the yarn into cotton piecegoods.

The decline of yarn exports was reflected in the increase in the ratio of looms to spindles in the industry as a whole and in the different rates of development of the different centres of cotton mills in India. In 1900, the cotton-mill industry was almost wholly concentrated in western India. It had grown up in and around the cities of Bombay and Ahmedabad, Bombay being much the bigger centre. In 1900–1, about 56% of the looms and 53% of the spindles in the whole of India were located in the mills of Bombay City. But during the period from 1900 to 1914, Ahmedabad grew much faster than Bombay. The mills of Ahmedabad were, even at the beginning of the century, geared primarily to the domestic market. They had a much higher ratio of looms to spindles than the mills of Bombay or India as a whole; they also produced on an average a much larger proportion of yarn of counts above 20s than did the mills of Bombay or India as a whole.[39] The rate of growth of looms and spindles was much higher in Ahmedabad than in Bombay or India as a whole. (See Table 7.4.)

It is interesting to notice that Bombay had a higher ratio of looms to spindles than India, excluding Ahmedabad, both in 1900–1 and 1913–14. The rates of growth of capacity were not widely different in Bombay and India excluding Ahmedabad. Since the weight of Bombay in the capacity

[38] The total exports of cotton twist and yarn from India had increased from 143.2 million lb. in 1889–90 to 242·6 million lb. in 1899–1900. There was then a sharp break in 1900–1 with exports declining to 119.3 million lb., because of the plague in Bombay. The exports of twist and yarn recovered and reached a peak of 298·5 million lb. in 1905–6. But after that there were declining exports: they amounted to 152·3 million lb. and 198.9 million lb. in 1911 and 1914 respectively.

[39] The following table showing the total production (in '000 lb.) of various ranges of counts of yarn during the five-year period from 1901–2 to 1905–6 illustrates the position quite well:

Output of yarn	Bombay City and Island	Ahmedabad	British India excluding Ahmedabad and Bombay City and Island
Counts 21 to 30	214,014	115,010	100,123
Counts 31 and above	16,305	45,652	16,444
Total of all counts	1,718,843	238,575	929,156

Source: Gov. India, CISD: *Financial and Commercial Statistics of British India*, 13th Issue (Calcutta, 1907), pp. 415–19. In this table, British India excludes native states.

of Indian cotton mills was very high in the beginning, and since Ahmedabad was the fastest growing centre of the mill industry, the location of the cotton-mill industry remained almost as concentrated in western India in 1913–14 as in 1900–1.

The growth of the cotton-mill industry in centres away from western India was primarily stimulated by the demand for coarse yarn on the part of handlooms. There were a few weaving mills, particularly in South India, but most of the other mills only spun coarse yarn.[41] Hence one can point to a pattern of specialization in which the needs of handlooms for better varieties of yarn were satisfied mainly by imports and by mills in western India, the needs of the coarse and medium varieties of piecegoods came increasingly to be supplied either by Indian mills in western India or by handlooms, and the bulk of the needs for finer varieties of cloth continued to be satisfied by imports from abroad. No simple assumption

TABLE 7.4 *Looms and spindles in India – distribution among the major centres, 1900–20*

	Ahmedabad		Bombay (city)		India (excl. Burma)	
	Looms	Spindles	Looms	Spindles	Looms	Spindles
1900–1	5,861	485,706	22,563	2,608,527	40,542	4,932,602
1901–2	6,240	487,969	22,968	2,581,684	41,815	4,964,979
1902–3	6,491	511,184	23,178	2,648,544	43,676	5,164,360
1903–4	6,643	509,928	25,359	2,638,830	46,421	5,213,344
1904–5	7,061	537,928	25,387	2,598,200	47,305	5,196,432
1905–6	8,188	577,680	28,538	2,617,393	52,281	5,293,834
1906–7	9,805	714,601	32,534	2,689,532	59,375	5,546,288
1907–8	12,679	871,745	34,782	2,704,578	66,178	5,763,710
1908–9	13,880	884,538	38,629	2,780,748	74,592	5,966,530
1909–10	15,179	914,631	41,389	2,824,350	80,171	6,142,551
1910–11	16,037	922,458	42,299	2,907,235	84,627	6,346,675
1911–12	16,616	935,080	43,062	2,919,474	87,640	6,427,181
1912–13	–	–	–	–	91,585	6,495,012
1913–14	18,359	963,093	47,790	3,044,148	96,688	6,620,576
1914–15	–	–	–	–	103,311	6,598,108
1915–16	21,871	1,028,928	53,168	2,990,769	108,417	6,675,688
1916–17	–	–	–	–	110,812	6,670,162
1917–18	22,250	1,065,717	58,061	2,896,316	114,805	6,614,269
1918–19	22,379	1,072,540	60,344	2,921,099	116,094	6,590,918
1919–20	22,731	1,074,886	60,475	3,031,953	117,558	6,714,265

Source: [Up to 1905–6] *Financial and commercial statistics of British India,* [up to 1911–12] *Statistics of British India,* Part I, *Industrial;* [from 1913–14 onwards] *Statistics of British India,* Vol. I, *Commercial Statistics* (Calcutta, annual). ['India' excludes native states.]

[41] In 1908, Cumming reported that 9 out of 14 cotton mills in Bengal were only spinning mills and only 2 out of 14 spun yarn of counts above 25. See Cumming [IPG pub.]: *Review.* In the United Provinces at the same date, out of 11 cotton mills only 4 combined weaving with spinning. See Chatterjee [IPG pub.]: *Notes,* p. 3.

of production for import substitution alone will explain the trend of investment in the cotton-mill industry during this period. Nevertheless, since Indian yarn exports to China were increasingly affected after 1905–6 by competition from Chinese and Japanese mills, investment for import substitution became the dominant element after the structure of the cotton industry in Bombay had been suitably adjusted. Further, since our figures of imports of cotton-textile machinery exclude those of imports of bleaching and dyeing machinery, whose importance increased over time, the figures of total investment for the years immediately preceding the First World War are underestimates in comparison with the figures for the first few years of the century. It is clear, however, that the tendency towards substitution of domestic goods for imports began to assert itself sufficiently strongly to offset the effects of declining exports of yarn to China only around 1913–14.

One can ask why in spite of the existence of a distinct cost advantage in favour of the coarser and medium varieties of goods, there was no absolute substitution of domestic production for foreign goods. First, one can point to the existence of long-established channels of trade in Manchester piecegoods, which resisted a rapid replacement of them by Indian piecegoods. Bengal was by far the biggest market for cotton piecegoods in India and the external and internal trade of Bengal was far more dominated than that of western India by British merchants and industrialists. Secondly, the lack of a policy of tariff protection on the part of the government made industrialists unsure about their future: there was no clear target to aspire to in the face of resistance by the dominant exporters – the industrialists of Manchester. In the case of any miscalculation or even any temporary difficulties there was no tariff wall to shield one, and there was no near prospect of one coming up either. Thirdly, the decline of the export trade in yarn weakened some big business groups of Bombay, such as Greaves, Cotton and Company and E. D. Sassoon and Company, which had in the past played a dynamic role; the poor returns of spinning mills and the rising costs of land and labour in the immediate vicinity of Bombay also probably discouraged the flow of funds into the industry. Finally there were insistent complaints voiced in the meetings of the Bombay Mill-owners' Association and in the pages of the *Indian Textile Journal*[42] about the lack of technical dynamism on the part of Bombay mill-owners and their inability to exploit new markets at home or defend old markets in China against Chinese and Japanese competition. There was a distinct feeling that they expected customers to come to them rather than to take goods to the

[42] See, for example, the editorial on the annual meeting of the Bombay Mill-owners' Association and the article, 'The Mill Industry in Bombay' in *ITJ*, April 1914, pp. 222 and 225 respectively.

customer.[43] In the face of aggressive marketing by the Japanese and established marketing channels favouring Manchester, the progress made by the Bombay mills was slow. The growth of the cotton-mill industry in other centres was probably hampered by the poor quality of local cotton, the lack of mobility of capital, and the (initial) lack of skilled technical personnel and managers.[44]

Sometimes the complaint was voiced that India did not produce long-staple cotton in large enough quantities, and this hampered the growth of output of fine spinning and finer varieties of cotton piecegoods. This complaint, however, had little foundation. A large proportion of the long-staple cotton (produced mainly in Madras) was exported. The producers on the European continent often mixed Indian short-staple cotton with American long-staple cotton to produce better-variety cotton goods which were then exported to India. There was nothing to prevent Indian mill-owners from importing American cotton, spinning finer yarn and producing woven goods of quality. The IIC during its investigation found that the production of long (or rather medium-to-long) staple cotton in India was limited primarily by the inadequate premium offered for cotton of long-staple varieties, which yielded less per acre than cotton of short-staple varieties.[45] Earlier Sir James MacKenna had written: 'At present there is a strong and increasing demand for the coarse cottons spinning under twenties, for the production of which India is particularly suited. So long as this demand continues, it would be difficult to persuade the cultivators to abandon their cultivation.'[46] Efforts had been made by the Bombay Mill-owners' Association, the Bombay Chamber of Commerce and the Department of Agriculture, Bombay, to try and improve the varieties of cotton produced in India,[47] but in the absence of a strong demand for long-staple cotton either at home or abroad (the biggest customer for Indian cotton, Japan, took mainly short-staple cotton), and in the absence of proper irrigation facilities in the cotton-growing tracts,

[43] Gov. India, CISD: *Review of the trade of India for 1899–1900* (Calcutta, 1900), pp. 23–4. This lethargy of the Bombay mill-owners was evident only in the case of the home market, particularly for woven goods. They had by contrast shown considerable energy in finding new markets in East Africa and the Levant. The explanation was probably that in the latter case the mill-owners were selling their established varieties of grey goods, whereas in order to exploit the home market better they would have to weave finer varieties of goods and meet stiff resistance from the established sellers of Lancashire goods in India. See *Report of the Mill-owners' Association, Bombay, for the Year 1901* (Bombay, 1902), pp. 7–8, for an account of the efforts of the mill-owners to extend their sales in the markets of East Africa and Western Asia.

[44] See the reports of Cumming and Chatterjee on the industries of Bengal and the United Provinces respectively in 1908.

[45] *Report of IIC* (PP XVII, 1919), Appendix B, 'Draft Note on the Industrial Aspect of Cotton Growing in India', particularly pp. 327–8.

[46] J. MacKenna [Gov. India pub.]: *Agriculture in India*, p. 37.

[47] Sulivan: *One Hundred Years of Bombay*, p. 132.

such efforts were bound to have only a marginal effect.[48] It may be interesting to quote here from the speech by Lalubhoy Samaldas, Chairman of the Indian Industrial Conference held at Karachi on 25 December 1913:

American cotton is being imported to a much larger extent than before, enabling the mills to spin finer counts of yarn. The production of woven goods has doubled itself in the last decade, and yet the imports of woven goods do not show any decrease. This is due to the fact that the production of white and bleached goods in this country is on so small a scale that it has not affected the imports to any appreciable extent. As long as we have to depend for our plant and machinery on foreign countries, as long as we are behind these countries in our knowledge of technological chemistry, and as long as we are not able to produce cotton equal in quality to American and Egyptian cotton, we shall find it difficult to compete on fair terms with Manchester or other centres of weaving industries.[48a]

7.3   FOREIGN COMPETITION AND TARIFF CHANGES FROM THE FIRST WORLD WAR TO 1939

During the First World War, owing to the shortage of shipping space, the shipment of low-quality piecegoods from Britain (which was the largest supplier of the Indian market) was curtailed by a decision of the British Cotton Control Board. The import duty on cotton piecegoods was raised from $3\frac{1}{2}\%$ to $7\frac{1}{2}\%$ in 1917, but the excise duty on cotton piecegoods remained unchanged at $3\frac{1}{2}\%$. The import of yarn, on which handlooms depended, fell because of the diversion of resources in Great Britain to the war effort and because of shortage of shipping. The combined effect of all these developments was a fall in imports of piecegoods and yarn, a fall in the output of handlooms and a rise in the output of cotton piecegoods by mills. The relative fall in the price of raw cotton also helped in the last development.

The war also led to the invasion of the Indian market by Japanese producers of cotton goods. It is certain that the war hastened the process of displacement of Manchester piecegoods in the Indian market by the products of Indian and Japanese mills. However, the increase in Japanese exports to India was due to the fact that the Japanese mills were overtaking and surpassing the Indian ones in efficiency. Indian yarn exports had been displaced from the Chinese market by Chinese and Japanese competition, and while Japan then went on to increase her exports of cotton piecegoods to China, the Indians failed to increase their exports. It is possible that the search for external markets led the Japanese to pay more attention than did the Indians to the local conditions of those

---

[48] Cf. Chapter 4 above.   [48a] *ITJ*, January 1914, p. 114.

TABLE 7.5 *Gross imports of cotton piecegoods into India, 1900–1 to 1939–40 (figures in million yards)*

Year	From the U.K.	From Japan	Total imports into India
1900–1	1,972	—	2,003
1901–2	2,154	—	2,190
1902–3	2,071	—	2,107
1903–4	1,997	—	2,033
1904–5	2,251	—	2,288
1905–6	2,415	—	2,463
1906–7	2,276	—	2,318
1907–8	2,487	—	2,532
1908–9	1,941	—	1,993
1909–10	2,141	—	2,193
1910–11	2,254	—	2,308
1911–12	2,379	1	2,438
1912–13	2,942	6	3,023
1913–14	3,104	9	3,197
1914–15	2,378	16	2,446
1915–16	2,049	39	2,148
1916–17	1,786	100	1,934
1917–18	1,430	95	1,556
1918–19	867	238	1,122
1919–20	976	76	1,081
1920–1	1,292	170	1,510
1921–2	955	90	1,090
1922–3	1,453	108	1,593
1923–4	1,319	123	1,486
1924–5	1,614	155	1,823
1925–6	1,287	217	1,564
1926–7	1,467	244	1,788
1927–8	1,543	323	1,973
1928–9	1,456	357	1,937
1929–30	1,248	562	1,919
1930–1	523	321	890
1931–2	376	340	753
1932–3	586	579	1,193
1933–4	415	341	761
1934–5	552	374	944
1935–6	440	496	947
1936–7	334 (309)	417 (370)	764 (699)
1937–8	267	306	591
1938–9	206	425	647
1939–40	145	393	579

Source: Gov. India, CISD: *Review of the trade of India* (Calcutta, annual). Up to 1930–1, the figures include imports of fents, which formed 1–1.5% of imports before say 1920–1, but increased in some later years to about 2–3% of total imports. Up to 1936–7, figures include imports into Burma, since that was the political entity for the purpose of tariffs; after that date the figures exclude imports into Burma. The figures within brackets show the imports into India excluding Burma, thus indicating the rough order of importance of imports into Burma.

markets,[49] and it is really because of a more flexible marketing organization that the Japanese did better than the Indians in the markets in which they competed directly. According to Lockwood,[50] there was little gain in labour efficiency in cotton spinning in Japan between 1913 and 1926, but beginning in 1926 there was a tremendous increase in labour productivity in both cotton spinning and weaving.[51] The superior marketing organization and the gains in efficiency at the plant level enabled Japan to become a major exporter of cotton textiles during the 1920s and during the 1930s she outstripped all other exporters.[52]

The relative movements of Japanese and British exports of cotton piecegoods are displayed in Table 7.5. The tariff policy of the Government of India in relation to the Indian cotton-textile industry after the end of the First World War was dictated by three considerations: (a) the need to raise revenue during the years immediately following the First World War, (b) the need to protect Indian production and the exports from the U.K. to India from Japanese competition, and (c) the need to preserve a large section of the Indian mill industry from extinction during the thirties. Japan became a far more serious competitor of Indian mills than Lancashire because: (i) many Indian mills enjoyed an advantage over Lancashire mills in respect of wage-cost per unit of output, whereas the position was reversed with respect to Japanese mills, and (ii) Japan also sold the coarser kinds of cloth in which the Indian mills specialized before 1930.[53]

In 1921, because of budgetary needs, the Government of India raised the general rate of import duty to 11%, and imports of cotton piecegoods were subjected to the same duty. At the same time, imports of textile machinery were subjected to a duty of $2\frac{1}{2}\%$ by value. In 1922, the general

[49] Cf. *ITJ*, January 1914, p. 127 ('The Textile Industry in Japan'). Among the advantages the Japanese were supposed to enjoy in the Chinese market were knowledge of the local language, ability to slip through into places where foreigners were not allowed (because of their similarity to the Chinese in appearance), and backing by their local consuls, which placed them at an advantage even in relation to the Chinese mill-owners and merchants.

[50] W. W. Lockwood: *The Economic Development of Japan* (Princeton, N.J., 1954), pp. 172–3.

[51] See, for example, G. C. Allen: *Japanese Industry: its Recent Development and Present Condition* (New York, 1931), p. 31. 'In the spinning mills output per operative rose from 5,700 lb. in 1926 to 7,000 lb. in 1929 and 9,300 lbs in 1935. In the weaving sheds belonging to spinning mills the average figures for the same years were 22,300 yards, 36,000 yards, and 49,500 yards respectively.'

[52] I. Svennilson: *Growth and Stagnation in the European Economy* (Geneva, 1955), Table 35.

[53] See, for example. A. S. Pearse: *The Cotton Industry of India, being the report of the journey to India* (Manchester, 1930), pp. 172–4. The Indian Tariff Board concluded in 1932 that the labour costs in India per unit of 'the staple lines of goods' were not generally higher than in Lancashire. See ITB: *Report regarding the grant of protection to the cotton textile industry* (Calcutta, 1932), p. 113. For comparison with Japanese costs see *ibid.*, p. 206 and Buchanan: *Development of Capitalistic Enterprise*, p. 381.

rate of import duty was raised to 15%, but the rate of import duty on cotton piecegoods was kept unchanged at 11%. Imports of cotton yarn were subjected to a duty of 5% for the first time since 1896. As a result of agitation precipitated by the depression in the cotton-textile industry, the Government of India suspended the excise duty on cotton piecegoods in 1925 and repealed it in 1926.

In 1927 the Indian Tariff Board conducted an enquiry into the cotton-textile industry. According to the Tariff Board the main troubles of the industry (particularly in Bombay) were due to 'unfair' competition from Japan: Japan enjoyed a cost advantage because of the general adoption of the double-shift system and the employment of women and children at night in contravention of the international labour convention. The two Indian members differed with the British president in their views regarding the required remedies. The former wanted a bounty on yarn of counts above 30s produced in Indian mills and an additional import duty of 4% on cotton piecegoods. The president thought that a duty on yarn imports from Japan coupled with an increase of 4% in the duty on imports of cotton piecegoods would meet the needs of the Indian industry.[54]

The Government of India was at first disinclined to accept the remedies proposed by either the president or the Indian members of the Tariff Board, and merely removed the duties on mill stores and textile machinery as a measure of partial relief. The deepening crisis in the mill industry, however, compelled it to take stronger measures: in 1927 the duty of 5% *ad valorem* on imported yarn was replaced by an alternative duty of 5% *ad valorem* or 1·5 annas per lb., whichever was higher. This had the effect of raising the *ad valorem* duties on imports of yarns below 50s, and in particular of raising the duty on yarn within the range of 30s and 40s where the competition between Indian and Japanese mills was keenest.[55]

The severity of competition from Japan was not abated by these measures. There were general strikes in Bombay in 1928 and 1929, and the Government of India appointed G. S. Hardy in 1929 to examine and report on the extent of foreign competition in the different classes of cotton piecegoods and the possibility of introducing a system of specific duties on cotton piecegoods. Hardy found the foreign competition between India and Japan keenest in piecegoods; he also found that Lancashire had a practical monopoly of the finer varieties of grey and coloured piecegoods, and of bleached goods. He recommended that protection should be given by means of specific duties on medium grades of cloth.

The Government of India acted only after budgetary difficulties had

[54] ITB: *Cotton Textile Industry Enquiry, 1927*, Vol. I, *Report* (Calcutta, 1927), Chapters XI–XIV and Minute of Dissent by the President.

[55] B. N. Adarkar [Gov. India pub.]: *The History of the Indian Tariff* (Studies in Indian Economics issued by the Office of the Economic Adviser, First Series, No. 2, Delhi, 1940), p. 28.

become apparent in 1930, when it raised the duty on cotton piecegoods from 11 to 15%. A minimum specific duty of $3\frac{1}{2}$ annas per lb. on imports of plain grey goods from non-British sources, and an additional *ad valorem* duty of 5% on all imports of cotton piecegoods from non-British sources were proposed by the government. The Legislative Assembly made the specific duty of $3\frac{1}{2}$ annas per lb. applicable also to imports from British sources. Thus the Indian mill industry received tariff protection in all plain grey goods of coarser and medium varieties.

In 1931 the duties on cotton piecegoods were further enhanced by 5%: thus the effective rates of duty on imports from British and non-British sources were raised to 20% and 25% *ad valorem* respectively. In September 1931, as a result of the surcharge of 25% on all import duties, the duties on British and non-British piecegoods were raised to 25% and 31·25% respectively; at the same time the duty on imports of cotton yarn rose from 5% to $6\frac{1}{4}$% or from $1\frac{1}{2}$ annas per lb. to $1\frac{7}{8}$ annas per lb. The advantage to the cotton-mill industry was offset to some extent by the restoration of duties on machinery and mill stores and the imposition of a duty of half an anna per lb. on imports of raw cotton.

In 1932 the depreciation of the Japanese yen again made possible increased imports of Japanese piecegoods, and the survival of a large section of the Indian industry was threatened. As a result of the recommendations made by the ITB after a special enquiry, the Government of India raised *ad valorem* duties on imports of non-British piecegoods from $31\frac{1}{4}$% to 50%. A comprehensive enquiry into the cotton-textile industry was carried out by the ITB in 1932. But the government did not have enough time to deliberate on the recommendations made by the Tariff Board, for events moved too fast. The increase in the duty on cotton piecegoods of non-British origin in August 1932 failed to check Japanese imports and the Government of India gave notice of six months for the denunciation of the Indo-Japanese Convention of 1904 which entitled Japan to the most-favoured-nation treatment. In June 1933, the duty on imports of cotton piecegoods not of British manufacture was raised to 75% *ad valorem* with a minimum specific duty on plain grey goods of $6\frac{3}{4}$ annas per lb. Japan in reply boycotted Indian raw cotton of which she was the major foreign customer. But the imposition of the high duties on imports of Japanese goods had the result of bringing Japan to the conference table, and in July 1934 a Trade Agreement was concluded between India and Japan. This imposed a quantitative restriction on imports of piecegoods from Japan. Japan also agreed to buy a minimum quantity of Indian raw cotton. In exchange it was agreed that the duty on Japanese piecegoods should not exceed 50% *ad valorem* or $5\frac{1}{4}$ annas per lb., whichever was higher, in case of plain grey goods, or 50% in the case of all other goods.[56]

[56] Adarkar [Gov. India pub.]: *History of the Indian Tariff*, p. 36.

At the end of 1933 an agreement was concluded between the British Textile Mission and the representatives of the mill-owners of Bombay, by which the latter agreed to accept a reduction in import duties on yarns. They agreed not to make 'fresh proposals with regard to the duties applicable to the United Kingdom imports', if the surcharge of 25% on all import duties were removed. The Indian representatives also accepted a substantial reduction (from 50% to 30% *ad valorem* or from 4 annas per square yard to $2\frac{1}{2}$ annas per square yard) in respect of import duties on piecegoods made of artificial silk, and a small reduction (from 35% or $2\frac{1}{4}$ annas per square yard to 30% or 2 annas per square yard) in case of fabrics made from cotton and artificial silk.[57] In return provisions were made for India to share in British quotas of exports to other countries when India did not have independent quotas, for Manchester to use its good offices to bring Indian manufacturers and importers together in markets where India did not have good marketing arrangements, and to popularize the use of Indian cotton by British firms.[58]

In 1934, the Government of India passed legislation to take account of the Tariff Board reports of 1932 on the cotton textile and sericultural industry, the Indo-Japanese Trade Agreement of 1934 and the Bombay–Lancashire (or Mody–Lees) pact of 1933. The duty on yarn of counts above 50s was abolished, that on imports of yarn of counts up to 50s from non-British sources was kept at the level of $1\frac{7}{8}$ annas per lb., and that on imports of yarns up to 50s from British sources was lowered to 5% *ad valorem* or $1\frac{1}{4}$ annas per lb. The duty on British cotton piecegoods was kept at 25% as against 50% on non-British piecegoods, as agreed upon in the Indo-Japanese Trade Agreement.

Another inquiry into the cotton-textile industry was made by the Indian Tariff Board in 1936. As a result of the recommendations of the Tariff Board, in June 1936, the import duty on grey cotton piecegoods of British manufacture was reduced from 25% *ad valorem* or $4\frac{3}{8}$ annas per lb., whichever was higher, to 20% *ad valorem* or $3\frac{1}{2}$ annas per lb.,

[57] In our narrative we have ignored questions of tariff protection against imports of artificial silk yarns and piecegoods or yarns and fabrics made of mixtures of artificial silk and cotton. Handloom weavers often used artificial silk yarn to improve the appearance of cloth produced by them, and foreign producers often used small mixtures of artificial silk in order to take advantage of lower import duties on fabrics or yarns of mixtures of cotton and artificial silk. This created difficult policy problems for the Government of India and the Indian Tariff Boards since they were generally unwilling to take any measures which would directly harm the handloom producer, even though they might be necessary in order to make tariff protection for the Indian cotton-mill industry really effective. But the general trend of policy was definitely towards imposing duties high enough to protect the mill industry, and helping the handloom industry by more direct methods, such as affording them better marketing facilities, subsidizing design centres and organizing weavers' co-operation. See in this connection, Adarkar [Gov. India pub.]: *History of the Indian Tariff*, pp. 27–46.

[58] Mehta: *The Cotton Mills of India*, pp. 181–2.

whichever was higher, and that on other kinds of cotton piecegoods and fabrics of British manufacture (with the exception of printed cotton piecegoods and printed fabrics) from 25% to 20% *ad valorem*. In 1939, in pursuance of the provisions of the Indo-British Trade Agreement, import duties on cotton piecegoods of British manufacture were reduced again. The new rates of import duty were $17\frac{1}{2}$% on printed goods, 15% *ad valorem* or 2 annas $7\frac{1}{2}$ pies per lb., whichever was higher, on grey goods and 15% *ad valorem* on all others. Provision was made for an increase in import duties if imports from Britain exceeded 500 million yards in any year and for a decrease in duties if they fell short of 350 million yards in any year. These concessions were linked to provisions for the U.K. importing minimum quantities of Indian raw cotton: if annual exports of raw cotton to the U.K. fell below 400,000 bales, up to 31 December 1940, or 450,000 bales subsequently, import duties on British piecegoods might be increased.

In April 1937, the revised Indo-Japanese Protocol continued the quantitative restrictions on imports of piecegoods from Japan. Further, some loopholes were closed by imposing new restrictions on imports of fents, by raising the duty on rayon goods and rayon mixture goods by one anna per square yard, and by completely prohibiting the import of rayon fents.

Apart from the tariff changes and the trade agreements, two other political events influenced the growth of imports of cotton piecegoods into India, although in both cases the effects were temporary. The civil disobedience movement in India had the effect of curtailing imports of foreign goods into India. The value of imports of cotton piecegoods fell by a much bigger percentage (viz., 57%) between 1929–30 and 1930–1 than the values of imports of sugar, metals and machinery (30%, 33% and 22% respectively).[59] Furthermore, although total domestic consumption fell in that year, the output of Indian cotton mills rose. Hence the boycott movement had a part to play in 1930–1.

The other political event of importance to the cotton-mill industry of India was the breaking out of large-scale hostilities between China and Japan in 1937. Japan was for a time fully engaged in finding resources for the war, so that shipping facilities for exporting cotton manufactures were limited; she also experienced difficulties with the yen. But Japan managed again in 1938–9 to export a larger volume of cotton piecegoods than in 1937–8 and 1936–7.[60]

[59] Gov. India, CISD: *Review of the trade of India for 1930–31* (Delhi, 1931), p. 18. Sir Sorabji Saklatwala, a member of the Tata group, estimated that the boycott was responsible for a reduction of 460 million yards in the imports of cotton piecegoods and nearly 6 million pounds in those of yarn. Mehta, *Cotton Mills of India*, p. 178. The non-co-operation movement of 1920–1 had had some impact on imports of a similar character, but it had been much less noticeable, mainly because the Indian mill industry had been less prepared to meet all the domestic needs.

[60] These comparisons relate to imports into India excluding Burma.

As our figures in Table 7.5 show, the substantial preference in favour of British piecegoods could not prevent a drastic decline in imports from the U.K. after 1934–5. The prices of goods of comparable quality exported by the U.K. and Japan were substantially higher for British goods and generally continued to increase during the period from 1935–6 onwards, whereas the movement was often the other way round (see Table 7.6) for Japan. The upward movement of foreign prices in later years also helped the Indian industry more easily to displace foreign goods. As our Table 7.7 indicates, the Bombay–Lancashire Pact does seem to have led to an increase in the use of Indian cotton by Britain, but the increase in the output of long-staple cotton in India also contributed to this development. Japan

TABLE 7.6   *Average declared value of piecegoods imported from the United Kingdom and Japan, 1931–2 to 1939–40*

	Grey		White		Coloured	
Year	U.K. R. a. p.	Japan R. a. p.	U.K. R. a. p.	Japan R. a. p.	U.K. R. a. p.	Japan R. a. p.
1931–2	0 2 7	0 2 6	0 3 1	0 2 6	0 4 2	0 2 9
1932–3	0 2 6	0 2 2	0 3 0	0 2 2	0 4 0	0 2 2
1933–4	0 2 5	0 1 11	0 3 2	0 2 0	0 4 0	0 2 2
1934–5	0 2 6	0 2 0	0 3 1	0 2 7	0 3 9	0 2 5
1935–6	0 2 6	0 1 11	0 3 2	0 2 4	0 3 11	0 2 1
1936–7	0 2 9	0 1 11	0 3 4	0 2 6	0 4 0	0 2 4
1937–8	0 2 11	0 2 2	0 3 6	0 2 5	0 4 5	0 2 7
1938–9	0 2 11	0 1 9	0 3 4	0 2 1	0 4 4	0 2 2
1939–40	0 3 6	0 1 10	0 3 8	0 2 5	0 4 7	0 2 5

Source: Gov. India, CISD: *Review of the trade of India* (Calcutta, annual): *1936–37*, p. 38; *1937–38*, p. 83; *1938–39*, p. 88; *1939–40*, p. 110.

TABLE 7.7   *Exports of raw cotton from India, 1929–30 to 1939–40 (figures in 'ooo bales of 400 lb.)*

Year	United Kingdom	Japan	Total
1929–30	270	1,640	4,070
1930–1	281	1,686	3,926
1931–2	166	1,080	2,369
1932–3	167	1,085	2,063
1933–4	342	1,022	2,740
1934–5	347	2,011	3,446
1935–6	456	1,759	3,397
1936–7	610	2,334	4,140
1937–8	395	1,359	2,731
1938–9	411	1,211	2,703
1939–40	473	1,056	2,948

Source: Gov. India, CISD: *Review of the trade of India* (Calcutta, annual).

remained the most important foreign consumer of Indian cotton but after 1936–7 her imports drastically declined.

In the above narrative we have mainly traced the course of the tariff policy of the Government of India as it affected the Indian cotton-mill industry. It can be argued that the interwar years marked a definite shift of the policy of the Government of India in relation to handlooms. Before the First World War, the provincial Departments of Industries concerned themselves largely with the handlooms. Further, when duties were imposed on imports of cotton piecegoods, imports of yarn were still not subjected to any duty. But cotton piecegoods produced in Indian mills were subjected to an excise duty of $3\frac{1}{2}\%$ *ad valorem*. Thus handloom-weaving enjoyed some fiscal protection both against foreign cloth and against Indian mill-produced cloth. The abolition of the countervailing excise duty on mill-made piecegoods effectively from 1925 and the imposition of the duty of 5% on imports of cotton yarn knocked out the fiscal props from under the handloom industry. Later legislation imposing duties on imports of artificial silk yarn and yarn using a mixture of artificial silk and cotton further increased the disadvantage of the handloom weaver.

However, as we have seen in Section 7.1, the proportion of handloom production to mill production had been declining even before the First World War. Further, even before the First World War, the Indian mills were a much more important supplier of yarn to handlooms than were foreign producers.[61] Since some handloom products used yarn of higher counts, which were mainly imported, the proportion of imported yarn to the total quantity of yarn used by handlooms does not fully indicate the importance of yarn imports to handlooms. But insofar as the effective tariff protection of cotton mills allowed them to produce yarns of finer counts, the handlooms suffered less in the long run than they did initially. The substantial absolute increase in the output of handlooms during the thirties is a pointer in this direction. Further, the efforts made by provincial governments towards the improvement of the methods of production and, more particularly, of marketing had some effect in maintaining and even increasing the total output of handlooms.

If we look at the figures of total internal consumption of cotton piecegoods in India, we find that it was 9,389·7 million yards for the three-year period 1900–1 to 1902–3, and 16,594·6 million yards for the three-year period 1936–7 to 1938–9, an increase of about 77%. The population of India grew by about 36% during the period 1901–41.[62] Thus there was a substantial increase in consumption of cloth per capita during this period.

[61] See Table 7.2. Hence the claim of the *Report of the Fact-finding Committee Handloom and Mills*) (Delhi, 1942), Chapter I, that protection caused great harm to handlooms, is open to question.
[62] Davis: *Population of India and Pakistan*, p. 27.

If we estimate the intercensal population by the usual methods, we find that the consumption of cloth per capita increased more or less steadily up to 1913–14, fell during the First World War, and just about recovered to the pre-war level during the last five years of the 1930s.[63] Both income and price factors seem to be responsible for this development. There are grounds for believing that income per capita was increasing during the period 1901–14 (cf. Chapter 3 above). The period of the twenties was relatively depressed, particularly after 1926, when prices of primary products fell absolutely and relatively to the prices of industrial products. The depression of the thirties led to the further decline of incomes of people directly dependent on agriculture. At the same time, however, the

TABLE 7.8 *Movement in relative prices of grey shirtings and all commodities, 1901–5 to 1911–15*

Period	The average index number of prices of grey shirtings (Calcutta) (1)	The average index number of prices of all commodities (Calcutta) (2)	Ratio of (2) to (1) (3)
1901–5	83.6	105.2	1.13
1906–10	91.6	130.0	1.42
1911–15	103.6	141.6	1.37

Source: Gov. India, CISD: *Index numbers of Indian prices, 1861–1931* (Delhi, 1933), Table v. Base: 1873=100.

TABLE 7.9 *Movement in relative prices of cotton manufactures and all commodities, 1914 to 1939–40*

Period	The average index number of prices of cotton manufactures (Calcutta) (1)	The average index number of prices of all commodities (Calcutta) (2)	Ratio of (2) to (1) (3)
1914	100	100	1.00
1919–23	259.0	185.0	.71
1924–28	185.8	154.6	.83
1929–33	130.8	106.2	.81
1934–38	113.2	93.3	.82
1939–40	114.0	114.0	1.00

Source: Statistical abstracts for British India (London, 1939 and 1943). Base: July 1914=100.

[63] Cf. the estimate of per capita consumption given in Gov. India, CISD: *Review of the trade of India in 1936–37* (Delhi, 1937), p. 43; 1932–3 was an exceptional year because of the large imports of cotton piecegoods, particularly from Japan.

price movements of cotton piecegoods in India tended to accentuate the effects of changes in income as the figures in Tables 7.8 and 7.9 illustrate.

The figures quoted in Tables 7.8 and 7.9 are necessarily crude and either ignore or conceal changes in relative prices of different types of cotton goods, and in relative prices of agricultural and industrial commodities in general. Yet, if we take prices of all the different kinds of cotton piecegoods, and prices of important agricultural commodities such as rice, cotton or jute, the general impression conveyed by our figures is confirmed, viz., that while before the First World War the prices of cotton manufactures went down relatively to the prices of other important commodities produced in India, after the First World War, they rose relatively to prices of such other goods. During the depression of the thirties, while the prices of cotton manufactures went down, they did not decline by as large a percentage as the prices of agricultural commodities. It was only when the Second World War boosted the demand for agricultural commodities again that the parity prevailing before the First World War was restored.

7.4   STRUCTURAL CHANGES IN THE COTTON-MILL INDUSTRY, 1919–39

Some of the structural changes which had already begun before the First World War continued during the interwar period. The proportion of looms to spindles continued to increase because of the growth of mills catering mainly to the home market for piecegoods and because of the curtailment of yarn exports from Bombay (to an annual average of 42 million yards during the period from 1926–7 to 1928–9, compared with an annual average of 245 million yards during the period from 1906–7 to 1908–9).[64] The proportion of Indian mill output of cotton yarn of counts up to 20s to total yarn output (by weight) decreased from above 80% during the first five years of the twentieth century to 72·7% in 1914, 67·8% in 1919, 65·3% in 1924, 59·2% in 1929, 57·3% in 1934 and 52·4% in 1937. The proportion of output of yarn above 40s to total yarn output (by weight) increased from 0·2% in 1901 to 0·3% in 1914, 0·5% in 1919, 0·8% in 1924, 1·9% in 1929, 4·4% in 1934, and 7·3% in 1937.[65] The proportion of coloured piecegoods produced by Indian mills to their total output of cotton piecegoods (by weight) increased from 16·4% in 1901 to 22·0% in 1914, 26·6% in 1919 and 27·4% in 1924. However, this proportion went down later because of the enormous increase in the output of *dhoties* and shirting, particularly of the superior varieties. In 1929 this proportion was 22·4%, in 1934 21·0% and in 1937 19·6% only.[66]

[64] Mehta: *Cotton Mills of India*, p. 163.
[65] Sastry: *Statistical Study of India's Industrial Development*, pp. 79–84.
[66] *Ibid.*, pp. 80–5.

These changes reflected a better adaptation of Bombay to the requirements of the domestic market, but more importantly, the higher rate of growth of centres such as Ahmedabad, Cawnpore, and Madras, which produced the better varieties of cloth, displacing the imports from the U.K. In Bombay, the process of adjustment was extremely sticky. The capital values of the mills had been unduly inflated owing to the boom of the war and immediate post-war years. Thirty out of the 80 mills in Bombay changed hands between managing agents and owners during the boom years from 1917 to 1922, and this contributed to the inflation of capital values.[67] The wages in Bombay were higher than in other centres of the Presidency and of the rest of India. All major centres of the cotton industry had had to grant wage increases after 1920; but, while in many other centres wages fell around the middle 1920s, in Bombay they remained high throughout the decade. Attempts to reduce wages and employment caused costly strikes in Bombay in 1928 and 1929. The fact that Bombay mills had to bring about a better deployment of labour in relation to machinery and a production structure better adapted to domestic needs in the face of a large absolute decrease in total production and employment during the 1920s made their task much more difficult than that of mills in Ahmedabad or Cawnpore, where there were large increases in production and employment.

It would, however, be misleading not to point to a basic failure of mill management in Bombay to understand the gravity of the situation and grasp the need for drastic changes in their methods. Arno Pearse observed that, while, in Ahmedabad, managing agents generally spent the whole day either in the mill office or in the mill, in Bombay, the representative of the managing agents visited the mill for only short periods, and not every day;[68] the large number of mills and other businesses under the umbrella of the same managing agents led to inadequate attention being paid to individual mills. Two other deficiencies mentioned by Pearse can also be attributed to the deficiency of management in the Bombay mills. The Bombay mills had a larger proportion of worn-out or obsolete machinery and they had less working capital than Ahmedabad mills. While it is true that the faster growth of Ahmedabad in recent years would have led to a capital structure made up of a larger proportion of capital goods of later vintages, this would have an economic significance only if the older capital stock of Bombay mills had ceased to yield any positive quasi-rent. If it had ceased yielding any current gross profits, then the rational procedure would be to replace it. Since the Bombay mills had made very large profits during the boom years, it would not have been financially impossible to do so, and a higher rate of plough-back

[67] Mehta: *Cotton Mills of India*, p. 156.
[68] Pearse: *Cotton Industry of India*, pp. 119–20.

of profits would also have taken care of the needs of working capital.[69] But this did not happen. The managing agency system tended to lead to an undue concentration on problems of finance rather than of production at the plant level. It also led to various malpractices such as payment of commission by sellers of cotton or of machinery to the managing agents. There were other abuses which were strictly illegal in character but could not be corrected until the situation of the mill had become hopeless. Some mills had become museums of machinery bought from firms for which the managing agents happened to be the selling agents in India at that moment, or which were willing to pay a commission to the managing agents.[70]

Within Bombay, the adjustment to heightened competition was achieved through the writing down of capital, both during the later years of the 1920s and during the early part of the 1930s.[71] There was also progress in the re-deployment of labour in Bombay; although, because of the opposition of organized labour, the mill-owners could not introduce in all mills a scheme for improving efficiency which might reduce labour costs (in 1932) by between 17% and 20% in weaving, the number of spindles and looms operated by a worker did go up in most mills. For example, between 1930 and 1933 Bombay mills managed to reduce their requirements of labour on every 100 looms from 94 men to 61 men.[72]

Other centres of industry also achieved higher productivity per unit of labour and raw materials. Harold Butler reported that (in 1937) in Bombay and Ahmedabad there existed mills in which weavers looked

---

[69] The complaint usually voiced about the excessive dividend payments of Bombay mills during the boom years acquires a rationale only if it can be shown that the profits they handed out could have been profitably invested in the cotton-mill industry itself and that they would not have been re-invested in the mill industry once the crisis had started in 1923. But whether the management of most mills would have employed the retained profits wisely, at least until after 1926, remains an open question. See ITB: *Cotton Textile Industry Enquiry, 1927*, Vol. I, *Report* (Calcutta, 1927), Chapters VI and VII.

[70] For the fiercest indictment of the managing agency system in cotton mills in India, see the evidence of the Bombay Shareholders' Association, Bombay, in ITB: *Cotton Textile Industry*, Vol. II, *Views of the Local Governments, etc.* (Delhi, 1934), pp. 180–251; for more balanced but hardly less severe judgements see ILO Studies and Reports, Series B, No. 27, *The World Textile Industry, Economic and Social Problems*, Vol. I (Geneva, 1937), pp. 198–200; ITB: *Cotton Textile Industry Enquiry, 1927*, Vol. I (Calcutta, 1927), pp. 85–90; Buchanan, *Development of Capitalistic Enterprise in India*, pp. 165–71.

[71] Mehta: *Cotton Mills of India*, pp. 169 and 180. The paid-up capital of Bombay mills was reduced from about Rs. 200 million in 1922–3 to less than Rs. 150 million in 1929–30 with little change in capacity. In 1933–4, a large number of Bombay mills failed, including the Currimbhoy group of mills, the largest group under a single managing agency house.

[72] ITB: *Report on cotton* (Calcutta, 1932), para. 110; Mehta, *Cotton Mills of India*, pp. 170 and 179.

after 2, 4 or even 6 looms.[73] The Special Tariff Board of 1936 reported a general increase in the length of cloth woven in relation to its weight in the mills of British India and native states.[74] Another development which is considered an improvement is more properly regarded as adaptation to the opportunity for replacing imports of finer varieties of piecegoods mainly from the U.K., viz., the growth of bleaching and printing facilities. One index of this growth in Bombay city is the consumption of water by Bombay mills which increased from 80·65 million gallons in 1929–30 to 227·90 million gallons in 1938–9. There were only about half a dozen mercerizing ranges in Indian mills in 1930; by 1940 another twenty had been added.[75] It is not possible to accept the imports of dyeing and bleaching machinery as affording a proper index of the growth of such facilities, since much of the bleaching and dyeing was carried out as a cottage industry with the use of very little machinery.

The adjustment to the challenge of Japanese competition, and to the opportunities afforded by the increase in the size of the domestic market open to Indian mills as a result of the loss of competitive power by the British industry, took place along two broad directions. First, there were improvements in efficiency in established centres such as Bombay and Ahmedabad. There was also a general growth in multiple-shift working in all the major centres in the 1930s right up to 1939, when mills were faced with increasing stocks and falling sales, and closed their night-shifts, until the war came to their rescue.[76]

Second, there was a spread of the industry to new locations which were nearer to the local markets and which also had lower wage costs. Since labour cost accounted for anywhere between 15 and 25% of total costs, and raw material costs were the same, mills in low-wage centres such as Cawnpore, Calcutta or Coimbatore were much more profitable than Bombay mills.[77] Since a sizeable proportion of the latter had been supplying low-quality yarn to Chinese markets, their equipment was less suitable for weaving finer goods, whereas their wage costs demanded that they should concentrate on more sophisticated goods, where the greater skill of the workers in Bombay would count. The movement away from

---

[73] ILO Studies and Reports, Series B, No. 29, Harold Butler: *Problems of Industry in the East with Special Reference to India, French India, Ceylon, Malaya and the Netherlands* (Geneva, 1938), pp. 22–3.

[74] ITB, Special Tariff Board: *Report on cotton* (Delhi, 1936), p. 22.

[75] Mehta: *Indian Cotton Textile Industry*, p. 21 and footnote on pp. 21–2.

[76] See Gov. India, CISD: *Review of the trade of India in 1939–40* (Delhi, 1940), p. 40.

[77] An idea of the differences in wages between Bombay and other centres at different times can be obtained from ITB: *Cotton Textile Industry Enquiry*, Vol. 1 *Report* (Calcutta, 1927), Table LXVI; *Report of the Cawnpore Textile Labour Enquiry Committee* (Allahabad, 1938), Table IV; and Labour Investigation Committee: *Report on an Enquiry into Conditions of Labour in the Cotton Mill Industry of India* by S. R. Deshpande (Delhi, 1946), pp. 5–129 and pp. 197–8.

Bombay was also thus induced by the spinning of finer yarn and weaving of finer varieties of cloth, in Ahmedabad and in the mills under the management of Binny and Company. Ahmedabad also had the advantage that bleaching and dyeing were carried out as a cottage industry without the use of expensive machinery.[78]

The changes in the locational pattern of the cotton industry led to certain interesting developments. Up to the middle of the 1920s, the general trend in the established centres had been towards the setting-up of combined spinning and weaving establishments, and towards an increase in the size of individual mills (mills in Ahmedabad were typically smaller in size than those in Bombay). During the thirties a number of purely spinning mills were set up round about Coimbatore in Madras, which was favoured by nearness to markets (handloom weavers of Madras were the main customers), raw materials and the cheapness of electric power.[79] Many of the units which were set up in the new centres were smaller than the mills in older centres. In the cotton-mill industry the optimum size depended to a large extent on the varieties of goods produced.[80] The Indian Tariff Board of 1932 found that there were no significant economies of scale in cotton spinning and weaving on the purely manufacturing side; it was in overhead costs of management and taxes, and in the cost of power, that a large-sized mill might be able to show some advantage over a smaller-sized one. They concluded:

It may be stated, therefore, that the determining factor in fixing the size of a mill in India is mainly the extent of economy which a large-sized mill may bring about in the cost of power. Where, as in Bombay, power is derived from an outside central source of supply, a larger load will mean on the average a smaller cost per unit of power. On the other hand, where power is generated by the mills themselves, as in Ahmedabad, it is found by experience that the maximum economy is obtained where the size of the mill is between 600 and 700 looms.[81]

If we remember the multi-product nature of a cotton mill, we can also see why good management becomes crucial for its success; Ahmedabad was in

---

[78] See ITB: *Cotton Textile Industry*, Vol. IV, *Oral Evidence given by the applicants for protection before the ITB* (Delhi, 1934), p. 3. Mr Saklatvala (representing the Bombay Mill-owners' Association): 'In Bombay, we can scarcely compete against Ahmedabad where the bleaching is done by local washermen. That is why in respect of bleached goods where there is coloured yarn, Ahmedabad has got the bulk of the trade.' On factors governing the dispersal of the mill industry in India after 1925, see Sastry: *Statistical Study of India's Industrial Development*, pp. 22–7; Mehta: *Structure of Indian Industries*, pp. 154–68.

[79] ITB: Special Tariff Board: *Report on cotton* (Delhi, 1936), p. 15.

[80] Mehta, *Indian Cotton Textile Industry*, Chapter I, shows the impossibility of fixing a unique optimum size for the cotton-mill industry at any moment of time, for all centres and all combinations of types of products produced.

[81] ITB: *Report on cotton* (Calcutta, 1932), para. 90.

this respect far better served than Bombay, for it was rare for any company to look after more than one mill or two.[82]

We have already noticed that Ahmedabad had from the beginning been adapted to the domestic piecegoods market and was in a better position to exploit the opportunities for import substitution. It is possible that her advantages increased still more in this respect in the early thirties, when, because of accelerated development of some industries in India, the movement of terms of trade in favour of industry and a general increase in the inequality of income distribution (increased debts of peasants being one reflection of this phenomenon), the rate of growth of finer varieties of goods was faster. Although no details of the way in which finer varieties of goods were made up are available, it is significant that, between 1930–1 and 1934–5, the proportion of yarn of counts above 30s to total yarn output increased from 10 to 14% in the whole of India; it increased from 20 to 26% in Ahmedabad, and from 12 to 17% in Bombay, over the same period. Similarly, the output of yarns above 50s was concentrated in Ahmedabad and expanded faster in that centre over the period from 1930–1 to 1934–5 than in other centres.[83]

The move to new centres of production was not always a move towards a greater degree of efficiency for the industry, particularly if one takes a long-term view. The use of second-hand machinery, which was often supposed to lower technical efficiency compared with older centres with up-to-date machinery, was often quite rational, given the lower wages, higher rates of interest and/or a low limit on the total amount of capital available, faced by the capitalists investing in units in the new centres. But there is no doubt that the mills were very often badly designed and badly managed, because of ignorance of the best technical conditions on the part of entrepreneurs and their managers.[84] Many of the mills in regions and centres such as Uttar Pradesh, Madhya Pradesh, Nagpur and Cawnpore came to show, after the Second World War, higher labour costs per unit of output than Bombay and Ahmedabad, in spite of lower wages.[85]

Many mills in the low-wage centres such as Cawnpore, West Bengal and Madhya Pradesh also experienced special financial difficulties after the Second World War when they had to replace obsolete equipment. The report of the Technical Subcommittee of the Working Party on the Cotton

[82] ITB: *Cotton Textile Industry*, Vol. IV, *Oral Evidence* (Delhi, 1934), p. 76.

[83] ITB, Special Tariff Board: *Report on cotton* (Delhi, 1936), pp. 19–20.

[84] See, in this connection, Buchanan: *Development of Capitalistic Enterprise in India*, p. 203. 'Many of the upcountry mills have been laid out to fit the pocket books and the cautious ambitions of the group of local residents who formed the companies, men usually lacking in knowledge of the business, and too anxious to economise.' See also the description of Mills No. 26 and 27, both up-country mills, in Pearse: *The Cotton Industry of India*, pp. 150–3.

[85] See Gov. India, Ministry of Commerce and Industry: *Report of the Textile Enquiry Committee, 1958* (Delhi, 1958), Chapter x.

Textile Industry (1952) gives the accompanying figures for the cost of replacement and renovation in different centres of industry:[85a]

Centre	No. of mills which submitted returns	Total no. of spindles in these mills	Total no. of looms in these mills	Approximate cost of renovation and replacement for spinning and weaving only (Rs.)
Ahmedabad	38	1,067,000	23,200	70,000,000
Bombay	38	2,200,000	50,000	300,000,000
Delhi – U.P.	10	476,000	9,500	48,000,000
Coimbatore	11	336,000	872	13,000,000
Madhya Bharat	8	217,000	5,600	20,000,000
Madhya Pradesh	6	256,000	5,300	46,000,000

Expressing the total cost of renovation and replacement in different centres as cost per spindle or cost per loom, we get the following figures:

Centre	Cost per spindle (Rs.)	Cost per loom (Rs.)
Ahmedabad	66	3,017
Bombay	136	6,000
Delhi – U.P.	101	5,053
Coimbatore	39	14,908
Madhya Bharat	92	3,571
Madhya Pradesh	180	8,679

It can be seen that excepting the case of cost per spindle for Coimbatore, the cost of replacement per loom or spindle in the high-wage centre of Ahmedabad is lower than in every other centre. The higher cost of replacement per loom or spindle in Bombay is due to the troubles of the Bombay industry during the interwar period.

7.5 RELATIVE EFFICIENCY OF INDIAN AND JAPANESE COTTON-MILL INDUSTRIES

In spite of the changes in the location of the industry, in the varieties of goods produced and in the efficiency of operation of machinery, and in spite of protective duties of up to 50%, Indian mills could not fully cope with Japanese competition. There were some mills in the country which even in

[85a] *Report of the Working Party for the Cotton Textile Industry* (Delhi, 1953), Annexure C, at p. 125.

1932 could probably compete on equal terms with the Japanese mills.[86] But the vast majority certainly could not survive in free competition with Japanese imports.

Of course, Japan was already at the end of the 1920s one of the lowest-cost producers in the world. During the 1930s the depreciation of the yen gave her even greater advantages, particularly because the wages of workers tended to lag behind the prices of goods, so that real wages of workers in all textile branches fell during the period from September 1933 to September 1936, and she was alone among the major cotton-textile producing countries (not including China and India, however) in this respect.[87] But Japan possessed other advantages which neither India nor Great Britain had. The vast majority of the mills in Japan were combined in the Japan Cotton Spinners' Association, which was able to introduce short-time working in periods of crisis, and which organized the import of raw cotton from India and later on from China.[88] The Association was able to raise the prices of cotton piecegoods for consumption at home by charging high prices for yarn, and to reduce the prices of goods for export by offering low prices to bleachers and finishers. But its power in this respect was challenged by the federation of weavers' guilds.[89] The Association was also able to hasten the diffusion of any new methods in the industry.

Secondly, 'most of the importing of raw cotton and a large part of the exporting of cotton cloth are in the hands of three big merchant houses'.[90] Thirdly, the export guilds established in 1925 had wide powers 'to regulate the volume of exports, to impose levies thereon and to allocate quotas'.[91] Fourthly, four mill combines in 1929 controlled 60% of the whole industry. Finally, the Japanese marketing methods were much more flexible than those of Indian or European firms: the rate of return charged on turnover was generally lower, and the selling organizations had a better knowledge of local market conditions.[92]

Apart from these specific advantages in commercial organization and marketing, the Japanese were also obtaining the results of a much higher degree of industrialization and literacy than India. Japan had introduced a number of improvements by the end of the 1920s, including the warp-stop motion which increased the productivity of a weaver plying ordinary looms by a very large percentage.[93] But she had also pioneered the use of new types of automatic looms, the most successful and most famous of which was the Toyoda automatic loom.

[86] See ITB: *Report on cotton* (Calcutta, 1932), para. 118.
[87] See ILO: *World Textile Industry*, Vol. 1 (Geneva, 1937), pp. 245–9.
[88] A. S. Pearse: *The Cotton Industry of Japan and China* (Manchester, 1929), pp. 25–6.
[89] ILO: *World Textile Industry*, Vol. 1 (Geneva, 1937), p. 202.
[90] *Ibid.*, p. 201.   [91] *Ibid.*, pp. 201–2.
[92] Pearse: *Cotton Industry of India*, pp. 1–14; and *idem: Cotton Industry of Japan and China*, pp. 142–3.   [93] *Ibid.*, p. 83.

In the beginning of the 1930s, a Japanese weaver (man or woman) usually operated six looms, whereas the typical weaver in Bombay operated only two looms. Although there was some improvement in the efficiency of the weavers in India, because of the higher degree of improvement in Japan the difference in labour costs was not eliminated, but probably tended to increase over time.[94] The technical backwardness of India is dramatically illustrated by the failure of the Indian mill industry to adopt automatic looms or automatic attachments on any large scale.

Arno Pearse in 1930 found that Binny Mills in Madras was employing automatic looms (it was the only cotton mill to do so) and commented: 'The goods produced on their 2,300 automatic looms (mostly Northrop looms), though nothing but Indian (shortstaple) cottons are used in the spinning of the yarn, are the most perfect which the writer has seen on his journey through India; they are mostly high-class cotton suitings as well made as any in the country.'[95] Pearse also describes the results of an experiment with 22 Toyoda automatic looms and 11 ordinary looms in Mill No. 4, which he visited. It was found that with the use of automatic looms the saving in total costs (including depreciation and interest charges) came to 0·5375 annas per lb. of cloth.[96] Binny Mills (merged in 1930 into Buckingham and Carnatic Mills Company) prospered throughout the 1930s. The Indian domestic market was one of the biggest in the world; there was a noticeable trend towards displacement of high-quality British cloth and yarn by goods of high quality produced domestically. Under these circumstances, one would have expected a rapid spread of automatic looms for purposes of producing standardized commodities which could be sold in a grey or bleached state or which could be made into coloured goods of various kinds.

---

[94] For a comparison of Japanese and Indian labour costs per unit of cotton yarn or piecegoods produced, see Buchanan, *Development of Capitalistic Enterprise*, p. 381 (the figures used by Buchanan related to 1928). Mr Sasakura of the Toyo Podar Mills, Bombay, gave evidence before the Fawcett Enquiry Committee confirming the observations of enquirers from outside the mill industry. See ITB: *Report on cotton* (Calcutta, 1932), para. 106. Colin Clark used the data collected by the Fuji Gas Spinning Company in the latter part of 1932 to estimate the labour costs in spinning of yarns up to 40s as 0.53 pence per lb. in Japan as against 2.20 pence per lb. in the U.K. and 2.43 pence per lb. in India. It is probable that the wage costs used as the basis for comparison referred to Bombay; the labour costs in other centres within India would probably be lower after allowing for lower wages and lower productivity than in Bombay. See ILO: *World Textile Industry*, Vol. 1 (Geneva, 1937), pp. 203–17, for a comparison of different elements of the total cost of production of cotton yarn and cloth in several countries, including the U.K., U.S.A., Japan and India. This study also reported (pp. 215–17 and 299–300) an increase in Japan in the productivity per spindle per hour and per loom per day from 1927 to 1932 and from 1932 to 1936 (latest date for which data were available). The data came from various sources and generally covered subperiods of the period 1923–36, but they all confirmed the general impression of a reduction in labour costs of yarn and cloth through an improvement in the efficiency per worker and per loom or spindle.

[95] Pearse, *Cotton Industry of India*, p. 9.　　　　[96] *Ibid.*, pp. 125–7.

The failure of the automatic loom to catch on in India is probably attributable to several factors, such as imitation of Lancashire methods by technical men brought up to admire the virtues of Lancashire, lack of familiarity with Japanese methods and machines, the high initial cost of automatic looms, and the lessening of the pressure to reduce costs after the denunciation of the Indo-Japanese Convention in 1933. A sizeable proportion of managers or supervisory personnel in the mills of Bombay had been trained in Lancashire itself; most of them had been trained (in the mills or at the Victoria Jubilee Technical Institute) by men brought up in the methods of Lancashire. The machinery came almost exclusively from the U.K. The automatic loom used in the trials, on the basis of which it was judged to be unprofitable under Indian conditions, by two Indian Tariff Boards was the Northrop loom; neither European nor Japanese looms were even considered.[97] On 1 January 1934 the percentage of ordinary looms to the total number of looms in place was 97·0 in the U.K. and 97·6 in India. On 31 July 1936 the proportion of ring spindles to the total number of spindles in place was 27% in the U.K., 93% in India, 99% in the U.S.A. and 100% in Japan. It was supposed to be the case that mule spindles were useful only for spinning high grades of yarn with highly skilled labour. In view of that, only attachment to Lancashire methods and/or failure to replace obsolete machinery can explain the survival of mule spindles (7% of all spindles in place) in India.[98]

The lack of literacy of Indian workers and their poor standards of physique were also considered by many observers to be barriers to the adoption of new techniques requiring constant attention and high speeds. In contrast, the very high standard of literacy and technical training among Japanese workers was considered to be a great help in this direction.[99] The fact that Japanese workers were not unionized whereas the Bombay workers could put up an effective fight against any increase in workload without an increase in wages, and against retrenchment, was probably also a factor in favour of Japan. But one must notice that the difficulties of Bombay were accentuated precisely because of the failure of mill-owners to take

[97] See ITB: *Cotton Textile Industry Enquiry*, Vol. I, *Report* (Calcutta, 1927), pp. 143–5, and ITB: *Report on cotton* (Calcutta, 1932), p. 65. In both the cases the number of automatic looms that a weaver was supposed to operate was very low: the number of Northrop looms that a weaver could operate was taken to be only 4 or 5, whereas in Binny Mills, according to Pearse, a weaver operated 6 of them. In Japan, a weaver could operate up to 50 Toyoda looms. It is fair to point out that the President of the Indian Tariff Board of 1932 was not convinced by the arguments of the representatives of the Bombay Mill-owners' Association about the uneconomic character of automatic looms. See ITB: *Cotton Textile Industry*, Vol. IV, *Oral Evidence* (Delhi, 1934), pp. 10–11.

[98] For data on spindles and looms, see ILO: *World Textile Industry*, Vol. I, pp. 48–56. For information on the imitation of Lancashire methods in Indian mills see also Buchanan, *Development of Capitalistic Enterprise*, pp. 203–5.

[99] See Pearse: *Cotton Industry of Japan and China*, pp. 11–12, and Butler, *Problems of Industry in the East*, p. 24.

advantage of increasing demand for domestic goods and expand production and employment, and that centres other than Bombay and (to a much lesser degree) Ahmedabad rarely faced any effective trade union resistance.

The diversity of conditions in the different centres of industry frustrated several attempts made by the Bombay mill-owners during the thirties to adopt uniform standards in production or to curtail production by working short time. The scheme of rationalization was not adopted uniformly even within Bombay. It is possible that tariff protection followed by quantitative restrictions on imports from Japan allowed many Indian firms to survive without decreasing costs. But it is difficult to see how, without some element of government supervision and compulsion, any movement for rationalization or short-time working could have succeeded when there were several hundred mills scattered throughout the country, with cost and production structures varying greatly from centre to centre.[100] Perhaps with production concentrated in the hands of half a dozen firms or in the hands of a group with the same social and political background (as in the case of the jute mills of Calcutta), effective group action might have come about; but that also would have required some government sanctions if interlopers tended to upset the apple cart (as was required in the case of Bengal jute mills and in the case of Bihar and United Provinces sugar mills at the end of the thirties).

Finally, one can ask whether the existence of a cotton-textile machinery industry would have helped the Indian cotton-mill industry to reduce its costs. The answer must be that as an isolated industry kept alive only by tariff protection it might in fact have increased costs. But with the existence of a heavy engineering industry with a tradition of training men for skilled adaptation, the picture might have been different. Even under the generally backward conditions of Indian industry, a home-based cotton-textile machinery industry, drawing its raw materials from other Indian industries, might have helped the situation during and after the First World War (and especially after the Second World War) by enabling mills to replace their equipment and by keeping down the cost of new machinery, which was inflated by the domestic pressures of the war-ravaged countries of Europe.

If we give up such speculation as unprofitable, we can still notice the effects of the different patterns of the economic growth of India and Japan on their cotton-textile industries. At the beginning of the twentieth century Japanese efficiency in the production of cotton yarn and cloth was supposed

---

[100] See ITB: *Report on cotton* (Calcutta, 1932), pp. 74–6, on the benefits that might have been reaped from the rationalization of production in individual mills, bulk purchase of cotton by a central organization and elimination of inefficient units. For a description of the attempts at rationalization of the industry and the reasons for their failure see P. S. Lokanathan: *Industrial Organization in India* (London, 1935), pp. 306–8 and *Report of the Textile Labour Enquiry Committee*, Vol. II, *Final Report* (Bombay, 1940), Chapters VIII and IX,

TABLE 7.10 *'Real' investment in the cotton-mill industry of western India, 1905–6 to 1938–9*

Year	Imports of cotton-textile machinery into Bombay (Rs. '000) (1)	'Adjusted' imports of cotton-textile machinery into Bombay (Rs. '000) (2)	Index numbers of prices of textile machinery exported from the U.K. to Bombay (1904=100) (3)	'Real' value of imports of cotton-textile machinery into Bombay (Rs. '000) (4)	'Real' value of gross investment in the cotton-mill industry of western India (5)
1905–6	107,26	107,21	100.38	106,80	164,47
1906–7	116,58	116,53	89.19	130,65	201,20
1907–8	142,74	142,68	89.81	158,87	244,66
1908–9	135,33	135,27	97.46	138,80	213,75
1909–10	113,07	113,02	93.68	120,64	185,79
1910–11	76,53	76,50	100.74	75,94	116,95
1911–12	77,82	77,78	100.14	77,67	119,61
1912–13	88,21	88,21	110.86	79,57	122,54
1913–14	158,14	158,14	101.40	155,96	240,18
1914–15	132,61	132,61	103.43	128,21	197,44
1915–16	108,80	108,80	109.14	99,69	153,52
1916–17	115,42	115,42	174.33	66,21	101,96
1917–18	106,53	106,53	253.93	41,95	64,60
1918–19	151,62	151,62	375.01	40,43	62,26
1919–20	98,76	98,76	295.54	33,42	51,47
1920–1	286,45	286,45	331.81	86,33	132,95
1921–2	607,78	607,78	362.88	167,49	257,93
1922–3	659,49	659,49	307.80	214,26	329,96
1923–4	446,62	446,62	242.33	184,30	283,82
1924–5	206,38	206,38	236.02	87,44	134,66
1925–6	183,61	183,61	208.15	88,21	135,84
1926–7	132,05	132,05	233.10	56,65	87,24
1927–8	149,23	149,23	262.24	56,91	87,64
1928–9	166,97	166,97	195.74	85,30	131,36
1929–30	155,41	155,41	188.65	82,38	126,87
1930–1	134,86	134,86	198.48	67,95	104,64
1931–2	158,95	158,95	—	—	—
1932–3	173,10	173,10	—	—	—
1933–4	142,61	142,61	—	—	—
1934–5	159,55	159,55	—	—	—
1935–6	128,37	128,37	—	—	—
1936–7	103,17	103,17	—	—	—
1937–8	178,60	178,60	—	—	—
1938–9	165,17	165,17	—	—	—

Sources and Notes: The price index is derived on the basis of figures of quantity and values of textile machinery given in *Annual statements of the foreign trade of the U.K.* (PP), Vol. I (up to 1919) and Vol. III (from 1920 onwards). The units for the prices are tons of textile machinery. The figures of imports of textile machinery into Bombay are obtained from *Annual statement of the seaborne trade of British India* for the relevant years (Calcutta, annual), Vol. I. Figures for cotton-textile machinery imports are available separately from textile machinery imports only since 1912–13. For deriving the figures before that, the proportion of the value of cotton-textile machinery imports to that of total textile machinery imports into Bombay was estimated for the years from 1912–13 to 1916–17, the years 1912–13 to 1914–15 being given on weight double that for the years 1915–16 and 1916–17. This proportion came to 0.99955, and this served as the multiplier for the figures in the first column up to 1911–12 for deriving the figures in the second column up to the same year. (The proportions are very similar for the sub-periods 1911–15 and 1916–18.)

The price indices related to calendar years and were applied to the figures for corresponding fiscal years (April–March), a three-month lag between exports from the U.K. and imports into India being quite realistic. The weights used for price indexes were quantities (by weight) of textile machinery of different kinds exported to Bombay; the classification was changed in 1914: So one series was constructed with 1904 quantities as the weights and another with 1904 quantities as the weights. The crude (aggregate) prices per ton of textile machinery exported to Bombay were calculated for 1914 and 1913. The two series were then merged by multiplying the series from 1914 to 1930 by the ratio of the price per ton of textile machinery exported to Bombay in 1914 to that in 1913. No direct check was available for the prices derived in this way. But from information supplied by Messrs. Howard and Bullough Limited, Globe Works, Accrington, England, we find the following figures for prices of carding engines:

Year	Price			Year	Price			Year	Price		
	£	s.	d.		£	s.	d.		£	s.	d.
1904	60	3	10	1910	57	2	11	1915	65	8	11
1905	60	5	3	1911	57	13	4	1916	83	4	7
1906	66	8	8	1912	62	2	1	1917	*		
1907	72	1	0	1913	65	7	8	1918	*		
1908	66	15	8	1914	59	13	9	1919	199	3	10
1909	63	17	5								

* No sales to India in 1917 and 1918. Apart from some divergence in the movement for individual figures, the above figures support the impression of stability of textile machinery prices before the war. They also support the impression of the very large increase in prices around the last half of the war, which continued after the war.

For converting the 'real' values of imports of cotton-textile machinery into 'real' investment in the cotton-mill industry in western India, we multiplied the figures in column (4) by 1.54, this being the average ratio of the block value of cotton mills in Bombay to the value of plant and machinery in those mills, as derived from the balance sheet data given in S. M. Rutnagur: *Bombay Cotton Industries: The Cotton Mills* (Bombay, 1927), pp. 363–7. The mills covered numbered 53 in 1914 and 67 in 1924, and the ratio came out as 1.54 in both cases. This is probably higher than the ratio of block value to the value of plant and machinery in centres away from Bombay port, for on the one hand, the value of land in other places would be lower than on the congested Bombay Island, and on the other hand, the cost of machinery would be higher since it would cover costs of transport from Bombay to inland centres such as Ahmedabad, Sholapur or Nagpur. From balance sheet data of Ahmedabad Advance Mills Limited for the year 1906–7, and of the Central India Spinning, Weaving and Manufacturing Company Limited for the years 1904–5, 1905–6, 1906–7 and 1908–9, the ratios of the block value of the mills to the values of plant and machinery were found to lie between 1.40 and 1.44. But our use of the ratio 1.54 is not likely to over-estimate the investment in the cotton industry before the war because (a) Bombay City and Island accounted for the major part of the investment as is evident from Table 7.5, (b) the textile machinery imports did not include bleaching and printing machinery producing power or supplying light, and (c) the cost of machinery would be higher inland than in Bombay. The risk of over-estimation is probably present to a larger extent for the post-war years since other centres away from Bombay forged ahead during that period, and Bombay was subjected to a speculative boom inflating land values. But there is no easy way of correcting such over-estimations. The official rates of exchange were used throughout. The series of 'real value' of investment could not be continued after 1930–1, for the *Annual statement of the foreign trade of the United Kingdom* do not give figures of exports of textile machinery for the different parts of British India separately after 1930.

TABLE 7.11 *Imports (in Rs. '000) of cotton-textile machinery into India as a whole (excluding Burma), 1905–6 to 1938–39*

Year	Imports of textile machinery (Rs. '000)	Imports of cotton and jute machinery (Rs. '000)	Imports of jute machinery (Rs. '000)	Imports of cotton machinery (Rs. '000)	Real value of cotton machinery imports (Rs. '000)	Price index of textile machinery exported to Bombay (1904=100)
1905–6	248,98	245,49	117,29	128,20	127,71	100.38
1906–7	227,45	224,27	95,50	128,77	144,38	89.19
1907–8	263,29	259,60	99,06	160,54	178,76	89.81
1908–9	287,60	283,57	127,65	155,92	159,98	97.46
1909–10	215,15	212,14	78,01	134,13	143,18	93.68
1910–11	163,96	161,66	71,06	90,60	89,93	100.74
1911–12	135,81	133,91	41,56	92,35	92,25	100.14
1912–13	204,31	199,94	86,42	113,52	102.40	110.86
1913–14	327,99	324,24	145,70	178,74	176,27	101.40
1914–15	241,44	238,52	87,62	150,90	145,90	103.43
1915–16	217,44	213,55	93,60	119,95	109,90	109,14
1916–17	238,64	236,55	107,81	128,74	73,85	174.33
1917–18	188,81	185,70	69,19	116,51	45,88	253.93
1918–19	229,36	222,38	57,06	165,32	44,08	375.01
1919–20	292,40	278,46	147,77	130,69	44,22	295.54
1920–1	669,68	641,98	277,67	364,31	109,79	331.81
1921–2	12,80,80	1,195,41	432,15	763,26	210,33	362,88
1922–3	10,59,99	1,020,30	179,08	841,32	273,33	307.80
1923–4	7,19,04	696,26	136,89	559,37	230,83	242.33
1924–5	3,80,61	360,28	92,84	267,44	113,31	236.02
1925–6	3,29,17	316,34	81,58	234,66	112,74	208.15
1926–7	2,51,52	235,10	64,67	170,43	73.11	233.10
1927–8	3,08,61	291,45	94,11	197,34	75,25	262.24
1928–9	364,82	345,21	129,88	215,33	110,01	195.74
1929–30	380,68	353,38	143,86	209,52	111,06	188.65
1930–1	282,38	259,16	81,33	177,83	89,60	198.48
1931–2	247,39					
1932–3	268,05					
1933–4	260,51					
1934–5	322,99					
1935–6	341,46					
1936–7	274,79					
1937–8	450,49					
1938–9	378,77					

Sources and Notes: The sources are the same as for Table 7.10, and the price index of textile machinery is the same as in that table.

to be lower than Indian efficiency in these directions.[101] But by the end of the 1920s the workers in Japanese mills had come to be recognized as far more skilled than the workers in Indian mills. India continued to be dependent on foreign countries for the supply of cotton-textile machinery whereas Japan had built up a cotton-textile machinery industry at home, producing equipment which was often superior to that produced by the British industry, which continued to be the main source of supply for India.

[101] See Mehta: *Cotton Mills of India*, pp. 78–9 and 164.

8

PRIVATE INVESTMENT IN THE JUTE
INDUSTRY IN INDIA

8.1 THE JUTE INDUSTRY, 1900–14

The jute industry in India was established within twenty years of its establishment in Dundee and by the turn of the century it had definitely outstripped its Dundee counterpart in production. Dundee did not give up its earlier supremacy without a struggle, which found its expression in the use not only of the usual economic weapons but also of political pressure. Around 1894 the Hastings Mills introduced a night shift and this sparked off protest by the Dundee Chamber of Commerce to the Secretary of State for India, alleging violation of the Factory Act and the lack of trained inspectors to enforce the observation of the Factory Act by Indian mills generally. Sir John Leng, the senior M.P. for Dundee, visited India and inspected Indian jute mills. He ended up with the tribute that 'the hands in these mills are among the best paid native workers in India. The silver ornaments worn by the women and girls show that they consider themselves amongst the aristocracy of labour.'[1] Not all Dundee interests were appeased by Sir John's acquiescence in the views regarding labour welfare held by the jute-mill managers in India; for a handbook on Dundee published in 1912 commented acidly on the 'unwisdom' of the growth of the jute-mill industry in India as shown by the short-time working in Indian mills.[2] However, Dundee had several firms strongly interested in the supplying of jute machinery to Indian mills[3] and there were probably firms interested in both the Dundee and the Indian jute industry. Dundee was also an important centre of *entrepôt* trade in jute. So the hostility did not break out into open warfare.

In India jute manufactures remained an industry almost completely dominated by British, more particularly Scottish, businessmen right up to the end of the Second World War. Among all the directors of jute mills listed in *IIYB, 1911* (First Issue), we find the name of only one Indian, viz. Luchmi Narain Kanoria, and he was on the board of directors of the smallest jute mill in existence, the Soorah Jute Mills Company Limited, with net fixed assets (net block expenditure) of Rs. 785,357 and 175 looms

---

[1] D. R. Wallace: *The Romance of Jute* (London, 1928), p. 57.
[2] *Handbook and Guide to Dundee and District* published for the Dundee meeting of the British Association, 1912 (Dundee, 1912), p. 278.
[3] *Ibid.*, pp. 279–301.

on 31 December 1910.[4] All the other jute mills were controlled by the big British or European managing agency houses, such as Andrew Yule and Co., Bird and Co., F. W. Heilgers and Co. (headed by a German), Thomas Duff and Co., Jardine, Skinner and Co., Anderson, Wright and Co., Kettlewell, Bullen and Co. All the companies which were formed after 1900 were rupee companies promoted by British or European managing agency houses located in India: it is difficult to find out the sources of their capital, but one can guess that most of it must have come from British businessmen, officials and military men, stationed in India or with close connections with India. But the jute industry was booming and some amount of Indian capital was also invested in it.[5]

What seems so mysterious, in view of the relative simplicity of processes involved in jute manufacture and the recognized monopoly India had in raw jute production, is the almost complete absence of Indian enterprise on the manufacturing side. It is not enough to say that enterprise was deficient among Bengalis or that Marwaris were interested only in trade; for after all, many of the Parsi and Gujarati industrialists on the other side of India had made their money in trade (often trade with China) and then invested in industry. Why was that process not repeated in the jute industry before the First World War?

Part of the explanation lies in the fact that jute was pre-eminently an export commodity both in its raw and in its manufactured state; unlike cotton, however, it was not the raw material for a consumer good the demand for which already existed. The market for jute manufactures had to be sought out,[6] and this search could be made only by businessmen who had an intimate contact with the export trade. Unlike in Bombay, the export trade in Bengal had almost entirely passed out of the hands of the Indians; no Indians in Bengal owned ships, for instance, whereas Indian businessmen owned ships in Bombay even at the turn of the century.[7] One might wonder whether the size of the minimum viable unit in the jute industry also

[4] The Soorah Jute Mills had been under Indian management for a number of years but had passed under the management of McLeod and Company in 1907. See Wallace: *The Romance of Jute*, p. 35 and *IITB, 1911*, p. 96.

[5] *Report of IIC* (PP 1919, XVII), p. 15.

[6] On the work done by mills such as Samnuggur (controlled by Thomas Duff and Company, with Scottish connections) and Hastings (controlled by Birkmyre Brothers who had previously a mill at Gourock in Scotland) in seeking out new markets for jute manufactures, see Wallace: *The Romance of Jute*, pp. 37–8.

[7] See Chapter 6 above. The only important shipping and steamer companies controlled by Indians before and after the First World War were registered in Bombay. The Bombay Steam Navigation Company Limited was registered in 1906; its managing agents were Killick, Nixon and Company, but there was an Indian majority on its board in 1913. At the latter date it had a net block expenditure of Rs. 6,603,000 and it had 25 steamers and 19 steam launches besides 178 smaller craft. The company was formed in 1906 to purchase as a going concern, owing to the indifferent health of the owner and vendor, Hajee Ismail Hassum, the navigation business known under the name of Shepherds Steamers. See *IITB, 1914*, pp. 400–2.

deterred the Indians: as we shall see later, the minimum investment needed in a new jute mill around 1910–12 certainly exceeded Rs. 2 million. Although this might definitely keep out small Indian capitalists, it should not have deterred the bigger fry, for after all, there *were* cotton mills under Indian management with total capital investments of Rs. 2 million and above. But again one can argue that the bigger Indian capitalists found a safer field for investment in the cotton industry anyway.

As we noted in Section 6.5, the Europeans in eastern India controlled the export and import trade in most commodities; they controlled river transport and coastal shipping;[8] the railways connecting Calcutta to the jute districts were managed by British officials of the Eastern Bengal Railways and another private British company;[9] the exchange banks (except for Eastern Bank founded in 1910 by the firm of E. D. Sassoon) were under exclusive European control. The biggest joint stock bank in Bengal, viz., the Bank of Bengal, enjoyed state patronage and was managed exclusively by Europeans; it never had any Indian directors after the first few years from its birth in 1806, and its Board of Directors generally included partners of the biggest managing agency houses of Calcutta,[10] which were interested in jute as in practically every other article of merchandise in eastern India. Some banks under Indian control came up in the wake of the Swadeshi movement but they did not have the capital or connections to challenge the supremacy of the European banks.

In the jute trade itself, European (and Armenian) businessmen were involved at almost every stage from the buying of jute from the peasant up to

[8] The main inland steamer companies in 1910 were the Bengal Assam Steamship Company, and Port Shipping Company Limited (both under the management of Andrew Yule and Company), Calcutta Steam Navigation Company Limited (under the management of Hoare Miller and Company), India General Navigation and Railway Company Limited (originally registered in 1844 under a slightly different name; registered under the present name in London in 1899, but full particulars were quoted in the 1911 edition of *Investor's Year Book*), and Rivers Steam Navigation Company (a sterling company). The India General had a working agreement with both the Rivers Steam, and the Bengal Assam companies. See *IIYB, 1922*, entry on India General. The British India Steam Navigation Company appears to have been the dominant company in coastal shipping; it enjoyed governmental patronage, in the form of mail-order contracts, almost all along the coast of India and Burma. See Blake: *B.I. Centenary 1856–1956*.

[9] The principal railway connecting Calcutta with the jute districts was the Eastern Bengal State Railway. But some jute also came from Assam and travelled part of the way by the Assam Bengal Railway which was managed by the Assam Bengal Railway Company (registered in England) from 1892 to 1942. The East Indian Railways which connected Calcutta to the less important jute districts of western Bengal and northeastern Bihar were also managed by a private joint-stock company registered in London until 1924. See Gov. India, Railway Department (Railway Board): *History of Indian Railways constructed and in progress, corrected up to 31st March 1945* (Delhi, 1947), p. 78.

[10] For instance, in 1903, the new directors of the Bank of Bengal in place of the resigning directors included J. C. Shorrock of George Henderson and Company, A. S. Gladstone of Gillanders, Arbuthnot and Company, and J. M. G. Prophit of Turner, Morrison and Company. See *Bankers' Magazine*, July–December 1903, p. 387.

the shipping of jute and jute fabrics to foreign countries. Long after Dundee had ceased to be the centre of jute industry, London continued to be the *entrepôt* for raw jute and the arbiter in the matter of standards for raw jute and jute fabrics.[11] In the internal trade in jute, the Europeans were the dominant element as soon as one left the villages and came to the big markets such as Serajgunj, Narayangunj, or Calcutta.[12] The Europeans were organized with trade associations at every stage. There were the Calcutta Jute Dealers' Association, Calcutta Jute Fabrics Brokers' Association, Calcutta Jute Fabrics Shippers' Association, Baled Jute Shippers' Association (which was renamed Calcutta Baled Jute Shippers' Association in 1926), Calcutta Baled Jute Association, and the Indian Jute Mills Association (Indian Jute Manufacturers' Association until 25 July 1902).[13] The Indian Jute Mills Association (IJMA) had representatives in many of the associated organizations, such as the Jute Fabrics Brokers' Association.

The ties which linked the members of all these different organizations to one another and to high officials of the government before the First World War were those of a common interest (with some conflicts which could be readily reconciled in a growing market), a common language, and above all,

---

[11] A. Wigglesworth: 'India's Commercial Fibres', *JRSA*, Vol. LXXIX, No. 4075, 26 December 1930, pp. 136–7. Disputes about the quality of jute were referred to the London Jute Association and the Dundee Jute Association, from Italy, the U.S.A., and other countries.

[12] Duffus, Steel, Landale and Clark, Ralli Brothers, Sarkies and Company, David and Company and R. Sim and Company, were some of the bigger merchants in jute centres such as Narayangunj, Serajgunj, Dacca, etc. They generally had presses for pressing jute into *kutcha* bales and sending it to Calcutta for use in the mills or for export, or into *pucca* bales for direct shipping overseas. The European merchants in these centres were organized into trade associations such as the Naraingunge Chamber of Commerce, and were strongly represented in the local bodies, so that they had considerable influence over local affairs. See C. C. McLeod: 'The Indian Jute Industry', *JRSA*, Vol. LXIV, No. 3292, 24 December 1915, pp. 110–11; Eastern Bengal District Gazetteers: *Dacca* by B. C. Allen (Allahabad, 1912), pp. 110–11, 188–9, 157–8; Bengal District Gazetteers: *Pabna* by L. S. S. O'Malley (Calcutta, 1923), p. 127. There were bales and presses in the chief jute-growing districts including Mymensingh, and many of these came to be owned by Marwari merchants, particularly after the First World War. See McLeod, 'The Indian Jute Industry'; Bengal District Gazetteers: *Pabna*, p. 61; and Bengal District Gazetteers: *Mymensingh* by F. A. Sachse (Calcutta, 1917), p. 74.

[13] See, for example, *Proceedings of the Interprovincial Jute Conference held at Calcutta from the 2nd to 4th August, 1915* (Calcutta, 1915), Appendix C. In the meeting of the representatives of the jute trade with the officials of the government, A. R. Murray, the Chairman of IJMA, took the lead for the jute trade. Again, when in 1917 the Dundee Chamber of Commerce and the London Jute Association addressed a memorial to the Bengal Chamber of Commerce advocating a duty on raw jute exported to countries outside the British Empire, it was IJMA which sent the reply on behalf of the jute trade. See Imperial Institute: *Indian Trade Enquiry Reports on Jute and Silk* (London, 1921), pp. 6–9 and 27–32. For a brief history of the various associations, practically all of which were housed in the same building as the Bengal Chamber of Commerce, see Tyson: *The Bengal Chamber of Commerce and Industry 1853–1953*, pp. 59–71. See also H. Sinha: 'Marketing of Jute in Calcutta', *Indian Journal of Economics*, Conference Number, January 1929, pp. 513–47, particularly pp. 534–9.

a common social distance from the Indians among whom they lived. The government was interested in increasing railway revenues from the traffic in jute; the merchants and the mill-owners would have no difficulty in approaching the officials of the government, particularly when they were concerned with directly productive departments such as agriculture, commerce and industry, or railways. If there was a shortage of wagons for jute, a simple meeting between the Committee of the Indian Jute Mills Association and a high official of the railway concerned would be enough to remove the shortage; if there was a difficulty about the space for storage of jute in the dockyards or jetties, another meeting with the official concerned could be arranged. (IJMA usually had a representative on the Calcutta Port Commissioners.)[14] In the face of such recognized mutuality of interests, no formal discrimination against Indian merchants was called for, and perhaps the Indian merchants knew better than to try to break into this nexus. Some of the associations did have rules restricting entry to Europeans,[15] but even without such explicit restrictions Indians would have found it difficult to penetrate these organizations, as the histories of the Bengal, Madras and Karachi Chambers of Commerce up to 1947 amply testify.

The quasi-homogeneous nature of the interests controlling trade in raw jute and jute manufactures did not depend only on the formal associations: many of the firms involved were as interested in the shipping of raw jute as in the manufacture of it.[16] In addition, Andrew Yule and Company floated two steamer companies to carry jute, tea and other cargo from eastern

[14] IJMA, *Reports of the Committee* for the years 1900 to 1914 contain illustrations of such amicable settlements almost every year.

[15] See, for example, Calcutta Jute Dealers' Association, *Report of the Committee from 1st January to 31st December 1927* (Calcutta, 1928), pp. 12–17 which give the articles of association. Among these articles were the following:

'4. All European persons directly connected, either as sellers or as brokers, with the trade in jute for local consumption shall be eligible as new members of the Association.'
'5. No person shall be admitted to membership unless proposed by two members of, and seconded by the committee of IJMA and elected by a majority of the members of that Association.'

The Appendices to the Reports of IJMA contained the lists of members of the Calcutta Jute Dealers' Association and of the Jute Fabric Brokers' Association. The cementing of the relationship between jute mills and steamer companies took the shape of Bengal Mills and Steamers Presbyterian Association whose accounts were published in the Reports of IJMA.

[16] For an example see Harrison: *Bird and Company of Calcutta*, pp. 82–7. Bird and Company were founding new jute mills and exporting large quantities of raw jute at the same time. In 1914 Bird and Company was the third largest shipper of jute bags (preceded by E. Meyer and Co. and Ralli Brothers, and immediately followed by Gillanders, Arbuthnot and Co., Moll Schutte and Co., and Andrew Yule and Co.). See IJMA: *Report of the Committee for the year ended 31st December 1914* (Calcutta, 1915), Statement XIX. Birkmyre Brothers had branched out from jute manufacture into trade in raw jute; see Playne and Wright: *Bengal and Assam, Behar and Orissa*, p. 85.

Bengal and Assam when their tea output and output of jute mills grew.[17] Most of the big managements also had a sizeable interest in coal and the European companies controlled the better and bigger mines before the First World War. They were organized in the Indian Mining Association; so they had some influence on the cost of fuel. The bigger managing agencies also had a substantial interest in tea, and hence they were familiar with the problems of recruitment of cheap labour from the poorer parts, both for tea plantations and for the coal mines, which were much bigger employers of labour than jute mills before the First World War. On the whole, the problems of recruitment of labour for jute mills were much less severe than those of recruitment of labour for tea plantations or coal mines, both because Calcutta had much better communication with and much better attraction for the districts from which the labourers came than the mining districts or the districts of tea plantations in Bengal and Assam, and because wages in jute mills were slightly higher than in tea plantations or coal mines. When the Government of Bengal set up a commission in 1895 to enquire into problems of labour supply in coal and again when there was a government labour enquiry in 1905, the jute mills did not show much interest: for the latter the only problem was to adjust to the shortage of labour during the three hot months of the year, and there was no question of a secular shortage.[18]

The European jute-mill owners had, of course, no direct control over the output of jute, on which their prosperity and the prosperity of the trade in raw jute depended. They were continually concerned about expanding this output.[19] They urged the government to try to extend the area of jute cultivation and to increase the average yield of jute: if necessary, the finances might be found by imposing a small export tax on jute. The Department of Agriculture in Bengal had not earned a good name for itself in the nineteenth century; money had been wasted in utterly useless experiments with expensive equipment and alien methods.[20] The Government of India had no direct interest in the improvement of yields since Bengal was permanently settled and government revenue demands were more or less fixed in perpetuity. For the same reason the government did not have adequate

[17] Andrew Yule were represented on the board of the India General Steam Navigation Company, which had absorbed their Inland Flotilla Company, and they had formed the Bengal Assam Steamship Company Limited in 1895. See Andrew Yule & Company: *Andrew Yule & Co. Ltd. 1863–1963.*

[18] See *Report of the Labour Enquiry Commission 1895* (Calcutta, 1896), p. 1, pp. 49–50; speech of J. Nicoll, Chairman, IJMA, at the annual general meeting of IJMA, in IJMA: *Report of the Committee for the year ended 31st December 1905* (Calcutta, 1906), pp. ii–iii.

[19] See, for example, the speech of J. D. Nimmo at the annual general meeting of the IJMA in *ibid.*, pp. ix–x; Nimmo quoted David Yule with approval on the necessity of encouraging the cultivation of jute.

[20] Mackenna: *Agriculture in India*, p. 12. Mackenna quoted from an official review of the work of the Department in 1893–4.

machinery for establishing close contact with the cultivator, for the revenue officials effectively made up whatever 'agricultural extension service' there was in India. Again, there was no immediate prospect of extending the cultivation of jute by increasing the area under irrigation, for government irrigation works in Bengal had proved quite unprofitable from a purely financial point of view. But the Government of India began to take a more active interest in agriculture with the opening of the twentieth century, when J. Mollison was appointed Inspector-General of Agriculture. Shortly afterwards the Agricultural Research Institute was established at Pusa, and R. S. Finlow was appointed the Fibre Expert in Bengal in 1904.[21]

Finlow and his assistants carried out experiments at Burdwan and at Cuttack on various aspects of jute cultivation; they classified the various strains of jute, clearly established the differences between the two main varieties, *corchorus capsularis* and *corchorus olitorius*. Finlow visited different parts of India testing the suitability of different districts for jute cultivation; his team also investigated the yields of different varieties of jute under different conditions (high or low land, with or without different types of manure). They found that on the Burdwan farm a variety called Kakya Bombai gave best results. But this variety did not give the highest yield per acre under all conditions, nor did the cultivators seem to be particularly keen on applying large amounts of manure, other than badly-prepared farmyard manure, to jute land. Hence despite encouragement by the European jute agents who helped in the distribution of jute seed, the average yield of jute in Bengal did not show much improvement up to the First World War.[22]

However, as far as the aggregate supply of the fibre in India was concerned, the Calcutta jute mills did not really have much cause for worry: the area under jute cultivation was quite sensitive to price, particularly to its price relatively to that of rice, since jute and rice were competitive crops so far as land use was concerned.[23] Further, although the area under jute seems to have reached a pre-war peak in 1907–8, the actual output was higher in 1912–13. Finally, the consumption of raw jute by mills in India increased almost steadily from 2,248,000 bales (1 bale=400 lb.) in 1899–1900, to 4,459,000 bales in 1909–10, and then, with a break in 1910–11 and 1911–12, rose again to exceed previous records.[24]

Ordinarily, the Calcutta jute mills did not have to interfere with either the jute trade or the position of the cultivator in order to get their raw

[21] *Ibid.*, pp. 1–4 and 60–4; *Idem*, 'Scientific Agriculture in India', pp. 537–9 and 542.
[22] On various aspects of the cultivation of jute in India, the best reference is N. C. Choudhury: *Jute and Substitutes* (Calcutta, 1933), and its predecessor volume, *Jute in Bengal* (Calcutta, 1908).
[23] See Narain: *Impact of Price Movements*, Chapter 5.
[24] IJMA: *Reports of the Committee* for various years. The figures of actual output and consumption by mills in India are taken from statistics appended to them.

material cheap. The cultivators were not organized into any association; there was hardly any co-operative movement among the cultivators of eastern Bengal, and the prices they obtained were entirely outside their control. But in 1914 we find the IJMA protesting against the proposal of the Collector of Dacca to lend Rs. 250,000 to the *ryots* of certain districts of Dacca to help tide them over the crisis caused by a disastrous drop in the price of jute. (The drop itself was due to the sudden cessation of more than 50% of the exports of raw jute because of Britain's entry into the First World War.) The main objection of the Committee was that such loans would enable the *ryots* to hold on to their jute and would create the impression that the government would come to their aid if prices of jute fell below certain limits. After the protest by the Committee, which was communicated through the Bengal Chamber of Commerce, the Government of Bengal decided to reduce the amount of the loans to Rs. 125,000.[25]

It would, of course, be distorting reality to say that the Calcutta jute mills had no other interests to contend with before the First World War. There were first of all problems of transport: the railway system in eastern India seems to have been extremely strained from the end of the nineteenth century, and the jute trade had to fight with other interests, such as the coal trade, for the allocation of wagons. But the mills generally had an edge over unorganized interests because of their ability to convince the right people with the right arguments.[26] IJMA generally had an agreement with the steamer companies about the terms and rates for transporting jute. Sometimes this agreement broke down, and then the individual mills had to arrive at separate agreements with the steamer companies.[27] But this was

[25] IJMA: *Report of the Committee for the Year ended 31st December 1914* (Calcutta, 1915), pp. 3–5 and 48–51. The original complaint was made to the Bengal Chamber of Commerce by the Naraingunge Chamber of Commerce, which was an organization of European traders at Narayangunj, and the Bengal Chamber had asked the views of IJMA. It is one index of the difference in the role of the government in agriculture in Bombay and in Bengal that in the former several crores of rupees were usually reserved as loans to peasants every year, whereas very few such loans were made by the Government of Bengal. The action of the Collector of Dacca was quite extraordinary in that respect and he had thought it necessary to inform the Naraingunge Chamber of Commerce before making the loan.

[26] On the extreme inadequacy of track and railway wagons, see for instance *Report of the Committee on the administration and working of Indian Railways* (PP 1921, x), pp. 7–8; for two specific instances of the priority secured by the jute trade over competing interests, see IJMA: *Report of the Committee for the Year ended 31st December, 1912* (Calcutta, 1913), pp. iv–v. The Agent of the Eastern Bengal State Railway assured the Committee that he would not allow any of the mills to stop for want of coal, that is, for shortage of wagons to transport coal; Sir Henry Burk, when faced with complaints of congestion in jute traffic, dealt with them by placing 700 wagons from the North-Western Railway at the disposal of the Eastern Bengal State Railway.

[27] The agreement seems to have broken down for some time in 1905 but a new agreement was reached after a short period of time. See the speech of the Chairman at the annual general meeting of the IJMA on 27 February 1905 in IJMA: *Report of*

rather an infrequent occurrence. Presumably the ability of the mill-owners to act as a body, the common interest of some managing agents in both jute and steamboats, and the competition from the railways decreased the probability of breakdown of agreement to a large extent. There were also occasional disagreements with the shippers of jute fabrics and other interests connected with the trade.

But in the face of all these conflicts, IJMA had one great strength: its ability to speak and act as a body. The most concrete expression of such unity was the short-time agreement. After a failure of price-fixing agreements to stabilize prices in 1885, the first short-time agreement was arrived at by the Indian Jute Manufacturers' (later Mills) Association (IJMA) on 30 December 1885.[28] This agreement among the mills took various forms, including the shutting down of given percentages of looms and spindles, closing the mills for specified numbers of days, working the mills for a certain maximum number of hours, and so on. An interesting part of the agreement was that mills or their managements agreed not to expand their production capacity in any way during the validity of the agreement except when specific permission was given. This was thus an attempt at controlling not only production but also investment in an expanding market. It is remarkable that the working-time agreement was successful for most of the period under consideration. The management committees generally recognized that the working-time agreement was the most important item on which a decision had to be made.[29] Thus, within the limits imposed by the entry of newcomers, the IJMA did operate as a quasi-monopolistic body for most of the period. The number of hours per week worked by mills before the First World War generally fluctuated between 75 and 90, but it went down briefly in 1910–11 to about 48 hours.[30] In the latter period many of the mills failed to adhere to the short-time agreement, since those mills which had bought large quantities earlier at rather high prices found it difficult – because of overhead costs and the large stocks of jute – to curtail production by curtailing working hours; but the aggregate production of all the

the Committee for the year ended 31st December 1904 (Calcutta, 1905), pp. viii–ix, and *Report of the Committee for the year ended 31st December 1911* (Calcutta, 1912), p. iv (speech of the Chairman who reported that a new agreement with the carrying companies had been signed for a further period of 5 years).

[28] See Wallace: *Romance of Jute*, pp. 47–51; section headed 'Decision' in IJMA: *Report of the Committee for the years before World War I*; Tyson: *The Bengal Chamber of Commerce and Industry*, pp. 67–8.

[29] See, for example, the Chairman's speeches at the annual general meetings of the Indian Jute Manufacturers' Association in 1902 and IJMA in 1929 in IJMA: *Report of the Committee for the years 1901, and 1928*, pp. 1 and 13 respectively.

[30] For a summary of the working-time agreements and their effects on the number of working hours, see *Report of the Jute Enquiry Commission* (Delhi, 1954), Appendix IV, and Sir Alexander R. Murray, 'The Jute Industry', *JRSA*, LXXXII, No. 4263, 3 August 1934, pp. 981–2.

mills taken together *was* effectively curtailed and the gunny market again looked up.[31]

The fortunes of individual mills depended to a large extent on the management of stocks of raw jute and of jute manufactures: prices of jute varied very greatly between the immediate post-harvest months and the immediate pre-harvest ones, and they also varied enormously from one year to the next. Under the circumstances, the ability to buy raw jute at the right times and in the right quantities was the most important factor in the determination of projects of individual mills and of groups of mills. One can, therefore, understand that mills were extremely concerned about the reliability of the annual jute forecasts made by the Government of Bengal.[32] For the same reason, stability in the jute trade was also crucial for the interests of the jute mills. But so long as the trade was primarily in the hands of Europeans, the mills seem to have regarded some speculation as entirely healthy.[33]

The jute industry had an almost unbroken record of prosperity from 1895 onwards: the rates of dividends on the face value of ordinary shares went up to 25% in boom years such as 1906 and 1907; for good companies, such as Budge-Budge (managed by Andrew Yule), Howrah (managed by Ernsthausen Limited), Fort Gloster (managed by Kettlewell Bullen), Standard (managed by Bird and Company), and Union (managed by Bird and Company), the average rate of dividend exceeded 12% for the years from 1901 to 1910.[34] *IIYB, 1911* (p. 68) was quite optimistic about the profitability of the industry, in spite of the liquidation of Seebpore Jute Company and the temporary depression of the industry:

The investor in the ordinary capital of a jute mill should look to the average return which he is likely to receive over a series of years rather than to the return obtainable in any particular year, and taking one year with another the investor who does not purchase at too high a price can be fairly certain of not less than 7% on his money.

---

[31] IJMA: *Report of the Committee for the year ended 31st September 1910* (Calcutta, 1911), pp. iii–iv, and *Report of the Committee for the year ended 31st December 1911* (Calcutta, 1912), p. iii.

[32] In 1907–8 the actual crop fell short of the forecast (9,760,000 bales) by 1,080,000 bales; in 1908–9 it exceeded the forecast by 2,380,000 bales (forecast: 6,400,000 bales) and in 1909–10 the crop exceeded the forecast (7,300,000 bales) by 1,470,000 bales. These discrepancies were probably a major factor in the depression of the jute industry during the years from 1910 to 1912.

[33] See, for example, McLeod (President of IJMA): 'The Indian Jute Industry', p. 107: 'Meantime the present system gives rise to a very healthy gamble in Calcutta and London, which gives those engaged in the trade an annual opportunity of making or losing large sums of money.' According to *IIYB, 1911*, p. 68: 'In the working of a jute mill there are three distinct operations, the buying of the raw jute, its manufacture into fabrics, and the sale of those fabrics. Of these operations the first and last are the most important and require the exercise of much judgement and foresight.'

[34] The information is derived from *IIYB, 1911*, p. 71.

This estimate of the average rate of return is borne out particularly by the fact that most companies had substantial blocks of preference capital (almost as much as ordinary capital), which carried a dividend of 7% per annum. (It was only in the case of a few companies that preference shares carried a dividend of 6%.)

Our estimates of fixed investment in the jute industry show three peaks in the nine years from 1905–6 to 1913–14 (see Table 8.1), with no distinct rising trend (although investment was highest in 1913–14, in either real or money terms). It is tempting to say that this pattern of expansion was due to the fact that the managing agency firms in Calcutta controlled the expansion more or less as a group: thus the capacity would be built up to the point where it was just a little more than the demand that was foreseen and then a period of adjustment would follow, until the demand again outstripped the capacity. But the pulsating pattern was also due to the fact that jute mills came in lumpy units: it was often difficult to expand the capacity of older units because of lack of space, or because too much had to be spent on redesigning the buildings; on the other hand, new units had to have a minimum capacity.[35] Between 1896 and 1900, ten jute mills were added: of these one (Delta) was reconstructed out of an old mill (Serajgunge), one (Gordon Twist mill) was absorbed by one of the new companies (Anglo-Indian), and one (Arathoon) went down in the crisis of 1910–11, along with Seebpore. Of these ten, Anglo-India was registered in the U.K. and Gondolpara in France; the rest were registered in India. From 1901 to 1908 another nine mills were added, all registered in India. Again, three mills were added between 1909 and 1914; of these one was an American mill, promoted by a former manager of the group of mills under Thomas Duff and Company.[36] While the new units were being floated, substantial expansion was also taking place in the older units.

[35] A mill with 400 looms seems to have been considered a safe size to begin with at the beginning of the century, judging by the capacity of the new units set up: the size limit of the plant could not have been determined by financial considerations, since the same management put up different units of more or less the same size. Thus Dalhousie, registered in 1903, and Auckland, registered in 1908, were both managed by Bird and Company; Auckland had 400 and Dalhousie 430 looms in 1909 (Dalhousie had started with 400). *IITB, 1911* estimated (p. 68) that an investment of Rs. 6,000 to Rs. 7,000 per loom was necessary for a jute mill in 1911; on that basis the minimum gross fixed investment for a jute mill at that date would work out at between Rs. 2,400,000 and Rs. 2,800,000, without taking into account the working capital. An article entitled 'Our Jute Mills' in *Capital* (Calcutta), 20 January 1912, however, points out that the cost of erecting a mill was going up, and a 400-loom mill would at that date cost Rs. 8,250 per loom (including 10% as the interest on the money during the construction period, the original cost being Rs. 7,500 per loom). In that case the cost of a viable unit would shoot up to Rs. 3,300,000.

[36] Wallace: *Romance of Jute*, pp. 63–70. All the mills registered in India were listed by *IITB*. Information about the history of the mills was also collected from *Capital* (Calcutta), 3 March 1904, 5 January 1905, 12 January 1905, 22 February 1906, 11 January 1906, 19 March 1908 and 20 June 1912.

TABLE 8.1 *An approximate measure of gross fixed investment in the jute industry in Bengal, 1905–6 to 1938–39*

Year	Imports of jute machinery into Bengal (Rs. '000) (1)	Adjusted imports of jute machinery into Bengal (Rs. '000) (2)	Index nos. of prices of textile machinery exported from U.K. to Bengal 1904=100 (3)	'Real' value of jute machinery imports into Bengal (Rs. '000) (4)	Estimated gross value of real investment in the jute industry (Rs. '000) (5)=(4)×1.72
1905–6	127,97	117,22	98.52	118,98	204,65
1906–7	104,21	95,45	100.32	95,15	163,66
1907–8	108,05	98,97	105.66	93,67	161,11
1908–9	139,26	127,56	109.21	116,80	200,90
1909–10	85,04	77,90	112.31	69,36	119,30
1910–11	77,50	70,99	125.68	56,48	97,15
1911–12	45,29	41,49	125.27	33,12	56,97
1912–13	86,36	86,36	112.20	76,97	132,39
1913–14	145,65	145,65	105.20	138,45	283,13
1914–15	87,43	87,43	100.99	86,57	148,90
1915–16	93,46	93,46	118.25	79,04	135,95
1916–17	107,59	107,59	152.38	70,61	121,45
1917–18	69,18	69,18	188.26	36,75	63,21
1918–19	56,61	56,61	185.96	30,44	52,36
1919–20	147,57	147,57	251.23	58,74	101,03
1920–1	260,58	260,58	301.62	86,39	148,59
1921–2	425,78	425,78	320.91	132,68	228,21
1922–3	170,35	170,35	264.02	64,52	110,97
1923–4	131,00	131,00	190.88	68,63	118,04
1924–5	92,59	92,59	190.09	48,71	83,78
1925–6	81,66	81,66	199.41	40,95	70,43
1926–7	64,47	64,47	194.41	33,16	57,04
1927–8	94,02	94,02	209.78	44,82	77,09
1928–9	129,56	129,56	177.94	72,81	125,23
1929–30	143,74	143,74	184.45	77,93	134,04
1930–1	81,33	81,33	199.75	40,72	70,04
1931–2	32,18				
1932–3	35,93				
1933–4	31,90				
1934–5	51,66				
1935–6	115,11				
1936–7	72,73				
1937–8	105,87				
1938–9	70,75				

Sources and Notes: The data on imports of jute machinery into Bengal are from Gov. India, CISD: *Annual statements of the seaborne trade of British India* (Calcutta, annual); the index numbers of prices (per ton of jute machinery exported to Bengal from the U.K.) were derived from *Annual statements of the foreign trade of the U.K.* (PP). The method of construction of the price index is similar to that for Table 7.10. There is no direct way of checking the value of the index numbers of machinery by weight; but we find from a letter written by the Secretary of the IJMA to the Secretary of the Indian Tariff Board (IJMA: *Report of the Committee for the year ended*

31st December 1923 (Calcutta, 1924) pp. 63–6) that the cost of fully equipping a jute mill then would come to about Rs. 16,000 per loom compared with about Rs. 6,000 per loom before the war. This gives a price index for machinery (assuming that machinery prices either rose in the same proportion as other costs or that machinery costs dominated the total costs) of 267 in 1923 with 1913–14 as base, and this does not compare badly with our estimates. In the same letter the Secretary of IJMA estimated that approximately 75 % of the block expenditure was required for constructional steel, machinery, engines and plant together. Again, this estimate is consistent with the ratio of total block expenditure to plant and machinery (excluding constructional steel, etc.) of 1.72 which we derived (in order to calculate our column (5)) from the balance sheets of the India Jute Company. This was the only company (registered in Scotland) for which we could obtain a breakdown of pre-war block expenditure into plant, and machinery and the rest obtainable. For 31st March 1920, figures of the gross cost of machinery, buildings and land were available for the Champdany Jute Company (another company registered in Scotland). The ratio of gross block expenditure to the cost of machinery worked out as 1.69. The Champdany was an older mill than India Jute and its buildings and land were likely to have been purchased at lower cost, whereas substantial additions were made to its looms or looms were replaced. Considering all this, the ratio of 1.72 derived from the balance sheets of India Jute is near enough to give us some confidence. The gross investment figures thus derived are probably under-estimates, since plant and machinery also included power and lighting plant which is not included in jute machinery imports.

There was also some construction and replacement of machinery done by the jute mills themselves in their own workshops. However, a list of purchases of pig iron from the IISCO during the four years 1930–33 showed that only one jute mill purchased more than 100 tons in any of the years (Kamarhatty Company in 1932) and the typical purchase for a jute mill was of the order of 40 tons a year. See ITB: *Statutory enquiry 1933, steel*, Vol. III (Delhi, 1935), pp. 502–3. Most of the machinery constructed in the jute mills with pig iron was naturally jute-textile machinery. Assuming that only moderate-sized or large jute mills would construct their own machinery, and assuming the total number of such mills to be ninety at the most, the total amount of machinery repaired or constructed by jute mills in a normal year would come to $90 \times 40 = 3,600$ tons; thus the proportion of investment represented by construction in the workshops of the jute mills could not have been more than 25 % of total investment in machinery. (The pig iron would lose a considerable portion of its weight before it was shaped into machinery.) It is possible that, because of increasing construction undertaken by jute mills and other engineering works, our series underestimates the total gross investment in the jute industry more in the later years (after 1920 or so) than in the earlier years. On the other hand, the requirements of replacement and maintenance also increased over time, since most of the industry was built up before 1914 and since the mills were overworked during the war years.

Hence our series should not give a gravely distorted picture of net investment over time unless the relation of other types of plant to spindles and looms in jute mills changed. In deflating the series of imports of jute machinery, the index for the calendar year 1905 was applied to the imports of machinery in the financial year 1905–6, and a similar procedure was used for the other years.

In deriving the series for 'adjusted imports of jute machinery' up to 1911–12, for which only figures of total imports of textile machinery into Bengal were available, the mean of the average ratios of jute machinery imports to total textile machinery imports for the years 1912–13 to 1914–15 and for the years 1912–13 to 1916–17 was used. The coefficient of adjustment was 0·916. The exchange rates used were the official ones: £1 = Rs. 15 up to 1918–19 and £1=Rs. 10 for 1919–20.

The series of real investment could not be continued after 1930–1, because the *Accounts of foreign trade of the U.K.* (PP) do not provide separate figures of textile machinery exports for the different ports of British India after 1930.

The capital for most of the mills came from investors resident in India: of the estimated nominal capital (equities plus debentures) of £10 million invested in the jute industry on the Hooghly in 1909, about £2·8 million was invested in eight companies registered in the U.K., but this latter amount had mostly been invested before 1900.[37] A large proportion of the initial capital probably came from the managing agents themselves. Some companies also found practically all the money needed for working capital in this way; but since the substantial volumes of working capital[38] regularly went up after the time of the jute harvest and went down a little before the next harvest, it was less costly to borrow the money from the banks, whose rates of interest were quite sensitive to the volume of the jute trade.[39]

8.2   THE JUTE INDUSTRY, 1914–29

Before the First World War more than half of the raw jute produced in India was exported to foreign countries, particularly those of continental Europe and the U.S.A. In most of these countries the industry had been built up by imposing import duties on manufactured jute, while raw jute was imported duty-free. The U.K. took between a quarter and a third of the exports of raw jute from India,[40] so the cutting off of the continental markets, particularly Germany and Austria-Hungary, meant a drastic drop in the demand for raw jute; the shortage of shipping aggravated the situation and the prices of raw jute collapsed.

The divergent movements of the prices of raw jute and jute manufactures during the war are quite evident from the figures in Table 8.2. The mills on

---

[37] *IIYB, 1911*, pp. 63–4.

[38] For the group of companies registered in Scotland, the amounts invested in stocks of unfinished and finished goods (including raw jute) and total assets for the years 1908 and 1909 are given below:

	Stocks in hand			Total assets		
	£	s.	d.	£	s.	d.
Champdany (30 April 1908)	296,690	18	3	496,315	6	6
Anglo-India (28 February 1909)	280,868	19	6	973,433	2	6
India Jute (31 December 1908)	131,623	10	1	408,866	3	11
Samnuggur (31 December 1908)	208,050	16	0	617,668	6	5
Titaghur (31 December 1908)	400,308	4	2	1,089,499	15	2
Victoria (31 December 1908)	223,525	15	0	618,591	12	10

[39] The jute companies could apparently borrow directly from the banks and it was unusual for managing agents to have to lend money to a company under their management. See *Capital* (Calcutta), 12 January 1905. For the responsiveness of the demand for money, and of the rates of interest charged by banks, to fluctuations in the jute trade, see, for example, the report of the activities of the Bank of Bengal in 1899 in *Bankers' Magazine*, January–June 1900, pp. 761–2; and in 1913, in *Bankers' Magazine*, January–June 1914, p. 646.

[40] After allowing for re-exports: about a third of the exports to the U.K. were re-exported, mostly to the European continent: see Imperial Institute: *Indian Trade Enquiry Reports on Jute and Silk*, p. 4.

TABLE 8.2   *Values of exports, prices of raw jute and prices of gunny bags,*
1911–12 to 1918–19

Year	Value of exports of raw jute from India (Rs. '000)	January	Prices of raw jute (picked) (Calcutta)			Prices of gunny bags (Calcutta)		
			Rs.	a.	p.	Rs.	a.	p.
1911–12	22,55,66	1912	55	0	0	36	0	0
1912–13	27,05,07	1913	68	0	0	39	4	0
1913–14	30,82,64	1914	93	0	0	42	8	0
1914–15	12,91,02	1915	54	0	0	34	0	0
1915–16	15,64,20	1916	62	0	0	43	0	0
1916–17	16,28,81	1917	68	0	0	44	8	0
1917–18	6,45,38	1918	53	0	0	68	0	0
1918–19	12,72,01	1919	95	0	0	58	0	0

Source: Gov. India, CISD: *Statistical abstract for British India from 1911–1912 to*
1920–1 [First Issue] (Calcutta, 1923), pp. 526–7. The unit of raw jute was a bale of
400 lb; the unit for gunny bags was a bag with the weight of $2\frac{1}{2}$ lb. and a size of
$44'' \times 26\frac{1}{2}''$.

the Hooghly had practically a captive supply of jute, and they also were
monopolists as far as jute manufactures were concerned. While the beginning of the war saw a weakening of the demand for jute manufactures for
peaceful purposes, with the intensification of the operations the demand
for sandbags, canvas, cornsacks, etc. more than compensated for the fall
in civilian demand. The mills obtained cheap labour which had been released by the stoppage of railway construction and other large public works
owing to the war; they could thus operate an eighty-hour week for most of
the war period.[41]

Naturally the result was that the jute mills made very large profits during
the war; it was calculated that the ratio of net profits (*excluding* interest) to
paid-up capital was 10 in 1914, 58 in 1915, 75 in 1916 and 49 in 1917.[42]
The dividends declared during these years were also very high by any
standard.[43] But because of shortage of shipping and because of the fact that
the whole engineering capacity of the U.K. was devoted to war work, there
was very little expansion of the capacity of mills during these years. This is
evident from our figures of real investment in the jute mills (see Table 8.1)
and the figures of looms and spindles in jute mills in India given in Table
8.3.

While the war enabled the Indian jute-mill industry to steal a march

[41] For the numbers of hours worked see Sir Alexander R. Murray: 'The Jute
Industry', *JRSA*, LXXXII, No. 4263, 3 August 1934, Fig. 1, p. 982; for other details see
Gov. India, CISD: *Review of the trade of India* (Calcutta) for the war years. See also
Indian Munitions Board, *Industrial Handbook, 1919* (Calcutta, 1919), pp. 363–7.

[42] Gov. India, CISD: *Review of the trade of India for 1917–18*, (Calcutta 1918), p. 21.

[43] See *IITB, 1921*.

TABLE 8.3   *Number of looms, spindles and persons employed in jute mills in India, 1900–1 to 1939–40*

Year	Number of looms in IJMA Mills ('000) hessian (1)	sacking (2)	Total (All India) number of looms (3)	spindles (4)	No. of persons employed (5)
1900–1	6.6	8.7	15,340	317,348	111,272
1901–2	8.2	8.4	16,119	331,382	114,795
1902–3	8.7	8.9	17,189	352,214	118,904
1903–4	10.6	9.3	18,400	376,718	123,869
1904–5	11.4	9.9	19,999	409,170	133,162
1905–6	12.8	11.1	21,986	453,168	144,879
1906–7	14.5	11.9	25,284	520,504	166,895
1907–8	16.4	12.6	27,244	562,274	187,771
1908–9	17.7	13.1	29,525	607,358	192,181
1909–10	18.3	13.4	31,418	645,862	204,104
1910–11	18.3	14.0	33,169	682,527	216,390
1911–12	18.7	14.0	32,927	677,519	201,324
1912–13	18.6	14.0	34,033	708,716	204,092
1913–14	21.0	15.8	36,050	744,289	216,288
1914–15	22.3	15.8	38,379	795,528	238,274
1915–16	22.6	15.8	33,890	812,421	254,143
1916–17	22.8	15.9	33,697	824,325	262,552
1917–18	23.2	15.9	40,639	834,055	266,038
1918–19	23.4	16.0	40,043	839,919	275,500
1919–20	23.4	16.1	41,045	856,307	280,431
1920–1	24.4	16.1	41,588	869,879	288,401
1921–2	24.5	16.4	43,025	908,359	288,450
1922–3	25.0	16.4	47,528	1,003,179	321,296
1923–4	28.1	17.5	49,038	1,043,417	330,408
1924–5	29.1	18.3	50,359	1,067,633	341,723
1925–6	31.1	18.3	50,503	1,063,700	331,326
1926–7	31.3	18.5	51,061	1,083,816	333,659
1927–8	31.0	19.2	52,221	1,105,634	335,804
1928–9	31.2	19.3	52,409	1,108,147	343,868
1929–30	31.5	19.5	53,900	1,140,235	343,257
1930–1	36.2	21.9	61,834	1,224,982	307,676
1931–2	36.2	21.9	61,426	1,220,586	276,810
1932–3	36.2	21.9	60,506	1,202,183	263,442*
1933–4	35.3	21.6	59,501	1,194,405	257,175
1934–5	35.3	21.6	61,387	1,221,786	263,739
1935–6	35.3	21.6	63,724	1,279,416	277,986
1936–7	35.3	21.6	65,273	1,300,077	289,136
1937–8	35.3	21.6	66,704	1,337,958	305,785
1938–9	35.3	21.6	67,939	1,350,465	295,162
1939–40	41.1	23.7	68,528	1,369,821	298,967

Sources: Gov. India, CISD: *Statistics of British India, 1913–14* (Calcutta, 1915) and subsequent issues for columns (3), (4), (5); IJMA: *Annual Reports of the Committee* for columns (1) and (2).

* From 1932–3 to 1939–40, figures of employment relating to the calendar years from 1932 to 1939 are used.

over its competitors in other countries,[44] and to amass huge profits, it also
ended the absolute control of the jute trade and industry by Europeans. The
jute mills had already been concerned about the speculation in jute carried
on by Indian traders (mainly Marwaris) just before the war.[45] The Committee of the IJMA had submitted a draft of a Bill to the Government of
Bengal aimed at suppressing the speculation in the *bhitar bazar*, but the
government rejected the proposal as impracticable. However, after the war
IJMA had to consider the question of the *futka* market, or *bhitar bazar*,
practically every year: the falling off of demand for jute fabrics was often
blamed on the operations of the futures market in jute and jute goods.[46]

During the war Indians also seem to have captured a large part of the
capital of the jute mills;[47] the explanation cannot be that Europeans were
keen to sell their shares in the companies concerned, for jute shares continued to carry very high dividends well up to 1926.[48] One plausible explana-

---

[44] The percentage of raw jute output processed in India showed a dramatic rise
during the war, although it had been rising earlier, as shown by the following figures:

Period	Percentage of the jute crop consumed by Indian mills
1893–7 (average)	31
1898–1902 (average)	39
1903–7 (average)	42
1908–12 (average)	47
1913	49
1914	59
1915	61
1916	63
1917	71
1918	65
1919	57
1920	66

Source: IJMA: *Report of the Committee for the year ended 31st December 1921*
(Calcutta, 1922), p. 163.

[45] See IJMA: *Report of the Committee for the year ended 31st December 1911*,
pp. 9–10, and *Report of the Committee for the year ended 31st December 1912*, pp. 5–6.
It was alleged that the contracts on pink and white forms for the sale and purchase
of jute were entirely fictitious, and that this speculation in the *bhitar bazar* was purely
a form of gambling. The 'gamblers', however, must have had considerable connections
with the jute trade, for otherwise fictitious transfers could not affect the course of jute
prices.

[46] See, for example, IJMA: *Report of the Committee for the year ended 31st December
1928* (Calcutta, 1929), pp. 18–19 and 120–1.

[47] See written evidence, given in 1922, of the Marwari Association, Calcutta, claiming
that while Indians held not less than 60% of the shares in jute mills, the European
managers did not buy jute through Indian traders, in *Evidence (Report of the Indian
Fiscal Commission)*, Vol. II (Calcutta, 1923), p. 419. See also Sections 6.9 and 6.10 above.

[48] The mills managed by Andrew Yule and Company, and by Bird and Company –
the two biggest groups – often declared dividends of 100% and above, per annum. Even a
new mill such as Caledonian (registered in 1916) declared a dividend of 150% for the
half-year ended November 1920. But they were not the only companies declaring high
dividends. Another mill, Fort Gloster, managed by Kettlewell, Bullen and Company,

tion is that during the war a large proportion of the British businessmen of Calcutta were either out in the front lines or engaged in other war work.[49]

Along with the European associations for different levels of the jute trade, there now grew up corresponding Indian associations: the Bengal Jute Dealers' Association, the East India Jute Association, the Hatkhola Banijya Sabha, and the Indian Jute Balers' Association, and so on.[50] The end of the war also saw the entry into the mill industry of the first Indian-managed mills, viz., the Birla Jute Manufacture and Hukamchand Jute Mills Ltd.

8.3   THE DEPRESSION IN THE JUTE INDUSTRY, 1929–30
TO 1938–9

The policy of controlled production and expansion of the jute industry pursued by IJMA before the war was continued after the war. The mills reached an agreement in 1921 to work only 54 hours a week and this was observed throughout the twenties. The world demand for jute manufactures was expanding during the twenties: countries such as Australia, the U.S.A., the Argentine, Cuba and New Zealand were importing larger quantities of gunny bags and gunny cloth. Naturally, both the output of jute and the capacity of mills continued to expand; although the expansion of capacity by members of the IJMA was subject to restrictions, firms outside the Association were free to set up new mills or expand their capacity. Since the profits of and dividends declared by the established jute mills were very high, and since Indians had by the end of the war become familiar with the jute trade in all its aspects, it was natural that new mills should be established.[51] 'Real' values of annual gross investment in the jute industry in the 1920s were, if anything, lower than during the pre-war years (see Table 8.1, column (4)). But because of the lumpy nature of investment in jute mills, as before the war, expansion led to problems of over-production of jute fabrics which were aggravated by wide fluctuations in the prices of raw jute: since many mills bought very large quantities of jute in advance, they found it difficult to cut their own prices if they had bought most of their jute dear.[52]

declared dividends which averaged 115.5% per year over the period from October 1920 to September 1925. Kinnison (managed by F. W. Heilgers and Company) declared a dividend of 350% per annum for the half-year ended 31 March 1921.

[49] See Tyson: *Bengal Chamber of Commerce and Industry*, p. 112.

[50] East India Jute Association Limited, Calcutta: *Annual Report for the year ended 30th June, 1928* (first report of the Association) (Calcutta, 1928), p. 2.

[51] Birla Brothers, Sir Sarupchand Hukamchand, Chhajuram, Adamji Haji Dawood, and other Indian firms began to figure prominently in the accounts of clearances of jute and jute fabrics after the war. In fact, in some years, Birla Brothers ranked second only to Ralli Brothers in the clearances of raw jute.

[52] See Gov. India, CISD: *Review of the trade of India in 1926–27*, pp. 58–9; *IIYB, 1926–7*, p. 181.

Although the total exports of jute manufacturers did not in fact fall much until the onset of the depression in 1929–30, as Table 8.4 clearly shows, they did not grow either; furthermore, the profits of many mills had been badly affected in some years by fluctuations in jute prices. With the coming of the world depression around September 1929, world agriculture and consequently the demand for both raw jute and jute manufactures declined drastically. (Most of the products of Indian jute mills were coarse materials used primarily for the transport of grain, wool, and other agricultural products.)

TABLE 8.4 *Exports of raw jute and jute manufactures from India, 1919–20 to 1939–40*

Year	Raw jute exports		Total value of jute manufactures exported ('ooo Rs.)
	Quantity ('ooo tons)	Value ('ooo Rs.)	
1919–20	592	246,995	500,155
1920–1	472	163,609	529,947
1921–2	468	140,492	299,957
1922–3	578	225,285	404,942
1923–4	660	200,006	422,836
1924–5	696	290,930	517,666
1925–6	647	379,457	588,398
1926–7	708	267,804	531,809
1927–8	892	306,626	535,643
1928–9	898	323,492	569,049
1929–30	807	271,738	519,268
1930–1	620	128,847	318,945
1931–2	587	111,881	219,243
1932–3	563	97,303	217,118
1933–4	748	109,327	213,749
1934–5	752	108,711	214,683
1935–6	771	137,076	234,895
1936–7	821	147,710	279,475
1937–8	747	147,190	290,776
1938–9	690	133,967	262,611
1939–40	570	198,333	487,214

Source: Gov. India, CISD: *Annual statement of the sea-borne trade of British India,* Vol. I (Calcutta, annual).

The coming of the depression accentuated four problems which had already been faced by the mills associated in the IJMA: the first was the problem of reaching an agreement about hours of work and the expansion of capacity between the stronger and weaker members of the Association, and even more, between the new mills and the member mills. Even in years of expanding demand, IJMA had kept the 54-hour week and the agreement about non-expansion of capacity, except under special permission. In 1928, the mills secured large profit margins because of the limitation of production; but then serious questions were raised about the wisdom of the policy when it was found that continental mills were expanding their capacity, and that new mills were coming up. As a result the Committee of IJMA decided in 1928 to allow mills to work 60 hours instead of 54, but the operation of the new agreement was postponed till 1 July 1929.[53] The agreement to work 60 hours lasted from 1 July 1929 to 30 June 1930 only.

In 1928, IJMA had to allow two mills, Waverley and Craig, set up during the war and managed by Begg, Dunlop and Company, to extend their capacity by 250 looms before they would agree to join the Association.[54]

With the onset of the depression, the problem of reaching working agreements between new mills and old mills became even more acute.[55] The new mills had mostly been set up during the era of very high prices for capital goods, and did not have the huge reserves which the older mills could fall back on. IJMA went back to working for 54 hours per week after 30 June 1930, in an effort to stop the fall of prices; from 1 October 1930 to 28 February 1931 the associated mills further agreed to work 54 hours but to close down for one week per month; and from 2 March 1931 they agreed to work only 40 hours a week and keep 15% of their looms sealed.

It was natural that the new mills should find it unprofitable to abide by the agreement, and in 1931 two mills broke away from IJMA, because the latter would not grant them special permission to work longer hours. The existence of the Association itself was threatened; it had less influence on total output than before, and the restriction scheme seemed to hurt only the member mills; the jute industry probably reached its worst state in 1932, even though stocks of jute manufactures on hand were reduced. Ultimately in May 1932, after the intervention of the Governor of Bengal, an agreement was reached between the member mills and the mills outside IJMA. The Association mills agreed to stick to the previous arrangement of working 40 hours a week with 15% of the looms sealed. The other provisions of the agreement were:

---

[53] *IITB, 1928-9*, p. 183.

[54] *Ibid.*, p. 183. Begg, Dunlop and Company were not newcomers to the management of jute mills; they were the managing agents of Alliance Jute Mills Company Limited, registered in 1895. The Alliance was a highly profitable enterprise and had declared dividends of 100% per annum even in 1925.

[55] Apart from the reserves shown on the books, many mills had hidden reserves in the form of stocks of jute 'at or under cost'; many also had more looms than were shown. The latter fact was confirmed by a census of looms carried out by IJMA in 1930, when it was found that as against 52,929 mills enumerated previously, the correct figure came to 58,639 looms, that is, there was an excess of 10·79% in the actual number of looms (including those under construction). IJMA *Report of the Committee for the year ended 31st December 1930* (Calcutta, 1931), pp. 21–3; *IITB, 1929–30*, p. 188.

(a) that outside mills would work 54 hours a week with their full complement of machinery;

(b) that the Agarpara Mill would be permitted to increase the number of its looms by 64;

(c) that no other mill should increase its capacity during the currency of the agreement;

(d) that the Premchand Jute and the Sree Hanuman Jute Mills (both under Indian management), which would continue to be the members of the Association, would be given the privilege of working with their full complement of machinery for 54 hours a week during the currency of the agreement and that IJMA would be at liberty to consider a similar claim from other mills of the Association provided that the privilege did not affect more than 4% of the total number of looms in mills within the Association, including the Premchand and the Sree Hanuman Mills.[56]

This agreement seems to have bettered the position of the Indian jute manufacturers as a whole, and from 1933 onwards there was an improvement in the profits of the industry, with a break in 1937 and 1938. The agreement is remarkable in two respects: it shows how side payments can be profitably offered by members of a coalition to induce members outside the coalition to observe certain rules of the game. The agreement also shows the usefulness of the government as an arbiter in bringing about monopolistic arrangements. The success of the working-time agreements of IJMA was to a large measure made possible by a low value of the short-term elasticity of demand for jute.[57]

The jute mills were able from 1 November 1934 to release $2\frac{1}{2}\%$ of the 15% of looms sealed earlier; there did not seem to be any immediate adverse effects on prices, and profits of jute mills appeared to improve in 1934 and 1935; there was a fall in prices of manufactures in 1936–7 and the agreement between members of the Association and outside mills about

---

[56] For details of the controversy and the agreement, see Gov. India, CISD: *Review of the trade of India in 1931–32*, pp. 82–4, and *idem: Review of the trade of India in 1932–33*, pp. 81–2; Bengal National Chamber of Commerce, *Report of the Committee for the Year 1932* (Calcutta, 1933), pp. 62–3.

[57] Chatterjee and Sinha found the elasticity of exports of raw jute with respect to prices of raw jute (First Marks) in London to be −0·37 and with respect to industrial production in the U.S.A. to be 0·45: T. P. Chatterjee and A. R. Sinha: 'A Statistical Study of the Foreign Demand for Raw Jute,' *Sankhyā*, Vol. 5, 1940–1, pp. 433–8. (The data used here were time series for 1920–38). Nanda K. Choudhry, in 'An Econometric Analysis of the Import Demand Function for Burlap (Hessian) in the U.S.A.', *Econometrica*, Vol. 26, 1958, pp. 416–28, found that the elasticity of demand for burlap with respect to (a) changes in ratios of burlap prices and prices of manila kraft wrapping paper was −0·306 for 1919–29 and −0·741 for 1930–40, (b) changes in U.S. sales of agricultural commodities was 0·267 for 1919–29 and 0·485 for 1930–40, and (c) changes in U.S. industrial output was 0·852 for 1919–29 and 1·314 for 1930–40.

working hours broke down. Progressively larger numbers of looms were released until, after 31 March 1936, all looms were released from restriction. The number of hours worked also went up. As a result prices fell, and in spite of total foreign demand responding well, profits of the mills were affected: they declined in 1936 and further in 1937. To check a further imbalance between supply and demand, the Government of Bengal promulgated an ordinance in September 1938 by which the working hours of all jute mills were restricted to 45 hours per week. Under the threat of legislation by the Government of Bengal, all the mills reached an agreement under the aegis of IJMA; under this agreement, with the exception of the smaller units, all mills were in effect restricted to a 45-hour week at a maximum. From the end of 1938, war demand began to exercise a strong influence on mill production; but by the end of the 1930s, it was obvious that under normal conditions the capacity of the world jute industry was in excess of the world demand for jute manufactures, since every attempt at complete relaxation of controls on total production in the Indian industry had led to unwanted accumulation of stocks (this happened even in 1939, a few months before the outbreak of the war).[58]

The second problem which the depression aggravated was that of the relation between the jute futures market or *futka bazar* and the jute-mill industry. The question of imposing legal restrictions on futures trading was raised by IJMA whenever raw jute prices seemed too high in relation to the prices of manufactured goods, but the problem did not seem to require any serious action until the years of the depression. An informal meeting of the jute interests was held in 1932 under the auspices of the Bengal Chamber of Commerce, to consider the question of the futures market.[59] The interests attending the meeting were more or less divided between those on the Indian side and those on the side of the Europeans. On behalf of the Indian traders N. R. Sarkar, President of the Bengal National Chamber of Commerce, urged the necessity for a futures market in jute to iron out discrepancies between seasonal supply and year-long demand. D. P. Khaitan complained that standards were tampered with by the mills so that 'rejections' were the highest standard of jute being sold. On the European side, Mr Luke, on

[58] There was a distinctly upward trend in Indian consumption of jute manufactures from 1931–2 onwards, with a break only in 1934–5; the figures of shipments up-country by members of IJMA rose from 60,000 tons in 1931–2 to 121,000 tons in 1938–1939 and 130,000 tons in 1939–40.

[59] The European interests were represented by the Bengal Chamber of Commerce, the Baled Jute Association, the Baled Jute Shippers' Association, the Calcutta Jute Dealers' Association, the Calcutta Jute Fabrics Shippers' Association, IJMA, and the Jute Fabrics Brokers' Association; on the Indian side were the Bengal Jute Dealers' Association, the Bengal Jute Growers' Association, the Bengal National Chamber of Commerce, the East India Jute Association, the Gunny Trades Association, the Indian Chamber of Commerce, the Jute Balers' Association and the Marwari Association. For reports of the proceedings see East India Jute Association Ltd, *Proceedings of the Sixth Annual General Meeting* (Calcutta, 1934), pp. 15–19.

behalf of the Calcutta Jute Dealers' Association, said that before the birth of the *futka* market, it was nearly always possible to buy jute in the *mofussil* and to sell it in Calcutta at a price which more than covered the cost; but since the *futka* market had grown up on such a large scale it had become impossible to buy in the *mofussil* at a price near the parity of the Calcutta price. This particular complaint seemed to be vindicated by the first report on the marketing of jute published by the Indian Central Jute Committee.[60] It was found that Calcutta merchants, when sending price information to their *mofussil* agents, also included the futures price, and this in turn influenced the prices paid by the *kutcha* balers. It was further stated: 'European balers, on the other hand, carry on business for the most part in accordance with the movements of genuine supply and demand, and are seldom entirely guided by *futka* which they do not regard as a true barometer of trade conditions.'[61] It is not clear what 'genuine supply and demand' means in this context, but presumably it means an estimate of the annual demand for and supply of jute manufactures; this latter estimate could probably be formed with greater certainty by dealers in close contact with the members of IJMA than by dealers who operated freelance.

The third problem, which had caused some public discussion before the depression, but became almost the single most controversial economic problem in Bengal throughout the thirties, was the relation between the mills and the growers of jute. Whereas the mills were organized into a highly effective cartel, the peasants operated under conditions of atomistic – though far from perfect – competition. There was some unofficial propaganda whenever it was felt that the growers were not getting their due share of the returns of the industry.[62] But after the disastrous fall in jute prices in 1930, vigorous propaganda was carried on to get the cultivators to restrict their jute areas drastically. This propaganda seems to have had very little effect: the area under jute fell by nearly 50% between 1930–1 and 1931–2, but went up by 25% in 1933–4, and maintained the same level in 1934–5, in spite of the fact that the price of raw jute continued to decline in 1932, 1933 and 1934.[63] The Bengal Jute Enquiry Committee of 1934 failed to arrive at a consensus about the proper methods of stabilizing the incomes of

[60] Indian Central Jute Committee: *Report on the marketing and transport of jute in India, First Report* (Calcutta, 1940), Chapter VII, 'Prices'.

[61] *Ibid.*, p. 204.

[62] We find the Committee of IJMA deliberating over the propaganda for reduction of the jute acreage by the Agricultural and Commercial Development Association – an unofficial body. The Committee (rightly) shrugged off such propaganda as inevitably ineffective, since it felt that the cultivator would be guided mainly by prices obtainable for competing crops: IJMA: *Report of the Committee for the Year ended 31st December 1921* (Calcutta, 1922), pp. 7–8.

[63] The summary data on the prices of jute and of areas under jute in British India have been conveniently reproduced in Narain: *Impact of Price Movements*, pp. 165–6 and 181–2.

the consumer. The Government of Bengal compromised by instituting from 1935 onwards a scheme for voluntary restriction: cultivators were told to cultivate given fractions of the areas sown by them in previous years. But in spite of some apparent success, it was obvious during the crisis of the years from 1936 to 1938 that any favourable effects must be attributed to factors such as a decline in prices in the previous year, or unfavourable weather conditions. The second Bengal Jute Enquiry Committee, reporting in 1939, recommended compulsory restriction, and the Government of Bengal instituted a system of licensing of jute acreage under the Regulation of Jute Area Act, 1940.

Looking back over this experiment, it seems clear that the government could not possibly succeed in what they were trying to do, first by propaganda, and then by some degree of compulsion, that is, to stabilize the incomes of the cultivators.[64] In the first place, the staff of the Department of Agriculture was quite inadequate for the work of instruction and persuasion that might be necessary. The Government of Bengal was not prepared, before the elected provincial government came in in 1937, to incur the small increase in cost which maintaining an adequate organization for compulsory crop restriction would involve. In the second place, any rational peasant could see that it would pay him to violate the government's instructions and increase the area under jute cultivated by him, if in fact jute prices went up because other peasants restricted their crop according to governmental instruction.

In the third place, even in normal years, the cultivator had to pay the middleman a large commission in one form or another, and an increase in prices in the Calcutta market was reflected in the prices obtained by the peasant only in an attenuated form. The commission paid in the first instance to the middleman was probably exaggerated: figures of 50% of the final price paid to the middleman were often quoted, and it was also believed that the share of the middleman in the revenue was higher in the case of jute than in the case of other agricultural products.[65] The First Marketing Enquiry of the Indian Central Jute Committee, however, found on the basis of several case studies that the prices paid to growers of jute in October 1937 were between 76·4% and 82% of the Calcutta landed price. By con-

---

[64] For a discussion of the problems of stabilization of prices and incomes with special reference to jute-growing in East Pakistan, see A. I. Macbean: 'Problems of Stabilization Policy in Under-developed Countries', *Oxford Economic Papers*, N.S., Vol. 14, 1962, pp. 251–66. Macbean does not pay sufficient attention to the divergences between the prices obtained by the peasants and the export prices, or to seasonal fluctuations of prices and their impact on the prices of manufactures.

[65] See, for example, the speech of B. Coventry, Agricultural Adviser to the Gov. India in *Proceedings of the Interprovincial Jute Conference Held at Calcutta from the 2nd to the 4th August, 1915* (Calcutta, 1915), p. 3; Bengal District Gazetteers, *Pabna*, p. 69; M. Azizul Huque: *The Man Behind the Plough* (Calcutta, 1937), Chapter IV, Jute (pp. 58–78).

trast, the producers of wheat and linseed received between 58·6 and 83·2%, and between 67·7 and 91·2% of the consumers' price respectively.[66] However, the handling charges of the middleman were often fixed in money terms; and the costs of transportation by rail and steamer were relatively inflexible during the years of the depression, and hence the percentage paid by the grower was higher in the years of low prices.

More serious than this was the fact that for various reasons, the grower of jute had little holding power. East Bengal had relatively poor rail communications, and the jute-growers had to try to transport the jute to the big markets before the streams dried up after the rains; also the storage facilities available to the grower were negligible; the risk of fire in the case of jute was great, and so was the loss of value because of loss of colour owing to bad storage. But an overriding factor was the need of the cultivator, who generally had a very small plot or owned no land at all, for cash. In the first marketing enquiry of the Indian Central Jute Committee it was found that

in the marketing season 1937–38 growers in East Bengal disposed of two-thirds of their jute during the months of July to October. In spite of the fact that river communications, which in this area form the most convenient means of transport, are adequate during these months, it was found that 38% of jute had been disposed of by the middle of September.[67]

The cultivator was generally heavily indebted, and the degree of indebtedness had probably increased during the years of the agricultural depression; since the money-lender was often also the local trader, his power over the cultivator was considerable. The revenue demands of the state or the landlord also coincided in time with the harvesting of jute, which was the main cash crop. All these factors combined to compel the cultivator to sell his jute crop as soon as the harvest came in, or even before the harvest if he had borrowed money on the security of the crop.[68]

The fact that the cultivator probably lost more by selling his crop at the harvest time than by selling it through the middleman is borne out by a comparison of the average harvest prices with the average prices of loose jute in Calcutta, published by IJMA.[69] The (unweighted) average harvest prices of jute in Bengal were as given in column (1) and the (unweighted) average prices of loose jute in Calcutta were as in column (2) below:

[66] Indian Central Jute Committee: *Report on the marketing and transport of jute in India, First Report*, pp. 216–18; the figures for wheat and linseed are quoted from Directorate of Marketing and Inspection, Agricultural Marketing Series: No. 1: *Report on the marketing of wheat in India* (Delhi, 1937), p. 440, and No. 8: *Report on the marketing of linseed in India* (Delhi, 1938), p. 328.

[67] Indian Central Jute Committee: *Report on the marketing and transport of jute in India, First Report*, p. 65.

[68] *Ibid.*, pp. 61–86.

[69] See, for example, IJMA: *Report of the Committee for the year ended 31st December 1949* (Calcutta, 1950), pp. 116–17.

	(1)		(2)	
Period	Rs.	a.	Rs.	a.
1911–12 to 1920–1	7	6	9	12
1921–2 to 1930–1	9	7	12	6
1931–2 to 1940–1	5	1	6	12

It can easily be seen that the prices of loose jute in Calcutta were higher than the harvest prices of jute in Bengal by 32%, 31% and 33%, for the periods from 1911–12 to 1920–1, from 1921–22 to 1930–1 and from 1931–1932 to 1940–1 respectively. The cultivator sold most of his jute at the time of the harvest when the price was often the lowest of the year, and he could not generally take advantage of increases in prices occurring later in the year. Allowing for the crudeness of the data and for the fact that the qualities of jute are not specified, it seems that the spread between the harvest prices and the weighted annual average of jute prices in Calcutta was on an average greater than the spread between prices in the *mofussil* and in Calcutta at the time of the harvest, as was found by the first marketing enquiry of the Indian Central Jute Committee, quoted earlier.

Thus it appears that a large part of the controversy about the stabilization of jute prices was not really about the return to the cultivator but about the division of the gains from arbitrage in jute between the mill-owner and the trader; in a period of falling prices each suspected the other of getting a bigger slice of the profit margin than before. This has a bearing on an analysis of investment in eastern India since a large part of the new investment was directly or indirectly financed by profits in the jute trade. Practically all of the new mills set up by Indians were not only promoted but also largely financed by people who were actively involved in the jute trade.[70]

The depression of the thirties finally raised serious doubts about the flexibility and the level of technical efficiency of the mills on the Hooghly. The jute industry had relied for its markets on the efforts of individual firms overseas; for recruiting men it had depended on its contacts with Dundee. Apprentices came out from the area near Dundee and served as the technical and managerial staff of the jute mills. So long as the mills were

[70] In this period the rationality of the cultivator's response was not doubted; there was no evidence of a perverse response to decreases in prices. A. R. Sinha found that the elasticity of supply of jute in Bengal with respect to a change in the preceding year's price of jute was 0·65. A. R. Sinha: 'A Preliminary Note on the Future Supply of Raw Jute', *Sankhyā*, Vol. 5, 1940–1, pp. 413–16. In a later analysis, Rabbani found that the equation best explaining the fluctuations of jute acreage in Bengal over the period from 1912–13 to 1938–9 was one which had as explanatory variables the acreage under jute in the previous year and the price ratio of jute and rice in the previous season. The 'adjustment model' can easily explain the relative inelasticity of jute supply after the drastic fall in 1931–2. Rabbani found the short-run and the long-run elasticities of jute acreage with respect to changes in the relative prices of jute and rice to be 0·52 and 0·90 respectively: Rabbani: 'Economic determinants of jute production in India and Pakistan'. See also Chapter 4 above.

riding an expanding market, no attention had been paid either to marketing research or technical research in jute. But with the coming of the depression it was found that the mills had been turning out too much of the coarse goods and too little of the finer varieties in which Dundee had specialized. Over time there had taken place a change of production away from sacking to hessian and from gunny bags to cloth; but both these changes were relatively simple ones, and had been prompted first by the expansion of the North American market and secondly by the fact that there were usually stiffer import duties on gunny bags than on hessian.

The depression found the jute industry in a critical situation. A sub-committee was appointed in 1933 by IJMA to look at the question of competition offered by substitutes. It was found that competition from paper bags, 'sisal-kraft', cotton bags and bagging, grain elevators, and fibres such as sisal and hemp had eroded the market for jute to a considerable extent.[71] It was also said that 'there is no industry in the world which knows so little about its business as the jute industry'.[72] The subcommittee suggested the formation of an advisory committee in London to look after the problems of jute marketing. Along with this, in 1934, Dr S. G. Barker, Director of Research, Wool Industries Research Association, was invited out to India to prepare a report on the manufacturing aspects of the jute industry.

Dr Barker found that the basic processes of jute manufacture were mainly mechanical in nature and had changed very little since the end of the nineteenth century. Many of the machines were very old, but quite well maintained and adequate for their simple purposes. The very simplicity of the processes and the fact that the supervisors had little scientific knowledge had led to a lack of initiative and technical development. The fact that the mills were completely dependent upon machine-makers in the U.K., which did not cater to the specifically Indian needs, contributed to the lack of development of the chemical engineering side. Dr Barker also found among the technical personnel of the mills a complete lack of knowledge of the chemical or other properties of the jute fibre itself. Finally, there was no agency for supplying technical, industrial, commercial or scientific intelligence to the industry. The distance from centres of industry and research in advanced countries created a sense of isolation which led to a complacent attitude among the technical personnel concerned with jute mills.[73]

[71] *Report of the Bengal Jute Enquiry Committee 1933* (Finlow Committee), Vol. I (Alipore, 1934), Appendix VII: 'Competition, Research and the Expansion of Markets for Jute Goods', Circular No. 64–D, dated 5 June 1933, from IJMA to all members of the association.   [72] *Ibid.*, p. 64.

[73] S. G. Barker: *Report on the scientific and technical development of the jute manufacturing industry in Bengal* (Calcutta, 1935), particularly pp. 38–40. See also Dr Barker's remarks at the meeting of the Royal Society of Arts at which Sir Alexander Murray read his paper on jute: *JRSA*, LXXXII, No. 4263, pp. 994–5.

Dr Barker's report is a very interesting piece of evidence, showing first that the dominance of the British managerial and technical personnel was not primarily due to the level of their technical knowledge,[74] and secondly that the basic conditions inhibiting any major technical breakthrough independently of the advanced countries applied as much to the foreign-controlled sector as to the sector controlled by Indians.

While the jute mills were looking belatedly at ways of improving the methods of manufacturing jute products and of introducing new products (Dundee had already specialized in the manufacture of the finer types of jute goods), the Government of India also made a move to improve the organization of information and research in the jute industry. The Royal Commission on Agriculture in India had already, in 1928, warned against regarding the monopolistic position of India in the jute trade too complacently, drawing a pointed analogy with the case of indigo. It therefore considered 'it most desirable that a Jute Committee which would watch over the interests of all branches of the trade from the field to the factory should be formed'.[75] It suggested that since the export duty on raw and manufactured jute brought in a large revenue (Rs. 45 million in 1926-7) for the Government of India, the expenditure on additional research and on the promotion of the interests of the trade generally should be met from central funds.[76]

The Government of India did not do anything until 1936, when it announced the formation of the Indian Central Jute Committee, representing all interests. The functions of the committee would be to 'undertake agricultural, technological and economic research, the improvement of crop forecasting and statistics, the production, testing and distribution of improved seed, enquiries and recommendations relating to banking and transport facilities and transport routes and the improvement of marketing in the interests of the jute industry in India'.[77] The Indian Central Jute Committee was actually constituted in January 1937. (The initial Government of India grant to the committee for 1936-7 was Rs. 250,000.) IJMA decided on the establishment of a small research laboratory and an information and statistical department in Calcutta and the appointment of representatives abroad with effect from 1937. Dr Barker was appointed Scientific Advisor to the Association. The cost of these proposals was not expected to

[74] The degree of scientific knowledge and technical skill required in the cotton-textile industry was in fact far higher, and Indians had succeeded in controlling the top jobs in cotton mills by the end of the nineteenth century. See Mehta: *Cotton Mills of India*, Chapter VIII; Buchanan: *Development of Capitalistic Enterprise*, pp. 210-11 and 254; Rutnagur: *Bombay Industries: The Cotton Mills*, pp. 288-314.

[75] RC on Agriculture in India: *Report* (London, 1928), p. 63.

[76] *Ibid.*

[77] IJMA: *Report of the Committee for the year ended 31st December 1936* (Calcutta, 1937), p. 292 (quoting from the resolution of the Government of India published in the Gazette of India of 28 May 1936).

be much more than Rs. 175,000. The research department of the IJMA collaborated with the Indian Central Jute Committee[78] but no remarkable results were obtained from such research before 1939.

[78] IJMA: *Report of the Committee for the year ended 31st December 1938* (Calcutta, 1939), p. 134.

9

THE GROWTH OF THE IRON AND STEEL INDUSTRY

9.1 THE FORCES BEHIND THE SURVIVAL AND GROWTH OF TISCO

The enterprise of the Tata Iron and Steel Company constitutes the single most important instance of pioneering by private enterprise in India during the twentieth century. The representatives of both the British government and the nationalists used superlatives in describing the achievements of the Tata Iron and Steel Company (TISCO) in the field of steel.[1] It grew up without tariff protection to guard its infancy, weathered the crisis of the years 1923–34 under the umbrella of protection and then dispensed with protection altogether. It is useful to enquire into the factors which allowed it to grow into a viable enterprise when the steel industry all over the world was passing through a general crisis.

The major factors which contributed to the survival of the steel company were (a) the initial advantages enjoyed in terms of location of the plant, (b) the initially favourable attitude of the government to the enterprise, possibly induced by the decline of British steel in the Indian market, (c) the grant of protection to the industry by the Government of India both as a reward for the loyal service of TISCO in the First World War and as an insurance against another major war, and (d) the steep reduction in costs effected by TISCO during the period 1923–33. We shall deal with these different aspects in turn. In our account we shall deal with iron and steel products together; for a steel plant is generally a multi-product one and can turn out both iron and steel products. In fact, in a small and fluctuating market, a measure of diversification will give it flexibility. We shall see later on that one of the major advantages of TISCO over other Indian enterprises producing only iron products lay precisely in this versatility and flexibility. Furthermore, we shall emphasize in the following account the political forces bearing on the growth of the steel industry, because these have previously been insufficiently stressed.[2]

---

[1] See, for example, the speech of the Viceroy, Lord Chelmsford, on the occasion of his first visit to the TISCO works at Sakchi on 2 January 1919, reprinted in Lovat Fraser: *Iron and Steel in India* (Bombay, 1919), pp. 103–4; this ardour of the government survived the Tata Company's demand for tariff protection. See, for instance, the speech of Sir Charles Innes in the debates on the Bill for granting tariff protection to steel (*Legislative Assembly Debates* (New Delhi), 27 May 1924, pp. 2327–8). For a sample of nationalist opinion see the speech of Pandit Madam Mohan Malaviya in the same debate (*ibid.*, pp. 2320–1).

[2] A more straightforward account of the growth of the iron and steel industry is to be

9.2 THE INITIAL ADVANTAGES ENJOYED BY TISCO
AND HURDLES IN ITS PATH

TISCO enjoyed initial advantages in respect of the cheapness of raw materials, including ore, coal and water. While the existence of good quality iron ore in abundance in India had been known for at least thirty years before the Tata Company began to produce steel, the finding of a suitable site for the erection of a modern steelworks needed many years of prospecting. If entrepreneurship is defined in the original Schumpeterian sense,[3] then what was achieved during the years from 1900 to 1905 must rank as work of a high order of entrepreneurial ability. But at least the technical experts – and after the mining regulations were revised, the government – did not offer any positive obstacle to the work of the prospectors.[4]

The major obstacles faced by the new Tata enterprise stemmed from a group of factors which can be traced to the colonial nature of the Indian political and economic organization. The refusal of the London money market or the technical experts in England to help the new enterprise[5] was due to the contemptuous belief that India would never make steel of saleable quality. This belief was flying in the face of the record of American and European steel production since 1865 onwards: every country which had usable iron ore and coal resources and had a home market for steel, had developed steel production. Most of the technical problems of treating iron ores of low or high phosphorus content had been solved and many other countries were competing sucessfully, and increasingly so, with the U.K. for world steel markets.[6]

The attitude of the British financiers and 'experts' cannot be explained, therefore, on grounds other than prejudice or, perhaps, self-interest narrowly

found in Buchanan: *Development of Capitalistic Enterprise in India*, Chapter XIII. Professor Amartya Sen has emphasized the international economic background to the political decision to grant tariff protection to Indian steel in 1924, in his important paper 'The Commodity Pattern of British Enterprise in Early Indian Industrialization, 1854–1914', in *Deuxième Conference Internationale D'Histoire Economique, Aix-en-Provence 1962* (Paris, 1965), pp. 780–828.

[3] J. A. Schumpeter: *The Theory of Economic Development* (Cambridge, Mass., 1934), particularly Chapter II, p. 66.

[4] The *Quinquennial Review* and other publications of the Geological Survey of India contain useful information on the minerals of British India; the geologists in charge, including Sir Thomas Holland, generally welcomed the development of the iron and steel industry in India.

[5] On the attempts of the Tata firm to raise money in London, see Fraser: *Iron and Steel in India*, pp. 51–2. On the failure of the Tatas to get blast furnaces or a manager for their steelworks in England see the evidence of Sir Fazulbhoy Currimbhoy in *Evidence* (*Report of IIC*), Vol. II (PP 1919, XVIII), p. 369.

[6] See, for example, Duncan Burn: *The Economic History of Steel-Making* (Cambridge, 1940). Chapters V–X.

conceived.[7] On the other hand, that Tata naturally turned first to the U.K. for supply of money and technical men was also due to the tight nexus of economic domination in which India was related to the U.K.

Although some British experts working in India were sympathetic to Tata enterprise, not all of them were. In particular, the experts of Indian railways, which were the largest single customer of steel products, were sceptical about the prospects of making good quality steel rails in India.[8] In other respects too, the environment was quite hostile to the starting of steel production in India under Indian management. Most of the big engineering concerns in India were in exclusively British hands, and these firms rarely employed Indians in supervisory capacities. The recruitment of engineers and other technical personnel for railways and public works took place largely in England, as we noted in Chapter 6, and in fact the Government of India maintained from the 1870s a Royal Indian Engineering College at Coopers Hill in Surrey, at great expense, for the purpose of training engineers intended for service in India. The prospectus of the college specifically excluded Indians from entry, except in special cases.[9] In general one can say that (a) there was no receptivity to Indian steel on the part of large customers in India because of their dominance by European experts and European managers,[10] and (b) there was no pool of skilled personnel in India from which TISCO could hope to recruit its supervisors and technicians.[11] The management of TISCO had, therefore, to work in this colonial environment. Their first move had been to secure

[7] It is possible in fact that British technical experts recognized in a new Indian steel industry a threat to their market for steel products in India. But why should those experts who were not managers or owners of plants be deterred by this consideration? And why should all financiers stay aloof because the profits of *some* British steel firms might go down? It is difficult to believe that capitalists as a class can in fact act together even on small matters and that there is no competition between individual capitalists. That the financiers might in fact have been prepared to go in if they could *control* the new enterprise is evidence that in fact they did tend to think of Indian enterprise in terms of *domination* and not profitable co-operation if they had anything to do with it. See Fraser: *Iron and Steel in India*, pp. 51–2.

[8] See H. M. Surtees Tuckwell: 'The Tata Iron and Steel Works: Their Origin and Development', *JRSA*, LXVI, No. 3402, 1 February, 1918, p. 193.

[9] See *Reports and correspondence relating to the expediency of maintaining the Royal Indian Engineering College, and other matters* (PP 1904, LXIV), particularly Appendix 1. See also Chapters 2 and 5 above.

[10] Even though there were railway apprenticeship schemes for training the lower-level supervisory staff in India, very few Indians, as distinct from Europeans resident in India or Eurasians were in fact accepted for such schemes. See the *Report of IIC* (PP 1919, XVII), pp. 103–4, *Report of the Committee appointed by the Secretary of State for India to enquire into the administration and working of Indian Railways* (PP 1921, X), paras. 182–4.

[11] Steel was being made by government ordnance factories in India. But Brigadier General H. A. Young, Director of Ordnance Factories in India from 1917 to 1921, stated categorically: 'There has been little attempt to train the Indian for posts of responsibility in the Ordnance Factories.' H. A. Young: 'The Indian Ordnance Factories and Indian Industries', *JRSA*, LXXII, No. 3,715, 1 February 1924, p. 181.

the goodwill of the Secretary of State for India and the Government of India;[12] Lord Crewe, the Secretary of State for India, visited Sakchi on 6 January 1911, when the works had already started producing pig iron.[13] The Government of India had in its turn helped the company in acquiring land for the works, and in constructing a railway line from Gurumaishini to Kalimati, and a short railway connection from Kalimati to Sakchi.[14] The Government of India also undertook to purchase on behalf of the state railways 20,000 tons of steel rails annually for a period of ten years, the conditions being that the rails must comply with government specifications, and the price be no more than that of similar goods delivered c.i.f. Indian ports.[15] Also concessions in rates were granted by railways on the freight of raw materials to the works and on all finished products dispatched for shipment from Calcutta.[16] (Such concessions for bulk freight were, however, nothing unusual and were enjoyed by many big concerns.)[17]

The incentive for establishing a steel industry in India is to be found in the widespread evidence of the existence of large reserves of very good iron ore, the increasing consumption of iron and steel products (including railway materials) at the beginning of the twentieth century (see Table 9.1), and the rising prices of iron and steel imported into India during the years from 1904 to 1906.[18] While the Bengal Iron and Steel Company had already established that the production of pig iron was highly profitable in India, the manufacture of steel was a much more difficult proposition altogether. But it was also clear that the future lay in steel and not in iron products, for there was a progressive substitution of steel for iron (e.g. in place of cast iron pipes, steel tubes were being used as water mains).[19] A company producing only pig iron would have to depend on a highly fluctuating export market, whereas a company producing steel could depend on a large internal market if only foreign competition could be overcome or

[12] Fraser: *Iron and Steel in India*, pp. 15–18.

[13] *Ibid.*, pp. 69–70.

[14] *Ibid.*, pp. 54–5. Similar facilities were given to the Indian Iron and Steel Company. See the evidence of G. A. Young, General Manager, Indian Iron and Steel Company Limited in RC on Labour in India, 1931, *Evidence*, Vol. v, part 2 (London, 1931), p. 32.

[15] Tuckwell: 'Tata Iron and Steel Works', p. 194; Cumming [*IPG pub.*]: *Review of the Industrial Position*, p. 23. As Keenan reports, however, the government's attitude may have been similar to that of 'the London comedian who some years later offered to give £5,000 to the widow of the Unknown Soldier'. J. L. Keenan: *A Steel Man in India* (London, 1945), p. 35.

[16] Anstey: *The Economic Development of India*, p. 243.

[17] See, for example, the oral evidence of G. H. Fairhurst, representing the Indian Iron and Steel Company, in ITB: *Evidence (Report on steel)*, vol. III (Calcutta, 1924), p. 157.

[18] See Gov. India, CISD: *Review of the trade of India, for the years 1904–5 to 1906–7* (Calcutta, annual): the paragraphs on imports of iron and steel.

[19] See *ibid.*

TABLE 9.1   *Iron and steel imports into India, 1894–5 to 1924–5 (figures in tons)*

Year	Private merchandise		Government stores		Total	
	From all countries	From the U.K.	From all countries	From the U.K.	From all countries	From the U.K.
1894–5	207,787	116,324	21,237	21,237	229,024	137,561
1895–6	285,125	159,502	28,892	28,892	314,017	188,394
1896–7	272,296	156,734	38,077	38,076	310,373	194,810
1897–8	289,700	177,150	40,350	40,300	330,050	217,450
1898–9	248,650	142,500	17,400	17,400	266,050	159,900
1899–1900	221,750	144,850	32,450	29,250	254,200	174,100
1900–1	262,600	149,350	23,950	23,950	286,550	173,300
1901–2	339,050	165,650	31,750	31,700	370,800	197,350
1902–3	367,300	200,050	37,550	37,350	404,800	237,400
1903–4	455,150	265,500	37,550	37,500	492,700	303,000
1904–5	467,450	283,000	27,850	27,850	495,300	310,850
1905–6	520,500	281,100	42,450	42,400	562,950	323,500
1906–7	523,750	334,300	34,050	34,050	557,800	368,350
1907–8	616,900	347,300	28,600	28,600	645,500	375,900
1908–9	611,000	345,350	23,350	23,250	634,350	368,600
1909–10	602,300	370,050	28,550	28,350	630,850	398,400
1910–11	642,750	385,050	24,650	24,550	667,400	409,600
1911–12	684,047	408,198	16,060	16,060	700,107	424,258
1912–13	729,311	436,922	16,211	16,211	745,522	453,133
1913–14	1,018,248	611,286	17,210	17,210	1,035,458	628,496
1914–15	608,635	421,503	16,166	15,977	624,801	437,480
1915–16	424,597	289,351	17,034	16,844	441,631	306,195
1916–17	257,169	176,725	16,881	16,881	274,050	193,606
1917–18	152,049	76,829	13,450	13,335	165,499	90,164
1918–19	181,406	76,932	15,303	15,131	196,709	92,063
1919–20	426,946	269,346	18,514	15,707	445,460	285,053
1920–1	711,890	498,291	25,016	24,926	736,906	523,217
1921–2	612,781	280,548	20,780	20,166	633,561	300,714
1922–3	746,467	359,393	24,730	23,959	771,197	383,352
1923–4	756,053	428,902	21,915	20,995	777,968	449,897
1924–5	868,923	439,430	19,914	16,470	888,837	455,900

Source: Accounts of the seaborne trade of British India, Gov. India, CISD: for the relevant years (Calcutta, annual). There were rounding errors in the figures for 1897–8 to 1910–11 because they were taken up to the nearest thousand cwt. and then converted into tons. Up to 1912–13, only 'iron' and 'steel' were distinguished. After that 'iron', 'iron or steel' and 'steel' were distinguished.

eliminated. In 1906, the year in which the house of Tata was trying to raise capital in London, the iron and steel industry was specially prosperous. 'Both in England and America the past twelve months has been a period of great prosperity in the iron and steel industries', wrote *The Economist* of 24 November 1906.[20]

[20] Quoted in Sen: 'The Commodity Pattern', p. 805.

9.3 THE SUPPLY OF RAW MATERIALS TO TISCO

The works were situated excellently from the point of view of access to raw materials and to the biggest market for steel in India, viz. Calcutta.[21] (Most of the British engineering firms, which were also the largest private workshops apart from the railway ones, were situated near Calcutta and Howrah.) Tatanagar (formerly Kalimati) station was about 155 miles west of Calcutta on the main line of the Bengal Nagpur Railways. TISCO owned or leased coalfields and iron-ore mines. The coalfields were north of the works, the distance by rail averaging about 115 miles. Ore was at first brought from the deposits (Gurumaishini being one of them) in Mayurbhanj, at an average distance of 50 miles or under, and was later on also mined from Noamundi in Singhbhum, which was about 80 miles south-west of Jamshedpur (formerly called Sakchi).[22] The flux for the blast furnaces was dolomite, which was obtained from Panposh in Gangpur state, about 100 miles west of Tatanagar. The dolomite was also mined at Rajgangpur, about 126 miles away. Moreover, the company had long-term contracts with another firm for the supply of dolomite.[23] The company owned a limestone quarry at Jukehi near Katni, about 500 miles away; from this source it obtained the limestone used as the flux for the steel furnaces. Later the Jukehi quarry was closed and limestone was bought from Katni. The company also owned limestone quarries near their dolomite quarries but the quality was not as good as at Katni.[24] The company was admirably located as far as the supply of water was concerned: the works were so planned as to be bounded on the north by the Subarnarekha river, and on the west by the Khorkai river. The former was never known to run dry in the hottest summer, and the risk of shortage of water was eliminated by putting across the Subarnarekha a low dam, creating a reservoir, and using a pumping system by which used water was cooled and returned to the reservoir.[25] It was actually the advantage in respect of water along with the difficulty of obtaining sufficient land at Sini, the originally chosen site, which led the consultants to choose Sakchi.[26] The company also possessed manganese mines at Balaghat, a distance of 32 miles by railway (a railway line was constructed for the purpose of bringing

---

[21] Gov. India, CISD: *Annual statements of seaborne trade*, Vols. I and II (Calcutta, annual).

[22] R. H. Mather: 'The Iron and Steel Industry in India', *JRSA*, LXXV, No. 3,886, 13 May 1927, pp. 600–16, at p. 604.

[23] ITB: *Evidence on steel*, Vol. I, *The Iron and Steel Industry* (Calcutta, 1924), p. 278; Harris: *Jamsetji Nusserwanji Tata*, pp. 204–5.

[24] Tuckwell: 'The Tata Iron and Steel Works', p. 194; ITB: *Evidence* (*Report on steel*), Vol. I (Calcutta, 1924), p. 278.

[25] Harris: *Jamsetji Nusserwanji Tata*, p. 192.

[26] *Ibid.*, pp. 191–2.

the ores), and these provided sufficient manganese not only for the use of the company but also for export.[27] The company finally owned magnesite mines in Mysore, 1,329 miles away from Tatanagar, but it found it cheaper to buy magnesite in Madras or from foreign sources.[28]

The greatest single advantage that TISCO possessed was probably the cheapness of iron ore. According to Julian Kennedy, of the firm of consulting engineers for the Tata Company, 'to make the ore for a ton of pig iron costs [before the First World War] 75 cents here, as against 8 dollars in Pittsburgh'.[29] It also possessed enormous advantages in being located on a river which had a perennial flow.[30] The distance of good-quality limestone might be considered a handicap but the limestone near Panposh, though of inferior quality, would be cheap enough to be used by TISCO, which probably did not suffer much because of this disadvantage.[31]

The situation as regards coking coal was not very satisfactory if one looked at the quality of the coal consumed. According to Tutwiler, the general manager of TISCO works, the ash content of the (coking) coal used at Jamshedpur was as high as 18%.[32] Thus the ash content was equivalent to that of several tons of British coking coal of the best quality. Further, the coking coal also contained a high percentage of phosphorus. It is this high percentage of phosphorus in the coking coal, rather than the percentage of phosphorus in the iron ore itself, which contributed a high percentage of phosphorus to the pig iron and therefore necessitated the use of the basic open-hearth process in the production of steel.[33]

[27] *Ibid.*, p. 205. But the company found it profitable, at least until 1923, to buy its requirements (20,000 tons a year) under a ten-year contract with the Central Provinces Syndicate. See ITB: *Evidence (Report on steel)*, Vol. 1 (Calcutta, 1924), p. 297.

[28] *Ibid.*, p. 279.

[29] Harris: *Jamsetji Nusserwanji Tata*, p. 204.

[30] For example, Mr H. Fitzpatrick, representing the Bengal Iron Company, on 8 November 1923, said that the Barakar river on which their works (erected much earlier than the Tata works) were situated dried up in the hot season, and that steel could be produced there only when storage facilities had been provided. See ITB: *Evidence (Report on steel)*, Vol. III (Calcutta, 1924), p. 218.

[31] ITB: *Report on steel* (Calcutta, 1924), pp. 13–14 and 102–3. According to the estimates of the United Steel Corporation of Asia Ltd, a company organized by Bird and Co. of Calcutta, and Cammell Laird and Co. of Sheffield, much less than a ton of limestone would be necessary for a ton of pig iron and the cost of limestone would be Rs. 1 - 8 out of a total works cost of Rs. 32 - 8. ITB: *Evidence (Report on steel)*, Vol. III (Calcutta, 1924), pp. 168–9 and 173. The cost of dolomite which was used as a flux by TISCO was Rs. 1 - 12·44 as., out of a total materials cost of Rs. 18 - 8·70 as. in 1916–17, and Rs. 3 - 4·64 as. out of a total materials cost of Rs. 34 - 7·52 as. in 1921–2. *Ibid.*, Vol. I (Calcutta, 1924), pp. 185–6. Hence neither limestone nor dolomite could be considered a dominating item of cost.

[32] *Ibid.*, Vol. I (Calcutta, 1924), p. 227.

[33] ITB: *Report on steel* (Calcutta, 1924), p. 97 (the report of Dr Fox of the Geological Survey of India), and p. 4. The basic Bessemer process could not be used because the percentage of phosphorus in the pig iron was not high enough; the phosphorus is needed in the basic Bessemer process to generate the heat. See, for example, Peter Temin: *Iron and Steel in Nineteenth Century America* (Cambridge, Mass., 1964), pp. 144–5. The

TISCO owned only small coal mines before 1917. (Jamadoba mine was bought in 1917 and Sijua in 1918.)[34] In order to protect itself it entered into contracts with various collieries. The price of coal in these contracts was geared to the price paid to the collieries by the Railway Board of the Government of India. As the cost of raising and moving coal increased, because of rises in wages of labour and because of lack of wagons available for the movement of the coal, the price of coal rose both in the open market and for the Railway Board, and hence for TISCO.[35]

It was alleged at the time of the tariff enquiry that the cost of coal purchased under contract by TISCO was too high, and that this cost could have been avoided if TISCO depended only on its own coal mines. This argument is invalid on two counts. First, since TISCO could not be sure of the supplies from its newly-bought coal mines, it was right to cover itself by entering into contracts with other firms. Since the railways were the largest single consumers of coal in India, it is natural that the terms offered to other firms by the collieries should be linked to, but less favourable than, the terms offered to the railways.[36] Secondly, the imputed cost of the coal from its own coal mines to TISCO could not be based on the historical cost of the mines; for a proper assessment of profitability of steel-making it must be based on the market price. The market price of coal sold by the Tata Company was in fact generally higher than the price Tata paid for its coal to other collieries.[37]

9.4 THE NATURE OF GOVERNMENT AND RAILWAY SUPPORT FOR TISCO BEFORE THE FIRST WORLD WAR

The fate of TISCO was linked to railways not only on the supply side but, even more importantly, on the demand side. The railways were again the biggest single consumer of steel products in India. For profitable operation of a steel plant it was necessary that it should obtain the patronage of the Railway Board, which was in charge of the state-managed railways, and of the other railway companies.[38] This was a difficult task because initially there was bound to be distrust of an Indian product

higher ash content also made for greater consumption of limestone. See ITB: *Evidence (Report on steel)*, Vol. III (Calcutta, 1924), p. 161 (the evidence of Mr Fairhurst of IISCO).

[34] ITB: *Evidence (Report on steel)* (Calcutta, 1924), p. 151.

[35] On the rise in the cost of raising, stocking and moving coal, because of shortage of wagons and other railway facilities, see the evidence of E. S. Tarlton, partner of Bird and Company, in *ibid.*, Vol. III, pp. 205–8.

[36] IISCO had a similar contract for the purchase of coal. *Ibid.*, Vol. III, p. 153.

[37] See Statements Nos. XXXVI (p. 149) and XLVIII (p. 161) in *ibid.*, Vol. I.

[38] Over the period from July 1912 to March 1923, the total output of finished steel of TISCO was 1,035,659 tons; of this 572,409 tons, that is well over 50%, was made up of rails, light rails and fishplates. *Ibid.*, Vol. I, p. 69.

even if it was of the same quality as the British standard product; the Railway Board and the company-managed railways habitually bought only British standard rails and did not consider other types of rails at all. To the question 'If you have purchased or propose to purchase Continental rails and fishplates, kindly state fully the considerations which have influenced you in doing so', the Eastern Bengal Railway and the East Indian Railway gave the uncompromising answers, 'No Continental rails have been purchased from the year 1921–2 to 1925–6 nor is it proposed to purchase such rails in the future' and 'No Continental rails were purchased during 1921–2 to 1925–6 and I am not aware of any future intention to purchase Continental rails', respectively. Most of the company-managed railways had boards of directors resident in Britain and it was the latter which decided on purchase policy. In the 1920s, with depreciation of the German currency, only a few thousand tons of rails seem to have been purchased from Germany. Before the war, there were some years, for example, 1903–4, 1909–10, and 1911–12, in which *all* the rails and fishplates imported on government account were from the U.K.; in all other years the proportion of imports of rails and fishplates from the U.K. constituted more than 90% of the total. A similar situation prevailed in respect of imports of rails and fishplates on private account, though perhaps a slightly higher percentage was bought from countries other than U.K.[39]

There was little scope for price competition or competition of any other kind unless one could make an inroad on this deep-seated prejudice. It is against this background that the attempt of TISCO to secure the patronage of the Government of India and thereby of the railways under the management of the Railway Board, must be viewed.

One could raise the question at this point whether the announced policy of the Government of India in favour of goods manufactured in India would not be sufficient for the purposes of the Tata Company. The answer must be 'No'. For, the announced policy of the Government of India had little bearing on the purchases made by the Stores Department of the India Office in London, which often called for tenders only within the U.K. This applied particularly to the iron and steel trades and affected the growth of Indian engineering firms, most of which were European-controlled.[40] The Bengal Iron and Steel Company's attempt to manufacture steel by the basic open-hearth process in 1904 was doomed not only by

---

[39] ITB: *Statutory enquiry in 1926: steel*, Vol. v (Calcutta, 1926): replies of the Railway Board (p. 2), Assam-Bengal Railway Company, Ltd (p. 101), Bombay, Baroda and Central India Railway Company Ltd (p. 108), Eastern Bengal Railway (p. 113), East Indian Railway (p. 115), Madras and Southern Mahratta Railway Company Ltd (p. 121), North Western Railway (p. 121), South Indian Railway Ltd (p. 124) to questions regarding the purchase of Continental rails and fishplates.

[40] On the deficiencies of the stores purchase policy of the Government of India from the point of view of fostering Indian industry, see *Report of IIC* (PP 1919, xviii); Chapter xii, p. 126–7. See also Sen: *Studies in Economic Policy*, pp. 19–20.

the smallness of the plant – of capacity 20,000 tons per annum – which in itself, one suspects, was the result of uncertainty about the market, but also by the great diversity of sections in the government orders for rails and other structural materials.[41] The Chairman of the Bengal Iron and Steel Company tried but failed to get the support of the Railway Board; the reply of one of the members of the Railway Board was 'We cannot help you in any way but our advice to you is that you should advertise your steel along the railways of India in the same way as you advertise tea'.[42]

The original change in the attitude of the Government of India may well have been associated with the displacement of British steel by Belgian and Continental steel over wide ranges of private merchandise, as Professor Sen has argued.[43] But it should be noted that in the field of government and railway purchases British iron and steel remained supreme, for the simple reason that government departments and railways refused to buy any other kind of steel. As Tables 9.1 and 9.2 show, there were vast differences in the control of different segments of the Indian market in iron and steel products by British producers. In the fields of private imports of iron and steel products for purposes other than use by the company-managed railways, British iron and steel products had largely been displaced by imports from the European continent. In particular, in the field of pure steel products, the British share of the market had fallen to about a fifth of the private purchases in 1911–12, when such products were separately shown for the first time in Indian foreign trade accounts.[44] In 1924–5 the share of imports from the U.K. was only about one-eighth of imports of steel products on private account.[45] However, the

---

[41] ITB: *Evidence (Report on steel)*, Vol. III (Calcutta, 1924), pp. 210 and 218–19. As an example of the lack of demand one can mention that the total government orders to the Bengal Iron and Steel Company amounted to about 600 tons of steel and included 70 different sections. Tuckwell: 'The Tata Iron and Steel Works', p. 190; and E. R. Watson [*IPG pub.*]: *A Monograph on Iron and Steel Work in the Province of Bengal* (Calcutta, 1907), pp. 56–7. The Bengal Iron and Steel Company received a subsidy of £1,500 from the government, on condition that Rs. 3 per ton had to be allowed as rebate for all steel purchased by the latter. But the company lost over £50,000 apart from the cost of the plant, which came to Rs, 1,750,000, and the experiment was stopped. See *ibid.*, p. 56, and Buchanan, *Development of Capitalistic Enterprise*, pp. 281–2. In 1904, the Bengal Iron and Steel Company was using lean iron ore (containing 46% iron) and it began to use the superior quality iron ore of Pansira Buru and Nota Buru only after 1910. But this was unlikely to have been the major factor in its failure to make steel. See IISCO: *Growth and Perspective* (Calcutta, 1968), pp. 5–10.

[42] ITB: *Evidence (Report on steel)*, Vol. III, p. 235. See also *ibid.*, p. 159, where Mr Fairhurst, representing IISCO complains that very often prices for the purpose of calling tenders were asked for only in England.

[43] Sen: 'The Commodity Pattern', pp. 803–7.

[44] In 1911–12, out of total imports of steel products on private account amounting to 156,782 tons, imports from the U.K. amounted only to 32,795 tons.

[45] In 1924–5 total imports of steel products on private account came to 228,267 tons; imports from the U.K. amounted to 27,954 tons.

TABLE 9.2   *Imports of railway materials made of iron and steel into India,
1894–5 to 1924–5 (figures in tons)*

| | Excluding 'other sorts' or construction materials | | Including 'other sorts' or construction materials | |
Year	From all countries	From the U.K.	From all countries	From the U.K.
1894–5	120,056	119,579	150,713	150,155
1895–6	162,818	161,503	206,680	205,336
1896–7	320,924	320,069	388,905	387,327
1897–8	252,550	247,900	335,650	330,950
1898–9	181,950	175,750	241,300	235,100
1899–1900	132,150	127,800	184,650	179,050
1900–1	99,400	89,550	133,150	123,150
1901–2	114,900	105,250	150,950	141,350
1902–3	149,450	148,250	174,400	173,150
1903–4	181,850	177,900	222,150	218,000
1904–5	212,050	203,400	283,300	273,350
1905–6	244,700	231,000	307,550	293,600
1906–7	176,900	172,000	256,950	251,900
1907–8	154,500	147,500	210,850	203,500
1908–9	177,950	165,900	224,800	212,300
1909–10	189,950	181,000	254,950	243,750
1910–11	181,700	180,000	232,700	230,050
1911–12	181,750	174,950	237,300	229,250
1912–13	224,550	221,450	288,350	275,650
1913–14	247,400	244,800	314,400	309,950
1914–15	240,600	239,000	286,950	283,900
1915–16	70,100	66,350	88,950	84,900
1916–17	21,181	18,347	31,449	28,059
1917–18	194	14	1,720	1,540
1918–19	61	61	511	509
1919–20	63,147	62,987	69,983	69,753
1920–1	71,500	71,227	91,842	89,624
1921–2	112,262	110,525	139,436	134,176
1922–3	176,032	165,271	200,533	187,858
1923–4	110,219	101,855	157,898	145,471
1924–5	49,095	42,752	80,764	65,634

Source: Gov. India, CISD: *Accounts of the seaborne trade of British India* (Calcutta,
annual). Up to and including 1896–7, 'other sorts' of materials did not specifically
distinguish wooden sleepers; furthermore, while the amounts of imports of other sorts of
materials were given both by value and by weight for private merchandise, for government stores only quantities by weight of the imports of 'other sorts' of materials were
given. Hence the quantities of imports of other sorts of materials on government account
were estimated by deflating the value figures by the average price per ton of imports of
other sorts of materials on government account for the years from 1897–8 to 1899–1900.
We also derived – from the figures relating to private merchandise – the prices per ton
of other sorts of railway materials imported on private account for the period 1894–1900.
All these prices were found to be increasing over time. Hence our method of deflation
may have underestimated the imports of other sorts of railway materials on government
account for the years from 1894–5 to 1896–7. On the other hand, the figure of price
per ton of government imports of other sorts of railway materials for the year 1897–8

appeared to be too low, and may have brought down the average price over the period 1897–1900. For all these reasons, the figures of imports of railway stores including other sorts of materials for the years 1894–7 are not strictly comparable with later figures. There are also rounding errors in the figures from 1897–8 to 1915–16 for the same reasons as in the case of Table 9.1.

The justification for including other sorts of railway materials is that they appear under the entry for metals and appear to have consisted mainly of iron and steel products. From 1911–12 onwards, figures for imports of bridgework were separated from those for imports of other railway materials in the case of private merchandise only. We added them in the item including other sorts of railway materials for the sake of comparability.

government rarely bought anything but British-made iron and steel products. Admittedly, the share of government imports of iron and steel products in total imports of iron and steel products for non-railway consumption was small. But this is not true of railway consumption: even if we do not include miscellaneous iron and steel products used for construction in total railway consumption of iron and steel, in a year like 1896–7, total railway imports of iron and steel products exceeded the private imports of iron and steel products by users other than the railways. (See Tables 9.1 and 9.2.) In the field of imports of railway products British suppliers ruled supreme. There was no question of competition here because in the eyes of the management of the railways, British would always be best. Thus the rebuke of the India Office to the Chamberlain Commission of 1895 expressed a simple consequence of the possession of an empire:

It is well known to the India Office that Belgian iron and steel are of inferior quality. In Lord Cross's Financial Despatch No. 3 dated 8th January 1891, it was enjoined us that for public purposes only English metal should be purchased in consequence of the inferiority of Continental iron and steel. These metals, are, however, regarded as sufficiently good by the Indian consumer and, the goods being cheap, the displacement of English by Belgian iron and steel in recent years has been very marked.[46]

That this policy was continued by private railways even after the government had taken a more favourable attitude towards the products of TISCO is sufficiently illustrated by the evidence of the privately-owned Indian railways before the Indian Tariff Board, constituted to enquire into the steel industry in 1926 (some of this evidence has been quoted on p. 299 above.)

One can argue from the figures given here that over time the ratio of imports of railway materials of iron and steel to total imports of iron and steel products tended to decline, and hence a protective tariff alone would have been enough for TISCO to capture the major share of the

[46] *Trade of the British Empire and Foreign Competition*, C.8449 of 1897, p. 577, quoted in Saul: *Studies in British Overseas Trade*, p. 199.

Indian market. The answer is that, first, the railways still remained – until net railway investment dwindled to zero in the early thirties – the most important single consumer of iron and steel products, and their attitude would definitely have influenced the markets for TISCO products. Secondly, much of the private imports of iron and steel products were in fact for public works, and there again, the attitude of the engineers and administrators in charge towards the products of TISCO would be a major factor influencing the purchases by private producers. The Government of India could conceivably have granted formal tariff protection to the indigenous steel industry and allowed the public works departments and the railways to use higher-cost British steel on the grounds of better quality. Alternatively, if the government did not want any competition for British steel in the reserved market and at the same time did not want the cost of construction in public works and railway departments raised, it could still have refused tariff protection to Indian steel or patronage to the Indian steel works: British iron and steel would, in spite of continental competition, retain a major share of the Indian market by virtue of administrative preference. It should be noted that the absolute amounts of steel imported from the U.K. were going up before the First World War.

Hence the Government of India cannot be assumed to have responded to the decline of British steel for private uses in India passively, in the form of tariff protection for Indian steel. There was a definite alteration of policy, if not before the First World War, when the government promised to buy 20,000 tons of rails from TISCO annually for ten years, then definitely after. The military importance of the TISCO works as the only iron and steel works under exclusive British control east of Suez (Australia had been largely self-governing for a long time) and the implicit promises exacted by the TISCO management probably determined the outcome as much as did the compliance with the conditions laid down under the policy of discriminating protection. The tide of the nationalist movement must have also influenced the decision.

9.5 TISCO DURING THE FIRST WORLD WAR
AND NEGOTIATIONS WITH THE GOVERNMENT

While the railway contract and other concessions by the government (including the acquisition of five square miles of land for TISCO by the government under the Land Acquisition Act)[47] gave the company the green light to go ahead, they did not by any means commit the government to a policy of helping the company if it ran into real trouble, as it was almost bound to do as soon as there was any depression in the world industry: the Indian industry being a pigmy in comparison with the

[47] Tuckwell: 'The Tata Iron and Steel Works', p. 193.

industries of Europe and the United States, it would exert little influence on the course of events and have little staying power in the form of customers' goodwill. One can regard the policy of the Tata Company throughout the war period as one of trying to commit the government implicitly to helping the company when it needed help.

During the First World War TISCO sold steel to the Government of India at prices of controlled steel in Britain. From the second year of the war onwards all the steel output was at the disposal of the government. The works supplied a variety of products to the government; rails, shell steel, and ferromanganese for a brief period in 1916, when a world shortage of the alloy developed.[48] The supplies of imported steel were cut off from India, first by the necessity of devoting all the British production to the war in Europe, and secondly by the action of submarines (a sizeable amount of construction materials and machinery for the extension of the Tata plant was lost through the action of German submarines), and thirdly by the shortage of shipping. During the latter half of 1918 the government took 90% of the Tata output, and in one month 97%. The steel supplied by the company had to meet British standard specifications, and the price allowed – the controlled rate in Britain – did not include the transport costs. The open market price of steel – even the steel rejected by the Government Inspector – came to between two and four times the price allowed (Rs. 150 a ton).[49] Since the total amount of steel supplied by the Tata company during these years came to 290,000 tons, it is obvious that the company had to give up a large amount of profit (Rs. 60 million was the estimate usually quoted[50]).

When the war began the steel production of TISCO rose to capacity: most of the pig iron produced during the period from July 1912 to June 1914 was sold, rather than used for the firm's own steel production.[51] Even during the year July 1914 to June 1915, out of a total of 160,587 tons of pig iron, 83,832 tons were sold outside. Some delay was unavoidable in starting up a plant for steel production (the company seems to have decided to push through the pig-iron production programme in the early stages because it was safer and therefore was more certain to

---

[48] *Ibid.*, p. 197.

[49] See the speech of Sir Thomas Holland at the meeting of the Royal Society of Arts at which Mather's paper 'The Iron and Steel Industry in India', was read: *JRSA*, LXXV, No. 3886, 13 May 1927, pp. 617–18. For accounts of losses to the Tata company through the hostile action of Germany during the war, see Harris: *Jamsetji Nusserwanji Tata*, p. 216.

[50] For the amount of steel supplied to the government see ITB: *Evidence (Report on steel)*, Vol. 1 (Calcutta, 1924), p. 17. The figure of Rs. 60 million as the saving to the government was obtained assuming that the steel would have cost at least Rs. 200 more per ton. This figure was quoted often in the Legislative Assembly debates on the Steel Protection Bill during the period from 27 May 1924 to 5 June 1924.

[51] *Ibid.*, Vol. 1, p. 69.

bring in some revenue, which would be needed to defray overhead and interest costs); there were also troubles arising from defects in the working of the open-hearth furnace.[52] In the beginning a very large percentage of the rails were rejected by the Railway Board; TISCO also had difficulty in selling its steel to the railways even when the steel had passed the specifications.[53]

As soon as the war started the difficulties of working the open-hearth plant multiplied because most of the operators were Germans; they were at first allowed to continue working, but according to Keenan, sabotage, or at least obstruction, was attempted even before the war had started, until the Germans were replaced by much more expensive Allied and American labour, and an American, Ralph Watson, had taken charge of the plant.[54] The supplies of steel from Europe and the United States drastically declined from 1915–16 onwards, and the needs of the Indian and British armies fighting in the Middle East increased enormously. TISCO responded to this increased demand in various ways: it produced shells, carriage wheels and at one stage ferromanganese; the blast furnaces, which were scheduled to produce 175 tons a day of pig, went on to produce 250 tons a day.[55] But the management saw the immense possibilities of expansion of steel production. An initial plan for expanding total output from 150,000 tons to 225,000 tons was revised[56] and came later to be known as Greater Extensions. The question of extending the plant capacity, by the provision of additional blowing power, additional open-hearth or duplex tilting equipment and a third blast furnace, had been mooted by Mr Perin, the consulting engineer, from 1915 onwards. At first the Government of India and the military authorities were content with encouraging the expansion scheme but 'did not actually assist it'.[57] As the war dragged on and as supplies from Europe fell more and more short of the military requirements of steel and ammunition, the Government of India took a more positive attitude towards the Greater Extensions scheme. On 19 January 1917, Mr Tutwiler, the General Manager of

[52] See the evidence of Dr A. McWilliam, Government Metallurgical Inspector, Railway Department, Railway Board, in *Evidence (Report of IIC)*, Vol. II (PP 1919, XVII). For corroboration of Dr McWilliam's statement see ITB: *Evidence (Report on steel)*, Vol. I (Calcutta, 1924), p. 226.

[53] See the exchange between Sir Fazulbhoy Currimbhoy and Dr McWilliam in *Evidence (Report of IIC)*, Vol. II (PP 1919, XVII), p. 370. See also V. Elwin: *The Story of Tata Steel* (Bombay, 1958), pp. 43–4.

[54] J. L. Keenan: *A Steel Man in India* (New York, 1943), pp. 39–44. The average wage (plus bonus) of covenanted labour in the open-hearth department jumped from Rs. 3,970·1 in 1914–15 to Rs. 9,036·4 in 1915–16. The figures are derived from ITB: *Evidence (Report on steel)*, Vol. I (Calcutta, 1924), p. 110.

[55] See Keenan: *A Steel Man*, Chapter IV; Harris: *Jamsetji Nusserwanji Tata*, pp. 217–218.

[56] See Keenan: *A Steel Man*, Chapter IV.

[57] ITB: *Evidence (Report on steel)*, Vol. I (Calcutta, 1924), p. 77.

TISCO, met General Bingley, Commander-in-Chief of the Army in India, Sir George Barnes, Secretary to the Department of Commerce and Industry, Government of India, and Sir Robert Gillam and Mr Anderson of the Railway Board; Tutwiler was asked to get on with the extension of steel output and was promised co-operation in all directions. In June 1917 the Foreign Office requested the U.S. authorities for priority for the supply of machines and materials required for the extension of steel plant. By January 1918 the Munitions Board of the Government of India had also agreed to recommend the issue of urgent war measure priority for all plant and material from England or America for the full extensions, including a plate mill and a duplex open-hearth furnace. But it still took a long time for the deliveries to be made, a large amount of equipment was lost through the action of the Axis powers, some essential equipment was commandeered for war purposes in England and the U.S.A., and the war was over in November 1918, after which all priority ratings were withdrawn. The Greater Extensions were ultimately completed only by 1924. (The government's approval of the Greater Extension Scheme was also expressed through the granting of a licence under the Indian Companies Restriction Act, 1918, dated 21 October 1918, for the increase of capital by a sum not exceeding Rs. 70 million.)[58]

The correspondence between TISCO and various bodies of the Government of India shows the former as skilled negotiators and enthusiastic collaborators with the Government of India in their military plans. 'With the ready consent of the management of TISCO, Government exercised complete control over the distribution of the output of steel, and obtained favourable rates for supplies on Government account, without having recourse to compulsion under the Defence of India Rules.'[59] Although the production of ferromanganese was astonishingly profitable the company stopped its production because the pig iron would be needed for the production of steel and ammunition.[60] When, in December 1917, the Government of India experienced a shortage of pig iron, the company voluntarily relinquished control of distribution of pig iron to the Munitions Board, although selling the pig iron on open market was far more profitable than selling it to the government at the price of Cleveland iron, not including the freight.[61]

As well as complying with the wishes of the government as regards the pricing and distribution of its major products, the company tried

[58] For a detailed account of negotiations between TISCO and the Government of India and the Secretary of State for India on the subject of Greater Extensions see *ibid.*, pp. 77–97.

[59] *India's contribution to the Great War* (Calcutta, 1923), pp. 128–9.

[60] Keenan: *A Steel Man*, Chapter IV.

[61] Harris: *Jamsetji Nusserwanji Tata*, p. 216, and *India's contribution to the Great War* (Calcutta, 1923), pp. 128–9.

to obtain the goodwill of the government for its plans for expansion even when it did not ask for help in any concrete form. On 30 November 1915, its representatives met Austen Chamberlain, the then Secretary of State for India, to explain to him its plans for expansion of output from 350 tons of shell steel a day to between 600 and 800 tons a day and ultimately to 3,000 tons, in order to provide a 'permanent armament reserve for the British Empire East of the Suez'. Mr Chamberlain was not enthusiastic, for understandable reasons. In particular, he was not prepared to concede to TISCO, the manufacturers of ammunition for a future war, the same assistance as was enjoyed by the actual manufacturers of munitions at that time. But he recommended that the subject might be taken up with the Government of India.[62]

Similarly, in September 1916, the whole scheme was placed before the Government of India, Commerce and Industry Department, as well as the Railway Board, not with the object of inviting any contribution from the government, 'but to bespeak their support and encouragement'.[63] When Mr Padshah, the representative of TISCO, met Mr Anderson, a member of the Railway Board, the former took 'the liberty of assuring him that the Steel Company are quite content with the prices which the Railway Board pay'. Mr Anderson acknowledged the saving of costs through the low prices charged by TISCO but wanted a 'counter-acknowledgement from the Steel Company that this reduction of its profits is just in view of the services rendered by the Government in fostering the Steel Company'. Mr Padshah went on to say that 'The steel company is more than content with the reduction [of profits], if the reduction be acknowledged, and kept on record by the Railway Board. When lean times come, this acknowledgement would be a help to the Steel company'.[64]

TISCO thus showed a remarkable degree of prescience in keeping on the right side of the government even at the cost of profits which would later be badly needed for replacement of worn-out and obsolete plant and expansion of the works. However, in an industry which was known to be subject to fluctuations Tata could expect trouble after the war when all the European and American producers came back to break its monopoly of the Indian market. Moreover, Tata was dependent on the goodwill of the government, for the reason that in India nine-tenths of its sales were 'ultimately in some form or other to Government, Railways, and public bodies'.[65]

[62] ITB: *Evidence (Report on steel)*, Vol. I (Calcutta, 1924), pp. 79–80.
[63] *Ibid.*, p. 81.   [64] *Ibid.*, p. 81.   [65] *Ibid.*, p. 229.

9.6 TARIFF PROTECTION FOR THE STEEL INDUSTRY: REASONS FOR TISCO'S DIFFICULTIES IN POST-WAR YEARS

The Tata Iron and Steel Company applied for tariff protection in 1923 (it had earlier made out a case for protection of the steel industry in its evidence before the Indian Fiscal Commission in March 1922) and was granted statutory protection and bounties on steel rails in 1924. It continued to be protected in one form or another up to the Second World War, although the degree of protection afforded by tariffs was drastically reduced in 1934.

In analysing the causes of the difficulties of TISCO one must distinguish clearly between the factors on the supply side, such as the efficiency of the plant and the personnel, the cost of labour, raw materials, fuel, technical personnel, and machinery, and the factors on the demand side, such as prices charged to railway companies under long-term contract, the competition from more efficient and larger plants in Europe and the U.S.A., the policy of price discrimination widely practised by the iron and steel producers of the world, the level of the demand generated by policies relating to public works and railway construction, and the distribution of that demand between the Indian producer and other suppliers.

It is clear from Table 9.3 that up to 1916–17 the works cost, which is defined as 'the cost of the labour employed and of the power and material used in the manufacture of steel, together with the expenditure on the salaries of the supervising staff',[66] declined, primarily owing to the fuller utilization of the plant and supervisory staff, including the fuel supplies which often did not vary proportionately with the output.[67] Then the costs began to go up. This rise, one has to infer, was not directly due to the rise in the wages of uncovenanted, that is Indian, labour, for there was no significant increase in wages per labourer until 1920–1.[68] There was a substantial increase in the wages plus bonus of covenanted labour in most departments from 1916–17 onwards; the impact of this was to some extent moderated by the replacement of covenanted labour by Indian skilled personnel, who were paid much less than what the Europeans or Americans had obtained earlier.[69] Even with such replacement, however, the increase in their wages was so great that in the crucial blast furnace department the cost of covenanted labour per ton of product increased a little between 1915–16 and 1922–3 and in the open-hearth department this cost increased substantially (by about 30%) between

[66] ITB: *Statutory enquiry 1926: steel*, Vol. I (Calcutta, 1927), p. 18.
[67] Burn: *Economic History of Steel Making*, p. 97 and Appendix II.
[68] ITB: *Evidence (Report on steel)*, Vol. I (Calcutta, 1924), pp. 109–11.
[69] R. D. Tata informed the Tariff Board in his oral evidence that trained Indians, when obtained at all, would not be paid more than two-thirds of the pay of a European

TABLE 9.3 Works costs per ton of steel in TISCO, 1912–13 to 1925–6 (Rs.)

	1912–13	1913–14	1914–15	1915–16	1916–17	1917–18	1918–19	1919–20	1920–1	1921–2	1922–3	1923–4	1924–5	1925–6
Open-hearth ingots	69·68	54·60	45·66	42·77	41·13	45·11	58·90	53·45	65·48	68·82	72·50	68·64	60·57	55·52
Duplex plant ingots	—	—	—	—	—	—	—	—	—	—	97·64	82·03	70·81	58·84
Blooming mill (old)	87·30	68·23	56·20	53·18	49·95	54·36	71·72	65·22	79·05	83·67	89·11	85·77	77·02	73·24
28 inch mill (old)	147·13	94·12	82·11	78·04	75·17	82·13	107·15	93·91	112·10	116·00	125·07	120·93	110·30	112·99
Bar mills (old)	150·57	118·92	97·32	86·59	81·99	87·79	111·61	102·27	123·72	135·50	138·53	132·55	123·27	125·10
Plate mill											145·84	142·13	145·76	124·33
New blooming mill												93·96	85·45	68·36
New rail mill													113·24	96·02
New bar mills												115·84	134·12	104·59
Sheet bar and billet mill													96·09	77·76
Black sheets													203·90	181·16
Galvanized plain sheets													332·09	298·88
Galvanized corrugated sheets													357·48	314·19
Sleepers														119·42

Sources: ITB: *Evidence (Report on steel), 1924,* Vol. I, p. 137 (Statement xx); ITB: *Statutory Enquiry 1926, steel,* Vol. II (Calcutta, 1927), p. 65 (Statement No. 5).
N.B.: In 1925–6, the costs on old 28-inch mill and old bar mills were higher because production was lower, the work being transferred to the new mills.

1915–16 and 1920–1.[70] But the major part of the increase was at first made up of an increase in the labour, fuel and raw material requirements of the plant, which was very intensively worked and therefore needed frequent overhauling and careful maintenance. Then from 1919–20 onwards the cost of coal began to increase substantially;[71] from 1920–1 the wages of Indian labour also began to go up (there were strikes by workers because of the substantially higher cost of living before wage increases were granted).[72] According to TISCO, the production per man fell after the war, owing to the facts that 'we were not driving our plant so hard, that the quality of the raw materials had fallen off and that the specifications had been tightened up for steel'.[73] The output per man was also affected by the strike of 1922–3. The company found it difficult to lay off redundant men for fear of strike action.

While the working of the existing plant was affected by the factors mentioned above, the new plant which was being installed turned out to be much more costly, because of delays in delivery from the U.S.A. and Europe, because of lack of synchronization of the arrivals of different units, and because of the phenomenal increase in prices of machinery just after the war.[74] This rise in prices of plant and machinery was a general phenomenon but nevertheless bore particularly hard on a company which needed to replace its obsolete and small plant by a more up-to-date and bigger unit, if it was to survive. While most of the plant for Greater Extensions was purchased at highly inflated prices, these prices came down considerably in 1923, so that the TISCO suffered a very great disadvantage with respect to firms in the advanced countries which were subject to less delays, had to pay lower transport costs, and could wait and purchase plants at much lower prices than before.[75] Of course, during

with the same position. *Ibid.*, Vol. I, p. 280. See also the evidence of Tutwiler who claimed that Americans and Europeans had to be paid 50% above what they would get in the U.S.A. or Europe; the imported labour also had to be granted their freight and extended paid leave for going home. *Ibid.*, p. 223, and Buchanan, *Development of Capitalistic Enterprise*, pp. 287–8. Gilbert Slater tells the story of how Santals, with wages of ten annas (less than a shilling) per day, had replaced Yorkshiremen in the work of straightening of steel rails: Slater: *Southern India*, pp. 235–6. See also Chapter 5 above.

[70] ITB: *Evidence (Report on steel)*, Vol. I (Calcutta, 1924), pp. 109–11.

[71] Apparently the quality of the coal also deteriorated, the ash content of the coke rising from about 20% to 24%. ITB: *Report on steel* (Calcutta, 1924), p. 31.

[72] ITB: *Evidence (Report on steel)*, Vol. I (Calcutta, 1924), pp. 109–11 and 149.

[73] *Ibid.*, Vol. I, p. 241.

[74] *Ibid.*, Vol. I, pp. 83–4. Of the total estimated cost of Rs. 132·9 million on Greater Extensions up to March 1924, expenditures of Rs. 18·4 million and Rs. 56·3 million only were incurred up to 31 March 1922 and 31 March 1923, respectively. Most of the orders, however, had been placed previously. *Ibid.*, p. 212.

[75] TISCO estimated the cost of one 200-ton open-hearth tilting furnace to be Rs. 5,575,000 in India as against Rs. 4,310,000 in the U.S.A., that of one 50-ton blast furnace to be Rs. 8,343,000 in India as against Rs. 5,976,000 in the U.S.A., and that of one 28-inch mill to be Rs. 18,242,000 in India against Rs. 15,392,000 in the U.S.A.

the years 1919 and 1920 TISCO enjoyed the advantage of a greatly appreciated rupee but much of that advantage vanished as the rupee began to find its older level.

In addition to these factors, there was the steep depreciation of the Continental exchange rates, so that, even without dumping, TISCO would have found it difficult to sell steel at the same price as these Continental countries. But dumping did occur (according to the evidence submitted by TISCO before the Tariff Board).[76] Finally, TISCO had entered into contracts with both the Railway Board and the so-called Palmer Railways (railways managed by private companies) for supplies of rails at prices which turned out to be much lower than the cost price of TISCO and than the c.i.f. prices of imported steel. While the Railway Board revised their prices upward, though by a much lower margin than the gap between the import prices and the contract prices, the Palmer Railways refused to raise their purchase prices at all; so there was a net transfer of resources from the private Indian company to the general public, to the government, and also to the British companies managing the railways.[77]

Along with the arguments based on the economic benefits rendered by TISCO to the government, to the railways and to the country generally, and on the disadvantages suffered by it because of the dearness of imported labour, the inclemency of the climate which requires special measures for protection against heat, the difficulties associated with the obsolescence of the old plant and the delay in the delivery of the new plant, the depreciation of Continental exchanges, and dumping by major steel producers, TISCO also emphasized the military importance of the works as a source of steel for the British Empire east of Suez, when it asked for a protective duty of $33\frac{1}{3}\%$ on all imported steel.[78] The ITB also

Ibid., Vol. I, pp. 216–18. The IISCO originally (in March 1918) budgeted for Rs. 15 million for its plant (two blast furnaces designed to produce 350 tons a day each), but had to spend Rs. 30 million in all and estimated in 1923 that it could put up the plant at a cost of between Rs. 15 million and Rs. 20 million. *Ibid.*, Vol. III, p. 160. The value of the plant of the TISCO was written down in 1925 from Rs. 30 million to Rs. 22.5 million, which was taken to be the cost of erection of the plant at current prices. ITB: *Statutory enquiry 1926: steel*, Vol. IV (Calcutta, 1927), pp. 7–8. The Indian Tariff Board estimated that the actual expenditure by TISCO on fixed capital for producing the output of 1921–2 was Rs. 40 million, whereas the replacement value of the plant was Rs. 60 million. It allowed depreciation on the basis of replacement value. See ITB: *Report on steel* (Calcutta, 1924), pp. 36–8. It pointed out, however, that an up-to-date plant costing Rs. 60 million would have much lower operating costs. *Ibid.*, p. 37.

[76] On the low prices of Continental and British steel see ITB: *Evidence (Report on steel)*, Vol. I (Calcutta, 1924), 14–15; on dumping see *ibid.*, pp. 52–6.

[77] *Ibid.*, Vol. I, p. 281 (oral evidence of Mr Peterson). The difference between the cost of rails on the basis of the price of imported rails and the cost actually paid to TISCO for the two years 1920–1 and 1921–2 came to Rs. 5,247,000 for the Railway Board and Rs. 8,955,000 for the company railways (the Palmer Railways, B. N. Railway and G.I.P. Railway) respectively. See *ibid.*, Vol. I, p. 25.

[78] See *ibid.*, Vol. I, pp. 13–18.

emphasized the strategic importance of the TISCO works when recommending a scheme of protective duties on steel and bounties for rails. The duties were specific and were expected to come to about 15% *ad valorem*, and this meant only a 5% increase in the general rate of duty on iron and steel. Since TISCO had to sell rails under long-term contract, at fixed prices which were very much lower than the fair selling price of Rs. 180 as calculated by the Tariff Board, and therefore could not benefit from duties, bounties of Rs. 32, Rs. 26 and Rs. 20 per ton were proposed for its sales of rails for the years 1924–5, 1925–6 and 1926–7 respectively. Duties were also proposed on fabricated steel at rates which ranged up to 25% *ad valorem* (on tariff valuations of 1924). But steamers, launches, barges, flat boats and other vessels were excluded from the operation of the duties, and their components, being rather bulky, were supposed to enjoy a natural advantage.[79] These proposals were made for a period of three years after which the position was to be reviewed. The government accepted them without any major modification. In this, it may have been influenced by the loss of ground suffered by British products. Iron and steel imports into India from all countries were considerably lower during the period 1919–24 than during the period 1909—14 (see Table 9.4, columns (4) and (5)). Further, while the share of the U.K. in total imports in the earlier period was 0·70, for the latter period it fell to 0·65. In comparison with the first decade of the twentieth century, the decline in the U.K.'s share in total Indian imports of iron and steel was even more striking.

However, the depression in the steel industry in European countries continued, there occurred a general depreciation of Continental currencies, and a rise in the sterling value of the rupee above 1*s*. 4*d*. (on which the provisions of the Steel Industry [Protection] Act [xiv of 1924] were based). TISCO applied for additional protection, and the government, in place of the off-setting duties recommended by the Tariff Board, which reported in October 1924, proposed to give bounties at the rate of Rs. 20 a ton of rolled steel, the total subsidy not exceeding Rs. 5 million in the aggregate from 1 October 1924 to 30 September 1925.

After a further enquiry, the Tariff Board in September 1925 recommended that further assistance to the Indian rolled-steel industry should be given in the form of bounties at the rate of Rs. 18 per ton on 70% of ingot production for a period of eighteen months.[80] The Government of India reduced the bounty from Rs. 18 to Rs. 12 per ton and the maximum amount of assistance from Rs. 9 million to Rs. 6 million.[81] The Tariff

[79] The plea for protection for the ship-building industry was rejected.
[80] ITB: *Report regarding the grant of supplementary protection to the steel industry* (Calcutta, 1925), p. 22.
[81] See ITB: *Statutory enquiry 1926: steel*, Vol. I (Calcutta, 1926), pp. 8–9.

TABLE 9.4 *Total imports of iron and steel and railway materials into India, 1894–5 to 1924–5 (figures in tons)*

| Year | Excluding 'other sorts' of railway materials | | Including 'other sorts' of railway materials | |
	From all countries	From the U.K.	From all countries	From the U.K.
1894–5	349,080	257,140	379,737	287,716
1895–6	476,835	349,897	520,697	393,730
1896–7	631,297	514,879	699,278	582,137
1897–8	582,600	465,350	665,700	548,400
1898–9	448,000	335,650	507,350	395,000
1899–1900	386,350	301,900	438,850	353,150
1900–1	385,950	262,850	419,700	296,450
1901–2	485,700	302,600	521,750	338,700
1902–3	554,250	385,650	579,200	410,550
1903–4	674,550	480,900	714,850	521,000
1904–5	707,350	514,250	778,600	584,200
1905–6	807,650	554,500	870,500	617,100
1906–7	734,700	540,350	814,750	620,250
1907–8	800,000	523,400	856,350	579,400
1908–9	812,300	534,500	859,150	580,900
1909–10	820,800	579,400	885,800	642,150
1910–11	849,100	589,600	900,100	639,650
1911–12	881,857	599,208	937,407	653,508
1912–13	970,072	674,583	1,033,872	728,783
1913–14	1,282,858	873,296	1,349,858	938,446
1914–15	865,401	676,480	911,751	721,380
1915–16	511,731	372,545	530,581	391,095
1916–17	295,231	211,953	305,499	221,665
1917–18	165,693	96,178	167,219	91,704
1918–19	196,770	92,124	197,211	93,683
1919–20	508,607	348,040	515,443	354,806
1920–1	808,406	594,444	828,748	612,841
1921–2	745,823	411,239	772,997	434,890
1922–3	947,229	548,623	971,730	571,210
1923–4	888,187	551,752	935,866	595,368
1924–5	937,932	498,652	969,601	521,534

Note: The 1st and 2nd columns are obtained by adding the 1st and 2nd columns of Table 9.2 to the 5th and 6th columns of Table 9.1 respectively. The 3rd and 4th columns are obtained by adding the 3rd and 4th columns of Table 9.2 to the 5th and 6th columns of Table 9.1 respectively.

Board also recommended an increase in the duty on fabricated steel from 25 to $32\frac{1}{2}\%$ *ad valorem* but the government did not accept this recommendation.

The Steel Industry (Protection) Act, 1924, had granted protection to the industry for a period of three years, ending on 31 March 1927. Hence in April 1926 the government asked the Tariff Board to enquire again into the conditions of the industry and to recommend appropriate measures of protection by tariffs or otherwise, if such help were still necessary. The recommendations of the Tariff Board were accepted and basic duties, generally at rates lower than those in force between 1924 and 1927, on different varieties of steel were imposed, but additional duties were imposed on Continental (as distinct from British) steel. Bounties on steel rails were dispensed with in the new scheme. The period of protection was fixed at seven years, primarily because this would be the time needed to assess the effects of the extension of capacity of the Tata plant from 420,000 tons to 600,000 tons of finished steel.[82]

The Steel Industry (Protection) Act of 1927 authorized the Government of India to vary the rate of duty on different kinds of steel if the prices of imported steel varied greatly. On an application from TISCO in September 1930 for an increase in the duty on galvanized sheets on the grounds that their import prices had fallen much below the figures on which the duties of 1927 were based, the Tariff Board, after an enquiry, recommended an increase in the contract price of rails paid by the government, since the total purchases made by the government had fallen substantially short of the purchases expected during the enquiry of 1926. The government accepted this recommendation.[83]

During 1933–4, there was another enquiry by the ITB, which in its report[84] recommended that duties be abolished on rails, steel sleepers, fish-plates, semis, and tested structural steel and plates from the U.K. Only in the case of Continental structural steel was a higher duty recommended. Since Continental steel was almost equivalent to untested steel and the latter was protected, the principle of Imperial preference, introduced in 1927, was continued. But the Tariff Board recommended in addition that requirements of Indian railways should be purchased in India at a fixed average price of Rs. 95 per ton under an arrangement lasting until 31 March 1941, which was also the date at which the existing scheme of protection would be reviewed.[85] In the event, this review never took place, as the war intervened and eliminated any need for protection.

9.7　FALL IN THE COST OF PRODUCTION OF STEEL UNDER
TARIFF PROTECTION

The recommendations of the ITB were throughout based on an average cost of production of steel during the period of protection, the mid-year of the period being generally chosen for computing the average. Since the calculation of the average cost hinged upon a successful prediction of output, any

---

[82] *Ibid.*, Chapters III and VI.
[83] B. N. Adarkar [Gov. India pub.] *The History of the Indian Tariff, 1924–39*, p. 15.
[84] ITB: *Report on the iron and steel industry* (Delhi, 1934).
[85] *Ibid.*, Chapter VI.

under-utilization of the steel plant led to a decrease in the effective degree of protection. The Tariff Boards worked on the assumption that costs per unit would fall as plants expanded and became better balanced, and as Indian supervisory staff replaced the foreign personnel. This assumption was again based on the claim of TISCO that it could reduce its costs if only the firm had a breathing space during which it could renovate, expand and re-organize its plant. In the event total costs per unit did fall almost continuously from 1923–4 to 1933–4, thus enabling the government to reduce the quantum of protection from 1927 onwards. But a part of the increase in works costs of TISCO over that predicted in the Tariff Board reports during the period from 1923–4 to 1933–4 was due to the drastic decline in the purchases of rails by the Railway Board, and to the lingering prejudice on

TABLE 9.5   *Purchases of steel rails by class I Indian railways*

Three-year period	Total purchases of steel rails (Rs. '000)	Percentage of purchases of steel rails of Indian manufacture to total purchases of steel rails
1922–3 to 1924–5	46,968	61.17
1925–6 to 1927–8	58,985	72.11
1928–9 to 1930–1	43,929	89.35
1931–2 to 1933–4	19,561	92.90
1934–5 to 1936–7	22,197	96.78
1937–8 to 1939–40	17,241	99.19

Source: Gov. India: *Railway Board: Administration Report*, Vol. II (Simla and Calcutta, annual). Up to and including 1936–7 the figures also cover the Burma railways.

TABLE 9.6   *Rail orders received by TISCO from the Indian railways, 1923–4 to 1933–4*

Year	Quantity ('000 tons)	Average price received by TISCO (Rs. per ton)	
1923–4	76.6	133.7	
1924–5	104.8	124.9	plus rail bounty Rs.32
1925–6	117.4	122.9	plus rail bounty Rs.26
1926–7	139.8	121.1	plus rail bounty Rs.20
1927–8	182.8	110.0	
1928–9	59.7	110.0	
1929–30	119.7	110.8	
1930–1	95.6	129.6	
1931–2	80.8	128.2	
1932–3	36.5	113.5	
1933–4	40.0	n.a.	

Source: ITB: *Statutory enquiry 1933: steel*, Vol. I: *Written evidence given by the Tata Iron and Steel Company Limited* (Delhi, 1934), p. 74.

the part of some company railways which continued to buy British rails. For purchases of Indian steel by Class I Indian railways see Table 9.5, and for the rail orders received by TISCO see Table 9.6. TISCO, in its representation before the Indian Tariff Board of 7 May 1926, complained that the Burma Railways, South Indian Railway and the Madras and Southern Mahratta Railway would not accept Indian rails even at the low price of Rs. 105 per ton; in the case of Burma Railways the company tendered at Rs. 100 a ton and the tender was not accepted.[86] In their evidence Burma Railways stated that the Home Board (i.e. the Board in the U.K.) placed all contracts for rails.[87] Madras and Southern Mahratta Railways reported that for 1926–7 they were buying about 87% of their requirements of rails and all their fishplates from the U.K.[87a] Both the Burma Railway and the Madras and Southern Mahratta Railway stated that Tata rails were inferior to British rails, without assigning any reasons.[87b] Doubts about the wearing quality of Tata steel were expressed by various railways and the Assam Bengal Railway considered the very fact that TISCO turned out material not satisfying British Standard specification (for other purposes) sufficient ground for suspicion.[87c] The Agent of the Great Indian Peninsula Railway in a letter to the Railway Board, however, reported that 'a comparison by weighment between the Tata and British rails . . . was made in 1925 and the results showed no appreciable difference in wear between the British and Indian rails'.[87d]

The degree of fall in works costs can be gauged from Table 9.3 above and Table 9.7. By comparing columns (6) and (9) of Table 9.7 we see that in several lines of production the actual reduction of works costs between 1926 and 1933 was greater than that postulated by the Tariff Board, in spite of the fact that full capacity production was never achieved during this period.

Many of the facilities, such as power or general supervision, were common to many lines of steel production, and since these costs are included in works costs and their allocation between the different items was largely a matter of rough judgement, too much should not be read into the exact relation of costs of different items. But since the fall in costs was in fact experienced by all lines of production, one can point out some general factors.

First, there were improvements in practice resulting from the installation of new plant: new bar mills, new blooming mills and new rail mills resulted in a fall in works costs below those of the old mills within a year or two of the commissioning of the new plant.[88] The reduction in costs of finished

---

[86] ITB: *Statutory enquiry 1926: steel*, Vol. II (Calcutta, 1927), p. 10.
[87] ITB: *Statutory enquiry 1926: steel*, Vol. V (Calcutta, 1927), p. 110.
[87a] *Ibid.*, p. 121.			[87b] *Ibid.*, pp. 111 and 121.			[87c] *Ibid.*, p. 127.			[87d] *Ibid.*, p. 5.
[88] ITB: *Statutory enquiry 1926: steel*, Vol. I (Calcutta, 1926), pp. 10–11, Tables I and II. A sheet mill installed in 1933 showed considerable reduction in works costs as compared with the older mills. ITB: *Report on the iron and steel industry* (Delhi, 1934), p. 31.

TABLE 9.7 *Works costs per ton of steel in TISCO, 1925–6 to 1940–1 (Rs.)*

	Actual, August 1926 (1)	Actual, 1934 (2)	1933–4 as estimated in 1934 (3)	1940–1 as estimated in 1934 (4)	1927–8 as estimated in 1926 (5)	1933–4 as estimated in 1926 (6)	Actual, 1925–6 (7)	Actual, 1927–8 (8)	Actual, Jan.–June 1933 (9)
Rails	79.6	56.00	61.6	44.23	63.2	54.5	89.7	72.7	66.2
Fishplates	116.4	86.52	90.0	69.00	95.2	82.9	112.9	119.6	95.0
Structural sections	105.3	60.00	69.1	48.23	73.2	62.0	102.4	95.3	67.4
Bars	99.0	59.63	77.0	49.00	80.2	69.9	99.9	84.5	72.0
Plates	103.3	62.57	80.3	50.58	84.2	73.2	113.6	88.5	72.0
Black sheets	164.0	85.54	122.0	65.12	135.2	114.9	170.0	134.2	98.0
Galvanized sheets	263.7	115.54	200.0	95.12	196.8	165.5	237.5	193.6	128.4
Sleepers	—	55.86	72.0	46.06	66.2	64.9	109.3	78.8	61.7

Sources and Notes: For columns (1) to (4), ITB: *Statutory enquiry 1926, steel*, Vol. I (Calcutta, 1926), p. 31, and *Report on the iron and steel industry* (Delhi, 1934), pp. 28, 29 and 34. For columns (5) to (9), ITB: *Statutory enquiry 1933, steel*, Vol. I: *Written evidence given by the Tata Iron and Steel Company Ltd* (Delhi, 1934), p. 34. The figures in columns (5) to (9) were arrived at after adjusting for a fall in the prices of coal and spelter between 1926 and 1933.

steel on the old mills over the years from 1922–3 to 1925–6 is largely illusory, since the cost of steel ingots declined by about Rs. 20 between 1923–4 and August 1926; hence in fact the continued operation of old mills led to increasing works costs.[89] (There was also a higher percentage of scrap used for open-hearth furnaces leading to a lowering of costs.)[90] Between 1926 and 1933 two of the blast furnaces were greatly enlarged and four blowers of 'unusually high capacity' installed. A third converter and a third finishing furnace were erected at the duplex plant, thus changing the relative efficiencies of the duplex process and the simple open-hearth process. New equipment was also installed at the new blowing mill and the new 28-inch mill. Other auxiliary equipment for the productive departments, and more rolling stock and power-generating machinery for the service departments were also erected. These changes enabled the company to retire the old blowing mill and the old 28-inch mill after May 1932, and this also had a beneficial effect on average costs.[91]

Apart from the increase in efficiency resulting from extensions in scale and improvements in the plant, there were also improvements resulting from 'learning by doing'. There were substantial improvements in practice – particularly in fuel consumption – at the coke ovens, blast furnaces and open-hearth furnaces between 1924 and 1926.[92] 'Learning by doing', and by training, partly had the effect of replacement of Europeans and Americans ('covenanted staff') in supervisory posts by Indians. Since a large number of new units was commissioned with the completion of Greater Extensions, the number of covenanted employees rose at first to a maximum of 224 in 1924, but went down to 161 on 1 June 1926 and gradually to 70 on 1 April 1933; apart from some on-the-job training, most of the Indian employees in supervisory positions were trained at the Jamshedpur Technical Institute. The average salary of the covenanted employees remained more or less the same, with a slight fall after 1930–1. But the Indians replacing them were employed at salaries which were only 50% to 70% of the salaries of covenanted employees. The gross saving in cost per unit of saleable steel through the decrease in the numbers of covenanted employees was Rs. 4 between 1927–8 and 1932–3. Along with this development, there was also a substantial economy in the number of men employed: the number in all departments went down from 26,290 in 1925–6 to 17,517 in January–June 1933. The number in so-called productive departments contracted much faster than in the service departments. The average wages (per annum) of non-covenanted employees rose from Rs. 497 in 1927–8 to Rs. 688 in 1932–3, but this rise also reflected the salaries of Indian supervisory per-

[89] ITB: *Statutory enquiry 1926: steel*, Vol. I (Calcutta, 1926), p. 11.

[90] *Ibid.*, p. 11, and ITB: *Statutory enquiry 1926: steel*, Vol. III (Calcutta, 1927), pp. 8–51.

[91] ITB: *Statutory enquiry 1933: steel*, Vol. I (Delhi, 1934), pp. 39–40.

[92] ITB: *Statutory enquiry 1926: steel*, Vol. III (Calcutta, 1927), pp. 8–51.

sonnel who were increasingly replacing the convenanted staff. The *net* decrease in the labour cost per ton of saleable steel (after deducting the gross decrease on account of replacement of covenanted employees by Indians) over the period from 1927–8 to 1932–3 was Rs. 3. Since the production of saleable steel remained more or less constant over the same period (it was 429,000 tons in 1927–8 and 427,000 in 1932–3), this movement reflects a genuine economy.[93]

The economies in labour as well as in other departments were effected partly through a conscious policy: there was a Retrenchment Committee and a monthly Cost Committee of all departmental heads presided over by the general manager. In 1925 a Metallurgical Department was set up and it scrutinized the quantity and quality of output of various products. A Fuel Economy Department was established in 1928 and a Lubricating Engineer a little later.[94] The proportion of good steel rolled from ingots at the rolling mills increased by amounts ranging from 0·7% to 8% on various mills (barring only the merchant mill), between the years 1927–8 and 1932–3. The consumption of coal per unit of product fell substantially in practically all the departments.[95] The company considered a saving of 20% in coal consumption a representative figure.[96]

In a way, the credit for a large part of the fall in the cost of production must be given to the successive Tariff Boards appointed by the Government of India: TISCO was compelled to reduce costs because at every stage the tariffs or bounties proposed were just enough to cover the prime costs of production plus given percentages of the replacement value of capital and the working capital the Tariff Board considered necessary.[97] At every stage allowance was made for the fall in works costs the Tariff Board considered reasonable. Over most of the period from 1924 to 1933, the prices charged by competitors and therefore the realized prices of TISCO were lower than those predicted by the Tariff Boards; on the other hand the demand for the steel output of TISCO was substantially lower than the predicted value, primarily because of the drastic decline in railway construction and public investment in general. Hence the profits of TISCO from steel production were in most cases lower than even the minimum provided for by the Tariff Board. TISCO therefore had to reduce working costs as much as possible if it was to survive.

That the company did survive, in spite of the partial failure of tariff protection, was due to several factors acting in conjunction with the drastic fall in works costs. In years of low demand for steel, it could and did sell substantial amounts of pig iron; the Indian market for pig iron was small,

[93] ITB: *Statutory enquiry 1933: steel*, Vol. I (Delhi, 1934), pp. 41–2, 56, 75–6 and 94.
[94] *Ibid.*, Chapter x, and p. 38 in particular.
[95] *Ibid.*, p. 81.   [96] *Ibid.*, p. 38.
[97] The rate of profit on fixed capital allowed was 8%; the rate of interest on working capital allowed was 7% or 6% (in the 1934 Report).

however, and most of the pig iron went overseas, Japan, the United States and the U.K. being the major consumers, in that order of importance. This export market was also extremely competitive, and the pig iron of TISCO was for a time subject to a countervailing duty in the U.S.A. because of anti-dumping legislation.[98]

Secondly, over the period from 1927 to 1933 the prices of coal and spelter fell, thus enabling the company to reap a larger surplus.

Finally, the financial position of the company was strong at the time it ran into trouble (around 1922). The company raised large amounts of capital through ordinary shares, deferred shares, and second preference shares (carrying a cumulative dividend of $7\frac{1}{2}\%$) between the years 1917 and 1922, so that while the share capital stood at Rs. 23,175,000 at the end of the financial year 1916–17, it stood at Rs. 103,228,000 at the end of the year 1922–3.[99] It also floated debentures (carrying a rate of interest of 7%) in 1917, 1918 and 1919 (the total amount thus raised being Rs. 9,900,000). It raised a further debenture loan (at a discount) of Rs. 31 million in 1922, and Rs. 1·5 million in 1923, the debenture loan of 1922 being used to liquidate the old debenture loan of Rs. 20 million.[100] Since the Tata shares were sold at very high premiums during the years from 1917 to well into 1922, the company could raise the needed capital at a low cost.[101] While the dividend

[98] As against the estimate of saleable pig iron of 40,000 tons for the period from 1924–5 to 1926–7 made by the ITB, the total production of saleable pig iron by TISCO during the same period came to nearly 450,000 tons. The surplus (of gross revenue over works costs) on this count came to Rs. 6,300,000 as against the Tariff Board estimate of Rs. 3,200,000. ITB: *Statutory enquiry 1926: steel*, Vol. I (Calcutta, 1926), p. 15. Again the surplus of pig iron produced for sale by TISCO during the period 1927–9 was considerably in excess of that estimated by the Tariff Board (60,000 tons a year) and the surplus realized thereon was also greater than that estimated by the Tariff Board. ITB: *Report on the removal of the revenue duty on pig iron including the evidence recorded during the enquiry* (Calcutta, 1930), pp. 6–7. The total sales of pig iron by TISCO during the years from 1928–9 to 1932–3 were as follows (in '000 tons):

| 1928–9 | 114·9 | 1929–30 | 143·3 | 1930–1 | 115·1 |
| 1931–2 | 174·0 | 1932–3 | 103·6 | | |

TISCO thus sold very much larger quantities of pig iron than were expected by the ITB, most of it abroad. See ITB: *Report on the iron and steel industry* (Delhi, 1934), pp. 137–8. The Indian consumption of pig iron was estimated at about 150,000 tons in 1925. ITB: *Report regarding the grant of supplementary protection to the steel industry* (Calcutta, 1925), p. 28. For evidence on action taken by the U.S. Government against pig iron sales by TISCO, see ITB: *Statutory enquiry 1926: steel*, Vol. VI (Calcutta, 1927), pp. 6–7 (the oral evidence of Mr Fairhurst of IISCO).

[99] *Annual Reports of the Tata Iron and Steel Company.*

[100] ITB: *Evidence (Report on steel)*, Vol. I (Calcutta, 1924), pp. 26–7, 66 and 71–2. Part of the debenture capital in 1922 was raised in London at an average rate of interest of 8·26%. *Ibid.*, pp. 247–8.

[101] As an illustration of the premiums enjoyed by ordinary and deferred shares it may be noted that over the period from 1 July 1916 to 31 March 1922, the highest price of an ordinary share (face value: Rs. 75) was Rs. 726 and the lowest Rs. 109 and the highest price of a deferred share (face value: Rs. 30) was Rs. 1,630 and the lowest Rs. 205. See *IITB 1925–6* (Calcutta, 1925), pp. 401–2.

on ordinary shares was quite low, the deferred shares often earned very high dividends (going up to 233%) since they shared in surplus profits on extremely favourable terms. But the argument was that one was allotted a deferred share only if one already held ten ordinary shares, so it was not arbitrary favouritism, and it enabled the company to earn very large premiums on its new issues.[102]

Further, TISCO followed an extremely cautious policy of depreciation so that, while up to 1921–2 the sum allowed by income tax authorities as depreciation was about Rs. 16 million, the company had written off more than that sum, and thus it had good reserves for financing the replacement of capital and its expansion.[103]

9.8 THE STRUCTURE OF THE STEEL INDUSTRY AND THE INFLUENCE OF GOVERNMENT POLICY

While the cautious policy of the Government of India may have had a favourable influence on the efficiency of operation of TISCO, it had an inhibiting effect on the growth of the steel industry and the growth of ancillary industries. It is not quite true to say that the government only wanted to guarantee the survival of TISCO and did not pay any attention to ancillary industries, for it did provide some protection for *existing* enterprises in some ancillary industries. But it refused to guarantee the protection of any new industry or firm whose setting up was proposed.

The Indian Iron and Steel Company was floated in 1918 with the object of producing pig iron and steel, although it was decided then that steel production would come only later. It was expected that all the steel for the Indian Standard Wagon Company, which started its shops alongside of IISCO, would be supplied by the latter.[104] Similarly, Bird and Co. of Calcutta and Cammell Laird and Co. Ltd, of Sheffield and London, joined together to organize (in 1921) the United Steel Corporation of Asia Ltd; the projected capacity of this company was 450,000 tons of rolled steel per annum, besides pig iron, ferromanganese, coke and by-products.[105] (Its projected output was thus more than twice the output of steel ingots of TISCO in 1921–2.) Both these firms were, however, deterred in their projects by the depression in the steel industry and both wanted protection, even though the works of the United Steel Corporation of Asia were planned on a large scale, embodying the latest improvements in technique.[106]

It was considered that in order to attract the necessary volume of capital from India, the investor would have to be assured a profit of 10 to 12%.[107]

---

102 ITB: *Evidence (Report on steel)*, Vol. I (Calcutta, 1924), pp. 220–2.
103 ITB: *Report on steel* (Calcutta, 1924) p. 36.
104 ITB: *Evidence (Report on steel)*, Vol. III (Calcutta, 1924), pp. 145–6.
105 *Ibid.*, pp. 166–7.   106 *Ibid.*, pp. 145, 147 and 169.   107 *Ibid.*, pp. 155–6.

The steel industry was protected for only three years from 1924, with no guarantee of further protection if required; further the Indian Tariff Board tried to ensure only a rate of profit of 8% on the invested capital of TISCO *after* taking into account the fall in works costs expected from greater efficiency in TISCO. Thus no allowance was made for the initial difficulties of any new firm wanting to enter the industry, nor was protection guaranteed for a sufficiently long period. In 1926, it was argued both by IISCO and by Bird and Co., representing the United Steel Corporation of Asia, that the guarantee of protection would have to be fixed for ten years. Although there were enough financial reserves available for investment in stocks and shares (the rise in the price of government paper being a pointer in that direction), the investing public would not put up any money for iron and steel works unless there was a reasonable chance of financial success.[108]

TABLE 9.8   *Consumption of steel in India, 1923–4 to 1932–3*

Year	Total steel consumption ('000 tons)	Percentage of TISCO despatches to total consumption	Year	Total steel consumption ('000 tons)	Percentage of TISCO despatches to total consumption
1923–4	839.6	17.6	1928–9	1145.9	23.7
1924–5	839.4	28.5	1929–30	1078.7	35.4
1925–6	1038.0	31.3	1930–1	811.4	51.2
1926–7	1004.6	37.3	1931–2	627.2	65.4
1927–8	1402.6	30.1	1932–3	574.1	72.3

Source: ITB: *Statutory enquiry 1933: steel*, Vol 1: *Written Evidence given by the Tata Iron and Steel Company Limited* (Delhi, 1934), pp. 57–8.

The expectation of a continuation in the growth of steel consumption in India at the pre-war rate had not materialized (see Tables 9.4 and 9.8), but the representative of Bird and Co. still considered that there was room for another steel works in India if only the government would protect it against foreign competition.[109] The government, however, refused to grant tariff protection for ten years, and on top of that there soon came the depression and a drastic fall in steel consumption, so that no new venture could be seriously considered until recovery had set in in 1937, when the Steel

[108] ITB: *Statutory enquiry 1926: steel*, Vol. VI (Calcutta, 1927), pp. 19 and 31. The ITB in its 1926 report stated: 'The uncertainty and depression in the Steel Trade have been so great in recent years that it is doubtful whether new capital will be forthcoming for investment in the industry unless the public is assured by a clear statement in the legislative enactment that protection will be continued so long as the circumstances, not merely of the pioneer Company but of the industry as a whole, indicate that such a course is necessary.' ITB: *Statutory enquiry 1926: steel*, Vol. I (Calcutta, 1926), p. 81.
[109] *Ibid.*, p. 30.

Corporation of Bengal was floated under the same management as controlled IISCO.[110]

The fate of the industry producing pig iron was connected with the fate of the steel industry and the engineering industries. Up to 1939, the Tata steel mills remained the only works producing pig iron and steel within the same plant. The earliest firm producing pig iron was the Bengal Iron and Steel Company (later the Bengal Iron Company), which was originally formed to acquire the property of the Barakar Iron Works.[111] It seems to have been a profitable concern from the start, producing and selling pig iron and also using the pig iron in its own foundry for various cast-iron products. But by 1920 its four blast furnaces were quite old and rather small in capacity (three with a capacity of about 90 tons a day and one a little larger).[112]

A new, English blast furnace was added in 1920 with a capacity of 150 to 250 tons a day.[113] Thus even the new blast furnace had a much smaller capacity than the new blast furnaces of TISCO or IISCO, which had rated capacities of 350–400 tons a day.

The Bengal Iron Company complained in its evidence before the Indian Tariff Board in 1923 that TISCO had undercut its prices of pig iron, particularly in foreign markets. It went on to complain later that 'the protective duties and the bounties on steel enable[d] the Tata Iron and Steel Company to sell pig iron at very cheap rates, and that the price at which they [were] offering pig iron at present, [was] below the cost of production.'[114] However, it was found on enquiry by the Indian Tariff Board that TISCO had never sold at a price lower than normal cost.[115] The fall in price had occurred primarily because of factors outside the control of TISCO. First, the capacity for producing saleable pig iron within India had been doubled by the setting up of blast furnaces by IISCO, capable of producing over

---

[110] For a rough indication of the trends in Indian steel consumption see Tables 9.8 and 9.9. (The figures in the two tables are not strictly comparable since they make different assumptions about the content of iron and steel imports as shown in the returns of the sea-borne trade of India.) It should be noted (in Table 9.8) that TISCO supplied an increasing fraction of a diminishing total consumption of steel during the depression years.

[111] See the Stock Exchange: *Burdett's Official Intelligence for 1890* (London, 1890), p. 1209.

[112] ITB: *Report regarding the grant of supplementary protection to the steel industry* (Calcutta, 1925), p. 29.

[113] *Ibid.*, p. 29. According, however, to the oral evidence of H. Fitzpatrick, representing the Bengal Iron Company, before the Indian Tariff Board on the Steel Industry in 1923, the capacity of the new blast furnace was 100 tons only. ITB: *Evidence (Report on steel*, Vol. III (Calcutta, 1924), p. 223.

[114] ITB: *Report regarding the grant of supplementary protection to the steel industry* (Calcutta, 1925).

[115] For long-period contracts, the prices were often substantially lower than current prices, but even then they were always remunerative. See ITB: *Evidence (Report on steel)*, Vol. I (Calcutta, 1924), p. 139.

300,000 tons a year (the capacity of the Bengal Iron Company was between 150,000 to 200,000 tons a year and the sales of pig iron over the period from 1912–13 to 1922–3 averaged about 75,000 tons a year). The main outlets of Indian pig iron were the home market, Japan and the U.S.A. The capacity of firms in Japan and under Japanese control in Southern Manchuria and China had recently increased, and the price of pig iron within the U.S.A. had fallen. The American price was the dominant one, since the U.S.A. levied prohibitive duties against firms suspected of dumping. Indian consumption was estimated at 150,000 tons, and this was affected by the general depression in engineering industries. The price of pig iron fell by more than 50% between 1920 and 1925, from around Rs. 85 a ton to around Rs. 40 a ton. Hence naturally the Bengal Iron Company found itself in a tight corner and had to close down pig-iron production first partially and then completely, although according to the ITB the all-in cost of pig iron from its new blast furnace was still less than the selling price, and even the cost on the older furnaces was within the limits of profitability.

After 1925, the two major producers of pig iron were TISCO and IISCO, but they had been joined by a small company, the Mysore Iron and Steel Works, with its plant at Bhadravati. This was set up to exploit the iron ore reserves of the Bababudan Hills (with an average iron content of 60% in the ore), and to use the large forest resources in the north of Mysore. (Limestone could also be found nearby.) It was one of the first large-scale industrial enterprises run by the state anywhere in India, as it was set up by the Government of Mysore; the consultant was C. P. Perin, the chief engineer and technical adviser of TISCO. The plant was designed to produce 28,000 tons a year (it started production in January 1923) and a wood distillation plant was set up to recover valuable by-products, such as wood-tar, methyl alcohol and calcium acetate, while converting the wood into charcoal for use in the blast furnace.[116] This may have been one of the last charcoal blast furnaces ever erected.

The cost of this plant was too high owing to the same set of factors as operated in the case of the Greater Extensions of TISCO works. Further, technological change made the production of chemicals by the wood distillation process uneconomical even while the plant was being erected. Finally, pig-iron prices collapsed. In spite of all this, however, the Mysore Government decided to carry on production at the plant and to find uses for its pig iron. First, in 1926, a mill for producing cast-iron pipes was put up. Then in 1934, two furnaces were set up with a rated capacity of 30,000

[116] See Mather: 'The Iron and Steel Industry in India', and Chatterton: 'Industrial Progress of the Mysore State'. Chatterton in 1925 predicted the closure of the plant because, after two years of production, the running costs exceeded the value of the iron produced; interest charges and depreciation would add at least another Rs. 100 per ton to the total cost. *Ibid.*, p. 730.

tons of steel per year to use the pig iron produced by the works. (The pipe mills and steel mills were both designed by German firms.)[117]

Meanwhile the two major producers of pig iron, IISCO and TISCO, along with the Bengal Iron Company, found it profitable to enter into an agreement about internal prices, but sales in foreign markets were often made at prices which were lower than internal prices.[118] It seems that at first the prices of pig iron charged by the combine, particularly to small consumers, were equal to import prices after allowing for the revenue duty of 10% *ad valorem*. But as a result of press criticism and competition from the Mysore Iron and Steel Works, they reduced their prices.[119] In response to representations received from consumers of pig iron the Government of India appointed a Tariff Board to look into the question of retention or abolition of the revenue duty on pig iron. The Board found that large consumers of pig iron were not likely to be affected by the abolition of the duty, since they were protected by their position and their long-term contracts. The prices for *bazar* sales (which accounted for 40,000 out of the total Indian consumption of 150,000 tons of pig iron) might come down by about Rs. 5. But this would reduce the profits of TISCO from sales of surplus pig iron by about Rs. 100,000.[120] Since such profits had already been taken into account in the scheme of protection for the steel industry recommended by the Tariff Board in 1926, the reduction of these profits would jeopardize that scheme. The Board also found that the manufacturers of machinery would benefit by only small amounts from the reduction of the duty on pig iron.[121] On these grounds the Tariff Board rejected the plea for abolition of the revenue duty on pig iron. It also hoped to ensure the survival of the Mysore Iron and Steel Works by this method.[122] It con-

[117] Baldwin: *Industrial Change in South India*, pp. 70–1.

[118] See ITB: *Statutory enquiry 1926: steel*, Vol. VI, p. 29 (oral evidence of G. H. Fairhurst, admitting that when IISCO opened the Japanese market, it sold pig iron in Japan at Rs. 28 per ton f.o.b. Calcutta when the prices in Calcutta were between Rs. 45 and Rs. 50 per ton). On the combine of pig iron producers see ITB: *Report on the removal of the revenue duty on pig iron including the evidence recorded during the enquiry* (Calcutta, 1930), pp. 2–4. On the differences between the domestic and export prices realized by TISCO, see *ibid.*, p. 7.

[119] *Ibid.*, p. 4.

[120] TISCO sold more to the *bazar* than the other two companies, since it had more low-grade surplus pig than the other two. *Ibid.*, pp. 145–7.

[121] The cost of a jute loom worth Rs. 650, for example, would come down only by Rs. 3 – 12 – 0, the cost of a jute cop worth Rs. 4,000 would come down by only Rs. 18–12–0. *Ibid.*, p. 5.

[122] The Tariff Board found that, even after reducing the book value of fixed capital from Rs. 20 million to Rs. 10 million and allowing depreciation at $3\frac{1}{2}$% and interest on working capital at 5%, the full cost per ton of pig iron produced by the Mysore Iron Works came to Rs. 51·42, whereas its average realized price came to Rs. 49 per ton. It was obviously sensible to operate the plant because the works costs came to only Rs. 30 per ton. It also provided healthy competition against the combine and supplied many consumers, particularly in the south and west of India, at prices that were much lower than import prices or the prices charged by the combine. One of the by-products

sidered that the monopolistic exploitation of the internal market by the pig-iron combine was unlikely, for internal prices were more favourable than export prices, and that the profitable course of action of the combine was to develop the internal market by offering attractive prices.[123]

Although the pig-iron combine agreed not to undercut the Mysore Iron Works in Ceylon, Mysore, Madras south of Bezwada, and Hyderabad State, this would not solve the latter's problem, since the total consumption in this area (excluding Ceylon and the railways) would not be more than 2,500 tons, whereas it had to find a market for a surplus production of 12,000 to 15,000 tons.[124] The problem of the Mysore Iron Works vividly illustrates the lack of a developed home market for pig iron in India and particularly in South India, which in its turn reflects the meagre development of engineering industries outside Bengal. The largest consumers of pig iron within India were the East Indian and North-Western Railways, and the only large consumer of pig iron anywhere near the Mysore Iron Works was the Great Indian Peninsula Railway;[125] the combine was quite easily keeping this market to itself.

The depression which began at the end of 1929 led to a contraction of both the home market and the export market for all Indian companies. The Mysore Iron Works joined the pig-iron combine of eastern India. The sale of pig iron by Indian producers was effected under an agreement by which all sales of pig iron in the Bombay Presidency (excluding Sind), Hyderabad State, Madras Presidency (up to Bezwada) and in the Indian States enclosed thereby, were diverted to the Mysore Iron Works, up to a maximum of 7,000 tons a year. All sales in other parts of India and in the southern area above 7,000 tons were allotted to the producers in eastern India. The necessary control was maintained by a differential quota, the difference being Rs. 4 per ton delivered at the buyers' nearest railway station. Sales not allotted to Mysore were divided equally between TISCO on the one hand and IISCO and the Bengal Iron Company on the other hand. The Bengal Iron Company ceased to produce pig iron in November 1931, on the understanding that IISCO (of whose pig iron it was the biggest customer and in which it had a financial interest) should supply all the pig iron needed at cost price. After that, TISCO shared equally in North Indian sales, usually by identical quotations. The sales to the engineering firms were allotted to IISCO and those to the smaller foundries to TISCO (which generally sold basic iron

produced by the Mysore Iron Works was acetate of lime, the basis of acetate, which was in turn an important constituent of modern explosives, and the Tariff Board strongly emphasized its importance in a future emergency. *Ibid.*, pp. 8–11.

[123] *Ibid.*, p. 6.

[124] See *ibid.*, p. 129 for the offer of the combine communicated by TISCO, and p. 38 for the estimate of demand in South India, which was placed at 2,500 tons (presumably excluding the railway demand).

[125] See the oral evidence of M. Veckatanaranappa on behalf of the Mysore Iron Works, on 12 November 1928, in *ibid.*, pp. 64–76, especially pp. 67–8.

with a lower silicon content than good foundry iron). The Mysore Iron Works was guaranteed about 6,000 tons of sales in southern India. It also entered into an agreement with the Bengal Iron Company, by which it secured a market for about 8,000 tons of pipes a year. (The capacity for cast iron production of the Bengal Iron Company was 60,000 tons and that of the Mysore Iron Works was 15,000 tons, after the enlargement of the pipe foundry.)[126]

The pig-iron combine also had explicit agreements about exports: the export business was almost entirely in the hands of TISCO and IISCO. The former exported more to the U.K. than the latter, whereas IISCO exported more to Japan than TISCO. Under the Ottawa agreement, TISCO's exports of pig iron to the U.K. were subject to a minimum of 70,000 tons a year, whereas IISCO were allowed to export approximately 30,000 tons a year.

The combine charged different internal and external prices, but according to the Indian Tariff Board this was not unusual. The internal prices of pig iron in India were substantially lower than the prices of imported pig iron; but the difference between the internal prices charged to small foundries in India and the prices at which pig iron was exported to Japan was still so great that it enabled Japan to use Indian pig iron and undercut the Indian producers of cast iron. The Tariff Board therefore suggested that 'provision should be made for supplying foundry iron at prices not different from those charged to the associated companies (producing cast iron pipes, cast iron sleepers, etc.) and not exceeding export prices by a margin of more than Rs. 10 per ton'.[127]

Most of the measures taken during this period can be regarded as defensive reactions to internal depression and adverse external trade conditions: the international demand was more price-elastic, thus justifying price discrimination; but the biggest customer for Indian pig iron, viz. Japan, imposed duties on Indian pig iron, thus increasing the difficulties of the Indian producers. The Bengal Iron Company was forced to give up pig-iron production and concentrate on producing cast iron products; the Mysore Iron Works diversified first into cast iron pipes and then into steel. Although the small capacity of the Mysore Iron Works made its position apparently more difficult during this period of disastrously falling total demand and declining prices, a larger capacity might have been more of an embarrassment than an asset, as is clearly shown by the case of IISCO. Only TISCO weathered the period well, because it had a dependable buffer in the market for protected steel. The Mysore Iron Works survived because of the willingness of the government to pour more money into it as a defensive investment when

---

[126] See ITB: *Statutory enquiry 1933: steel*, Vol. III (Delhi, 1935), pp. 349–60; ITB: *Report on the iron and steel industry* (Delhi, 1934), Chapter XII, pp. 136–8.
[127] *Ibid.*, p. 143.

the supposed advantages of charcoal iron and wood distillation products had been wiped out by technical change and the depression.[128]

9.9 REDUCTION IN PROTECTIVE TARIFFS AND THE FOUNDING OF THE STEEL CORPORATION OF BENGAL

In 1934 the Indian Tariff Board recommended the reduction of protective duties on a whole range of steel products. For most products the ordinary revenue duties were considered enough. Protective duties on imports of rails, fishplates, semis and sleepers from all countries, and on imports of tested structurals and plates from the U.K., were abolished altogether. In case of bars, black sheets and galvanized sheets, differential protective duties ranging from 10% to 39% were recommended for imports from the U.K. and from the continental countries.[129] Only in the case of structurals imported from continental Europe was a raising of the duty recommended (to 43% *ad valorem*). The Tariff Board was confident that Indian producers of steel, with the enormous advantage of a very low cost of production of pig iron, would be able to hold their own not only against British but also against Continental producers, if the latter charged an 'economic', that is, full cost, price for their products.

[128] Up to 1935, the works had cost the state over Rs. 40 million. The government sanctioned the installation of steel plant at a cost of Rs. 2,100,000 after the ITB had reported in 1934 that the consequential results of the addition of a steel plant would, after meeting interest charges on the capital, 'leave a balance of Rs. 800,000 to meet depreciation and profit'. See C. Ranganatha Rao Sahib: 'The Recent Industrial Progress of Mysore', *JRSA*, LXXXIII, No. 4292, 8 March 1935, p. 384.

[129] Up to 1926 galvanized sheets came almost exclusively from the U.K. and were charged a duty of Rs. 30 per ton under the Steel Industry Protection Act, 1927. When in 1928–9 galvanized sheets began to be imported from Belgium at extremely low prices the duty was raised to Rs. 67 per ton. In September 1931, with the surcharge of 25%, the duty was automatically raised to Rs. 83–12–0 per ton. In 1932, after the conclusion of the Ottawa Pact, an agreement was reached by which lower duties were imposed on imports of sheets made in the U.K. than on imports of sheets made in other countries. According to the terms of the Ottawa Agreement itself, there was to be a difference of Rs. 30 per ton between duties on imports of sheets from the U.K. and those on imports of sheets from other countries; in addition, special preference was given to galvanized sheets made in the U.K. from Indian sheet bar, so that the imports of this category were charged only Rs. 30 per ton as against the duty of Rs. 83 per ton on imports of sheets from countries other than the U.K. This measure was designed to provide a new outlet for Indian sheet bar. In addition, in 1932 special preference was given to the import of Indian foundry iron. The Tata company also entered into an agreement with the Oriental Company of the U.K., guaranteeing that the latter would use the output of the former for producing sheets for the Indian market, and that the sheets thus made would be the property of the Tata company. This supplementary agreement was terminated in 1934; but imports of British galvanized sheets continued to enjoy a measure of preference after an assurance had been obtained from the Government of the U.K. that Indian pig iron would continue to be allowed free. Very soon, however, the Tata company was able to supply a major part of the Indian market in galvanized sheets. See Adarkar [Gov. India Pub.]: *History of the Indian Tariff*, pp. 16–22.

The Government of India accepted the recommendation of the Tariff Board, but it proceeded to impose an excise duty of Rs. 4 per ton on steel ingots so as to make up for the loss expected from the lowering of the customs duties. Hence in order to give the steel industry the same measure of protection as the Tariff Board had intended, it added to the duty recommended by the Tariff Board an amount equal to $1\frac{1}{2}$ or $1\frac{1}{3}$ times the excise duty. Tariff protection in this form was extended for seven years from 1934. A minimum revenue duty of 10% was imposed on iron and steel products, and a minimum preferential margin of 10% was allowed to imports from the U.K., by the imposition of a revenue duty of 10% on imports of steel products from any country other than the U.K., whenever such products were not subject to a protective duty.[130]

TABLE 9.9 *Consumption of saleable steel in India, 1931–2 to 1938–9 (figures in '000 tons)*

Year	Production TISCO	MISW	Imports	Exports and re-exports	Approximate consumption
1931–2	456	—	369	15	810
1932–3	431	—	324	30	725
1933–4	535	—	323	47	811
1934–5	610	—	367	1	976
1935–6	661	—	446	2	1,105
1936–7	680	3	360	3	1,040
1937–8	674	15	365	26	1,028
1938–9	715	23	264	24	978

Source: W. A. Johnson: *The Steel Industry of India* (Cambridge, Mass., 1966), pp. 14–15. MISW stands for Mysore Iron and Steel Works. The consumption figures are crude because they relate to current production rather than actual use and disregard changes in stocks altogether.

The prediction of the ITB turned out to be right as far as TISCO was concerned. As Table 9.9 shows, the consumption of saleable steel in India, after falling to a minimum of 725,000 tons in 1932–3, began to increase again. TISCO was able to increase its dividend on second preference shares from Re. 1 in 1932–3 to Rs. 5 per share (face value: Rs. 100) in 1932–3, Rs. 15 in 1933–4 and Rs. 22 - 8 - 0 in 1934–5. In 1935–6 it was also able to declare a dividend of Rs. 6 per share on ordinary shares (nominal value: Rs. 75).[131] TISCO was also increasing its output every year; but imports had not fallen below 300,000 tons of saleable steel even in the worst years, and in spite of the increase in output by TISCO imports increased in 1934–5 and 1935–6.[132] Hence it was obvious that there was room for a plant

[130] *Ibid.*, pp. 19–20.
[131] The figures are taken from the *Fifty-ninth annual report* (*1965–6*) of the Tata Iron and Steel Company Limited.
[132] TISCO spent Rs. 85 million between 1934 and 1941 expanding the capacity of

producing around 250,000 or 300,000 tons, if that could be considered a minimum economic size.

It was also well-known that the Mysore Iron Works (later Mysore Iron and Steel Works) wanted to produce steel primarily in order to find a use for the pig iron produced by it. Even if it wanted to put up a larger plant, Bhadravati could not be considered an ideal site for it. The capacity of the proposed steel plant was 20,000 tons of finished steel.[133]

Given these circumstances and given the pressure for diversification which we have already noticed, it is not surprising that the management of IISCO should decide to float a new steel plant. The Steel Corporation of Bengal was registered in 1937. The timing of the flotation was connected both with the prosperity of TISCO and the general economic recovery all over the capitalist world.[134] The prospectus of the new company fully explained its *raison d'être*. It pointed out that there was room for a new steel plant in India. The promoters were obviously being conservative: the initial capacity of the plant was planned to be 200,000 tons of finished steel. The plant of the Steel Corporation of Bengal (SCOB) was situated near that of IISCO at Hirapur. SCOB entered into an agreement with IISCO for the supply of water, electricity and gas and the use of town facilities. There was also a strong financial interlinking of IISCO, SCOB and Burn and Company – the managing agents who managed both IISCO and SCOB. IISCO and SCOB entered into agreements for the purchase of all the pig iron needed by the latter from the former. It was claimed that 'the costs of production of iron by the Indian Company were probably lower than those of any other iron-producing company in the world' and that the corporation would get the benefit of these low costs.[135] The promoters of SCOB hoped to net a return of 11% on ordinary capital, taking only the revenue duties on steel products into account.

The size of the plant was probably determined by the size of the Indian market for steel expected to be left unsupplied by TISCO. Financial restrictions were unlikely to have been decisive, both because of the strong financial position of the business group (Burn and Company and Martin and Company) promoting the company,[136] and because of the standing of iron and

its plant and its output of saleable steel expanded from 611,000 tons in 1934–5 to a war-time maximum of 839,000 tons in 1941–2. See ITB: *Report on the continuance of protection to the iron and steel industry* (Bombay, 1947), pp. 8–9, Appendix v. By the beginning of the Second World War the steel plant of TISCO had a capacity of a little under 800,000 tons of saleable steel. See Elwin: *The Story of Tata Steel*, p. 78.

[133] ITB: *Report on the iron and steel industry* (Delhi, 1934), p. 145.

[134] The figures for consumption of steel in India do not tell the whole story. Because of re-armament in most countries of the world, there was very little surplus steel available for export to other countries, including India. The price of steel in India began to rise from November 1936, when the index was 77; it rose finally to 130 in November 1937.

[135] *IITB, 1938–9*, pp. 476–8.

[136] Martin Burn emerged as the third largest business group in independent India: *Report of the Monopolies Inquiry Commission 1965* (Delhi, 1965), p. 119.

steel securities in the market at the time of the flotation of SCOB. Between September 1933 and March 1937 the index number of prices of iron and steel securities rose from 135·5 to 581·3 (Base: 1928–9 = 100). The prices dropped later on, but never below 300, and they began to rise again from May 1939 until they reached 562 in December 1939.

Whatever the reasons for the size of the plant of SCOB,[137] it was almost certainly too small from a long-term point of view and raised the cost of production far above the lowest possible levels. Further, the organizational and physical separation of IISCO and SCOB – the reasons for which were probably the inability of the managing agent to tackle the problem of getting the shareholders of IISCO to merge their interests in a new company or to persuade the investing public to invest in IISCO, which had not been a very profitable concern in the recent past – increased the cost of production of steel unnecessarily. The establishment of SCOB certainly helped the Government of India during the Second World War, when most of the steel was commandeered for military purposes; it also helped the Indian industrial consumer in the immediate post-war days when most countries were busy reconstructing. But the small size of the plant and its non-optimal layout created enormous problems for the future; these problems have to be laid at the door of the lack of public planning and the inability of the share-holders to let bygones be bygones. The slow rate of growth of demand in an industry which was subject to strongly increasing returns to scale aggravated the problems.[138]

[137] The plant did not actually produce any steel until 1940.

[138] It can be easily shown that the higher the rate of growth of demand the more it pays to build in advance of demand and lower current operating costs, and conversely.

10

THE GROWTH OF PRIVATE
ENGINEERING FIRMS

The earliest engineering firms in India, such as Jessop and Company and Burn and Company, seem to have grown up in response to the demand for construction of houses, boats and various other structures as the British consolidated their position in India.[1] With the growth of the jute industry in Bengal and the cotton industry in Bombay, the demand of the mills for various types of structure naturally spurred the growth of engineering. But the general engineering firms came to depend mainly on public works such as roads, bridges and irrigation channels, and on the railways – public and private – for sustenance, particularly when famine or trade depression affected the level of private demand.

Practically all of the more important engineering firms were owned and controlled by Europeans. But they by no means had easy access to the work on the various public works projects and railways. When the East Indian Railway was due to start, the carriages for the railway were lost at the Sandheads in the Hooghly estuary; John Hodgson, the enterprising Locomotive Chief Engineer of the East Indian Railway, then set about building the carriages with the help of two local coach-building firms, and it was with carriages made in India that the first trip from Howrah to Pundooah was made in 1854.[2] This beginning, however, was not followed up with any energy: the railways built their own workshops, in which repairs, reconstruction and assembly-work were mainly undertaken; under stress (for instance, during the two world wars) they even built their own locomotives, but most of the essential rolling stock and locomotives were imported from the U.K. throughout the nineteenth century.[3] Rails and sleepers and keys of iron and steel were also imported almost exclusively from the U.K.; but in some

---

[1] Jessop and Company had been started about 1820, although its business had been carried on before under another name. The domicile of the firm was changed from India to England in 1901. In 1923 most of the shareholders were English but they had lived all their lives in India and retained their interests. See ITB: *Evidence (Report on steel)*, Vol. II (Calcutta, 1924), p. 446. Burn and Company had been started either in 1774 or 1781. It had at first been concerned with building and contracting work, but it had a foundry from the start. It had emerged as a leading railway contractor after the coming of the railways to India. It entered the field of mechanical engineering with the construction of the Howrah Works: *Burn & Co. Ltd, Howrah* (Martin Burn Ltd. Calcutta, 1961). See also Playne & Wright, *Bengal and Assam*, pp. 91–5.

[2] Sahni [Gov. India pub.]: *Indian Railways, One Hundred Years, 1853 to 1953*, p. 5.

[3] *Ibid.*, Chapters XIV and XV.

years large amounts of sleepers and keys of iron and steel were also imported from Australia.

The Government of India was at first quite unwilling to buy manufactures of iron and steel in India, even after a new stores purchase policy had been announced in 1883, and the local engineering firms through the Engineering and Iron Trades Association exerted continuous pressure on the government so that they should be able to tender for engineering stores.[4] The government often took shelter behind the argument that the engineering concerns used mostly imported components or raw materials and so their products could not be regarded as of *bona fide* Indian manufacture. But it was obvious that without the hope of some continuity of orders, and without the assurance that orders would normally be substantial enough, the engineering firms could not invest in machinery and equipment on a scale large enough to compete successfully with their British counterparts, nor could the accessory industries grow up if the industries manufacturing the final goods for the government were themselves stunted.

The engineering firms gradually won the right to tender for the simpler types of structural work, such as small spans of railway girders, through the agitation of firms such as Burn and Company in Calcutta and Richardson and Cruddas in Bombay.[5] While the local officials of the Government of India and provincial governments were often sympathetic to the demands of the engineering firms in India,[6] and while significant advances had been made by 1898 in local purchases of engineering stores, further progress was blocked by the opposition of John Morley, the Secretary of State for India.[7]

Although in theory, under the new policy, government officers were asked to look for Indian manufactures, a clause in Rule 8 (dated 12 September 1912) stated:

In cases, however, in which stores have to be obtained through the India Office, every effort should be made to foresee requirements so that indents may be

---

[4] Sen: *Studies in Economic Policy and Development*, pp. 19–21.

[5] See the evidence of Sir Francis J. E. Spring, Chairman and Chief Engineer, Madras Port Trust Board, *Evidence (Report of IIC)*, Vol. III, (PP 1919, XIX), pp. 68–9.

[6] See, for example, Watson [IPG pub.]: *Monograph on Iron and Steel Work*, pp. 54–7.

[7] Sen: *Studies in Economic Policy and Development*, pp. 19–20. The initial stimulus for the setting-up of the wagon-building divisions of Burn and Company and Jessop and Company seems to have come from the increasing expenditure on railway rolling stock budgeted by the Government of India. The budgeted expenditure on rolling stock was as follows:

	Rs. million
1903–4	29·1
1904–5	29·2
1905–6	27·9
1906–7	38·2
1907–8	56·8

See *Indian financial statement for 1907–8 and proceedings* (PP 1907, LVIII), pp. 198 and 216.

despatched in ample time. Persistent failure of any officer to make such efforts should be brought to notice by the Local Government or other authority, which may, at its discretion, cancel or reduce the powers of sanction entrusted to the officer at fault.

Thus the threat was directed primarily against officers failing to make indents through the India Office, and hence many officers found it safer and easier (as it saved the trouble of scrutinizing tenders) to make indents directly through that Office.[8] The local engineering firms in many cases thus obtained only rush orders or infrequent orders in small batches.[9] This situation continued until the First World War when the enormously increased demands of the government changed the situation radically.

During the war, engineering firms were occupied primarily in supplying the military requirements of the government, including the manufacture of cases for shells, various types of castings and other foundry products, and a large number of rivercraft.[10] Although this demand kept most of the engineering works fully occupied and stimulated the establishment of new firms, the virtual cornering of all steel by the government for its own requirements meant sometimes that the engineering works could not carry out any work for lack of raw materials.[11]

Although the industrial census taken during the population censuses of 1911 and 1921 cannot be fully relied on for obvious reasons (such as lack of rigorous definition of different occupations and of different classes of workers, the inability to reflect seasonal fluctuation of either perennial or seasonal occupation), it does show, for what it is worth, that between 1911 and 1921 the number of persons employed in machinery and engineering workshops increased from 23,147 to 82,182, and that of persons engaged in metal industries increased from 71,045 to 169,693. Taking figures on a comparable basis, the number of persons employed in metal industries increased from 71,045 in 1911 to 164,680 in 1921, and persons employed in metal, machinery, etc., workshops increased from 23,147 in 1911 to 81,598 (the growth was due more to an increase in the number of factories than to in-

[8] See the evidence of H. D. Gill, partner in the firm of Richardson and Cruddas, in *Evidence (Report of IIC)*, Vol. IV (PP 1919, XIX), pp. 76–8, and particularly the exchange between Gill and the President, Sir Thomas Holland, p. 78.

[9] Burn and Company of Calcutta, for example, received no orders for wagons or carriages at all in 1903–4; there was an upward, but not steady, trend in the orders received by the company for wagons and carriages from 1907–8 to 1913–14; in the former year the company received orders for 147 wagons and 40 carriages and in the latter for 1354 wagons and 96 carriages. The situation changed radically during the war since the reconstruction and expansion programmes of the railways were rudely interrupted. See ITB: *Evidence (Report on steel)*, Vol. II (Calcutta, 1924), pp. 316–18. The other wagon-building firm, Jessop and Company, did not receive any orders at all for wagons or carriages. *Ibid.*, p. 435.

[10] See *India's Contribution to the Great War* (Calcutta, 1923).

[11] See, for example, evidence of Jessop and Company Limited in ITB: *Evidence (Report on steel)*, Vol. II (Calcutta, 1924), p. 435.

creases in the average number employed in a factory, although the latter also increased).[12]

Just after the war a large number of new companies were formed in the engineering industries, either to take over old firms and expand them or to start new enterprises. Some of the new enterprises were established with a view to manufacturing textile machinery, machine tools, and so on. A number of companies were set up as subsidiaries to the Tata Iron and Steel Company's works at Jamshedpur. TISCO did not have a direct financial stake in all the companies: it generally leased the requisite land to the companies concerned, and entered into long-term contracts for the supply of power, water and raw materials, which consisted largely of iron and steel ingots or rolled steel. The list of the companies thus set up by 1923 is as follows: (1) Enamelled Ironware Limited, (2) The Indian Cable Company Limited, (3) The Tinplate Company of India Limited, (4) The Calmoni Engineering Company Ltd (for manufacturing jute-textile machinery), (5) the Agricultural Implements Company Limited, (6) the Indian Steel Wire Products Limited, and (7) the Peninsular Locomotive Company Limited. There were even more ambitious projects in 1918, but it appears that the attraction of external economies was not powerful enough to overcome the misgivings about the volume of internal demand and the stiffness of foreign competition.[13] The competition from European countries in structural steel; the fall in the prices of base metals and machinery; the faltering policy of reconstruction of the government, which was embarrassed by budgetary difficulties, the wild fluctuations in exchange rates and the lack of government support of any kind up to 1924 led to the liquidation of many of the new companies.[14]

At about the same time as TISCO applied for the statutory protection of Indian steel against foreign competition, many engineering firms, including those manufacturing or proposing to manufacture structural or fabricated steel (Burn and Company Limited, Jessop and Co. Ltd), wagons for rail-

[12] Gov. India, CISD: *Statistical abstract for British India*, 7th Issue (1913–14) (Calcutta, 1915), and *Statistical abstract for British India 1913–14 to 1922–3* (Calcutta, 1924). Only persons working for factories employing 20 persons or more were included in the 1911 census, and persons working for factories employing 10 persons or more were included in the 1921 census. See *Census of India, 1921*, Vol. I, *Report* (Calcutta, 1924), p. 266.

[13] ITB: *Evidence (Report on steel)*, Vol. I (Calcutta, 1924), pp. 66 and 70; for the plans of 1918, *ibid.*, p. 87.

[14] Angus and Company and Fairbairn, Lawson, Combe and Barbour (India) Limited were two of the textile machinery manufacturers: the total requirement of steel of the former when working at capacity was given as 2,000 tons, and that of the latter as 200 tons. See *ibid.*, Vol. II, pp. 9–11 and 540. Among the engineering companies which flickered into existence and then died out between 1919 and 1920 were Automatic Tools Limited (Calcutta), the Bengal Bridge and Bolt Company Limited (in its unincorporated state it was one of the biggest engineering firms managed by an Indian company, Messrs J. C. Banerjee and Company), Bengal Lead Mills Company (which was formed for manufacturing lead lining for tea chests) and the Dock Engineering Company Limited.

ways (such as Burn and Company Ltd, Jessop and Company Ltd, Indian Standard Wagon Co. Ltd), enamelled ironware (Enamelled Ironware Ltd of Jamshedpur and Pioneer Enamel and Iron Works Ltd, of Salkia in Howrah district), tinplate (the Tinplate Company of India Ltd), wire and wire nails (the Indian Steel Wire Products Ltd), agricultural implements and miners' equipment (the Agricultural Implements Company Limited and Kiroloskar Brothers), locomotives (the Peninsular Locomotive Company Ltd) and steel castings (Hukamchand Steel Works Company, Calcutta), applied to the Indian Tariff Board for substantive or at least compensatory protection (in case statutory protection were granted to the steel manufactured in India). The Indian Engineering Association, representing the large engineering concerns of India, wanted protection to be give to the steel industry but only in the form of bounties: if the TISCO works were to close down for lack of protection 'the industrial development of India would be set back by certainly a quarter of a century'.[15] The Association also wanted the protection of engineering industries to be given preferably in the form of guaranteed Indian prices rather than by import duties or bounties.[16]

The case of the engineering industry catering for Indian railways was examined in 1923 by a committee of members of the Indian Legislative Assembly who were appointed to consider 'what steps should be taken by the Government of India to encourage the establishment of necessary industries so that as large an amount as possible of the [Rs. 1,500 million] proposed to be set aside for the rehabilitation of the railways during the next five years be spent in India'.[17] The Committee approved of the relaxation of the rules governing government purchases, which had been undertaken following the recommendation of the Stores Purchase Committee of 1920. It recommended that the price of all stores purchased should be fixed after taking account of the cost of transport and any import tariffs ruling, but this was already recognized in principle in Rule 10 of the existing Stores Purchase Rules.[18] However, the committee pointed out that the application of the Rules posed difficulties in the case of those industries 'which involve fabrication and the employment of large bodies of skilled labour'. 'The principal difficulty is that described in paragraph 65 of the Report of the Fiscal Commission. Industries of this kind require a considerable period for their development.'[19] They also required considerable initial capital, had small outputs and large overhead costs initially, and necessitated the import of skilled labour from abroad. 'In fact, industries newly started in India for the manufacture of railway material of a fabricated nature cannot in the initial stage compete without assistance against established industries abroad'.[20] After citing the example of a recent tender for 3,132 wagons

[15] ITB: *Evidence (Report on steel)*, Vol. II (Calcutta, 1924), pp. 583–4.
[16] *Ibid.*, p. 585.   [17] *Report of the Railway Industries Committee* (Delhi, 1923), p. 1.
[18] *Ibid.*, pp. 3–4.   [19] *Ibid.*, p. 4.   [20] *Ibid.*, p. 4.

placed by the Railway Board for which the lowest satisfactory Indian tender was 50% higher than the lowest English tender, even after taking account of c.i.f. charges and customs duty, the committee concluded: 'We see no escape from the conclusion that the industries which we are now discussing, if they are to be developed – or rather kept alive – in India, must temporarily get some form of protection or assistance from Government.'[21] Thus by 1923 it was recognized publicly that the Indian engineering industry needed government assistance if it was to be preserved from extinction.

The capital invested in the bigger firms of the engineering industry represented by the Indian Engineering Association was estimated at Rs. 120 million in 1923; including the smaller works, the total number employed in the industry was estimated at 75,000.[22] The Indian Tariff Board considered the industry deserving of protection on these grounds and on the ground that it provided a potentially large home market for Indian steel; also the industry had rendered service to India for a long period.

The Board had difficulty in arriving at estimates of the average cost of different types of engineering products, because of the multiplicity of products, the lack of relation between accounting practice and true cost, and the secretiveness of the firms, caused by fear of competition. It had, therefore, to take the cost of fabrication on trust from bigger firms, such as Burn and Company Limited, and Jessop and Company Limited; it found that among fabricated steel products, it was in the case of bridgework and buildings that foreign competition was keenest, and Indian firms found it difficult to hold their own. But it also included steel works using plates – such as colliery tubs – in its scheme of protection, since this provided a market for Indian plate, which was going to be turned out by TISCO.

It estimated the average import price of bridgework as Rs. 250 per ton, and the average cost of such Indian work at Rs. 310 per ton, and proposed a uniform duty of 25% on all fabricated steel. Out of the duty of Rs. 62 per ton, Rs. 33 merely compensated for the duty on unfabricated steel. The balance (Rs. 29) was the measure of protection given to the fabricating industry. (The duty on all iron and steel products and raw materials had already been raised from $2\frac{1}{2}$% to 10% in 1922.)[23]

The Indian Tariff Board considered the railway wagon-building industry separately. Although Burn and Company and Jessop and Company in Calcutta, and Herman and Mohatta in Karachi, had built wagons as part of their general engineering work before the war, the real beginning of a separate wagon-building industry was made with the establishment of the Indian Standard Wagon Company Limited in 1918, under the management of Burn and Company. This development was directly stimulated by the *communiqué* of the Government of India, dated 1 March 1918, in which

[21] *Ibid.*, p. 5.   [22] ITB: *Report on steel* (Calcutta, 1924), p. 112.
[23] *Ibid.*, pp. 113–15.

it guaranteed to purchase in India 2,500 broad-gauge and 500-metre or narrow-gauge wagons annually for 10 years.[24] The works were adjacent to the Burnpur works of IISCO, with which it had agreements for the supply of pig iron. The Indian Standard Wagon Co. found that it could not compete with British producers in price and lost valuable railway contracts in 1922; it could not reduce costs to a sufficient extent to compete with British producers if it could not produce at least 1,500 wagons per annum, and it could not reach that target if it did not receive special terms from the railways in the initial stage.[25] The Railway Board, however, refused to grant such special terms; prices of imported wagons declined further, and so all the wagon-building firms applied for government assistance in the form of tariff protection or bounties.

The Indian firms had claimed that they could compete successfully with British firms up to 1914; but now they found that the lowest British tender for a certain (standard) type of wagon came to Rs. 3,500 as against the lowest Indian cost of Rs. 5,000 for the same type in 1923, in spite of the fact that wages had risen faster in Britain than in India. The Indian firms claimed this to be evidence that British producers had deliberately set out to kill the Indian wagon-building industry.

The ITB, however, pointed out that before the war the Indian firms had obtained only rush orders or orders which were on too small a scale for it to be worthwhile for British producers to tender. Moreover, the Indian firms had omitted to take into account the advances which had taken place in methods of wagon-building in Britain, which had allowed British producers to cut their costs drastically and quote low tenders. The ability of the British producers to buy their raw materials cheaply in times of keen competition had also to be taken into account.

The ITB recommended government assistance for the wagon-building industry in the form of bounties, for otherwise the costs of railways would go up. They thought that it was essential that the Indian manufacturers should have some assurance of continuity of orders, and, as the capacity for carrying out work would increase as time went on, that the numbers ordered in India should gradually rise. They also expected that as experience was gained and output went up the cost of production would fall. With these aims in mind they recommended the scale of bounties on the manufacture of railway wagons in India shown in Table 10.1.[26]

When it came to the problem of whether or not to recommend tariff protection for the locomotive industry in India, the ITB came up sharply against the Indian Fiscal Commission's condition that an industry must have a large home market in order to qualify for protection. The Peninsular

---

[24] ITB: *Evidence (Report on steel)*, Vol. II (Calcutta, 1924), p. 315.
[25] *Ibid.*, pp. 317–18.
[26] ITB: *Report on steel* (Calcutta, 1924), pp. 117–20.

TABLE 10.1 *Scale of bounties for railway wagons proposed by the ITB in 1924*

	Number of wagons on which bounty would be payable	Amount of bounty per wagon Rs.	Cost of bounty (Rs. thousand)
1st year	800	850	680
2nd year	1,000	700	700
3rd year	1,200	580	696
4th year	1,400	500	700
5th year	1,600	400	704

Locomotive Company was formed as a direct response to the *communiqué* of the Government of India dated 30 September 1921, in which the government gave a general undertaking that tenders would be invited annually in India for all the railway locomotives and locomotive boilers required by the government during the twelve years commencing in 1923. The government estimated that its average annual requirements would be 160 locomotive engines and 160 additional boilers during 1923 and 1924, and thereafter 400 locomotives and 400 additional boilers.[27]

The Peninsular Locomotive Company Ltd was established on 6 December 1921 with a capital of Rs. 6 million, under the management of Kerr, Stuart and Company, a British wagon- and locomotive-building firm with works at Stoke-on-Trent. The company hoped ultimately to produce 300 locomotives per year. The initial cost of erection of the works of the company (Rs. 5 million) was approximately 35% in excess of the cost of putting up the same plant in Great Britain. The cost of the 2–8–0 type locomotive and tender f.o.b. English port was estimated in 1923 at £6,400. The additional cost in India was estimated by the company to be £2,753 (though the ITB considered this too high an estimate). Initially, the company would have to import a large proportion of the parts of a locomotive (in particular, boilers) but more than 50% by weight would be either produced by the company in its own works or obtained from Indian firms producing steel and iron castings and other foundry and forge products. But the company hoped to produce a larger proportion of locomotive parts in India with the passage of time, and to bring down the cost of production through expansion of output, experience and increasing Indianization of superior staff. In the meantime, it was not able to quote competitive prices and received no orders and so had not brought over the supervisory staff and technical personnel whom it had already engaged in the U.K. It was at this stage that the company applied for tariff protection or bounties.[28]

[27] ITB: *Evidence (Report on steel) 1924*, Vol. II, p. 288.
[28] *Ibid.*, pp. 280–93.

The ITB supported most of the arguments in favour of protection for the locomotive industry in India, and conjectured that the protection needed might not be greater than had been found necessary for the protection of the locomotive industries in countries such as Australia (with $27\frac{1}{2}\%$ duty *ad valorem* on imported locomotives) and Canada (where the duty was $22\frac{1}{2}\%$). It pointed out, however, that the demand situation had radically changed since 1921, for, acting on the recommendations of the Inchcape Committee on Retrenchment, the government had revised the capital programme of the railways and had effected drastic cuts in it. Mr Hindley, giving evidence for the Railway Board before the Tariff Board, had stated that the requirements of the railways during 1924–5 would be only 60 locomotives, and that it was doubtful whether the requirements in any one of the next five years would be as high as 100 locomotives.

A locomotive factory, in order to be economic, must produce at least 200 a year, whereas the estimated demand of the railways fell far short of this; even if the locomotive works secured the order for the whole Indian railway system it could not produce at a reasonable cost, particularly since the locomotives would have to fit a large number of designs meant for the three main gauges in India. There was no prospect whatsoever of the demand increasing in the near future. Hence the ITB could not recommend tariff protection for the locomotive industry and in the event no private (or public) locomotive works were established in India until after independence.[29]

The ITB refused to recommend tariff protection in the case of two other branches of engineering, viz., steel castings and enamelled ware. Steel castings were manufactured by using two different processes; in one (the 'converter' process) the raw material was pig iron with very low phosphorus content, and in the other (the electric process) the raw material was steel scrap. The Tariff Board considered that the 'converter' process did not satisfy one of the requirements for protection, viz., that it should use Indian raw materials, for it was unlikely that pig iron with a very low phosphorus content would be ever produced in India. In the case of the electric steel, the raw material was available in sufficient quantities from railways and other industries round about Calcutta, and its average price (Rs. 30 per

[29] See ITB: *Report on steel* (Calcutta, 1924), Third Report, Ch. II, pp. 169–71. It may be pointed out that locomotives had been manufactured off and on since 1896 in the Ajmer workshops of G. I. P. Railways and since 1899 in the Jamalpur workshops of East Indian Railways. This production was particularly valuable during the two world wars. However, 'despite these successful attempts, locomotive manufacture on a large scale was not adopted as a part of railway policy', although combined with a proper programme of rehabilitation and expansion between the wars, self-sufficiency in locomotive production would have resulted in very great economies in expenditure and foreign exchange. See Sahni [Gov. India pub.]: *Indian Railways*, pp. 107–9; and Lehmann: 'Great Britain and the Supply of Railway Locomotives for India'.

ton) was 'lower than the prices prevailing for similar material in other countries'.[30] But the Tariff Board found it difficult to estimate the demand for steel castings in India; taking into account the actual manufacture of steel castings by various railway workshops, and the probable rate of growth of railway wagon-building (steel castings were parts of railway wagons and coaches), it doubted whether the probable demand could keep the two main producers of steel castings (with a combined monthly output of 450 tons) fully occupied. But apart from this, it faced the problem that steel castings were always parts of something else. Without a policy for protection of machinery for locomotive production and without any policy regarding the differential treatment of machines and their parts, the Tariff Board could not make any general recommendations. It summed up by saying: 'The output of steel castings must clearly be limited by the demand, and at the same time the cost of production is largely determined by the output. Unless some estimate can be formed of the output, it is hardly possible to determine the cost of production, or to assess the amount of protection needed. For this reason we are unable to make any general recommendation at present.'[31]

In the case of enamelled ware, the reasons for refusal of tariff protection were summarized by the ITB as follows:

The market is not a large one, and, if it were to be further restricted, the prospects of the industry would be prejudiced and not improved. Nor are we able to support the proposal that the firms should be allowed to import the steel sheets they require free of duty. The practical difficulties would be great for no means has been suggested by which the firms would receive a rebate of customs duties paid by them on imported sheets in proportion to their output of finished goods. It would, however, be wholly inconsistent with protection for the steel industry to exempt from duty sheets of the kind which is likely to be produced at Jamshedpur. The TISCO are under contract with Enamelled Ironware, Ltd., to supply them with sheet suitable for enamelling and the doubt that has been expressed as to their ability to do this is not, we think, well founded. The Tinplate Co. are already manufacturing from steel made at Jamshedpur sheets of a similar quality to the kind required and there is no reason why the TISCO should not be successful.[32]

Apart from the reasons thus explicitly given, it was also clear, from the rest of the argument of the Tariff Board in the relevant chapter, that it was impressed neither by the financial capacity of the actual producers (three firms whose combined capital was less than the capital (Rs. 900,000) of the subsidiary of TISCO at Jamshedpur, Enamelled Ironware Limited) nor by the ability of these firms to forecast their own demand. It also

[30] ITB: *Report on steel* (Calcutta, 1924), p. 176.
[31] *Ibid.*, p. 179. The total amount of capital invested in the two major steel casting firms, Hukamchand Electric Steel Co., and the Kirtyanand Iron and Steel Works Ltd, came to about Rs. 2 million in 1923. [32] *Ibid.*, p. 182.

probably surmised that all these small firms would be in difficulties once the TISCO subsidiary got into its stride. It was very rare indeed for small firms, not backed by a powerful association, to succeed in an application for tariff protection between the wars.[33]

The only producer of tinplate in India was the Tinplate Company of India Ltd, a joint subsidiary of the Burmah Oil Company, the biggest consumer of its output, and TISCO, the sole Indian supplier of sheet bars,

TABLE 10.2 *Private consumption of tinplate in India, 1911–12 to 1932–3* *(figures in tons)*

Year	Imports	Sales of Tinplate Company of India	Total consumption
1911–12	42,337	—	—
1912–13	43,093	—	—
1914–15	52,836	—	—
1915–16	50,442	—	—
1916–17	47,400	—	—
1917–18	44,126	—	—
1918–19	31,966	—	—
1919–20	42,169	—	—
1920–1	49,934	—	—
1921–2	24,747	—	—
1922–3	43,621	—	—
1923–4	44,090	—	—
1924–5	36,529	—	—
1925–6	29,758	—	—
1927–8	—	42,806	66,663
1928–9	—	35,150	62,124
1929–30	—	35,681	66,768
1930–1	—	37,868	55,097
1931–2	—	38,306	45,890
1932–3	—	38,967	45,970

Sources: For 1911–12 to 1925–6, ITB: *Evidence* (Report on steel), Vol. II (Calcutta, 1924), p. 24 and *Statutory enquiry 1926: steel*, Vol. I (Calcutta, 1926), p. 170; for 1927–8 to 1932–3, ITB: *Statutory enquiry 1933: steel*, Vol. III (Delhi, 1935), p. 238.

from which tinplate is made. India was importing large quantities of tinplate even before the First World War, as Table 10.2 indicates. It was natural that the biggest consumer of tinplate in India, the Burmah Oil Co., should enter into an agreement for its manufacture with TISCO soon after the latter had set up facilities for the production of steel. The Burmah Oil Co. had also entered into an agreement with the Tinplate Co. to purchase (if the oil company needed it) all its output for twenty-five years at the price

[33] *Ibid.*, pp. 180–4. The Tariff Board recommended that the application of these firms to be allowed to import the essential raw materials for glazing steel sheets duty-free should be seriously considered, but it did not make any concrete proposals.

of imported tinplate. TISCO had agreed to supply sheet bar at the price f.o.b. Swansea of sheet bar, subject to an adjustment for the average cost of production of tinplate, such that if the latter exceeded the price of imported tinplate, TISCO would make good half the loss, whereas if it fell short of the price of imported tinplate, TISCO would receive half the profit. Clearly, in the initial stages, and until the Tinplate Company could compete with the Welsh manufacturers, TISCO would have to subsidize the Tinplate Company quite heavily.

The Tinplate Company suffered from two basic disadvantages in relation to South Wales: first, it had to incur a much heavier capital expenditure, to make continuous manufacture in the hot weather physically possible; secondly, it had to incur a much heavier expense on supervisory and skilled personnel since no experienced Indian workmen were available. The latter disadvantage was expected to disappear through time. But tariff protection would clearly be necessary, seeing that India was a very important market for the tinplate industry of South Wales and that manufacture of tinplate had failed in several countries, such as Italy, Spain, Canada, Norway, Russia and Japan; and that it had succeeded in the U.S.A. only after heavy duties had been imposed on imported tinplate after the passing of the McKinley Tariff Act in October 1890.[34]

There were further complications in the situation: an increase in the cost of tinplate would probably mean an increase in the cost of kerosene which would harm the poorer classes. For some time to come, the Burmah Oil Company might be the sole beneficiary of protection since the eventual capacity of the Tinplate Company was 28,000 tons, whereas the consumption of the Burmah Oil Company alone was 21,000 tons; the oil companies (along with the Standard Oil Company) consumed about 28,000 tons of tinplate, which was about half the total Indian consumption. So even with full production, the Tinplate Company could supply only 20% of the open market (after supplying 21,000 tons to the Burmah Oil Company). But, of course, there was no reason to suppose that the Tinplate Company would not expand its capacity or that new firms would not come up once the production of tinplate had been proved economical in India.[35]

The ITB considered that it was important to build up a tinplate industry in India, and with a more or less assured market for the output of the Tinplate Company, there were good prospects for reduction of costs once full production could be undertaken. The Tinplate Company would also provide a welcome outlet for the sheet bars of TISCO, whose fortunes were in any case tied up with those of the Tinplate Company

---

[34] ITB: *Evidence (Report on steel)*, Vol. II (Calcutta, 1924), pp. 16–20.
[35] ITB: *Evidence (Report on steel)*, Vol. III (Calcutta, 1924), pp. 729–30.

through the existing long-term contract for the supply of sheet bars. But since little experience had been gained, it recommended only a minimum degree of protection, viz., a duty of Rs. 60 per ton on all imported tinplate, and this duty was imposed by the Steel Industry (Protection) Act, 1924. In February 1926, following an enquiry by the Indian Tariff Board, the government raised the duty to Rs. 85 per ton and at the same time replaced the existing duty of 15% *ad valorem* on imported tin by a specific duty of Rs. 250 per ton, which meant a reduction of Rs. 305 per ton in comparison with the previous *ad valorem* duty of 15%.[36]

In the statutory enquiry of 1926, the ITB found that 'the Tinplate industry affords a notable illustration of the industrial progress attainable within a comparatively short period under the policy of discriminating protection adopted by Government'.[37] Starting production at the end of 1922, and with a plant originally designed to produce 28,000 tons, the Tinplate Company had produced just over 9,000 tons in 1923, 20,763 tons in 1924, and 29,555 tons in 1925, while output was expected to be 35,000 tons in 1926. The works costs per ton of tinplate fell from Rs. 459 in 1924 to Rs. 313 in 1926; abstracting from the fall in the price of tinbar, the remaining works costs fell from Rs. 213 to Rs. 138. A large part of this fall in costs (amounting to Rs. 44·9 per ton) was accounted for by the fall in labour costs, which had been achieved partly by the decline in the number of European covenanted employees, and partly through an improvement in the skill of Indian workers. The number of European covenanted employees declined from 84 in 1924 to 71 in 1925, and to 59 in 1926. Indian labour costs per ton of tinplate fell from Rs. 58 in 1924 to Rs. 34 in 1926.[38]

The tinplate output of the Tinplate Co. of India went up to 41,521 tons in 1927, but it was affected in 1928 by the strike at TISCO and then in 1929 by the strike in its own works; for the next two years the output was affected by limited demand but it recovered to 42,151 tons in 1932.[39]

The Tinplate Company estimated that at the end of 1933 the works costs would come to Rs. 285 per ton; the Indian Tariff Board, however, considered this a high figure and suggested improvements in practice as regards consumption of tinbar and Indian labour and estimated the 1933 works costs to be Rs. 279·1 per ton. The Indian Tariff Board chose Rs. 293 as the average works costs over the seven-year period; this figure was slightly below the arithmetical average of Rs. 310·6 (the 1926 works costs after allowing for reduction in duty on tinbar) and Rs. 279. In arriving at the fair selling price of tinplate, the Indian Tariff Board reduced the book value of the Tinplate Company's works and town from Rs. 16·2

---

[36] ITB: *Statutory enquiry 1926: steel*, Vol. I (Calcutta, 1926), p. 101.
[37] *Ibid.*, p. 107.   [38] *Ibid.*, Ch. XIV and XV.
[39] ITB: *Statutory enquiry 1933: steel*, Vol. III (Delhi, 1935), p. 234.

million to Rs. 8·5 million, the latter representing the fair replacement value of the company's works. In arriving at this figure, the ITB adopted the same procedure as it had applied in reducing the book value of the 'Greater Extensions' part of TISCO's works from Rs. 150 million to Rs. 100 million, and for the same reason: viz., that the plant had been bought at greatly inflated prices during the period of the post-war boom. On this basis the fair selling price came to Rs. 368·22 per ton, and the import price to Rs. 320 per ton (disregarding the rise in British prices due to the stoppage of coal production).[40] The Tariff Board recommended a reduction in the specific duty from Rs. 85 to Rs. 48 per ton. It could not recommend any discrimination in favour of Wales, since it was with Welsh tinplate that the Indian tinplate had mainly to compete.[41] The Government of India accepted this recommendation, and this was given effect to by the Steel Industry (Protection) Act, 1927. The duty was increased to Rs. 60 per ton as a result of the surcharge of 25% imposed in 1931.

When the ITB conducted its statutory enquiry in 1933, it found that the progress in output and efficiency had been maintained. The total output in 1932 had exceeded 46,000 tons, including 4,000 tons of galvanized sheets as against the estimated capacity of 36,000 tons. The depression of the thirties had an adverse effect on Indian consumption of tinplate, but the sales of tinplate by the Tinplate Co. were not greatly affected (see Table 10.2). Thus, while the sales of the Tinplate Co. constituted between 50 and 60% of total Indian consumption up to 1929–30, by 1932–3 they had come to form more than 80%.[42] In the meantime, the number of covenanted employees had been reduced from sixty in 1927 to twenty-three in 1932, less than 1% of the total number of employees. The works costs had fluctuated during 1927–9 because of strikes, but after that they had fallen steadily so that works costs of tinplate stood at Rs. 227·5 in 1932 compared with Rs. 292·1 in 1927 (see Table 10.3).

In 1926 the Board anticipated economies which would by 1934 reduce the cost excluding that of metal to Rs. 117 as against Rs. 138 per ton in 1926. By 1932 the cost above metal had fallen to Rs. 83. The fall in the price of steel and tin accounted for about Rs. 30 per ton and the fall in prices of stores for another Rs. 15 per ton, still leaving an improvement in practice equivalent to Rs. 10 per ton.[43] Most of this fall appears to

[40] The Tinplate Co. actually carried out a reconstruction of capital in 1927 so as to bring down the block value of its property from Rs. 16,159,736 at the end of 1925 to Rs. 12,000,000 in 1927; corresponding adjustments were made in the nominal values of debentures and ordinary shares. See ITB: *Statutory enquiry 1933: steel*, Vol. III (Delhi, 1935), p. 243.

[41] *Ibid.*, Chapters xv, xvi and xix.

[42] Compare the share of the sales of TISCO to the total Indian consumption of steel before and during the depression of the thirties.

[43] ITB: *Report on the iron and steel industry* (Delhi, 1934), pp. 106–7.

TABLE 10.3 *Cost of production of tinplate in India, 1927 to 1932*

Date	Tinplate produced (tons)	Works costs (Rs. per ton)	Total costs of tinplate per ton (Rs.)
1927	41,521	292.138	294.243
1928	36,815	271.991	274.817
1929	33,113	298.199	300.848
1930	38,482	254.594	256.742
1931	37,320	229.814	232.627
1932	42,151	227.514	230.499

Source: ITB: *Statutory enquiry 1933: steel*, Vol. III (Delhi, 1935), p. 231.

have been due to the fall in wage costs owing to the replacement of European by Indian labour and a slight reduction in the labour force, for the total number of employees was 2,990 in 1927 and 2,951 in 1932 whereas the wage costs per ton of tinplate were Rs. 55 in 1927 and Rs. 46 in 1932 (the tinplate output was slightly larger in 1932).[44] The company did not anticipate any further reduction in costs through more intensive exploitation of the plant and improvement in practice. The ITB suggested a revision of the agreement between TISCO and the Tinplate Company, since the price of tinbar supplied by the former was fixed with reference to the price of Welsh tinplate, whereas in actual fact it could supply tinbar at a much lower price.

The Tariff Board recommended a reduction in this duty: imports of tinplate from the United Kingdom would be subject to a duty of Rs. 38 per ton and imports from all other countries would pay a duty of Rs. 59 per ton. (The main competitors other than the U.K. were the U.S.A., Germany and Italy.)

Another branch of engineering, the production of wire and wire nails, had a rather shaky beginning, for although Indian Steel Wire Products Limited was set up in 1919, and although the Indian wire and wire nail industry had been granted tariff protection in 1924 (a specific duty of Rs. 60 per ton was imposed on wire (other than barbed or stranded wire) and wire nails and a similar duty of Rs. 40 per ton was imposed on wire rods), the sole Indian company got into difficulties because it had to import wire rods from abroad. With increased European competition, the duty on wire and wire nails was increased to Rs. 90 per ton and later, on the recommendation of the ITB, the specific duty on wire rod was replaced by an *ad valorem* revenue duty of Rs. 10 per ton, since wire rod was not yet manufactured by TISCO or any other Indian company. Indian Steel Wire Products Limited, however, got into financial

[44] ITB. *Statutory enquiry 1933: steel*, Vol. III (Delhi, 1935), p. 242.

difficulties, and worked only intermittently; tariff protection was withdrawn by the government in 1928 on the liquidation of the company. The works at Jamshedpur were bought at a very low price by a new company, Indian Steel and Wire Products, Tatanagar, and production began again in 1928. By the time of the statutory enquiry of 1933, one other firm, Messrs Devidas Jethanand of Karachi, had begun manufacturing wire, wire nails and screws, and the Indian Hume Pipe Company of Bombay had been drawing wires for use in the manufacture of reinforced concrete pipes. Most of the wire and nails were, however, imported from countries outside the British Empire. In 1931 after a fresh enquiry ITB proposed a specific duty of Rs. 45 on wire and wire nails, while recommending the continued exemption of imported wire rod from duty on the understanding that the Indian Steel and Wire Products set up a rod mill, since TISCO had stated its inability to produce wire rod.

In 1934 the Tariff Board found that the claim of the major company for protection was justified since the rod mill had been installed and started functioning in September 1933. The capacity of the main company for wire and wire nails production was about 12,000 tons whereas imports of the same, excluding fencing materials, amounted to 22,829 tons even in 1932–3; hence there was obviously an ample home market for its output. The company was also equipped to produce about 30,000 tons of small bars and sections and had a galvanizing plant capable of dealing with 2,000 tons of wire. The consumption of small bars and sections was estimated at 70,000 tons for all India and 20,000 tons for Bengal alone. Hence there was a sufficiently large market for these other products also.

Indian Steel and Wire Products did not ask for protection against British wire and wire nails. The ITB recommended for wire rod, small bars and sections the same duties as they had fixed for bars of the classes already protected, viz., Rs. 10 on imports from the U.K. and Rs. 39 on imports from other countries. They recommended a duty of Rs. 25 per ton on imports of wire and wire nails from the U.K. and Rs. 60 on those from other countries. The severest competition in wire products was offered by Japan and the Tariff Board proposed that dumping prices lower than those it had assumed should be dealt with by the operation of the provision for off-setting duties.[45]

In the field of general engineering, which included structural steel, most of the firms in eastern and northern India had a hard time of it throughout the twenties since the earlier hopes of a continuation of the immediate post-war boom did not materialize. Most of the firms worked below capacity. But the real crisis came with the depression, since public works including railway structural work were drastically cut down; even a firm

[45] ITB: *Report on the iron and steel industry* (Delhi, 1934), Chapter xi and *Statutory enquiry 1933: steel*, Vol. iii (Delhi, 1935), pp. 266–326.

of the standing of Burn and Co. Ltd, was forced to stop dividends on its ordinary shares for all the years from 1931 to 1934; according to the *IITB* of 1931–2, 1931 was the third year in the history of Burn and Co. Ltd, in which it was forced to pass the dividend on ordinary shares.

The ITB after its enquiry in 1926 recommended a basic duty of 17% *ad valorem* on fabricated steel in place of the duty of 25% *ad valorem* imposed in 1924. The reason for the decrease was that the import price of fabricated steel had not changed in the same proportion as Indian costs. The Tariff Board in 1926 found that none of the firms which applied for protection was working up to its full capacity output; this, however, was due rather to the general increase in producing capacity of engineering firms than to increased European competition. The Tariff Board hoped for a steady increase in the business of engineering firms as the programme of railway construction developed.[46] However, the demand provided by increased railway construction proved to be short-lived and a crisis in the engineering industry of eastern India developed with the onset of depression. In 1934, the Tariff Board considered that substantive protection for the fabricated steel industry would be not merely unnecessary but positively harmful since it might attract fresh capital into the industry and further aggravate the problem of excess capacity. The Tariff Board estimated that the total fabricating capacity in the country was probably well over 150,000 tons a year while the average consumption in 1931–2 and 1932–3 was approximately 70,000 tons. It considered the real need of the industry to be the development of demand for fabricated steel, which could not be brought about by the grant of tariff protection. The Tariff Board, in an unusual foray into the field of general government economic policy went on:

The credit of the Government of India in the capital market is exceptionally high and money is both plentiful and cheap. A bold policy of public loans for capital expenditure would at this juncture afford enormous assistance in stimulating the market for capital goods like structural steel. We believe that the effect of such a policy would not be confined to the steel industry, but would be felt in every aspect of the country's economic life.[47]

The ITB found that the integration of steel production and structural steel work in some firms in the U.K., such as Dorman Long, gave them a special advantage over their Indian competitors. Hence a duty in the nature of an anti-dumping measure had to be imposed on British structural steel as well. It recommended a duty of Rs. 40 on imports of fabricated steel from all countries.[48]

[46] *Statutory enquiry 1926: steel*, Vol. 1 (Calcutta, 1926), p. 88.
[47] ITB: *Report on the iron and steel industry* (Delhi, 1934), pp. 97–8.
[48] *Ibid.*, Chapter ix.

General engineering firms in Bombay (such as Alcock, Ashdown and Co., Jost's Engineering, etc.) seem to have fared a little better than their counterparts near Calcutta, probably because they had been less dependent on government and railway orders in the first place and also because the cotton-mill industry was less affected by the depression than the jute industry, which suffered a severe fall in world demand from 1928 onwards. The tea and coal industries also suffered badly from the depression, thus adding to the troubles of the engineering firms in eastern India. The engineering firms in the sugar belt, such as Arthur Butler and Company of Muzaffarpur and Saran Engineering Company, began to flourish as soon as the sugar industry developed in Bihar and the United Provinces.

After the adoption of the proposals of the ITB with regard to the wagon-building industry, the wagon-building firms were able to exploit economies of scale and to spend large sums on extension and improvement, owing to a guaranteed market. The bounty was already reduced to Rs. 228 per wagon in 1926, as against the original recommendation of Rs. 580 per wagon in the third year made by the ITB.[49] The railways gradually adopted the policy of placing all orders for wagons and undertrains with Indian manufacturers. In 1934, it was estimated that the annual require-ments for rolling stock were 3,000 wagons, as against the total capacity of Indian Manufacturers, which was estimated to be not less than 8,500 wagons. In spite of that, the leading manufacturer of railway wagons in India, the Indian Standard Wagon Company, declared dividends from 5% to 20% *per annum* throughout the thirties, although its earlier perform-ance had been admittedly poorer.[50] (Its stablemates Burn and Co. Ltd, and Indian Iron and Steel Company Ltd, fared much worse.)

One branch of engineering which was inadvertently protected at first by the ITB was ship-building, or rather inland steamer-building. The ITB in 1924 explicitly exempted the building of steamers, tugs, flats, barges, etc., from the operation of the enhanced tariffs on steel (up till then fabricated steel had been subjected to a tariff of 10% *ad valorem* and machinery to a tariff of $2\frac{1}{2}\%$ *ad valorem*) on the ground that this branch of manufacture had nothing to fear from foreign competition. But a difficulty arose in enforcing the operation of the new tariff schedule since ships or steamers were rarely imported whole but came in sections. Under a ruling of the Central Board of Revenue, unless the hulls of vessels were imported entire or in built-up sections which could be launched separately and fastened together in the water, the fabricated steel from which the hull was made was liable to a protective duty of 25%. However, what normally passed through the Custom House was a collection of fabricated plates, angles,

---

[49] *Statutory enquiry 1926: steel*, Vol. IV (Calcutta, 1927), pp. 101–2.
[50] ITB: *Report on the iron and steel industry* (Delhi, 1934), p. 104. The dividend statistics are taken from various issues of the *IIYB*.

beams, and sheets, and vessels were not imported in any other way. The result of the ruling, therefore, was to subject every inland vessel imported into India to a protective duty which the Tariff Board did not recommend.[51]

Representations were made to the Government of India against the ruling of the Central Board of Revenue by the Irrawaddy Flotilla Company Limited, which controlled practically the whole inland water transport of Burma in modern vessels, and by the India General Navigation and Railway Company Limited, which was the biggest inland water transport company of eastern India. The engineering firms of India such as Burn and Company Limited, the Shalimar Works Limited and John King and Company Limited, building steamers, tugs, etc., opposed this representation mainly on the ground that the duty on steel and fabricated steel had been raised in 1924, thus raising the cost of construction of vessels in India.

The ITB in 1926 found that the ship-building industry in India had not required any protection before the war and that it did not require any substantive protection now, but that the engineering firms had to be compensated for a rise in the rate of exchange and for a rise in the duty on unfabricated steel. It proposed that the duty on the fabricated steel parts of ships and other inland vessels should be fixed at 10% but subject to the proviso that the duty should in no case be less than Rs. 35 a ton (the last provision was to guard against adverse exchange fluctuations). There would then be no danger of the Indian builder paying a higher duty on the material he purchased than the importer paid on the finished product.[52]

The ship-building industry did not in fact develop in India to any considerable extent before independence. It is doubtful whether a mere imposition of duty on imported vessels would have served the purpose. The basic condition for the existence of a sizeable ship-building industry, viz., a large Indian merchant marine, was not there. Most of the steam vessels on inland waterways in eastern India and Burma were under the control of companies under British management or companies registered in Britain. In 1921 about 90% of the coastal trade and 98% of the foreign trade of India were carried in foreign ships.[53] Indian lines faced stiff and unfair competition from liners' conferences and from old inland steamer companies which employed devices such as deferred rebates, drastic price-cutting and so on. Some coastal trade came to be handled through Indian companies based in Bombay, such as Bombay Steam Navigation Company Limited and Scindia Navigation Company Limited, but they had to join liners' conferences in order to survive; they also needed

[51] ITB: *Report regarding the grant of protection to the ship-building industry* (Calcutta, 1926), pp. 1–3.

[52] *Ibid.*, pp. 1–13.

[53] S. N. Haji: *State Aid to Indian Shipping* (Indian Shipping Series, Pamphlet No. 1, Bombay, 1922), p. 6.

very large financial resources (on 30 June 1936 the net block plus liquid assets of Scindia Navigation was Rs. 19,579,461 and that of Bombay Steam Navigation was Rs. 11,003,752). The little government help that there was went to British concerns, such as British India Steam Navigation Company and the Peninsular and Oriental Steam Navigation Company, in the form of subventions for carrying mail. The Indian Mercantile Marine Committee in 1923 recommended the encouragement of Indian ship-building and Indian shipping in the form of nationalization of a major British line, reservation of coastal shipping to Indian lines, mail contracts and such other measures as were commonly employed by the U.K. (in earlier days and in wartime), the U.S.A., Japan, Italy, and other independent advanced countries, but no action was taken on any of the major recommendations. A Bill introduced by S. N. Haji in the Central Legislative Assembly for encouragement of Indian shipping failed because of government opposition. Hence without any positive measures for fostering Indian shipping and ship-building nothing could be achieved in these directions until independence.[54]

In conclusion, it may be pointed out that there were important differences between different branches of engineering as regards their dependence on the levels of investment – public and private – in the economy. The depression of the thirties had an adverse effect on all branches of the capital goods industries in India – however small in absolute size and however young. But those products which could count on a domestic market of a minimal absolute size (because they entered directly or indirectly into consumption or inescapable expenditure for maintenance of productive assets – such as tinplate or crude steel) somehow managed to hold on to a larger share of a shrinking, but not altogether vanishing, domestic market. Those products, such as various types of fabricated steel, which depended directly on the level of public investment fared worst, because public investment was drastically cut, particularly by the central government, under the guidance of an extremely orthodox financial policy. Since tariff protection for some products, such as cotton textiles, paper and sugar, tended to keep private investment relatively buoyant, some engineering firms managed to eke out their normal business with construction for private industry, but private investment could not entirely fill the gaps that had been opened up by the fall in public investment. In so far as there occurred some movement of industry away from the ports and into the interior of India, and in so far as investment by provincial and local authorities fell less than investment by the central government, small, locally-based private engineering firms probably did

---

[54] *Ibid.*, pp. 7–18; *IIYB, 1936–7*; the memorandum of the Indian National Steamship Owners' Association, Bombay in *Evidence of the Fiscal Commission, 1949–50*, Vol. III (Delhi, 1952), pp. 185–276.

not do as badly as the larger concerns, and in some areas they may have actually prospered in spite of the depression. But this small and problematic gain in diffusion of crude engineering skill could not offset the major retardation that capital goods industries suffered during the period of the depression of the thirties because of the pursuit by the Government of India of a perverse, cyclical financial policy.

11

THE CEMENT INDUSTRY

The Portland cement industry developed rather late in India.[1] Although, as is shown in Table 11.1, the consumption of cement in India in 1914 was low (166,668 tons only), it would have been enough to support several plants of the right size at that time. It can be conjectured that it required a substantial change in the building methods in India and a substantial volume of demand for cement in western India before Indian or European capitalists would venture on the setting up of cement plants. What is certain is that the first three companies manufacturing cement on a large scale, viz., the Indian Cement Company Ltd, Katni Cement Company Ltd, and Bundi Portland Cement Company Ltd, were floated by managing agency houses in Bombay (Tata Sons, C. MacDonald and Co., and Killick, Nixon and Co., respectively) and had their works near Bombay (at Porbandar in Kathiawar, at Katni in the Central Provinces and at Bundi in Rajputana).[2] The pioneering cement company had been built in Madras in 1904 by South India Industrials Limited, but its basic raw material had been shells, and its capacity was only 10,000 tons per year; it had become practically defunct a few years after the end of the First World War.[3] The market in south India was small. Hence, although

[1] For early history, see H. A. P. Musgrave and H. F. Davy: 'The Portland Cement Industry' in Indian Munitions Board, *Industrial Handbook*, 1919, pp. 313–18. The vertical kiln process of manufacture of cement had been in existence since 1851 and 'the more modern rotary kiln processes had been in operation in other countries since 1885'.

[2] In 1914 all the directors of Katni Cement except one were Indian, although the name of the managing agency house was C. MacDonald and Company; similarly, a majority of the directors of Bundi Cement, floated by Killick, Nixon, were Indian. See *IITB*, 1914 and 1922, 'Miscellaneous Companies'. The works of Katni Cement Company were 673 miles from Bombay and 674 miles from Calcutta in 1925, but the factories of the other two companies were considerably nearer Bombay than Calcutta. ITB: *Report regarding the grant of protection to the cement industry* (Calcutta, 1925), p. 50.

[3] ITB: *Report on cement* (Calcutta, 1925), p. 4; and the evidence of Ian Scott Mackenzie in *Evidence (Report of IIC)*, Vol. III (PP 1919, XIX), p. 39. See also *Report of the Department of Industries, Madras, for the year ended 31 March, 1920* (Madras, 1921), p. 11. The question of a possible cement factory at Bezwada (now in Andhra Pradesh) had been under consideration for some time; the minimum size of an economic unit for cement production in 1920 was taken to be 25,000 to 30,000 tons per year whereas the average annual imports into Madras for the four years ending 1915–16 came only to about 22,000 tons. Even though the eventual consumption of cement might be higher, obviously there was not yet a large enough market for a cement factory, and so the Department hoped that the scheme for development of the Vizagapatam harbour would provide the extra demand. The Bezwada Cement Company, which was floated in 1922, and the Kistna Cement Co. Ltd, which was registered in 1920, both had to stop mainly because of financial difficulties.

TABLE 11.1 *Production, imports and consumption of cement in India, 1914 to 1938 (figures in tons)*

Year	Indian production	Total (private and government) imports into India	Total Indian consumption
1914	945	165,723	166,668
1915	17,912	142,469	160,381
1916	38,672	97,543	136,215
1917	73,728	85,594	159,322
1918	84,344	27,177	111,521
1919	86,812	92,787	175,599
1920	91,253	138,698	229,951
1921	132,812	129,813	262,625
1922	151,336	136,920	288,256
1923	234,936	124,822	359,758
1924	263,746	117,950	381,696
1925	360,549	134,292	494,841
1926	388,000	106,916	495,000
1927	478,000	121,299	599,000
1928	558,000	137,428	695,000
1929	561,000	129,878	691,000
1930	563,929		
1930–1	570,000	120,575	691,000
1931–2	583,000	91,744	675,000
1932–3	592,531	85,485	678,016
1933–4	642,944	65,915	708,859
1934–5	780,794	69,111	849,905
1935–6	890,683	58,796	949,479
1936–7	997,414	52,164	1,049,578
1937–8	1,169,894	31,916	1,201,810

Sources and notes: Before 1937–8, figures also include Burma, but there was no cement factory in Burma. Imports relate to fiscal years: for instance, imports in 1924 means imports during the period 1 April 1924 to 31 March 1925. Figures of production up to 1924 are derived from ITB: *Report on cement* (Calcutta, 1925). Figures of imports up to 1923–4 are derived from the same report, and later figures are derived from Gov. India, CISD: *Annual statements of seaborne trade* (Calcutta, annual). Sources for the figures of production after 1924: from 1926 to 1931–2, Sastry, *Statistical Study of India's Industrial Development*; for 1925 and 1930, *The History of the Cement Industry in India*, published by the Associated Cement Companies in 1937, quoted in Mukerjee and Dey: *Economic Problems of Modern India*, p. 39: all other figures are from Gov. India, CISD: *Statistical abstracts for British India* for the relevant years (Calcutta, annual).

raw materials were available, and the Department of Industries, Madras, was ready to help with information and advice, no cement company was started until the Coimbatore Cement Company Ltd came into existence at Madukarai, Coimbatore.[4]

[4] *Report of the Department of Industries, Madras for the year ended 31 March 1924* (Madras, 1925), p. 12. The Coimbatore Cement Company was apparently floated by a

In north and central India, however, in response to the growth in consumption of cement and the short post-war boom in investment and construction, cement factories sprang up fast. It was already known before the First World War that Portland cement could be manufactured profitably in many localities of northern India where raw materials were available, but the war held up investment.[5] After the war, with investment taking place at a rapid rate, excess capacity developed in the industry, which applied for tariff protection. At the time of the enquiry by the ITB, the total Indian demand was not quite 390,000 tons, whereas the capacity of the Indian cement factories was already 550,000 tons and was expected to be 600,000 tons as soon as the works of the Shahabad Company (managing agents, Tata Sons) were completed. Imports from abroad curtailed the Indian market: there was a strong preference for British cement (but not apparently for cement from other European countries) on the part of users in India.

The problem here was not simply one of deficiency of demand in relation to some optimum scale of plant; excess capacity developed mainly because private investors invested largely independently of one another. Each investor over-estimated the extent of the market available and the advantages to be enjoyed by the location of the plant in a new area. This over-estimation was natural since transport costs formed such a large fraction of the costs of cement. Tariff protection alone would hardly have solved the problem. If anything, the consequent rise in price in the presence of stagnant incomes would have curtailed the demand still further, particularly because cement was a relatively new building material and would be substituted by older types of building materials. On the other side, because of the increasing awareness on the part of builders of the possibilities of cement as a building material, one could in the 1920s expect a secular rise in the consumption of cement.[6] This secular rise in demand cannot be attributed either to an increase in the level of industrial

West Indian business group to serve the area which could not be profitably reached by the Shahabad factory. In 1936–7 the Andhra Cement Company was floated. The Department of Industries had apparently little to do with either of these enterprises, although it had earlier pointed out the potential for a cement industry in Madras. (In the few years up to 1928, the imports of cement into Madras had averaged about 25,000 tons.) See *Report of the Department of Industries, Madras*, for 1927–28 and 1936–37, pp. 14 and 27 respectively.

[5] See, for instance, the evidence of John White, of Christie White and Co., before the IIC in 1916, pointing out that there was 'a good future for up-to-date cement works at Dehri-on-Sone in Shahabad'. *Evidence (Report of IIC)*, Vol. vi, *Confidential Evidence* (Calcutta, 1918), pp. 21–2.

[6] See ITB: *Report on cement* (Calcutta, 1925), pp. 6–10. Tariff protection was not granted to the Indian cement industry because the Tariff Board considered excessive internal competition rather than foreign competition to be the real problem of the industry (in 1924) and because the industry enjoyed natural protection owing to the high cost of transport of cement.

investment or to a rise in agricultural income, but it may have been due partly to the fall in the price of Portland cement relative to the prices of other cementing materials.

If we compare the figures of consumption of cement in India (Table 11.1) with imports of industrial machinery, we find that while cement consumption *rose* from about 230,000 tons in 1920 to about 691,000 tons in 1929, the value of industrial machinery imported fell from Rs. 107 million in 1920–1 to Rs. 77 million in 1928–9. The decline in imports of industrial machinery between the triennial period 1920–1 to 1922–3 and the triennial period 1926–7 and 1928–9 contrasts even more sharply with the rise in cement consumption between these periods.

Again, between 1931–2 and 1936–7, the total consumption of cement increased from about 678,000 tons to more than a million tons, while the price of cement remained constant up to May 1936.[7] During the same period the value of imports of industrial machinery increased from Rs. 49 million to Rs. 64 million. Altogether, it appears that during the interwar years the rate of rise in the consumption of cement was much faster than that of the imports of industrial machinery, either in money or real terms, and that the rise was taking place even when the price of cement was not declining.

Taking all these considerations together, it seems justifiable to treat the increase in the consumption of cement as largely independent of the development of other industries. Changes in the 'technology' of building seem to have been more responsible for generating the increase in demand for cement than industrial development as such.[8] The growth in consumption of cement between 1922 and 1925 was connected also with a decline in the price of Indian cement. The price fell from upwards of Rs. 70 per ton in 1922 to Rs. 25 per ton in some cases in January 1925.[9] This fall was mainly due to internal competition and the existence of excess capacity, and the prices ruling in 1925 were 'wholly unremunerative', according to the Indian Tariff Board,[10] and did not even cover works costs. The ITB estimated the fair selling price of Indian cement as being between Rs. 46 and Rs. 60 per ton for various companies.[11]

The Indian cement industry had in fact worked with excess capacity almost from the beginning of the 1920s. In 1924 the total production of the cement companies was 264,000 tons, whereas the capacity was 561,000 tons. Thus even on the basis of the capacity observed in 1924, it was not until 1929 that Indian companies reached full capacity output.

---

[7] See Gov. India, CISD: *Review of the trade of India, 1937–8* (Calcutta, 1938), p. 54.
[8] See in this context the discussion of how far lime could be substituted by cement in the *Report on cement* (Calcutta, 1925), pp. 9–10.
[9] *Ibid.*, p. 11.
[10] *Ibid.*, p. 11.   [11] *Ibid.*, pp. 27–8.

According to one estimate,[12] the manufacturing capacity of the industry had by 1936–7 grown to 1·465 million tons, whereas actual production was less than a million tons. The Dalmia group of companies began to operate in 1938 and the total capacity rose to 2·5 million tons in 1940, whereas production in that year was only 1·5 million tons.[13]

As a result of internal competition, the price of cement continued to fall after 1925 and three companies went into liquidation. A series of quasi-monopolistic organizations came into existence: the Indian Cement Manufacturers' Association in 1926, the Concrete Association of India and the Cement Marketing Company of India Limited in 1930. This last organization was responsible for the sale of almost all the companies and it succeeded in stabilizing the price of cement, but it had no control over total production.[14]

In 1936, Associated Cement Companies (ACC) was formed by the merger of ten out of twelve existing companies. During the six years the Cement Marketing Company of India was in existence, it provided each factory with a minimum offtake in accordance with a prearranged quota and it was also able to spend a considerable amount of money in propagating the use of Portland cement, rather than the use of any particular brand. But the fixed quotas made for an inefficient use of existing capacity, and led to unnecessary increases in transport costs. Hence the scheme to merge the cement companies was undertaken, primarily under the leadership of F. E. Dinshaw.[15] The board of directors of the newly-constituted Associated Cement Companies Limited represented practically all the major business groups of western India (Sir Purshotamdas Thakurdas, Sir Chunilal Mehta, Ambalal Sarabhai and several Parsi businessmen were on the board);[16] but this company soon faced a challenge to its monopolistic position from a business group in eastern India – the Dalmia Jain group. Although some cement companies had done badly up to 1936, some had done very well even in the years of the depression. In 1934 and 1935 the dividends of cement companies such as Bundi, Indian, Katni, Shahabad and Okha had ranged between 10% and 20%.[17] Since the initial capital cost of a new unit in the cement factory was not prohibitive, it was natural that the monopolistic position of the Associated Cement Companies should be soon challenged.

With the coming into production of factories of the Dalmia group in May 1938, the price of cement dropped sharply from Rs. 43 per ton

[12] M. C. Munshi (assisted by K. P. Karnik): *Industrial Profits in India (1936–44)* (New Delhi, 1948), p. 207.
[13] See George Rosen: *Industrial Change in India* (Glencoe, Illinois, 1958), p. 21.
[14] See B. S. Rao: *Surveys of Indian Industries*, Vol. 2 (Madras, 1958), pp. 189–90.
[15] *Indian Finance Year-Book, 1936* (Calcutta, 1936), pp. 282–3.
[16] *IIYB, 1938–39*, p. 363.
[17] *Indian Finance Year-Book, 1936*, p. 283.

(in Calcutta) to Rs. 30 per ton in October 1938; it recovered to Rs. 33 eventually, but the fall in prices and sales was reflected in the net profits of ACC, which fell from Rs. 7,630,000 in the year ended 31 July 1938 to Rs. 3,178,000 in the next year and to Rs. 3,606,000 in the year ended 31 July 1940. Eventually an agreement was reached between ACC and the Dalmia Cement Company to set up a joint selling organization; prices were to be fixed by the joint organization and total sales were to be divided between the two concerns on an agreed basis.[18]

Thus we observe the same development of quasi-monopolistic organizations and agreements in response to an actual or potential threat of production in excess of existing demand as we observe in the cases of the sugar and steel industries.[19]

The history of the development of the Indian cement industry raises some questions for the policy-maker in a partially planned economy. Should the government have attempted to control the expansion of the industry in view of the obvious appearance of excess capacity and wastage of scarce capital? It is difficult to say 'Yes', because during the Second World War the cement industry was worked fully to capacity, the government absorbing as much as 90% of total production in some years.[20] The answer to the problem of excess capacity was expansion of demand rather than curtailment of investment, especially in a situation in which investment in this industry remained profitable in relation to investment in other industries and shortages of capital or foreign exchange did not depress the social profitability of such investment below its private profitability.

[18] The above account is based on Gov. India, CISD: *Review of the trade of India* and *Statistical abstract for British India* (Calcutta, annual); and Munshi: *Industrial Profits in India,* Chapter VIII.

[19] There was an agreement between TISCO and SCOB for joint distribution of output as soon as the latter began to market its products.

[20] See Rosen, *Industrial Change,* p. 22.

12

THE GROWTH OF THE SUGAR INDUSTRY

12.1 THE SUPPLY OF SUGAR-CANE
AND THE DEMAND FOR SUGAR
BEFORE THE FIRST WORLD WAR

India used to export large quantities of sugar, primarily unrefined, up to the middle of the nineteenth century, but even in those days she used to import some sugar from China and Egypt. The export trade to Britain had then been considerably hampered by a higher import duty on (East) Indian sugar (amounting to about 30s. per cwt.) than on West Indian sugar; with the abolition of slavery in the West Indies and with the equalization of import duties on Indian and West Indian sugar there was a revival in the export trade, the high point being reached in 1840–5. Then the British Government introduced free trade in sugar, and India could no longer compete with countries outside the British Empire; the growth of the beet-sugar industry fostered by government patronage was a factor contributing to India's decline.[1]

TABLE 12.1 *Index numbers of imports of sugar into India* (Base: average for the years from 1884–5 to 1888–9 = 100)

Annual average for the period or year	Quantity			Value		
	Refined	Unrefined	Total	Refined	Unrefined	Total
1884–5 to 1888–9	100	100	100	100	100	100
1885–6 to 1890–1	121	183	123	120	188	121
1890–1 to 1895–6	141	220	145	146	165	146
1895–6 to 1900–1	242	496	253	219	361	219
1900–1 to 1905–6	396	827	415	327	931	335
1906–7	608	2,670	697	422	3,309	456
1907–8	626	2,398	702	450	3,105	481
1908–9	654	3,086	758	523	4,411	569
1909–10	718	2,425	792	579	2,447	601

Source: F. Noel-Paton: *Notes on Sugar in India* (Calcutta, 1911).

[1] Noel Deerr: *The History of Sugar*, Vol. 1 (London, 1949), Chapter v; Sir James MacKenna: 'The Indian Sugar Industry', *JRSA*, LXXVII, No. 3970, 21 December 1928, pp. 142–4; Hilton Brown: *Parry's of Madras*, pp. 82–3; and B. C. Burt: 'The Indian Sugar Industry', *JRSA*, LXXXIII, No. 4318, 16 August 1935, p. 921. According to the report of the Select Committee of the House of Commons on Sugar and Coffee Planting, published in 1848, referred to by Burt, India supplied about one-quarter of England's total sugar requirements during the years from 1839 to 1847, the average annual exports to England being 59,373 tons.

However, it appears that for most of the nineteenth century the imports of refined sugar into India remained insignificant. India produced and consumed her own varieties of unrefined sugar. From the end of the nineteenth century sugar imports began to increase at a rapid rate. The figures in Table 12.1 illustrate the growth in imports of sugar into India (including Burma) after 1884–5.

The reasons for this growth are quite simple: there was a high rate of technological progress in the major beet-sugar and cane-sugar industries of the world. This progress related as much to the methods of cultivating, as to those of extracting sucrose from, beet and sugar-cane. Furthermore, many of the major exporting countries, particularly those producing beet sugar, had bounties or export subsidies supporting their own sugar industries. In most of these countries, the government had taken a hand in propagating and actively assisting better methods of producing beet or sugar-cane or in improving the varieties available; in places such as Java and Formosa the government had also helped the mill-owners by compelling or inducing cultivators to produce cane in concentrated blocks so as to make central factories economically viable.

In contrast, in India there had been practically no progress in the methods of cultivating, or of extracting sucrose from, sugar-cane. Apart from Madras, where some work had been done by the Department of Agriculture in propagating new varieties of sugar-cane, the governments at the centre and in the provinces had taken no part in assisting the growth of the sugar-cane industry in any positive fashion.

The first step taken by the Government of India in checking the imports of sugar into India was to impose, in March 1899, a duty on imported sugar countervailing the bounties enjoyed by the sugar industry in the exporting countries. This step was taken in response to representations by sugar refiners in India, Mauritius and the West Indies.[2] The effect of this legislation was to decrease the imports of beet sugar from Europe but to increase the imports of cane sugar from Mauritius, Java, and China. The countervailing duties were further raised in May 1902 to counteract the increase in bounties created by the sugar cartels; but the Brussels Convention of 1903 led to the virtual abolition of bounties on sugar in the countries which ratified the convention, and in December 1903 the countervailing duties were abolished except on imports of sugar from some countries, such as Denmark, Chile, Argentina and Russia, which had not observed the provisions of the Brussels Convention. In spite of the countervailing duties and even more after the abolition of the latter, imports

[2] Gov. India, CISD: *Review of the trade of India, 1901–02* (Calcutta, 1902), p. 5. The immediate stimulus to the increased supply of beet sugar from foreign countries was apparently provided by the closing of the U.S. market to bounty-fed sugar in 1897. See MacKenna, 'The Indian Sugar Industry', p. 144.

of sugar, mainly from Java, Mauritius and other sugar-cane-producing lands, increased at a rapid rate, as Table 12.1 shows.

The impact on the indigenous sugar industry was adverse but not dramatic. The indigenous industry used inefficient methods at each stage. By the beginning of the twentieth century over most of India, the older crushers made of wood or stone had been replaced by iron-roller mills, but the latter were generally inefficient. Although in some cases three-roller mills were used, more often farmers used single- or two-roller mills which often extracted only about 60% of the juice of the sugar-cane. Furthermore, in converting the juice into *gur* or unrefined sugar, a large part was lost through evaporation, through inversion of sucrose into glucose and through sheer wastage owing to lack of co-ordination of the processes. The refineries which converted *gur* or *rab* (thickened juice) into white sugar further contributed to the wastage through inefficient processing.[3]

The increasing imports of sugar from countries using more efficient methods however did not kill the indigenous industry (production of unrefined sugar fell, as is indicated by some shrinkage in the area under sugar-cane in most provinces of India). This tenacity is accounted for by several factors: first, to some extent at least, refined sugar and gur had different markets. Gur was often preferred because it was mixed with glucose matter and was supposed to be more nutritious than sugar. It was used for making sweets and was preferred to white sugar because it had a better adhesive quality.

There were, however, two other factors which explain the survival of the indigenous industry. First, sugar-cane was grown by peasants on small and scattered plots of land. Although the methods they used might be inefficient compared with modern methods, the peasant's total earnings might still be greater than the profit he would make by selling the cane to a sugar mill or a refinery or *khandsari* (the refinery using older methods). Furthermore, the peasant would continue to grow sugar-cane on the land using his family labour so long as producing sugar-cane remained the best use for his labour and land, although if he paid his labour the wages ruling in the market he might show a loss.[4]

[3] MacKenna ('The Indian Sugar Industry', p. 147) estimated that while the value of *gur* produced in India was about Rs. 350 million, the value of refined sugar on the basis of the same output of sugar-cane but with efficient methods would come to Rs. 698 million; thus the wastage at that date amounted to fully 100%. Before the First World War the wastage would probably have been even greater because of the use of even more primitive methods.

[4] It is interesting that Disraeli in 1846 had recognized the small-peasant character of sugar production in India and the advantage in terms of increased income enjoyed by the peasant because of his control over production, in spite of the use of inefficient methods. See *Hansard*, 1846, lxxxiii, p. 151, quoted by Deerr, *The History of Sugar*, Vol. I, p. 57. Disraeli was a champion of preferential duties for sugar imported into the U.K. from India.

The second factor explaining the persistence of *khandsari* production was the hold that the *khandsari* had over the cultivator either directly as landlord, money-lender, or trader (the *khandsari* often combined all the three functions) or indirectly through the landlord who acted as middleman between the *khandsari* and the cultivator.[5] Thus, both positive incentives on the part of the peasants and compulsion on the part of landlords and traders helped to keep the indigenous industry going, particularly in the United Provinces, Punjab and Bihar. There was, however, a decline in the total area under sugar-cane in British India with the increase in competition from imported sugar.[6]

Attempts were made by officials in various parts of the country to improve the indigenous methods of manufacture. The most famous of the improved methods was called the Hadi process, after Syed Muhommad Hadi, an official of the Department of Agriculture in the United Provinces. This process consisted of an improved method of crushing the cane, using a steam-engine, a more elaborate process of boiling, and refining the sugar by means of a small centrifugal machine. Although the quantity of sugar extracted from cane was higher than in the indigenous process, it required more capital expenditure, and it could not compete in efficiency with centralized sugar-cane mills, which extracted up to 90% of the sucrose content of the cane and which prevented 'inversion' of sucrose into glucose.[7] In the event, the Hadi process was not adopted widely, although it was claimed to be a financial success.[8]

12.2 THE GROWTH OF THE WHITE-SUGAR INDUSTRY UP TO THE FIRST WORLD WAR

After the middle of the nineteenth century, white sugar continued to be produced in Madras at the Nellikuppam factory and in the United Provinces

[5] See, for example, District Gazetteers of the United Provinces of Agra and Oudh: Vol. XIII, *Bareilly* (Allahabad, 1911), p. 40; District Gazetteers of Agra and Oudh: Vol. XVIII, *Shahjahanpur* (Allahabad, 1910), pp. 54–5.

[6] See W. H. Moreland's note on MacKenna's paper, 'The Indian Sugar Industry', *JRSA*, LXXVII, No. 3970, 21 December 1928, p. 157.

[7] For a description of the Hadi process, see Ghosh: *The Advancement of Industry*, pp. 101–5. According to Hadi's statement, quoted by Ghosh, the cost of the complete plant would not be more than Rs. 5,000; but it was considered that landlords or small capitalists adopting the process would have to persuade tenants, by loans if need be, to bring their cane or juice to them, unless they themselves happened to have large areas of land under sugar-cane. For the methods used generally in the United Provinces, see Chatterjee [IPG pub.]: *Notes*, pp. 91–5. Among the sources of waste in indigenous methods, Chatterjee noted the fact that the iron mills used were often worn out, soon got out of order and could not be quickly repaired. On the methods used in the Punjab, see Latifi [IPG pub.]: *The Industrial Punjab: A Survey of Facts, Conditions and Possibilities* (Bombay and Calcutta, 1911), Chapter XIII. Latifi was not as enthusiastic about the Hadi process as Ghosh or Chatterjee, mainly because it brought about a small improvement at a relatively large cost.

[8] See Moreland's note on MacKenna's paper, 'The Indian Sugar Industry'.

at the Rosa factory, with the help of relatively advanced methods: it appears that the cane was crushed or *gur* was refined, depending on the availability of cane, the relative price of cane and *gur*, and the state of demand for the refined product. The refining of sugar was generally carried on with the distillation of spirits.[9] In south India, after Binny and Company had been compelled to transfer their sugar interests to Parry and Company, the latter came to hold a practically monopolistic position in respect of the production of white sugar and spirits. In the case of white sugar this monopoly was largely illusory because of foreign competition; in the case of the supply of spirits there was some element of monopoly, since Parry and Company became the sole suppliers of many local governments.

The major developments in the sugar industry, however, took place in the United Provinces and Bihar. Some factories which had been set up by Europeans for manufacturing sugar were converted into indigo factories when indigo had become the more profitable crop; these again went back to the cultivation of cane and sugar-refining when natural indigo became an unprofitable crop as a result of the growth of the synthetic dye industry at the end of the nineteenth century.[10]

Although some indigo planters went on to become owners or managers of sugar refineries, most of them in fact remained planters or virtually became landlords, with land rented out to sub-tenants; many of them took to the cultivation of sugar-cane to supply the sugar factories.[11] In Bihar and the United Provinces a major pioneer of central sugar factories after 1900 was Begg, Sutherland and Company of Cawnpore. They had started as indigo-seed and general produce merchants, and had then entered industry in a big way. They set up the Cawnpore Sugar Works in 1894 which refined *gur* by a process which did not use bone charcoal, so that the sugar would be acceptable to orthodox Hindus. Many other sugar refineries were later set up, mostly by Indians, with the same purpose. Begg, Sutherland and Company set up a sugar factory in Barrah in the district of Saran in Bihar

[9] Hilton Brown: *Parry's of Madras*, pp. 83–6, 138–46, 159–71. Playne and Wright: *Southern India*, pp. 166–8. Binny and Company used to refine only *jaggery*, mainly made from palmyra juice.

[10] Bengal District Gazetteers: *Champaran* (Calcutta, 1907), pp. 72 and 102. During the brief boom of the Indian sugar industry in the middle of the nineteenth century some indigo planters had gone back to sugar, but they reverted to indigo when the boom collapsed. See D. J. Reid: 'Indigo in Behar' in Playne and Wright: *Bengal and Assam, Behar and Orissa*, p. 255.

[11] The Bengal Tenancy Act of 1885 allowed Europeans to become occupancy tenants, and they used this right to take out land on a long, or sometimes a virtually irrevocable, lease. As one development we find some Europeans becoming *zemindars* in the Indian style, with land leased from other *zemindars*. This happened for instance in the case of the Naraipur estate: see Playne and Wright: *Bengal and Assam, Behar and Orissa*, p. 329. Many indigo-planters became heavily indebted at the time of the crisis of 1897, which was brought about by the marketing of German synthetic dyes. This also partly explains why planters found it difficult to become major entrepreneurs in the sugar industry. See in this connection, Reid: 'Indigo in Bihar'.

in 1905 (Champarun Sugar Company Limited) and a branch of the Cawnpore Sugar Works was opened at Marhourah in the district of Saran in Bihar in 1905. In 1913 it floated the Ryam Sugar Company Limited with a factory at Ryam in the district of Durbhanga in Bihar. All these three factories crushed cane grown on the land owned by themselves or by planters or ordinary tenants, and refined it into sugar.[12] Before the enterprises of Begg, Sutherland and Company, there had been in existence in the district of Shahjahanpur a European-owned factory called the Rosa factory, which had been at first devoted only to the refining of sugar and distillation of spirits. After 1902, the factory acquired cane-crushing facilities which could deal with between ten and twelve thousand maunds of cane daily. The location of the Rosa factory was dictated by the fact that Shahjahanpur had been a major cane-growing district for a long time.[13] There were other large sugar works which were private concerns (rather than joint-stock companies): around 1916 the Durbhanga Sugar Company was supposed to have the largest mill. The mill had been situated at Ottar near Muzaffarpur but it was not financially a success and so it was moved to the Durbhanga district which had a larger cane-growing area.[14]

Although the United Provinces had a much larger cane-growing area than Bihar, most of the sugar factories started before the First World War were located in Bihar.[15] The explanation is probably (a) that Meerut and Bareilly already had a large *khandsari* industry, and sugar factories would find it difficult to compete for sugar-cane with the *khandsaris* because of the hold of the latter on the tenant, (b) that Bihar had a system of Permanent Settlement with *zemindars* controlling very large blocks of land which could be leased out to sugar mills or to cultivators supplying sugar mills, (c) that with the decline of the indigo industry, which was more important in Bihar than in the United Provinces, many planters turned to the cultivation of sugar-cane, often becoming managers of sugar-cane for the mills,[16] and (d) that the price of *gur* was generally lower in Bihar than in the United Provinces, so that sugar mills found it cheaper to buy either *gur* for refining or cane for crushing and converting into sugar.[17]

[12] The information is derived from District Gazetteers of the United Provinces of Agra and Oudh: Vol. xix, *Cawnpore* (Allahabad, 1909), pp. 81–3; *IITB, 1911*, pp. 301–302; 304; ITB: *Evidence (Report on sugar)* (Calcutta, 1932), Vol. i, pp. 93–105.

[13] District Gazetteers of the United Provinces of Agra and Oudh: Vol. xvii, *Shahjahanpur* (Allahabad, 1910), pp. 56–7.

[14] See the evidence of J. Henry, Manager, Durbhanga Sugar Company Limited, in *Evidence (Report of IIC)*, Vol. i (PP 1919, xvii), p. 385.

[15] According to the figures given by Noel-Paton, there were nine sugar factories in the districts of Bihar as against four in those of the United Provinces. Noel-Paton [Gov. India pub.]: *Notes on Sugar in India*, pp. 52–9.

[16] See the evidence of J. Henry, G. R. Macdonald and H. C. Finzel in *Evidence (Report of IIC)*, Vol. i (PP 1919, xvii), pp. 382–96.

[17] See ITB: *Report on sugar* (Delhi, 1938), pp. 51–3, for evidence that prices of *gur* were normally lower in Bihar (Bhagalpur) than in the United Provinces (Meerut).

The total investment in sugar factories and refineries before the First World War was, however, small, and the capacity of typical individual factories or refineries was also small.[18] The governmental effort at encouraging the industry was limited to the countervailing duties which were imposed in 1899, and lifted in 1903, and the establishment of the small experimental factory at Nawabgunge after agitation in the Indian Legislative Council in 1911. Dr Barber had begun his efforts as sugar-cane expert but not much had come out of them as yet. As a result of the establishment of central sugar factories in some areas cane production tended to be concentrated round the factories and there even occurred some increase in cane cultivation in individual cases.[19] The planters who took to cane cultivation generally used more manure and practised a more elaborate rotation of crops than ordinary cultivators. There were also attempts by men like MacGlashan to cultivate sugar-cane on an extensive scale, with some government concessions. But in the absence of a definite improvement in the sugar-cane crop, the planters' rate of return on the older varieties tended to diminish; and without tariff protection for sugar-cane the factory industry could not grow quickly, even had adequate supplies of cane been available within a reasonable distance from the factory.

12.3   THE SUGAR INDUSTRY FROM THE FIRST WORLD WAR
UP TO 1930

The white-sugar industry in India was effectively protected during the First World War by the fall in imports of sugar from foreign countries. As a result, both the output of white sugar and the area under sugar-cane went up, although the increases were only moderate. The supplies of machinery from abroad were restricted and this acted as a limiting factor in the sugar industry as in other cases.[20] The war, however, also stimulated the interest of the Government of India in the industry. Sir James MacKenna, Agricultural Adviser to the Government of India, submitted a scheme for a Sugar Bureau, which would include 'a factory expert, an engineer, a chemist, and agriculturalist and botanist, with an officer as Secretary of the Bureau'.[21] Eventually only the Secretary to the Bureau was appointed, and he did some valuable work in assembling a mass of information on the trade side, and in spreading information about the Coimbatore canes in Bihar.[22]

In 1919, the Committee of the Indian Sugar Producers' Association at

[18] See the evidence of J. MacGlashan in *Evidence (Report of IIC)*, Vol. II (PP 1919, XVIII), pp. 684–704.

[19] See the evidence of MacGlashan in *ibid.*, p. 691.

[20] See S. G. Panandikar: *Some Aspects of the Economic Consequences of the War for India* (Bombay, 1921), Chapter III, for the effect of the war on Indian industrial development.   [21] MacKenna: 'The Indian Sugar Industry', p. 148.

[22] See the evidence of Dr C. A. Barber in RC on Agriculture in India, Vol. x, *Evidence taken in England* (Calcutta, 1927), p. 752.

Cawnpore prodded the Government of India into appointing a Sugar Committee which was to advise on all the aspects of the development of the sugar industry in India. The Committee found that the smallness and inefficiency of Indian factories were mainly attributable to their difficulty in obtaining adequate supplies of cane. At the time of enquiry by the Committee there were 22 factories in India working mainly with sugar-cane; of these 10 were located in Bihar, 5 in the United Provinces and 3 in Madras. The production from the 18 factories which actually worked during 1919–20 was only 23,100 tons of sugar, and approximately equal to the output of three average factories in Java. None of the Indian factories worked up to full capacity, and half of them crushed only half the cane their mills could deal with.[23] But the Committee also found that many of the factories used inefficient methods of handling cane, used too much fuel, and had very old plants. It considered that the first essential for improving efficiency was better chemical control and supervision, and the second was greater economy of labour. It found *gur* refineries unpromising for development or improvement.

The Committee had to tackle the vexed questions of acquisition of land for central sugar factories or reservation of specified areas for individual factories on the models of Java and Formosa.[24] It agreed that compulsory acquisition of land for sugar factories was bad policy both because of the principle involved and because of the practical difficulties. However, it was prepared to endorse the acquisition of blocks of land for purposes of demonstration of improved methods of sugar-cane cultivation. There were two dissenters from the majority: Wynne Sayer, the Secretary to the Sugar Bureau, wanted to have reservation of areas for individual mills, and B. J. Padshah, of Tata Sons and Company Limited, wanted a much more forceful policy for the development of sugar-cane production for sugar factories. Among other things, he wanted the government to exercise its power of compulsory acquisition of land. He also wanted better administration of existing canals with more incentive for the cultivator to use his water wisely, and a much bigger investment in irrigation and drainage to increase the area in which sugar-cane could be economically grown.[25] Both Padshah

[23] *Report of the Indian Sugar Committee 1920* (Simla, 1921), Chapter XIX.

[24] The models of Formosa and Java were constantly cited as worthy of emulation by India: see, for example, *Report of the Indian Sugar Committee 1920* (Simla, 1921), Chapter II, and Noel-Paton [Gov. India pub.]: *Notes on Sugar in India*. It is not clear, however, that these models, which implied a drastic curtailment of the freedom of the cultivator over the disposition of his land, would leave the latter better off. Initially at least, he might easily be worse off. See G. F. Keatinge: *Agricultural Progress in Western India* (London, 1921), pp. 35–6.

[25] *Report of the Indian Sugar Committee 1920* (Simla, 1921), pp. 408–62. Padshah's note is one of the ablest statements of the Indian capitalists' attitude to economic policy during this period. Of course, the Government of India could not pursue the policy recommended, because it would have led to conflict with the vast majority of the population.

and Sayer also wanted sugar factories to be licensed by the government so that they were properly located and were built on a sufficiently large scale.

The recommendations of the Indian Sugar Committee were rather mild: it wanted the government to set up a Sugar Board with five official and six non-official members; a Sugar Research Institute with three divisions, agricultural, chemical and engineering; a pioneer model sugar factory in northern India, and Sugar Schools to train sugar technologists. It also wanted the government to fix a scale of prices for sugar-cane producers so that the latter were protected against exploitation by sugar factories.

None of the recommendations of the Indian Sugar Committee was implemented during the next ten years. The development of the industry was very slow up to 1931, as is amply indicated by the figures in Table 12.2. The revenue duty on the sugar industry had been increased from 5% *ad*

TABLE 12.2 *Imports of sugar machinery into India, 1920–1 to 1939–40*

Year	Imports of sugar machinery (Rs. '000) (1)	Price index of sugar machinery (measured in tons) (2)	Imports of sugar machinery in Rs. at constant prices (Rs. '000) (3)
1920–1	1,755	100.00	1,755
1921–2	8,846	106.65	8,294
1922–3	1,689	77.40	2,182
1923–4	1,278	57.73	2,214
1924–5	1,662	57.70	2,880
1925–6	1,597	51.84	3,081
1926–7	621	45.68	1,359
1927–8	913	64.05	1,425
1928–9	1,752	47.62	3,679
1929–30	921	50.19	1,835
1930–1	1,368	61.06	2,240
1931–2	3,014	62.92	4,790
1932–3	15,311	41.89	26,550
1933–4	33,639	38.63	87,080
1934–5	10,545	44.21	23,852
1935–6	6,572	41.27	15,924
1936–7	9,516	44.18	21,539
1937–8	6,986	47.76	14,627
1938–9	6,137	64.17	9,564
1939–40	5,084	59.74	8,510

Sources: For column (1), Gov. India, CISD: *Annual statement of the seaborne trade of British India* (Calcutta, annual); for column (2), *Annual statements of the trade of the United Kingdom.*

Notes: (a) The price index series is related to calendar years; the price index for calendar year 1920 is applied to the import series of 1920–1, and similarly for other years. (b) Figures in column (3) are derived by dividing column (1) by figures in column (2) and multiplying by 100.

valorem to 10% in 1916; it was further increased to 15% in 1921, 25% in 1922 and Rs. 4 - 8 - 0 in 1925, which implied a duty of more than 50% *ad valorem*.[26] These changes were mainly motivated by the Government of India's needs for higher revenue. There was no guarantee of government protection in the future. Moreover, over these years the prices of imported sugar were falling.

Improved varieties of sugar-cane also spread rather slowly during the twenties. The existing supply of water from rainfall and irrigation could not support some of the high-yielding but less hardy varieties of cane with the methods of cultivation practised on ordinary peasants' holdings; the planters of Bihar were generally able to spend more on sugar-cane cultivation and practise a proper system of rotation. But the Indian Sugar Committee of 1920 reported

There are, in fact, already signs that the planter's system of cane cultivation is in danger of outrunning the cane he cultivates. In the comparative absence of work, either by the planters themselves or by the local Agricultural Department, on the introduction and acclimatisation of medium and thick exotic varieties, the planters' more intensive methods have been applied to the best of the indigenous canes, with the result that, when very high yields of cane have been obtained, . . . the sucrose content of the cane has been proved in the factory to fall far short of what the same cane yields under less intensive cultivation.[27]

The Royal Commission on Agriculture in India reported that, in 1925–6 and 1926–7, the areas under improved varieties of sugar-cane were 6·5% and 7·2% of the total cultivated areas under sugar-cane in the respective years.[28] The speed of diffusion of improved varieties accelerated considerably during the thirties. It may be that the development of the Sarda Canal in the United Provinces was a contributory factor; it is also probable that the newer varieties produced by the cane-breeding stations of the government led by the one at Coimbatore were much more obviously superior to the older 'improved' or indigenous varieties, and the cultivator could adopt them without any basic change in his methods of cultivation.[29]

[26] Dey: *The Indian Tariff Problem*, Chapter VIII.

[27] *Report of the Indian Sugar Committee 1920* (Simla, 1921), pp. 71–2.

[28] RC on Agriculture in India: *Report* (Calcutta, 1928), p. 95.

[29] Compare Dr C. A. Barber's opinion in RC on Agriculture in India: Vol. x, *Evidence taken in England* (Calcutta, 1927), p. 754: '. . . the new kind of cane must be quite *obviously* better than that being grown, and its growth should, if possible, at first entail little alteration in the cultivator's time-honoured methods.' (According to Burt, although S.48, an improved variety produced at Shahjahanpur, proved suitable for the United Provinces, it was not until 1927, when Co.290, produced at Coimbatore, proved its value, that a cane better than S.48 was forthcoming.) See Burt, 'The Indian Sugar Industry', p. 926. (The Director of Agriculture, United Provinces, in his evidence before the ITB in 1937, produced figures showing that, while in the districts which had obtained the benefits of tubewells (Muradabad), the Sarda Canal (Hardoi) or cane factories (Gorakhpur), the areas under cane had expanded by between 75% and 130%

There is little doubt, however, that the push given to the development of the sugar industry by statutory tariff protection in 1931 was quite critical in speeding up the spread of improved varieties of cane and substantially raising the yield per acre of sugar-cane in practically all the cane-growing provinces. The power of tariff protection to increase the output of white sugar and raise the area under sugar-cane was wildly underestimated in official circles. Thus Sir James MacKenna asked

Those who held the view that the limit of tariff had not been reached, what tariff rate would they propose to suggest [*sic*] which would keep out Java's efficiency? The success of Java had been entirely built up on its efficiency. Notwithstanding that India's tariff barrier had been raised again and again against Java's sugar, steadily and annually Java's imports of sugar increased.[30]

It is possible to argue that even with the prevailing inefficiency in the cultivation of sugar-cane, India should have been able to compete with other major sugar-producing countries, if only the factories were sufficiently large and efficient: India had probably the lowest labour costs among the major sugar-cane-growing countries, including Java.[31] But there were at least three factors militating against the growth of a white-sugar industry without tariff protection: (a) sugar prices were falling in the world market,[32] and this would inhibit investment on a large scale, particularly when equally high rates of return could be obtained with greater certainty from other industries or trades; (b) unlike other countries, where sugar production was backed up by well-organized research sponsored or financed by the government, India had no sugar research bureau properly speaking; (c) the competition among sugar factories was already pushing up the price of the raw material in most localities; without either an extension of the area under sugar-cane or a large increase in the yield of sugar-cane per acre, large factories would find it difficult to obtain their supplies of cane.

12.4 TARIFF PROTECTION AND THE GROWTH OF THE SUGAR INDUSTRY

The situation radically changed with the coming of the depression. The Government of India at first increased the rate of duty on imported sugar

over the period from 1929–30 to 1935–6, in Benares a typical district which had obtained neither irrigation facilities nor the stimulus of cane factories, the area under sugar-cane had increased only by a small percentage.) See ITB: *Evidence (Report on sugar)* (Delhi, 1938–9), Vol. III A, *Replies received from the Local Governments and Indian States*, p. 180.

[30] MacKenna's reply to the discussion on his paper, 'The Indian Sugar Industry', *JRSA*, LXXVII, No. 3970, (21 December 1928), p. 156.

[31] Cf. Barber's comment on MacKenna, *ibid.*, p. 153.

[32] The price of sugar at Cawnpore fell from Rs. 38 per maund in August 1920 to Rs. 12 - 6 - 0 per maund in March 1926. See the evidence of Wynne Sayer, Secretary, Sugar Bureau, Pusa, in RC on Agriculture in India, Vol. I, Part II, *Evidence of Officers Serving Under the Government of India* (Calcutta, 1927), p. 176.

to Rs. 6 per cwt. in 1930; this measure was taken entirely for revenue purposes. The Government of India had addressed all local governments, that is, the provincial governments, in 1929 on the subject of the sugar industry. The three provincial governments most interested in the sugar industry, namely the Governments of the Punjab, the United Provinces, and Bihar and Orissa, together with the Government of Bombay, had asked for an enquiry by the Tariff Board. On receipt of the replies to the government's letter the question had been examined by a specially qualified Committee appointed by the Imperial Council of Agricultural Research. On the receipt of the report of this Committee, the Imperial Council of Agricultural Research resolved 'that the Government of India be asked to refer the general question of the import duties on sugar for investigation by the Tariff Board'. It was this resolution which led to the appointment of the Indian Tariff Board to examine the question of according statutory protection to the sugar industry. At the enquiry itself, the Imperial Council of Agricultural Research strongly supported the case for protection of the Indian sugar industry, primarily on the ground that protection of the sugar industry was essential for the development of sugar-cane cultivation in India, and that this development was essential to maintain even a reasonable standard of living for cultivators. It was also argued by them that statutory protection was essential for the growth of all branches of the sugar industry, for revenue duties as such did not inspire confidence.[33] In May 1930 the question of protecting the Indian sugar industry was referred to the Indian Tariff Board, and the latter reporting in 1931, recommended tariff protection for the industry. According to the Tariff Board, protection for the sugar industry was necessary as much to provide an outlet to the cultivators of sugar-cane, particularly those in the United Provinces, who had put a larger area under it, as to ensure the survival and growth of the white-sugar industry.

The Tariff Board recommended tariff protection for fifteen years: the rate of duty should be Rs. 7 - 4 - 0 per cwt. for the first seven years and Rs. 6 - 4 - 0 per cwt. for the next eight years. It justified the long period of protection on the ground that a reduction in the cost of cane, which formed such a large proportion of the cost of production of sugar, demanded a widespread adoption of the improved varieties of sugar-cane by the cultivators, and such adoption was likely to be a lengthy process.

The government accepted the Tariff Board's recommendation with the qualification that the position would be reviewed by a statutory enquiry before the end of the seven years of protection; the Select Committee of the Legislative Assembly, however, inserted a declaration in the preamble of the Indian Sugar (Protection) Bill of 1932 to the effect that protection was to continue until 31 March 1946, and that the statutory enquiry before 31

[33] See ITB: *Evidence* (*Report on sugar*) (Calcutta, 1932), Vol. I, pp. 1–2, 18–60.

March 1938 would only determine the form in which and the extent to which protection was to be given.

The duty on the superior grades of sugar was raised to Rs. 7 - 4 - 0 in the Finance Act of 1931; with the supplementary budget of 1931, which imposed a surcharge of 25% on a wide range of customs duties, the duty on sugar was raised to Rs. 9 - 1 - 0 per cwt. The Sugar Industry (Protection) Act, 1932, gave statutory force to the recommendations of the ITB, transferring the sugar and sugar candy duties from revenue to protective tariffs. But the rates of duties remained higher than those recommended by the Tariff Board. The effective rates of duty were around 185% *ad valorem* on the basis of a price of Rs. 15 - 0 - 0 per cwt. of Java sugar in Bombay, including the duty and landing and handling charges.[34]

The effect of the high protective duty on imported sugar was immediately felt, both in a drastic reduction of the imports of sugar and in a phenomenal increase in imports of sugar machinery. This is shown by our Tables 12.3 and 12.2 respectively. The net imports of sugar fell from 933,000 tons in 1929–30 to 510,000 tons in 1931–2 and 366,000 tons in 1932–3. Part of this decline was due to the depression, but not the whole: even in 1930–1, the total Indian consumption of white sugar was higher than in the twenties. The imports of sugar machinery rose from an average level of Rs. 1,160,000 per year during the years from 1925–6 to 1929–30, to a value of Rs. 15,311,000 in 1932–3 and Rs. 33,639,000 in 1933–4, that is, nearly thirty times the level of imports of sugar machinery in the last five years of the 1920s. Throughout the thirties the value of imports of sugar machinery stayed at a level much higher than any that was attained before the grant of protection. The drop in the prices of machinery, combined with the fact that most other industries of India were depressed, also contributed to the growth in investment in the sugar industry.[35] The increase in the real value of imports of sugar machinery during the thirties is very much greater than the increase in the money value because of the large drop in prices of sugar machinery as indicated by our crude price index.

The imposition of the tariff on imported sugar, in conjunction with the diffusion of improved varieties of sugar-cane, also led to a growth in the acreage under sugar-cane for India as a whole.[36] In the thirties, the prices of most agricultural crops fell drastically. Hence, in the sugar-cane tracts, the profitability of sugar-cane improved in relation to that of other crops, when a substantial measure of tariff protection was introduced for sugar, while most other crops did not enjoy either direct or indirect protection of any kind. This improvement in profitability was reflected in an extension of

[34] See Dey: *The Indian Tariff Problem*, Chapter VIII.
[35] Cf. Burt, 'The Indian Sugar Industry', p. 934.
[36] For the effects of these developments on the different provinces see Chapter 4 above.

TABLE 12.3 *Production and consumption of white sugar and gur in India, 1926–7 to 1939–40 (figures in '000 tons)*

Year (1)	Production of sugar direct from cane (2)	Production of sugar refined from gur (3)	Total production of factory sugar (4)=(2)+(3)	Production of khandsari sugar (5)	Net production of gur (6)	Net imports of white sugar into India (7)	Indian consumption of white sugar (8)=(4)+(7)
1926–7	63	58	121	n.a.	2,313	815	936
1927–8	68	52	120	n.a.	2,276	706	826
1928–9	68	31	99	n.a.	1,778	859	958
1929–30	90	23	113	200	1,837	933	1,046
1930–1	120	30	150	200	2,241	898	1,048
1931–2	159	62	221	250	2,758	510	731
1932–3	290	78	368	275	3,240	366	734
1933–4	454	65	519	200	3,486	249	768
1934–5	578	44	622	150	3,701	220	842
1935–6	932	48	980	125	4,101	198	1,178
1936–7	1,111	26	1,137	100	4,268	−17	1,120
1937–8	931	17	948	125	3,364	−35	913
1938–9	651	15	666	100	2,131	−4	662
1939–40	1,242	27	1,269	125	2,441	198	1,467

n.a. denotes 'not available'.

Sources: (a) *Reviews of the sugar industry of India,* Annual Supplements to the *Indian Trade Journal;* (b) for net production of gur from 1930–1 to 1939–40, ITB: *Report on Sugar,* Vol. I (Bombay, 1950), p. 62.

Up to 1935–6, India includes Burma; the net exports after 1935–6 are primarily accounted for by land frontier trade with Burma.

Explanatory Note: *Gur* is congealed cane juice made with the help of bullock-drawn or power-driven small presses. *Khandsari* is an indigenous process of manufacture of sugar from *gur*. Both these processes of production are much less efficient than factory production in extracting sucrose from sugar-cane. Again, in the factory production of sugar, refining from *gur* is a much less efficient process than production of white sugar direct from cane.

With the growth of production of sugar in India the extractive efficiency of *khandsari* and factory production of sugar increased. The average efficiency of extraction of white sugar in factories producing direct from cane increased from 6.85% (by weight) at the time the Indian Sugar Committee reported (1920) to 9.07% in 1929–30. This average increased to 10.28% in 1942–3, although it declined subsequently and stayed close to 10%. The percentage of recovery for *khandsari* increased from 4%, as estimated by the Indian Sugar Committee, to 5.25% round about 1930, largely because of the introduction of new machinery. The following table, derived from the ITB, *Report on sugar* (Calcutta, 1931), indicates the position round about 1930:

Process	Output (tons) per 100 tons of sugar-cane	Sucrose content (per cent)	Output (tons) sucrose per 100 tons of sugar-cane
Gur	9 to 10·88	65 to 75	6 to 7
Factory			
(i) Direct production from cane		99 to 100	8·90 to 10·12
(ii) Refining from gur		99 to 100	5·5 (maximum)
Khandsari			5·25

the area under sugar-cane in India as a whole from 2·7 million acres in 1928–9 to about 4·6 million acres in 1936–7. This area declined again during 1937–40 but still remained substantially higher than during the 1920s (see Table 12.4).

One of the first problems the Government of India had to tackle after protecting the sugar industry was that of the relationship between the cane-growers and the sugar factories. A major reason for tariff protection was the hope that it would improve the position of the cultivator by increasing the demand for his product. In actual fact, however, the cultivator was in a very weak bargaining position *vis-à-vis* the mill-owner, particularly in those areas in which the practice of *gur*-making was not widespread or had been discontinued. Cane could not be sold in places which were very far from the factories because of the high transport costs and because of the fact that the sucrose content of cane that had been cut fell rapidly with time. Moreover, factories often had agreements about zones, so that there was no real competition for the cane of the cultivator. The area under improved varieties of sugar-cane at first tended to expand faster than the effective capacity of cane factories.

Some of these difficulties arose because the white-sugar industry was growing very fast and yet was not keeping up with the growth of sugar-cane production, but some were peculiar to the cultivation of sugar-cane as a crop. These difficulties were aggravated by the condition of the small peasant

TABLE 12.4 *Production of raw sugar in India, 1925–6 to 1939–40*

Year	Area under sugar-cane ('000 acres) (1)	Production of raw sugar (in '000 tons) (2)
1925–6	2,806	3,143
1926–7	3,075	3,420
1927–8	3,105	3,376
1928–9	2,719	2,827
1929–30	2,624	2,885
1930–1	2,905	3,359
1931–2	3,077	4,116
1932–3	3,425	4,859
1933–4	3,422	5,055
1934–5	3,602	5,292
1935–6	4,154	6,102
1936–7	4,582	6,932
1937–8	3,997	5,579
1938–9	3,270	3,572
1939–40	3,788	4,849

Source: Reviews of the sugar industry of India, Supplement to the *Indian Trade Journal*
Raw sugar is the *gur* equivalent of sugar-cane.

in northern India: he was too poor generally to do without loans to tide him over the season between harvests. The fact that sugar-cane occupied the land for between eighteen months and two years meant that the cultivator of sugar-cane had to borrow even more heavily than the cultivator of other crops. He borrowed from the money-lender, the trader, the landlord or from the mill-owner. Whatever the source of the loan, his indebtedness made him subject to pressures which weakened his competitive position. As a result, the prices realized by the cultivator in the United Provinces and Bihar often went down to 3 annas per maund, which did not even recoup his total current expenses.[37]

The Government of India convened a Sugar Conference in the summer of 1933 which disclosed, among other things, the very rapid rate at which the sugar industry was growing, the reduction in the cost of sugar-cane that had taken place as a result of the spread of improved varieties of canes, and the unremunerative prices paid for cane by many factories. In order to give some measure of protection to the cultivator the Government of India in 1934 passed the Sugar-cane Act, which permitted the provincial governments to fix minimum prices for sugar-cane and to make these prices effective by framing appropriate rules. The governments of the United Provinces and Bihar accordingly fixed minimum prices for cane in their respective

[37] See general representation by the All-India Sugar Merchants' Conference to the Tariff Board, in ITB: *Evidence (Report on sugar)* (Delhi, 1938–9), Vol. III B, pp. 377–8.

provinces (the rules were made applicable only to North Bihar because most of the sugar factories in Bihar were located north of the Ganges). The minimum prices of cane were at first fixed at 5 annas per maund for vacuum-pan factories, on the assumption that the average price of first-grade sugar would be Rs. 8 - 8 - 0 per maund; a sliding scale was then adopted so that for every rise or fall in the price of sugar by eight annas per maund, the price of cane would be raised or lowered by 3 pies per maund. For *khandsaris* and open-pan factories, a lower minimum price was fixed, at 3 annas and 6 pies per maund, the rise or fall in the price of cane for delivery to *khandsari* or open-pan factories being fixed at two-thirds of the corresponding rise or fall in the minimum price of cane for delivery to vacuum-pan factories. For the enforcement of the Sugar-cane Rules, Cane Inspectors were appointed in both the provinces.[38]

It seems that the fixing of minimum prices by the governments of Bihar and United Provinces was not very effective in stabilizing sugar-cane prices. In 1935–6, the harvest of sugar-cane was short relative to the capacity of sugar factories in many areas, and the prices paid by vacuum-pan factories were apparently higher than the prescribed minimum prices. However, in 1936–7, when the sugar-cane crop was abundant, the actual sugar-cane prices were even lower than the prescribed minimum prices,[39] and the prescribed minimum prices had themselves been lowered by the governments concerned in order to induce the sugar factories to lengthen their crushing season and deal with the abundant crop.

The imbalance between the demand for and supply of sugar-cane in 1937 was accentuated by the increase in the excise duty levied by the Government of India to Rs. 2 - 0 - 0 per cwt. In 1934 the Government of India had imposed an excise duty of Rs. 1 - 5 - 0 per cwt. on sugar produced by vacuum-pan factories. The amount of duty was the difference between the import duty of Rs. 9 - 1 - 0 per cwt. in force at the time and the recommended duty of Rs. 7 - 12 - 0. (The ITB had recommended in 1931 that the import duty should be increased by 8 annas when the ex-duty price of Java sugar fell below Rs. 4 per maund in Calcutta, and hence the prescribed duty in 1934 was Rs. 7 - 12 - 0 and not Rs. 7 - 4 - 0.) The excise duty was imposed primarily to recoup the losses in customs revenue caused by the drastic fall in sugar imports; but a secondary aim was also to check the growth of the sugar industry, which was considered too rapid.

The excise duty of 1934 probably did not affect the sugar industry so as to cut into its normal profits; but it probably eliminated the supernormal profits which had been reaped since the end of 1931.[40] There was a drastic

---

[38] *Ibid.*, Vol. III B, pp. 66–70 (letter dated 18 August 1937 from the Imperial Council of Agricultural Research). [39] *Ibid.*, Vol. III B, pp. 54–65, 69.

[40] See in this connection the evidence of the Revenue Department, Government of Bihar, the Director of Industries, United Provinces, and the Director of Agriculture, United Provinces, in *Ibid.*, Vol. III A, pp. 62–205.

decline in the imports of sugar machinery in 1934–5; but one would have expected some decline anyway, after the hectic build-up of capacity during 1932 and 1933. In 1934, a small part of the excise duty was passed on to the consumer in the shape of higher prices, but this was a temporary phenomenon. In 1937, when the government imposed the higher excise duty, the prices of factory sugar had already been declining for some time, and many factories had delayed their crushing. There had also been serious disagreements between the sugar merchants and sugar factories about the prices contracted for future delivery. In anticipation of the Italo-Abyssinian conflict developing into a serious international situation many sugar merchants had contracted for delivery of sugar at relatively high prices. When the international situation eased and sugar prices fell, the sugar merchants refused to take delivery[41] and the Government of United Provinces had to step in and bring about a settlement between sugar factories and sugar merchants.

When the sugar-cane crop of 1937 proved excessive in relation to the demand for it, the governments of United Provinces and Bihar had to lower the minimum prices of cane in successive fortnights from 4 annas 9 pies per maund in November 1936, to 3 annas and 6 pies per maund in United Provinces and to 3 annas in Bihar in May 1937.[42] The scale of minimum prices had also to be revised downwards in April 1937 in order to allow for the increased excise duty on sugar. In Bihar the minimum price of cane was reduced by 3 pies per maund for delivery to vacuum-pan factories and by 2 pies per maund for delivery to open-pan factories.[43] In the United Provinces similar revisions were made.[44]

The price of sugar did not rise after the imposition of the excise duty. Thus the increased duty was almost wholly borne by the cane-growers and factories, and factories in turn were able to pass on most of the duty to the cane-growers in the form of lower prices for cane.

As a result of the low prices realized by sugar-cane growers in 1937, sowings fell that year, and the prices paid to the growers rose. The crop in 1938–9 was even lighter because of adverse monsoons and floods, and the minimum prices of cane touched high levels: cane-growers in United Provinces got prices ranging from 6 to $8\frac{1}{2}$ annas per maund of cane. In the season, factories had to pay a tax of 6 pies per maund of cane to the government and an additional 3 pies per maund for cane bought from co-operative societies. But since sugar prices were high, factories were not hard hit.[45]

---

[41] See *Ibid.*, Vol. I, *Indian Sugar Mills Association and Individual Mills in the United Provinces*, pp. 104–5. [42] *Ibid.*, Vol. III B, pp. 68–9, and Vol. III A, p. 66.
[43] *Ibid.*, Vol. III A, p. 70. [44] *Ibid.*, Vol. III A, pp. 216–17.
[45] See *The administration report of the Department of Industries, United Provinces for the year ending 31 March 1937* (Allahabad, 1937), pp. 3–4; *for the year ending 31 March 1938* (Allahabad, 1938), pp. 8–9; and *for the year ending 1 March 1939* (Allahabad, 1940), pp. 5–6.

It would then seem that the policy of the government in fixing minimum prices could neither protect the cultivator against monopsonistic exploitation by factories nor prevent severe fluctuations in the areas under sugar-cane. In many cases, the minimum price became in effect the maximum price.[46] The cultivators were also cheated by dealers underweighing their cane, and deducting too large an amount for the alleged dryness of cane; they were made to pay commissions or tips to dealers, cane managers or the subordinate staff of the mill. The contracts drawn up by the mills were generally one-sided in that, while they compelled the cultivator to sell his cane to the contracting mill, the mill in its turn was not bound to buy the cultivator's cane. There was no definite schedule of delivery from different sugar-cane fields to the sugar mills, and generally the cultivators suffered because of this since they had to wait long hours at the factory gate, lose money on account of the drying of cane and pay tips to subordinate staff of the mill for early purchase. Neighbouring mills often had zoning agreements so that cultivators within the zone of a mill were generally at the mercy of that mill.[47]

But the Sugar-cane Rules with their enforcing agency in the form of Cane Inspectors did serve to protect the interests of the cultivators to some extent, in that the latter received a larger part of the legal minimum price than they would have received without any enforcing agency. The legally prescribed minimum price probably also prevented actual prices from declining even more drastically in 1937. The Co-operative Departments of the local governments also did some good work in organizing co-operative societies for delivery of cane; but factories sometimes refused to deal with such societies, and most of the ordinary cultivators remained outside them.

12.5 THE RELATIONS BETWEEN THE GOVERNMENT AND THE SUGAR INDUSTRY, 1931–9

The ITB recommended in 1931 that Rs. 1 million should be set aside by the Government of India for sugar research. The Government of India did not give legislative effect to this recommendation but assured the central Legislative Assembly that adequate funds would be made available for research into the problems of the sugar industry. A sugar technologist had already been appointed in 1930 by the Imperial Council of Agricultural Research and the Sugar Bureau had been transferred into his charge. A grant of Rs. 125,000 was also made to the Sugar Technology Section of the Harcourt Butler Technological Institute at Cawnpore, for setting up a

---

[46] See ITB: *Evidence (Report on sugar)* (Delhi, 1938–9), Vol. III A, p. 86.
[47] For a list of the difficulties faced by ordinary cultivators, see the evidence of various departments of the Governments of Bihar and United Provinces in *ibid.*, Vol. III A, esp. pp. 100–1, 139–40, 201–2.

small factory for purposes of training, and a recurring grant of Rs. 20,000 per year was made to the same section on condition that a certain number of free students should be admitted from other provinces on the nomination of the Imperial Council of Agricultural Research. In 1936 the Government of India merged the Sugar Section of the Harcourt Butler Technological Institute and the office of the sugar technologist into an All-India Imperial Institute of Sugar Technology. This Institute was responsible both for the training of sugar technologists and research into various branches and aspects of the sugar industry.[48]

After the imposition of the excise duty in 1934, a Sugar Excise Fund was set up by the Government of India out of which grants were made to provincial governments for financing approved schemes, which included schemes of research, regulation of prices of sugar-cane, spread of improved varieties and improved methods of cultivation, and co-operative marketing of sugar-cane. The sums thus allotted came to a total of Rs. 972,500 for the two years 1934–5 and 1935–6, and Rs. 835,500 in 1936–7; by the middle of 1937 the governments of Bengal and Madras, which had been allotted a total amount of Rs. 134,000 for the three years, had not formulated any suitable schemes at all.[49]

The research work conducted by the government cane-breeding stations at Coimbatore, Shahjahanpur and other provincial centres was also expanded from 1930 onwards. This was the work which had the greatest impact on the sugar industry, since it brought down the cost of production of sugar-cane, particularly in northern India, by increasing yields per acre with little increase in the cost of production. The Indian Sugar Mills Association complained that the Imperial Institute of Technology could not render any assistance that was beyond the powers of the sugar technologists of large mills;[50] the sugar technologist in his turn complained that 'the staff and laboratory equipment of the Harcourt Butler Technological Institute were inadequate for any elaborate researches' on processes appropriate for vacuum-pan factories and that there was 'practically no demand for investigation into particular problems from the sugar industry'.[51]

But it is possible that the open-pan factories, that is the *khandsaris*, and *gur* refineries and small factories did benefit from research conducted by various government agencies and by the information supplied by the office of the sugar technologist. Mr Syed Muhammad Hadi had been active for many years in propagating the use of improved rollers for crushing the cane, a system of continuous boiling of the juice and centrifugal machines

---

[48] Burt, 'The Indian Sugar Industry', pp. 932–3; a fuller account is given in the evidence of R. C. Srivastava, Director, Imperial Institute of Sugar Technology, in ITB: *Evidence (Report on sugar)* (Delhi, 1938–9), Vol. III B, pp. 104–18.

[49] *Ibid.*, Vol. III B, pp. 32–3.

[50] *Ibid.*, Vol. I, pp. 39–40 and *ibid.*, Vol. IV, pp. 5–7.

[51] *Ibid.*, Vol. III B, p. 108.

to separate the sugar from molasses.[52] This improvement was partly responsible for the survival of *khandsaris* up to the period of tariff protection. The local governments were generally not in a position to provide any direct financial or technical help to large sugar factories (cf. Chapter 2). It is symptomatic that the only sugar factory to which the Government of Madras gave a loan after 1930 was Sri Ramakrishna Sugar Mills Ltd, Kirlampudi, which had a capacity of 80 tons a day; the loan was to be utilized to pay off a debt and to extend the capacity to 120 tons a day. The capacity of the factory was far below what was considered a minimum economic size for a sugar factory, viz., 400 tons a day.[53]

The position of the *khandsaris* and the *gur* industry in relation to the central sugar factories definitely worsened with the grant of tariff protection and with the rapid expansion of sugar production by central factories. It was estimated by Wynne Sayer that in 1928, of the total Indian sugar-cane crop of about 30 million tons, only about 2·5% was utilized for white-sugar manufacture by modern methods, 7·5% by *gur* refineries (including *khandsaris*) and the rest was utilized for making *gur* or for use as seeds or for chewing.[54] According to Table 12.3, in 1929–30, the output of *khandsaris* was about 200,000 tons, and that of modern factories about 90,000 tons; by 1934–5, the output of factory sugar had gone up to 578,000 tons and that of *khandsaris* had shrunk to 150,000 tons.[55] It is possible that the figures for *khandsari* production are overestimates; only a fraction of the *khandsaris* ranked as factories, and the output of the rest had to be guessed. From a careful survey of *khandsari* production in the United Provinces conducted by the sugar technologist, the output was found to be a little less than 100,000 tons in 1933–4. Since most of the *khandsaris* were concentrated in the United Provinces, the total Indian production would be less than 200,000 tons, contrary to the estimate of the Imperial Council of Agricultural Research, which is regarded as official. On the other hand, *khandsaris* were astute businessmen and would be anxious to conceal their real output in view of the liability of firms classed as factories to the excise duty. So in spite of cross-checks some underestimation was bound to occur in the survey. Moreover, *khandsari* was probably less affected in areas in which the capacity of sugar factories had not expanded as much as in the United Provinces. How one balances these conflicting biases is to some

[52] See Burt, 'The Indian Sugar Industry', p. 923; the evidence of S. M. Hadi in ITB: *Evidence (Report on sugar)* (Delhi, 1938–9), Vol. III B, pp. 703–6, and the evidence of the Government of United Provinces in the same volume, p. 196 and pp. 226–32.

[53] ITB: *Evidence (Report on sugar)* (Delhi, 1938–9), Vol. III A, p. 502.

[54] ITB: *Evidence (Report on sugar)* (Calcutta, 1932), Vol. I, p. 206.

[55] See 'Report on Production of Khandsari Sugar, Rab and Gur in the United Provinces' in ITB: *Evidence (Report on sugar)* (Delhi, 1938–9), Vol. III B, pp. 98–102; the evidence of the Imperial Council of Agricultural Research in the same volume, pp. 71–2; and the evidence of the Director of Industries, United Provinces, in *ibid.*, Vol. III A, p. 223.

extent arbitrary. The net production of *gur*, however, did not shrink noticeably; the cane factories came to account for between a third and a fifth of total cane production, but *gur* remained the predominant form in which sugar-cane was used. (The amounts of white sugar and *gur* realized from sugar-cane were roughly one-tenth of the weight of cane in each case, although the sucrose content of *gur* was, of course, much lower.)

When the excise duty of Rs. 1 - 5 - 0 per cwt. was imposed on white sugar manufactured by vacuum-pan factories, the duty imposed on *khandsari* sugar was only 10 annas per cwt. In 1937, while the excise duty on sugar manufactured by vacuum-pan factories was increased to Rs. 2 - 0 - 0 per cwt., that on sugar manufactured in open-pan factories was increased only to Rs. 1 - 5 - 0 per cwt. The rate of excise duty on *khandsari* sugar was later reduced to Rs. 1 - 0 - 0 per cwt. Many *khandsaris* split up their operations so as to employ less than twenty men at any place and so escape registration as factories and the excise duty.[56] Furthermore, the *khandsaris* also enjoyed concessions in the form of substantially lower minimum prices for cane delivered to them.

The survival of the *khandsari* industry owed something to the policy of the government. Although after the first two or three years after protection *khandsari* production must have declined, as is shown by the large-scale closure of open-pan factories from 1934–5, the statement in *The administration report of the Department of Industries, United Provinces, for the year ended 31st March, 1939*[57] that 'the industry is gradually being driven out by the modern sugar refineries', which represented the predominant opinion, was premature, as later events were to prove. The small capitalist who was generally the *zemindar* or money-lender or trader turned capitalist had too much power over the suppliers of cane and some of the local inhabitants had too persistent a habit of preferring the *khandsari* product for the industry to die quickly or gracefully.

The continued strength of the *gur* industry owed little to government policy. The farmer obviously found it useful to have a bargaining counter against the mill-owner in the form of *gur*-making facilities. The prices of *gur* often followed a course which was largely independent of sugar prices.[58] Finally, apart from considerations of bargaining or making a profit out of high *gur* prices, the farmer would also want to retain a part or the whole of his sugar-cane output for self-consumption in the form of *gur*. But it is probable that with the better integration of local sugar and *gur* markets, *gur* and factory sugar came more directly into competition, particularly when the prices of sugar-cane delivered to factories rose, as a result of short harvests

[56] *Ibid.*, Vol. III A, p. 223.

[57] Allahabad, 1940, p. 10.

[58] See, for example, the tables of prices of sugar and valley *gur* at Patna in ITB: *Evidence (Report on sugar)* (Delhi, 1938–9), Vol. III A, pp. 72–3, and the evidence of the Government of United Provinces in the same volume, pp. 194–6.

and high relative prices of sugar. This is indicated by the relatively large fluctuations in the figures of *gur* production in the closing years of the thirties. The factory sugar industry was helped by what appears to have been a secular increase in the consumption of white sugar per head.

The provincial governments of United Provinces and Bihar came to play a major role in relation to the factory sugar industry after the crisis of 1936–7, which was caused by a large harvest of sugar-cane, low sugar prices, and the increase in excise duty. The sugar mills set up the Indian Sugar Syndicate on 30 June 1937. This was essentially a selling syndicate. By the beginning of October 1937, 92 mills had joined the syndicate, but 19 big factories and 17 smaller factories in north India, 4 factories in Bombay and all the factories in Madras had stayed out. The member factories were supposed to sell all the sugar they manufactured to the syndicate: the syndicate was in its turn to release the stocks (kept with the factories though sold to the syndicate) in specified quantities during the selling periods of a fortnight or a month. The selling price was fixed at a higher level than that prevailing in the market at the time. There was rather a slow take-off of sugar from the syndicate during the first three months after its formation, because of accumulated stocks and competition from member mills. Although the syndicate did succeed in raising the price of sugar by about a rupee, it could not finally succeed so long as a large number of mills remained outside its fold. Hence the Governments of Bihar and United Provinces got together and gave the syndicate a legal status by providing that only members of the Indian Sugar Syndicate would be given licences to crush cane.[59]

The Sugar Syndicate used its monopolistic position to push up prices, until by early 1939 the prices had doubled by comparison with the lowest levels reached in 1937. In June 1940, the Governments of United Provinces and Bihar repealed the law requiring sugar factories crushing cane to be members of the Sugar Syndicate. This led to a flood of resignations from the syndicate, and there was a crisis in the industry, with stocks of sugar piling up and many factories facing great financial difficulties. The syndicate pleaded with the governments concerned to restore recognition to it. This plea was granted on condition that the release of stocks and fixing of sugar prices would be controlled by the governments. Thus ended one of the few efforts at voluntary regulation of an industry, and government help was needed to check the rapacity of member firms and the tendency of individual firms to gain at the expense of the majority, who were restrained by the agreement underlying the coalition.[60]

[59] See *ibid.*, Vol. I, pp. 122–3, and Vol. IV, pp. 47–8.
[60] See the sections on the sugar industry in CISD: *Review of the trade of India* for the years 1937–8 to 1940–1 (Calcutta, annual). See also Leon V. Hirsch: *Marketing in an Underdeveloped Economy: the North Indian Sugar Industry* (Englewood Cliffs, N.J., 1961), pp. 76–7.

12.6 THE EFFICIENCY OF THE SUGAR INDUSTRY IN THE THIRTIES

The existence of a technically optimum size of plant in an industry does not imply the existence of an optimum size of the firm equal to the technical optimum. Economies in marketing and finance will often lead to a size of firm which is different from the size of the technically optimum unit.[61]

In industries in which there are significant economies of scale, the concept of the optimum size of the firm becomes very imprecise. One can then talk about the size which will allow a firm to earn normal profits if the current cost and market conditions continue. This is the sense in which the phrase the 'economic size' of a plant was often used by the ITB. The ITB of 1931 had taken a plant with a capacity for crushing 400 tons of sugar-cane a day as the economic unit; the ITB of 1938 took 500 tons of crushing capacity as the economic size.[62]

It was recognized by all the witnesses at the tariff enquiries that there could be no unique economic size for a sugar mill. The size would depend on (a) the concentration and cost of cane in the locality, (b) the transport costs of cane and sugar, (c) the distance of the market from the mill, (d) the length of the crushing season, determined by the availability of early- and later-ripening varieties of cane and the keeping quality of cane, and (e) the relative importance of overhead costs. Two processes of manufacture of white sugar were available, the sulphitation process and the carbonitation process. In the case of the carbonitation process, the quality of sugar produced was superior, and more uniform and less susceptible to damage by unfavourable weather, since the process could be controlled more easily than in the case of the sulphitation process; the yield was also higher, but both the capital and operating costs per unit of output were higher for the carbonitation process. The very high freight on limestone was also a factor increasing the cost of the carbonitation process. It was used where limestone was relatively cheap. For India as a whole, the sulphitation process was found to be much more widespread than the other process by the Indian Tariff Boards of 1931 and 1939. There was no evidence of significant interaction between the process and the size of the plant, so we shall ignore the former in the rest of this section.

Intimately connected with the question of the size of the plant was the question of its location. For cane-growing purposes, the whole of India could be divided into two regions – the subtropical and the tropical. The United Provinces, Bihar, Punjab and Bengal comprised the subtropical region, and Bombay, Mysore and Madras made up the tropical region. Around 1937, more than 90% of the total area under cane was in the sub-

[61] See E. A. G. Robinson: *The Structure of Competitive Industry* (London, 1931).
[62] ITB: *Report on sugar* (Delhi, 1938), Chapter v.

tropical region and the rest in the tropical region.[63] The tropical region enjoyed the advantage that the crushing season was longer there, so that, other things being equal, a firm could operate a smaller factory than in the subtropical region and break even. Furthermore, since in both Bombay and Madras the local consumption far exceeded the local production, the factories could usually market the product with much lower transport costs on the average than the north Indian mills which had to seek markets in western, eastern and southern India, besides selling in the north Indian market. Finally, the yield of cane per acre and the sucrose content of the cane were much higher in Madras, Bombay and Mysore than in north India.[64]

However, apart from the fact that the United Provinces and Bihar started with large sugar-cane areas which naturally attracted factories to these provinces, the costs of cultivation of cane per acre were lower in these provinces than in Bombay or Mysore. This is shown by the following table of average costs of cane per acre given by the Indian Tariff Board of 1938:

Province	Average cost of sugar-cane per maund (Rs.)
United Provinces	0 - 3 - 7
Bihar	0 - 3 - 4
Punjab	0 - 5 - 0
Bengal	0 - 4 - 0
Bombay	0 - 5 - 10
Madras	0 - 5 - 0

Source: ITB: *Report on sugar* (Delhi, 1938), pp. 33–6.

There are many difficult problems in calculating the cost of cultivation of sugar-cane or, for that matter, of any other crop cultivated under conditions of small-peasant farming. The peasant usually applies a considerable amount of family labour to his land and he also uses the labour of the bullocks or other draught animals which he owns for various operations connected with the cultivation of sugar-cane. It would be misleading to calculate the cost of all such family inputs at the market prices, for much of the cost is incurred in the slack season, when the alternative to spending the family inputs on the family farm would be unemployment. Ideally, one would like to impute only the alternative costs incurred to the cost of cultivation. But nobody took the trouble to find out the exact distribution of family inputs over the different parts of the farming season or to calculate

[63] *Ibid.*, p. 20.

[64] The climatic and hydrological factors influencing the distribution of sugar-cane cultivation are described and analysed in T. R. Sharma: *Location of Industries in India* (Bombay, 1946), Chapters VII and VIII. Sharma points out that within northern India, the United Provinces and north Bihar are placed favourably in relation to other areas, because of the mildness of the seasons, the presence of irrigation facilities, and the prevalence of relatively long crushing periods and of a comparatively high percentage of extraction of sucrose from the sugar-cane.

the additional costs incurred through the working of the family (including the draught animals) during the slack season. Again, difficulties arise in calculating the rent of the land that the peasant owns; the peasant is often willing to accept a lower return on the land cultivated by himself than would a profit-maximizing capitalist, because land is the essential factor needed to keep the peasant and his family as fully employed as possible. The Imperial Council of Agricultural Research published during the years 1938–40 the results of their investigations of the cost of cultivation in the principal sugar-cane- and cotton-producing tracts of India, in nine main volumes and nine supplementary volumes. Their calculations also suffer from the defects we have mentioned. Their figures support the relative magnitudes of the costs of cultivation in tropical and subtropical regions given in the ITB: *Report on sugar* of 1938[65] so long as allowance is made only for the out-of-pocket expenses for making *gur* and not for the imputed costs of family labour, bullocks, and so on. Comparison has to be made between the costs of *gur* because the cost of sugar-cane is not given separately for different regions for Madras. The average costs of *gur* per maund in the districts of Coimbatore, Bellary, and Vizagapatam in Madras for the years from 1933–4 to 1935–6 were Rs. 4 - 1 - 9, Rs. 3 - 5 - 2 and Rs. 3 - 0 - 1 respectively. The average costs of production of sugar-cane per maund in the Patna and Saran districts of Bihar over the years from 1934–5 to 1936–7 were Rs. 0 - 3 - 3 and Rs. 0 - 4 - 5 respectively. Multiplying the latter costs by 10 (on the assumption that ten maunds of cane are needed for one maund of *gur*) and adding in the average out-of-pocket expenses of making one maund of *gur* during the same period in the Patna district, we get Rs. 2 - 2 - 1 and Rs. 2 - 14 - 3 as the costs of production of *gur* in the Patna and Saran districts of Bihar. Adding in the imputed costs of family labour and bullocks, these costs rise to Rs. 3 - 3 - 2 and Rs. 3 - 14 - 10 respectively.[66]

The doubts about the meaningfulness of calculating the cost of cultivation on the basis of the scanty information available have a bearing on the decisions of the industrialists. It was recognized by many capitalists that, under conditions of small-peasant farming, the price that would be accepted by the peasant as economic could not be accepted by the capitalist, who would charge an economic rent for the land, and the full market wages of labour, and who would have to include explicit charges for supervision.[67]

[65] Delhi, 1938.

[66] See Imperial Council of Agricultural Research, *Report on the cost of production of crops in the principal sugarcane and cotton tracts in India*, Vol. IV, *Madras* (Delhi, 1938), p. 36 and Vol. V, *Bihar* (Delhi, 1938), pp. 21–3.

[67] Thus Parry's of Madras, the managing agents controlling the largest group of sugar factories in south India, found that even when they spent more money on better methods of cultivation and more fertilizers, their cost of cultivation was higher than that of the peasant, and they therefore diminished the area under their own cultivation considerably. See ITB: *Evidence (Report on sugar)* (Delhi, 1938–9), Vol. IV, p. 126.

Assuming that the biases introduced into the figures for costs of cultivation of cane in the different regions are the same in all parts of India, it follows that a sugar mill could obtain cane more cheaply in Bihar and the United Provinces than in other parts, under the prevailing conditions.[68] It does not follow that if cane was cultivated under different conditions, the same distribution would be the most economic from the point of view of the factories. If cane could be grown in large blocks owned by the factories, probably the least-cost location of factories would be found to be in the tropical regions. The factories could spend more money on cultivation and on manuring than ordinary farmers, and could use the managerial staff of the mills for purposes of supervision. In Bombay, the growth of cane factories was encouraged by the Government of Bombay after 1932 by the device of making compact blocks of land available to the mills in the tract served by the Deccan canals.[69] Similar developments also took place in Mysore and Hyderabad.[70] Generally speaking, when no special assistance was given to sugar factories by the provincial governments or governments of native states, it was profitable to set up central sugar factories only in areas in which a sizeable fraction of the cultivated area was already under sugar-cane. Once a factory was set up in a tract in which sugar-cane was a major crop, the cultivators found it cheap to sell their sugar-cane directly to the factory. Hence we find a rough correlation between the ratio of the area under sugar-cane to the total cultivated area in a province and the ratio of the cane delivered at factory gates to the total quantity of cane crushed.[71] And hence, under conditions of peasant farming, which was the dominant mode of cultivation of sugar-cane, the existing distribution of sugar factories in India was approximately right from the point of view of the capitalist.[72]

[68] Sharma points out (*Location of Industries in India*, Chapter VIII) that one important factor behind the difference in the costs of production of sugar-cane as between the tropical and subtropical regions was the difference in the cost of irrigation. Whereas in north India the irrigation charges per acre were not more than Rs. 10 or 11, in the Bombay Deccan they were as high as Rs. 60.

[69] The Government of Bombay appointed the Deccan Canals Improvement Committee (the Kamat Committee) to suggest ways of improving the irrigation revenue from the canals, and the committee came to the conclusion that the development of sugar factories would be a good way of doing it. The cane estates of the sugar factories in the Deccan canals area covered over 12,000 acres in 1937. See ITB: *Evidence* (*Report on sugar*) (Delhi, 1938–9), Vol. II, pp. 401–2 (evidence of the Deccan Sugar Factories, Bombay); *ibid.*, Vol. V, pp. 41–8 (evidence of C. E. Aitken, Superintending Engineer, Deccan Irrigation Circle); ITB: *Report on sugar* (Delhi, 1938), pp. 26–7.

[70] *Ibid.*, pp. 28–9.

[71] Sharma: *Location of Industries in India*, pp. 126–7.

[72] Propaganda was carried on by the Departments of Agriculture and Industries, Madras, to induce the cultivator to cultivate more sugar-cane. But, apart from the fact that the direct costs of cultivation of sugar-cane per acre in most districts of south India were too heavy for the cultivator, there were often more paying alternative crops such as bananas, coconuts or turmeric available to him. Even if the direct costs of cultivation of sugar-cane per maund were lower in the south Indian districts than in the north, it would not follow that cultivators in either region would have benefited from the shift of

This conclusion is strengthened when we find that the cost of manufacture of sugar from sugar-cane was also generally lower in the subtropical than in the tropical region. The following are the relevant figures:

Region	Cost of manufacture per maund (Rs.)
Western United Provinces	1 - 0 - 7
Central United Provinces	1 - 3 - 8
Eastern United Provinces	1 - 2 - 6
North Bihar	1 - 4 - 2
South Bihar	1 - 7 - 6
Bombay	1 - 10 - 7
Madras	2 - 3 - 8
Mysore	1 - 3 - 10

Source: ITB: *Report on sugar* (Delhi, 1938), p. 67.

Of course, within the United Provinces and Bihar, the location of factories was completely unplanned, and there was a considerable degree of divergence between the optimum locational pattern and the actual one. There were areas which had an excess of cane in relation to the capacity of sugar factories and there were other areas in which there was a shortage of cane for the factories. Transport costs could have been lowered, and peasants' incomes could have been increased, by a systematic planning of location. But, at least up to 1937, there was no general overcrowding of factories in the United Provinces and Bihar.[73]

We can now take up the question of the economic size of factories directly. It is true that under special circumstances, such as the existence of a compact block of land under sugar-cane under the control of the factory and a market very near the factory for all the sugar produced by it, a small factory with a capacity of, say, 300 tons might do better than a large factory, whose capacity was not fully utilized because of shortage of cane, or which had to import cane from long distances and sell its sugar in distant markets; but it was generally admitted in 1937 that larger factories did better than smaller ones, because of economies in overhead costs. Many witnesses

cane cultivation and sugar factories from the north to the south. See ITB: *Evidence* (*Report on sugar*) (Delhi, 1938–9), Vol. III A, pp. 484–564 (letter from the Secretary, Development Dept, Madras, including estimates of comparative profitability of different cash crops in different regions of Madras). A serious misconception underlying much of the calculation of the cultivator's costs made by the ITB ought to be cleared up here. The fact that the factory could often get cane from the cultivator just by paying the latter his out-of-pocket expenses does not mean that he *ought* to have been paid a price which covered only those expenses (plus a nominal interest charge on the capital). For a start, the cultivator would often have to borrow money at rates of interest far higher than the Tariff Board would ever allow in its calculation. Secondly, the factory could often use its monopsonistic position to beat down the price in the locality. Thirdly, the price they calculated did not take into account the prices of alternative crops, which were particularly important in Bengal, Madras, and Bombay.

[73] See ITB: *Evidence* (*Report on sugar*) (Delhi, 1938–9), Vol. III A, pp. 64–5, 211–12, 217.

thought that under the prevailing conditions of low prices for sugar no mills could break even.[74] The Director of Agriculture, Bihar, considered that the economic size of the factory should be so defined that it yielded at least 10% return on capital in normal years; he thought that a factory with a crushing capacity of 650–800 tons daily would satisfy that requirement.[75] But neither he nor any of the other witnesses gave the full reasoning for picking on a particular capacity as the economic one.

One could try to find out the actual rates of return earned by the factories and see whether they varied significantly with size. A scrutiny of 29 sugar mills listed in *IIYB* for the years 1936–7 and 1941–2 revealed wide divergences between rates of dividends declared, both between individual sugar mills and between sugar mills managed by or associated with the same business group. Begg, Sutherland and Company managed the largest number of sugar companies – Balrampur, Cawnpore, Champarun, Purtabpore, Ryam and Samastipur. Of these only Balrampur was registered after 1930 (in 1932). For this company the average yearly rate of dividend for the years from 1934 to 1940 came to 5·18%. For the other five, the average rates of dividend over the decade from 1931 to 1940 were as follows (% per year): Cawnpore, 16·55; Champarun, 11; Purtabpore, 3.5; Ryam, 12; Samastipur, 2·75. Among the other groups, companies managed by or associated with Narang Brothers declared the highest rates of dividends. Thus the average annual rates of dividend for Basti Sugar and Punjab Sugar, both established before 1930, for the decade 1931–40 were 17·9% and 22·1% respectively. But Nawabganj Sugar, registered in 1932, declared an average rate of dividend of 8⅝% over the period 1935–40. The two companies under the management of Parry and Company, EID, and Deccan Sugar and Abkhari, earned average rates of 9·25% and 17·5% per year respectively. Among the other companies, South Bihar (managed by N. K. Jain and Company), Mysore Sugar, Belapur (managed by W. H. Brady and Company), and Raza and Buland (both managed by Govan Brothers) were highly profitable ones. In general, it appears that mills which had been operating before 1931 or 1932 and were of a minimum economic size were able to make very high rates of profit in the first few years; the rate of profitability was higher than is indicated by the rates of dividend, since much of the expansion of capacity was financed out of internal funds. Companies started after 1933 or 1934 were not generally outstandingly profitable, and even some companies managed by reputable managing agents, such as James Finlay (Belsund) or Andrew Yule (New Savan), failed to show good results.

However, some of the most successful companies, such as the Durbhanga Sugar Company and Saraya Sugar Factory, were private companies or

[74] See the evidence of Sir William Wright, of Parry and Company, in *ibid.*, Vol. IV, p. 141.
[75] *Ibid.*, Vol. III A, p. 127.

partnerships, and for the rest of the companies sufficient data are not available. I have tried instead to see how the size distribution of factories had actually altered from the detailed list of factories submitted by the Indian Sugar Mills Association in 1937.

TABLE 12.5   *Change in the size-distribution of sugar factories over time*

Range of sizes of sugar factories by crushing capacity (tons per day)	Original distribution (i.e. distribution when each of the factories was founded)	Distribution in April 1937
0–100	11	10
101–200	14	8
201–300	14	11
301–400	33	10
401–500	18	13
501–600	6	18
601–700	8	6
701–800	3	18
801–1,000	4	22
1,001–1,500	3	7
1,501–2,000	—	6
Above 2,000	—	1
Total	114	130

Source: ITB: *Evidence (Report on sugar), 1938*, Vol. I, pp. 2–8.

It is obvious from Table 12.5 that the proportion of large-sized factories increased significantly with time.[76] The table understates the difference between the old distribution (which was composed of factories of all ages from the oldest to the new-born) and the new because many 'old' factories had come into being only shortly before. Many of the factories which had started with a capacity of 400 tons or above increased their capacity to 600 tons or above. More importantly, it is generally the larger factories which managed to increase their capacity significantly. Few of the factories in the two lowest ranges of capacity climbed out of them. Apart from the diseconomies of scale this was also probably due to the fact that the smaller factories generally occurred outside the main sugar-cane belt of the United Provinces and Bihar. The tendency for moderate-sized factories to become

[76] There is a discrepancy between the size distribution indicated by the list submitted by the Indian Sugar Mills Association, on which our table is based, and the distribution of factories by size given by the ITB: *Report on sugar* (Delhi, 1938), p. 60, for out of 140 factories in the latter list there are 76 with a size of 500 tons or below, whereas there are only 62 such factories in April 1937, according to our table. Even if we assume that the 10 factories missing from our list were all of 500 tons or below, we get a total of 72 factories within that size range. This discrepancy is probably due to differences in (a) the coverage of the two lists and (b) the dates on which the capacities reported were effective.

bigger becomes more pronounced if we confine our attention to the United Provinces and Bihar.

There were two influences acting on the expansion of the factories. First, the factories or business groups which made very large profits during the first two or three years after tariff protection had easy access to finance for expansion. Secondly, with falling sugar prices in 1936–7, it was only by expanding capacity and spreading overheads that factories could break even or cut losses. In so far as tariff protection provided the stimulus for the entry of new firms and the creation of large-sized factories, one can claim that a high rate of protection proved more efficacious in bringing down costs of manufacture than a low rate of protection would have been.

The location and size of factories were determined mainly by the availability of cane and the rapidity with which cane production and yield per acre increased. In general, the proportion of smaller-sized factories was higher in provinces other than the United Provinces, Bihar and Bombay. Although a tropical province such as Madras could yield a much higher output of sugar-cane per acre with proper cultivation, the cost of cultivation was also high, and there were a large number of alternative cash crops. Also, the yield per acre did not improve noticeably, mainly because it had already been high. Hence, in spite of repeated exhortations by the Departments of Agriculture and Industries, cane cultivation did not spread, and small factories remained small. There was a demand for regulation of the growth of factories on the part of administrators as well as mill-owners, but it is not clear that a better location of factories could have been brought about without interfering with peasant farming or with the free choice of crops by the peasants:[77] regulation of location of plants might merely have restricted competition without improving the position of the cultivator or the efficiency of the industry.

The ITB in 1938 found that the policy of discriminating protection for the sugar industry had succeeded in increasing production beyond expectation, so that imports of foreign sugar had entirely ceased. The production of white sugar in 1936–7 was estimated to be 1,254,000 tons, 53,000 tons in excess of the estimated consumption. This was to prove rather an exceptional year, because of large harvests, but also because of the more intimate relationship that was brought about between the production of *gur* and the production of sugar, by the elimination of foreign competition.[78] The ITB enquiry also established that an improvement in the operating efficiency of Indian factories had taken place, mainly through an increase in scale,

[77] For a plea for regulation of sugar mills made out by sugar-mill interests see the evidence of the Indian Sugar Producers' Association, Cawnpore, in ITB: *Evidence (Report on sugar)* (Delhi, 1938–9), Vol. III B, pp. 371–5.

[78] See in this connection, P. N. Nayer and P. S. B. Pillai: 'An Analysis of Sugar and Gur Prices in India in the Post-Protection Period', *Sankhya (The Indian Journal of Statistics)*, Vol. 4, Part 4, 1938–40, pp. 473–8.

which brought about a better balance between types of operations within a mill and which led to lower overhead costs per unit of output, but also through economies in fuel costs in northern India, which were effected by more extensive use of *bagasse*. Finally, the cost of production of sugar-cane had gone down considerably, because of the introduction of improved varieties and the increase in yields per acre. The fair price of sugar-cane delivered at factory gate was worked out as 5 annas 6 pies per maund as against 8 annas per maund in the 1931 Tariff Board enquiry.

The ITB of 1938 recommended a protective duty of Rs. 7 - 4 - 0 per cwt. on Indian sugar for the next eight years. The Government of India considered the period of a fixed duty too long, and on the basis of revised estimates of the likely price of Java sugar and allowance for difference in quality, fixed the protective duty at 6 - 12 - 0 per cwt. and made the rate of duty operative only for the period from 1 April 1939 to 31 March 1941.[79] (The old rate of duty was operative during the financial year 1938–9.)

[79] India became a party to the International Sugar Agreement in 1937, but this had little bearing on the fortunes of the Indian sugar industry during the thirties.

13

THE DEVELOPMENT OF THE INDIAN
PAPER INDUSTRY

13.1 THE INDUSTRY UP TO 1924

The origins of the machine-made paper industry in India go back to the early part of the nineteenth century when a paper mill was set up at Serampore by the Christian missionaries.[1] The Bally Paper Mills was started under British management in 1870, with one machine. The company was floated in England. The first mill managed by Indians was set up about 1878 in Lucknow. But the entry of British capital on a large scale was probably precipitated by the new policy of the Government of India, favouring the purchase of local stores, proclaimed in 1883; it also owed something to the prices of paper ruling in the world market, because of the spread of literacy among the masses in advanced and advancing countries, including the U.K., the U.S.A., western Europe, and Japan. The local market in India for machine-made paper was also expected to develop through the replacement of hand-made paper and the spread of literacy.[2]

Both British and Indian entrepreneurship played their part in the birth of the industry. The Upper India Couper Paper Mills Company Ltd, was registered as a joint stock company in 1878 and started production in its mills in Lucknow in 1882. It owed its origin to a group of Indian businessmen in Lucknow and had an Indian board of directors almost all through. (In 1912, it had only one European director, Rev. L. C. Bare.)[3] With the exception of 1883 (second half of the year), 1884 and 1896, it managed to pay a dividend of between 4 and 10% per annum during all the years up to 1914, even though the severity of foreign competition increased greatly after the turn of the century. The mill seems to have depended to a large extent on the local demand for high-grade paper; some paper was exported

---

[1] There is some doubt as to whether machines or manual methods were employed at Serampore. See M. J. Cogswell: 'Paper making in India' in Indian Munitions Board: *Industrial Handbook, 1919*, p. 247. Cogswell claims that the first paper mill on European lines was set up in 1716 at the Danish settlement of Tranquebar in the Tanjore district, but this mill was about a century earlier than the basic inventions in paper-making by Robert and Fourdrinier.

[2] W. W. Hunter: *The Indian Empire: its Peoples, History and Products* (London, 1893), p. 721 (on the replacement of hand-made by machine-made paper); J. C. Eddison: *A Case Study in Industrial Development – the Growth of the Paper and Pulp Industry in India* (Centre for International Studies, M.I.T., Cambridge, Mass., 1955), p. 216; S. K. Sen: 'Government Purchase of Stores for India (1858–1914)', *Bengal Past and Present*, January–June 1961, pp. 47–64.   [3] See *IITB, 1913*, p. 440.

from the United Provinces to the neighbouring provinces. But the local demand for low-grade paper was supplied by imports from Germany and other Continental countries. The mill mainly supplied the government, and did not advertise its products.[4] It also managed gradually to Indianize its staff so that in 1924 it had only three European supervisors and by 1931 all the managing and supervising staff were Indians. But the burst of entrepreneurship which had seen its birth had apparently exhausted itself quite early on: in spite of changed circumstances after the First World War and a protected market, it failed either to expand its capacity significantly or to change its processes of production. The two types of failure were connected; for, with the old methods of production which utilized *sabai* grass, jute, hemp, rags and waste paper as primary raw materials, its cost of production per ton was very much higher than that of the India Paper Pulp Company, Titaghur Paper Mills, and Bengal Paper Mill, although the last two had to pay higher freight on *sabai* grass, which was their primary raw material (along with wood-pulp) in the beginning.[5] It also appears that the company had a very limited knowledge of the market, and because it supplied a small fraction of the local demand for many different kinds of paper, its prices were at the mercy of quotations of imported paper and of the paper supplied by the Bengal mills, which was often 'dumped' in the upcountry markets.[6]

By far the most important of the Indian paper mills at the beginning of the century were the Titaghur Paper Mills and the Bengal Paper Mill. The former was established in 1882 and began manufacturing paper in 1884. It took over two of the machines of the Bally Mills in 1905, when the latter went into liquidation. The Titaghur Mills also took over the Kankinara Mill of the Imperial Paper Company (established between 1892 and 1894) in 1903, when the latter was liquidated. The Bengal Paper Mill Company Ltd was formed in 1889, and its mill at Raniganj commenced production in 1891. The Titaghur Paper Mills Company was controlled by the managing agency firm of F. W. Heilgers and Co., which also controlled jute mills. The Bengal Paper Mill Company was controlled by the managing agency firm of Balmer, Lawrie and Co., which had extensive interests in tea. The figures for the average annual output of Titaghur Paper Mills, Bengal Paper Mill and Upper India Couper Paper Mills during the years 1911–14 were 17,135 tons, 6,061 tons and 3,000 tons respectively.[7] Apart from these

    [4] See Chatterjee [IPG pub.]: *Notes*, p. 82.
    [5] See ITB: *Evidence (Report on paper and paper pulp)* (Calcutta, 1925), Vol. 1, pp. 34–593; ITB: *Evidence (Report on paper and paper pulp)* (Delhi, 1939), Vol. 1, pp. 17–295, 351–419, for the comparative histories of the three Bengal companies (Titaghur, Bengal Paper and India Paper Pulp) and the Upper India Couper Paper Mills.
    [6] See ITB: *Evidence (Report on paper and paper pulp)* (Calcutta, 1925), Vol. 1, esp. pp. 90–1 and ITB: *Report on paper and paper pulp* (Calcutta, 1925), p. 22.
    [7] ITB: *Report on paper and paper pulp* (Calcutta, 1925), p. 107.

three there were other smaller paper mills, most of which were managed by Indians and were not very successful in financial terms. The difficulty in many cases was an inadequate appreciation of the capital requirements of the company. This is illustrated by the case of the Travancore Paper Mills Company, which was floated in 1887 with the financial participation of the Travancore Government. But the company needed more capital (particularly working capital) than was anticipated and after several stages of financial help in the form of loans and orders by the government, it was wound up in 1893.[8] The total capital invested in the enterprise was Rs. 558,000 altogether, whereas the paid-up capital plus debentures alone of the Titaghur Paper Mills on 31 December 1913 totalled Rs. 4,585,000 and at the same date the corresponding figure for the Bengal Paper Mill Company came to Rs. 1,108,000.[9]

After aiding in the birth of the major units of the paper industry through

TABLE 13.1 *Total value and government purchases of Indian paper, 1901 to 1913*

Year ended 31 March	Government purchases of Indian paper and pasteboard (Rs. '000) (1)	Calendar year	Value of Indian paper production (Rs. '000) (2)
1901	28,85	1901	65,84
1902	28,75	1902	64,38
1903	26,98	1903	59,15
1904	22,58	1904	61,49
1905	27,75	1905	51,87
1906	27,10	1906	63,11
1907	32,14	1907	72,90
1908	40,86	1908	75,87
1909	38,11	1909	79,12
1910	38,69	1910	81,52
1911	39,30	1911	80,04
1912	35,95	1912	77,06
1913	34,52	1913	80,37

Sources and notes: Column (1): Sen, 'Government purchases'. Column (2): Gov. India, CISD: *Statistical abstract for British India* (Seventh Issue) (Calcutta, 1915). It is probable that not all Indian paper and pasteboard purchased by the Government was manufactured in India since the Indian Tariff Board in ITB: *Report on paper and paper pulp* (Calcutta, 1925), p. 13, stated that Indian mills did not make pasteboard, millboard and cardboard.

[8] See the written evidence of C. A. Innes, Director of Industries, Madras, in *Evidence* (*Report of IIC*), Vol. III (PP 1919, XIX), p. 147.

[9] Gov. India, CISD: *Statistical abstract for British India* (Seventh Issue), Vol. I (Calcutta, 1915).

its changed policy towards the purchase of local stores in the 1880s, the Government of India took no further interest in it beyond purchasing a sizeable fraction of the output of the industries. Government purchases of Indian paper and pasteboard between the years 1901 and 1914 normally accounted for a little less than half of Indian production, as is shown by the figures in Table 13.1.

The help of the government was certainly crucial during pre-war years, when the very existence of the industry was threatened by competition from European paper manufactured from cheap wood-pulp. The more successful mills were those which managed to get government contracts for the supply of various kinds of paper.[10]

The survival of the Titaghur Paper Mills and Bengal Paper Mill during the period 1901–14 also owed something to the fact that they began to co-ordinate their pricing and production policies from an early date, and the area of co-operation between the two companies included the supply of the basic raw material, viz., *sabai* grass.[11] The two companies were formally associated in the Indian Paper Makers' Association.

The First World War and its aftermath increased the profits of the paper mills; the dividends paid by the three major companies during the years 1914 to 1922 are shown in Table 13.2.

By the end of 1922, however, the competition from European paper had started in earnest, and profits had dwindled to zero or had become negative

TABLE 13.2   *Dividends paid by Indian paper mills, 1914 to 1922 (%
per annum)*

	Upper India Couper Paper Mills	Bengal Paper Mill Company	Titaghur Paper Mills Company
1914	7	6	nil
1915	10½	8	nil
1916	24¼	10	6
1917	59	52	20
1918	58	52	55 (15 months 1918–19)
1919	65	52	50 (1919–20)
1920	50	52	50 (1920–1)
1921	50	25	15 (1921–2)
1922	32	nil	nil (1922–3)

Source: IITB for the relevant years.

[10] See in this connection the written evidence of H. W. Carr, representing Balmer, Lawrie & Co., Managing Agents, Bengal Paper Mill Company Limited, *Evidence (Report of IIC)*, Vol. II (PP 1919, XVIII), pp. 140–1.

[11] For evidence of co-ordination of price policies see ITB: *Report on paper and paper pulp* (Calcutta, 1925), p. 21; see also Eddison: *Growth of the Pulp and Paper Industry in India*, p. 217.

(the dividends paid by the Upper India Couper Paper Mills in 1922 came out of reserve funds).

The Government of India came to the aid of the paper industry again. This aid was given, first, in the form of the development of a bamboo pulping process at the Forest Research Institute, Dehra Dun, which was handed over to private enterprise, and secondly in the shape of grant of tariff protection to the paper and pulp industry in 1925. Before the establishment of the India Paper Pulp Company, the main raw materials used by the Indian paper mills were *sabai* and *moonj* grasses, rags, jute, hemp, waste paper and imported wood-pulp. Of these, *sabai* grass was the most important material. By the end of the war, however, the known sources of *sabai* grass were pretty well tapped by the existing mills, and the cost of collection of grass had gone up enormously. The Titaghur and Bengal Paper Mills had to get their grass supplies from Nepal, the Punjab, United Provinces, Bihar and Orissa, and Central Provinces, so that this bulky raw material sometimes travelled more than 900 miles to come to the mill (it took $2\frac{1}{2}$ tons of *sabai* grass to make a ton of *sabai* pulp). It was doubtful under these circumstances whether the existing mills could rapidly expand their production of paper if they had to depend on supplies of *sabai* grass.[12]

The introduction of the bamboo-pulping process delivered the paper manufacturers from this impasse. The technical possibility of pulping bamboo had been demonstrated by the experiments of R. W. Sindall, conducted under the auspices of the Government of India between 1900 and 1904, but the process was not commercially successful.[13] In the meantime, W. Raitt, who was the mill manager of the Bengal Paper Mill Company, became interested in bamboo pulping and developed a small pulping unit. He received no encouragement from his employers, but is said to have impressed the Viceroy, and was employed in the Forest Research Institute at Dehra Dun to conduct experiments in bamboo pulping. The Government of India also deputed (in 1909) R. S. Pearson, forest economist, to make an extended survey of the forest areas, including bamboos, of India and Burma. Pearson's report[14] was a valuable source of information on the bamboo forests which could be exploited for the purpose of pulp-making. In

---

[12] See the oral evidence of R. S. Pearson, Forest Economist, Forest Research Institute, Dehra Dun, in *Evidence* (*Report of Indian Fiscal Commission*) (Calcutta, 1923), Vol. II. After Pearson had expressed his opinion before the Fiscal Commission that the *sabai* grass supply had reached its limit, the manufacturers even went up to the Punjab hills for their grass, and thus increased their supplies. But there is little doubt that the limits of economic working had been reached by the twenties, given the prices of paper then prevailing. See the oral evidence of personnel of the Forest Research Institute, Dehra Dun, in ITB: *Evidence* (*Report on paper and paper pulp*) (Calcutta, 1925), Vol. II, pp. 440–79.

[13] V. Podder: *Paper Industry in India 1959* (Delhi, 1959), p. 15.

[14] R. S. Pearson: 'Note on the utilization of bamboo for the manufacture of paper-pulp', in *Indian Forest Records*, Vol. 4, Part 5 (Calcutta, 1913).

1919, the Government of India decided that the success of Raitt's laboratory experiments justified the setting up of a pilot plant, which was put into operation in 1924. The enlargement of the scale of production from the laboratory to the pilot plant in fact helped in the solution of many technical problems.[15] In 1922 the India Paper Pulp Company started production by the sulphite process, before the semi-sulphate process had been tried out at the pilot plant of the Forest Research Institute, but the possibility of making pulp from bamboos had already been clearly established at Dehra Dun.[16] However, the initial success of the Forest Research Institute in the production of bamboo pulp was not followed up either by the government or by private enterprise for quite a number of years. The government did not have any plans for the production of paper on a commercial scale: and it refused to endorse the proposal of the Indian Tariff Board of 1925, that the government should grant private enterprise financial assistance for the development of bamboo pulping in its initial stage.[17]

13.2   GOVERNMENT TARIFF PROTECTION AND THE GROWTH OF THE PAPER INDUSTRY

The claim to protection was originally submitted to the Government of India in June 1923 by the Indian Paper Makers' Association, which, as we have already noted, consisted of the Titaghur Paper Mills Company Ltd and the Bengal Paper Mill Company Ltd, and the question was referred to an Indian Tariff Board in June 1924. The report of the Board was submitted in February 1925, and the principle of protection was accepted. The Board recommended protection primarily because it considered that bamboo pulp could provide the basis for the long-term development of an Indian paper industry, and that 'If no assistance is given, it is probable that the manufacture of paper in India will cease, with a somewhat remote prospect of revival when wood pulp has grown very dear'.[18] The Board considered that mills using *sabai* grass did not have a bright future, first because the supplies of *sabai* grass from known sources were rather limited, and secondly because the two Bengal mills which were the major producers of paper were situated far from the sources. Hence the Board considered it inadvis-

[15] See Podder, *Paper Industry in India*, p. 15; and the written evidence of Forest Research Institute, Dehra Dun, in ITB: *Evidence (Report on paper and paper pulp)* (Calcutta, 1925), Vol. II, pp. 437–8.

[16] See the oral evidence of R. S. Pearson, the written statement of the Indian Paper Pulp Company and the oral evidence of Mr Courtenay, *Evidence (Report of the Indian Fiscal Commission)* (Calcutta, 1923), Vol. II, pp. 401–2, 552–4; and the written evidence of the Indian Paper Pulp Company Ltd, ITB: *Evidence (Report on paper and paper pulp)* (Calcutta, 1925), Vol. I, pp. 468, 480–2, 504.

[17] See ITB: *Report on paper and paper pulp* (Calcutta, 1925), Chapter VI; ITB: *Report on paper and paper pulp* (Calcutta, 1931), Chapter I.

[18] ITB: *Report on paper and paper pulp* (Calcutta, 1925), p. 104.

able for the government to commit itself firmly to the protection of the paper and pulp industry, until the bamboo-pulping process had really proved itself commercially. It suggested that the government should help the only mill then producing bamboo pulp, viz., the India Paper Pulp Company, by providing the capital (either in the form of a loan, or by guaranteeing a public issue of debentures) for an extension of its capacity from 2,500 to 5,000 tons a year. Secondly, it recommended that, in place of the existing 15% *ad valorem* duties on printing paper and writing paper, a specific duty of 1 anna per lb. should be imposed on all writing paper, and on all printing paper other than newsprint containing 65% or more of mechanical pulp.[19]

The Board also stressed, somewhat inconsistently, that a guarantee of assistance in some form would be necessary to enable the firms to raise the capital needed for experiments with the bamboo-pulping processes.

The Government of India rejected the Board's recommendation for the grant of financial assistance to the mills conducting experiments with bamboo for the following three reasons. Firstly, the India Paper Pulp Company was a private Company; secondly, the sulphite process which was to be tested with the assistance of the subsidy was covered by patent rights held by one of the members of this private company; and thirdly, financial assistance to an industry should assist equally all competitors within that industry and should not benefit one mill alone and thereby give it an undue advantage over its rivals.[20]

The Government proceeded instead to extend the period of protection from the five years recommended by the Board to seven years (up to 31 March 1932) and calculated that the India Paper Pulp Company and the Carnatic Paper Mills Ltd (later the Andhra Paper Mills Ltd), Rajamundhry, would as a result gain approximately the same total sum of money as under the scheme of subsidy and tariffs recommended by the Board. Only two major changes took place in the tariff schedules between 1925 and 1931: for purposes of exemption from tariff duty the percentage of mechanical pulp in paper was calculated on the basis of net fibre content from 1927 onwards; also in 1927, in order to remove the discrimination in favour of printing paper and writing paper, the tariff schedule was amended so as to render 'ruled or printed forms (including letter paper with printed headings) and account and manuscript books and the binding thereof' liable to a duty of one anna per lb. or 15% *ad valorem*, whichever was higher.[21] The *ad valorem* duty was raised from 15% to 20% on 1 March 1931 (printing paper except ruled or printed forms and account and manuscript books continued to be subject to a specific duty of 1 anna per lb.). In November 1931, surcharge of 25% was levied on the existing revenue and protective duties on different classes of paper, thus raising the specific protective duty to 1 anna 3 pies per lb. and the alternative *ad valorem* duty to $18\frac{3}{4}\%$.

[19] *Ibid.*, p. 106.   [20] ITB: *Report on paper and paper pulp* (Calcutta, 1931), p. 30.
[21] *Ibid.*, p. 4.

(This was thus a general rise in the rate of protective duties as against the rise in March 1931 in protective duties on certain classes of paper only.)

The net effects of the tariff protection given to the paper and pulp industry in 1925 were examined in detail in Chapter II of the *Report* of the ITB, appointed in 1931 to enquire into the desirability of extending the period of protection for the paper and pulp industry.[22] Total Indian consumption of all varieties of paper increased from 111,963 tons in 1924–5 to 175,627 tons in 1929–30, i.e. by 56·86%, and the consumption of 'protected' paper increased from 43,331 tons in 1924–5 to 53,584 tons in 1929–1930, or by a mere 23·66%. (The year 1930–1 was exceptional, since it reflected the effects of both the world-wide depression and the increased import duty on most types of protected paper.) So protection was primarily effective in restricting the consumption of certain classes of paper, but a substitution of unprotected for protected varieties took place. The share of Indian production in total consumption of paper (including pasteboard) decreased from 24·13% in 1924–5 to 21·98% in 1929–30, whereas its share in the 'protected' varieties of paper increased from 53·84% in 1924–1925 to 62·52% in 1929–30.[23] So, viewed from the narrow point of view of increasing Indian production in relation to total consumption of paper tariff protection was not much of a success, though it did succeed in increasing the Indian share in the consumption of protected paper, which was falling as a proportion of the total consumption of paper.

One of the effects of the protection of finished paper was a rise in the proportion of imported wood-pulp used in the manufacture of paper. This was natural because the bamboo-pulping process developed very slowly and in fact only one mill, the India Paper Pulp Company, succeeded in developing it to any extent. (Even in the case of the India Paper Pulp Company, imported wood-pulp accounted for 63·04% by weight of the finished paper produced in 1930–1, as against 21·02% in 1924–5.) All the major companies were using a higher percentage of wood-pulp in 1930–1 than they had done in 1924–5.[24] Furthermore, the cost of imported wood-pulp went

---

[22] *Ibid.*, pp. 6–28. [23] *Ibid.*, pp. 6–7.

[24] For four leading paper mills, viz., Titaghur, Bengal, India Paper Pulp and Upper India Couper, taken together, indigenous materials accounted for 17,169 tons of finished paper in 1924–5 and 19,843 tons in 1930–1. The corresponding figures for finished paper manufactured from imported wood-pulp were 7,976 tons in 1924–5 and 17,529 tons in 1930–1. Thus between 1924–5 and 1930–1 the use of both indigenous and imported materials for paper production increased absolutely, but there was a drastic decline in the ratio of indigenous to imported materials used. Apart from the exemption of imported wood-pulp from protective duties when such duties were imposed on imported paper, another factor which favoured the use of imported as against indigenous materials was that it took a much larger quantity of indigenous materials to produce the same quantity of paper; since the Indian mills had often to transport indigenous materials over long distances inland, imported wood-pulp coming by sea may have enjoyed an advantage in terms of effective transport costs. See ITB: *Report on paper and paper pulp* (Calcutta, 1931), Tables VI and VII, pp. 14–15.

down in relation to that of traditional raw materials, such as *sabai* grass, rags, hemp, waste paper, and so on. The government could not very well in 1925 protect a practically non-existent bamboo-pulping industry.[25] Giving financial help to one company or two companies might also have been considered unfair. The only feasible alternative left, viz., the development of the bamboo-pulping processes invented at the Forest Research Institute for commercial purposes, was ruled out by the absolute refusal of the government to undertake industrial activity directly.

The immediate effect of the grant of tariff protection to the paper industry on the structure of the Indian industry was not marked. At the time of the first enquiry by the ITB of 1924, there were nine paper mills in India, three with four machines each, one with two and the rest with one each. Of these mills, two were owned by the Titaghur Paper Mills Company Ltd, which had eight paper machines altogether and in 1923 had a capacity of 20,000 tons and an output of 15,585 tons. This company and the Bengal Paper Mill Company Ltd, with four machines (capacity, 8,400 tons) and an output of 6,565 tons in 1923, were clearly the leaders of the industry. They were also the lowest-cost producers, apart from the India Paper Pulp Company, which, though it had started production only in 1922, already showed lower works costs than the Bengal and the Titaghur Paper Mills.[26]

13.3 THE LOSERS IN THE PAPER INDUSTRY

Among the other established paper mills the Tariff Board managed to get information only from Upper India Couper Paper Mills and Deccan Paper Mills. Deccan Paper Mills was obviously a submarginal concern even before the war, and Upper India Couper Paper Mills became submarginal after the war:[27] both of these mills depended heavily on the local market and in particular the patronage of the local provincial governments. Deccan Paper Mills was established near Poona in 1885 to take advantage of the Bombay market, the cheap and pure water at Poona and the very cheap labour; it

[25] One is not on absolutely sure ground here, for, after all, the grant of protection to the bamboo-pulp industry in 1932, when the latter was in a stage of infancy, did lead to a very rapid development of the industry. So in fact the results might have been beneficial, if the government had protected the bamboo-pulping industry at an earlier stage. But this step would probably have been vehemently opposed by most of the producers of paper in 1925.

[26] The actual works costs of India Paper Pulp, Titaghur Paper and Bengal Paper in 1923–4 (1923 in the case of Bengal Paper) were Rs. 457·12, Rs. 540·48 and Rs. 519·09 per ton respectively. The future works costs with full output were expected to be lowest for India Paper Pulp and highest for Bengal Paper, though the works costs of all of them were expected to be much lower than in 1923–4. See ITB: *Report on paper and paper pulp* (Calcutta, 1931), p. 108.

[27] Cogswell remarked on the increasing decrepitude of its two paper machines just after the war. Cogswell, 'Paper Making in India', p. 248.

used primarily rags, gunny, jute, waste paper and similar materials. But then considerable improvements were made in wood-pulping in Europe and the mill just managed to survive. Although it was designed to be a two-machine mill a second machine was never installed. Hence it had too high a level of overhead costs all through.[28] The dividends paid by the company were 5% per year from 1890–1 to 1908–9 and 6% per year from 1909–10 to 1917–18 (it had paid no dividends up to 1888–9 and a dividend of 4% in 1889–90). Even during the war its fortunes did not noticeably improve: its output was limited by the scarcity of materials for making the kinds of paper the government and other consumers wanted. Its rate of dividends did go up from 1918–19 onwards, but this was obviously a period of capital consumption, for the mill had to be let out to D. Pudumjee and Sons and it had to close down in 1924. The company only managed to accumulate a reserve fund of Rs. 93,116, against a minimum estimated cost of Rs. 300,000 for the replacement of worn-out machinery and expansion of the plant by installing another paper machine.[29] With the coming of tariff protection, however, a serious effort was made to change the fortunes of the company, by increasing the share capital from Rs. 500,000 to Rs. 925,000, and by converting the mill from a one-machine to a three-machine plant (one of these machines, however, was situated in Bombay). The increase in capital was entirely due to the acquisition of the property of the D. Pudumjee Paper Mill, Bombay. This policy seemed to pay until 1931, when the next measure of protection was introduced. Thus the output of the mill increased continuously from 876·6 tons in 1924–5 to 2,290·4 tons in 1930–1 (the total effective capacity of the two mills was 4,000 tons, although the paper machines themselves had a capacity of 5,700 tons). Under the new dispensation, the policy regarding dividends was altered: no dividends at all were paid from 1924–5 to 1929–30.[30] The output was expanded, however, both by increasing the supplies of domestic materials and by increasing the use of imported pulp, and the proportion of the latter increased continuously from 1925–6 to 1930–1.[31] Hence when duties on imported wood-pulp were imposed at fairly stiff rates, by the Bamboo Paper Industry (Protection) Act of 1932, the mill was very hard hit. The profits made from 1931–2 up to 1934–5 were not enough even to cover the depreciation on the buildings and machinery at the usual rates. The mill could not economically draw on supplies of cheap bamboo or *sabai* grass from which to make pulp.[32]

[28] ITB: *Evidence (Report on paper and paper pulp)* (Calcutta, 1925), Vol. I, pp. 688–692.
[29] *Ibid.*, pp. 672–3.
[30] See written evidence of the Deccan Paper Mills Company Ltd, Bombay, in ITB: *Evidence (Report on paper and paper pulp)* (Calcutta, 1932), Vol. I, pp, 531–4, 553.
[31] *Ibid.*, p. 535.
[32] ITB: *Evidence (Report on paper and paper pulp)* (Delhi, 1939), Vol. I, pp. 461–4.

The other pre-war paper mill, the Upper India Couper Paper Mills managed by Indians, was equipped to produce 4,000 tons per year at full capacity. But the maximum output it attained up to 1923 was 3,678 tons, in 1906. Financially, however, it was much more successful than the Deccan Paper Mills. It paid dividends of 10% per year over the period 1891–5 and also over the period 1900–2 and it often paid dividends of more than 6% before the war. During the war it paid dividends up to 59% per year, and it continued paying dividends at very high rates even after profits had practically disappeared altogether, from the latter half of 1922 onwards. The Upper India Couper Paper Mills, being situated in Lucknow, enjoyed certain advantages: water and labour were cheap and the supplies of *sabai* grass were quite near. Also it was far from the ports and was to some extent protected by distance. But, at the time of the first enquiry by the Tariff Board, it appeared quite clearly that shareholders were trying to get as much out of the company as possible, without any consideration whatsoever for its future: the company had total 'reserve funds' of Rs. 2,123,000, part of which must have been used as working capital, as against the estimated cost of Rs. 4,000,000 for replacement and expansion of the plant, so as to bring it up to date. The company had refrained from making the necessary replacement in 1922 because the quotations of machinery prices were too high.[33]

After protection had been accorded to the paper industry in 1925, the output of the mill increased, from 1,693 tons in 1924 to an average of about 2,600 tons up to 1930, but this expansion was due entirely to better utilization of existing capacity, rather than to any expansion of capacity. The works costs were also reduced, from Rs. 505·22 per ton in 1924 to Rs. 401·57 per ton in 1930, but this again was almost entirely due to more intensive utilization of existing plant rather than to any actual improvement in the methods of manufacture.[34] The company did, however, purchase a modern steam and power plant, and this was expected to bring down the cost of power and actual power consumption quite considerably. It followed a more conservative financial policy than before, declaring no dividends in 1924 and then declaring dividends of between 6% and 10% from 1925 to 1930.[35] The quality of the paper also improved and with the installation

[33] ITB: *Evidence (Report on paper and paper pulp)* (Calcutta, 1925), Vol. I, pp. 50 and 78–93. It is interesting to notice, however, that the company still managed to ward off foreign competition and hold the contract of the Government of Bihar and Orissa even in 1924. It is not clear whether this was due to market-sharing arrangements with the Titaghur and Bengal Paper Mills. See *ibid.*, p. 191 (evidence of H. W. Carr, representing the Bengal Paper Mill).

[34] ITB: *Evidence (Report on paper and paper pulp)* (Calcutta, 1932), Vol. I, pp. 481–482. Practically the whole reduction in the cost of production took place between 1924 and 1925, when the output went up from 1,694 tons to 2,469 tons and the works costs went down from Rs. 505·32 to Rs. 428·17 per ton.

[35] *Ibid.*, pp. 469 and 481.

of *sabai* grass screening, washing and bleaching plant after 1932 the quality improved further. But no expansion in the capacity of the plant took place. The financial policy of the company continued to be conservative. No dividend was declared in 1932 and between 1931 and 1936 (excepting 1932) the rate of dividend varied between 2% and 5½%. The works costs of finished paper came down from Rs. 394·42 per ton in 1931 to Rs. 328·50 per ton in 1936.

13.4 STAGNATION AND GROWTH IN THE PAPER INDUSTRY, 1932–8

The period from 1932 to 1937 was a surprisingly stagnant one for the Indian paper and pulp industry; although total production went up every year, this was due more to the better utilization of existing capacity under the stimulus of higher duties, than to any marked increase in the capacity of the mills. The rate of protective duty on paper was effectively raised in 1932 from 18¾% to 30% *ad valorem*, with a preferential rate of duty of 20% for articles manufactured in the U.K. This was the result of a new tariff classification after the Ottawa trade agreement.[36]

There was also considerable progress in the substitution of indigenous pulp, made from bamboo and other materials, for wood-pulp; this was primarily the result of the imposition in 1932 of a specific duty of Rs. 45 per ton on imported pulp (by the Bamboo Paper Industry (Protection) Act of 1932). Since all protective duties were subject to the revenue surcharge imposed in November 1931, the effective rate of specific duty on imported pulp came to Rs. 56·25 per ton. The substitution of imported pulp by domestically produced pulp was also facilitated by the solution of the problem of the mechanical treatment of bamboos; at the time of the 1931 enquiry by the ITB only the Titaghur Paper Mills seemed to have succeeded in reducing the nodes of bamboo for proper chemical digestion.[37]

The progress of the Indian industry between the Tariff Board enquiries of 1931 and 1938 can be judged from Tables 13·3 and 13·4 on pages 403–4 below. These tables show that, even in 1931–2, imported pulp accounted for more than half of the total pulp consumption of the paper mills in India, but this proportion was reduced to less than 25% by 1936–7. The second interesting feature is the sizeable increase in total Indian consumption of paper other than newsprint: between 1931–2 and 1937–8 total consumption increased from about 83,000 tons to about 114,000 tons. The surprising

---

[36] ITB: *Report on paper and paper pulp* (Delhi, 1938), pp. 1–7.

[37] See evidence of India Paper Pulp Company: 'the progress [in the new process of bamboo pulping] we have made has been chiefly confined within what may be defined as experimental limits' (ITB: *Evidence (Report on paper and paper pulp)* (Calcutta, 1932), Vol. I, p. 22); and the evidence of Titaghur Paper Mills, *ibid.*, p. 171. At the time of the Tariff Board enquiry of 1931, the Bengal Paper Mill had only started experimenting with the production of bamboo pulp (*ibid.*, p. 395). Other mills mainly used *sabai* grass, rags, etc.

TABLE 13.3   *Indian production and imports of paper and paper pulp, 1931–2 to 1936–7*

Year	Number of mills working	Quantity of pulp used (tons)		Imported pulp as per cent of total	Consumption of paper including boards but excluding old newspapers, other kinds of paper and newsprint (tons)			
					Indian		Imported	
		Indigenous	Imported		Protected	Not protected	Protected	Not protected
1931–2	8	17,571	20,081	53.33	35,738	4,820	12,393	29,784
1932–3	8	17,718	21,424	54.74	35,370	4,847	11,490	45,592
1933–4	8	21,867	20,016	47.79	38,151	5,507	13,005	37,378
1934–5	8	23,126	19,737	46.05	40,084	4,517	11,163	44,789
1935–6	9	30,288	16,615	35.43	42,839	5,260	12,096	59,096
1936–7	9	35,374	10,976	23.68	43,364	5,167	11,840	53,283

Source: ITB: *Report on paper and paper pulp* (Delhi, 1938), p. 8.

TABLE 13.4 *Quantities of pulp made from indigenous materials and of imported pulp used, 1931–2 to 1936–7 (tons)*

Year	Bamboo pulp used (1)	Grass pulp used (2)	Pulp of other indigenous materials used (3)	Total (4)= (1)+(2)+(3)	Imported pulp used (5)
1931–2	5,228	9,049	3,294	17,571	20,081
1932–3	5,429	9,632	2,657	17,718	21,424
1933–4	6,721	11,377	3,769	21,867	20,016
1934–5	9,225	11,340	2,561	23,126	19,737
1935–6	14,441	12,280	3,567	30,288	16,615
1936–7	19,281	11,510	4,583	35,374	10,976

Source: *Ibid.*, p. 18.

thing is that the existing Indian mills failed to take advantage of this increase: they were supplying a smaller percentage of the market at the end than in the beginning. Of course, most of the increase had occurred in the so-called non-protected varieties. But one would have expected Indian mills to take advantage of their protection to invade the field of non-protected consumption also. This phenomenon cannot be explained by any lack of profitability of the Indian mills. The Titaghur and Bengal Paper Mills

TABLE 13.5 *Dividends declared by the leading Indian paper mills, 1929 to 1938*

Bengal Paper Mill		Titaghur Paper Mills	
Half-year ended	Dividend (% per annum)	Half-year ended	Dividend (% per annum)
31 Dec. 1929	20	31 Mar. 1930	40
30 June 1930	20	30 Sept. 1930	35
31 Dec. 1930	20	31 Mar. 1931	35
30 June 1931	20	30 Sept. 1931	35
31 Dec. 1931	20	31 Mar. 1932	35
30 June 1932	20	30 Sept. 1932	45
31 Dec. 1932	20	31 Mar. 1933	45
30 June 1933	20	30 Sept. 1933	45
31 Dec. 1933	20	31 Mar. 1934	45
30 June 1934	20	30 Sept. 1934	45
31 Dec. 1934	20	31 Mar. 1935	50
30 June 1935	25	30 Sept. 1935	55
31 Dec. 1935	25	31 Mar. 1936	55
30 June 1936	25	30 Sept. 1936	55
31 Dec. 1936	25	31 Mar. 1937	60
30 June 1937	29	30 Sept. 1937	$32\frac{1}{2}$
31 Dec. 1937	29	31 Mar. 1938	$32\frac{1}{8}$
30 June 1938	29	30 Sept. 1938	$32\frac{1}{8}$

Source: *IIYB* for the years 1931–2 to 1939–40.

were the leaders of the Indian market and they declared the dividends on ordinary capital during the relevant years shown in Table 13.5.

Another possible explanation might be that although the existing paper mills were highly profitable, they were faced with rather steeply increasing variable costs; this explanation might sound particularly plausible for Bengal Paper Mill, which had depended far more than Titaghur on pulp made from grass or on imported pulp. One would expect this to be reflected in the works costs of Bengal Paper. Our table of works costs of the different mills (Table 13.6) does not, however, bear this out. After the First World War, the Titaghur Paper Mills started with higher works costs than any of the other four mills, but it soon succeeded in bringing down its works costs below those of most other mills; the Bengal Paper Mill was slower in adapting its plant and processes, but it had managed to reduce its works costs below the level of those reached by Titaghur in 1930. This difference, however, should not be taken too seriously, for the Bengal Paper Mill typically produced a smaller percentage of the better varieties of paper than

TABLE 13.6 *Works costs of finished paper of Titaghur, Bengal, Deccan, India Paper Pulp and Upper India Couper Paper Mills, 1913 to 1936 (Rs. per ton)*

	Titaghur Paper Mills	Bengal Paper Mills	India Paper Pulp	Upper India Couper Paper	Deccan Paper
1913	261.121	243.84*	—	297.84*	350.54
1921	774.818	667.52	—	699.25	—
1922	689.232	588.05	—	621.38	—
1923	540.481	519.09	457.12	681.00	—
1924	431.065	—	457.63	507.36	307.1
1925	377.515	463.837	463.84	445.36	330.1
1926	387.409	401.389	419.32	421.82	320.6
1927	384.572	387.536	378.81	436.20	298.72
1928	367.084	358.321	346.03	410.72	328.7
1929	355.080	364.444	326.92	426.00	327.07
1930	360.075	350.827	330.65	417.54	—
1931	337.949	—	313.84	408.61	320.89
1932	316.203	—	317.38	477.01	321.87
1933	300.780	—	318.79	375.10	291.40
1934	296.647	—	302.19	382.09	283.97
1935	294.206	—	294.83	345.07	277.03
1936	292.459	243†	299.33	341.18	272.66

Sources: ITB: *Evidence (Report on paper and paper pulp)* (Calcutta, 1925), Vol. 1; ITB: *Evidence (Report on paper and paper pulp)* (Calcutta, 1932), Vol. 1; and ITB: *Evidence (Report on paper and paper pulp* (Delhi, 1939), Vol. 1.

N.B. For Titaghur Paper Mills, India Paper Pulp and Deccan Paper Mills, 1921 refers to 1921–2, 1922 refers to 1922–3 and so on. The works costs sometimes included depreciation, head office expenses, selling expenses, etc.; these have been eliminated as far as possible.

* 1914.

† ITB: *Evidence (Report on paper and paper pulp)* (Calcutta, 1939), Vol. 1, p. 274.

Titaghur.[38] Again, while Bengal Paper was hard hit by the new duty on imported pulp imposed in 1931, it managed to reduce its works costs drastically, primarily by finding new sources of *sabai* grass, and solving the problems of producing bamboo pulp.

Hence we find in the case of the two leaders a determination to retain their share of the Indian market by reducing the works costs as much as possible on the output of the existing, that is, mainly protected, varieties of paper, but an unwillingness to venture into new lines of production. The record of profitability of the two companies attracted the attention of Indian entrepreneurs who began to set up new units from 1936 onwards. Some of the new mills, such as Orient Paper Mills, and the paper mill unit of Rohtas Industries, were set up primarily to manufacture kraft paper, a type that was not covered by the scheme of protection, although there were high import duties on it.[39] But it was not only the high profits of existing mills and the existence of markets in the field of 'unprotected' varieties of paper which attracted new units: they were also attracted by the prospects of expanding demand for paper through the spread of education under the new provincial governments which began to operate in 1937.[40]

The years from 1936 onwards marked the entry into the industry of Indian businessmen with an adequate command over capital. The new units which they proposed to set up generally had a capacity of 6,000 tons or above (Shree Gopal Paper Mills had a capacity of 7,500 tons). The Orient Paper Mills were set up by the Birla group, Rohtas Industries were controlled by the Dalmia group, and Shree Gopal Paper Mills were set up by Karam Chand Thapar. All these groups would figure prominently in independent India, for their control over large sectors of industry and their high rates of expansion.[41]

In Table 13.7, the estimated works costs of the new units have been tabulated against their capacities. The Orient and Mysore Paper Mills appear to have the lowest works costs; Shree Gopal Paper Mills had taken

[38] ITB: *Evidence (Report on paper and paper pulp)* (Calcutta, 1939), Vol. I, pp. 120 and 247–8. Of the total production of paper, *badami* accounted for 8·28% in the case of Titaghur in 1936–7, and for 14·35% in the case of Bengal Paper over the years 1934–6. At the other end, while cream laid and woven and white printings accounted for more than two-thirds of the output of Titaghur, they made up only half of the output of Bengal Paper.

[39] *Ibid.*, pp. 323 and 346–7. Orient Paper Mills were going to produce kraft paper; the estimated landing price of kraft paper was Rs. 274 per ton; the duty in 1938 was Rs. 140 plus Rs. 35 (surcharge imposed in 1931)=Rs. 175 per ton. While the imports of kraft paper were 10,000 tons, the plant of Orient Paper Mills was designed to produce 6,000 tons. The plant could alternatively be used to produce white printing paper.

[40] See the evidence of Rohtas Industries in *ibid.*, p. 325.

[41] See Hazari: *The Corporate Private Sector in India*. Orient, Rohtas and Shree Gopal had reached the capacities of 31,000 tons, 16,000 tons and 15,000 tons respectively by December 1953, and had thus expanded at faster rates than the older Indian units. See Eddison, *Growth of the Pulp and Paper Industry in India*, p. 11, for the figures of capacity in December 1953.

TABLE 13.7 *Expected capacity and works costs of new units in the paper industry set up after 1937*

		Capacity (tons)		Block capital (Rs. million)	Works cost per ton (Rs.)	
		Pulp	Paper		Pulp	Paper
1.	Rohtas Industries	25 a day (17 from bamboo, rest grass)	20 a day (6,000 a year)	4·0	117 (all overheads shifted to paper)	337.0
2.	Orient Paper Mills		6,000 of kraft paper a year	4·8	n.a.	302·63
3.	Star Paper Mills, Saharanpur		6,000 per year (steam and power plant for 20,000 a year)	n.a.	n.a.	n.a.
4.	Shree Gopal Paper Mills		7,500 a year	3·3 (+ 0·08)	224·90	377·76
5.	Gujarat Paper Mills*		2,500 a year (not effective capacity)	0·3	n.a.	294·50
6.	Andhra Paper Mills,* Rajamundhry	3,000 from bamboo	3,000	1·4 (3·4 real expenditure)	n.a.	304·38
7.	Mysore Paper Mills	17 in 24 hours from bamboo	15 a day (4,500 a year)	3·4	n.a.	385·4 (total cost of bone dry paper)

Source: ITB: *Evidence (Report on paper and paper pulp)* (Delhi, 1939), Vol. I.
* Both Gujarat and Andhra Paper Mills were established before 1937, Andhra had not produced any paper from 1931 to 1937. It was expected to start again in 1938. Gujarat had operated only a rag plant since May 1935, producing 758 tons of paper during 1936–7. Its projected capacity of 2,500 tons of paper had not yet been erected although some of the machinery had been bought. See ITB: *Evidence (Report on paper and paper pulp)* (Delhi, 1939), Vol. I, p. 527.

over the mills of Punjab Paper Mills, which had an old plant, and also had to bring its grass from a considerable distance and at a higher price than other mills, since it had lost to Star Paper Mills the control of the areas producing *sabai* grass in the Western Circle[42] of the United Provinces. But this disadvantage of high works costs was partially outweighed by the low cost of the fixed capital.[43] The works costs of Gujarat Paper Mills were lower

[42] A rough territorial division used by forestry officials and paper manufacturers.
[43] ITB: *Evidence (Report on paper and paper pulp)* (Delhi, 1939), Vol. I, pp. 431–60, for the written and oral evidence of Shree Gopal Paper Mills. See also Eddison, *Growth of the Pulp and Paper Industry in India*, pp. 226–8.

than those of other new mills but this estimate should not be taken too seriously, for it was only working a small rag pulp unit at the time of the Tariff Board enquiry.[44] The Andhra Paper Mills had been reconstructed in 1938. It had not worked from 1931 to 1937. Mysore Paper Mills were aided substantially by the Government of Mysore: the latter contributed part of the capital as shareholders,[45] and undertook to supply bamboo at the cheap rate of Rs. 12 per ton delivered at the mill sidings.[46] It was also in the natural course of events an important customer for the output of the paper mills. But since the demand for paper was expected to fall short of the capacity of 17 tons per day, it was proposed to sell 2 tons of pulp outside.[47]

The works costs of the older units cannot be compared directly with those of the new units because of the enormous variation in the qualities of paper: the proportion of common *badami* to total output in 1936–7 was 45·35% in the case of Deccan Paper Mills and only 8·28% in the case of Titaghur Paper Mills.[48] (The reduction in the works costs of Deccan Paper Mills over the years from 1931 to 1936 was accompanied by a rise in the proportion of *badami* to total output from 39·40% in 1931–2 to 45·35% in 1936–7.) But judging roughly, the product-mix which the bigger of the new mills proposed to manufacture would not be inferior to the product-mix of the Bengal Paper Mill: it appears then that the bigger new units (with the exception of Shree Gopal) would have works costs which were fairly comparable with those of India Paper Pulp and Titaghur, but definitely lower than those of Upper India Couper Paper Mills and Deccan Paper Mills (after allowing for the low quality of the paper produced on the average by the latter mills).[49]

Around 1937, there also took place that development of chemical industries ancillary to the paper industry which Cogswell, in his survey of the Indian paper industry in 1919, had considered essential.[50] In the north, Imperial Chemical Industries proposed to set up a plant to manufacture chlorine and caustic soda;[51] in the south, Mysore Chemicals and Fertilizers

[44] ITB: *Evidence (Report on paper and paper pulp)* (Delhi, 1939), Vol. I, pp. 527–53.
[45] R. Balakrishna: *Industrial Development of Mysore* (Bangalore City, 1940), p. 210.
[46] ITB: *Evidence (Report on paper and paper pulp)* (Delhi, 1939), Vol. I, p. 584.
[47] Balakrishna: *Industrial Development of Mysore*, p. 92.
[48] ITB: *Evidence (Report on paper and paper pulp)* (Delhi, 1939), Vol. I, pp. 463 and 120 respectively.
[49] Andhra Paper Mills, Upper India Couper Mills, Deccan Paper Mills and Gujarat Paper Mills failed to expand between 1938 and 1953. See Eddison, *Growth of the Pulp and Paper Industry in India*, p. 11.
[50] Cogswell: 'Paper Making in India', pp. 246–53.
[51] ITB: *Evidence (Report on paper and paper pulp)* (Delhi, 1939), Vol. I, p. 420. The Star Paper Mills, which had planned to set up an electrolytic bleaching plant, held off after they learned about ICI's plans. Actual production by the subsidiary of ICI, the Alkali and Chemical Corporation of India Limited (with a plant at Rishra near Calcutta), began in April 1940. See ITB: *Report on the Caustic Soda and Bleaching Powder Industry* (Bombay, 1946), p. 4.

Ltd was set up in 1937 with financial participation by the Government of Mysore as a shareholder. This plant was expected to produce Glauber's salt and titanium dioxide, which were used by the paper mill.[52] In 1936, the Mettur Chemical and Industrial Corporation was floated, and it obtained a plant for the manufacture of caustic soda by the electrolytic process. This plant went into production around the middle of 1941.[53] Although the consumption of chemicals by the paper mills probably did not provide the main market for these chemical plants, it must have played an important role in the decision to invest in these industries.

The new paper mills which were set up around 1938 naturally provided increased competition for the existing Indian mills and the prices of paper went down during 1938–9. This fall in price was also partly the result of increased foreign competition in paper. The reduction in prices was accentuated by the further increase in production and the effective reduction in the rates of protective duty on imported pulp and paper from 1 April 1939. The prices reached just before the outbreak of the Second World War in September 1939 were said to be the lowest for several years.

The ITB, in its report on the pulp and paper industry, submitted in 1938, recommended some protection for the grass-pulp industry as well as for the bamboo-pulp industry, although on an average grass pulp cost decidedly more (Rs. 173 per ton) than bamboo pulp (Rs. 144 per ton). Since the cost of imported pulp was Rs. 126 per ton, the duty required for bamboo pulp would be Rs. 18 per ton and for grass pulp Rs. 47 per ton. Ultimately a duty of Rs. 30 per ton, or 25% *ad valorem*, whichever was higher, was imposed on imported wood-pulp.

On paper the rate of duty recommended by the ITB was 11 pies per lb., this being the difference between the import price of Rs. 133 per ton and the fair selling price of Rs. 381 per ton calculated by the ITB. The Government of India pointed out an element of double-counting (amounting to Rs. 32 per ton) in the calculations of the Tariff Board and reduced the duty to 9 pies per lb. on imported paper. In order that this duty should not be too low for certain expensive kinds of paper, an alternative duty of 25% *ad valorem* was applied to them. The period of protection was reduced from seven to three years.[54]

The growth in investment in the paper industry over the years from 1931 to 1939 can be broken down into three components: (a) the investments by

[52] ITB: *Evidence (Report on paper and paper pulp)* (Calcutta, 1939), Vol. 1, p. 588; see also Baldwin: *Industrial Growth in South India*, pp. 87–93, particularly for the markets of Mysore Chemicals and Fertilizers and for its relations with the government.

[53] ITB: *Report on the Caustic Soda and Bleaching Powder Industry* (Bombay, 1946), p. 4.

[54] ITB: *Report on paper and paper pulp* (Delhi, 1938); Adarkar [IPG pub.]: *The History of the Indian Tariff*, pp. 53–5; Gov. India, CISD: *Review of the trade of India in 1938–39* (Delhi, 1939), pp. 52–5, and *Review of the trade of India in 1939–40* (Delhi, 1940), pp. 71–4.

existing firms for changing over from imported pulp to bamboo pulp or grass pulp; (b) the investments by existing firms for extending production so as to retain the share of the market in the protected varieties of paper; (c) investments by new firms for capturing the expanding domestic market in paper, both of protected and of 'unprotected' varieties. The first and third elements seem to have been the most important.

The paper industry illustrates the importance of the emergence of new entrepreneurial groups for industrial investment; in this case the rise of the new groups was probably intimately connected with the rise of provincial autonomy and the passing of political power in the provinces into Indian hands.

13.5   DEMAND, PRODUCTION, AND INVESTMENT IN THE
PAPER INDUSTRY

The paper industry typically produced a large number of varieties of paper; some of these varieties – such as newsprint – could not be produced in India without direct governmental help, and some could not be produced without a much higher degree of protection than the ITB was prepared to recommend or the Government of India to grant in 1925. Hence one must be careful to define the conditions assumed in order meaningfully to estimate the extent of the potential market for Indian-produced paper. The ITB in its estimates compared the Indian output of paper with either the imports of the 'protected' varieties of paper or total imports of paper and pasteboard.[55] Neither of these two latter quantities would indicate the true potential demand for the industry under the prevailing conditions: on the one hand, the imports of 'protected' varieties of paper could and did vary with the degree of protection afforded; on the other hand, there were, as has already been pointed out, some varieties of paper which could probably be produced only by a government enterprise or by a larger private firm receiving massive government aid in the form of bounties, loans or guarantees. Again, the ITB of 1938 took the total imports of 'paper including boards but excluding old newspapers, other kinds of paper and newsprinting paper' as the standard of comparison.[56] This standard leaves out too much; for many of the varieties of 'other kinds of paper' could be and were being produced in Indian mills. While the total quantity of paper and the major types of paper that could be produced in a mill were fixed, the quantities of different types of paper could be varied within limits by using different types of raw materials and by adopting different finishing methods.[57]

[55] See, for example, ITB: *Report on paper and paper pulp* (Calcutta, 1931), pp. 6–7.
[56] ITB: *Report on paper and paper pulp* (Delhi, 1938), pp. 7–9.
[57] See for example the plans of the Orient Paper Mills, as summarized in *ibid.*, p. 58: 'The company is itself not certain of success in the manufacture of Kraft paper and has so arranged its purchase of plant that, if the manufacture of Kraft paper is a failure, the manufacture of ordinary paper can be substituted.'

Hence we have defined a category – competitive imports of paper – consisting of imports of packing paper, writing paper, printing paper and envelopes excluding newsprint, other kinds of paper excluding old newspapers and paper manufactures and, finally, including imports on government account. The quantities and values of imports of this category can

TABLE 13.8 *Quantities of imports of paper into India, 1923–4 to 1939–40 (figures in tons)*

	Total imports of paper into India excluding Burma* (1)	Competitive imports of paper into India† (2)	Private imports of 'protected' paper into India† (3)
1923–4	35,611.1	27,540.3	—
1924–5	45,415.3	30,140.3	20,000
1925–6	44,115.2	33,092.7	17,000
1926–7	51,754.6	33,653.0	16,826
1927–8	45,921.1	38,198.1	18,090
1928–9	59,382.5	45,546.6	19,065
1929–30	69,151.0	48,959.0	20,093
1930–1	55,369.9	37,606.2	14,179
1931–2	51,415.1	34,085.6	12,393
1932–3	59,958.2	40,057.5	11,490
1933–4	61,065.5	38,366.3	13,005
1934–5	63,950.8	38,698.9	11,163
1935–6	79,945.2	47,891.0	12,096
1936–7	76,451.0	45,492.2	11,840
1937–8	102,542.3	58,003.0	14,780
1938–9	79,727.7	46,375.6	13,471
1939–40	76,619.5	42,806.5	17,519

Sources: For columns (1) and (2), Gov. India, CISD: *Annual statement of the seaborne trade of British India* for the relevant years (Calcutta, annual); for column (3), ITB: *Report on paper and paper pulp* (Calcutta, 1931), pp. 6–7, ITB: *Report on paper and paper pulp* (Delhi, 1938), p. 8, and Gov. India, CISD: *Annual statement of the seaborne trade of British India* for the relevant years (Calcutta, annual).

* Total imports of paper excludes import of old newspapers.

† Includes Burma up to and including 1936–7.

Notes: The table begins with 1923–4, for before that year the figures for quantities of writing paper imported on government account are not available; and before 1921–2, the figures for quantities of writing paper imported on private account were not available either. The figures of competitive imports have been computed for the years 1923–4 to 1934–5 by taking the figures of total imports of paper on private and government account, and subtracting the figures of imports of old newspapers, paper manufactures and newsprint. Since newsprint was not separately classified after 1934–5, the figures of imports of newsprint have had to be estimated from the figures of printing paper. This was done by taking the average ratio of figures of imports of newsprint to those of printing paper for the three years from 1932–3 to 1934–5, which came to 0.69, and applying it to total imports of printing paper for the corresponding years. Since there was an upward trend in the ratio of quantities (and value) of imports of newsprint to those of printing paper (from 1923–4 to 1934–5), this may lead to underestimation of the imports of newsprint.

TABLE 13.9 *Values of imports of paper into India, 1912–13 to 1939–40 (figures in Rs.)*

	Competitive imports of paper into India including Burma (1)	Total private imports of paper into India excluding Burma (2)	Total government imports of paper into India excluding Burma (3)	Total imports of paper into India excluding Burma (4)=(2)+(3)
1912–13	8,825,748	10,422,615	430,590	10,853,205
1913–14	10,028,930	11,521,815	637,980	12,159,795
1914–15	7,912,154	9,011,130	451,320	9,462,450
1915–16	8,797,769	10,305,075	458,295	10,763,370
1916–17	14,403,326	17,478,705	598,260	18,076,965
1917–18	12,616,675	15,736,695	850,980	16,587,675
1918–19	14,945,603	18,770,850	797,070	19,567,920
1919–20	13,339,990	15,075,533	933,160	16,008,693
1920–1	47,241,590	55,638,324	963,030	56,601,354
1921–2	14,844,420	15,195,976	2,153,569	17,349,545
1922–3	17,816,971	20,092,564	899,464	20,992,028
1923–4	17,083,201	18,749,276	1,064,402	19,813,678
1924–5	17,376,005	21,498,357	514,056	22,012,413
1925–6	17,712,688	19,472,314	1,379,233	20,851,547
1926–7	17,733,072	22,101,869	1,337,013	23,438,882
1927–8	19,675,733	21,266,048	1,699,911	22,925,959
1928–9	22,230,495	23,611,777	2,224,561	25,836,338
1929–30	23,791,482	26,724,895	2,540,765	29,265,660
1930–1	18,047,740	20,470,794	2,216,279	22,687,073
1931–2	14,793,043	17,542,051	1,231,713	18,773,764
1932–3	15,425,433	19,196,806	558,430	19,755,236
1933–4	14,179,273	18,140,224	607,656	18,747,880
1934–5	14,115,960	18,022,374	902,478	18,924,851
1935–6	16,030,222	20,668,426	1,130,892	21,799,318
1936–7	14,732,548	19,246,352	881,847	20,128,199
1937–8	22,465,283	31,209,235	1,410,649	32,619,884
1938–9	17,928,122	23,976,087	989,822	24,965,909
1939–40	18,780,163	25,109,467	1,188,086	26,297,553

Source: Gov. India, CISD: *Annual statement of the seaborne trade of British India* for the relevant years (Calcutta, annual).

Notes: In arriving at values of competitive imports, values of private imports of packing paper; writing paper and envelopes; printing paper, excluding newsprint; and other kinds of paper, excluding old newspapers and paper manufactures, were added to the values of government imports of paper. The series begins in 1912–13 mainly because before that date packing paper was not separately classified. For the years from 1923–4 to 1934–5 the imports of newsprint, old newspapers and paper manufactures (which form the main items of non-competitive imports) were separately classified. But newsprint ceased to be separately classified from 1935–6 onwards; paper manufactures were classified only from 1918–19 onwards and old newspapers and newsprint were separately classified only from 1923–4 onwards. Hence the imports of these items were estimated for the years for which they were not separately classified. First, estimates of imports of newsprint: the average ratios of values of imports of newsprint to total imports of newsprint were estimated for each of two three-year periods 1923–6 and 1932–5; these came to 0.42 and 0.57 respectively. The former ratio was used to estimate the imports of newsprint for the years up to 1922–3 and the latter ratio was used to estimate the imports of newsprint after 1934–5. The average ratio of imports of other kinds of paper to imports of other kinds of paper plus imports of old newspapers, and the average ratio of imports of other kinds of paper to imports of other kinds of paper plus imports of old newspapers plus imports of paper manufactures, were computed for the years from 1923–4 to 1925–6: these ratios came to 0.40 and 0.30 respectively. The former ratio (0.40) was used to estimate competitive imports of other kinds of paper for the years 1918–23 (when paper manufactures were separately classified), and the latter ratio (0.30) was used to estimate competitive imports of other kinds of paper for the period 1912–18 (when both old newspapers and paper manufactures were included in other kinds of paper).

Our methods almost certainly lead to an overestimation of imports of non-competitive varieties of paper and hence an underestimation of imports of competitive types of paper up to 1922–3.

In the first place, because of the exemption of paper containing a high ratio of mechanical pulp and some initial confusion in the classification of paper for tariff purposes, a considerable amount of competitive paper could be imported duty-free as newsprint; hence at least up to 1927 there were excess imports of newsprint. There is also a rising trend in the ratio of the value of imports of newsprint to the value of imports of printing paper from 1923–4 to 1934–5. Hence, by applying the ratio of imports of newsprint to the imports of printing paper for 1923–6, we overestimate the imports of newsprint during the earlier years. Apart from the exemption of paper containing mechanical pulp, because of the selective taxation of imports of paper after 1925, a considerable degree of substitution took place between protected varieties and unprotected varieties, which were mainly subsumed under 'other kinds of paper'. This would also tend to increase the importance of 'other kinds of paper' immediately after protection was introduced, and to lead to some underestimation because of the years we have chosen as the base for comparison. Rough checks (such as extending the period over which the ratio of imports of other kinds of paper to imports of paper of all kinds is computed and taking account of the time trend in the ratio of newsprint imports to total imports of printing paper) indicate that the degree of underestimation is between 5% and 10% of the estimated value of competitive imports.

In arriving at the values of total imports of paper into India excluding Burma on private account, we subtracted the values of old newspapers. To arrive at the values of old newspapers before 1923–4, we took the average ratio of the values of old newspapers to other kinds of paper, including old newspapers and paper manufactures, for the years from 1923–4 to 1925–6 and used it as the multiplier (0·44) for the total values of imports of other kinds of paper from 1912–13 to 1922–3.

be obtained directly from the *Annual statements of seaborne trade*[58] only for the years from 1923–4 to 1934–5, but the values can be estimated, under certain assumptions, for earlier years also. For the purposes of construction of this series Burma is included, since up to 1936–7 the same protective duties applied also to Burma. In order to estimate the total consumption of paper (excluding pasteboard, millboard, etc.) in India, we have taken the total imports of paper and subtracted the imports of old newspapers. The results are given in Tables 13.8 and 13.9.

We can see from Tables 13.8 and 13.9 that whereas the quantity of output of Indian mills increased by 57% between 1923 and 1929, between 1923–4 and 1929–30 the quantities of competitive imports of paper and of total imports of paper (excluding old newspapers) increased by 78% and 94% respectively. There may have been some substitution between imports of competitive paper and imports of other kinds of paper (especially those

[58] Gov. India, CISD: *Annual statements of the seaborne trade of British India*, for the relevant years (Calcutta).

containing a high percentage of mechanical pulp, which often passed as newsprint). Hence some paper not included in our category of competitive imports may have been in effect competitive with Indian paper. If we compare the increases in values (see Table 13.9) we find that while the value of output produced in Indian paper mills increased by 33% between 1923 and 1929, the values of competitive imports and of total imports each increased by 48% between 1923–4 and 1929–30. Thus it is clear that the output of Indian mills was not keeping pace with either the total consumption of competitive varieties of paper in India including Burma or the total consumption of all kinds of paper in India excluding Burma. Furthermore, the average price of competitive imports of paper fell in relation to the average price of Indian-produced paper over the years 1923–9, and the average price of all kinds of paper fell in relation to the average price of both competitive imports of paper and, even more, Indian mill-produced paper. This development was at least partly the result of the policy of selective protection recommended by the ITB and adopted by the Government of India.

The ITB in its 1925 Report was quite discouraging about the prospects for development of the industry. After casting doubt on the ability of Indian mills to manufacture either high-quality or low-quality papers, the ITB estimated that the additional demand the Indian mills could conceivably capture under a protective system was 20,000 tons. The Report went on: 'If our estimate is a reasonable one, it is clear that no great expansion of the paper industry is possible in the near future.'[59] It also predicted that the increase of the protective duties to Rs. 140 a ton of paper would not encourage 'indiscriminate investment in new paper-making enterprises', for the reason that

the protection we have proposed falls greatly short of the amount required to make paper-making in India profitable under present conditions. It is possible, however, that the duties may facilitate the raising of capital by the Punjab Paper Mills Company for their projected mill near Saharanpur, and also perhaps by others for the manufacture of bamboo pulp near Cuttack. If this came about, there would be no cause for regret, for the natural conditions are apparently more favourable to cheap production in these two places than anywhere else in India.[60]

The predictions of the ITB turned out to be remarkably accurate – particularly its more negative forecasts (which goes to show that it is much easier to predict slow growth in a slow-growing economy than to predict spurts of growth in it!). The Punjab Paper Mills Company did not start working until 1929 and then it closed down after only nine months for lack of adequate finance. The Andhra Paper Mills at Rajahmundhry which had

[59] ITB: *Report on paper and paper pulp* (Calcutta, 1925), p. 15.
[60] *Ibid.*, p. 101.

TABLE 13.10 *Imports of paper-mill machinery into India, 1920–1 to 1938–9*

Year	Value of imports of paper-mill machinery into India excluding Burma (Rs. '000) (1)	Price per ton of paper-making machinery exported from the U.K. to British India (£) (2)	Three-year moving average of price of paper-making machinery (£) (3)	Index numbers of prices of paper-making machinery average (1920–3= 100.00) (4)	Value of paper-mill machinery imported into India at constant prices (Rs. '000) (5)
1920–1	1,293	261.26	—	—	—
1921–2	2,228	185.20	208.95	100.00	2,228
1922–3	1,394	180.38	170.86	81.77	1,705
1923–4	616	146.99	212.25	101.58	607
1924–5	721	308.39	227.80	109.02	662
1925–6	331	227.02	214.13	102.48	323
1926–7	669	105.98	139.67	66.84	1,002
1927–8	943	86.01	101.56	48.60	1,941
1928–9	3,460	112.69	115.33	55.20	6,268
1929–30	686	147.30	123.76	59.23	1,159
1930–1	732	111.29	119.22	57.06	1,283
1931–2	632	99.06	135.29	64.75	977
1932–3	531	195.53	131.11	62.75	847
1933–4	1,103	98.75	124.75	59.70	1,847
1934–5	897	179.96	121.11	57.96	1,547
1935–6	806	84.61	134.73	64.48	1,250
1936–7	785	139.61	105.66	50.57	1,553
1937–8	4,489	92.75	112.28	53.74	8,354
1938–9	2,767	104.49	117.04	56.01	4,939

Sources: Column (1), Gov. India, CISD: *Annual statement of the seaborne trade of British India* for the relevant years (Calcutta, annual), Vol. I; column (2), *Annual statement of the foreign trade of the U.K.*, Vol. III.

Notes: (1) Exports of paper-making machinery to Burma from the U.K. were not shown separately in the accounts until 1937; the actual exports of paper-making machinery to Burma were nil or negligible during the years 1937–9. There is also no reason to believe that the prices of paper-making machinery exported to Burma and to the rest of British India would be systematically different.

(2) For the years from 1936 to 1939, the values and quantities of exports of paper-machine (Fourdrinier) wires are separately shown in the accounts. They have been merged with the values and quantities of other paper-making machinery and the average prices have been derived on that basis in order to preserve continuity with the earlier years.

(3) The figures of U.K. exports relate to calendar years; in the above table it has been assumed that the figure for 1920 is applicable to the financial year April 1920 to 31 March 1921, and similarly for figures relating to other years.

been partially constructed in 1924 worked only fitfully.[61] It was not until 1938 that the Orient Paper Mills was set up to exploit the bamboo resources of Orissa. The failure of the Government of India to grant tariff protection

[61] ITB: *Report on paper and paper pulp* (Calcutta, 1931), pp. 7–8.

for the manufacture of indigenous pulp or to aid the manufacture of paper from bamboo through subsidies also led to an increasing import of wood-pulp into India.

How were these developments reflected in the imports of paper-mill machinery? Table 13.10 provides a partial answer. As can easily be seen from the table, the price of paper-mill machinery by weight fluctuated widely from year to year, and smoothing the series by taking three-year moving averages still leaves a large amount of variation. Furthermore, imports of paper-mill machinery were very diverse in character, particularly when mills were moving from the use of *sabai* grass to the use of imported wood-pulp and back (after 1931) to the use of grass and bamboo, and when the use of bamboo required new types of equipment.[62] However, it is of some comfort to notice that the peaks in imports of paper-mill machinery at 'constant prices' coincide with peaks in imports of paper-mill machinery at current prices: a small peak in 1921–2 is followed by a larger peak in 1928–9 and by a still larger one in 1937–8; and in 1938–9 the value of imports of paper-mill machinery exceeds the value in any other year except 1928–9 and 1937–8. Our qualitative analysis in the earlier sections is consistent with this finding; the only surprising feature is perhaps the spurt in imports of paper-mill machinery in 1928–9: the explanation seems to lie in (a) the reasonable profits made by the leading paper companies after 1925–6,[63] which allowed them to experiment with the manufacture of bamboo as a preliminary to expansion of capacity, (b) the new investment made by the Punjab Paper Mills and (c) the attempt of the Andhra Paper Mills to adapt their plant, which had originally been designed for the manufacture of kraft and similar papers from straw, to the manufacture of paper from bamboo.[64]

The developments after 1931 have already been described in earlier sections. It will be noticed (see Tables 13.8, 13.9 and 13.11) that the growth of imports during the period from 1931 to 1937 was not more rapid than that of output of Indian mills, either by weight or by value. Furthermore, the quantity of imported pulp used in Indian mills decreased noticeably. Hence tariff protection on paper at the higher rates of 1931, combined with protection of indigenous pulp manufacture, was successful in the limited sense of checking the growth of imports. But massive investment in the paper industry had to wait for the revival of world trade and Indian industrial production, and the granting of provincial autonomy, which led

---

[62] See Table 13.3 for the changes in the proportions of indigenous and imported materials used for the production of paper from 1931–2 to 1936–7. The proportion of bamboo pulp to the total amount of indigenous pulp used increased from an average of 13% over the period from 1924–5 to 1930–1, to 30% in 1931–2 and 55% in 1936–7. See ITB: *Report on paper and paper pulp* (Calcutta, 1931), p. 14 and Table 13.4 on p. 404 above.

[63] ITB: *Report on paper and paper pulp* (Calcutta, 1931), pp. 22–3.

[64] *Ibid.*, pp. 9–10.

TABLE 13.11   *Quantity and value of output of paper mills in India, 1900 to 1939*

Year	Quantity (tons)	Value (Rs.)	Year	Quantity (tons)	Value (Rs.)
1900	20,509	6,251,748	1920	29,363	22,275,902
1901	20,854	6,583,724	1921	28,689	23,069,996
1902	20,828	6,438,319	1922	23,928	15,047,456
1903	19,479	5,914,799	1923	25,970	14,056,801
1904	20,133	6,149,446	1924	25,670	13,612,912
1905	19,708	5,186,729	1925	28,596	14,173,747
1906	21,198	6,310,940	1926	32,144	15,830,192
1907	24,650	7,290,385	1927	33,943	16,498,612
1908	25,369	7,587,267	1928	38,142	18,233,767
1909	25,409	7,911,943	1929	40,787	18,700,984
1910	26,340	8,151,537	1930	39,817	17,431,266
1911	26,500	8,004,482	1931	40,714	18,549,492
1912	26,900	7,706,000	1932	40,606	18,809,244
1913	27,100	8,037,000	1933	43,443	18,026,907
1914	28,700	8,212,000	1934	44,505	17,201,821
1915	30,400	8,962,000	1935	47,619	19,064,708
1916	31,922	12,485,000	1936	48,486	19,302,356
1917	31,900	18,786,000	1937	57,050	24,931,461
1918	31,400	21,118,000	1938	60,803	24,777,237
1919	30,900	20,943,000	1939	73,138	31,132,526

Source: Gov. India, CISD: *Statistics of British India* [later, *Statistical abstracts for British India*] for the relevant years (Calcutta, annual).

to a greater volume of demand for paper for educational purposes and the entry of Indian entrepreneurial groups with a sufficient financial strength into the industry. As has already been noted, many of the new units were set up to produce varieties of paper which had not previously enjoyed tariff protection. For example, the imports of kraft paper increased from 9,544 tons in 1935–6 (when they were first classified separately) to 13,805 tons in 1937–8; the Orient Paper Mills was planning to produce 6,000 tons and applied for tariff protection on kraft paper.[65] The ITB refused to recommend tariff protection for kraft paper (preferential revenue duties were already being imposed on imports of kraft paper) on the ground that they were not satisfied that the paper could be manufactured 'in a satisfactory quality at a reasonable price'.[66] The Government of India in its resolution concurred in this. But some of the problems arising from the policies pursued by the government were solved by the coming of the Second World War.

In Chapter 1 the hypothesis was advanced that the level of investment in a particular industry was proportional to the difference between the desired

[65] ITB: *Evidence (Report on paper and paper pulp)* (Delhi, 1939), Vol. I, p. 342.
[66] ITB: *Report on paper and paper pulp* (Delhi, 1938), pp. 58–9.

capital stock and the actual capital stock. How does that hypothesis perform in explaining investment behaviour in the paper industry? If we take the desired capital stock to be given by the total Indian consumption of paper multiplied by the marginal capital – output ratio for the paper industry, then the hypothesis does not stand up very well. There were long intervals over which the total output of paper in India was not expanding faster than total Indian consumption, and the year-to-year variations in investment did not follow a simple pattern such as that shown in Figure 1.1 above (see Table 13.10, columns (1) and (5)). Several complications have to be introduced into our simple hypothesis in order to convert it into something like a complete explanation.

First, the paper industry is an essentially multi-product industry. Even before the First World War, Indian mills were supplying the major portion of some varieties (mainly the simpler ones, neither too fine nor too specialized) of paper. When tariff protection for Indian paper was introduced, it at first covered only a part of the spectrum of qualities of paper consumed in India, and left a number of loopholes through which qualities of paper which were meant to be protected could still be imported into India after paying only the revenue duties. This meant that (a) for the purpose of computing the 'desired' capital stock in the Indian paper industry, only a part of the total Indian consumption of paper could be considered; and that (b) the size of the desired capital stock would be smaller than that which could be computed on the basis of the pre-protection consumption of protected varieties of paper, since unprotected varieties would be substituted for protected varieties and since many varieties of imported paper would slip into the category of 'unprotected' varieties.

Similarly, because of economies of scale and indivisibilities, a paper mill had to reach a rather large size (by Indian standards) before it could break even. For example, all the mills set up after 1937 had block capital exceeding Rs. 3 million (see Table 13.7). Hence some lumpiness in the flow of investment was to be expected. Since older (British-managed) paper mills would not venture into the manufacture of new (mainly unprotected) varieties of paper, it was left to Indian entrepreneurs to do so. These entrepreneurs, however, waited for a suitable opportunity (in the form of a recovery of economic activity after the depression of the thirties and the spread of education under popularly-elected provincial governments) before undertaking investment. This factor accentuated the peak of 1937–8 (see Table 13.10).

Finally, the profile of investment was also influenced by the technical changes taking place in the paper industry. Indian timber resources were poor from the point of view of developing a low-cost wood-pulp industry. Further, the paper industry was relatively capital-intensive, and characterized by rather inflexible combinations of inputs. Hence Indian producers could not respond to the threat of cheaper wood-pulp and paper imports from Europe either by producing wood-pulp cheaply in India, or by extensive substitution of labour for capital (or chemicals) in the manufacture of paper. Moreover, in the twenties, the major indigenous material for the production of paper – *sabai* grass – was in short supply in relation to the level of demand likely if import substitution were to be carried through fully in the industry. The development of the bamboo pulping process was the Indian producers' answer, and this development in turn affected the profile of investment in the paper industry.

Despite all these qualifications, our hypothesis that investment in the paper industry was primarily determined by the difference between domestic consumption and domestic production is valid if we take a long view. An early attempt at import substitution in the industry was choked off before the First World War by the rapid progress of the wood-pulping process in Europe. The process of import substitution was set going again in the middle of the 1920s when protective duties were imposed on imports of some varieties of paper. It was held up for a time by the inadequate coverage of the protective duties, the conservative attitude of the leading, British-controlled, firms in the paper industry, and the difficulty of augmenting the supplies of domestic materials for the manufacture of paper. All these difficulties were overcome as soon as tariff protection against imports of major varieties of paper and paper pulp was introduced. The bamboo-pulping process, although theoretically known for a long time, was actually developed for manufacturing purposes after tariff protection had become effective. This new technology was mainly embodied in the new mills, but it was also adopted by the older mills in response to the rise in the costs of grass or rag pulp. Indian entrepreneurs stepped into the shoes of the British entrepreneurs when the latter were not prepared to supply the existing Indian markets in protected and unprotected paper to the full. Thus it was the pull of Indian demand for paper which was responsible in the long run for the growth of capital in the industry. That this growth was not very fast was due to the basically stagnant nature of the economy and society as a whole

14

BRITISH IMPERIAL POLICY AND THE SPREAD OF MODERN INDUSTRY IN INDIA

14.1 PRIORITIES OF THE IMPERIAL ORDER

India was the richest prize of the era of colonialism and the British held on to her well beyond the age of imperialism, in which Britain ceased effectively to be the leader of world capitalism. India occupied a special position in the British imperial order, and much of Britain's long-term policy with regard to India in the period covered in this book can be explained in terms of an effort to keep her in such a position. Up to 1914, India formed the biggest single foreign market for traditional British exports – particularly for cotton textiles, but to a lesser extent for engineering goods; India's exports to hard currency areas provided the critical balancing item in the current balance of payments of the British Empire and more particularly, of Britain, with the rest of the world;[1] the payments for 'home charges', the profits on capital accumulated in India by British nationals and the payments for the financing and transport of Indian exports and imports served as the mechanism for the transfer of the surplus from India to Britain. India was useful less as a field for the reinvestment of profits made by British nationals elsewhere than as the dependable source from which part of the needed surplus for maintaining the British-controlled gold standard and the political apparatus of *Pax Britannica* was derived.

This special position of India was maintained by a policy of exclusiveness which has often escaped the notice of economic historians marvelling at the policy of free trade pursued by Britain in India. As Maurice Dobb has noticed, 'the aphorism that "Trade Follows the Flag" embodies the essential truth that a significant aspect of the rôle of colonies in international economics is that they constitute in large part "private markets" for the interests of the national group which controls them, even where the policy of the "Open Door" prevails'.[2] Exports by other manufacturing nations to India were discouraged by government policy; government patronage was extended almost exclusively to British manufacturers alone; imports of non-British manufacturers were probably even more effectively discouraged by

---

[1] See Chapter 2 above and the references to A. E. Kahn's book in the later sections of this chapter.

[2] Maurice Dobb: *Political Economy and Capitalism: some Essays in Economic Tradition* (London, 1940), Chapter VII, p. 240.

the prevailing ethos. Most of the British civil servants, bankers, and merchants were convinced of the superiority of British goods over others.

In order to preserve India's usefulness as a source of scarce foreign currency for the British Empire and lend credence to the professed policy of free trade, India, alone among the bigger colonies of Britain (excluding of course, the colonies of black Africa), was prevented from adopting the policies of state patronage for industry (including tariff protection against imported goods) which helped to industrialize Canada, Australia and South Africa.[3] One consequence of this policy was that, while the so-called 'new' colonies of Canada, Australia and South Africa normally had an import surplus with Great Britain, India always had an export surplus with Britain.[4] The further ironical consequence was that these new colonies, as they grew richer, attracted British capital from abroad, whereas most of the foreign investment in India (with the possible exception of investment in railways) consisted of reinvestment of part of the profits made or salaries earned by Europeans in India.[5]

This 'Open Door' policy in India was buttressed by an ideology which had implicitly or explicitly racialist overtones. Indians were excluded from most 'positions of profit' by government policy, private business practices, or prejudice that transcended official or non-official instructions, so that the last large field of 'free and profitable employment' of Britons outside Britain could not be entered by indigenous Indians.[6]

Naturally the economic policy of the Government of India, throughout the period from 1900 to 1939, remained geared to the purpose of preserving the British imperial order. The top priority was attached to the maintenance of stability in the imperial system: the interests of individual industries in Great Britain or of British industrialists in India were subordinated to that overriding objective. As a concrete example of how this priority system worked, let us take the case of the extension of the railway system in India at the end of the nineteenth century. It was believed in Britain that a more

[3] See, e.g. H. G. J. Aitken (ed.): *The State and Economic Growth* (Social Science Research Council, New York, 1959), Chapters 2 and 3 for an account of the role of the state in the economic growth of Australia and Canada.

[4] For evidence that British merchants and policy-makers were aware of this fact see Sir Charles H. Armstrong, late Chairman of the Bombay Chamber of Commerce: 'Indian Trade and the War', *JRSA*, LXIII, No. 3263, 28 May 1915, pp. 645–7; and D. T. Chadwick: 'The Trade of India with Russia, France and Italy', *JRSA*, LXVI, No. 3397, 28 December 1917, pp. 96–107.

[5] Professor Nurkse had already noticed the fact that most British investment flowed to temperate lands in his article 'The Problem of International Investment Today in the Light of Nineteenth Century Experience', *Economic Journal*, LXIV (December 1954), p. 750; Matthew Simon provided detailed confirmation of this rough guess in his paper 'The Pattern of New British Portfolio Investment 1865–1914' in J. H. Adler (ed.): *Capital Movements and Economic Development* (London, 1967), pp. 33–66.

[6] Cf. J. M. Maclean: 'India's Place in an Imperial Federation', *JSA*, LII, No. 2665, 18 December 1903, pp. 81–90. For evidence of racial prejudice working against technically trained Indians, see Chapters 5 and 6 above.

active policy of expansion of the railway system would ultimately widen the market for British goods in India, increase directly the demand for British-manufactured railway materials in India and finally increase the flow of exports from India, thus benefiting British trade and industry all round. Hence many British politicians and businessmen advocated such a policy. However, the Government of India (or rather, the Secretary of State for India) was not prepared to sanction such a policy if it would endanger the financial balances of the Government of India and thus impede, directly and indirectly, the processes of remittance of funds from India to Great Britain, since the smooth working of the latter was crucial for the stability or equilibrium of the imperial system of balances of payments (and of the gold standard). In general, the interests of large British industries, such as the cotton textile, shipping and engineering industries, and of British banks coincided with the requirements of imperial policy before 1914, so that it was often assumed that British interests were in fact *identical* with the interests of Lancashire.

Such homogeneity of interests of the different partners in imperial power did not, however, always prevail, nor was it to be expected in an ever-changing economic situation. The conflict between British imperial policy and the short-term interests of British businessmen in India was quite obvious in many cases: cotton mills in India controlled by British industrialists would have benefited from tariffs on the imports of cotton piecegoods. We find most British businessmen joining the Indian mill-owners in protesting against the imposition in 1896 of an excise duty on Indian mill-made cotton piecegoods to 'countervail' a revenue duty on imports of piecegoods from abroad (mainly Britain).[7] Again, British engineering firms would have benefited from a more liberal stores purchase policy on the part of the Government of India.[8] British industrialists in India realized that fiscal autonomy for India might in fact benefit the established industrialists most, at least in the beginning. We find, for example, Ernest Cable (later Lord Cable) of Bird and Company and the Bengal Chamber of Commerce wanting fiscal autonomy for India in 1904.[9] There were demands by British businessmen and their representatives before and during the First World War for tariff protection for the paper and sugar industries, which were then mainly under British control.[10]

European (British) businessmen in India also feared the prospect of control of local industry by British finance capital based in Britain: in 1918, when Lloyds Bank wanted to absorb the National Bank of India, the Secretary of State for India vetoed the move, and was warmly supported

[7] See Chapter 7 above.
[8] See Chapter 10 above.
[9] See his speech in *Indian financial statement and proceedings* (PP 1904. LXIII), p. 255.
[10] See Chapters 2, 12 and 13 above.

by British business interests in India.[11] But on the whole, they were quite happy with the existing arrangements under which they had the major share of external trade, organized banking and finance, industries catering for the export markets, and industries depending primarily on government patronage. Protectionist policies might after all encourage the growth of indigenous Indian entrepreneurship and force the Europeans to compete with the Indians on somewhat more equal terms in the home market. The interests of Indian business or of Indian economic development inevitably received a low priority in the imperial scheme, and could be sacrificed in order to safeguard the other interests involved in the preservation and smooth working of the system.

The factors which have been outlined above would constitute a sufficient explanation for the industrial backwardness of India before 1918. The alternative explanations that are often encountered in the literature generally ignore the facts of the exploitative relationship of Britain with India and of the relationship of racial dominance between Europeans (particularly British nationals) and Indians, fostered and maintained by the British rulers. Professor Habakkuk, for example, writes: 'The contrast of Japan with India is certainly one which requires explanation, since India had many of the basic conditions of industrialization – a merchant class, banking and transport facilities, considerable production for the market – and perhaps in this case difference in character and quality of the native entrepreneurs was the decisive factor.'[12] As we have seen in Chaper 6, the emergence of Indian entrepreneurship in most parts of India was systematically discouraged by the political, administrative and financial arrangements maintained by the British rulers, and in the few cases before 1914 in which 'native' entrepreneurship had emerged, it was no less enterprising or interested in industry than were British businessmen in India. If anything, Indians showed a greater degree of courage, since they did not have many of the tangible advantages that British businessmen enjoyed because of their birth.

Another favoured explanation for the industrial backwardness of India, which attempts to by-pass the question of imperial domination, adduces the shortage of capital. This attempt cannot succeed because the growth of

[11] See *Capital* (Calcutta), 2 August 1918, pp. 231–9, 9 August 1918, pp. 291–3 and 16 August 1918, pp. 351–2, articles entitled 'India's Banking Machinery'. These articles also reflect the rivalry between the Bank of Bengal and the Bank of Bombay, and the misgivings of British businessmen about the proposed merger of the three Presidency Banks. It was feared that the greater control over the affairs of the Bank of Bombay exercised by Indians would be translated into a major share of control over the affairs of the Imperial Bank of India. These fears proved to be largely illusory.

[12] H. J. Habakkuk: 'The Historical Experience on the Basic Conditions of Economic Progress' in Leon H. Dupriez (ed.): *Economic Progress*, Papers and Proceedings of a Round Table held by the International Economic Association (Louvain: Institute de Recherches Economiques et Sociales, 1955), pp. 149–69, at p. 158.

capital is ultimately dependent on the levels of investment. If, as we have maintained, India functioned primarily as the source of surpluses for the British empire and as the market for the staples of Britain, rather than as a field of investment, much of the potential investment out of profits and high salaries did not in fact take place in India. Hence if capital was in short supply in relation to population, this shortage was at least partly caused by the working of the imperial mechanism.

There is in fact little evidence of shortage of capital in India in relation to the demand for capital for investment in industry under the stunted conditions for growth of the market for domestically produced industrial goods that prevailed in India before 1914. The capital market was, as in almost every other under-developed or semi-developed country, imperfect, and smaller industrialists naturally complained about the shortage of 'industrial finance'. But neither European managing agency houses nor the larger Indian business houses complained about such shortage.[13] When the profitability of investment in a particular field was judged to be low, of course, capital would not be forthcoming for investment in it. But it was not just a shortage of the right kind of financial institutions which held up industrial development.[14] The level of internal demand for manufactured goods was low because of the poverty of the ordinary people and the high degree of inequality of distribution of incomes. The cost of production of goods requiring a high degree of skill and ability to adapt techniques to local conditions was higher than in more advanced countries because the level of education of the workers was low.[15] The slow development of consumer goods industries and the lack of government orders for indigenously produced capital goods virtually eliminated the possibility of building up capital goods industries. Naturally, when capital goods were in short supply in western economies – during and immediately after the First World War – industrial production in India was hindered by the stringent supply conditions of capital goods. But these shortages of domestic and foreign capital goods or skills were more the result than the basic cause of industrial stagnation.

Before the First World War, modern factories in India constituted an 'enclave' economy. There were only two major centres of industrial production – Calcutta and Bombay. Most of the British and European enterprise was engaged in extractive industries in eastern India. For reasons that have been analysed by Singer, Nurkse and Baldwin,[16] the effects of foreign invest-

---

[13] See Chapter 6 above.

[14] Cf. the experience of the short-lived Tata Industrial Bank, referred to in the concluding section of Chapter 2. See also Chapters 9 and 13.

[15] See Chapter 7.

[16] R. E. Baldwin: 'Patterns of Development in Newly Settled Regions', *Manchester School of Economic and Social Studies*, May 1956; R. Nurkse: 'Some International Aspects of the Problem of Economic Development', *American Economic Review*, May

ment in plantations and extractive industries did not spread widely among the indigenous population. In the case of the jute industry, the growth of indigenous manufacture did create some degree of prosperity for the farmers of Bengal – primarily those of modern East Pakistan – but for reasons that we have analysed in detail in Chapters 6 and 8, the concentration of economic and political power in European hands prevented the growth of any substantial Indian business class. It was only in Bombay and Ahmedabad that Indian entrepreneurs survived the era of British political domination, but they had to wait till after the First World War before they could become the dominant business group even in western India.

One concomitant of this lopsided development was the emergence of distinct divisions between industrially developed and industrially backward regions. As we shall see in later sections, these divisions were only partially mitigated by the slight quickening of industrial change in the 1930s. Looking back, one is tempted to say that the seeds of the partition of India along ostensibly religious lines were sown before the First World War, but they might not have germinated without the aid of subsequent mistakes of policy, both in the economic and in the political field, on the part of leaders who did not want India to be divided.

14.2 INDIAN OPINION ON ECONOMIC POLICY AFTER THE FIRST WORLD WAR

As we saw in Chapters 2 and 3, radical changes took place during our period in the relations of Great Britain with the rest of the world, including India, and in the economic policy pursued by the Government of India.[17] Indian interests still remained subject to imperial interests, but the links between the Indian economy and the imperial economy were weakened. In particular, Japan emerged as a major competitor with Britain in the field of the most important British export to India, namely, cotton piecegoods.[18] At the same time, Indian mills had also begun to supply a much larger fraction of the home market than before. Britain's grip on the international payments mechanism was loosened by the impact of the First World War and the doldrums of the twenties, and the U.S.A. emerged as the leader of world capitalism. Along with these global and local economic changes, a movement for fundamental political change in India had gathered momentum under the leadership of Mahatma Gandhi. Under these circumstances, the

---

1952; H. W. Singer: 'The Distribution of Gains between Investing and Borrowing Countries', *American Economic Review*, May 1950.

[17] For accounts of the working of the payments mechanism of the British imperial system before and after the First World War, see S. B. Saul: *Studies in British Overseas Trade* and A. E. Kahn: *Great Britain in the World Economy* (Columbia University Press, New York, 1946).

[18] See Chapter 7 above.

British rulers were persuaded to grant some economic concessions to privileged Indians, and in particular to Indian businessmen: the real cost of granting such concessions was much lower when Britain was in any case losing her closed market in India to foreign competitors, and the rulers had to find new allies in India, however undependable they might be in the long run.

What comes as a surprise was that articulate Indian opinion on economic policy remained so little ahead of British economic policy in India after the First World War. The demand for greater state patronage for industries and for a measure of industrialization under the banner of private enterprise was never to be more persuasively argued by any Indian publicist after Ranade. Looking back, one can see that the measures which might have sufficed when the major competitors of Britain – Prussia, France, the U.S.A. and Japan – were just beginning on the road to industrialization would not have sufficed when several capitalist countries had already advanced far along that road. Moreover, the depression of the twenties was not a propitious period to venture on a path of industrialization under the auspices of private enterprise. Again, the problems of development of the backward regions of India or the advancement of the less privileged communities within India could be tackled only if essentially socialist measures, of redistribution of incomes on more egalitarian lines and diffusion of opportunities of development among all sections of society, were carried out. But Indian business had already tasted profit in the China trade in yarn and opium, and in the scarcity conditions of the First World War, and it was unwilling to leave the safe anchorage of free enterprise; no other section of society emerged to effectively challenge the leadership of business in the field of economic and social policy. Hence we find Indian business opinion and vocal public opinion often on the side of caution in the field of economic policy.

Caution then dictated financial orthodoxy to the British rulers, and Indian businessmen acquiesced. The Indian Retrenchment Committee had a number of Indian members: they were as enthusiastic in recommending measures of drastic retrenchment as their British colleagues. Indian business opinion *was* critical of the slow and halting progress of tariff protection in the twenties. It was also generally critical of what it considered to be extreme monetary deflation, which was enforced to keep the external value of the rupee at 1s. 6d. But their views did not advance beyond such mercantilist platitudes. The removal of the basic obstacles to industrial development in India in the 1920s would have required the adoption of a framework of socialist planning: the Government of India would certainly not have encouraged any such revolutionary development, nor would the Indian capitalists have risked stirring up the whole social order in this fashion. Hence they contented themselves by demanding tariff protection, which would be profitable to them in the short run and which would be granted by the then Government of India – under pressure. The pattern that was thus initiated at the beginning of the 1920s became set in the thirties: industrial development was limited almost entirely by what would be permitted in a framework of tariff protection excluding all other kinds of government action.[19] This limited industrialization combined with the depression of the thirties to increase the disparity between the more backward regions and the relatively industrialized pockets, and between the commercially prosperous and the commercially backward communities.

There was some opposition from landlords or spokesmen for the more backward provinces to measures of tariff protection, as there were demands from representatives of industrial labour in the Legislative Assembly, such as Chaman Lal or N. M. Joshi, that measures of tariff protection should be coupled with measures to improve the standard of living of workers. But the spokesmen of labour rarely had much influence on economic policy in a broader sense. The opposition of the landlords or of the predominantly agricultural provinces to tariff protection for industry is understandable since it generally involved a redistribution of income in favour of industrialists and of the relatively industrialized urban centres. But, as we have seen in Chapters 6 and 12, the opposition of landlords or capitalist farmers to tariff protection could not be absolute, for (a) they often invested in industry, and (b) in a time of depression, the protection of an industry depending on an agricultural raw material could benefit the producers (or the interests connected with the producers) of such material.

During the economic depression of the 1930s, more and more politicians and publicists began to talk or write about economic planning. The All India Congress Committee went to the length of setting up a National Planning Committee under the chairmanship of Jawaharlal Nehru. But most of the discussion on planning assumed a basically capitalist order of institutions,[20] and often envisaged collaboration with British or other foreign capitalists. 'Planning' was taken in a very loose sense, and was equated more with *étatisme*, as in modern Turkey or Prussia under Bismarck, than with a rational reorganization of the whole productive system on basically socialist

---

[19] The growth of Indian capitalism was thus stunted and it became subservient to capital in more advanced countries. Since no social transformation took place in India and the rate of growth of the economy was very low, the conditions for technical dynamism did not exist, and the Indian economy remained extremely vulnerable to changes originating in advanced capitalist economies. India shared this status of 'dependent capitalism' with Latin American countries such as Argentina, Brazil and Mexico.

[20] See, for example, M. Visvesvaraya: *Planned Economy for India* (Bangalore, 1934), p. 8 and 230–2 and N. R. Sarkar: 'Economic planning in India' in Mukerjee and Dey (eds.): *Economic Problems of Modern India*, Vol. 2, pp. 191–213. Visvesvaraya (p. 8) stated explicitly: 'The Indian plan should avoid *communistic* tendencies; its basic policy should be to encourage collective effort without interfering with individual initiative. The developments should be more on the lines followed in the United States of America and Turkey' (italics in the original).

principles. In the case of the most ambitious effort by the nationalist party, the Congress, we find big business represented along with socialists and 'near Communists' on the National Planning Committee. According to the most enthusiastic and most influential organizer of this effort, Jawaharlal Nehru, the deliberation of the Committee had 'an air of unreality about it'.[21]

Thus for all practical purposes Indian economists and politicians remained imprisoned by some of the basic presuppositions of the British imperial system even after the First World War: a capitalist order of society, international collaboration between capitalists of all countries, avoidance of drastic social changes and respect for the fundamental rights of property. No major social forces emerged to challenge these basic presuppositions effectively. The only forceful challenge to the miniature capitalist system built up by the dominant Indian capitalist groups was a secessionist one; the Muslim League demanded a separate State in the name of the Muslims of India. The success of the Muslim League in forcing the partition of the country on the nationalist leaders is a measure, on the one side, of the contradictions inherent in the system of dependent capitalism which had grown up, and on the other of the narrowness of the social values guiding most nationalist and Muslim League leaders in their struggle against the British.

14.3 SOME FACTORS BEHIND THE DEMAND FOR A SEPARATE STATE OF PAKISTAN

The roots of the secessionist movement leading to the partition of India are diverse and tortuous. There were basic differences in world outlook between believing Hindus and believing Muslims; there were the social differences aggravated by the obsessively hierarchical practices of the Hindu caste system; there was the deliberate policy of 'divide-and-rule' practised by British administrators who felt their position in India altered by the massive nationalist movement which had grown up since the beginning of the twentieth century; there were the divisive tendencies inherent in the anti-Muslim attitudes (generated partly as a reaction to the British policy of encouraging Muslim leaders to carry on loyalist propaganda) of many early nationalist leaders, including revolutionaries.[22] The divisive tactics and the

---

[21] See J. Nehru: *The Discovery of India* (third edition, Calcutta, 1947), pp. 331–7, at p. 331.

[22] See Maulana Abul Kalam Azad: *India wins Freedom* (Bombay, 1959), p. 4. Rabindra Nath Tagore wrote the novel *Gharey Bairey* (published in 1916 in the Bengali periodical 'Sabuj Patra') which had as background the movement of revocation of the partition of Bengal in 1905. In this novel, the extreme nationalists were either *zemindars* or young men from the middle classes, and the people resisting the boycott of foreign goods (which were cheaper than indigenous goods) came from the poorer classes and were mainly Muslim in religion. Tagore had written an essay ('Lokahit') a little earlier (in

secessionist ideology thrived on the underlying movement tending to aggravate the economic disparity (a) between the more backward districts, many
of which (particularly in East Bengal and Punjab) had a majority of
Muslims, and the less backward districts, and (b) between the Hindu
entrepreneurial and professional groups which dominated commerce, industry and the professions, and the Muslim upper classes. The latter naturally
tried to find an independent base from which to attack the barriers set up by
the more established Hindu upper and middle classes.

In Chapter 4 we have referred to the tendency of the different land-
tenure systems of India to converge to a situation in which a large proportion of the real cultivators were without any legal right to their land. In
East Bengal the majority of the cultivators were Muslims and the majority
of landlords were Hindus. Hence there were potent seeds of conflict along
communal lines. The jute and rice economy of East Bengal was hard hit
by the agricultural depression of the thirties; successive provincial governments, including the 'popular' one which was elected under the Government
of India Act of 1935, failed to improve the condition of peasants,[23] who
became more and more discontented. The recommendations of the Bengal
Land Revenue Commission, which was appointed in 1938 and which in its
report advocated the abolition of the Permanent Settlement and the granting of some rights to ordinary cultivators including share-croppers, were
not put into effect.[24] In the Punjab and in the north-west of India generally,
a large majority of the traders were Hindus, although the majority of the
people were Muslims. This created communal tensions between the Hindu
traders and money-lenders and the Muslim cultivators. A series of legal and
other measures were taken to ameliorate the conditions of ordinary
peasants, but these did not lead to a permanent improvement in the
situation.[25] Hence mass discontent was added to the discontent of the tiny

the year 1321 according to the Bengali calendar, around 1914 or 1915) pointing out that
the call for unity and evocation of brotherly relations during the Swadeshi movement
(starting in 1905) rang a little false when Hindus were used to discriminating against
Muslims in a blatant fashion in their daily lives.

[23] See Chapter 8.

[24] See Sir Frederick A. Sachse: 'The work of the Bengal Land Revenue Commission',
JRSA, LXXXIX, No. 4596, 19 September 1941, pp. 666–77.

[25] In some ways, the history of the British administration of the Punjab provides the
most ironic commentary on the efforts of men who believed themselves to be the true
friends of the underdog – the Sikh or Muslim cultivator – as against the Hindu money-
lender or trader and who did not or would not understand the functional use of the
money-lender in the British system of revenue collection and extraction of the surplus.
Thorburn's name comes first to mind in this connection. But Thorburn was not alone.
There was Sir Denzil Ibbetson, the man who framed the bill for introduction of co-
operative societies, there were F. L. Brayne, Malcolm Darling and Sir Michael O'Dwyer
of the Jallianwallabagh fame in the same tradition. See S. S. Thorburn: *Musalmans and
Money-lenders in the Punjab* (Edinburgh and London, 1886); M. L. Darling: *The Punjab
Peasant in Prosperity and Debt* (London, 1928), Chapters IX–XII; H. K. Trevaskis: *The
Land of the Five Rivers* (London, 1928), pp. 307–44 ('The Economic Dictatorship of the

Muslim middle class in Bengal, who felt themselves debarred from any offices of importance by the predominant position of the Hindus.

If the pace of industrial development in the rest of India had been fast enough, it is possible that the sheer pull of the market would have led to a betterment of the prospects of both the cultivators and the middle classes. But the pace of development was slow. It was obvious that both East Bengal and the Punjab had an economic base for the development of those industries which had grown up in the two industrial poles of Calcutta and Bombay. The Punjab produced cotton of better and better quality in ever larger quantities as irrigation progressed and as the domestic cotton-mill industry of India expanded, and East Bengal was practically the only source of jute, which was in its turn the base for the single most important item in India's export trade. Moreover, the regional markets of the Punjab and East Bengal were by no means small. An average peasant of East Bengal was probably more prosperous in a normal year than an average peasant of the heartland of India.[26] A Punjabi peasant, however oppressed by money-lenders and traders, was certainly more prosperous than a peasant from almost any other province of India.

The demographic changes in the twentieth century further increased the weight of the Muslim-majority districts in the political arithmetic of India. The proportion of Muslims to the total population of India had gone up steadily since 1881.[27] Bengal and Assam were the only provinces which had experienced uninterrupted growth in population from 1901 to 1941; apart from Assam, the rate of growth of population in Bengal was the highest among the provinces. A large part even of the growth of population in Assam was accounted for by the immigration of peasants – mainly Muslim – from East Bengal. Bengal was the most populous province in India, with a population of 42 million in 1901 and 60 million in 1941. Thus, even if the proportion of Muslims to Hindus in Bengal had remained the same, the proportion of Muslims to Hindus in the whole of India would have gone up. There is, in fact, evidence that the natural rate of increase of Muslims was higher than that of Hindus in the districts of the Gangetic delta which already had a majority of Muslims in the population at the beginning of the century.[28] Finally, during the twenties, Punjab and Sind

Money-Lender'); F. L. Brayne: *The Remaking of Village India* (London and Bombay, 1929); and H. Calvert: *The Wealth and Welfare of the Punjab* (Second edition, Lahore, 1936), Chapters XIII and XVIII. See also Philip Woodruff: *The Men who Ruled India*, Vol. II, *The Guardians* (London, 1963), pp. 159–63, 187–9, 235–43.

[26] See Chapters 5 and 8.

[27] *Census of India, 1931*, Vol. I, *India*, Part I, *Report* by J. H. Hutton (Delhi, 1933), p. 387; *Census of India, 1941*, Vol. I, Part I, *Tables* by M. W. M. Yeatts (Delhi, 1943), pp. 102–3. The number of Muslims per 10,000 of the population of India went up from 1,974 in 1881 to 2,122 in 1901 and 2,384 in 1941.

[28] See S. G. Panandikar: *The Wealth and Welfare of the Bengal Delta* (Calcutta University Press, Calcutta, 1926), pp. 231–3, for an attempted explanation of the differential rates of increase in the numbers of Hindus and Muslims in the Bengal Delta.

also experienced a high rate of growth of population.[29] Thus the population of provinces or districts with Muslim majorities increased in relation to the population of the rest of the country throughout the period under consideration.

Thus the economic, social and demographic bases for a separatist movement along communal lines among the Muslims grew stronger as the twentieth century wore on. To call this movement a 'feudal' or anti-capitalist reaction against modernization would be to mistake its origins or its aims. The more perceptive of the Indian nationalist leaders knew that any solution would have to incorporate a drastic alteration of the political and social relations between Hindus and Muslims. Thus C. R. Das, the Swarajist leader, had declared that when the Congress came to power in Bengal, it would reserve 60% of all new appointments for the Muslims until they achieved parity of representation with the Hindus according to population. In the case of appointments to the Calcutta Corporation he would reserve 80% of the seats for the Muslims for the same purpose. But with the untimely death of Das, his proposals were buried, never to be seriously considered again.[30]

Jawaharlal Nehru, in practically all his books, made perceptive comments on the differences in industrial growth between the regions of India, on the economic domination of Muslim cultivators by Hindu landlords, money-lenders and traders, on the difficulties preventing the Muslim *bourgeoisie* from making headway against the competition of the better-entrenched Hindu middle classes, and so on. In his *Glimpses of World History*, he went so far as to say that the exploitation of the Muslim weaver or tenant in Bengal and in India as a whole by the *bania* or the landlord was the 'root cause of the tension between Hindu and Muslim'.[31] In his autobiography he pointed out that communal politicians (in the 1920s and 1930s) were wrangling for jobs for the middle-class intelligentsia. Behind this struggle lay, according to him, the economic (class) difference between Hindus and Muslims in the Punjab and in Bengal, since the former tended to come from richer, more urban, and exploiting classes. He also pointed out that the Hindu Mahasabha (a communal party) had consistently opposed measures for reducing the burden of rural debt in the provinces, since the bankers and *banias* were almost always Hindus.[32] In the *Discovery of India*, written in 1945, Nehru specifically discussed provincial differences in the growth of industry, and the differences in the characteristics of ordinary and educated people associated with differences in provincial

[29] See Table 4.9 above for variations in the populations of the major provinces of British India from 1901 to 1941.

[30] Maulana Abul Kalam Azad: *India wins Freedom*, pp. 20–1.

[31] J. Nehru: *Glimpses of World History* (Bombay, 1967; originally published by Kitabistan, Allahabad, 1934), p. 452.

[32] Nehru: *An Autobiography*, pp. 466–7.

development. He noted that a Bengali Muslim was far nearer to a Bengali Hindu than he was to a Punjabi Muslim.[33] He also noticed that while Bombay became the 'centre and headquarters of Indian-owned industry, commerce, banking, insurance, etc.', Calcutta continued to be 'the chief centre of British capital and industry', although the British were 'being caught up by Marwaris and Gujratis'.[34]

But Nehru failed to draw the right conclusion from these observations: the differences in opportunity between different religious groups, between different economic classes or between provinces in different stages of development could not be eliminated or even mitigated significantly, by assuring a fair deal to the minorities or by talking about the need for balanced development of all regions in a market-dominated economy. The community which suffers under economic and social handicaps cannot advance if only the obvious legal or social discriminations against it are eliminated: it has actually to be accorded very strong preferences in opportunities for economic and social advancement in order to overcome the unfavourable initial conditions. The provinces or regions which are economically backward have to receive more than their 'fair' share of public investment in a free enterprise economy because there is a tendency for private investment to flow into the more developed regions.[35]

In any case, there was little recognition of the economic and social roots of Muslim separatism in the thinking of most of the leaders of the Congress party. The willingness to make the drastic sacrifices necessary to improve the social and economic position of Muslims or of the more backward provinces was totally absent from the programmes of the more advantageously placed business or professional classes which formulated the policies of the party. A socialist solution for the problems of disparate development of communities or regions, was, of course, unthinkable, according to most of the nationalist or separatist leaders. Hence the so-called 'feudal' (really big landlord) elements and the lawyers leading the Muslim League were provided with ammunition for their struggle to create a separate state of Pakistan. The real issue involved in their struggle, however, was neither the restoration of the pre-capitalist order nor the uniform betterment of the conditions of Muslims through the abolition of economic classes, but the hedging off of a part of India from competition by the established Hindu business groups or professional classes so that the small Muslim business class could thrive and the nascent Muslim intelligentsia

[33] Nehru: *The Discovery of India*, pp. 275–8, at p. 278.
[34] *Ibid.*, p. 277.
[35] For a discussion of the processes of 'cumulative disequilibrium' working against under-privileged communities or backward regions under conditions of free enterprise see G. Myrdal: *Economic Theory and Underdeveloped Regions* (London, 1957) and *Value in Social Theory* (London, 1958).

could find employment.[36] In the process, of course, some Muslim tenants of East Pakistan got a little more out of the value of the land they tilled, but this beneficial effect was neither general nor permanent. In retrospect, it appears that much of the mass discontent against the colonial capitalist path of development that India was treading before independence was dissipated through the struggle for the creation of two different nation states, and thus the struggle for a radical revision of the social structure of the subcontinent along socialist lines was further postponed.

We have seen in Chapter 6 that in undivided India, the new entrepreneurs came from groups which had connections with trade and finance, rather than from the westernized professional classes. In Pakistan also, the people who took advantage of the state patronage of industrialization were groups which traced their origins to various 'trading castes' although they were Muslims.[37] As in India, so in Pakistan, development has taken place along capitalist lines: it has been limited by social and political factors rather than by any immutable endowment of natural resources.[38] Economists who underestimate the influence of political arrangements on economic growth have been surprised by the 'explosion' of private investment in Pakistan. They may have other surprises in store for them if, as is likely, the capitalist path of development in Pakistan is blocked in its turn by internal social and political hindrances and by international political developments.

In the remaining sections of the chapter we summarize some major features of the limited industrial growth that had taken place in India up to 1939.

14.4 THE SPREAD OF MODERN INDUSTRY IN DIFFERENT REGIONS OF INDIA

Between 1900 and 1939, India more or less completed the 'textile revolution'; she became nearly self-sufficient in the production of cotton textiles,[39] and emerged as a major exporter of cotton piecegoods during the Second World War. Several new industries, run on modern techniques, grew up in this period: of these, steel and cement could be roughly classed as producer goods industries. The production of refined sugar in large-scale units employing modern methods had started before 1900, but the total output remained insignificant until the latter half of the period. By the

---

[36] See in this connection, P. Moon: *Divide and Quit* (London, 1961), Chapter xiv, especially p. 288.

[37] See G. F. Papanek: 'The Development of Entrepreneurship', *The American Economic Review*, lii, 2, May 1962, pp. 46–58 and *Pakistan's Development: Social Goals and Private Incentives* (Cambridge, Mass., 1967), Chapter ii.

[38] Kingsley Davis had, in common with many other economists, considered the prospects of industrial development of Pakistan to be rather dim because of the supposed lack of mineral resources. See Davis: *Population of India and Pakistan*, Chapter 20.

[39] See Chapter 7.

end of the period the capacity of the sugar industry was large enough to satisfy the internal demand for refined sugar in India.[40] Among other notable industries employing large-scale units should be mentioned the match and paper industries.

Large-scale production employing modern methods remained confined to the consumer goods industries and the crude producer goods industries. India in 1939 was almost entirely dependent on imports from abroad for her requirements of machinery and machine tools, and for chemicals. By 1939 a beginning had been made in the production of some heavy chemicals, such as caustic soda and sulphuric acid. But the real beginning of an industry producing cotton-textile machinery was made only after the Second World War had started.[41] While some crude machinery and machine tools had been produced during the First World War, practically all the facilities had been dismantled after the war, because of lack of demand and of government support in any form.

Before the First World War, industrial investment was almost exclusively confined to the two 'nodes', Bombay and Calcutta, but Ahmedabad in the Bombay Presidency was emerging as a centre of cotton mills. During the first few years after the First World War as well, it was the investment in the cotton mills of Bombay and Ahmedabad and the jute mills on the Hooghly that dominated total industrial investment. But with the rise of the cement industry to serve the different regions of India, the depression in the cotton-mill industry of Bombay from 1923 onwards and the jute mills of Bengal from 1928 onwards, and the rise of the sugar industry in the United Provinces and Bihar, there was some spread of industry to other regions of India. In this diffusion, the cotton-textile industry continued to play a leading role. The total number of spindles and looms in the cotton mills of India rose from 6·62 million and 96·7 thousand respectively in 1914 to 10·06 million and 202·4 thousand respectively in 1939. The total number of spindles and looms in Bombay City and Ahmedabad taken together rose from 4·01 million and 66·1 thousand respectively in 1914 to 4·75 million and 114·1 thousand respectively in 1939.[42] Thus it can be seen that the cotton-mill industry, particularly the spinning section of it, expanded much faster in centres away from Bombay and Ahmedabad. The expansion was particularly rapid in Delhi, the United Provinces (mainly Cawnpore) and Madras (mainly Coimbatore, Madura, and Madras).

This spread of industry was aided by the relative cheapness of labour in the new centres and the availability of cheap sources of hydroelectric power,

---

[40] See Chapter 12.

[41] The Textile Machinery Corporation was floated under the management of Birla Brothers in 1941: *ITJ*, February 1941, p. 115.

[42] The figures for 1914 are given in Table 7.4 above; the figures for 1939 are taken from Sir Ness Wadia: 'The Industry in Retrospect', *ITJ, 1890–1940, Jubilee Souvenir* (Bombay, 1941), p. 18.

particularly in south India. But it was also helped by the creation of local markets through tariff protection for the whole of India.[43] The sources of entrepreneurship in new industries and centres were also to a large extent, but not entirely, local. In the south, many communities which had earlier been involved in trade moved into industry: the Chettiars were the most famous community among the traders, but entrepreneurship was not confined to, or even dominated by, the Chettiar community.[44] In most of Central Indian States, such as Gwalior, Bhopal, and Indore, the Jains and Marwaris had been the most important trading communities before the First World War,[45] and naturally they were heavily involved in the new textile mills that sprang up in these states. Ahmedabad continued to grow at a faster rate than Bombay, and, by the end of the thirties, the number of looms and spindles in the former city was more than two-thirds the number of looms and spindles in place in the mills of Bombay. The capitalists of Ahmedabad devoted most of their energy to developing the cotton mills, but eventually they moved into other fields, such as cement, sugar and chemicals. Baroda, which was contiguous with Ahmedabad, witnessed an inflow of entrepreneurship from the latter city in the development of its cotton mills. Although Bombay declined relatively to other major industrial cities, such as Coimbatore, Cawnpore or Ahmedabad, as a centre of textile production, the capitalists of Bombay, headed by the house of Tata, continued to play a large part in other fields, such as iron and steel, cement, shipping and chemicals.

In the north of India, the sugar industry was probably the single most important field of investment of capital. It provided new opportunities for investment, both to established business groups, such as Begg, Sutherland and Company, and Juggilal Kamlapat, and to new business groups, such as the Narangs, Dalmia Sahu Jain, and Birla Brothers. One major part of India which remained relatively untouched by the dispersion of industry was that comprising Punjab, Sind and the North-Western Frontier Provinces – roughly the region which came later to form West Pakistan.[46] It is

[43] The established centres did not generally have enough capacity at the onset of tariff protection to supply all the regional markets of India, and therefore local entrepreneurs could set up new capacity in advance of, or in competition with, older Indian centres of production, when tariff protection restricted imports from abroad.

[44] The Southern India Mill-owners' Association was represented before the Special Tariff Board by J. Doak, C. S. Ratnasabapathy Mudaliar, R. Venkataswamy Naidu and G. N. Sirur – none of them Chettiars. Further, in a list of eight highly profitable Coimbatore cotton mills we find the names of only two Chettiar firms as managing agents. See ITB: Special Tariff Board: *Oral Evidence*, Vol. III, p. 71 and *Written Evidence*, Vol. II (Delhi, 1937), p. 92.

[45] The Central India State Gazetteer series, *Gwalior State Gazetteer*, p. 77; *Indore State Gazetteer*, p. 127; *Bhopal State Gazetteer*, p. 55. See also Chapter 6 above.

[46] When we talk about the relative lack of industrial development we mean only the lack of development of modern large-scale units of production. If we look at the percentage of the occupied labour force engaged in industry in 1931, including cottage and small-

difficult to find any satisfactory explanation for this lack of industrial development. One factor may have been the relative lack of power – coal was almost entirely absent in this region and there was no development of hydroelectricity comparable to what occurred in south India. Another inhibiting factor may have been that, although the extension of irrigation facilities in the Punjab and Sind increased the prosperity of the peasant to some extent in the twenties, he was much harder hit by the agricultural depression than peasants in most other parts of India (that is, with the possible exception of Bengal), for exports formed a much larger fraction of the total agricultural output of Punjab and Sind than of that of most other parts of India. The third factor may have been that there was no regional entrepreneurial group with the extensive connections, capital and experience comparable to those of the groups that existed in central, southern or even eastern India.[47] The case of the Punjab and Sind illustrates very well that industrial development is *not* automatically triggered off by increasing agricultural production in a region.

The lack of industrial development in the Punjab and Sind – the major source of long-staple cotton in India – and in East Bengal – the major source of jute – and thus together in the most important raw material base of the two biggest manufacturing industries of undivided India, provided a powerful argument for those who wanted to create a separate state for the Muslims of India. In the Punjab, the demand for political control over industrial policy also had a powerful argument in the relative prosperity of the Punjabi peasant – particularly in the canal colonies – and the dynamism of the small entrepreneur. During the twenties and thirties many small foundries and other workshops catering to the needs of the farmers had sprung up in the Punjab.[48] These small industrialists could not, however, compete with the large business houses in the rest of India. When the State of Pakistan came into being, the political insulation of the north-west

scale industries, Punjab would appear to be better developed than all other large Indian provinces except Delhi. See *Census of India, 1931*, Vol. II, Part I, *Report* (Delhi, 1933), p. 307. But in 1930 the number of workers employed in the factories of Punjab was 44,724 as against 381,349 in Bombay and 480,349 in Bengal; the populations of Punjab, Bombay (including Aden) and Bengal in 1931 were 23,581,000, 21,931,000 and 50,114,000 respectively. See Gov. India, CISD: *Statistical abstract for British India from 1922–3 to 1931–2* (Calcutta, 1933), pp. 812–13, and *Census of India, 1931*, Vol. I, Part I, *Report* (Delhi, 1933), p. 35. The number of workers in manufacture per 100 male workers in 1931 was 4·1 in East Bengal (Pakistan) as against 10·4 in West Bengal and 8·4 in the Indian Union as a whole. See Alice and Daniel Thorner: 'The twentieth century trend in employment in manufacture in India – as illustrated by the case of West Bengal', in C. R. Rao *et al.* (eds.): *Essays on Econometrics and Planning* (Calcutta, 1964), p. 306.

[47] The importance of political factors in allowing the latent entrepreneurial potential of trading groups to express itself in industrial investment is dramatically illustrated by the experience of Pakistan since independence.

[48] See *Census of India, 1921*, Vol. XV, *Punjab and Delhi*, Part I, *Report* (Lahore, 1923), pp. 78, 352–5; *Census of India, 1931*, Vol. XVII, *Punjab*, Part I, *Report* (Lahore, 1933), pp. 41–2.

from the rest of India would provide a large market for the local industrialists who would have time to develop because of immunity from competition.

14.5   TWO PHASES IN THE DEVELOPMENT OF INDIAN
ENTREPRENEURSHIP AND INDUSTRY

One can clearly divide the interwar period into two phases, so far as the
importance of Indian entrepreneurs in Indian industry and the relationship
of the Indian economy to the British economy are concerned: up to 1929 or
so, although new Indian business houses had emerged and new industries
such as cement and iron and steel were being established, Indian industrial investment was still dominated by older entrepreneurial groups and centres. The
imports of jute-textile machinery formed more than a third of the total
imports of textile machinery during the years from 1919–20 to 1921–2
and between a fourth and a third of the total imports of textile machinery
during the years from 1919–20 to 1923–4. Up to 1930–1, in fact, the imports of jute-textile machinery rarely fell below a quarter of the total imports of textile machinery into India. The corresponding proportion declined
to between $\frac{1}{8}$ and $\frac{1}{5}$ in the thirties. The value of imports of textile machinery
was between a third and a half of the total imports of industrial machinery
for the years from 1919–20 to 1923–4.[49]

If we take into account the imports of boilers and prime-movers which
were installed in textile mills, but which were included in the general category of machinery and mill-work, rather than in the specific category of
textile machinery, the proportion of imports of textile machinery to total
imports of industrial machinery becomes even higher during these years.
In the later years of the twenties and in the thirties, however, the proportion
of imports of textile machinery to total industrial machinery imports often
fell below the one-quarter mark. The relative decline in imports of textile
machinery from 1926–7 onwards was even greater in real terms: for the
prices of all industrial machinery fell after the boom years of the early
twenties, but the prices of textile machinery fell less than those of sugar and
paper machinery.[50]

The greater importance of investment in the textile industries in the early
twenties meant that the European capitalists who were already entrenched
in the jute industry and the established Indian (and European) capitalists of
Bombay and Ahmedabad played a larger role in industrial investment. New
Indian industrial groups had already begun emerging, as we have seen in

[49] All the comparisons are based on figures from Gov. India, CISD: *Annual statement
of the seaborne trade of British India* (Calcutta, annual). The figures for imports of industrial machinery are given in Chapter 3 above (Table 3.2).
[50] For the price indices of textile and sugar machinery see Tables 3.2 and 12.2.

Chapter 6; Birla Brothers had established one jute mill and at least two cotton mills between 1919 and 1921, and acquired another (Kesoram Cotton Mills, registered in 1919) by 1925; in the north, Sri Ram was building up his group around the Delhi Cloth and General Mills, and Juggilal Kamlapat was moving into the cotton, sugar and vegetable oil industries in a big way. But there was not yet the explosion of local entrepreneurship which took place in the 1930s.

In many respects, the twenties were a period of waiting for the growth of Indian industrial capitalism.[51] In the first place, although discriminating protection was granted to the iron and steel and paper industries, the Government of India had not yet been forced into granting tariff protection to all consumer-goods industries. In the second place, although the external economic relations of Britain and India had changed substantially since 1914, India was still playing some of the balancing role she traditionally played in the British imperial system. In 1929, for instance, India had a positive net trade balance of £19 million with the U.S.A., which went part of the way towards meeting Britain's large deficit balance with the latter.[52] Another part of India's enormous transfers to Britain was effected through her credit balance with other countries of the British Empire, such as Ceylon, Malaya, and South Africa.[53] The relative size of India's adverse balance on account of current visible trade with the U.K. had fallen, mainly because of the curtailment of imports of cotton piecegoods from the latter. But it was still very large absolutely. This large adverse balance with the U.K. on current account was accompanied during the first four or five years of the 1920s by a net inflow of capital from the U.K.[54]

Thus in spite of the agricultural depression, the substantially diminished roles of imports into India from the U.K. and of Indian contributions of the hard currency earnings in the British imperial system, the pre-war trade and capital inflow relations remained qualitatively unchanged during the twenties. Indian entrepreneurs advanced by taking advantage of the (limited) opportunities for import substitution, and by exploiting the changed political relations between India and the United Kingdom. However, no

[51] See also Chapter 3.

[52] Kahn: *Great Britain in the World Economy*, p. 233. Malaya in 1929 had a positive balance of £46 million with the U.S.A.; thus she had largely replaced India as the main source of dollars for Britain in meeting her deficit balance in current trade with the U.S.A.

[53] Kahn: *Great Britain in the World Economy*, p. 232.

[54] In many of the traditional textbook accounts of international capital movements, a continuing adverse balance of trade with the creditor country is in fact accompanied by an equivalent net outflow of capital from the creditor to the debtor country. This, however, overlooks the multilateral character of world trade and, in particular, the crucial role that India played in the imperial payments system: her balancing role could be successfully played only if she had a continually favourable balance with the group of countries with which the U.K. had an adverse balance on current account. See also Saul: *Studies in British Overseas Trade*.

decisive and irreversible advance was made until the coming of the depression.

The depression of the 1930s radically altered the character of trade relations between India and the U.K. India moved closer to a situation of bilateral balance with the U.K.; the position of the U.K. *vis-à-vis* the U.S.A. improved in spite of the restrictionist measures taken by the latter. On the other side, British exports to India declined drastically, whereas the share of Britain in exports from India increased both because of the fact that Britain was less affected than other advanced capitalist countries by the depression and because of Imperial Preference. Britain's relations with other countries of the Empire became closer; although the share of the U.K. in India's imports fell substantially between 1929 and 1939 and India's share in British exports also fell, the share of the Empire countries together in British exports rose from 39·5% in 1929 to 45·6% in 1938.[55] This latter development was accounted for both by Imperial Preference and by the fact that India's income rose more slowly than did those of many of the other countries of the Empire.

Not only was there a greater degree of bilateral equilibrium in current trade between India and the U.K.; also the Government of India repaid during the years from 1931 to 1935 a substantial amount of the capital it had earlier raised in London and became independent of the London money market for the raising of long-term capital.[56]

Some of the shift in the trade relations between the U.K. and India was brought about by the policy of tariff protection for Indian industry which was forced upon the Government of India by the adverse impact of the depression, on the traditional sources of government revenue.[57] The expanded home markets for domestic producers led to a rapid growth of the textile industry in the smaller centres, and of industries such as sugar and paper. Changes in the political climate also led to a change in the position of the European businessman *vis-à-vis* the Indian businessman. It can be argued that the systematic preference for the European businessman, built into the political administrative and financial framework before the First World War,[58] acted as a system of quotas for investment and production such that the agreed quota for Indian businessmen at any moment of time was zero: Indian businessmen could only enter fields in which the whole of Indian production had not already been entirely allocated by administrative and political preference to European businessmen. Economists inferring equal opportunities for all entrepreneurs from a system of formal free trade seem to have overlooked this aspect of systematic bias towards one group of entrepreneurs.

[55] Kahn: *Great Britain in the World Economy*, pp. 244 and 211 (including footnote).
[56] Banerji: *India's Balance of Payments*, pp. 186–96.
[57] See Chapter 2 above.   [58] See Chapter 6 above.

During the 1920s, and more particularly during the 1930s, this bias was gradually mitigated by a greater degree of Indianization of the civil and military administrations and by a greater degree of participation by (mainly well-to-do and educated) Indians in the political process. Indian entrepreneurs were not slow to realize the advantages of participation in the government of the country: the Kumara Rajah of Chettinad (M. A. Muthiah Chettiar) in Madras, Sir Jwala Prasad Srivastava in the United Provinces, Sir Gokul Chand Narang in the Punjab and Sir Bejoy Prosad Singh Roy in Bengal served as ministers in the respective provincial governments up to 1937.[59] The coming of the popular provincial governments under the Government of India Act of 1935 further increased the opportunities for Indian entrepreneurs to influence the formulation and the execution of the policy of the provincial governments.

Before we end this section, we should notice that the emergence of new entrepreneurial groups in India is far better understood if we connect them with trade and the opening up of opportunities in particular fields and regions, than with specific castes. As was pointed out in Chapter 6, tariff protection for modern industries made production for the home market more profitable than trade, at least up to a point. The agricultural depression, with its severe effects on the fortunes of peasants, made money-lending less attractive than before: many capitalists found idle money in their hands and invested it in industry. It is true that the most important group of entrepreneurs – the Marwaris – claimed to belong to the Bania castes; but many of them were Jains, that is, were really outside the accepted framework of Hinduism. In Punjab and north-western India in general, the entrepreneurs were mainly Aroras and Khatris who claimed Kshatriya (military caste) status. Finally, most of the groups which became prominent industrialists in Pakistan after independence came from Muslim trading castes.[60] What seems to be common to most of the entrepreneurial groups is that they had been connected with trade or construction before entering industry.[61]

14.6   THE UPSHOT OF STUNTED INDUSTRIALIZATION IN INDIA

In 1939, Indian industry had developed far enough for India to be more or less self-sufficient in the production of consumption goods such as cotton

---

[59] The information is derived from various issues of the *Indian Year Book* and *Debrett's Peerage, Baronetage, etc.*

[60] Papanek: 'The Development of Entrepreneurship' and *Pakistan's Development*, Chapter 11.

[61] Walchard Hirachand's family in Sholapur had been prominent in trade and money-lending and they had entered construction later; in Bengal Sir Rajendranath Mookerjee first made his name and money in civil engineering and then moved into the iron and steel industry. Mookerjee was a Brahman by caste. So was Laxmanrao Kirloskar, who founded the house of Kirloskar.

cloth, sugar and matches. But the development of the capital goods industries was extremely meagre, and the share of modern industry in total national income was low. The employment created in the modern industrial sector was very limited indeed. The total employment in all perennial factories in British India, including native states, was 1,421,377 in 1937, 1,521,219 in 1938 and 1,528,028 in 1939; including seasonal factories the figures of employment rise to 1,958,879 in 1937, 2,036,758 in 1938 and 2,050,231 in 1939.[62]

The shift in economic power between Britain and India after 1929–30 did have some effects on industrial investment. As we have seen in Chapter 3, total industrial investment remained surprisingly stable in real terms during the years of the depression of the thirties. Furthermore, there also seems to have occurred a marginal shift in the occupational structure between 1931 and 1941. According to some calculations made by Alice and Daniel Thorner, the percentage of workers in manufacture, mining and construction in the Indian Union declined from 10 to 9 between 1911 and 1931 and rose again to 10 in 1951. Although they have not yet released their estimates of the change between 1931 and 1941 for the whole of India, they have given figures for the four selected states of Baroda, Central Provinces, Madras and United Provinces, and for West Bengal separately. In all these cases, we observe a slight decline in the proportion of the working force engaged in manufacture, mining and construction between 1901 and 1931 and a slight increase in the same between 1931 and 1941.[63] Thus in spite of a wider spread of investment in the twenties and thirties, West Bengal, a relatively industrialized region, shared in the general Indian movement towards greater industrialization in the thirties.

The private entrepreneurial base supporting this development was rather small. In our discussion of the supply of entrepreneurship we have primarily devoted our attention to large entrepreneurial groups, not because they were the most important in the development of the economy or even in the development of all the modern sectors of the economy, but because they were the only ones which counted in the development of the industries we have selected. Throughout the country small businessmen had been busy since before the First World War in the setting up of cotton gins and presses, rice and oil mills, jute presses, open-pan processes of sugar manufacture (*khandsaris*), and small powerloom or handloom factories. Sometimes their efforts in the development of their enterprises were assisted by joint-stock banks as rice mills in the Guntur district were helped by the Bank of

[62] *Statistical abstracts for British India* (statistics collected under the Factories Act, 1934). The total population of India and Pakistan in 1941 was 388,998,000.
[63] Alice Thorner: 'The Secular Trend in the Indian Economy, 1881–1951', *The Economic Weekly*, Special Number, July 1962; and Thorner: 'Twentieth century trend in employment in manufacture in India'.

Madras.[64] More often, it was mainly local capital which helped in the development of the small-scale industries.[65]

But these small capitalists did not start an industrial revolution. They did not pioneer any new methods of production or any new industries. The industries that grew up under the umbrella of tariff protection were generally controlled by capitalists with a large amount of capital; but the latter also depended entirely on western countries for their techniques of production. We have seen in our chapters on the iron and steel, sugar and paper industries that tariff protection did not lead to inefficiency in the usual textbook sense, but in fact helped the industrialists to expand their plants, and improve their methods of production. But these improvements took place in the context of a borrowed technology and a very narrow basis of technical personnel. There were no major technical improvements pioneered in India and applied to the solution of industrial problems.

Thus in 1939 the economy of India remained poor, basically agricultural and colonial. The social structure had not adapted to the requirements of capitalistic growth. In most parts of India the land-tenure system was extremely cumbersome, with an enormous number of layers or intermediary rights between the state and the cultivator. There was little 'capitalist farming' in the true sense. The administrative system was colonial, geared primarily to the maintenance of law and order.

Industry had developed only to a limited extent; practically all the development was confined to consumer-goods industries.[66] Although indigenous capitalists had managed to get a much larger share of modern industry than they had before 1914, foreign capitalists were firmly in control in the staple industries. Moreover, there was already a shadow of the shape of things to come in the penetration of Indian industry by large foreign firms, controlled from abroad by foreign capitalists. Unilever, ICI, Dunlop, General Motors and other such firms established their branches or subsidiary companies in India.[67] Thus even before Indian capitalists had wrested control over the economy from the pre-capitalist elements and from the old European-controlled Indian firms, they had to witness the invasion of new fields of industry by international cartels. Moreover, the capitalist groups in

[64] See the written evidence of Sir W. B. Hunter, Appendix II (prepared by W. R. T. Mackay, the inspector of branches of the Bank of Madras in charge of the rice-mill industry in the delta districts of Kistna and Godavari), *Evidence (Report of IIC)*, Vol. III (PP 1919, XIX), pp. 277–9.

[65] See the evidence of Rao Bahadur R. N. Mudholkar, in *Evidence (Report of IIC)*, Vol. II (PP 1919, XVIII), pp. 467, 475–6.

[66] According to a United Nations calculation, in 1936 67% of the total volume of employment in factories in India was in consumer-goods industries, 18% in industries producing intermediate materials (wood, paper, chemicals, etc.) and 15% in other finished goods (mostly capital goods). See U.N.: *Processes and Problems of Industrialization in Underdeveloping Countries* (New York, 1955), p. 138.

[67] D. R. Gadgil: 'Indian Economic Organization' in Simon Kuznets *et al.* (eds.): *Economic Growth, Brazil, India, Japan* (Durham, N.C., 1955), pp. 448–63, at p. 456.

different regions were in very different stages of development – some having already become established industrialists and some not having emerged from the stage of 'primitive accumulation' through commerce. In this situation, there were naturally conflicts between them for the control of resources and markets, which contributed, among other things, to the partition of India. Meanwhile, however, the struggle of ordinary people against British rule continued. When independence came, the capitalist class in India and Pakistan, however small numerically and weak financially, was still in a far better position than before to utilize the advantages of an independent State for furthering its own interests.

BIBLIOGRAPHY

PRIMARY SOURCES:

ARCHIVES AND OFFICIAL PUBLICATIONS

I. ARCHIVES
A. National Archives of India, New Delhi
Government of India, Department of Revenue and Agriculture: Emigration, 'A' Proceedings, 1899–1902.

Government of India Proceedings, Department of Industries and Labour: Inter-provincial migration files 1924–6.

B. Office of the Regional Director, Company Law Board, Eastern Region, and Registrar of Companies, West Bengal, Calcutta
Memoranda of association of jute companies registered in India.

Copies of agreements of mortgage (for cash, credit and overdraft facilities) between jute and sugar companies and the Bank of Bengal.

Lists of shareholders of the Ryam Sugar Company at various dates between 1914 and 1949.

C. Office of the Registrar of Companies, Scotland, Edinburgh
Balance-sheets of the Anglo-India Jute Mills Company Limited, the Champdany Jute Company Limited, the India Jute Company Limited, the Samnuggur Jute Factory Company Limited, the Titaghur Jute Factory Company Limited, and the Victoria Jute Company Limited, from 1908 to 1920.

D. Office of the Shareholders' Association, Bombay
Balance-sheets and directors' reports of the Ahmedabad Advance Mills Limited, and the Central India Spinning, Weaving and Manufacturing Company Limited, 1904–10 (broken series).

2. OFFICIAL PUBLICATIONS: UK
A. UK Parliamentary Papers
Indian financial statements and the proceedings of the Legislative Council of the Governor-General thereon, from 1900–1 to 1909–10: PP 1900 LVII;

445

PP 1901 XLIX; PP 1902 LXX; PP 1903 XLVI; PP 1904 LXIII; PP 1905 LVII; PP 1906 LXXXI; PP 1907 LVIII; PP 1908 LXXIV; PP 1909 LXII.

(*Return of the*) *Indian financial statement and budget of the Governor-General in Council*, from 1929–30 to 1935–6: PP 1929–30 XXIII; PP 1930–1 XXIII; PP 1931–2 XIX; PP 1932–3 XX; PP 1933–4 XX; PP 1934–5 XVI.

Indian tariff and the cotton duties: papers relating to the Indian Tariff Act and the Cotton Duties Act 1894; and *Representations made to the Government of India, in March 1894, against the exclusion of cotton manufactures from import duties* . . . : PP 1894 LXXII.

(*Papers relating to the*) *Indian Tariff Act 1896, and the Cotton Duties Act 1896*: PP 1896 LX.

Progress of education in India, 1902–7, Vol. I, Fifth quinquennial review; and Vol. II, Maps and statistical tables: PP 1909 LXIII.

Report of a Committee appointed by the Secretary of State for India to inquire into the system of state technical scholarships established by the Government of India in 1904: PP 1913 XLVII.

Report of the Committee on Indian Railways finance and administration: PP 1908 LXXV.

Report of the Committee appointed by the Secretary of State for India to enquire into the administration and working of Indian Railways: PP 1921 X.

Report of the Indian Industrial Commission, 1916–18: PP 1919 XVII.
   Minutes of Evidence, Vols. I–V: PP 1919 XVII; PP 1919 XVIII; PP 1919 XIX; PP 1919 XX. [Vol. VI, *Confidential Evidence* (Calcutta, 1918) is not included in PP.]

Report of the Indian Irrigation Commission 1901–3, Part I General; Part II Provincial; Part III Maps; and Part IV Appendix: PP 1904 LXVI.

Report of the Textile Factories Labour Committee appointed by the Government of India, Dec. 1906. . . : PP 1907 LIX.

Report and correspondence relating to the expediency of maintaining the Royal Indian Engineering College; and Evidence taken before the Committee: PP 1904 LXIV.

Robertson, Thomas (Special Commissioner for Indian Railways): *Report on the administration and working of Indian Railways:* PP 1903 XLVII.

Royal Commission on Indian finance and currency:
   Appendices to the interim report of the Commissioners, Vols. I and II; *Final report of the Commissioners; Evidence taken before the Royal Commission,* Vol. II; and *Appendices to the final report of the Commissioners:* PP 1914 XX.

Royal Commission on Opium: *Minutes of Evidence taken between 18 November and 29 December 1893*, Vol. II: PP 1894 LXI.
   Minutes of Evidence taken from 29 January to 22 February 1894, Vol. IV: PP 1894 LXII.

Royal Commission on Public Services in India: *Report:* PP 1916 VII.

(*Statements exhibiting the*) *moral and material Progress and condition of India* (later called *India 1922–23*, etc.) from 1898–9 to 1933–4: PP 1900 LVII; PP 1901 XLIX; PP 1902 LXXIII; PP 1903 XLVI; PP 1904 LXIII; PP 1905

LVIII; PP 1906 LXXXII; PP 1907 LIX; PP 1908 LXXV; PP 1909 LXII; PP 1910 LXVII; PP 1911 LV; PP 1912–13 LXI; PP 1913 XLVI; PP 1914 LXIII; PP 1914–16 XLIX; PP 1916 XXI; PP 1917–18 XXIV; PP 1918 XVIII; PP 1919 XXXVIII; PP 1920 XXXIV; PP 1921 XXVI; *PP 1922* XVI; PP 1923 XVIII; PP 1924–5 XI; PP 1927 XVIII; PP 1928 XVIII; PP 1928–9 XV; PP 1929–30 XXIII; PP 1930–1 XXIV; PP 1931–2 XIX; PP 1933–4 XX; PP 1934–5 XVII; PP 1935–6 XX.

Statistical abstracts relating to British India
from 1911–12 to 1920–1: PP 1924 XXV.
from 1917–18 to 1926–7: PP 1928–9 XXII.

Statistical abstracts for British India and certain Indian States
from 1918–19 to 1927–8: PP 1929–30 XXIX.
from 1921–2 to 1930–1: PP 1932–3 XXVI.
from 1929–30 to 1938–9: PP 1941–2 VIII.
from 1930–1 to 1939–40: PP 1942–3 X.

(Annual statements of the) trade of the United Kingdom with foreign countries and British Possessions, Vols. I and II, from 1902 to 1920: PP 1903 LXIX, LXX; PP 1904 XC, XCI; PP 1905 LXXIX, LXXX; PP 1906 CXVI, CXVII; PP 1907 LXXXII, LXXXIII; PP 1908 CII, CIII; PP 1909 LXXXIII; PP 1910 LXXXVII, LXXXVIII; PP 1911 LXXIX, LXXX; PP 1912–13 LXXXV; PP 1913 LX; PP 1914 LXXXII, LXXXIII; PP 1914–16 LXIV, LXV; PP 1916 XXV, XXVI; PP 1917–18 XXVIII, XXIX; PP 1918 XXI, XXII; PP 1919 XLIII, XLIV; PP 1920 XLI, XLII; PP 1921 XXXII, XXXIII.

Annual statements of the foreign trade of the United Kingdom, in 3–4 vols., were published separately – not as part of the Parliamentary Papers — with effect from 1920 onwards.

B. Other official UK publications

Royal Commission on Indian currency and finance:
Vol. I, *Report;* and Vols. II–IV, *Appendices and evidence* (Cd. 1687, London, 1926).
Royal Commission on Labour in India: *Report;* and *Evidence,* Vols. I–VIII, X (Parts 1 and 2 each), and Vols. IX, XI (London, 1931).

3. OFFICIAL PUBLICATIONS : GOVERNMENT OF INDIA
A. Listed under collective authors

Census of India, 1911, Vol. I, Part I: *Report* by E. A. Gait (Calcutta, 1913).
Vol. V, *Bengal, Bihar and Orissa, and Sikkim,* Part I, *Report* (Calcutta, 1913).
Vol. VII, *Bombay,* Part I, *Report* by P. J. Mead and G. L. Macgregor (Bombay, 1912).
Vol. VII, *Bombay,* Part II, *Imperial tables* by Mead and Macgregor (Bombay, 1912).
Census of India, 1921, Vol. I, *India,* Part I, *Report* by J. T. Marten (Calcutta, 1924).
Vol. V, *Bengal,* Part I, *Report* and Part II, *Tables* (Calcutta, 1923).
Vol. VII, *Bihar and Orissa,* Part II, *Tables* (Patna, 1923).

Vol. XIII, *Madras*, Part I, *Report* (Madras, 1922).

Vol. XV, *Punjab and Delhi*, Part I, *Report* (Lahore, 1923).

Census of India, 1931, Vol. I, *India*, Part I, *Report* by J. H. Hutton (Delhi, 1933).

Vol. VI, *Calcutta*, Parts I and II (Calcutta, 1933).

Vol. XVII, *Punjab*, Part I, *Report* (Lahore, 1933).

Census of India, 1941, Vol. I, *India*, Part I, *Tables* by M. W. M. Yeatts (Delhi, 1943).

Departments of the Government of India

Commercial Intelligence and Statistics Department [CISD] (Department of Statistics up to 1902–3): *Annual statements of the (seaborne) trade (and navigation) of British India with the British Empire and foreign countries* (with foreign countries), Vols. I and II (Calcutta, annual).

Estimates of area and yield of principal crops in India (Calcutta, annual).

Financial and commercial statistics of British India (Calcutta, annual); afterwards *Statistics of British India* (in several volumes, Calcutta, annual); afterwards *Statistical abstract for British India* (Calcutta, annual).

Index numbers of Indian prices, 1861–1931 and annual supplements through 1939 (Calcutta).

Joint-stock companies in British India and in the Indian States of Hyderabad, Mysore, Baroda, Gwalior, Indore and Travancore (Calcutta, annual).

Prices and wages in India (Calcutta, annual).

Review of the sugar industry of India (annual supplement to the *Indian Trade Journal*, Calcutta).

Review of the trade of India (Calcutta, annual).

Finance Department: *Report(s) upon the operations of the (Paper) Currency Department during the year(s) 1910–11*, and *1911–12* (Calcutta, 1911 and 1912).

Home Department (Education): *Review of education in India in 1886, with special reference to the report of the Education Commission*, by Sir A. Croft (Calcutta, 1888).

Mines Department: *Report of the inspection of mines in India* (annual, Calcutta); from 1901 onwards, *Report of the Chief Inspector of Mines in India* (Calcutta, annual).

Public Works Department: *Review of irrigation in India, 1911–12*, and *1913–14* (Simla, 1914 and 1915).

Railway Department (Railway Board): *Administration Report*, Vols. I and II (annual, Simla, up to 1923; Calcutta, from 1924 onwards).

History of Indian Railways constructed and in progress, corrected up to 31 March 1945 (Delhi, 1947).

Statistics Department: see under Commercial Intelligence and Statistics Department.

Directorate of Marketing and Inspection, Agricultural Marketing Series: No. 1: *Report on the marketing of wheat in India* (Delhi, 1937). No. 8: *Report on the marketing of linseed in India* (Delhi, 1938).

Imperial Council of Agricultural Research: *Report on the cost of production of crops in the principal sugar-cane and cotton tracts in India, Vols.* I–V (Delhi, 1938–9).

Imperial Gazetteer of India: *The Indian Empire*, Vol. III, *Economic* (Oxford, 1907).

India Office, London: *India Office List* (London, annual).

Indian Central Cotton Committee: *Annual report(s)*, 1937–41 (Bombay).

Indian Central Jute Committee: *Report on the marketing and transport of jute in India* (Calcutta, 1940).

Indian Factory Labour Commission 1908: Vol. I, *Report and appendices*; and Vol. II, *Evidence* (Simla, 1908; also PP 1908, LXXIV).

Indian Munitions Board: *Industrial handbook 1919* (Calcutta, 1919).

India's Contribution to the Great War (Calcutta, 1923).

Indian Tariff Board: Reports and Minutes of Evidence

Report on the caustic soda and bleaching powder industry (Bombay, 1946).

Report regarding the grant of protection to the cement industry (Calcutta, 1925).

Cotton Textile Industry Enquiry, 1927: Vol. I, *Report;* and Vols. II–IV, *Evidence* (Calcutta, 1927).

Report regarding the grant of protection to the cotton textile industry (Calcutta, 1932).

Cotton Textile Industry, Vols. I–IV, *Evidence* (Delhi, 1934).

[Special Tariff Board] *Report and Evidence on the enquiry regarding the level of duties necessary to afford adequate protection to the Indian cotton textile industry against imports from the United Kingdom of cotton piecegoods and yarn etc. . .,* Vol. I, *Report;* and Vols. II–III, *Evidence* (Delhi, 1936–7).

Report regarding the grant of protection to the paper and paper pulp industries; and *Evidence*, Vols. I–II (Calcutta, 1925).

Report regarding changes in the tariff entries relating to printing paper, 1927 (Calcutta, 1929).

Report on the grant of protection to the paper and paper pulp industries (Calcutta, 1931); and *Evidence*, Vols. I–II (Calcutta, 1932).

Report on the grant of protection to the paper and paper pulp industries (Delhi, 1938); and *Evidence*, Vols. I–II (Delhi, 1939).

Report on the removal of the revenue duty on pig iron including the evidence recorded during the enquiry (Calcutta, 1930).

Report regarding the grant of supplementary protection to the steel industry (Calcutta, 1925).

Report regarding the grant of protection to the steel industry; and *Evidence*, Vols. I–III (Calcutta, 1924).

Report regarding the grant of supplementary protection to the steel industry (Calcutta, 1925).

Statutory enquiry 1926: steel industry, Vol. I: *Report regarding the continuance of protection to the steel industry;* and *Evidence*, Vols. II–VII, (Calcutta, 1927).

Statutory enquiry 1926: steel industry, Vol. VIII, *Report regarding the grant of protection to the manufacture of wagons and underframes, component parts thereof, and wire and wire nails, including supplementary evidence recorded in 1927* (Calcutta, 1927).

Statutory enquiry 1933: steel industry, Vols. I–IV, *Evidence* (Delhi, 1934–5).

Report on the iron and steel industry (Delhi, 1934).

Report on the continuance of protection to the iron and steel industry (Bombay, 1947).

Report on the sugar industry (Calcutta, 1931); and *Evidence,* Vols. I–II (Calcutta, 1932).

Report on the sugar industry (Delhi, 1938); and *Evidence,* Vols. I, II, III A, III B, and IV (Delhi, 1938–9).

Report on the continuance of protection to the sugar industry, Vol. I (Bombay, 1950).

Labour Investigation Committee: *Report(s) on an enquiry into conditions of labour in* (a) *the cotton mill industry of India* and (b) *the jute-mill industry of India* by S. R. Deshpande (Delhi, 1946).

Legislative Assembly proceedings, 1924–34.

Proceedings of the Inter-provincial Jute Conference held at Calcutta from the 2nd to 4th August, 1915, with Appendices (Calcutta, 1915).

Reports of miscellaneous committees, commissions etc.

Reports of Currency Committees (Calcutta, 1931).

Report of the Fact-finding Committee (Handloom and Mills) (Delhi, 1942).

Report of the Fiscal Commission, 1949–50 (Delhi, 1950); and *Evidence,* Vol. III (Delhi, 1952).

Report of the Indian Cotton Committee (Calcutta, 1919).

Report of the Indian Fiscal Commission 1921–22 (Simla, 1922); and *Evidence,* Vols. I–III (Calcutta, 1923).

Report of the Indian Retrenchment Committee (Delhi, 1923).

Report of the Indian Sugar Committee (Simla, 1920).

Report of the Jute Enquiry Commission (Delhi, 1954).

Report of the Monopolies Inquiry Commission 1965, Vols. I and II (combined) (Delhi, 1965).

Report of the Railway Industries Committee (Delhi, 1923).

Report of the Textile Enquiry Committee (Delhi, 1958).

Report of the Working Party for the cotton textile industry (Delhi, 1953).

Reserve Bank of India: *Banking and monetary statistics of India* (Bombay, 1954).

Report on currency and finance for the years 1935–6 and 1936–7 (Bombay, 1937).

Royal Commission on Agriculture in India: *Report* (London, 1928); and *Evidence,* Vol. I (Parts 1, 2, 3), Vol. II (Parts 1, 2), and Vols. III–XIII (London, 1927–8).

B. Listed under individual authors [Gov. India pub.]

Adarkar, B. N. *The history of the Indian tariff* (Studies in Indian Economics issued by the Office of the Economic Adviser, First Series, No. 2) (Delhi, 1940).

Clow, A. G. *The State and Industry* (Calcutta, 1928).

Datta, K. L. *Report on the enquiry into the rise of prices in India*, Vols. i–v (Calcutta, 1914).

Gorrie, R. Maclagan. *Forestry development and soil conservation in the Upper Damodar Valley* (Damodar Valley Corporation, Alipore n.d.; *c.* 1952).

Hardy, G. S. *Report on the import tariff on cotton piecegoods trade* (Calcutta, 1929).

MacKenna, J. *Agriculture in India* (Calcutta, 1915).

Noel-Paton, F. *Notes on sugar in India* (Third edition, Calcutta, 1911).

Pearson, R. S. 'Note on the utilization of bamboos for the manufacture of paper pulp', *Indian Forest Records*, Vol. 4, Part 5 (Calcutta, 1913).

Sahni, J. N. *Indian Railways, one hundred years, 1853 to 1953* (New Delhi, 1953).

Sethi, B. L. 'History of cotton' in B. L. Sethi and others: *Cotton in India*, Vol. 2 (Indian Central Cotton Committee, Bombay, 1960), pp. 1–39.

4. OFFICIAL PUBLICATIONS: INDIAN PROVINCIAL GOVERNMENTS
A. Listed under collected authors
Assam

Report on immigrant labour in the Province of Assam (Shillong, annual).
Resolution on immigrant labour in Assam (Shillong, annual).

Bengal

Report on the Administration of Bengal (Calcutta, annual).

Bengal District Gazetteers: *Champaran* by L. S. S. O'Malley (Calcutta, 1907).
Dacca (in the Eastern Bengal District Gazetteers series) by B. C. Allen (Allahabad, 1912).
Hooghly by L. S. S. O'Malley and Monmohon Chakravarti (Calcutta, 1912).
Howrah by L. S. S. O'Malley and Monmohon Chakravarti (Calcutta, 1909).
Mymensingh by F. A. Sachse (Calcutta, 1917).
Pabna by L. S. S. O'Malley (Calcutta, 1923).
Santal-Parganas by L. S. S. O'Malley (Calcutta, 1910); second edition, in the Bihar District Gazetteers series, by S. C. Mukherji (Patna, 1938).
24-Parganas by L. S. S. O'Malley (Calcutta, 1914).

Report of the Bengal Jute Enquiry Committee 1933 (Finlow Committee), Vol. 1 (Alipore, 1934).

Report of the Bengal Jute Enquiry Committee (Fawcus Committee) (Alipore, 1940).

Report of the Labour Enquiry Commission 1895 (Calcutta, 1896).

Bombay

Report on (Bombay, a review of) the administration of the (Bombay) Presidency (Bombay, annual).

Report of the Bombay Development Committee 1914 (Bombay, 1914).

Gazetteers of the Bombay Presidency: *Bombay City and Island* (see below under Secondary Sources, Edwardes, S. M.).

Vol. II, *Gujarat: Broach and Surat* (Bombay, 1877).

Vol. IV, *Gujarat: Ahmedabad* (Bombay, 1879).

Vol. VII, *Baroda* (Bombay, 1880).

Department of Industries, Bombay: *Annual report, 1917–18* (Bombay, 1919) and subsequent issues up to 1922–3.

Labour Office, Bombay: *Wages and unemployment in the Bombay cotton textile industry: Report of the Departmental Enquiry* (Bombay, 1934).

Labour Office, Bombay: *General wage census*, Part I, *Perennial factories, Third Report* (Bombay, 1937).

Report of the Textile Labour Enquiry Committee, Vol. II, *Final Report* (Bombay, 1940).

Central Indian States

The Central Indian State Gazetteer Series: Vol. I, *Gwalior State Gazetteer*, Text and Tables (Calcutta, 1908).

Vol. II, *Indore State Gazetteer*, Text and Tables (Calcutta, 1908).

Vol. III, *Bhopal State Gazetteer*, Text and Tables (Calcutta, 1908).

Madras

Madras, a review of the administration of the Presidency (Madras, annual).

The Madras Provincial Banking Enquiry Committee, Vol. I, *Report*; and Vols. II–IV, *Written and Oral Evidence* (Madras, 1930).

Report of the Department of Industries, Madras, for the year ended 31st March 1920 (Madras, 1921), and subsequent annual issues up to 1939.

Punjab

Punjab District Gazetteers: Vol. V A, *Delhi District with Maps* (Lahore, 1913).

The United Provinces

The UP Provincial Banking Enquiry Committee, 1929–30, Vol. I, *Report* (Allahabad, 1930); and Vols. II–IV° *Evidence* (Allahabad, 1930–1).

District Gazetteers of the United Provinces of Agra and Oudh (compiled and edited by H. R. Nevill, ICS.): Vol. IV, *Meerut* (Allahabad, 1904).

Vol. XIII, *Bareilly* (Allahabad, 1911).

Vol. XVIII, *Shahjahanpur* (Allahabad, 1910).

Vol. XIX, *Cawnpore* (Allahabad, 1910).

Vol. XXXVIII, *Lucknow* (Allahabad, 1904).

Report of the Cawnpore Textile Labour Inquiry Committee appointed by the Government of the United Provinces (Allahabad, 1938).

The administration report of the Department of Industries, United Provinces, for the year ending 31 March 1937 (Allahabad, 1937), and subsequent annual issues.

B.   Listed under individual authors [IPG pub.]

Chatterjee, A. C. *Notes on the Industries of the United Provinces* (Allahabad, 1908).

Chatterton, A. *Note on Industrial Work in India* (Madras, 1905).

Collin, E. W. *Report on the Arts and Industries of Bengal* (Calcutta, 1890).

Cumming, J. G. *Review of the industrial position and prospects in Bengal in 1908 with special reference to the industrial survey of 1890, Part II of special report* (Calcutta, 1908).

Finlow, R. S. *General Report on Jute in Bengal for 1904–5* (Calcutta, 1906).

Latifi, A. *The Industrial Punjab: A Survey of Facts, Conditions and Possibilities* (published for the Punjab Government by Longmans, Green & Co., Bombay and Calcutta, 1911).

Mitra, A. *An Account of Land Management in West Bengal 1870–1950, Census 1951, West Bengal* (Alipore, 1953).

Moreland, W. H. *Notes on the Agricultural Conditions and Problems of the United Provinces, revised up to 1911* (Allahabad, 1913).

Raghavaiyangar, S. Srinivasa. *Memorandum on the Progress of the Madras Presidency during the Last Forty Years of British Administration* (Madras, 1893).

Watson, E. R. *A Monograph on Iron and Steel Work in the Province of Bengal* (Calcutta, 1907).

5.   OFFICIAL PUBLICATIONS: INTERNATIONAL ORGANIZATIONS AND OTHER GOVERNMENTS

ILO Studies and Reports Series B, No. 29, Butler, Harold: *Problems of Industry in the East with Special Reference to India, French India, Ceylon, Malaya, and the Netherlands India* (Geneva, 1938).

ILO Studies and Reports Series B, No. 27: *The world textile industry, economic and social problems*, Vol. 1 (Geneva, 1937).

League of Nations: *The Causes and Phases of the World Economic Depression* (Geneva, 1931).

(Nurkse, R. and Brown, W. A., Jr.) *International Currency Experience* (League of Nations, 1944).

United Nations: *Processes and Problems of Industrialization in Underdeveloped Countries* (New York, 1955).

U.S. Bureau of the Census: *Historical Statistics of the United States, Colonial Times to 1957* (Washington, D.C., 1960).

6.   PUBLICATIONS OF UNOFFICIAL (OR SEMI-OFFICIAL) ORGANIZATIONS, AND PERIODICALS

The Bankers' Magazine (London, monthly).

Bengal National Chamber of Commerce and Industry: *Report of the Committee for the year 1932* (Calcutta, 1933).

Bengal National Chamber of Commerce and Industry 1887–1962 (Souvenir Volume) (Calcutta, 1962).

The Bombay Investor's Year-Book 1940 (First edition, Bombay, 1940).

Calcutta Jute Dealers Association: *Report of the Committee from 1st January to 31st December 1927* (Calcutta, 1928).

Capital (Calcutta, weekly).

Debrett's Peerage, Baronetage, Companionage, etc. (London, annual).

East India Jute Association Limited, Calcutta: *Annual Report for the year ended 30th June 1928* (Calcutta, 1928) and subsequent annual reports.

Handbook and Guide to Dundee and District published for the Dundee meeting of the British Association 1912 (Dundee, 1912).

Imperial Institute: *Indian Trade Enquiry reports on jute and silk* (London, 1921).

Indian Chamber of Commerce: *Annual Report of the Committee for the year 1928* (Calcutta, 1928) and subsequent annual reports.

Indian Finance Year-Book 1931 (Calcutta, 1931) and subsequent annual issues.

Indian Jute Mills Association (up to 1901, Indian Jute Manufacturers' Association): *Report of the Committee for the year ended 31st December 1901* (Calcutta, 1902) and subsequent annual reports.

The Indian Textile Journal [ITJ] (Bombay, monthly).

The Indian Textile Journal 1890–1940, Jubilee Souvenir (Bombay, 1941).

Indian Year-Book (Bombay, annual).

Investor's India Year-Book [IIYB] (Calcutta, annual; first edition, 1911).

Issues advertised in the Times (London, 1894–8).

Millowners' Association, Bombay: *Annual Report* (Bombay) from 1895 onwards.

Murray's Handbook for Travelling in India, Burma and Ceylon (London, annual; fifteenth edition, 1938).

The Stock Exchange: Burdett's Official Intelligence (later, *The Stock Exchange: Official Intelligence*) (London, annual).

Tea Producing Companies 1914, and *Tea Producing Companies 1923–4*, compiled by the Mincing Lane Tea and Rubber Share Brokers' Association Limited and the Indian Tea Share Exchange Limited (London, 1914 and 1924).

SECONDARY SOURCES: BOOKS AND ARTICLES

Adarkar, B. N. 'The Ottawa Pact' in Radhakamal Mukerjee (ed.): *Economic Problems of Modern India*, Vol. I, pp. 378–95.

Adler, J. H. (ed.). *Capital Movements and Economic Development* (London, 1967).

Aitken, H. G. J. (ed.). *The State and Economic Growth* (New York, 1959).

Aldcroft, D. H. (ed.). *The Development of British Industry and Foreign Competition 1875–1914* (London, 1968).

Allen, G. C. *Japanese Industry: Its Recent Development and Present Condition* (New York, 1931).

'The Industrialization of the Far East' in H. J. Habakkuk and M. Postan (eds.): *Cambridge Economic History of Europe*, Vol. VI, Part II, pp. 873–923.

Allen, G. C. and Donnithorne, A. G. *Western Enterprise in Indonesia and Malaya* (London, 1957).

Alva, J. *Men and Supermen of Hindustan* (Bombay, 1943).

Andrew Yule and Co. *Andrew Yule and Co. Ltd* (Printed in Great Britain for private circulation, 1963).

Anstey, V. 'Economic Development' in O'Malley (ed.): *Modern India and the West*, pp. 258–304.

The Economic Development of India (London, 1957).

Antrobus, H. A. *The Jorehaut Tea Company Ltd* (London, 1949).

A History of the Assam Company 1839–1953 (Edinburgh, 1957).

Armstrong, Sir Charles H. 'Indian Trade and the War', *JRSA* LXIII, No. 3, 262, 28 May 1915, pp. 645–57.

Atkinson, F. J. 'A statistical review of the Income and Wealth of British India', *Journal of the Royal Statistical Society*, Vol. LXV, Part II, June 1902, pp. 209–72; discussion on the above paper by W. Digby, pp. 272–5.

Arrow, K. J. 'Towards a Theory of Price Adjustment' in Moses Abramovitz *et al.* (eds.): *The Allocation of Economic Resources* (Stanford, California, 1959).

Azad, Maulana Abul Kalam. *India Wins Freedom* (Bombay, 1959).

Bagchi, K. *The Ganges Delta* (Calcutta, 1944).

Bain, J. S. *Barriers to New Competition* (Cambridge, Mass., 1956).

Balakrishna, R. *Industrial Development of Mysore* (Bangalore City, India, 1940).

Baldwin, G. B. *Industrial Growth in South India* (Glencoe, Illinois, 1959).

Baldwin, R. E. 'Patterns of Development in Newly Settled Areas', *Manchester School*, Vol. 24, May 1956, pp. 161–79.

Banerjee, A. K. *India's Balance of Payments: Estimates of Current and Capital Accounts from 1921–22 to 1938–39* (Bombay, 1963).

Barker, S. G. *Report on the Scientific and Technical Development of the Jute Manufacturing Industry in Bengal* (Indian Jute Mills Association, Calcutta, 1935).

Barna, T. 'On Measuring Capital' in D. C. Hague and F. A. Lutz (eds.): *The Theory of Capital* (London, 1961), pp. 75–94.

Batten, G. H. M. 'The Opium Question', *JSA*, XL, No. 2054 (1 April 1892), p. 444–67; discussion on the paper, pp. 467–94.

Bensusan-Butt, D. *On Economic Growth* (Oxford, 1960).

Bergstrom, A. R. *The Construction and Use of Economic Models* (London, 1967).

Bhattacharya, S. 'Laissez Faire in India', *The Indian Economic and Social History Review*, II (1), January 1965.

Bickerdike, C. F. 'The Theory of Incipient Taxes', *Economic Journal* XVI (4), December 1906, pp. 529–35.

Binani, G. D. and Rama Rao, T. V. *India at a Glance: A Comprehensive Reference Book on India* (Calcutta, 1954).

Bird and Company of Calcutta. *A History produced to mark the firm's centenary 1864–1964* by G. Harrison (Bird and Company, Calcutta, 1964).

Blackett, Sir Basil P. 'The Economic Progress of India', *JRSA*, LXXVIII, No.

4,028 (31 January 1930), pp. 313–27; discussions on the paper, pp. 328–336.

Blake, George, *B.I. Centenary* (London, 1956).

Blyn, G. *Agricultural Trends in India 1891–1947: Output, Availability and Productivity* (University of Pennsylvania Press, Philadelphia, 1966).

Bompas, C. H. 'The Work of the Calcutta Improvement Trust', *JRSA*, LXXV, No. 3868, 7 January 1927, pp. 200–13; discussion on the paper, pp. 213–19.

Bose, A. 'Foreign Capital' in V. B. Singh (ed.): *Economic History of India, 1857–1956* (Bombay, 1965), pp. 484–527.

Bose, S. K. *Capital and Labour in the Indian Tea Industry* (Bombay, 1954).

Brayne, F. L. *The Remaking of Village India* (Bombay and London, 1929).

Broughton, G. M. *Labour in Indian Industries* (London, 1924).

Brown, Hilton. *The Sahibs* (London, 1948).

Parry's of Madras: A Story of British Enterprise in India (Madras, 1954).

Buchanan, D. H. *The Development of Capitalistic Enterprise in India* (New York, 1934; reprinted, London, 1966).

Buckland, C. E. 'The City of Calcutta', *JSA*, LIV, No. 2776, 2 February 1906, pp. 275–94.

Bull, H. M. and Haksar, K. N. *Madhav Rao Scindia of Gwalior 1876–1925* (Gwalior, 1926).

Burkhead, Jesse. 'The Balanced Budget', *Quarterly Journal of Economics*, May 1954, reprinted in A. Smithies and J. K. Butters (eds.): *Readings in Fiscal Policy* (London, 1955), pp. 3–27.

Burn & Co. Ltd, Howrah (published by Martin Burn Ltd, Calcutta, 1961).

Burn, Duncan L. *The Economic History of Steel-Making 1867–1939* (Cambridge, U.K., 1940).

Burnett-Hurst, A. R. *Labour and Housing in Bombay* (London, 1925).

Burt, B. C. (later Sir Bryce Burt). 'The Indian Sugar Industry', *JRSA*, LXXXIII, No. 4317, 16 August 1935, pp. 919–40; discussion on the paper, pp. 940–943.

'Agricultural Progress in India during the Decade 1929–39', *JRSA*, XC, No. 4602, 20 February, 1942.

Calvert, H. C. *The Wealth and Welfare of the Punjab* (London, 1936).

Chadwick, D. T. 'Agricultural Progress' in S. Playne (compiler) and A. Wright (ed.): *Southern India* (London, 1915), pp. 745–54.

'The Trade of India with Russia, France and Italy', *JRSA*, LXVI, No. 3397, 28 December 1917, pp. 96–107.

'The Work of the Indian Tariff Board', *JRSA*, LXXVI, No. 3921, 13 January 1928, pp. 195–205.

Chandra, Bipan. *The Rise and Growth of Economic Nationalism in India* (New Delhi, 1966).

Chatterjee, T. P. and Sinha, A. R. 'A Statistical Study of the Foreign Demand for Raw Jute', *Sankhya*, Vol. 5 (1940–1), pp. 433–8.

Chatterji, R. *Indian Economics* (Calcutta, 1959).

Chatterton, Sir Alfred. 'Weaving in India', *The Hindustan Review* (Allahabad), XV, No. 91, March 1907, pp. 235–49.

'The Weaving Competitions in Madras', *The Indian Trade Journal*, Vol. IX, No. 106, 9 April 1908, pp. 54–7.

'The Industrial Progress of the Mysore State', *JRSA*, LXXIII, 26 June 1925, pp. 714–37; discussion on the paper, pp. 737–47.

Chaudhuri, K. C. *The History and Economics of the Land System in Bengal* (Calcutta, 1927).

Chaudhury, N. C. *Jute in Bengal* (Calcutta, 1908).

Jute and Substitutes (Calcutta, 1933).

Choudhry, N. K. 'An Econometric Analysis of the Import Demand Function for Burlap (Hessian) in the U.S.A., 1919–53', *Econometrica*, Vol. 26, July 1958, pp. 416–28.

Chowdhury, B. *Growth of Commercial Agriculture in Bengal (1757–1900)*, Vol. I (Calcutta, 1964).

Cooke, C. N. *The Rise, Progress and Present Condition of Banking in India* (Calcutta, 1863).

Cooper, A. T. 'Recent Electrical Progress in India', *JRSA*, LXXVII, No. 3994, 7 June 1929, pp. 739–58.

Coupland, Sir Reginald, *India: A Restatement* (London, 1945).

Coyajee, Sir J. C. 'Money reconstruction in India (1925–7)', *Annals of the American Academy of Political and Social Science*, Vol. 145, Part II, 1929, pp. 101–14.

Crane, R. I. 'Technical Education and Economic Development in India before World War I' in C. A. Anderson and M. J. Bowman (eds.): *Education and Economic Development* (London, 1966), pp. 167–201.

Creighton, Charles, M.D. 'Plague in India', *JSA*, LIII, No. 2743, 16 June 1905, pp. 810–26.

Cumming, Sir John (ed.): *Modern India* (London, 1931).

Cunningham, J. R. 'Education' in L. S. S. O'Malley (ed.): *Modern India and the West*, pp. 138–87.

Dantwala, M. L. *Marketing of Raw Cotton in India* (Bombay, 1937).

A Hundred Years of Indian Cotton (Bombay, 1948).

Darley, Sir Bernard. 'Irrigation and Its Possibilities' in Radhakamal Mukerjee (ed.): *Economic Problems of Modern India*, Vol. I (London, 1939), pp. 148–67.

Darling, M. L. *The Punjab Peasant in Prosperity and Debt* (London, 1928).

Das, N. *Industrial Enterprise in India* (London, 1938).

Das, R. K. *Factory Labour in India* (Berlin, 1923).

Plantation Labour in India (Calcutta, 1931).

Dasgupta, A. 'The Jute Textile Industry' in V. B. Singh (ed.): *Economic History of India, 1857–1956*, pp. 260–80.

Davis, Kingsley. *The Population of India and Pakistan* (Princeton, N.J., 1951).

Dayal, Hari Har. 'Agricultural Labourers: An Inquiry into their Condition in the Unao District' in Radhakamal Mukerjee (ed.): *Fields and Farms in Oudh* (Calcutta, 1929).

Deane, P. and Cole, W. A. *British Economic Growth 1688–1959: Trends and Structure* (2nd ed. Cambridge, U.K., 1967).

Deerr, N. *The History of Sugar*, Vol. I (London, 1949).

Desai, Ashok V. 'Origins of Parsi Enterprise', *Indian Economic and Social History Review*, Vol. v (4), December 1968.

Desai, R. C. *Standard of Living in India and Pakistan 1931–2 to 1940–1* (Bombay, 1953).

Dey, H. L. *The Indian Tariff Problem in Relation to Industry and Taxation* (London, 1933).

Dey, H. L. and Mukerjee, Radhakamal (eds.). *The Economic Problems of Modern India*, Vol. ii (London, 1941).

Dickinson, A. 'Water Power in India', *JRSA*, lxvi, No. 3,417, 17 May 1918, pp. 417–22; discussion on the paper, pp. 422–6.

Digby, W. *'Prosperous' British India* (London, 1901).

Dobb, M. *Political Economy and Capitalism: Some Essays in Economic Tradition* (London, 1940).

Doraiswamy, S. V. *Indian Finance, Currency and Banking* (Madras, 1915).

The Duncan Group. *Being a Short History of Duncan Brothers & Co. Ltd, Calcutta and Walter Duncan and Goodricke Ltd, London, 1859–1959* (London, 1959).

Dunn, G. O. W. 'The Housing Question in Bombay', *JRSA*, lviii, No. 2989, 4 March 1910, pp. 393–405; discussion on the paper, pp. 405–13.

Dupriez, L. H. (ed.). *Economic Progress, Papers and Proceedings of a Round Table held by the International Economic Association* (Louvain, 1955), pp. 149–69.

Dutt, R. C. *The Economic History of India in the Victorian Age* (London, 1904; reprinted, Delhi, 1960).

Dutt, R. P. *India Today* (Bombay, 1949).

Eddison, J. C. *A Case Study in Industrial Development – the Growth of the Pulp and Paper Industry in India* (Centre for International studies, M.I.T., Cambridge, Mass., 1955).

Edwardes, S. M. *The Gazetteer of Bombay City and Island*, Vol. i (Bombay, 1909).

Memoir of Rao Bahadur Ranchhodlal Chhotalal, CIE (Exeter, U.K., 1920).

Elwin, V. *The Story of Tata Steel* (Bombay, 1958).

Feldman, H. *Karachi through a Hundred Years, the Centenary History of Karachi Chamber of Commerce and Industry 1860–1960* (Karachi, 1960).

Ferber, R. 'The Anatomy and Structure of Industry Expectations in relation to those of Individual Firms', *Journal of the American Statistical Association*, June 1958, pp. 317–35.

Forrest, L. R. Windham. 'The Town and the Island of Bombay – Past and Present', *JSA*, xlix, 14 June 1901, pp. 569–84; discussion on the paper, pp. 584–8.

Fraser, Lovat. *India Under Curzon and After* (London, 1911).

Iron and Steel in India (Bombay, 1919).

Fremantle, S. H. 'The Problem of Indian Labour Supply', *JRSA*, No. 2947, 14 May 1909, pp. 510–19; discussion on the paper, pp. 519–24.

Fuhrer, A. 'Parsees or Parsis', *Encyclopaedia Britannica*, 9th ed. (Edinburgh, 1885), Vol. xviii, p. 327.

Furnivall, J. S. *An Introduction to the Political Economy of Burma* (Rangoon, 1931).

Gadgil, D. R. *The Industrial Evolution of India in Recent Times* (Bombay, 1944).

'Indian Economic Organization' in S. Kuznets and others (eds.): *Economic Growth Brazil, India, Japan* (Durham, N.C., U.S.A., 1955), pp. 448–463.

Ganguli, B. N. *Reconstruction of India's Foreign Trade* (New Delhi, 1946).

Gerschenkron, A. *Economic Backwardness in Historical Perspective* (New York, 1962).

Ghosh, H. H. *The Advancement of Industry* (Calcutta, 1910).

Ginwala, Sir Padamji P. 'India and the Ottawa Conference', *JRSA*, LXXI, No. 4,175, 25 November 1932.

Glass, D. V. 'World Population 1800–1950' in H. J. Habakkuk and M. Postan (eds.): *Cambridge Economic History of Europe*, Vol. VI, Part I (Cambridge, U.K., 1965), pp. 56–138.

Goodwin, R. M. 'Secular and Cyclical Aspects of the Multiplier and the Accelerator' in *Income, Employment and Public Policy* (Essays in Honour of Alvin H. Hansen) (New York, 1948).

'The Nonlinear Accelerator and the Persistence of Business Cycles', *Econometrica*, 19, 1951, pp. 1–17.

Gordon, L. A. 'Social and Economic Conditions of the Bombay Workers on the Eve of the 1908 Strike' in I. M. Reisner and N. M. Goldberg (eds.): *Tilak and the Struggle for Indian Freedom* (New Delhi, 1966), pp. 471–544.

Greenberg, M. *British Trade and the Opening of China* (Cambridge, U.K., 1951).

Grimston, F. S. 'The Indian Ordnance Factories and their Influence on Industry', *JRSA*, LXXIX, No. 4,103, 10 July 1931, pp. 777–89; discussion on the paper, pp. 789–92.

Growth and Perspective (published for the Indian Iron & Steel Co. Ltd by Martin Burn, Calcutta, 1968).

Gurtoo, D. N. *India's Balance of Payments (1920–1960)* (Delhi, 1961).

Habakkuk, H. J. 'The Historical Experience on the Basic Conditions of Economic Progress' in L. H. Dupriez (ed.): *Economic Progress*, Papers and Proceedings of a Round Table held by the International Economic Association (Louvain, 1955), pp. 149–69.

Habakkuk, H. J. and Postan, M. (eds.): *The Cambridge Economic History of Europe*, Vol. VI, Parts I and II (Cambridge, U.K., 1965).

Haji, S. N. *State Aid to Indian Shipping* (Indian Shipping Series, Pamphlet No. 1, Bombay, 1922).

Harris, F. R. *Jamsetji Nusserwanji Tata: A Chronicle of His Life* (Bombay, 1958).

Harrison, G. *Bird and Company of Calcutta, A History produced to mark the firm's centenary 1864–1964* (Calcutta, 1964).

Havell, E. B. 'Art Administration in India', *JRSA*, LVIII, No. 2985, 4 February 1910, pp. 274–84.

Hazari, R. K. *The Structure of the Corporate Private Sector: A Study of Concentration, Ownership and Control* (Bombay and London, 1966).

Heady, Earl O. and Kaldor, Donald R. 'Expectations and Errors in Forecasting Agricultural Prices', *Journal of Political Economy*, Vol. 62, February 1954, pp. 34–47.

Heaton, H. 'Industrial Revolution', *Encyclopaedia of the Social Sciences*, Vol. VIII (New York, 1935), pp. 3–13.

Helm, Elijah. 'An International Survey of the Cotton Industry', *Quarterly Journal of Economics*, 1903, pp. 417–37.

Hirachand, Lalchand. 'Indian Sugar Industry' in *Bombay Investor's Year Book 1940* (Bombay, 1940), 71–2.

Hirachand, Ratanchand. 'Constructional Engineering in India' in ibid., pp. 75–7.

Hirachand, Walchand. 'Why Indian Shipping Does Not Grow' in ibid., pp. 58–66.

Hirsch, Leon V. *Marketing in an Underdeveloped Economy: the North Indian Sugar Industry* (Englewood Cliffs, N.J., 1961).

Hope, G. D. 'The Tea Industry of Bengal and Assam' in S. Playne (compiler) and A. Wright (ed.): *Bengal and Assam, Behar and Orissa* (London, 1917).

Howard, A. 'The Improvement of Crop Production in India', *JRSA*, LXVIII, Nos. 3,530 and 3,531, 16 July and 29 July 1920.

Howard, Louise. *Sir Albert Howard in India* (London, 1953).

Hubbard, G. E. *Eastern Industrialization and Its Effect on the West* (London, 1938).

Hunt, N. G. 'Banks and the Indian Cotton Textile Industry' in *The Indian Textile Journal, Jubilee Souvenir 1890–1940* (Bombay, 1941).

Hunter, W. W. *The Indian Empire, Its Peoples, History and Products* (London, 1893).

Huque, M. Azizul. *The Man Behind the Plough* (Calcutta, 1939).

Husain, S. A. *Agricultural Marketing in Northern India* (London, 1937).

Imlah, A. H. *Economic Elements in the Pax Britannica* (Cambridge, Mass., 1958).

'The Indian Mill Hands: A Movement on their behalf', *ITF*, October 1913, p. 32.

Islam, N. *Foreign Capital and Economic Development: Japan, India and Canada* (Rutland, Vermont, U.S.A. and Tokyo, 1962).

Ito, Shoji. 'A Note on the "Business Combine" in India – with special reference to the Nattukottai Chettiars', *The Developing Economies* (Tokyo) IV (3), 1966, pp. 367–80.

Jack, J. C. *The Economic Life of a Bengal District* (Oxford, U.K., 1916).

James, Sir Frederick. 'The House of Tata – Sixty Years of Industrial Development in India', *JRSA*, XCVI, No. 4,776, 27 August 1948, pp. 612–20.

James, R. C. 'Labour Mobility, Unemployment, and Economic Change, An Indian Case', *The Journal of Political Economy*, LXVIII (6), December 1959, pp. 545–59.

James Finlay and Company Limited: Manufacturers and East India Mer-

chants, 1750–1950 (published privately by Jackson Son and Company, Glasgow, 1951).

Jenks, L. H. *The Migration of British Capital to 1875* (first published New York, 1927; reprinted, London, 1963).

Johnson, W. A. *The Steel Industry of India* (Cambridge, Mass., 1966).

Jones, Gavin. 'The Rise and Progress of Cawnpore', in S. Playne (compiler) and A. Wright (ed.). *The Bombay Presidency, United Provinces, Punjab, etc.* (London, 1920), pp. 497–99.

Joshi, L. A. *The Control of Industry in India* (Bombay, 1965).

Kahn, A. E. *Great Britain in the World Economy* (New York, 1946).

Kanitkar, N. V. and Mann, H. H. *Land and Labour in a Deccan Village, Study No. 2* (London and Bombay, 1921).

Kannappan, S. 'The Tata Steel Strike: Some Dilemmas of Industrial Relations in a Developing Economy', *The Journal of Political Economy*, LXVII, October 1959, pp. 489–507.

Karaka, D. F. *History of the Parsis*, Vol. 2 (London, 1884).

Keatinge, G. F. 'Agricultural Progress in Western India', *JRSA*, LXI, No. 3,141, 13 January 1913, pp. 267–73.

Agricultural Progress in Western India (London, 1921).

Keenan, J. L. *A Steel Man in India* (New York, 1943; London, 1945).

Kennedy, R. E. 'The Protestant Ethic and the Parsis', *The American Journal of Sociology*, 68 (1962–3), pp. 11–20; reprinted in N. J. Smelser (ed.): *Readings in Economic Sociology* (Englewood Cliffs, N.J., 1965), pp. 16–26.

Keynes, J. M. Review of T. Morison: *The Economic Transition in India* (London, 1911) in *Economic Journal*, XXI, September 1911, pp. 426–31.

Indian Currency and Finance (London, 1913).

The General Theory of Employment, Interest and Money (London, 1936; reprinted 1949).

Kidron, M. *Foreign Investments in India* (London, 1965).

Kindleberger, C. P. *Economic Development* (2nd edition, New York, 1965).

Kling, B. 'The Origin of The Managing Agency System in India', *The Journal of Asian Studies*, XXVI (1), November 1966, pp. 37–48.

Knowles, L. C. A. *Economic Development of the British Overseas Empire* (London, 1924).

Kosambi, D. D. 'The Bourgeoisie Comes of Age in India', *Science and Society*, Vol. x, 1946, pp. 392–8.

Krishna, Raj. 'Farm Supply Response in India – Pakistan', *Economic Journal*, LXXIII, September 1963.

Kuczynski, J. 'Condition of Workers' in V. B. Singh (ed.): *Economic History of India 1857–1956* (Bombay, 1965), pp. 609–37.

Kuznets, S. and others (eds.): *Economic Growth: Brazil, India, Japan* (Durham, N.C., 1955), pp. 448–63.

Lall, S. 'Industrial Development in the Indian Provinces', *JRSA*, LXXXIX, No. 4,579, 24 January 1941, pp. 134–45; discussion, pp. 145–7.

Landes, D. S. *Bankers and Pashas: International Finance and Economic Imperialism in Egypt* (London, 1958).

Leacock, S. and Mandelbaum, D. G. 'A Nineteenth Century Development

Project in India: the Cotton Improvement Program', *Economic Development and Cultural Change* (Chicago), III (4), July 1955, pp. 334–51.

Leake, H. Martin. *The Foundation of Indian Agriculture* (Cambridge, U.K. 1923).

Lehmann, F. 'Great Britain and the Supply of Railway Locomotives of India: A Case Study of "Economic Imperialism"', *The Indian Economic and Social History Review*, II (4), October 1965.

Lewis, W. A. *Economic Survey 1919–1939* (London, 1949).

'Economic Development with Unlimited Supplies of Labour', *The Manchester School of Economic and Social Studies*, XXII, 1954, pp. 139–91.

The Theory of Economic Growth (London, 1955).

Lindsay, H. A. F. 'World Tendencies Reflected in India's Trade', *JRSA*, LXXV, No. 3,876, 4 March 1927, pp. 384–94; discussion on the paper, pp. 394–399.

Lockwood, W. W. *The Economic Development of Japan* (Princeton, N.J., 1954).

Lokanathan, P. S. *Industrial Organization in India* (London, 1935).

Lovett, Pat. *The Mirror of Investment 1927* (Calcutta, 1927).

Macbean, A. I. 'Problems of Stabilization Policy in Underdeveloped Countries', *Oxford Economic Papers*, N.S. Vol. 14, 1962, pp. 251–66.

Mackenna, J. (later Sir James Mackenna). 'Scientific Agriculture in India', *JRSA*, No. 3,316, LXIV, 9 June 1916, pp. 537–46.

'The Indian Sugar Industry', *JRSA*, LXXVII, No. 3,970, 21 December 1928, pp. 140–52; discussion on the paper, pp. 152–8.

Mackenzie, Sir Compton. *Realms of Silver: One Hundred Years of Banking in the East* (London, 1954).

Maclean, J. M. 'India's Place in an Imperial Federation', *JSA*, LII, No. 2,665, 18 December 1903, pp. 81–90; discussion on the paper, pp. 90–5.

McLeod, C. C. 'The Indian Jute Industry', *JRSA*, LXIV, No. 3,292, 24 December 1915, pp. 105–18; discussion on the paper, pp. 113–20.

Mahindra, K. C. *Sir Rajendra Nath Mookerjee* (Calcutta, 1933; reprinted, Calcutta, 1962).

Majumdar, S. C. *Rivers of the Bengal Delta* (Calcutta, 1941).

Mann, H. H. 'The Progress of Agriculture' in S. Playne (compiler) and A. Wright (ed.): *The Bombay Presidency, United Provinces, Punjab etc.* (London, 1920), pp. 540–7.

'The Agriculture of India', *Annals of the American Academy of Political and Social Science*, Vol. 145, Part II, 1929, pp. 72–81.

'The Economic Results and Possibilities of Irrigation', *Indian Journal of Agricultural Economics*, 13 (2), 1958, pp. 1–6.

Mann, H. H. and Kanitkar, N. V. *Land and Labour in a Deccan Village*, Study No. 2 (London and Bombay, 1921).

Marx, Karl. *Capital: A Critical Analysis of Capitalist Production*, Vol. 1 (translated by Edward Aveling and Samuel Moore and edited by Frederick Engels) (London, 1957).

Masani, R. P. *N. M. Wadia and His Foundation* (Bombay, 1961).

Mather, R. 'The Iron and Steel Industry in India', *JRSA*, LXXV, No. 3,886, 13 May 1927, pp. 600–16; discussion on the paper, pp. 616–24.

Meek, D. B. (later Sir David B. Meek). 'Indian External Trade', *JRSA*, LXXXIV, No. 4,362, 26 June 1936, pp. 835–69.
'World Economic Controls and India's Part in These', *JRSA*, LXXXVII, No. 4,508, 14 April 1939, pp. 554–69.
Mehta, M. M. *Structure of Indian Industries* (Bombay, 1955).
Mehta, S. D. *The Indian Cotton Textile Industry: An Economic Analysis* (Bombay, 1935).
The Cotton Mills of India 1854–1954 (Bombay, 1954).
Meston, Lord. 'Public Finance' in Sir John Cummings (ed.) *Modern India* (London, 1931).
'The Mill Industry in Bombay', *ITJ* April 1914, p. 222.
Misra, S. and Singh, B. *A Study of Land Reforms in Uttar Pradesh* (Calcutta, 1964).
Misra, B. B. *The Indian Middle Classes* (London, 1961).
Mitra, Kishori Chand. *Dwarakanath Tagore* (in Bengali) (Calcutta, 1962).
Modigliani, F. 'New Developments on the Oligopoly Front', *Journal of Political Economy*, LXVI, June 1958, pp. 215–32; discussion on the above paper by F. M. Fisher, D. E. Farrar and C. F. Phillips, Jr., and reply by F. Modigliani, *Journal of Political Economy*, LXVII, August, 1959, pp. 410–419.
Mody, Jehangir R. P. *Jamsetjee Jejeebhoy – the First Indian Knight and Baronet* (Bombay, 1959).
Moon, P. *Divide and Quit* (London, 1961).
Moore, Barrington, Jr. *Social Origins of Dictatorship and Democracy* (London, 1967).
Moraes, Frank. *Sir Purshotamdas Thakurdas* (Bombay, 1957).
Morarjee, Seth Narottam. 'Indian Mercantile Marine', *Annals of the American Academy of Political and Social Science*, Vol. 145, Part II, 1929, pp. 68–71.
Moreland, W. H. *The Agriculture of the United Provinces: An Introduction for the Use of Landowners and Officials* (Allahabad, 1904).
The Revenue Administration of the United Provinces (Allahabad, 1911).
'The Indian Peasant in History: An Introduction to the Linlithgow Report', *JRSA*, LXXVII, No. 3,988, 26 April 1929, pp. 605–13; discussion on the paper, pp. 613–19.
Morison, Sir Theodore. *Economic Transition in India* (London, 1911).
The Industrial Organization of an Indian Province (London, 1911).
Morris, M. D. *The Emergence of an Industrial Labour Force in India* (University of California Press, Berkeley, 1965).
Mukherjee, Haridas and Uma. *The Origins of the National Education Movement* (Jadavpur University, Calcutta, 1957).
Mukerji, K. 'Trend in Real Wages in Cotton Textile Mills in Bombay City and Island, from 1900 to 1951', *Artha Vijnana* (Poona), 1 (I), March 1959.
'Trend in Real Wages in the Jute Textile Industry from 1900 to 1951', *Artha Vijnana*, 2 (I), March 1960.
'Trend in Real Wages in Cotton Textile Industry in Ahmedabad from 1900 to 1951', *Artha Vijnana*, 3 (2) June 1961.

'Trend in Textile Mill Wages in Western India: 1900 to 1951', *Artha Vijnana*, 4 (2), June 1962.

Mukerjee, Radhakamal. *The Indian Working Class* (Bombay, 1945).

Mukerjee, Radhakamal (ed.). *Fields and Farms in Oudh* (Calcutta, 1929).

Economic Problems of Modern India, Vol. 1 (London, 1939), particularly *idem*: 'Land Tenures and Legislation', pp. 218–45.

Mukerjee, Radhakamal and Dey, H. L. (eds.): *Economic Problems of Modern India*, Vol. 2 (London, 1941).

Munshi, M. C. (assisted by K. P. Karnik). *Industrial Profits in India (1936–1944): An Inductive Study* (New Delhi, 1948).

Muranjan, S. K. *Modern Banking in India* (Bombay, 1940).

Murray, Sir Alexander R. 'The Jute Industry', *JRSA*, LXXXII, No. 4,263, 3 August 1934, pp. 977–92; discussion on the paper, pp. 992–5.

Myers, C. A. *Labour Problems in the Industrialization of India* (Cambridge, Mass., 1958).

Myrdal, G. *Economic Theory and Underdeveloped Regions* (London, 1957). *Value in Social Theory* (London, 1958).

Naigamwalla, N. K. D. *Stars of the Dawn: A Historical Memoir* (Bombay, 1946).

Nanavati, M. B. and Anjaria, J. J. *The Indian Rural Problem* (Bombay, 1945).

Narain, D. *The Impact of Price Movements on Areas under Selected Crops in India*, 1900–39. (Cambridge, U.K., 1965).

'Agricultural Change in India' (review of Blyn: *Agricultural Trends in India*), *Economic and Political Weekly* (Bombay), II (6), 11 January 1967, pp. 359–60.

Nayer, P. N. and Pillai, P. S. B. 'An Analysis of Sugar and Gur Prices in India in the Post-protection Period', *Sankhya*, Vol. 4, Part 4, 1938–40, pp. 473–8.

Neale, W. C. *Economic Change in Rural India: Land Tenure and Reform in Uttar Pradesh 1850–1955* (New Haven, Conn., 1962).

Nehru, J. *Glimpses of World History* (Bombay, 1967; originally published by Kitabistan, Allahabad, 1934).

An Autobiography (London, 1936; reprinted Calcutta, 1962).

The Discovery of India (3rd edition, Calcutta, 1947).

Nerlove, M. 'Time Series Analysis of the Supply of Agricultural Products' in Earl O. Heady *et al.* (eds.): *Agricultural Supply Functions – Estimating Techniques and Interpretation* (Iowa State University Press, Ames, Iowa, 1961).

Nurkse, R. 'Some International Aspects of the Problem of Economic Development', *American Economic Review*, May 1952.

'The Problem of International Investment in the Light of Nineteenth Century Experience', *Economic Journal*, LXIV, December 1954, pp. 744–58.

O'Conor, J. E. 'The Economic and Industrial Progress and Condition of India', *JSA*, LII, No. 2,691, 17 June 1904.

O'Malley, L. S. S. (ed.). *Modern India and the West* (London, 1941).

Painton, A. C. *The Bombay Burmah Trading Corporation Limited, 1863–1963* (London, 1964).

Panandikar, S. G. *Some Aspects of the Economic Consequences of the War for India* (Bombay, 1921).
The Wealth and Welfare of the Bengal Delta (Calcutta, 1926).
Panckridge, H. R. *A Short History of the Bengal Club (1827–1927)* (Calcutta, 1927).
Pandit, Y. S. *India's Balance of Indebtedness 1898–1913* (London, 1937).
Papanek, G. F. 'The Development of Entrepreneurship', *The American Economic Review*, LII (2), May 1962, pp. 46–58.
Pakistan's Development: Social Goals and Private Incentives (Cambridge, Mass., 1967).
Pasinetti, L. L. 'On Concepts and Measures of Changes in Productivity', *Review of Economics and Statistics*, Vol. 4, August 1959, pp. 270–286.
Patel, S. J. 'Long-term Changes in Output and Income in India: 1896–1900' in *Essays on Economic Transition* (London, 1965).
Patwardhan, R. P. and Ambekar, D. V. (eds.). *Speeches and Writings of Gopal Krishna Gokhale* (Poona and London, 1962).
Pavlov, V. I. *The Indian Capitalist Class* (New Delhi, 1964).
Pearse, A. S. *The Cotton Industry of Japan and China* (Manchester, 1929).
The Cotton Industry of India, being the report of the journey to India (Manchester, 1930).
Phillips, A. W. 'Stabilisation Policy in a Closed Economy', *Economic Journal*, LXIV, June 1954, pp. 290–323.
'Stabilisation Policy and the Time-form of Lagged Responses', *Economic Journal*, LXVII, June 1957, pp. 265–77.
'A Simple Model of Employment, Money and Prices in a Growing Economy', *Economica*, N. S. Vol. 28, November 1961.
Pigou, A. C. *Aspects of British Economic History 1918–1925* (London, 1947).
Pillai, P. P. *Economic Conditions in India* (London, 1925).
Playne, S. (compiler) and Wright, A. (ed.). *Southern India* (London, 1915).
Bengal and Assam, Behar and Orissa (London, 1917).
The Bombay Presidency, United Provinces, Punjab, etc. (London, 1920).
Podder, V. *Paper Industry in India 1959* (Delhi, 1959).
Pointon, A. C. *The Bombay Burmah Trading Corporation Limited 1863–1963* (London, 1964).
Power, Beryl M. le. 'Indian Labour Conditions', *JRSA*, LXXX, No. 4153, 24 June 1932, pp. 763–76; discussion on the paper, pp. 776–82.
Rabbani, A. K. M. Ghulam. 'Economic Determinants of Jute Production in India and Pakistan', *Pakistan Development Review*, Vol. 5, 1965, pp. 191–228.
Ranade, M. G. *Essays on Indian Economics* (2nd ed., Madras, 1906).
Rangnekar, D. K. *Poverty and Capital Development in India* (London, 1958).
Rao, B. Shiva, *The Industrial Worker in India* (London, 1939).
Rao, B. Srinivasa. *Surveys of Indian Industries*, Vols. 1 and 2 (Oxford University Press, Indian Branch, 1957 and 1958).
Rao, Shama. M. *Modern Mysore (From the Coronation of Chamaraja Wodeyar X in 1868 to the Present Time)* (Bangalore, 1936).

Rao, V. K. R. V. 'Handloom vs. powerloom', *ITJ*, 1890–1940, *Jubilee Souvenir* (Bombay, 1941).

Rao, V. K. R. V. *et al.* (eds.). *Papers on National Income and Allied Topics*, Vol. i (London, 1960).

Rao, C. Ranganatha Sahib. 'The Recent Industrial Progress of Mysore', *JRSA*, LXXXIII, No. 4,294, 8 March 1935, pp. 372–89; discussion on the paper, pp. 390–94.

Ray, P. K. *India's Foreign Trade since 1870* (London, 1934).

Redford, A. *Manchester Merchants and Foreign Trade*, Vol. ii, *1850–1939* (Manchester, 1956).

Reid, D. J. 'Indigo in Behar' in S. Playne (compiler) and A. Wright (ed.), *Bengal and Assam, Behar and Orissa* (London, 1917).

Rippy, J. F. *British Investments in Latin America, 1822–1949* (Hamden, Conn., 1966).

Robinson, E. A. G. *The Structure of Competitive Industry* (London, 1931).

Rosen, G. *Industrial Change in India* (Glencoe, Illinois, 1958).

Rosenberg, N. 'Capital Goods, Technology and Economic Growth', *Oxford Economic Papers*, N. S. Vol. 15, 1963, pp. 216–27.

'Technological Change in the Machine Tool Industry, 1840–1910', *Journal of Economic History*, XXIII, 1963, pp. 414–43.

Roth, Cecil. *The Sassoon Dynasty* (London, 1941).

Rutnagur, S. M. *Bombay Industries: The Cotton Mills* (Bombay, 1927).

Sachse, Sir Frederick A. 'The Work of the Bengal Land Revenue Commission', *JRSA*, LXXXIX, No. 4, 596, 19 September 1941, pp. 666–77.

Sanyal, N. *Development of Indian Railways* (Calcutta, 1930).

Sarkar, J. N. *The Economics of British India* (Calcutta, 1911).

Sarkar, N. R. 'Economic Planning in India' in Radhakamal Mukerjee and H. L. Dey (eds.): *Economic Problems of Modern India*, Vol. 2, pp. 191–213.

Sarkar, Sumit 'Swadeshi Movement in Bengal, 1903–1908' (thesis approved by the University of Calcutta in 1969 for the degree of D.Phil.).

Sastry, N. S. R. *A Statistical Study of India's Industrial Development* (Bombay, 1949).

Saul, S. B. *Studies in British Overseas Trade 1870–1914* (Liverpool, 1960).

'The Engineering Industry' in D. H. Aldcroft (ed.): *The Development of British Industry and Foreign Competition 1875–1914*.

Schumpeter, J. A. *The Theory of Economic Development* (Cambridge Mass., 1934).

'The Decade of the Twenties', *American Economic Review*, Supplement, May 1946.

Schuster, Sir George. 'Indian Economic Life: Past Trends and Future Prospects', *JRSA*, LXXXIII, No. 4,306, 31 May 1935, pp. 641–69.

Schwartzberg, J. T. 'Agricultural Labour in India: A Regional Analysis with Particular Reference to Population Growth', *Economic Development and Cultural Change* (Chicago), Vol. 11, July 1963.

Sen, A. K. 'The Commodity Pattern of British Enterprise in Early Indian Industrialization, 1854–1914', in *Deuxieme Conference Internationale*

D'Historie Economique, Aix-en-Provence 1962 (Paris, 1965), pp. 780–828.

'Surplus Labour in India: A Critique of Schultz's Statistical Test', *Economic Journal*, Vol. LXXVII, March 1967, pp. 154–61.

Sen, S. K. 'Government Purchase of Stores for India (1893–1914)', *Bengal Past and Present*, January–June 1961, pp. 47–64.

Studies in Economic Policy and Development of India, 1848–1926 (Calcutta, 1966).

Shah, K. T. *Sixty Years of Indian Finance* (London, 1927).

Sharma, T. R. *Location of Industries in India* (Bombay, 1946).

Shirras, G. F. *India's Finance and Banking* (London, 1920).

'Public Finance in India', *Annals of the American Academy of Political and Social Science*, Vol. 145, Part II, 1929, pp. 115–23.

Simon, M. 'The Pattern of New British Portfolia Investment 1865–1914', in Adler (ed.): *Capital Movements and Economic Development*, pp. 33–66.

Singer, H. W. 'The Distribution of Gains between Investing and Borrowing Countries', *American Economic Review*, XL (2), May 1950.

Singh, V. B. (ed.). *Economic History of India 1857–1956* (Bombay, 1965).

Sinha, A. R. 'Interrelation between Supply and Price of Raw Jute', *Sankhya*, Vol. 4 (1938–40), pp. 397–400.

'A Preliminary Note on the Effect of Price on the Future Supply of Raw Jute', *Sankhya*, Vol. 5 (1940–1), pp. 413–16.

Sinha, A. R., Sinha, H. C. and Thakurata, J. R. Guha. 'Indian Cultivators' Response to Price', *Sankhya*, Vol. I, Parts 2 and 3, May 1934.

Sinha, H. *Early European Banking in India* (London, 1927).

'Marketing of Jute in Calcutta', *Indian Journal of Economics*, Conference Number, January, 1929, pp. 513–47.

Sinha, N. K. *The Economic History of Bengal*, Vol. I (Calcutta, 1961) and Vol. II (Calcutta, 1962).

'Indian Business Enterprises: Its Failure in Calcutta (1800–1848)', *Bengal Past and Present*, Diamond Jubilee Number July–Dec. 1967, pp. 112–23.

Sivasubramonian, S. 'Estimates of Gross Value of Output of Agriculture for Undivided India, 1900–1 to 1946–7', in V. K. R. V. Rao *et. al.* (eds.): *Papers on National Income and Allied Topics*, Vol. I, pp. 231–44.

National Income of India, 1900–01 to 1946–47 (mimeographed, Delhi School of Economics, Delhi, 1965).

Slater, G. *Southern India* (London, 1936).

Slater, G. (editor). *Some South Indian Villages* (London, 1918).

Soni, H. R. *Indian Industry and Its Problems*, Vol. I (London, 1932).

Spodek, H. 'The "Manchesterisation" of Ahmedabad', *Economic Weekly* (Bombay), XVII (11), 13 March 1965, pp. 483–90.

Stuart-Williams, S. C. 'The Port of Calcutta and Its Postwar Development', *JRSA*, LXXVI, No. 3,948, 20 July, 1928, pp. 891–900; discussion on the paper, pp. 900–6.

Sulivan, R. J. F. *One Hundred Years of Bombay* (Bombay, 1937).

Tagore, Rabindranath. 'Lokahit', first published in B.S. 1321 (1914 or 1915 A.D.) and reprinted in *Kalantar* (first published, B.S. 1344; 1937 A.D.).

Gharey Bairey (first published in B.S. 1322, in *Sabujpatra*).

My Reminiscences (London, 1917).

The Tata Iron and Steel Company Limited: *Annual Reports*.

Temin, Peter. *Iron and Steel in the Nineteenth Century America* (Cambridge, Mass., 1964).

Thavaraj, M. J. K. 'Capital Formation in the Public Sector in India: A Historical Study 1898–1938' in V. K. R. V. Rao *et al.* (eds.): *Papers on National Income and Allied Topics*, Vol. I, pp. 215–30.

'The Textile Industry in Japan' (anonymous), *ITJ*, January 1941, p. 127.

Thomas, P. J. *The Growth of Federal Finance in India* (Oxford University Press, Indian Branch, 1939).

Thompson, E. and Garratt, G. T. *Rise and Fulfilment of British Rule in India* (London, 1934).

Thorburn, S. S. *Musalmans and Moneylenders in the Punjab* (Edinburgh and London, 1886).

Thorner, Alice. 'The Secular Trend in the Indian Economy, 1881–1951', *The Economic Weekly* (Bombay), XIV, *Special Number*, July 1962.

Thorner, Daniel. 'Great Britain and the Development of India's Railways', *The Journal of Economic History*, XI (4), Fall 1951, pp. 389–402.

'The Pattern of Railway Development in India', *The Far Eastern Quarterly*, XIV (2), February 1955, pp. 201–16.

Thorner, Daniel and Alice. *Land and Labour in India* (Bombay and London, 1962).

'The Twentieth Century Trend in Employment in Manufacture in India – as illustrated by the case of West Bengal' in C. R. Rao *et al.* (eds.): *Essays on Econometrics and Planning* (Calcutta, 1964).

Tiwari, S. G. *Economic Prosperity of the United Provinces* (Bombay and Calcutta, 1951).

Townend, Sir Harry (compiler). *A History of Shaw Wallace & Co., and Shaw Wallace & Co., Ltd* (Calcutta, 1965).

Tozer, H. J. 'The Manufacturers of Greater Britain – II. India; *JSA*, LIII, No. 2,741, 2 June 1905, pp. 333–54.

Tressler, K. 'Industries' in S. Playne (compiler) and A. Wright (ed.). *Southern India* (London, 1915).

Trevaskis, H. K. *The Land of the Five Rivers* (London, 1928).

Tripathi, A. *Trade and Finance in the Bengal Presidency* (Bombay and Calcutta, 1956).

Tripathi, S. D. *The Kanpur Money Market* (Delhi, 1966).

Tuckwell, H. M. Surtees. 'The Tata Iron and Steel Works: Their Origin and Development', *JRSA*, LXVI, No. 3402, 1 February 1918, pp. 190–202; discussion on the paper, pp. 202–5.

Tyson, Geoffrey, *The Bengal Chamber of Commerce and Industry, 1853–1953. A Centenary Survey* (Calcutta, 1953).

100 Years of Banking in Asia and Africa: A History of National and Grindlays Bank Limited 1953–1963 (London, 1963).

Vakil, C. N. and Maluste, D. N. *Commercial Relations between India and Japan* (Calcutta, 1937).

Venkatasubbiah, H. *The Foreign Trade of India 1900–1940: A Statistical Analysis* (New Delhi, 1946).

Visvesvaraya, M. *Planned Economy for India* (Bangalore, 1934).

Wadia, Sir Ness. 'The Industry in Retrospect', *Indian Textile Journal 1890–1940, Jubilee Souvenir* (Bombay, 1941).

Wallace, D. R. *The Romance of Jute* (London, 1928).

Weston, A. T. 'Technical and Vocational Education', *Annals of the American Academy of Political and Social Science*, Vol. 145, Part II, 1929, pp. 151–160.

Wigglesworth, A. 'India's Commercial Fibres', *JRSA*, LXXIX, 26 December 1930, pp. 134–52; discussion on the paper, pp. 152–8.

Williamson, A. V. 'Irrigation in the Indo-Gangetic Plain', *Geographical Journal*, Vol. 65, 1925, pp. 141–53.

'Indigenous Irrigation Works in Peninsular India', *Geographical Review*, Vol. 21, October 1931, pp. 613–26.

Woodruff, P. *The Men Who Ruled in India*, Vol. II, *The Guardians* (London, 1963).

Woodruff, W. *Impact of Western Man* (London, 1966).

Young, Brigadier-General H. A. 'The Indian Ordnance Factories and Indian Industries', *JRSA*, LXXII, No. 3715, 1 February 1924, pp. 175–85; discussion on the paper, pp. 185–8.

Zachariah, K. C. *A Historical Study of Internal Migration in the Indian Subcontinent, 1901–1931* (London, 1964).

INDEX

471